Gender and Politics in India

Themes in Politics Series

GENERAL EDITORS

Rajeev Bhargava
Partha Chatterjee

The Themes in Politics series aims to bring together essays on important issues in Indian political science and politics—contemporary political theory, Indian social and political thought, and foreign policy, among others. Each volume in the series will bring together the most significant articles and debates on each issue, and will contain a substantive introduction and an annotated bibliography.

Gender and Politics in India

Edited by

Nivedita Menon

OXFORD
UNIVERSITY PRESS

OXFORD
UNIVERSITY PRESS

YMCA Library Building, Jai Singh Road, New Delhi 110001

Oxford University Press is a department of the University of Oxford. It furthers the
University's objective of excellence in research, scholarship, and education
by publishing worldwide in

Oxford   New York

Athens Auckland Bangkok Bogota Buenos Aires Cape Town
Chennai Dar es Salaam Delhi Florence Hong Kong Istanbul
Karachi Kolkata Kuala Lumpur Madrid Melbourne Mexico City Mumbai
Nairobi Paris Sao Paolo Singapore Taipei Tokyo Toronto Warsaw

with associated companies in

Berlin Ibadan

Oxford is a registered trade mark of Oxford University Press
in the UK and in certain other countries

Published in India
By Oxford University Press, New Delhi

ISBN 0 19 5658930

Typset by Eleven Arts, Keshav Puram, New Delhi 110035
Printed at Pauls Press, New Delhi 110020
and published by Manzar Khan, Oxford University Press
YMCA Library Building, Jai Singh Road, New Delhi 110 001

Note from the General Editors

Teaching of politics in India has long suffered because of the systematic unavailability of readers with the best contemporary work on the subject. The most significant writing in Indian politics and Indian political thought is scattered in periodicals; much of the recent work in contemporary political theory is to be found in inaccessible international journals or in collections that reflect more the current temper of Western universities than the need of Indian politics and society.

The main objective of this series is to remove this lacuna. The series also attempts to cover as comprehensively and usefully as possible the main themes of contemporary research and public debate on politics, to include selections from the writings of leading specialists in each field, and to reflect the diversity of research methods, ideological concerns and intellectual styles that characterize the discipline of political science today.

We plan to begin with three general volumes, one each in contemporary political theory, Indian politics and Indian political thought. A general volume on international politics and specific volumes of readings on particular areas within each of these fields will follow.

RAJEEV BHARGAVA
PARTHA CHATTERJEE

Acknowledgements

The publishers would like to thank the following for granting permission to reprint the articles included in this volume:

Kali for Women for Vandana Shiva, 'Colonialism and the Evolution of the Masculinist Forestry' in *Staying Alive: Women, Ecology, and Survival in India,* 1988; and Nandita Shah and Nandita Gandhi (eds), *The Issues at Stake,* 1993.

Kumkum Sangari and Sudesh Vaid for 'Institutions, Beliefs, Ideologies: Widow Immolation in Contemporary Rajasthan' in Kumari Jayawardene and Malati de Alwis (eds), *Embodied Violence,* 1996.

Friedrich Ebert Stiftung and UNDP for Bina Agarwal, 'The Gender and Environment Debate: Lessons from India' and Rohini Hensman, 'Impact of Technological Change on Industrial Women Works' in N. Rao, L. Rurup and R. Sudarshan (eds), *Sites of Change,* 1996.

Amrita Basu and Westview Press for Radha Kumar, 'From Chipko to Sati: The Contemporary Indian Women's Movement' in Amrita Basu (ed.), *The Challenge of Local Feminisms: Women's Movements in Global Perspective,* 1995.

Nandita Shah, Sujata Gothoskar, Nandita Gandhi, Amrita Chhachhi and *Economic and Political Weekly* for 'Structural Adjustment, Feminization of Labour Force and Organizational Strategies', *EPW,* 30 April, 1994.

Ratna Kapur and Brenda Cossman and *National Law School Journal* for 'On Women, Equality and the Constitution: Through the Looking Glass of Feminism' in *NLSJ,* vol. 1, 1993.

Vidya Rao and *Economic and Political Weekly* for '*Thumri* as Female Voice' in *EPW,* 28 April, 1990.

Gabriele Dietrich and Horizon Books India for 'Women, Ecology and Culture' in *Reflections on the Women's Movement,* 1992.

Ilina Sen and *Economic and Political Weekly* for 'Feminists, Women's Movement and the Working Class' in *EPW,* vol. 24, no. 29, 1989.

Ruth Vanita and *Seminar* for 'Thinking Beyond Gender in India'.

Contents

Contributors

Bina Agarwal is Professor of Economics at the Institute of Economic Growth, University of Delhi. Her books include *Mechanisation in Indian Agriculture* and *Cold Hearths and Barren Slopes: The Woodfuel Crisis in The Third World.*

Amrita Chhachhi is Lecturer in Women, Gender Relations and Development Studies at the Institute of Social Sciences, the Hague. Her research has focused on women and industrialization and she is co-editor of *Confronting State, Capital and Patriarchy: Women Organising in the Process of Industrialisation* (Macmillan: 1996)

Brenda Cossman is currently Associate Professor at the Faculty of Law, University of Toronto. She has been Associate Professor at Osgoods Hall Law School, York University where she was also Director of the Institute of Feminist Legal Studies.

Gabriele Dietrich is a Professor at the Centre for Social Analysis, Madurai. She has also been working with pennurimai Iyakkam (movement for women's rights) in Tamilnadu for nearly twenty years and is at present one of the national convenors of the National Alliance of People's Movement.

Veena Das is Professor of Sociology at Delhi School of Economics. She is the author of *Structure and Cognition: Aspects of Hindu Caste and Ritual* (Oxford India Paperbacks: 1995) and has edited *Mirrors of Violence: Communities, Riots and Survivors in South Asia* (Oxford India Paperbacks: 1993)

Nandita Gandhi has been active in the women's movement since twenty years. She has written books, articles and held training workshops on many issues connected to women and women's studies especially the movement, labour and development issues. She has written a book *When Rolling Pins Hit the Streets: A Study of the Anti-Price Rise Movement in Maharashtra.*

Sujata Gothoskar is active in the women's and the trade union movement, is part of the Blue Star union, and has researched on these issues for fifteen years.

Rohini Hensman is a free lance researcher and writer, and is affiliated with the Union Research Group, a small voluntary group which does research on and for trade unions. She is also a Director of Women Working Worldwide, based in Manchester, UK.

Ratna Kapur is a legal researcher and Co-Director of the Centre for Feminist Legal Research. She is the co-author of *Subversive Sites: Feminist Engagements with Law in India* (Sage: 1996) with Brenda Cossman; and editor of *Feminist Terrains in Legal Domains: Interdisciplinary Essays on Woman and Law in India* (Kali: 1997).

Radha Kumar is a Fellow at the Council on Foreign Relations in New York and works on ethnic conflict, partition and post-conflict reconstruction.

Nivedita Menon teaches politics at Lady Shri Ram College, University of Delhi, and formerly was Visiting Fellow at the Centre of Developing Studies, Delhi. She has been actively involved with forums for democratic rights.

Tejaswini Niranjana is Director and Senior Fellow, Centre for the Study of Culture and Society, Bangalore.

Vidya Rao is a thumri singer and also writes on music and the performing arts. She works as a senior editor with Orient Longman, New Delhi.

Kumkum Sangari is Professorial Fellow at the Centre for Contemporary Studies, Nehru Memorial Museum and Library.

Ilina Sen has been actively associated both with the women's and mineworkers' movements, most recently with the Chhattisgarh Shramik Sangh in Madhya Pradesh. She has been affiliated both with the Indian Council for Social Science Research and the Centre for Women's Development Studies, and has published widely on demography, women's work and theory and practice of the women's movement in India.

Nandita Shah comes from a background of professional social work, the women's studies and women's movement. She has been able to combine them in teaching, training, writing and organizing around the issues of women and youth. She is one of the founders of Akshara, a women's resource centre, has written many papers, and co-authored a book *Issues at Stake: Theory and Practice in the Contemporary Indian Women's Movement.*

Vandana Shiva trained as a physicist but later shifted to inter-disciplinary research in science, technology and environmental policy. She is widely recognized for her contributions to the fields of women and environment, biodiversity, technology and intellectual property rights and ecological issues related to agriculture.

Susie Tharu is Professor, Department of English, Central Institute of English and Foreign Languages, Hyderabad. She is co-editor of *Women Writing in India* (2 vols; Oxford India Paperbacks: 1994)

Sudesh Vaid teaches English at the Department of English at Indraprastha College, New Delhi.

Ruth Vanita is Associate Professor, Liberal Studies and Women's Studies, University of Montana.

Introduction

Nivedita Menon

It is by now generally accepted that there is no one women's movement in India, but rather, several women's movements. That is, when we consider movements that specifically raise questions of gender, it is clear that in terms of political understanding, ideology, social base and modes of action, there are rich, complex and contentious debates that rage among them. In addition, 'the women's movement' is often used also to refer to women's participation in politics in general and not just to the specific interventions in politics which challenge various forms of patriarchy and gender injustice. These features have contributed towards outlining a field which is remarkable for its dissonances and disputes as much as for what still holds it together—so that it is possible after all, to refer to 'the women's movement' in India—a concern with gender inequity, however that is defined.

This volume will present a view of feminist theory and politics in India by identifying some key issues in terms of opposing or at least, differing positions on them from within the movement. There are seven sections. In the first section on *environment and gender*, the discussion centres around Vandana Shiva's conception of ecofeminism and critiques of it by Gabriele Dietrich and Bina Agarwal on the grounds of its silence on caste hierarchies and its essentializing of 'women'. In the next section on *work* Nandita Shah et al. address the debates on structural adjustment and its debilitating impact on women, while Rohini Hensman asks whether feminism ought to have a more positive, nuanced attitude to new technology. In the third section on *law*, Ratna Kapur and Brenda Cossman argue for a reconceptualization of 'equality' so that the actual conditions of women's subordination can be taken into account, while Nivedita Menon makes a more fundamental critique of law, suggesting that feminist politics needs to rethink altogether the terms of its engagement with legal discourse. Next, in the section on *the women's movement*, three extracts from the work of Nandita Gandhi and Nandita Shah, Radha Kumar and Ilina Sen, reflect on the forms of organizations within the women's movement, the trends within the movement up to the last decade, and the possibilities of a dialogue between Marxism and feminism in the Indian context. In the section on *women, community and rights*, two essays by Kumkum Sangari and Sudesh Vaid, and by Veena Das, explore in different ways the manner in which feminist politics must engage with the state on the one hand and with community on the other, in a context in which nationhood, community identity and women's rights are in extremely contested relationships with one another. In the sixth section, the extracts map out debates within the terrain of a question central to feminist politics, that of women's agency. While Vidya Rao's looks at *thumri* as a confined space whose limits have nevertheless been creatively subverted by women singers, thus raising questions for broader feminist practice as struggle, Susie Tharu and Tejaswini Niranjana address the dilemma for feminist politics arising from the visible presence of active women in Hindu right-wing and upper-caste movements that are in direct confrontation with the broad democratic ideals of the women's movement. In the final section on *sexuality*, a paper by Ruth Vanita presses for the need for the women's movement to rethink fundamentally the very idea of gender, and the anthropomorphism with which it is conceived.

In this introductory chapter, we will present a picture of Indian politics, in broad strokes, derived from the large body of feminist scholarship spanning decades. We will focus on shared understandings, so that we can place the differences, when we get to them, in perspective.

Feminist Critiques of 'The Golden Vedic Age'

It has come to be commonly believed among the middle classes that the Vedic period was the golden age of Indian womanhood. It is accepted that the status of women was very high in that period, and that it was only with the coming of invaders, especially Muslims, that restrictions began to be placed on women. All the evils of the nineteenth century—purdah, sati, female infanticide—

were explained as outcomes of fears for women's safety which had their origins in a time of invasions.

Contemporary feminist scholars argue that such a history is the product of the nineteenth century interaction between colonialism and nationalism. A significant tool used by colonial ideology to prove the inferiority of the subject population was the question of the status of women. The moral inferiority of Indians, especially Hindus, was supposed to be demonstrated by the barbaric practices followed against women—this was argued by Christian missionaries as well as by historians like James Mill. Writing in the nineteenth century, Mill considered Hindu civilization to be crude and immoral. Thus, colonial historians justified British rule in India by arguing that Hindu women required the protection and intervention of the colonial state.

The reaction to this kind of characterization of Indian/Hindu society took the form of a school of nationalist history writing by historians like Altekar and R.C. Dutt, who challenged colonial history writing by presenting the argument outlined above, that the evils of Indian society were attributable to Muslim invasions. That is, the patriarchal features of Hindu society were explained entirely as a response to external threats.

Historians like Uma Chakravarty (1993, 1989) and Kumkum Roy (1995) question this construction of the past at several levels. First, they point out that the evidence used by nationalist historians is exclusively drawn from brahmanical sources, and is therefore, a partial history at best. Moreover, even if, as they argue, the status of upper caste women was high, which is contested by feminist historians, it was at the expense of the exploitation of non-Aryan peoples, especially women.

Second, Vedic texts focused on specific geographical areas, early texts referred to the North-West of the subcontinent, later texts to the east around the mid-Gangetic valley and the Manusmriti to India north of the Vindhyas. From these texts, nineteenth century historians extrapolated a picture of 'Vedic India', an unsustainable generalization because 'India' as an entity came into being only in the nineteenth century through the encounter with colonialism. Thus, defining the past in terms of a 'Vedic India' presents a falsely homogeneous picture, a homogeneity which is then violated apparently, only by external interventions.

Third, even from the brahmanical sources alone, there is sufficient evidence to show that the structure of institutions that ensured the subordination of women was complete long before Muslims as a religious community had even come into being.

Referring specifically to the two features which the nationalist argument uses—scholarship and property—contemporary feminist historians of ancient India explode the myth of the superior position of women in the Vedic period. Regarding scholarship, they point out that less than one per cent of the one thousand hymns of the Rig Veda are attributed to women, which clearly shows the marginal position of women scholars. Further, Uma Chakravarty points out that the famous and oft-repeated story about the debate between Gargi and Yajnavalkya, celebrated as an example of the learning allowed to women, is an episode in which Gargi is finally silenced and eliminated from the contest by Yajnavalkya, not by the force of his arguments but because he threatens her—'Gargi, do not question too much, lest your head fall off ....'

As for property, women not only did not own property, they were considered to *be* property, the bride, for example, being gifted to the groom along with other goods. Women were excluded from participating in a variety of material transactions, from giving and receving *dakshina* on ritual occasions, to giving and receiving tribute and taxes. Women had a certain limited recognition only as wives and mothers within the patriarchal kinship structure.

Clearly then, the golden age of Indian womanhood was a selective picture of the past created in the context of the politics of the nineteenth century.

Social Reform Movements of the Nineteenth Century

There was no one uniform movement for social reform, but different campaigns on locally specific issues which were taken up at different times. By and large, these movements as well as the resistance to such reform were decisively shaped by the colonial encounter. Prominent sections of the bourgeoisie were intent on reforming what colonial discourse presented as primitive and barbaric aspects of Hindu society, while resistance came from revivalist nationalists who challenged the colonial interventions into 'Indian tradition'. Although reformists and revivalists defined themselves in opposition to one another, they also shared more than they would recognize. For instance, Ashis Nandy (1983) has shown how both shared the ideal of the anti-imperialist hero as 'manly', in the terms set by Victorian ideology, rejecting the more ambiguous, androgynous qualities which marked Indian traditions of the ideal man—Krishna, Ram, and the ideals of Sufi and Bhakti traditions, because Indian traditions were dismissed contemptuously as 'effeminate' by the British. Similarly, both reformers and revivalists shared a belief in a glorious pre-colonial pre-Muslim past where women were worshipped, and both used nationalist arguments, though mobilizing this picture of the past in different ways—reformers to demonstrate that Indians still had the capacity to meet the enlightened standards of the West, and thus, were fit for self-government, and revivalists to assert that Indian/Hindu 'traditions' had the inner resources to deal with its problems, and did not need foreign/imperialist intervention.

The focus of social reform movements reflected the concerns of the upper castes who constituted the bourgeoisie (Kumar, 1993). The issues the movements raised—widows' oppression, purdah, growing gender gap in education—did not affect the majority of Indian women. The majority of the total female population was involved in agrarian, manufacturing and trading activities, whether as part of household or family based enterprises or as independent workers, producers and traders. The status of these women was generally governed by local or community customs, which often gave more freedom than was available to higher-caste women, governed by the Manusmriti. As for education, the sex ratio among the illiterate population was almost the same, and the gender gap in traditional institutions for elementary education was not as high as it became under the English system.

Similarly, in the case of Sati, recent historical research suggests that the nineteenth century Sati abolition movement created the myth of a widespread practice when it seems to have been rather exceptional (Yang, 1987). The only evidence of widespread incidence of Sati is for the early decades of the nineteenth century in Bengal, for which there may be specific reasons. First, the majority of these incidents were recorded at the height of the Sati abolition movement in the province governed by the chief British opponent of Sati, William Bentinck. It is possible that these figures conflate suicide by widows with ritual Sati—partly out of ignorance and partly deliberately, to prove the gravity of the problem. In response to this picture presented by the colonial government, there may indeed have been a rise in incidents of Sati in Bengal, as part of the deliberate assertion of a supposed 'tradition' by a community perceiving itself to be in crisis. The practice was largely found among urban upper classes of Calcutta, a city which had the longest interaction with colonialism. In other words, it was not necessarily an existing custom, but an aggressive–defensive reaction to colonial rule. When the Sati Abolition Act was finally passed in 1829, there was eventually less protest from the Hindu orthodoxy than was feared (Kumar, 1993).

It has been argued by historians like Lata Mani (1989) that the struggle over the abolition of Sati by the British became less about women and their status and more about what constituted 'authentic' cultural tradition. Under colonial rule, the reconstitution of tradition was largely carried out through debating the status of women. Both British and Indian campaigners against Sati used the strategy of referring to the Shastras to show that Sati did not have religious sanction. Thus Brahminic scriptures were increasingly seen to be the basis of 'authentic' tradition. The point then, that some feminist historians like Mani make is that we must understand the practice of Sati as well as the campaign against and for it, not simply in terms of attitudes to women, but in the larger, more complex context of the encounter between colonialism and the Indian élites. This encounter produced Sati as *the* trope for Indian womanhood, so that the attack on the practice as well as its defence had little relation to its actual incidence or to beliefs about the status of women, and more to do with justifications of colonial rule and different forms of resistance to it, whether this resistance mobilized 'tradition' ('We're different from you') or modernity ('We're as civilized as you'). In this whole debate, it is suggested, the horror of the burning of women was not really the issue.

The argument has been made by Partha Chatterjee in an influential and controversial essay (1989), that while 'The Women's Question' was a central issue in the debates over social reform in nineteenth century Bengal, the issue disappears from the agenda of public debate by the end of the century. The reason for this, according to him, is the refusal of nationalism to make the women's question an issue of political negotiation with the colonial state. In other words, the bourgeois leadership of the national movement chose to contest imperialist domination by simultaneously defining the public ('outer') sphere of the citizen as that where 'we' are the same as or equal to the imperialist masters, and the private ('inner') domain as that where 'we' are different, thus justifying practices which were discriminatory to women. In his words, 'Nationalism

..., located its own subjectivity in the spiritual domain of culture, where it considered itself superior to the West and hence undominated and sovereign.' The nationalist position was based on the premise that the reform of the lives of women was an area where the nation was acting on its own, outside the guidance of the colonial state. Thus the 'new patriarchy' which nationalist discourse set up as a hegemonic construct distinguished itself not only from the West but from the mass of its own people, for its argument about preserving the 'difference' in the 'inner' realm was relevant only to sections of the middle classes. For the non-Hindu middle classes and other sections of Indian society which felt excluded from the idea of the nation produced by the nationalist leadership, the 'resolution' of the women's question was necessarily problematic (1993: 132–4).

The era of social reform in the nineteenth century then, must be seen as articulating complex and contested inter-relationships between 'women' on the one hand and on the other, the emerging notions of citizen, nation and community.

The National Movement and Women

The political economy of colonial rule had a specific impact on women because of new developments like lower wages, exclusion from some sectors which had been open to women before, and loss of usufructory rights to community property and resources through forest laws and the introduction of private property in land. In addition, the subordination of women was specially significant in maintaining the British Empire, as the position of women in Indian society was one of the major factors that legitimized British rule. The British government thus selectively intervened in changing the position of women—on some issues it liberalized the law, on others it increased constraints. Thus while by maintaining women's subordination the British could show that India was not fit for independence, by liberalizing it could at the same time demonstrate the superiority of Western culture (Kasturi and Mazumdar, 1994).

Women began to work collectively against male supremacy at the beginning of the twentieth century, and the analysis they made of their oppression linked patriarchal practices and imperialism. Thus the women's movement in India has a history of linking patriarchy with other structures of oppression. One of the landmarks in the rise of an organized women's movement is the formation of the All India Women's Conference in 1927. Originally, it was set up to discuss the issue of female education, but it soon found this question could not be addressed without looking at other issues such as purdah and child-marriage. From here came the realization that these questions could not be separated from India's political subjection. Thus, the AIWC came to a point where it stressed the political goal of national self-government as a means to achieve women's aspirations (Kumar, 1993).

The issue of votes for women was first raised in 1917, and rejected by the British government on the grounds of conservatism of Indian culture and because it would be premature when most Indian men were not educated enough to use the vote responsibly. Of course, the British could not possibly have directly enfranchised Indian women in 1919 when it was only in 1938 that British women got the vote. When it became clear that the major Indian political organizations supported the demand, the 1919 Government of India Act which enfranchised a tiny percentage of men, allowed the Provincial Assemblies to drop the clause excluding women if they wished. Most of them did. The Congress report of 1928 on self-government (the Nehru Report) fully endorsed the demand of the women's organizations for universal adult suffrage and sex equality. But the 1935 Government of India Act only gave the vote to wives and widows of men qualified to vote. This was strongly protested by women's organizations, and Kamaladevi Chattopadhyaya wrote, 'We do not think that woman's rights as a citizen should depend on her marriage ...' (Kumar, 1993).

As we have seen, apart from the feminist agenda, women in India also had a nationalist agenda. Women joined the Indian National Congress committees, took part in all forms of civil disobedience and were prominent in the communist party and revolutionary terrorist groups. The massive presence of women in the national movement was a challenge both to the British claim of moral superiority, because police and army were quite prepared to be as brutal with women as with men, as well as to British stereotypes of Indian women as passive and sheltered (Liddle and Joshi, 1985).

The self-identified women's movement had hitherto been largely middle-class, but in the 1920s, a new perception of women as workers emerged. However, attempts to expand the scope of nationalist activity to include poor women were based on the image of women as nurturers rather than as workers themselves. Thus, when nationalist women made attempts at employment generation along swadeshi lines, they assumed women's wage work to be subsidiary to the male wage. Hence they did not try to ensure a living wage for the women involved in such activities. At the same time, women were becoming prominent in workers' movements and women workers began to be consciously organized. In the Bombay textile strike of 1928–9, the presence of women was outstanding.

The question has been raised by later scholars and feminists as to how far women in the national movement were 'feminist' as opposed to being 'nationalist'. Certainly the women's movement did not call itself feminist, because that would imply priority to women's liberation, so it stressed rather, the joint struggle for national and gender equality. At this time it was imperialism rather than the family that was focused upon as the root of inequality, but nevertheless, as is clear from the demand for female suffrage and guarantees of sexual equality in the constitution, there was a clear feminist agenda as well.

Notable examples of this period of women participating in large numbers in a general movement against exploitation are the Tebhaga movement, a peasant struggle in Bengal for the right to one-third of the crop and the Telengana struggle against feudal exploitation (Kannabiran and Lalita, 1989). However, in the course of these movements, women also raised questions of oppression of women in the family by their own men.

Gandhi and Women

Gandhi's role in mobilizing women in an unprecedented way is unquestioned, although there might be differences in the assessment of the impact and limitations of this. Gandhi explicitly focused on 'feminine' qualities as having the strength to combat imperial power. He associated 'femininity' with spiritual and moral courage—the heroines he chose for women to emulate were Sita and Draupadi rather than, the Rani of Jhansi. His ideal stressed women's superior capacity for suffering and self-sacrifice rather than forceful intervention to protect their interests. However, Gandhi also insisted on the absolute personal dignity and autonomy of women in the family and society. This understanding that women had the right to the inviolability of their bodies challenged the basis of marriage as an institution. But the alternative he offered was asceticism and celibacy, not a freeing of sexuality in any other way.

The two central symbols that Gandhi used to generate a new life in the anti-imperialist struggle—khadi and salt—were both explicitly derived from women's life-sustaining activities in the 'private' realm, linking these, in a revolutionary manner, to the 'public'.

In his mobilizing of women Gandhi was clearly torn by contradictions generated by his class, caste and gender. Thus, while he continually exhorted women to be politically active, he seemed also to link their activism to their traditional roles and what he saw as the essential spirituality of women (Kumar, 1993: 81–5; Kishwar, 1985).

Religion and Feminist Politics

It is generally accepted within the feminist understanding that there are fundamental similarities among the religious patriarchies, although they have substantive differences (Sangari, 1995). The religious communities are governed by their own Personal Laws, which cover rights within marriage and inheritance, and all of them discriminate against women. As legal subjects, women are envisaged as non-productive and dependent, have little custodial or guardianship rights over children, and inheritance is invariably patrilineal. In all cases, women become the symbols of community identity and any attempt to change the position of women gets perceived as an assault on the community—the Personal Laws get defended as part of ancient religious tradition, although they were codified into their current forms only in the colonial period. As Zoya Hasan has pointed out in a volume which brings together essays on the inter-relationship of gender, communities and patriarchal practices of the State in relation to Muslim women, there is a need for 'nuanced understanding of the complex way in which identity is constructed, the manner in which gender and community intersect and cross-cut each other, and the ways in which these ..., intersect with state policy'. (1994: ix)

In the women's movement, the debate on religion has shifted over the years. Gabriele Dietrich (1994) characterizes the debate in the following way. Till the mid-eighties religion was considered to be a patriarchal construct, to be ignored or at best to be resisted and challenged. There was also the position that religion should not be ignored as it is present among people as a cultural force, and that progressive elements should use it for emancipation. By the mid-eighties there was an attempt to distinguish between the oppressive aspects of religion and moves to communalize it, from its potential to sustain women and give them room for self-expression. Now there arose the attempt to deal with 'faith' and its elements seriously, not just to use religion instrumentally, but to work for genuine religious reform. This debate took place at a time when the communalization of religion was already apparent— the Shah Bano judgement followed by the opening of the locks of the temple at Ayodhya.

Even more disturbing was the realization that communal organizations were drawing in women in large numbers, using the slogans of the Left and the women's movement. Not just prominent women like Uma Bharati and Sadhvi Rithambhara were involved here, but large numbers of ordinary women were in the forefront of the communal mobilizing prior to the demolition of the Babri Masjid and in the violence that followed (Agnes, 1995). Some of this was due to the concerted effort on the part of communal and fundamentalist groups to draw women in. Tanika Sarkar (1991) has described how the RSS and VHP have made enormous efforts to bring women in, train them in yoga and martial arts, and give them a role in their political campaigns. However this was done while reaffirming patriarchal family ideology—indeed, these organizations project themselves as extensions of the family. They stress complementarity rather than equality. Thus by giving women a public role, status and skills within a structure that reaffirms the patriarchal ideology, the Hindu right-wing organizations have been able to mobilize women without threatening the community.

Many feminist scholars argue that over the past few years it has become clear that caste and religious community are more powerful in women's lives than gender, especially in highly polarized situations (Omvedt, 1994, Dietrich, 1994). Thus the present climate of heightened violence against Dalits and minority communities strengthens patriarchal controls within the community. Women's link with caste and community is made through the family—as Dietrich puts it, the production of life itself takes place within patriarchal institutions. Thus, women are crucial to the process by which culture is transmitted—family, caste and community are key elements of patriarchal social organization in India (1994). The family is the source of continuing emotional and material support to which women's groups have been unable to provide an alternative, for women in struggle. This is where Hindu right-wing organizations have been successful, because they have politicized women without disturbing the family system.

Feminist Assessments of the Political Economy

Most feminists characterize the Indian state as both a class and patriarchal state. Nevertheless like other social movements, the women's movement also continues to put pressure on the state to yield to its demands; that is, the understanding is that the pressure of democratic movements can act on the state despite its esssentially class and patriarchal character.

There is no specifically feminist analysis of the class character of the Indian state, and it is the Marxian view that is generally accepted. As with other post-colonial societies, the Indian state at independence inherited a vast and well-developed state apparatus, that is, a civil and military bureaucracy, which had served the colonial purpose. Thus the state had at independence the potential to be more than merely an 'instrument of the ruling class', a potential further enhanced by the fact that colonial policies had resulted in a comparatively weak and unstable bourgeoisie which is incapable of controlling the state apparatus on its own. It is therefore a coalition of ruling classes which controls the state, and the contradictions between the interests of fractions of the ruling classes are as crucial in determining state policy as are the contradictions between the ruling class and the ruled. Nevertheless the bourgeoisie does exercise a leadership function in this coalition because the non-capitalist sectors and types of production in the Indian economy have been subsumed, economically and politically, under the logic of the reproduction of capital. The other components of the ruling class are rich farmers, the bureaucracy and the urban professional middle classes.

Another reason for the relative autonomy of the state is that since the bourgeoisie is weak, and capital resources low, the state is the only agency which can draw together scarce capital resources and invest these in basic infrastructural areas which need large initial investments and yield slow profits. Within the constraints posed by the dominant propertied classes therefore, it is possible for the state to act autonomously, for it is an important part of the economic base itself (Bardhan, 1984; Kaviraj, 1988).

This explains the 'socialistic' pattern of development adopted by the Indian state in the first three decades after independence with active intervention of the state in the economy. Sudipta Kaviraj (1988) has used the Gramscian notion of 'passive revolution' to explain the pattern of development adopted by the Indian state. That is, for a thoroughgoing bourgeois revolution to be effected, for industrialization to take place, a domestic market must be built up by reducing poverty in the countryside. This can only be done by land reforms, for which legislation was passed in the 50s, but which could never be implemented because of the the influence of the landed interests in the coalition of ruling classes. The entire planning process has therefore been an exercise in trying to promote industrialization without radical transformation of agriculture. Instead, short-term poverty alleviation measures have been followed, but investing resources in these—i.e. employment generation, loans, technical training for the educated unemployed—would require diverting resources from incentives for private capital, thus depressing rates of growth. At the same time, if these distributive policies are not followed, high growth rates would be impossible to sustain because of mass poverty and consequent low demand for goods. Since fundamental agrarian transformation has been ruled out, any attempt to resolve the crisis could only be in these self-contradictory terms.

In 1980 the beginning of the directional change in domestic industrial policy was made with the Industrial Policy Document, the two main features of which are *liberalization* and *export promotion*. The theory behind the first three decades of planning was that redistribution of incomes and property was necessary to create a market for goods and services. Since 1980 however, the rationale has been that development can be achieved even on a limited market. A small enclave was to be created, with enhanced purchasing power by: (a) raising salaries and perquisites of selected strata in services, trade and manufacturing, (b) tax exemptions and reductions and (c) using public money to provide loans and subsidized interest rates in order to create a market for luxury goods. In addition, the international market was to be opened up for

Indian industry through incentives for export promotion (Kurien, 1994).

The implications for a feminist understanding from such an analysis of the state arises from the fact that, of the 24 per cent of the female population classified as workers, the majority, 76 per cent, is in the agricultural sector. Since there has been a consistent refusal by, indeed, inability of, the state to transform agrarian relations, women are the worst hit by poverty and landlessness, since most women workers are concentrated here. But more fundamentally, the figures for women classified as workers is suspect to begin with, because non-paid work in subsistence activities including agricultural labour, is not recognized as 'work'. That is, the state and its agencies do not recognize the work of women as contributing to national income. Feminist economists have pointed out that planning in India did not consider women as productive workers except with reference to middle class working women (Ghosh, 1994, 1996). It was only in 1974 that the Committee on the Status of Women in India raised the matter of the invisibility of women workers, but even after that, it was as recently as the 1993 census that an attempt was made to redefine work in the context of women.

There are very grim prognoses of the consequences for women workers in the wake of liberalization/structural adjustment. Structural adjustment implies a set of policies which include: (a) incentives for the private sector, (b) privatization of government-owned units, (c) delicensing and deregulation of industry, (d) disciplining of labour, and (e) cutting down on government expenditure. On the whole, such policies—already tried in Latin America and Africa—have failed to generate growth of income and employment. The balance of payment situation may improve, exports may rise provided world demand is high, but the majority of the people have been seen to be pushed further into poverty. Studies carried out by UNICEF show that women and children of poorer families are hardest hit, in terms of nutrition, workload and mortality (Shah et al., 1994).

In addition, such programmes tend to shrink women's employment opportunities in the organized sector, while generating low-paying jobs which usually go to women, in the unorganized sector, in decentralized small units. This is called the feminization of the workforce, and some economists believe that this will increase work-participation rates of women and help in alleviating poverty (Deshpande and Deshpande, 1992). However, the counter-argument is that such workers do not have permanent status, are paid low wages, and deprived of statutory rights—these trends are evident in the new export promotion zones in Bombay and in garment industries in Delhi (Shah et al., 1994).

In any case, micro-level studies have shown an overall decline in the employment of women, not just in their conditions of work. For example, in the textile mill sector over the last two decades, in Ahmedabad and Bombay, automation has replaced women, and similar processes are evident in mining and chemical sectors (Jhabvala, 1985; Savara, 1982). A significant feature of structural adjustment is privatization to make industry more efficient and profitable. Privatization would have significant implications for women's employment. Between 1974 and 1988, women's employment rose more in the public than in the private sector and privatization usually means drastic cuts in the workforce, of which the main target is women (Shah et al., 1994). This has to do with the clear sexual division of labour in the production process whereby women are assigned only specific tasks (primarily assembly and packing) while men are given a wider range of jobs, including supervision and maintainence. However this sexual division itself has to do with the patriarchal ideology shared by workers and employers alike, and has no economic rationale. Men are considered to be 'better' workers, and any skills that women develop, such as nimbleness of fingers, required for microelectronic assembly lines for example, is defined as 'natural' to women and therefore not deserving of the higher wages paid for skilled work. It is a universal trend that whenever production is reorganized due to technical changes or when there is improvement in wages and working conditions, men take over women's jobs (Gothoskar, 1992).

With liberalization and the 'retreat of the state', the women's movement, like other democratic movements, finds itself in the position of turning increasingly to the state to protect and guarantee employment rights, while votaries of the market valorize what they call 'civil society', which is defined as the sphere free from state controls. This in effect means unrestrained freedom for employers, and all social movements which represent marginalized interests recognize this as dangerous. Thus they find themselves pressing for restoring state controls while continuing to characterize the state as repesenting propertied and socially/culturally dominant interests. This is a dilemma faced all over the world by movements which have hitherto been sharply critical of the state, and it is unlikely to be resolved in the immediate future.

The Patriarchal Character of the Indian State

In the laws on rape and marriage, women's rights to property, custody and guardianship of children, the Indian state shows itself to be the protector of patriarchal values.

Marital rape is not recognized, and only penetration by the penis is considered to be rape, any other form of sexual assault however grievous, being considered a lesser crime. Feminists argue that this kind of understanding of rape is clearly based on the value of women's chastity for patriarchal systems of property and descent, and has nothing to do with the notion of women as individuals with the right to bodily integrity.

As for laws governing marriage and inheritance, religious communities have their own personal laws, and all of these discriminate against women. The Directive Principles of state policy call for the state to enact a uniform civil code, but successive governments have not so far done so, because the personal laws are protected by the Fundamental Right to freedom of religion. Some feminists see this as a prominent example of the way in which the state protects patriarchal interests. Archana Parasher (1992), for example, points out that legal discrimination against any other group would not be tolerated on religious grounds, for example, the state has passed laws against untouchability. Its refusal to enact a uniform civil code is therefore, evidence of its commitment to a patriarchal system. This understanding that a uniform civil code is a staightforward feminist demand would not be acceptable now to many feminists because the issue has become implicated in the politics of communalism and community identity, and has to be understood in a much more complex way, as we shall see in a later section.

Archana Parasher's argument is nevertheless important, becasue she tries to theorize the relationship between patriarchy and ruling class interests in the context of the Indian State. The argument she advances is that that there is no consistency in this relationship— in one sense the patriarchal structure shored up by religion is functional for capitalism, for industrialization requires a pool of cheap labour, and women fulfil this function because of unequal property relations and the sexual division of labour. In another sense, however, religion, which is one aspect of patriarchal ideology, acts as a barrier to the establishment of modern capitalist society. Religion as an institution, argues Parasher, tends to reinforce conservatism and status quo, and therefore in order to mobilize the population for rapid industrialization, the state must loosen the hold of religion and enhance its own controls. This aspect of the state is demonstrated in the Indian context by the provisions in the constitution which guarantee freedom of religion while subjecting this to constitutional restrictions, and which abolished certain religious practices held to be incompatible with modern values.

This way of approaching the intersection of patriarchal and class interests in the arena of the state enables us to recognize that different structures of oppression do not merely overlap and reinforce one another, they also act in opposition to one another, one undercutting the interests of the other. A classic instance which illustrates the often contradictory relationship between patriarchy and capitalism is the issue of protective legislation. This issue highlights the fact that from a feminist perspective, the history of production under capitalism is not only the class struggle between the producer and the owner of the means of production, it is also the relationship of the sexual division of labour to that struggle. Protective legislation—restricting of women's employment in hazardous work, reduced hours of work for women workers, maternity benefits and so on—has often been used by the male working class to restrict competition for male workers. Michele Barrett (1984) has shown how in Britain the male leadership of the labour movement resisted the unrestricted entry of women into the workforce and argued for this in terms of disruption of family life and the particular vulnerability of women. Feminists urged instead that the focus should be on extension of protective legislation and better conditions of work for all workers rather than the use of this to restrict women's employment. For capitalists on the other hand, protective legislation is not desirable because it restricts the pool of labour, thus pushing up wages for men. In India too, it has been recognized that protective legislation has been used to restrict the employment of women, and Nandita Gandhi and Nandita Shah

(1992: 193–8) point to the ambivalence on the issue among organizations involved with women workers. That is, while it is agreed that women need protective legislation, it is also recognized that demands for such legislation and the existence of such measures can lead to the employment of fewer women. Although empirical studies have shown that the actual expenditure by employers under this head is negligible, it is nevertheless used as a justification for not employing women. Many groups contest the understanding that only women need to be protected from hazardous and heavy work, that maternity and child benefits are meant for women, rather than for society as a whole, and that women cannot do night shifts, all of which assume the sexual division of labour and some 'natural' weaknesses of women.

Thus there are ambiguities and contradictions generated at the interface of different structures and relations of oppression. Feminist politics finds itself having to negotiate these in the terrain of the state. As we have seen, the relationship of women's organizations with the state is often contradictory—on the one hand, the state is seen as the primary agent perpetuating oppression of women, and on the other, the state is treated as the agent of change and potential protector of powerless sections of society. Gandhi and Shah (1992: 271–2) feel that the focus on the state in feminist campaigns is because it is easier than confronting the family, which, as we have noted in an earlier section, provides a form of institutional support women's organizations are unable to replace.

History of the Women's Movement in India

In Gandhi and Shah's view (1992), the movement can be seen in the form of three 'waves'. The first can be said to have begun with the mass mobilization of women during the national movement. After independence, for over a decade, there was a lull in political activity by women. The legitimacy accorded to the post-independence state and the developmental programmes launched by the government blunted the edge of militancy. Gradually however, the economic policies adopted by the ruling classes was unfolding its logic. Growing unemployment and rising prices led to mass uprisings, especially in Gujarat and Bihar. This period, from the late 60s onwards, can be called the second wave, with a resurgence of political activity by women. The Indian Left splintered in the early 70s, and there was a questioning of earlier analyses of revolution. In Maharashtra, the United Women's Anti Price-Rise Front, formed in 1973 by Socialists and Communists, rapidly became a mass women's movement for consumer protection. The movement spread and linked up with the students' agitation against corruption in Gujarat, and it became a massive middle class movement which soon shifted its focus to an overall critique of the Indian state. The struggle was crushed by brutal police repression and the declaration of the Emergency.

During this period there was a growth of middle-class women's organizations in urban areas as well as organizations of working women fighting for their right to independent livelihood and basic resources like credit, training and access to technology. The Self Employed Women's Association (SEWA) in Ahmedabad and Working Women's Forum in Madras were formed in this period, organizing women in the informal sector. The Bodh Gaya movement in 1978 is another landmark, which confronted a local *muth* owning most of the village land. During the struggle, women were very active and militant, and tried to combine the issue of land rights with specifically women's right to resources. However finally when the government intervened and distributed land, both the male leadership and the government rejected the women's demand that land should be given in their names. Ultimately, very little of the land was given to women.

This second wave saw mass participation of women in popular upsurges against the government, and power structures in general, but the third wave which can be said to emerge in the late 70s, had a specific feminist focus. There was the growth of 'autonomous' women's groups in towns and cities, without party affiliations or formal hierarchical structures, although individual members often had party connections. The debate in the women's movement in the late 70s/early 80s was about how feminist politics could best be conducted. The critique from women in the Left parties was that these 'autonomous' groups were urban and middle-class and therefore could not represent Indian women, and the role of feminists was therefore, to raise questions within mass organizations. However, feminists within autonomous groups pointed out that Left parties and trade unions were as patriarchal as any other and so it was necessary to stay independent while allying on a broad platform. Feminist campaigns of this period were dominated by these new city-based groups. There were nation-wide campaigns on dowry and rape, and women's resource centres were set up in several cities.

Taking this notion of 'waves' into the late 80s and further, we may note the emergence of a new feature which has transformed the landscape of the women's movement. This is the large-scale availability of funding, both from government and international sources, so that most 'autonomous' groups are now actually funded non-governmental organizations. Since the 80s, there has been a large scale co-option of feminist rhetoric by the state, and 'empowerment of women' is a slogan glibly rattled off in government documents. However, it is increasingly being recognized that this kind of government programme aims at empowering women only to the extent that it would serve the purposes of education for population control through, for example, drives against child marriage. This has resulted in a distinct shift from 'struggle' to 'development' in the agenda of womens' organizations. At the same time, the women who participate in these programmes become politicized , and often exceed the limits set by their employer, generating forces unwelcome to government functionaries. As a result, when these women go beyond the limited degree of resistance to feudal structures acceptable to the government, they end up being victimized by their employers. An example of this is the Women's Development Programme (WDP) in Rajasthan, which dismissed six employees for attending the Fourth National Conference of Women's Movements in India, held in December 1990. They were charged with having tarnished the prestige of the WDP by attending a political meeting which was critical of the government. The dismissed women made this into an issue for the wider women's movement by contacting women's groups from all over the country. A team representing six organizations from Delhi and Bombay investigated the situation, and came to the conclusion that the WDP had been successful in reducing people's distrust of the state by appropriating the legitimacy garnered by the women's movement in a larger context. The report felt that schemes patterned on the WDP were becoming the norm for women's development in the country, and urged a serious consideration of the implications of this. At the same time it felt the necessity of ensuring support from the wider movement for trade union activities by employees of such programmes (Saheli et al., 1991).

As regards funding by international agencies, in addition to the danger of co-option, the compulsions of taking up and 'successfully' completing specific projects has meant that there is hardly any serious thought given to what constitutes 'feminism'. It is as if these agencies have a clear understanding of what feminism is, and the groups funded by them only need to apply it to specific instances. Thus, autonomous womens' groups, which began as an attempt to create spaces outside the orthodoxies of party women's wings, are now far from autonomous of the compulsions of getting and retaining funding.

This growing statism and NGO-ization of the women's movement has been noted within the movement itself, leading to often acrimonious debates.

In the 90s, another feature is that a common platform has emerged at the national level with the women's wings of national level political parties—All India Democratic Women's Association, All India Women's Conference, National Federation of Indian Women, Mahila Dakshata Samiti—and three national level women's organizations, that is, the YWCA, the Joint Women's Programme and Centre for Women's Development Studies, getting together on specific issues such as, for example, the recent Bill on reservations for women in Parliament.

As one historian of the women's movement, Radha Kumar (1995), sees it, the contemporary women's movement encompasses and links up a range of issues—work, environment, ecology, civil rights, health. It is also a network which encompasses party-based, professional and independent groups.

Issues in the Women's Movement

Development

The sixth national conference of women's movements, held in Ranchi in December 1997, passed a resolution which declared, 'We fundamentally question the development model itself....' This model has resulted in the increasing impoverishment of large sections of working people, and caused a severe ecological crisis, while serving the interests of the 'dominant class/caste groups'. The resolution recognized struggles like those against the Narmada Dam and mechanized aquaculture at the Chilka Lake, against nuclear bases and against the promotion of the tourism industry at the cost of the basic needs of the local people and of the ecological balance. Such struggles, it was stated, present alternative modes of managing natural resources which are more equitable as well as being ecologically sustainable.

The New Economic Policy is sharply criticized by the resolution, for its assumption that the path of maximum profit for capital is the best course for economic development. The restructuring of industry has led to women losing their jobs and being forced into the low-paid and insecure informal sector. All marginalized sections are being further exploited in the interests of capital. The resolution states that all policy changes should be widely debated in public forums, and people's responses considered in making policy.

Sexual Violence/Violence Against Women

This came into the public view from the 80s onwards, and soon became an issue of high media visibility, with women's groups making alliances with broad democratic platforms. Today the campaign against violence includes domestic violence, rape and sexual harassment, degrading portrayal of women in the media, and the practice of selective abortion of female foetuses.

The issue of sexual violence is raised by both autonomous women's groups as well as women's wings of political parties in terms of: (a) the fundamental rights of women, (b) the failure by the state to contain sexual violence because of its lack of political will, by not taking interest in improving public services like street lighting, women's lavatories, public transport, and (c) the need to have better laws which recognize sexual violence as a crime, which have as their basis a belief in the rights of women to their bodily integrity, and not the protection of patriarchal property systems.

There is the growing recognition of sexual harassment, especially at the workplace, as a serious issue. In 1997 feminist lobbying resulted in the Supreme Court issuing a suggested Code of Conduct at the workplace to check sexual harassment (during the 'Vishakha' judgement), and as a consequence, there has been a directive from the University Grants Commission to put this into effect in universities. However, this move has not been uniformly welcomed by feminists, because there has been no attempt on the part of university authorities to take seriously the views of women's groups in campuses which have been working on this issue. As a result, the kind of committees which are on the anvil seem hastily conceived and bureaucratic, and have no provision for democratic participation from the university community as a whole. Quite apart from the efficacy or otherwise of such committees, Ratna Kapur and Shomona Khanna have pointed to a more disturbing aspect of this drive to penalise a broad range of sexual conduct (1998). They argue that while the judgement is significant because of its recognition of sexual harrassment as a widespread problem for women at the workplace, there is a danger that regulatory codes will reinforce a conservative sexual morality in which women's sexual rights will be the first casualty. They urge therefore, that feminists must adequately address the question of women's sexual autonomy and freedom of association while attempting to ensure women's equal rights at the workplace.

This emerging discussion highlights the fact that the feminist critique of the sexual commodification of women is increasingly finding it necessary to define a space in opposition to critiques of sexual freedom and autonomy coming from conservative, particularly Hindu right-wing, sections.

Dowry and dowry-related murders have been an important issue for the women's movement, especially in the 80s. The campaign launched at the time resulted in legislation which required any death of a woman within seven years of marriage to be investigated as murder. However, dowry murders and suicides raise the more fundamental question for the women's movement, of marriage as an institution. The movement has mounted an attack on growing commercialization which has accentuated the pressure for conspicuous consumption during the marriage ceremony and exacerbated the objectification of women. What has not achieved equal visibility is a feminist critique of the family as an oppressive institution.

Abortion as such has never been at the centre of much debate because of the discourse on poverty as resulting from overpopulation, so that abortion has had legitimacy as a form of family planning. Abortion became an issue for the women's movement in 1975 when for the first time, amniocentesis, used to detect foetal abnormalities, was used to selectively abort female foetusues. Women's groups formed a broad front with democratic and human rights organizations, and were successful in getting legislation passed, first in the state of Maharashtra in 1988, and then central legislation in 1994, banning sex determination tests. However, the legislation has disappointed the campaigners, because there are several loopholes in the Act which enable such tests to continue to be conducted.

Health

Feminists as well as civil rights groups in general have expressed concern at the coercion, insensitivity and medical dangers of the family planning programme, which is the best provided and often the only, medical service for women. Family planning is organizationally linked to reproductive health, and women are often denied services relating to the latter if they do not agree to forms of contraception or sterilization. Programmes of international agencies such as UNICEF and WHO also operate on the premise that women's primary role in society is that of being mothers and keepers of family health. It is assumed that it is women's ignorance which leads to high rates of infant and maternal mortality, rather than poverty, malnutrition and lack of medical facilities. So the focus is on education of mothers along with providing of services in top-down schemes which ignore the structural constraints in which poor women work. For example, the government campaign on breast-feeding is not accompanied by measures to make breast-feeding a feasible option for working mothers. There is an increasing trend to link up relief work or employment schemes with pressure for family planning; for example, the Rajasthan government gives famine relief on a priority basis to those who get themselves sterilized.

The government has also been pushing a range of hormonal contraceptives manufactured by multinational companies, despite their being banned in the West. These include injectible contraceptives like Depo Provera and Net-En. The testing of these is shrouded in secrecy and women who volunteer for the trials are only told that this will stop them from conceiving, not that this is an experiment nor that there might be serious side-effects. Women's organizations, human rights and medical practitioners have been engaged in a nation-wide campaign against such drugs and in 1986 three groups (Stree Shakti Sangathana of Hyderabad, Chingari of Ahmedabad and Saheli of Delhi), along with doctors and a journalist filed a petition in the Supreme Court against Indian Council of Medical Research, Ministry of Health and the State of Andhra Pradesh, demanding a halt to Net-En trials, full and complete information on the drug, and an enquiry into the issue.

The petition is still with the Supreme Court, but in the meanwhile, the drug is already in use by health workers. It is being recognized that the campaign cannot afford to focus on specific contraceptives, and will have to evolve a more comprehensive critique of birth control and family planning.

More importantly, the women's movement is aware that it has to break out of the framework limiting women's health to reproductive issues alone. The resolution passed at the sixth national conference of women's movements in 1997 defined health as 'socio-cultural and economic well-being of the individual,' not just as absence of disease, and noted that there have been active campaigns against gender discrimination which results in lower health status of women. At the same time, women's reproductive health has been a focal point of struggle, with simultaneously, a resistance to the view that women are reproductive beings alone, a view embodied in 'the state-controlled and eugenic population policies which try to achieve their targets through manipulation and coercion.' The resolution puts forward as its vision, 'health education, self-help, safe contraception, easy access to medical facilities and support for alternate systems of healing.'

Sexuality

It is only recently that sexuality has become a publicly articulated issue for the women's movement. Earlier, attempts to challenge the supposed 'naturalness' of heterosexuality were resisted, not only by relatively conservative sections within the movement, but also by leftist groupings which denounced such critiques as élitist, trivial and diversionary. As late as the fifth Conference on Women's Movements held in 1994 in Tirupati, an attempt to pass a resolution recognizing alternative foms of sexuality was confronted by great hostility. However, at the sixth conference in Ranchi, in 1997, the resolution states,

We seek the right to make choices about our lives, our bodies, our sexuality and our relationships. Some of us are single, some of us are married. Some of us have our primary emotional/sexual/physical/intimate relationships with men, others with women, and some with both. Some of us do not have sexual relationships. We feel that we must evolve supportive structures that can make all of these choices a meaningful reality.

I have argued (1996) that feminist politics needs to take the issue of sexuality beyond the question of 'choice'. To consider homosexuality as an 'alternative' lifestyle is to leave unquestioned institutionalized heterosexuality as the norm. The recognition and validation of the gay/lesbian experience would require feminism to radically rethink what 'genderedness' itself is and to question the naturalness of two biological sexes. We would then be led to a recognition that the boundaries of the apparently stable self are cultural and historical constructs, not an immutable reality we are irrevocably faced with. Such a recognition could lead feminist practice into an emancipatory dislocation from sterile engagement with legal discourse and hegemonic cultural productions of selfhood. We would be forced then to constantly interrogate the processes by which we construct the 'women' who are the subjects of our feminist political practice.

Work

There is a trend of decline in women's participation in non-agricultural sectors of the economy, and the majority of the female workforce (94 per cent according to the 1981 census) is concentrated in the unorganized sector. Women's jobs in industry are those that men do not care for—unskilled, semi-skilled, low grade office jobs, or assembly lines. In addition, when manual jobs traditionally performed by women are mechanized, men take up that work, and women have no alternative training or employment. For example, electrically operated flour mills replacing the traditional work of hand-pounding of grains by women, or nylon fishing nets made by machines replacing those traditionally hand-made by women. On the one hand, women are considered to be unfit for heavy manual labour, but both in informal sector and in household work, they do the heaviest of jobs—carrying headloads of water, grinding corn, heavy headloads in mining, construction etc. On the other, when mechanization makes a job lighter, then women are considered to be unfit to be trained to use the machinery. We have already noted in an earlier section, that women's jobs are increasingly being shifted from the formal to the informal sector, where there is no security of employment, lower wages, more work and no trade union rights.

The Equal Wages Act was passed in 1975, assuring equal pay for 'equal work or work of a similar nature'. This law is nowhere effective, because whenever there is a struggle to implement the Act, employers respond by re-classifying the jobs done by women to show it is not 'work of a similar nature'. In any case, a tradition exists of women's work and men's work, which determines skill training. So already women are segregated into specific jobs which can then be defined as differentially paid because it is different work, not because women are doing it. The issue for women struggling in the area of work and equal wages is therefore, how to break the equation between women, inferior work and low wages.

Persistent issues for struggle have been security of employment, living wage, regulation of hours of work, discriminatory treatment and the right to organize. Women workers and unions have also adopted legal strategies and won important victories—pharmaceutical workers in the 60s getting the 'no marriage' clause struck down, Air India hostesses in 1981 obtaining the striking down of validity of regulations terminating employment on pregnancy, and in 1983, against the Kerala Government, striking down of policies designating jobs as male (Gothoskar, 1992).

Women have also had to struggle within unions against patriarchal assumptions and sexist attitudes (Gothoskar, 1992: 31–7; Menon, 1992).

Reservations for Women in Representative Institutions

The percentage of women in the Lok Sabha has fluctuated between 8.1 per cent in 1984 and 3.4 per cent in 1977, and in 1996 was 7.1 per cent. The issue of reservations for women had come up in the Constituent Assembly but had been rejected by women representatives as it was felt to be unnecessary and underestimated the strength of women to compete as equals. Twenty-five years later the Committee on the Status of Women in India considered the same question. It was agreed that rural women's empowerment and problems had remained undervalued and invisible. The Committee therefore unanimously recommended the establishment of statutory women's panchayats. The Panchayat Acts of most states had reserved one or two seats for women, to be filled by nomination if no woman was returned by election. But this had remained a token gesture and CSWI recommended instead, that the reserved seats be occupied by elected office-bearers of the women's panchayats. However, the CSWI by a majority decided to uphold the position taken in the Constitutional Assembly that there should be no reservations in Legislative Assemblies and Parliament.

The arguments made for reservations were mainly: (a) Parties were reluctant to sponsor women candidates because of the overall patriarchal character of Indian politics, (b) Reservations would increase the number of women at one go and the inhibitions arising from their minority status would disappear faster, leading to increase in political participation, and (c) Presence of more women in legislatures would lead to changes in direction of debates and policy.

Arguments against reservations included: (a) Women cannot be equated to socially backward communities as women are not a socially homogeneous group, (b) Women's interests could not be isolated from those of other economic and social strata, and (c) Such a measure would lead to demands from other groups/ communities, which could pose a threat to national integration (*Towards Equality,* 1975).

In 1987, Karnataka pioneered the step of reserving 25 per cent of seats for women in panchayats and zilla parishads (PRI), and this was extended nation-wide by the 73rd and 74th Constitutional Amendment Acts in 1992. Studies on the experience of Karnataka show that reservations for women has only strengthened the entrenched power of the dominant castes (UMA Resource Centre 1995). Male relatives usually coach women to speak at meetings, and do the actual paper work when the women are illiterate. There has been no significant reallocation of domestic work in the families of women panchayat members. Studies in Gujarat, Kerala and Karnataka (Nair, 1997) have shown that the more effective participation has come from women in the age group of 25 to 40, for whom child-bearing and rearing responsibilities are less pressing. The lack of training in political work is a severe impediment, governments have taken no responsibilty to impart training, and thus it is only taken up sporadically by concerned NGOs. A study of West Bengal demonstrates that dalit and tribal males have gained from reservations in PRI, but women have gained little, their chances growing even more limited if they are both poor and dalit (ibid.).

At the same time, in many cases women have acquired confidence and managed to make some noticeable effects in local power structures. Women have also been successful in raising specific issues with a gender dimension, for example, the need for covered toilets. Where reservations in PRI have been most succcessful has been in villages where there is active politicization through women's groups. In other words, there is no alternative to political activism, equality cannot be legislated into existence.

The most recent attempt has been to reserve 33 per cent of seats in parliament for women, as embodied in the 81st Amendment Bill of 1996. Despite the fact that all national political parties formally endorse this demand, the Bill could not even be tabled in parliament due to overall opposition and its future remains uncertain.

It is possible, in my opinion, to discern, in the recent debate on this issue, two kinds of arguments for and against reservations—feminist arguments for and against, and caste-based arguments for and against.

Feminist arguments for reservations are made in terms of the need for affirmative action, reaffirming the principle of equal rights, and making a link between presence of women in parliament and gender justice. This kind of argument is made by Left parties and women's groups.

Feminist arguments against reservations are made in the light of the experience of reservations in PRI which, as we have seen, has not been favourable. This argument is made principally, by the Shetkari Mahila Aghadi from Maharashtra, which has been campaigning instead for full panels of women candidates in panchayat elections.

Caste-based arguments against reservations appear to be misogynist—for example, the infamous statement by Sharad Yadav that reservations would only benefit *parkati mahilaen* (women with cropped hair), that is, the stereotype of urbanized 'westernized' women. However, this remark is better understood as an expression of the fear that the composition of parliament would be radically altered in favour of upper classes and castes. In the last decade, the character of Parliament has dramatically changed with growing Backward Caste assertion, and reservations for women would definitely, at least in the short term, swing the balance back.

Caste-based arguments for reservations for women which are made in apparently feminist terms, by for example, the Bharatiya Janata Party, must be understood in the context of its equally strong protests about the Mandal Commission reservations. It then becomes clear that the real concern is to contest Backward Caste assertion.

The Uniform Civil Code

It is important to note that the debate on the UCC has rarely surfaced in public consciousness as a feminist issue. Both in the media and in judicial pronouncements, the need for a UCC has invariably been cast in terms of the integrity of the nation, which is seen to be under threat from the existence of plural systems of legality. Conversely, resistance to the UCC comes from community leaders on the grounds that it destroys the cultural identity of minorities, the protection of which is the bedrock of democracy. Thus the UCC debate has polarized around the twin axes of State and Community, rendering invisible the issue of gender justice.

The argument of national integrity as the rationale for a UCC is deeply problematic for feminists, for two reasons. The immediately disturbing one is that underlying this argument is the explicit assumption that while the 'other' communities continue to cling to diverse and retrogressive laws, threatening the integrity of the nation state, Hindus have willingly accepted reform.

It is however, misleading to claim that Hindu Personal Law was reformed. It was merely codified, and even that was in the face of stiff resistance from Congress leaders. Moreover, these new acts were by no means an unqualified advance for women's rights. On the contrary, codification put an end to the diversity of Hindu law as it was practiced in different regions, in the process destroying existing, more liberal provisions in many cases (Kishwar, 1994).

The more fundamental problem with the national integrity argument emerges from the first point, that is, from the recognition of the homogenizing thrust of the Hindu Code. The rejection of practices and lifestyles which did not conform to a particular North Indian, upper caste construction of the family was legitimated on the grounds that these other practices were not 'Indian'. It is increasingly being felt that feminists, as advocates of democratic politics more generally, must resist the process of constituting 'the nation' as an objective entity which is beyond questioning. As suggested by the discussion on the coming into being of the Hindu Code, this entity is constructed only through the marginalization and exclusion of a multiplicity of other interests and identities. In every way that the nation is constituted by dominant discourses, the powerless and the marginal are defined out of its boundaries. The discourse of 'development', for example, violently excludes the hundreds of thousands of people whose lives and livelihoods must be destroyed by large projects so that 'the nation' may progress.

On the other hand, feminists cannot accept the unqualified rights of communities to their cultural identity, although the providing of space for such identity is crucial for a democratic polity. For one thing, the 'community' identity that is claimed today as natural and prior to all other identity is no more primordial than the nation is. The Personal Laws being defended in the name of 'religious' freedom are constructions of the nineteenth–twentieth centuries. The Hindu Code in 1955 completed the process of congealing 'Hindu' identity begun in the nineteenth century, by establishing as 'Hindu' all those who were not Muslim, Christian or Parsi. Similarly the Shariat Act of 1937 drew the boundaries of the 'Muslim' community while earlier, customary law had been widely followed.

Feminists also feel the need to reject community identity as an overriding one for another reason. This is the fact that the rights claimed by communities vis-à-vis the state—autonomy, selfhood, access to resources—are denied by communities to 'their' women. In other words, the discriminatory provisions of the personal laws are based on the same logic of exclusions that characterise the coming into being of the nation and must be rejected on the same grounds.

The demand for a Uniform Civil Code for all religious communities was first made by the All India Women's Conference in 1937. Sixty years later, this demand is certainly not made by the Indian women's movement with the same confidence. By 1993, at the Northern Region Nari Mukti Sangharsh Sammelan (Women's Liberation Struggle Conference) held in Kanpur, there were two resolutions put forward for debate, one calling for a UCC, and the other for a rethinking of the notion of uniformity, keeping in mind the use of the demand for a UCC by the right-wing forces of the majority community. Finally, the resolution that was unanimously passed was meant to incorporate both views. And at the Fifth National Conference of Women's Studies held in Jaipur in 1995, what emerged was a broad range of positions, from the reassertion of the demand for a UCC, to outright rejection of such a move, and calling instead for reforms within personal laws.

Many Indian feminists see this shift merely as a nervous reaction to Hindu communalism. However, for others it reflects a deeper dilemma at this historical conjuncture for feminist politics, and in general for secular/democratic politics. It might be more productive, in other words, to map the shifts in the trajectory of feminist thinking on the UCC, in terms of the troubled attempts at different levels to re-engage with notions of citizenship, nation and gender.

Conclusion

Feminist 'theory' has always resisted the implied dichotomy with 'practice', and has therefore continuously been in a dynamic relationship with politics on the ground. Thus, there are very real stakes involved, and the debates and disagreements within the women's movement in India are as significant as its opposition to what it struggles against. Nevertheless, despite these complex internal critiques, it is possible to discern a shared concern about the ways in which 'gender' gets defined, institutionalized and mobilized in perpetuating inequality and injustice. It is this concern which marks out a field which can be called feminist politics.

References

Feminist Critiques of 'The Golden Vedic Age'

Chakravarty, Uma, 1993, 'Conceptualising Brahminical Patriarchy', *EPW,* 3 April, p. 579.

———— 'Beyond the Altekerian Paradigm: Towards a new Understanding of Gender Relations in Early Indian History', in A. Suryakumari (ed.), *Women's Studies: An Emerging Discipline,* Gyan Publishing House, New Delhi, pp 1–12.

———— 1989, 'Whatever Happened to the Vedic Dasi?', in Kumkum Sangari and Sudesh Vaid (eds), *Recasting Women,* Kali for Women, New Delhi.

Roy, Kumkum, 1995, 'Where Women are Worshipped, There the Gods Rejoice', in Urvashi Butalia and Tanika Sarkar (eds), *Women and the Hindu Right,* Kali for Women, New Delhi, p. 10

Social Reform Movements of the Nineteenth Century

Chatterjee, Partha, 1989, 'The Nationalist Resolution of the Women's Question', in Kumkum Sangari and Sudesh Vaid (eds), *Recasting Women,* Kali for Women, New Delhi.

———— 1993, *The Nation and its Fragments,* Oxford University Press, New Delhi.

Kumar, Radha, 1993, *The History of Doing,* Kali for Women, New Delhi, Ch. 2.

Mani, Lata, 1989, 'Contentious Traditions: The Debate on Sati in Colonial India', in Kumkum Sangari and Sudesh Vaid (eds), *Recasting Women*, Kali for Women, New Delhi.

Nandy, Ashis, 1983, *The Intimate Enemy*, Oxford University Press, New Delhi.

Yang, Anand, 1987, 'The Many Faces of Sati in the Early Nineteenth Century', *Manushi* No. 42–3.

The National Movement

Kannabiran, Vasanth and K. Lalita, 1989, 'That Magic Time: Women in the Telengana Peoples' Struggle', in Kumkum Sangari and Sudesh Vaid (eds), *Recasting Women*, Kali for Women, New Delhi.

Kasturi, Leela and Vina Mazumdar, 1994, 'Women and Indian Nationalism', Occasional Paper, Centre for Women's Development Studies, New Delhi.

Kishwar, Madhu, 1985, 'Gandhi on Women', *EPW*, 5 October, p. 1691.

Kumar, Radha, 1993, *The History of Doing*, Kali for Women, New Delhi, Chs. 4, 5.

Liddle, Joanna and Rama Joshi, 1985, 'Gender and Imperialism in British India', *EPW*, 26 October, WS-72.

Religion and Feminist Politics

Agnes, Flavia, 1995, 'Redefining the Agenda of the Women's Movement within a Secular Framework', in Urvashi Butalia and Tanika Sarkar (eds), *Women and the Hindu Right*, Kali for Women, New Delhi, p. 136.

Dietrich, Gabriele, 1994, 'Women and Religious Identities in India after Ayodhya', in Kamla Bhasin, Ritu Menon and Nighat Said Khan (eds), *Against All Odds: Essays on Women, Religion and Development from India and Pakistan*, Kali for Women, New Delhi.

Hasan, Zoya, (ed.), 1994 *Forging Identities: Gender, Communities and the State*, Kali for Women, New Delhi.

Omvedt, Gail, 1994, 'Reconstructing the Methodology of Exploitation. Class, Caste and Gender as Categories of Analysis in Post-colonial Societies', in Neera Chandoke (ed.), *Understanding the Postcolonial World. Theory and Method*, Sterling Publishers, New Delhi.

Sangari, Kumkum, 1995, 'Politics of Diversity. Religious Communities and Multiple Patriarchies', *EPW*, 23 December, p. 3287.

Sarkar, Tanika, 1991, 'The Woman as Communal Subject', *EPW*, 31 August, p. 2057.

Of Related Interest

Anon, 1995, 'Oppressed Castes and Communities', in *Lokayan Bulletin*, July–October, pp 137–40.

Chhachhi, Amrita, 1989, 'The State, Religious Fundamentalism and Women: Trends in South Asia', *EPW*, 18 March.

Engineer, Asghar Ali, 1994, 'Status of Muslim Women', in *EPW*, 5 February.

Kapur, Ratna and Brenda Cossman, 1993, 'Women, Legal Discourse and the Saffron Agenda', *EPW*, 3 April, WS-35.

Sangari, Kumkum and Sudesh Vaid, 1991, 'Widow Immolation in Contemporary Rajasthan', *EPW*, 27 April, WS-2.

Feminist Assessments of the Political Economy

Bardhan, Pranab, 1984, *The Political Economy of Development in India*, Oxford University Press, New Delhi.

Deshpande S. and L.K. Deshpande, 1992, 'New Economic Policy and Female Employment', *Economic and Political Weekly*, 10 October.

Ghosh, Jayati, 1994, 'Gender Concerns in Macro Economic Policy', *EPW* 30 April, WS-2.

——— 'The Human Development Report 1995: A Consideration from an Indian Perspective', in Nitya Rao, Luise Rurup and R. Sudarshan (eds), *Sites of Change*, Friedrich Ebert Stiftung and UNDP, New Delhi, 1996.

Gothoskar, Sujata (ed.), 1992, *Struggles of Women at Work*, Vikas, New Delhi, Introduction

Jhabvala, Renana, 1985, *Closing Doors*, SETU Publications, Ahmedabad.

Kaviraj, Sudipta, 1988, 'A Critique of the Passive Revolution', *EPW*, Annual Number.

Kurien, C.T., 1994, *Global Capitalism and the Indian Economy*, Orient Longman, New Delhi.

Savara, Meera, 1982, *Changing Trends in Women's Employment*, Himalaya Publishing House, Bombay.

Shah, Nandita, Sujata Gothoskar, Nandita Gandhi and Amrita Chhachhi, 1994, 'Structural Adjustment, Feminisation of Labour Force and Organisational Strategies', *EPW*, 30 April (included in this reader).

Of Related Interest

Anon, 1995, 'The Impact of New Economic Policies', *Lokayan Bulletin*, July–October, pp 75–88.

Chakravarty, Sukhamoy, 1987, *Development Planning: The Indian Experience,* New Delhi, Oxford University Press.

Chaudhuri , Maitrayee, 1996, 'Citizens, Workers and Emblems of Culture: An Analysis of the First Plan Document on Women', in Patricia Uberoi (ed.), *Social Reform, Sexuality and the State,* Sage, New Delhi.

Dewan, Ritu 1995, 'Gender in Neo-classical Economics', *EPW,* 29 April, WS-46.

Jones, Jan Sinclair, 1996, 'Women and Technology', *EPW,* 20–27 April, WS-31.

The Patriarchal Character of the Indian State

Barrett, Michele, 1984, *Women's Oppression Today. Problems in Marxist Feminist Analysis,* Verso, London.

Gandhi, Nandita and Nandita Shah, 1992, *The Issues at Stake, Theory and Practice in the Contemporary Women's Movement in India,* Kali for Women, New Delhi, Chs 5 and 6.

Parasher, Archana, 1992, *Women and Family Law Reform in India,* Sage, New Delhi, Introduction, Ch. 1.

History of the Women's Movement in India

Gandhi, Nandita and Nandita Shah, 1992, *The Issues at Stake: Theory and Practice in the Contemporary Women's Movement in India,* Kali for Women, New Delhi, Chs 2 and 7. (Chapter 7 is included in this reader.)

Kumar, Radha, 1993, *The History of Doing,* Kali for Women, New Delhi, Ch. 6.

Saheli, Sabala Sangh, 1991, Action India, Disha, Women's Centre, Forum Against Oppression of Women, Awaz-e-Niswan, *Development for Whom—A Critique of Women's Development Programmes.*

Issues in the Women's Movement

Gothoskar, Sujata (ed.), 1992, *Struggles of Women at Work,* Vikas, New Delhi, Introduction.

Kapur, Ratna and Shomona Khanna, 1998, 'Women's Right to Law', *The Hindu,* Sunday, 26 April.

Kishwar, Madhu, 1994, 'Codified Hindu Law: Myth and Reality', *Economic and Political Weekly,* 13 August.

Kumar, Radha, 1993, *The History of Doing,* Kali for Women, New Delhi, Chs 7–12.

Menon, Nivedita, 1992, 'Women in Trade Unions: A Study of AITUC INTUC and CITU in the Seventies', in Sujata Gothoskar (ed.), *Struggles of Women at Work,* Vikas, New Delhi.

—— 'Destabilising Feminism', 1996, *Seminar* 437, January.

Nair, Janaki, 1997, 'An Important Springboard', *Seminar* 457, September.

UMA Resource Centre, 1995, 'Challenge and Opportunity: A Study of Women Panchayat Representatives in Karnataka', Occasional Paper Series 1.

Of Related Interest

Agnes, Flavia, 1995, 'Women and Law Reform: A Historical Perspective', in *State, Gender and the Rhetoric of Law Reform,* SNDT University Bombay, pp 188–228.

Agnihotri, Indu and Veena Mazumdar, 1995, 'Changing the Terms of Political Discourse', in *Lokayan Bulletin,* July–October.

Menon, Nivedita, 1998. 'Women and Citizenship' in Partha Chatterjee (ed.), *Wages of Freedom,* Oxford University Press, New Delhi.

—— 1996, 'The Impossibility of 'Justice': Female Foeticide and Feminist Discourse on Abortion', in Patricia Uberoi (ed.), *Social Reform, Sexuality and the State,* Sage, New Delhi.

Omvedt, Gail, 1993, Reinventing Revolution, New York, M E Sharpe Inc., Ch. 9.

Seminar, 1997, Issue on the Women's Reservations Bill , 457, September.

Tharu, Susie, 'Towards a Historiography of Women in People's Struggles', in A. Suryakumari (ed.), *Women's Studies: An Emerging Discipline,* Gyan Publishing House, New Delhi, pp. 89–104.

Gender and Environment

The extract from Vandana Shiva is a statement of her celebrated 'ecofeminism' critique of development in the context of government policy on forests. Her argument is that through movements like Chipko, what is reflected is a struggle in Indian society between two fundamentally different world-views. On the one hand is the life destroying and masculinist perspective of the commercial forestry system, which treats forests as a resource to be exploited for its monetary value, and which sets up private property in forest wealth. This perspective has the backing of agencies of the state, and has also colonized, 'cognitively, economically and politically', the local men. On the other hand is the feminine life-conserving principle embodied in seeing the forest as a diverse and self-reproducing system, shared as a commons by a diversity of social groups.

Gabriele Dietrich, from her perspective as a political activist in a women's group in Madurai for fifteen years, takes this argument forward, suggesting that we need to think both in terms of ecology and culture, and of how these two aspects are linked in terms of feminist politics. The question then is both to create a mode of production which does not depend on the exploitation of nature but works in harmony with it, as well as to create a counter-culture which 'arrests both the trends towards uniformity and towards fragmentation'. While drawing upon the work of Shiva which establishes the connection between ecological destruction and capitalist growth as a patriarchal project, Dietrich is troubled by its silence on two crucial questions of culture.

One, Shiva tends to unproblematically take the 'feminine principle' as expressed in upper-caste Hindu terms, which leaves open the question of what this can mean for non-Hindu and lower-caste world-views. Moreover, given the communalization of the polity in recent times, Dietrich points to the possibility of the appropriation of this notion by the Hindu Right.

Two, Shiva is blind caste as a mediating factor in the relationship of class and patriarchy. Dietrich argues that an ecologically sustaining system is perfectly compatible with a hierarchical and patriarchal society based on caste division of labour, and that this is in fact what obtained in pre-capitalist Indian society.

Bina Agarwal's critique of Shiva's analysis points both to its essentializing of 'women' which bypasses the question of the material rooting of the relationship of men and women to nature, and to its focus on Western science as the epistemological underpinning of colonialism which is supposed to have destroyed hitherto democratic forms of community. Agarwal holds that this view misses out on the precolonial forms of power and property relations which were unequal and unjust, and suggests an alternative framework, which she calls environmental feminism.

1

Colonialism and the Evolution of Masculinist Forestry

Vandana Shiva

When the British colonized India, they first colonized her forests. Ignorant of their wealth and of the wealth of knowledge of local people to sustainably manage the forests, they displaced local rights, local needs and local knowledge and reduced this primary source of life into a timber mine. Women's subsistence economy based on the forest was replaced by the commercial economy of British colonialism. Teak from Malabar was extracted for the King's Navy, and the *sal* of Central India and the conifers of the Himalaya were exploited for the railway system. Although it is always local people who are held responsible for deforestation, it is commercial demands that have more frequently resulted in large-scale forest destruction. In the Himalayan region there is evidence that it was the needs of the Empire and not of the local people that led to rapid forest denudation. According to Atkinson's *Gazetteer*,

The forests were denuded of good trees in all places. The destruction of trees of all species appears to have continued steadily and reached its climax between 1855 and 1861, when the demands of the Railway authorities induced numerous speculators to enter into contracts for sleepers, and these men were allowed, unchecked, to cut down old trees very far in excess of what they could possibly export, so that for some years after the regular forest operations commenced, the department was chiefly busy cutting up and bringing to the depot the timber left behind by the contractors.[1]

[1] E.T. Atkinson, *Himalayan Gazetteer*, vol. III, Allahabad: Government Press, 1882, p. 852.

When the British started exploiting Indian timber for military purposes, they did it rapaciously and in ignorance, because the

great continent appeared to hold inexhaustible tracts covered with dense jungles, but there was no apparent necessity for their detailed exploration, even had this been a possibility. In the early years of our occupation the botany of the forests, the species of tress they contained and their respective values was an unopened book.[2]

To the colonial government and its officials the critical role that forests play in nature and the great influence they exercise on the physical well-being of a country went unrecognized. In view of the large forest wealth that existed, the government for some years obtained its full requirement without difficulty, while local needs were also met. The early administrators appear to have been convinced that this state of affairs could go on for an unlimited period. In many localities forests were viewed as an obstruction to agriculture, which was taxed, and were seen therefore as a limiting factor to the prosperity of the colonizer. The policy was to extend agriculture and the watchword was to clear the forests with this end in view. Virgin forests of the Doon Valley were thus clearfelled for land grants made exclusively to British settlers.[3]

The military requirement for Indian teak led to an immediate proclamation declaring that the royalty right in teak trees claimed by the former government in the south of the continent was vested in the East India Company. In the year 1799 alone, 10,000 teak trees were brought down the Beypur River in Malabar. Under further pressure from the Home Government to ensure the maintenance of the future strength of the King's Navy, a decision was taken to appoint a special officer to superintend forest work—his duties were to preserve and improve the production of teak and other timber suitable for shipbuilding. Captain Watson of the police was appointed the first Conservator of Forests in India on November 10, 1806. Under the proclamation of April 1807, he wielded great powers. He soon established a timber monopoly throughout Malabar and Travancore and furnished the government, as did his immediate successors, with a plentiful supply of cheap

[2] E.P. Stebbing, *The Forests of India* (reprint), New Delhi: A.J. Reprints Agency, 1982, p. 61.

[3] J. Bandyopadhyay et al., *The Doon Valley Ecosystem*, mimeo, 1983.

timber. But the methods by which this was done were intolerable and gradually gave rise to seething discontent amongst both local peasants as well as proprietors. The feeling rose to such a pitch that the Conservatorship was abolished in 1823.[4]

The introduction of colonial forestry was thus established not because of superior forestry knowledge or scientific management, but through dominant military need and power. It was only after more than half a century of uncontrolled forest destruction by British commercial interests that an attempt was made to control exploitation. In 1865 the first Indian Forest Act (VII of 1865) was passed by the Supreme Legislative Council, which authorized the government to declare forests and wastelands (*benap* or unmeasured lands) as reserved forests.

The introduction of this legislation marks the beginning of what is called the 'scientific management' of forests; it amounted basically to the formalization of the erosion both of forests and of the rights of local people to forest produce. Commercial forestry, which is equated with 'scientific forestry' by those narrow interests exemplified by western patriarchy is reductionist in intellectual content and ecological impact, and generates poverty at the socio-economic level for those whose livelihoods and productivity depend on the forest. Reductionism has been characteristic of this forestry because it sunders forestry from water management, from agriculture and from animal husbandry. Within the forest ecosystem it has reduced the diversity of life to the dead product, wood, and wood in turn to commercially valuable wood only. A commercial interest has the primary objective of maximizing exchange value on the market through the extraction of commercially valuable species—forest ecosystems are therefore reduced to the timber of such species. By ignoring the complex relationship within the forest community and between plant life and other resources like soil and water, this pattern of resource use generates instabilities in the ecosystem and leads to counterproductive use of nature as a living and self-reproducing resource. The destruction of the forest ecosystem and the multiple functions of forest resources in turn hurts the economic interest of those groups of society, mainly women and tribals, who depend on the diverse resource functions of the forests for their survival. These include soil and water

[4] Stebbing, op. cit., p. 65.

stabilization and the provision of food, fodder, fuel, fertilizer, etc. In the alternative feminine forestry science which has been subjugated by the masculinist science, forests are not viewed as merely a stock of wood, isolated from the rest of the ecosystem, nor is their economic value reduced to the commercial value of timber. 'Productivity', 'yield' and 'economic value' are defined for nature and for women's work as *satisfying basic needs through an integrated ecosystem managed for multipurpose utilization.* Their meaning and measure is therefore entirely different from the meaning and measure employed in reductionist masculinist forestry. In a shift from ecological forestry to reductionist forestry all scientific terms are changed from ecosystem-dependent to ecosystem-independent ones. Thus while for women, tribals and other forest communities a complex ecosystem is productive in terms of water, herbs, tubers, fodder, fertilizer, fuel, fibre and as a genepool, for the forester, these components are useless, unproductive waste and dispensable. Two economic perspectives lead to two notions of 'productivity' and 'value'. As far as women's productivity in survival and overall productivity are concerned, the natural tropical forest is a highly productive ecosystem. Examining the forests of the humid tropics from an ecological perspective Golley has noted, 'A large biomass is generally characteristic of tropical forests. The quantities of wood especially are large in tropical forests and average about 300 tons per ha. compared with about 150 tons per ha. for temperate forests.'[5] However, in reductionist commercial forestry, overall productivity is subordinated to industrial use, and large biomass to species that can be profitably marketed—industrial and commercial biomass prevail; all the rest is waste. As Bethel, an international forestry consultant says, referring to the large biomass typical of forests in the humid tropics:

It must be said that from a standpoint of industrial material supply, this is relatively unimportant. The important question is how much of this biomass represents trees and parts of trees of *preferred species that can be profitably marketed....* By today's utilisation standards, *most of the trees in*

---

[5] F.B. Golley, *Productivity and Mineral Cycling in Tropical Forests' Productivity of World Ecosystems*, Washington: National Academy of Sciences, 1975, pp. 106–15.

these humid tropical forests are, from an industrial materials standpoint, clearly weeds.[6]

The 'industrial materials standpoint' is the standpoint of a capitalist and patriarchal reductionist forestry which splits the living diversity and democracy of the forest into commercially useful dead wood which it valorizes, and ecologically valuable weeds which it characterizes as waste. This waste, however, is the wealth of biomass that maintains nature's water and nutrient cycles and satisfies the needs of food, fuel, fodder, fertilizer, fibre and medicine of agricultural communities.

Since it is women's work that protects and conserves nature's life in forestry and in agriculture, and through such conservation work, sustains human life through ensuring the provision of food and water, the destruction of the integrity of forest ecosystems is most vividly and concretely experienced by peasant women. For them forestry is married to food production; it is essential for providing stable, perennial supplies of water for drinking and for irrigation, and for providing the fertility directly as green manure or as organic matter cycled through farm animals. Women's agricultural work in regions like the Himalaya is largely work in and with the forest, yet it is discounted both in forestry and in agriculture. The only forestry-related work that goes into census data is lumbering and tree-felling; cutting trees then becomes a source of *roti* or food for the men engaged in lumbering operations; for the women however, forests are food, not in death, but in life. The living forest provides the means for sustainable food production systems in the form of nutrients and water, and women's work in the forest facilitates this process. When, for example, women lop trees they enhance the productivity of the oak forest under stable conditions and under common ownership and control. While an unlopped tree has leaves that are too hard for cattle, lopping makes them soft and palatable, especially in early spring. Maintaining the diversity of living resources is critical to the feminine use of the forest: thus oak-leaf along with a mixture of dried grasses and agricultural by-products is fed to cattle through the late autumn, winter and into spring. In the monsoon, the green grass becomes the dominant fodder, and in October and November, agricultural

[6] James A. Bethel, 'Sometimes the Word is "Weed"', in *Forest Management*, June 1984, pp. 17–22.

waste such as rice straw, *mandua* straw and *jangora* straw become the primary supply of fodder. Lopping has never been viewed as a forest management strategy for using tree produce while conserving the tree. Yet, as Bandyopadhyay and Moench[7] have shown, lopping under appropriate conditions can actually *increase* the forest density and fodder productivity of the forest. Groups of women, young and old, go together to lop for fodder, and expertise develops by participation and through learning-by-doing. These informal forestry colleges of the women are small and decentred; creating and transferring knowledge about how to maintain the life of living resources. The visible forestry colleges by contrast are centralized and alienated: they specialize in a forestry of destruction, on how to transform a living resource into a commodity and subsequently, cash.

The dispossession of the local people of their rights, their resources and their knowledge has not gone unchallenged. Forest struggles have been taking place throughout the country for over two centuries to resist the colonization of the people's forests in India. The access and rights of the people to forests were first severely encroached upon with the introduction of the Forest Acts of 1878 and 1927. The following years witnessed the spread of forest satyagrahas throughout India, as a protest against the reservation of forests for exclusive exploitation by British commercial interest, and their concomitant transformation from a common resource into a commodity. Villagers ceremonially removed forest products from the reserved forests to assert their right to satisfy their basic needs. The forest satyagrahas were especially successful in regions where survival of the local population was intimately linked with access to the forests, as in the Himalaya, the Western Ghats, and the Central Indian hills. These non-violent protests were systematically crushed by the British; in Central India, Gond tribals were gunned down for participating in the protests; in 1930 dozens of unarmed villagers were killed and hundreds injured in Tilari village in Tehri Garhwal, when they gathered to protest against the Forest Laws of the local rulers. After enormous loss of life, the satyagrahis were successful in reviving some of the traditional rights

[7] Bandyopadhyay and M. Moench, 'Local Needs and Forest Resource Management in the Himalaya', in Bandyopadhyay et al., *India's Environment: Crisis and Responses*, Dehradun: Natraj Publishers, 1985, p. 56.

of the village communities to various forest products.[8] The Forest Policy of post-colonial India continued on the colonial path of commercialization and reductionism, and with it continued people's resistance to a denial of their basic needs, both through alienation of rights and through ecological degradation.

In the mountain regions of the Himalaya, the women of Garhwal started to protect their forests from commercial exploitation even at the cost of their lives, by starting the famous Chipko movement, embracing the living trees as their protectors. Beginning in the early 1970s in the Garhwal region of Uttar Pradesh, the methodology and philosophy of Chipko has now spread to Himachal Pradesh in the north, to Karnataka in the south, to Rajasthan in the west, to Orissa in the east, and to the Central Indian highlands.

The Women of Chipko

Women's environmental action in India preceded the UN Women's Decade as well as the 1972 Stockholm Environment Conference. Three hundred years ago more than 300 members of the Bishnoi community in Rajasthan, led by a woman called Amrita Devi, sacrificed their lives to save their sacred *khejri* trees by clinging to them. With that event begins the recorded history of Chipko.[9]

The recent Chipko movement has popularly been referred to as a women's movement, but it is only some male Chipko activists who have been projected into visibility. The women's contribution has been neglected and remains invisible, in spite of the fact that the history of Chipko is a history of the visions and actions of exceptionally courageous women. Environmental movements like Chipko have become historical landmarks because they have been fuelled by the ecological insights and political and moral strengths of women. I will dwell at some length on some of these exceptional women because I have personally been inspired by my interaction with them, and because I feel that it is unjust that the real pillars of the movement are still largely unknown. The experience of these powerful women also needs to be shared to remind us that we are not alone, and that we do not take the first steps: others have walked before us.

[8] J. Bandyopadhyay and V. Shiva, 'Chipko: Politics of Ecology' in *Seminar*, No. 330, 1987.

[9] R.S. Bishnoi, *Conservation as Creed*, Dehradun: Jugal Kishore, 1987, letter from Gandhi to Mirabehn, 16 January 1948.

In the history of social and political movements, the evolution is generally neglected, and only the end result focused on. This creates two problems: first, future organizational work does not benefit from the lessons of perseverence and patience born of years of movement building; people start looking for instant solutions because it is the instant successes that have been sold through pseudo history. Second, while the historical evolution of movements involves significant contributions from thousands of participants over extended periods, their climaxes are localized in space and time. This facilitates the appropriation of the movement by an individual or group who then erases the contributions of others. Movements are major social and political processes, however, and they transcend individual actors. They are significant precisely because they involve a multiplicity of people and events which contribute to a reinforcement of social change.

The Chipko process as a resurgence of woman power and ecological concern in the Garhwal Himalaya is a similar mosaic of many events and multiple actors. The significant catalysers of the transformations which made Chipko resistance possible have been women like Mira Behn, Sarala Behn, Bimala Behn, Hima Devi, Gauri Devi, Gunga Devi, Bachni Devi, Itwari Devi, Chamun Devi and many others. The men of the movement like Sunderlal Bahuguna, Chandi Prasad Bhatt, Ghanshyam Shailani and Dhoom Singh Negi have been their students and followers. Mira Behn was one of Gandhi's closest disciples who moved to the Himalayan region in the late 40s. Between Rishikesh and Hardwar she started a cattle centre called Pashulok, because cattle are central to sustainable agriculture. Writing to Mira Behn fifteen days before his death, Gandhi said:

I see that you are destined for serving the cow and nothing else. But I seem to see a vital defect in you. You are unable to cling to anything finally. You are a gypsy, never happy unless you are wandering. You will not become an expert in anything and your mother is also likely to perish in your lap. The only person, and that a woman, who really loves the cow, will fail her. Shall I pity you, the cow or me, for I, the originator of the real idea of serving and saving the cow for humanity, have never cared or perhaps never had the time to become even a moderate expert.[10]

[10] *The Collected Works of Mahatma Gandhi*, vol. 90, New Delhi: Government of India Publications, 1984.

As Gandhi had expected, Mira Behn moved on, from the ecology of the cow to the ecology of forests and water, to the links between deforestation and water crises. As she recollected later,

Pashulok being situated as it is at the foot of the mountains, just where the Ganga emerges from the Himalayan valleys, I became very realistically aware of the terrible floods which pour down from the Ganga catchment area, and I had taken care to have all the buildings constructed above the flood high-mark. Within a year or two I witnessed a shocking flood: as the swirling waters increased, [there] came first bushes and boughs and great logs of wood, then in the turmoil of more and more water came whole trees, cattle of all sizes and from time to time a human being clinging to the remnants of his hut. Nothing could be done to save man or beast from this turmoil; the only hope was for them to get caught up somewhere on the edge of an island or riverbank prominence. The sight of these disastrous floods led me each summer to investigate the area north of Pashulok whence they came. Merciless deforestation as well as cultivation of profitable pines in place of broad-leaf trees was clearly the cause. This in turn led me to hand over charge of Pashulok to the government staff and to undertake a community project in the valley of the Bhilangana. Here I built a little centre, Gopal Ashram, and concentrated on the forest problem.[11]

During her stay in Garhwal Mira studied the environment intimately and derived knowledge about it from the local people. From the older ones she learnt that, earlier, Tehri Garhwal forests consisted largely of oak, and Garhwali folksongs, which encapsulate collective experience and wisdom, tell repeatedly of species such as *banj* and *kharik*.* They create images of abundant forests of banj, grasslands and fertile fields, large herds of animals and vessels full of milk. In Mira's view the primary reason for degeneration in this region was the disappearance of the banj trees. According to her, if the catchment of the Ganga was not once again clothed with banj, floods and drought would continue to get aggravated.

The issue was not merely one of planting trees, but of planting *ecologically appropriate* trees. As Mira Behn pointed out, the replacement of banj and mixed forests by the commercially valuable pine was a major reason for the increasing ecological instability of the Himalaya and the growing economic deprivation of Garhwali women, since pine failed to perform any of the ecological and economic functions of banj.

[11] Mira Behn, 'Something Wrong in the Himalaya', mimeo, undated.
* *Quercus incana* and *Celtis australis*.

Mira Behn's ecological insights were inherited by Sunderlal Bahuguna who had worked with her in the Bhilangana valley. Bahuguna had joined the independence struggle at the tender age of 13, and was Congress Secretary of Uttar Pradesh at the time of Independence. In 1954 he married Bimla Behn, who had spent eight years with Sarala Behn, another close disciple of Gandhi's. Sarala Behn had started an ashram for the education of hill women in Kausani and her full-time commitment was to make them recognize that they were not beasts of burden but goddesses of wealth since they rear cattle and produce food, performing 98 per cent of all labour in farming and animal husbandry. Influenced by Sarala Behn's ideas of women's freedom, Bimla agreed to marry Sunderlal Bahuguna only if he left the Congress Party and settled down in a remote village so that they could awaken the hill people by living with and through them. Writing twelve years after the establishment of the Silyara Ashram, Sunderlal and Bimla Bahuguna wrote: 'One of us, Sunderlal, was inspired to settle in a village by Mira Behn and the other, Bimla, was inspired by living continuously with Sarala Behn.'[12] Sunderlal Bahuguna, in turn, drew in other activists like Ghanshyam Raturi, Chandi Prasad Bhatt and Dhoom Singh Negi to lend support to a movement generated by women's power. As he often says 'We are the runners and messengers—the real leaders are the women.'

In the early stages of the Chipko movement, when the exploitation of forest resources was carried out by non-local forest contractors, the women's special concern with forestry for survival, which provided the base for Chipko, was temporarily merged with a largely male concern for raw material supply for saw-mills and resin factories set up by local cooperatives.[13] These male cooperatives, set up by Gandhian organizations, saw the Chipko demand primarily as one of the supply of resin and timber for their industrial units. Among the many small scale forest industries that mushroomed in the hill regions in the 1960s were those run by Dasholi Gram Swaraj Sangh, Purola Gram Swaraj Sangh, Gangotri Gram Swaraj Sangh, Berinag Gram Swaraj Sangh, Kathyur Gram Swaraj Sangh, Takula Gram Swaraj Sangh, etc. Soon,

[12] Bimla and Sunderlal Bahuguna, 'Twelve Years of Working in Villages', in *Uttarakhand Smarika*, Chamba: Uttarakhand Sarvodaya Mandal, 1969.

[13] *Uttar ke Shikharo Mein Chetna ke Ankur*, New Delhi: Himalaya Seva Sangh, 1975, p. 129.

however, a new separation took place between local male interests for commercial activity based on forest products, and local women's interests for sustenance activity based on forest protection. Bahuguna has been an effective messenger of the women's concern. He has developed these insights into the philosophy of natural forests as life-support systems and the Chipko struggle as a struggle to conserve them. It is largely through listening to the quiet voices of the women during his *padyatras* that Bahuguna has retained an ability to articulate the feminine–ecological principles of Chipko. When asked in 1977 why he did not set up resin units and saw-mills like other voluntary agencies in Garhwal, he replied:

If you had proposed the setting up of saw-mills as hill development six years ago, I would have considered it. But today I see clearly that establishing saw-mills in the hills is to join the project to destroy Mother Earth. Saw-mills have an endless appetite for trees and wipe out forests to satisfy their appetite.[14]

While the philosophical and conceptual articulation of the ecological view of the Himalayan forests has been done by Mira Behn and Bahuguna, the organizational foundation for it being a women's movement was laid by Sarala Behn with Bimla Behn in Garhwal and Radha Bhatt in Kumaon.

In a commemorative column dedicated to Sarala Behn on her 75th birthday (which coincided with International Women's Year in 1975), the activists of Uttarakhand called her the daughter of the Himalaya and the mother of social activism in the region. Sarala Behn had come to India in search of non-violence. As a close follower of Gandhi, she worked mainly in the hill areas during the independence movement. Reflecting on the Gandhian legacy in her 75th year, she wrote:

From my childhood experience I have known that law is not just; that the principles that govern humanity are higher than those that govern the state; that a centralised government, indifferent to its peoples, is a cruel joke in governance, that the split between the private and public ethic is the source of misery, injustice and exploitation in society. Each child in India understands that bread (*roti*) is not just a right to the one who has money in his pocket. It is a more fundamental right of the one

[14] S.L. Bahuguna, 'Water is the Primary Product of the Hill Forests', interview in *Henwalika*, Yuvak Sangh, Jajal, Tehri Garhwal, 1980–1.

whose stomach is hungry. This concept of rights works within the family, but is shed at the societal level. Then the ethics of the market reigns, and men get trapped in it.[15]

Sarala Behn knew that the ethics of sharing, of producing and maintaining life, that women conserved in their activity, was the countervailing force to the masculinist morality of the market which came as 'development' and created a cash economy, but also created destitution and drunkenness. The early women's movement in Uttarakhand was therefore an anti-alcohol movement aimed at controlling alcohol addiction among men who earned cash incomes from felling trees with one hand and lost the cash to liquor with the other. For the women, drunkenness meant violence and hunger for their children and themselves, and it was the organizational base created among them through the anti-alcohol movement that was inherited by Chipko. In 1965 the women of Garhwal raised their voice for prohibition in Ghansyali. In November that year, when thousands of women in Tehri demonstrated and picketted at shops, prohibition came into effect in five districts—Tehri, Uttarkashi, Chamoli, Garhwal and Pithoragarh. In 1978 Sarala Behn wrote her *Blueprint for Survival* in which she reiterated the women's Chipko demand:

We must remember that the main role of the hill forests should be not to yield revenue, but to maintain a balance in the climatic conditions of the whole of northern India and the fertility of the Gangetic Plain. If we ignore their ecological importance in favour of their short-term economic utility, it will be prejudicial to the climate of northern India and will dangerously enhance the cycle of recurring and alternating floods and droughts.[16]

Sarala Behn established the Laxmi Ashram in Kausani primarily to empower the hill women. Bimla Behn who spent seven years with her, widened her project and established the Navjivan Ashram in Silyara, which then became the energizing source for Chipko.

The organizational base of women was thus ready by the 1970s, and this decade saw the beginning of more frequent popular protest

[15] Sarala Behn, 'From Revolt to Construction', in *Uttar ke Shikharo Mein Chetna ke Ankur.*

[16] Sarala Behn, 'A Blueprint for Survival of the Hills', supplement to *Himalaya: Man and Nature*, New Delhi: Himalaya Seva Sangh, 1980.

concerning the rights of the people to utilize local forest produce. Nineteen seventy-two saw widespread, organized protests against the commercial exploitation of forests by outside contractors: in Purola on 11 December, in Uttarkashi on 12 December, and in Gopeshwar on 15 December. It was then that Raturi composed his famous poem:

Embrace our trees
Save them from being felled
The property of our hills
Save it from being looted.

While the concept of saving trees by embracing them is old, as recalled by the case of the Bishnois, in the context of the current phase of the movement for forest rights, this popular poem is the earliest documentary source of the now famous name, 'Chipko'.

The movement spread throughout Garhwal and into Kumaon, through the totally decentred leadership of local women, connected to each other not vertically, but horizontally— through the songs of Ghanshyam Raturi, through 'runners' like Bahuguna, Bhatt, and Negi who carried the message of Chipko happenings from one village to the next, from one region to another. For hill women, food production begins with the forest. Disappearing forests and water are quite clearly an issue of survival for hill women, which is why thousands of Garhwal women have protested against commercial forestry which has destroyed their forests and water resources.

In March 1973, when 300 ash trees which had been auctioned to a manufacturer of sports goods, were to be felled in Mandal the villagers went to the forest, beating drums. They declared that they would embrace the trees and not allow them to be cut. The labourers withdrew, but the manufacturer obtained an alternative contract in the Rampur Fata forest in Kedar Ghati. On receiving this information, people started walking towards Kedar Ghati. Seventy-two year-old Shyama Devi, who in 1975 had picketted a wine shop in Chandrapuri, brought her leadership experience to Kedar Ghati and mobilized the local women; the forest of Rampur Fata resounded with Chipko slogans from June to December, when the contractor finally withdrew.

Chipko now shifted to the Alakananda Valley, to the village Reni, that lies on the road from Joshimath to Niti Ghati.

Devastation in the Alakananda Valley had been the first major signal that the Himalaya was dying when, in 1970, a major flood inundated several villages and fields for miles together. The women of Reni had not forgotten the Alakananda disaster; they linked the landslide that blocked the river and aggravated the floods with the felling of trees in the catchment area. In 1973, a woman grazing her cows spotted a few persons with axes in their hands; she whistled and collected all her companions who surrounded the contractor's men and said: 'This forest is our mother. When there is a crisis of food, we come here to collect grass and dry fruits to feed our children. We dig out herbs and collect mushrooms from this forest. You cannot touch these trees.'[17] The leadership to protect the Reni forest was provided by 50-year old Gauri Devi and 52-year old Gunga Devi, with co-workers Rupsa, Bhakti, Masi, Harki, Malti, Phagli and Bala Devi. Together, in small groups, they formed vigilance parties to keep an eye on the axemen till the government was forced to set up a committee, which recommended a 10-year ban on commercial green-felling in the Alakananda catchment.

The Chipko movement then started mobilizing for a ban on commercial exploitation throughout the hill districts of Uttar Pradesh because the overfelling of trees was leading to mountain instability everywhere. In 1975, more than 300 villages in these districts faced the threat of landslides and severe erosion. Genvala, Matli and Dharali in Uttar Kashi, Pilkhi and Nand Gaon in Tehri, Chimtoli and Kinjhani in Chamoli, Baghar and Jageshwar in Almora, Rayer Agar and Jajardeval in Pithoragarh are evident examples. The movement for a total ban was spurred by women like 50-year old Hima Devi who had earlier mobilized public opinion against alcoholism in 1965, and was now moving from village to village to spread the message to save the trees. She spoke for the women at demonstrations and protests against auctions throughout the hill districts:

My sisters are busy in harvesting the kharif crop. They are busy in winnowing. I have come to you with their message. Stop cutting trees. There are no trees even for birds to perch on. Birds flock to our crops and eat them. What will we eat? The firewood is disappearing: how will we cook?[18]

[17] Quoted in Bimla Bahuguna, 'Contribution of Women to the Chipko Movement', in *Indian Farming*, November 1975.
[18] Quoted in Bimla Bahuguna, op. cit., 1975.

In January 1975 women of the hill regions started a 75-day trek from Uttarkashi to Kausani and another 50-day trek from Devprayag to Naugaon to mobilize public opinion on women's increasing workload due to deforestation. Bimla Behn and Radha Bhatt were part of these padyatras. In June 1977 a meeting of all the activists in the hills held in Sarala Behn's ashram further strengthened the movement and consolidated the resistance to commercial felling as well as to excessive tapping of resin from the pine trees. In the Gotar forests in the Tehri range the forest ranger was transferred because of his inability to prevent the illegal overtapping of pine resin. It was in this period that the methodology of hugging trees to save them from being felled was actually used for the first time by Dhoom Singh Negi in Salet forest near the village of Pipleth in Henwal.

Among the numerous instances of Chipko successes throughout the Garhwal Himalaya in the years to follow, are those of Adwani, Amarsar, Chanchnidhar, Dungari, Paintoli and Badiyagarh. The auction of the Adwani forests took place in October 1977 in Narendernagar, the district headquarters. Sunderlal Bahuguna undertook a fast against the auction and appealed to the forest contractors and the district authorities to refrain from their mission. The auction took place despite expressions of popular discontent, and the forests were scheduled to be felled in the first week of December 1977. Large groups of women, led by Bachhni Devi (the wife of the local village headman; himself a contractor) gathered together. Chipko activist Dhoom Singh Negi supported the women's struggle by beginning a fast in the forest itself. The women tied sacred threads to the trees as a token of their vow of protection. Between December 13 and 20, a large number of women from 15 villages guarded the forests while discourses from ancient texts on their role in Indian life went on uninterruptedly.

The axe-man withdrew, only to return on 1 February 1978, with two truckloads of armed police. The plan was to encircle the forests with their help in order to keep the people away during the actual felling. Even before they reached the area, the volunteers of the movement entered the forest and told their story to the forest labourers who had been brought in from distant places. By the time the contractors arrived with the policemen, each tree was being guarded by three volunteers. The police, having been defeated in their own plan and seeing the determination and awareness of the people, hastily withdrew.

There are in India, today, two paradigms of forestry—one life-enhancing, the other life-destroying. The life-enhancing paradigm emerges from the forest and the feminine principle; the life-destroying one from the factory and the market. The former creates a sustainable, renewable forest system, supporting and renewing food and water sources. *The maintenance of conditions for renewability is its primary management objective*, while the maximizing of profits through commercial extraction is the primary management objective of the latter. Since the maximizing of profits is consequent upon the destruction of conditions of renewability, the two paradigms are cognitively and ecologically incommensurate. The first paradigm has emerged from India's ancient forest culture, in all its diversity, and has been renewed in contemporary times by the women of Garhwal through Chipko.

It is these two distinct knowledge and economic systems which clashed in 1977 in Adwani when the Chipko movement became explicitly an ecological *and* feminist movement. The women, of course, had always been the backbone of Chipko and for them the struggle was ever the struggle for the living, natural forest. But in the early days when it was directed against removing the non-local forest contractors, local commercial interest had also been part of the resistance. Once non-local private contractors were removed and a government agency (the Forest Development Corporation) started working through local labour contractors and forest cooperatives, *the women continued to struggle against the exploitation of the forests*. It did not matter to them whether the forest was destroyed by outsiders or their own men. The most dramatic turn in this new confrontation took place when Bachni Devi of Adwani led a resistance against her own husband who had obtained a local contract to fell the forest. The forest officials arrived to browbeat and intimidate the women and Chipko activists, but found the women holding up lighted lanterns in broad daylight. Puzzled, the forester asked them their intention. The women replied, 'We have come to teach you forestry.' He retorted, 'You foolish women, how can you who prevent felling know the value of the forest? Do you know what forests bear? They produce profit and resin and timber.' And the women immediately sang back in chorus:

What do the forests bear?
Soil, water and pure air.
Soil, water and pure air
Sustain the earth and all she bears.

The Adwani satyagraha created new directions for Chipko. The movement's philosophy and politics now evolved to reflect that needs and knowledge of the women. Peasant women came out, nly challenging the reductionist commerical forestry system o. the one hand and the local men who had been colonized by that system, cognitively, economically and politically, on the other.

Afforestation Projects and Reductionism

The main thrust of conservation struggles like Chipko is that forests and trees are life-support systems, and should be protected and regenerated for their biospheric functions. The crisis mind on the other hand sees the forest and trees as weed, valued commercially, and converts even afforestation into deforestation and desertification. From life-support systems, trees are converted into green gold—all planting is motivated by the slogan, 'Money grows on trees.' Whether it is schemes like social forestry or wasteland development, afforestation programmes are conceived at the international level by 'experts' whose philosophy of tree-planting falls within the reductionist paradigm of producing wood for the market, not biomass for maintaining ecological cycles or satisfying local needs of food, fodder and fertilizer. All official programmes of afforestation, based on heavy funding and centralized decision making, act in two ways against the feminine principle in forestry—they destroy the forest as a diverse and self-reproducing system, *and* destroy it as commons, shared by a diversity of social groups with the smallest having rights, access and entitlements.

'Social' Forestry and the 'Miracle' Tree

Social forestry projects are a good example of single-species, single commodity production plantations, based on reductionist models which divorce forestry from agriculture and water management, and needs from markets.

A case study of World Bank sponsored social forestry in Kolar district of Karnataka[19] is an illustration of reductionism and

[19] V. Shiva, H.C. Sharatchandra and J. Bandyopadhyay, *The Social, Ecological and Economic Impact of Social Forestry in Kolar* (mimeo), Indian Institute of Management, Bangalore, 1981; V. Shiva, H.C. Sharatchandra and J. Bandyopadhyay, 'The Challenge of Social Forestry', in W. Fernandes and S. Kulkarni (eds), *Towards a New Forest Policy*, New Delhi: Indian Social Institute, 1983; and V. Shiva, H.C. Sharatchandra and J. Bandyopadhyay, 'No Solution Within the Market', in *Ecologist*, October 1982.

maldevelopment in forestry being extended to farmland. Decentred agro-forestry, based on multiple species and private and common tree-stands, has been India's age-old strategy for maintaining farm productivity in arid and semi-arid zones. The *honge*, tamarind, jackfruit and mango, the *jola, gobli, kagli** and bamboo traditionally provided food and fodder, fertilizer and pesticide, fuel and small timber. The backyard of each rural home was a nursery, and each peasant woman the sylviculturalist. The invisible, decentred agro-forestry model was significant because the humblest of species and the smallest of people could participate in it, and with space for the small, *everyone* was involved in protecting and planting.

The reductionist mind took over tree-planting with 'social forestry'. Plans were made in national and international capitals by people who could not know the purpose of the honge and the *neem*, and saw them as weeds. The experts decided that indigenous knowledge was worthless and 'unscientific', and proceeded to destroy the diversity of indigenous species by replacing them with row after row of eucalyptus seedlings in polythene bags, in government nurseries. Nature's locally available seeds were laid waste; people's locally available knowledge and energies were laid waste. With imported seeds and expertise came the import of loans and debt and the export of wood, soils—and people. Trees, as a living resource, maintaining the life of the soil and water and of local people, were replaced by trees whose dead wood went straight to a pulp factory hundreds of miles away. The smallest farm became a supplier of raw material to industry and ceased to be a supplier of food to local people. Women's work, linking the trees to the crops, disappeared and was replaced by the work of brokers and middlemen who brought the eucalyptus trees on behalf of industry. Industrialists, foresters and bureaucrats loved the eucalyptus because it grows straight and is excellent pulp-wood, unlike the honge which shelters the soil with its profuse branches and dense canopy and whose real worth is as a living tree on a farm. The honge could be nature's idea of the perfect tree for arid Karnataka. It has rapid growth of precisely those parts of the tree, the leaves and small branches, which go back to the earth, enriching and protecting it, conserving its moisture and fertility. The eucalyptus, on the other

---

* *Pongamia globra, Azadirachta indica, Tamarindus indica, Autocarpus integrifolia, Mangifera indica, Acacia fernesiana* and *Acacia catechu.*

hand, when perceived ecologically, is unproductive, even negative, because this perception assesses the 'growth' and 'productivity' of trees in relation to the water cycle and its conservation, in relation to soil fertility and in relation to human needs for food and food production. The eucalyptus has destroyed the water cycle in arid regions due to its high water demand and its failure to produce humus, which is nature's mechanism for conserving water. Most indigenous species have a much higher biological productivity than the eucalyptus, when one considers water yields and water conservation. The non-woody biomass of trees has never been assessed by forest measurements and quantification within the reductionist paradigm, yet it is this very biomass that functions in conserving water and building soils. It is little wonder that Garhwal women call a tree *dali* or branch, because they see the productivity of the tree in terms of its non-woody biomass which functions critically in hydrological and nutrient cycles within the forest, and through green fertilizer and fodder in cropland.

In the context of ecological cycles and of the food needs of people and livestock, the eucalyptus actually makes negative contributions. It is destructive to nature's work and women's work in agriculture, for by destroying the water and land and organic matter base for food production, women's productivity in sustenance is killed. Kolar, which is the most successful social forestry district in Karnataka, has already lost more than 13 per cent of its agricultural land to eucalyptus cultivation; most of this has been at the cost of its staple food, the millet, *ragi*, and associated food crops. Table 1.1 gives the decline in the area under ragi cultivation since the beginning of the social forestry programme. Today Kolar is the most severely hit by drought and food scarcity, for eucalyptus undermines not just food production but the long-term productivity of the soil.

TABLE 1.1 Area and Production of Ragi in Kolar District

Year	Area (ha.)	Production (tons)
1977–8	1,41,772	1,75,195
1978–9	1,46,361	1,65,174
1979–80	1,40,862	99,236
1980–1	48,406	13,340

Malur, a region in Kolar district which has 30 per cent of its land under eucalyptus was compared to Korategere in neighbouring Tumkur where indigenous farm forestry continues to provide a diversity of organic inputs to agriculture. Table 1.2 shows how eucalyptus has induced food and nutrition deficiencies in Malur.

TABLE 1.2 Food Availability Per Day Per Individual

Land holdings (ha.)	Korategere		Malur	
	Cereals (gms)	Pulses (gms)	Cereals (gms)	Pulses (gms)
1 ha.	0.55	0.06	0.21	0.03
1–2 ha.	0.58	0.07	0.29	0.01
2–4 ha.	1.23	0.07	0.47	0.03
4 ha.	3.65	3.65	1.60	0.06

'Greening' with eucalyptus is a violence against nature and its cycles, and it is a violence against women who depend on the stability of nature's cycles to provide sustenance in the form of food and water. Eucalyptus guzzles nutrients and water and, in the specific conditions of low rainfall zones, gives nothing back but terpenes to the soil. These inhibit the growth of other plants and are toxic to soil organisms which are responsible for building soil fertility and improving soil structure.[20] The eucalyptus certainly increased cash and commodity flows, but it resulted in a disastrous interruption of organic matter and water flows within the local ecosystem. Its proponents failed to calculate the costs in terms of the destruction of life in the soil, the depletion of water resources and the scarcity of food and fodder that eucalyptus cultivation creates. Nor did they, while trying to shorten rotations for harvesting, see that tamarind, jackfruit and honge have very short rotations of one year in which the biomass harvested is far higher than that of eucalyptus, which they nevertheless declared a 'miracle' tree. The crux of the matter is that fruit production was never the concern of forestry in the reductionist paradigm—it focused on wood, and wood for the market, alone. Eucalyptus as an exotic, introduced in total disregard of its ecological appropriateness, has thus become an exemplar of anti-life afforestation.

[20] V. Shiva and J. Bandyopadhyay, *Ecological Audit of Eucalyptus Cultivation*, Dehradun, EBD Publishers, 1985.

Women throughout India have resisted the expansion of eucalyptus because of its destruction of water, soil and food systems. On 10 August 1983, the women and small peasants of Barha and Holahalli villages in Tumkur district (Karnataka) marched en masse to the forest nursery and pulled out millions of eucalyptus seedlings, planting tamarind and mango seeds in their place. This gesture of protest, for which they were arrested, spoke out against the virtual planned destruction of soil and water systems by eucalyptus cultivation. It also silently challenged the domination of a forestry science that had reduced all species to one (the eucalyptus), all needs to one (that of the pulp industry), and all knowledge to one (that of the World Bank and forest officials). It challenged the myth of the miracle tree: tamarind and mango are symbols of the energies of nature and of local people, of the links between these seeds and the soil, and of the needs that these trees—and others like them—satisfy in keeping the earth and the people alive. Forestry for food—food for the soil, for farm animals, for people—all women's and peasants' struggles revolve around this theme, whether in Garhwal or Karnataka, in the Santhal Parganas or Chattisgarh, in reserved forests, farmlands or commons. Destruction of diversity and life, and colonization of the commons is built into reductionist forestry and its new avatar, 'wasteland development'.

The Approaching Tragedy of the Commons

Recovering five million hectares of the commons in India each year could signal the end of rural poverty and a reversal of the ecological collapse of critical life-support systems like soil, water and vegetation. Yet the wasteland development programme, far from being a recovery of the commons project, will in fact, privatize the commons, accentuate rural poverty and increase ecological instability. In one stroke it will rob the poor of their remaining common resource, the only survival base to which they have access. The usurpation of the commons which began with the British will reach its final limit with the wasteland development programme as is. Chattrapati Singh of the Indian Law Institute argues:

It is evident that till the end of the last century and in all historical periods before that, at least 80 per cent of India's natural resources were common property, with only 20 per cent being privately utilised.... This extensive common property has provided the resource base for a non-cash, nonmarket economy. A whole range of necessary resources has been freely available to the people. Thus commonly available wood, shrubs and cowdung have been utilised for cooking and heating; and mud, bamboo and palm leaves for housing, wild grass and shrubs as animal fodder, and a variety of fruits and vegetables as food.[21]

These free commons have historically been the survival base for rural India and the domain of productivity of women. With the reservation of forests a century ago the first step towards the privatization of commons took place. Today, 'wasteland development' constitutes the last step in their disappearance. N.S. Jodha, who has worked extensively on common property resources, has shown how women's work and the livelihoods of poorer sections of rural society are intimately linked to trees and grasslands in the commons, which support the farm animals and thus take pressure off cropland, while increasing organic inputs to crop through animal waste.[22] Small peasants and landless labourers can own livestock largely because of the existence of the commons. Further, in arid zones, traditional farming systems partly derive their stability and viability from the commons which allow for an integrated and diversified production strategy using crops, livestock and trees, which cushion the dry-land economy by supplying food, fodder and fuel in years of crop failure. Nearly ten per cent of the nutrition of poorer families has been found to come directly from the commons. Women's work in the sustenance economy of the poorest groups is thus closely tied to the existence of the commons.

The privatization of the commons through wasteland development is not an aberration but an outcome of the dominance of development agencies like the World Bank, and their indifference to the needs of nature and vulnerable social groups. For such organizations and agencies, self-provisioning is not economic activity. In 1984, the World Bank wrote up a National Forestry Project for India, a significant component of which was the privatization of wastelands. In 1985, it floated a Tropical Forestry Action plan of eight billion dollars based on the same logic of the corporate takeover of commons. In 1985 the Wasteland Development Board was set up with the laudable objective of bringing five million

[21] Chattrapati Singh, *Common Property and Common Poverty*, Delhi: Oxford Publishing House, 1985, p. 2.

[22] N.S. Jodha, 'Common Property Resources', mimeo, 1986.

hectares of wasteland under tree cover annually. The regeneration of ecologically appropriate tree cover with socially appropriate community control could help rebuild people's resource base, and re-establish their control over the commons. Yet the Wasteland Board schemes will primarily privatize the commons by transferring rights and control from the community as a whole, to the World Bank, private business and a few local people. The Wasteland Board had recommended the entry of the corporate sector in wasteland development, and proposals have been cleared for a variety of industries from strawboard and paper to plastics and polythene. This attempt at appropriating the commons is being facilitated by a number of confusions: (a) the confusion between wastlands as commons and wastelands as ecologically degraded land, private or common; and (b) tree planting as foresty. In afforestation of wastelands risks arise both from what is understood as wasteland and as afforestation. Ecologically, wastelands are lands which have lost their biological productivity, a process also known as desertification. It is this meaning that is invoked to undertake a massive afforestation programme. However, a second meaning is invoked to administer the programme, and this meaning has nothing to do with whether or not the land is currently unproductive in the ecological sense.

The Colonial Heritage: Commons as 'Wasteland'

'Wastelands' as a land use category is, like much else, a part of our colonial heritage, loaded with the biases of colonial rule, where meaning was defined by the interest of the rulers. The colonial concept of wastelands was not an assessment of the biological productivity of land, but of its revenue generating capacity: 'wasteland' was land that did not pay any revenue because it was uncultivated. Under such wasteland came the forested districts of Chittagong, Darjeeling, Jalpaiguri, Chota Nagpur and Assam—and the vast trail of forest land towards the mouth and delta of the Hooghly and other rivers, known as the Sundarbans. These lands were taken over by the British and leased to cultivators to transform into revenue generating lands. While in the Gangetic plains 'wastelands' were allotted to villages, in the heavily forested region of Dehradun, Mirzapur, etc., forest tracts were retained as 'government waste'. In Punjab, 20 per cent of the cultivated area of a village was given away as village waste. These lands were kept partly as forest and grazing lands, and partly intended for the extension of cultivation. In 1861, under the viceroyalty of Lord Canning, the wasteland rules were formulated to administer the non-revenue generating, but often biologically productive, lands. As Baden–Powell records, 'The value of state forests—to be made out of the best and most usefully situated wooded and grasslands— was not even recognized, and the occupation of the 'waste' by capitalists and settlers was alone discussed.'[23] Rich forests were also considered waste in the early colonial period: the large scale destruction of the primeval forests of the Doon Valley for land grants to Britishers is one example of how an administrative category of waste actually created an ecological one. What was not economically of value to the British was declared value-less, inspite of high ecological and local use value.

The extensive clearfelling of forests for agricultural land use was a typically colonial view of turning waste into wealth, created by the notion of agricultural surplus as an important source of revenue. As the *Eighth Settlement Report* of the Doon Valley admitted:

Perhaps no mistake was more common in the early days of British rule than to suppose that the extension of the cultivation, wherever culturable land could be found, and the clearing of forest and jungle to extend cultivation, must necessarily benefit the country and the government, and should be pushed as much as possible.[24]

It was not until later in the nineteenth century that the value of forests was realized. Ecological considerations were not, however, the central objective of the reservation of forests through the notification of the Forest Act of 1878. It was the revenue generating capacity of forests which led to their reservation, and protection was defined as the exclusion of villagers' access to forests as a common resource. Forests in themselves now constituted a property of great value and might be made to yield an annual revenue equal to cultivation. The shift in the colonial perspective of seeing forests as wealth and not waste also led to their conversion from a common resource for local use, under local community control, to a

[23] B.H. Baden–Powell, *Land Revenue in British India*, London: Oxford, 1907.
[24] J. Baker, *Eighth Settlement Report*, Dehradun, 1888.

commodity for commercial use under bureaucratic control. This robbery of the commons was seriously resisted through 'forest satyagrahas' throughout the country.

A second robbery of the commons is now under way through 'wastelands development', which is a euphemism for the privatization of the commons. The last resource of the poor for fodder and fuel will now disappear through privatization. As usual, in every scheme that worsens the position of the poor, it is the poor who are invoked as beneficiaries. Leases to some token landless people are aimed at covering up the large-scale appropriation of the common resources of the majority of the poor.

Mannu Rakshana Koota: Saving the Soil, Protecting the Commons

An example of how such a scheme goes awry can be taken from the Karnataka experience. Village commons in Shimoga and Chikmagalur are being taken away from people for wasteland development. These village commons are C and D class lands in revenue records. Categorized as wastelands, they are meant for fulfilling the basic needs of villagers, for whom 'wastelands' are their common wealth, supporting their agricultural ecology. Attempts to change the vegetational and land use characteristics of these village commons are, in their perception, attempts at robbing their land of its biological wealth. There is a proposal for transferring all these village commons, within a radius of 100 km of Harihar Polyfibres, and utilizing about 45,000 acres of commons for growing eucalyptus and selling it to Harihar Polyfibres. The commons are to be leased individually to a few landless beneficiaries.

The people of the affected villages have protested by uprooting newly planted eucalyptus seedlings from these 'wastelands' in large numbers. (Some of the wastelands are in fact, under natural evergreen or semi-green forests, and the average tree population has been found to be 50–200 per acre of diverse tree species.) The cultivation of eucalyptus in the village commons consisting of these C and D class lands is seen by the people as a programme for the *creation* of wastelands, not a programme for their development. The conversion of ecologically productive village commons to feedstock for the wood and fibre industry is in direct conflict with the basic biomass needs of the local villages, and their diversion to industrial plantations through a project for wasteland development has generated a major popular resistance movement for the protection of the commons, called 'Mannu Rakshana Koota' or 'Movement for Saving the Soil'. The government seems determined to take over the commons and manage them commercially throughout the country. Poor people's needs and the need for ecological stability are to be sacrificed in this ultimate privatization of the commons.

The national programme for privatizing the commons is the tree *patta* scheme of breaking up the commons and leasing them out to individuals or groups of individuals for tree planting. The scheme will have a far-reaching social and ecological impact—largely detrimental to the poorest who have traditionally sustained themselves on the commons, a shared resource to which *all* in the local community have access. Privatization amounts to closing off the access of large numbers, granting exclusively to some. On paper, preference will be given to the landless; in practise, we know how beneficiaries are identified in the absence of community check and control. The World Bank National Social Forestry Plan admits that such schemes could at most benefit 10 per cent of landless and marginal farmers and remains silent about the 90 per cent who no longer have a commons to survive on. The planting will be financed through government loans. Since such loans must be paid back, the lessee will be forced to plant commercially and to harvest at short rotations. This has already been the trend of the tree patta scheme in West Bengal's World Bank funded project. The economics of the market will, as always, exclude those who have no purchasing power, and whose zero cost biomass sources in the commons have been usurped to create a commodity. The economy of the commons does not need purchasing power, the economy of the market does. Local needs will therefore be less satisfied through tree pattas than through commons. Further, since the banks which give the loans will also design the afforestation package, permanent and sustainable forestry can hardly be expected to be the outcome. Short-term commercial wood production, which mines soil nutrients and moisture, will result. The market, and not the needs of local people or local ecosystems will determine the planting pattern. As the report of the group constituted to evolve guidelines for tree pattas states, 'NABARD Banks and the implementing agencies could consider preparing some model schemes for adoption in different areas so that technical feasibility and economic viability are given due consideration.' The expertise for forestry has now shifted further away from the life of the forest and the lives of those who depend on forestry for survival. There is no reference in the new projects to *ecological* viability or issues of entitlements and rights for those for whom the panchayat and community lands were a free common resource. We have enough evidence to show that whenever this happens poor people are further deprived and ecosystems further degraded. The 'eucalyptization' phenomenon has shown how the people (especially women) and nature can be wounded simultaneously with inappropriate tree planting. The wasteland development programme as it stands today is merely a plan that will destroy the commons for the rule of the market. And with the commons will be destroyed the survival base of those who depend on them for their subsistence, and the production base for womanly work in sustenance.

There is, of course, the popular *triage* thesis that the poor have no right to survival and should be dispensed with. Hardin's tragedy of the commons scenario emerges from male reductionist assumptions about nature and the logic of triage that such reductionism and its principles of exclusion and dispensability entail.[25] Hardin is just a symbol of the new trend in reductionist science which uses the language of ecology and conservation to unleash another attack of violence against nature. More centralization, more uniformity, more manipulation become new and false prescriptions for overcoming the ecological crisis. Yet neither nature nor people can be saved when the destruction of the former and the dispensability of the latter are the presupposition for creating the new reductionist science of nature.

Breeding 'Super-Trees': The Ultimate Reductionism

The forest crisis was an outcome of a reductionist forestry which viewed the forest as a timber mine, not as a central mechanism in soil and water conservation. The separation of the life-giving and life-maintaining functions of the forest from its commercial value has thus led to the destruction of the essential ecological processes to which forests and trees contribute.

[25] G. Hardin, 'The Tragedy of the Commons', in *Science*, vol. 162, December 1968, pp. 1243–48.

The struggles of women, tribals and peasants, guided by a perception of the forest as a life-support system, are coinciding with failed projects of maldevelopment—of non-sustainable agricultural and energy policies. It is easy to invoke the environmental crisis and the poor people's energy crisis to open up new avenues for reductionist science and commodity production. The entry of bio-technologies in forestry for instance has been explained thus:

the incentive provided by the knowledge that fossil fuels must run out and that a need exists for new commodities to improve the profitability of agriculture, encourages the development of new biomass crops as energy sources for the future. Most projections for increased crop production rely on the new biotechnologies that promise to introduce the grand period of the 'science power' phase of agriculture. Hence, land and other resources should not constrain the development of biomass as a renewable energy source for the future.[26]

The new technologies and the new aid programmes in forestry are motivated by the future existence of markets for biomass-based industrial and commercial energy of the era beyond fossil fuels. As Flavin predicts in the 1986 *State of the World* report, 'Oil will have been largely eliminated as a fuel for power plants and many industries.[27]

The fuel-gathering Third World woman will once again be bypassed by the new sources of energy which will be produced on the land which gave her food and fodder and fuel. Industrial energy from weeds will be derived at the cost of sustenance needs that land in the Third World now satisfies.

The reductionist mind further entrenches colonization. The disjunction process, which underlies the existing ecological and economic chaos, is then applied at newer and deeper levels to resolve the chaos; all it achieves, instead, is further irreversible chaos. The breakdown of ecological cycles for example, is reduced to the problem of planting trees. The cycles recede, trees become a universal solution, and as a universal solution can only be engineered for a market which must go against nature, hastening the breakdown

[26] W.H. Smith, 'Energy from Biomass: A New Commodity', in J.W. Rosenblum (ed.), *Agriculture in the 21st Century,* New York: John Wiley and Sons, 1983.
[27] C. Flavin, 'Moving Beyond Oil', in *State of the World,* Washington: World Watch, 1986, pp. 78–97.

and making recovery less possible. Ecological crises signal the breakdown of scientific arrogance—the crisis mind turns this into yet another domain for its colonization, promising new miracles and inducing the closure of options even while they exist. Tissue culture—as opposed to forest culture—is now proposed as the afforestation strategy of the future in India. But this solution works only through the logic of uniformity or indifference to the diversity of life in nature. Tissue culture will be the ultimate triage of the earth in its diversity, and of her people in their diversity.

The organic recovery of nature cannot be a recovery of reductionism. The machine cannot be a metaphor for nature without sundering it apart, because nature is not mechanistic and Cartesian. The ecological crisis suggests the indispensability of nature and the impossibility of substituting its life-support processes. The reductionist response to eco-crises assures an extension of the logic of dispensability: it presupposes that life-support can be manufactured in the laboratory and factory. In fact, in the reductionist response to the ecological crisis, the lab and factory merge, the distinction between science and business blurs. With engineering entering the life-sciences, the renewability of life as a self-reproducing system comes to an end. Life must be engineered now, not reproduced. A new commodity set is created as inputs, and a new commodity is created as output. Life itself is the new commodity. Linkages that lay within nature to create conditions for self-renewal are destroyed, and in their place come linkages of the market and multinationals. The ultimate masculinist perception of trees as money is captured in Greenwood's statement, 'Knocking even one year off this interval has a net present value well into millions of dollars for organisations that own and plant large acreages.[28]

The breeding strategy is to search for trees with 'superior' characteristics. From nature providing its own seed, the laboratories of multinationals will become the new monopolies for the supply of seed and seedlings. This centralized, global control leads to a new colonization of nature and its commons, and will lead to new degrees of homogeneity and uniformity. In clonal propagation, all members of a clone are genetically identical. This uniformity in trees as resources allows the Taylorism logic to enter forest

[28] M.S. Greenwood, 'Shortening Generations', in *Journal of Forestry,* January 1986, p. 38.

management at an even deeper level than the monoculture plantation of the same species. The uniformity assumes a greater dispensability of species that the market and industry consider 'inferior'. And linked with the imperative of genetic engineering to dispense with species other than its favourites, is the political economy of dispensing with the small person and her needs for survival. As Hollowell and Porterfield point out, for the genetic 'improvement' of tree stands, a land base of 150,000 to 200,000 acres or more is required to assure an acceptable rate of return.[29] According to them,

... gains in desired traits are most meaningful when converted to economic gains. Growth gains may be expressed as obtaining more volume per acre for a given rotation or reaching rotation volume and/or desired piece size at an earlier age. Economics will favour the shorter rotation. Straightness improvement is reflected in increased yield of lumber or veneer per unit volume of raw material. Increases in wood specific gravity can result in improved fibre yields or higher grade lumber.

Once quantified, incremental gains can be converted into higher expected values using a forecast of future produce prices. Timing of expected gains is necessary to construct a cash flow stream for economic analysis.

Resource flows to maintain nature's cycles and local needs of water and diverse vegetation have been replaced by cash flows as a measure of 'yield' and 'growth'. Nature's ecology, its yields and growth are further pushed aside. The market and factory define the 'improvement' sought through the new biotechnologies. This reductionism induced by global markets for wood resources is the ultimate violence, when super-firms decide which super-trees are useful. Nature's integrity and diversity and people's needs are thus simultaneously violated.

Susan Griffin, in *Woman and Nature*, parodied the reductionist mind when she wrote:

The trees in the forest should be tall and free from knot-causing limbs for most of their height. They should be straight. Trees growing in the forest should be useful trees. For each tree ask if it is worth the space it grows in. Aspen, scrub pine, chokeberry, black gum, scrub oak, dogwood, hemlock, beech are weed trees which should be eliminated.

[29] R.R. Hollowell and R.L. Porterfield, 'Is Tree Improvement a Good Investment? Yes, if You've Got the Time and Money', in *Journal of Forestry*, February 1986, p. 46.

For harvesting trees, it is desirable that a stand be all of the same variety and age. Nothing should grow on the forest floor, not seedling trees, not grass, not shrubbery.[30]

She contrasts this uniformity with the logic of diversity in the forest as feminine. The voices of women join the voices of nature:

The way we stand, you can see we have grown up this way together, out of the same soil, with the same rains, leaning in the same way towards the sun.... And we are various and amazing in our variety, and our differences multiply, so that edge after edge of the endlessness of possibility is exposed. You know we have grown this way for years. And to no purpose you can understand. Yet what you fail to know we know, and the knowing is in us, how we have grown this way, why these years were not one of them heedless, why we are shaped the way we are, not all straight to your purpose, but to ours. And how we are each purpose, how each cell, how light and soil are in us, how we are in the soil, how we are in the air, how we are both infinitesimal and great and how we are infinitely without any purpose you can see, in the way we stand, each moment heeded in this cycle, no detail unlovely.

It is such a recovery of life in diversity, of a diversity shared and protected that the invisible Chipko struggles for. Giving value and significance to Prakriti, to nature as the source, to the smallest element of nature in its renewal, giving value to collective needs, not private action, women in Kangad, Sevalgaon, Rawatgaon work in partnership with nature to recreate and regenerate. Without signboards, without World Bank loans, without wire-fencing, they are working to allow nature's play in reproducing the life of the forest—grasses and shrubs, small trees and big, each useful to nature if not to man, are all coming alive again.

Recovering Diversity, Recovering the Commons

At an altitude of 6,000 ft, deep in the Balganga Valley in Garhwal lies Kangad, a hamlet of 200 families. In 1977, the already degraded forest of Kangad was marked for felling by the forest department. The women, who had to walk long distances for fuel, fodder and water, were determined to save the last patch of trees. The men of Kangad were employed by the forest department for felling operations. With the gender fragmentation of the interests

[30] Susan Griffin, *Woman and Nature,* London: The Women's Press, 1984.

of the village community—the women representing the conservation interests, and the men representing the exploitation demand—launching Chipko was not easy. The women contacted Bimla Bahuguna in Silyara, just 15 km from Kangad. Bimla Behn, with Chipko activists Dhoom Singh Negi and Pratap Shihar, came to support the women's struggle. After four months of resistance, the women succeeded in saving their forest.

The women's organization, the Mahila Mandal Dal, then decided to regenerate the degraded forests. On the basis of cattle owned by each family, contributions were raised to support a village forest guard who was paid Rs 300 per month. For three years the arrangement worked and then failed because the watchman became inefficient and corrupt: he would allow some people to extract fodder and fuelwood. Once the women learnt of this, they unanimously decided to abolish the post of the forest guard and guard the forest themselves.

Now the Mahila Mandal has allocated duties to a group of village women. About ten or twelve women are on duty every day, allocated in such a manner that the work is distributed among all the families. Thus the duty for one family or group of women comes in a cycle of 15 to 20 days. As one woman said, 'On these days we leave our own work and protect the forest because our oak trees are like our children.' Oak trees are now generating naturally in Kangad.

Once, when a Gujjar grazier allowed his goats to graze in the regenerated area, the women confiscated the goats and fined the Gujjar Rs 200. Villagers are fined upto Rs 50 per person for lopping the regenerating oak and Rs 100 for cutting trees for firewood. On another occasion, when a fire threatened to destroy the forest, all the women joined hands to put out the forest fire. As one woman reported, 'The men were at home, but they decided to stay back rather than join with us to put out the fire. The men are least bothered about saving trees.' In 1986, the Mahila Mandal decided to assist the forest department in tree planting. They dug 15,000 pits but found that the forest department wanted to plant only poplars. The women refused to plant this exotic, and forced the forest department to bring diverse indigenous fodder species instead.

The strength of nature and the strength of women is the basis of the recovery of the forest as commons in Kangad. The capital is not debt and aid. The market is not the guiding force. Nature's and women's energy are the capital, and local needs of water, food, fodder and fuel provide the organizing principle of managing a shared, living resource. This is merely a renewal of the conservation ethic and conservation work of hill women, that they think of the needs of their families. This is symbolized by their putting aside some leaves for Patna Devi (the goddess of the leaves) each time they go to collect fodder. These are small, perhaps invisible, but significant steps towards the recovery of the feminine principle in the forest. This recovery re-establishes the integration of forestry with food production and water management and it allows the possibility of a re-emergence of the diversity and integrity of life in the forest, of fauna and flora, of plants big and small, each crucial to the life of the forest, each valuable in itself, each having a right to participate in the democracy of the forest's life, and each contributing in invisible, unknown ways to all life. Diversity of living resources in the forest, natural or in an agro-ecosystem, is critical to soil and water conservation, it is critical for satisfying the diversity of needs of people who depend on the forest, and the diversity of nature's needs in reproducing herself.

The annihilation of this diversity has destroyed women's control over conditions of producing sustenance. The many colonizations —through 'reserved' forests, through 'social forestry', through 'wasteland' development—have implied not forest development but the maldevelopment of both forestry and agriculture. A maldeveloped forestry has meant new resources and raw material supplies for industry and commerce; for nature and women it has meant a new impoverishment, a destruction of the diverse means of production through which both provide sustenance in food and water, and reproduce society. The Chipko struggle is a struggle to recover the hidden and invisible productivity of vital resources, and the invisible productivity of women, to recover their entitlements and rights to have and provide nourishment for sustained survival, and to create ecological insights and political spaces that do not destroy fundamental rights to survival. Chipko women provide a non-violent alternative in forestry to the violence of reductionist forestry with its inherent logic of dispensability. They have taken the first steps towards recovering their status as the *other* silviculturists and forest managers, who participate in nature's processes instead of working against them, and share nature's wealth for basic needs instead of privatizing it for profit.

2

Women, Ecology and Culture

Gabriele Dietrich

In grappling with the crisis of ecology and of culture, we face two questions of great depth and magnitude: one, the problem of survival and identity, secondly, the problem posed by the limits of physical and spiritual endurance. The ecological crisis forces itself on our attention through the daily reports of droughts and floods, starvation deaths, poisoning through pesticides and chemical industries, soil salinity, water logging etc. The cultural crisis surfaces daily in communal and caste clashes, in the struggles of Dalits and Adivasis, and in the whole debate on secularism and freedom of religion.

It is no exaggeration to say that both the ecological and the cultural crises have affected women more deeply than men. It has been pointed out again and again that women are the worst victims of ecological deterioration since their working day has been drastically lengthened by scarcity of water, fuel and fodder, and their traditional skills and occupations have been adversely affected by new technologies in agriculture, artisanal work and marketing, while new opportunities have not sufficiently developed.[1] It has also been documented that women are adversely affected in situations of communal riots and that the whole communal battle about personal laws, freedom of religion etc., is largely fought out on the backs and at the cost of women.[2]

[1] See Anil Agarwal and Sunita Narain, *The State of India's Environment: A Second Citizen's Report,* Centre for Science and Environment, New Delhi, 1985.

[2] See, for example, the documentation on the anti-Sikh riots in November 84 in Delhi carried by *Manushi,* No. 25, and the debate on personal laws documented in A.R. Desai (ed.), *Women's Liberation and Politics of Religious and Personal Laws in India,* C.G. Shah Memorial Trust Publication (16), Bombay.

However, there are *two new moves* which have to be taken into account in the debate: from the side of the women's movements, we must raise the question of *how to go beyond victimization, how to draw on the vital experiences and skills of women to reverse the situation.*[3] The overriding question is how to create a mode of production which does not depend on the exploitation of nature and labour power but which, in harmony with nature, provides for the survival needs of all. We must also ask how we can create a counter-culture which arrests both the trends towards uniformity and towards fragmentation, and the growing communalization of daily life. Women have practical skills and mental resources which need to be discovered and mobilized for this vast task. The second step, which logically follows from the first one of mobilizing women's material and spiritual skills, is *to work out the connection between the ecological and the cultural crises* caused by a development model which is neo-colonial, capitalist, patriarchal and violently assaults the base for human material and spiritual survival, and which is destructive of both nature and culture. This connection has not been made sufficiently because the feminist analysis has been focusing more on reorganization of material culture.[4] At the same time, the cultural debate on decolonization, religion and secularism has been ambiguous as far as the women's question is concerned.[5] Ashis Nandy, who has raised many relevant questions on the model of science and technology underlying the prevailing development concept, has run into trouble by taking a cultural stand which could be co-opted by violently anti-feminist defenders

[3] In the field of ecology, this question has been raised powerfully by Vandana Shiva, *Staying Alive: Women, Ecology and Survival in India,* Kali for Women, New Delhi, 1988. As far as the cultural debate is concerned, a vigorous discussion is going on in the women's movement. See the interview with Romila Thapar, 'Traditions Versus Misconceptions', in *Manushi,* No. 42–43, September–December 1987. See also *Seminar,* No. 342, February 1988 on sati, and Chapter 2 of my book *Reflections on the Women's Movement in India* (Horizon India Books, New Delhi, 1992).

[4] This is particularly true of Maria Mies, *Patriarchy and Accumulation on a World Scale: Women in the International Division of Labour,* Zed Books, London, 1986. Vandana Shiva in *Staying Alive* has dealt with questions of spirituality and religion implicitly but has not related them to the overall situation of rising communalism.

[5] See Ashis Nandy, *The Intimate Enemy: Loss and Recovery of Self Under Colonialism,* Oxford University Press, New Delhi, 1983; Ashish Nandy, *Traditions, Tyranny, and Utopias: Essays in the Politics of Awareness,* Oxford University Press, New Delhi, 1987.

of sati[6] a company not of his choice but nevertheless raising questions of accountability.

My contention is that tackling the ecological crisis and the crisis of culture is a survival issue, not only because environmental destruction is close to reaching a level where it is irreversible but also because the cultural crisis can lead either to fascism or to fragmentation and disintegration, both of which would be destructive of any liberation movement. It is also crucial to tackle both these crises *together* because they are connected in their root-causes. My contention is also that a feminist perspective can give important impulses for a deeper analysis of class, caste and environmental destruction and for reconciliation with nature.

Ecological Crises, Capitalism, Patriarchy and Colonialism

In the recent debate, a clear connection has been established between ecological crisis, capitalism, patriarchy and colonialism. This is not to deny that ecological crisis also exists with equal gravity in socialist countries but it is based on the insight that the predominant concept of industrialism, and of science and technology, originated in the overdeveloped capitalist Western countries and has largely been imitated in Eastern Europe. Even in the People's Republic of China, where appropriate technology was more developed, technological and scientific options were taken under the pressure of military conflict with the USSR and alliance with USA. The events cannot be understood without the history of fascism and Stalinism, of hot and cold war. I am not saying this by way of apology for socialism but to draw attention to an important factor in the analysis of material reality.

Actually, the two books of Maria Mies and of Vandana Shiva, on which I am going to draw, do not really go into this overall context. Maria Mies in *Capitalism and Accumulation on a World Scale* goes into a global analysis which is preoccupied with the

---

[6] Ashis Nandy, 'Anti-Secular Manifesto', in *Seminar,* 314, October 1985. Ashis Nandy, 'The Human Factor', in *Illustrated Weekly,* 17–23 January 1988, pp. 20–23. For a feminist critique of Nandy see Kumkum Sangari, 'Perpetuating the Myth', in *Seminar,* 342, February 1988, pp. 24–30 and Sujata Patel/Krishna Kumar, 'Defenders of Sati', in *EPW,* vol. XXIII, (4), 28 January 1988.

overriding question of how it is that feminism and women's movements have, to a large extent, been co-opted by capitalists governments, and development policies, being not only classist but also inherently patriarchal, cannot deliver the goods. She also analyses the origins of the sexual division of labour and the role of violence, and connects these aspects with colonial division of labour, and the role of colonial and sexual violence. She ends with a perspective of a feminist, ecologically viable society which will also be classless, decentralized, anti-consumerist, largely self-sufficient and based on a different science and technology.

Vandana Shiva's *Staying Alive* gives us a history of the Chipko movement within the context of a very thorough study of the connections between forestry, agriculture and water management. She shows, through an evaluation of a large number of studies in the different fields, how a technocratic approach to development, which she flatly calls maldevelopment, has fragmented and separated these spheres and has been destructive of nature, of women's skills and expertise; of the survival base of the poor and of sustenance of life as a criterion for production. She emphasizes strongly the colonial and patriarchal character of this imported development concept and projects a feminist indigenous culture which she expresses in terms like 'feminine principle', *shakti* and *prakriti*, and characterizes by features like holism, decentralization, plurality and inter-dependence. She also raises the question of the relocation of the sacred, and emphatically demands that the sacredness of life has to replace the sacredness of science and technology, and of developmentalism. She sees the pseudo-worship of modernity and 'progress' as more harmful than the traditional worship of nature and life-sustaining forces.

Though both Maria Mies and Vandana Shiva do not go into this connection, it is important to keep in mind that communalism as a political phenomenon is both a result of colonialism[7] and a backlash against it, and goes together with the development of capitalism and parliamentary democracy. It has often been pointed out in the discussion on communalism and secularism that both the claims to universalism and nationhood are actually alien to Hinduism and a foreign import. They are often taken to connote a certain 'Semiticization' of Hinduism. I have heard this term 'Semiticization',

[7] See notes 3 and 4.

which I consider a misnomer, from people as different as Romila Thapar, M.M. Thomas and Ashis Nandy. I consider it a misnomer because such a term plays on existing anti-Jewish and anti-Muslim sentiment, and characterizes these religions as predominantly conquering and militant. Though both religions have an ideology of Holy War in their scriptures, Judaism has not had a corresponding history until Zionism turned communal under the impact of the fascist liquidation of Jews and British divide-and-rule policies, while Islam has had long and fruitful periods of non-militarized peaceful co-existence with other religions in many parts of the world, including the south of our own country. What has indeed happened today is that the Hindu religion, which had its own dialectics of plurality and universalism in the fragmentation of sects and castes, alongside of religious tolerance as long as these fragmentations remained accepted, has turned communal, in a situation of neo-colonial impact which was trying to overcome caste by *sanskritization* and class conflict by appeal to religious nationalism. This leaves capitalism and existing development concepts intact while it obscures the reality of the increasing neo-colonial dependence by offering a pseudo-religious identity surrogate.

The extent to which communalism is patriarchal can be seen in the blatant anti-women statements[8] of communalist organizations, in the communal battle against a gender-just secular family law, and in the recent attempts to use women in the forefront of communal struggle even though such struggles are a direct attack on women's anti-communalist unity in the women's movement.[9]

Science and Technology as a Patriarchal Colonial Project

In order to understand Maria Mies' and Vandana Shiva's contribution better, it is crucial to go into their critique of modern

---

[8] At this point I agree with Bipan Chandra, *Communalism in Modern India* (Vikas, Delhi, 1984) though I would feel that his definition of communalism as ideology and 'false consciousness' does underestimate the material reality of threat to life and livelihood, often enough across class lines, in the situation of communal clashes.

[9] An analysis of such statements can be found in Ish Narain Misra, 'The Women's Question in Communal Ideologies: A Study of the Ideologies of Rashtriya Swayam Sevak Sangh & Jamat-e-Islami', in *Teaching Politics*, vol. XIII, No. 1, 1987.

science and technology as a patriarchal colonial project. This is an important contribution to the debate on the question whether modern Western science and technology is 'universal' and 'neutral', implying that the only crucial question is who controls and uses it. The latter position has been taken by Marxist parties in power or close to power, including our own parliamentary Marxist parties and by people's science organizations close to them like Shastra Sahitya Parishad. That science and technology as ideology can be highly authoritarian and oppressive in great contrast to its claims of enlightenment, was pointed out in detail by members of the Frankfurt School.[10] Of course, the protest against industrialism itself was alive among machine-storming Luddites, Utopian Socialists,[11] critics and reformers like William Morris[12] and, very importantly, in the anti-colonial struggle of the Gandhian Movement. It was the Nehruite ideology of scientific temper which destroyed this heritage after independence. A critical Indian Marxist voice on science and technology is today rediscovered in D.D. Kosambi[13] who, despite more orthodox approaches in various other fields, pleaded powerfully for developing solar energy instead of nuclear energy. The authoritarian and fragmenting colonial character of Western science and technology, and its inherent violence, has also been worked out at length over many years by Ashis Nandy.[14] That Asian scientific and technological discoveries have been in greater harmony and interdependence with nature and, thus, are more conducive to a holistic ecological approach, has been convincingly established by Claude Alvares by contrasting them with colonial concepts.[15]

[10] For example, Jurgen Habermass, *Science and Technology as Ideology* (German), Suhrkamp, Frankfurt, 1968.

[11] Bastiaan Wielenga, *A History of the Working Class Movement*, ISI, Bangalore, 1978.

[12] E.P. Thompson, *William Morris: Romantic to Revolutionary*, Merlin Press, London, 1977.

[13] Most recently in *Traditions, Tyranny and Utopias*, especially the chapters 'The Traditions of Technology' and 'Science, Authoritarianism and Culture. On the Scope and Limits of Isolation Outside the Clinic'.

[14] D.D. Kosambi, *Science, Society and Peace* (Academy of Political and Social Studies, Pune, 1986), collected from publications in various journals.

[15] Claude Alvares, *Homo Faber: Technology and Culture in India, China and the West 1500–1975*, Allied Publishers, New Delhi, 1979.

What is new in the approach of Maria Mies and Vandana Shiva is the strong emphasis on the *patriarchal* character of Western science and technology which was much less evident in the earlier studies. They show how substitution of an organic perception of life by mechanistic, technocratic paradigms has contributed to exploitation of nature and displacement of women. They also establish more clearly the connection between ecological destruction and the capitalist 'growth' concept as a patriarchal project. This contribution is crucial since it gives a final blow to the myth of neutrality, objectivity and universality of scientific categories, and methods of experimentation. However, there is a certain drawback in their conceptualization as well.

Since both Maria Mies and Vandana Shiva draw heavily on Western feminist research on the Renaissance and the industrial revolution,[16] and since they are preoccupied with pinpointing colonial connections—which is in itself an extremely important contribution—they end up virtually suggesting that patriarchy, as a full-fledged mechanism of exploitation, is a product of the Renaissance and scientific revolution. This is particularly true of Vandana Shiva's line of argument.

While the connection between witch hunting and the development of modern science is extremely important,[17] it should *not* obscure the much earlier roots of patriarchy in antiquity[18] and, in our own civilization, in Vedic and pre-Vedic culture. Also, it is important to emphasize with Maria Mies that earlier forms of patriarchy are not just a cultural category resulting from religious ideology but that they had a material base in the organization of production of life from very early times. The way Vandana Shiva has taken Mies' analysis and reduced the problem to the Renaissance and to scientific imperialism is not enlightening for the understanding of the development of class, caste and patriarchy in the Indian context. Both Mies and Shiva are in danger of

[16] For example, studies like Carolyn Merchant, *The Death of Nature—Women, Ecology and the Scientific Revolution,* Wildwood House, London, 1980. Evelyn F. Keller, *Reflections on Gender and Science,* Yale University Press, New Haven, 1985. Susan Harding, *The Science Question in Feminism,* Cornwall University Press, Ithaca, 1986.

[17] Maria Mies, op. cit., Carolyn Merchant, op. cit., Chapter 5.

[18] *The Creation of Patriarchy,* Oxford University Press, 1986.

contributing to an ideology of patriarchy reductionism which resembles the class reductionism of the traditional left in reverse. They also have a tendency to extrenalize patriarchy as a primarily Western and modern category, which leaves out the age-old connection between patriarchy and caste in Indian society. Despite such words of caution, I feel that both Maria Mies and Vandana Shiva have given a very crucial impetus to the debate on science and technology and on ecology, not only by showing the destructive effects of a fragmented reductionist approach but also by drawing on the traditional skills of women. This is very inspiring in Vandana's narration of the Chipko movement, in which the skills of integrating forestry, agriculture and water management are combined with a philosophy of nature and of knowledge which poses an alternative to modern specialization and the promise of technocratic mechanistic solutions.

Vandana Shiva also makes an implicit contribution to the debate on women and religion by describing the ferment of local religious culture in the Chipko movement which enhance women's dignity and allows them to express their creative relationship with nature. At the same time she singles out the shakti aspects of religion, but does not mention any of the religious controls over women. Neither does she go into the problem that, what she describes as the religious 'feminine principle', is largely expressed in Hindu terms which coincide with *Sankhya* philosophy. This leaves open the question as to what the feminine principle may imply for Dalits, tribals, Muslims, Sikhs, Christians etc. One would also need to include in the debate communal attempts to appropriate ecological and women's issues and how to counter them. Also, when do religious interpretations of such issues turn communal? Heated debates on these issues arose during the Save the Western Ghats March (SWGM), between the contingents from Kerala and from Karnataka, once the march had entered South Kanara where RSS forces are very active in the environmental movement.[19]

Another point which strikes one is the fact that there was a historical alliance between chauvinistic patriarchal religion and patriarchal science and technology during the witch hunts of the post-Renaissance period. The witch hunters could be catholics or

[19] See the mimeographed statement of the Kerala section of SWGM distributed at the final meeting at Panaji, Goa, circulated by SAHYADRI, 16 Vanchi Lodge, Trichur-21.

protestants or enlightened scientists, but their ideologies were complementary to one another in controlling women, depriving them of skills and even killing them.

We can observe a contemporary version of such an anti-women alliance in the current debates on *sati* and on amniocentesis. If the Shankaracharya of Puri advocates sati and asks: 'If bodies are not equal how can rights be equal?[20] Then he is fundamentally in the same beat as modern enlightened scientists who offer sex-determination and sex pre-selection as a technological 'pro-women' solution to social discrimination, cheerfully contributing to further decimation of an already 'scarcer half'.[21] The patriarchal character of the state can be seen in the fact that both the central legislation on sati and the Maharashtra Act against sex-determination punish the women victims together with those who subject them to the crime. This connection between religious fanaticism and 'modernity' does not manifest itself only in women's issues in the narrow sense but also operates in counterpoising RSS virility versus Gandhiji's 'feminity', and Brahmin values versus Shudra values in the assassination of Mahatma Gandhi by Nathuram Godse, as Ashis Nandy has repeatedly pointed out.[22]

Reconceptualizing Productivity—The Production of Life *vs.* the Production of Profit

Apart from deepening the feminist dimension of the debate on science and technology, both Maria Mies and Vandana Shiva have contributed in an important way to the debate on productivity, redefinition of labour, and reassessment of subsistence production. This debate had earlier focused on emphasizing 'production of life' vs. the concept of 'reproduction',[23] and it also finds expression in the debate on the 'invisibility' of women's work since it often cannot

---

[20] *Illustrated Weekly,* 1–7 May 1988, pp. 26–29. But see also Swami Agnivesh's critique in the same issue, pp. 30–33.

[21] More detailed references can be found in my earlier article mentioned in note 3.

[22] See for example, 'Final Encounter: The Politics of the Assassination of Gandhi', in *At the Edge of Psychology,* Oxford University Press, Delhi, 1980, pp. 70–98; also 'From Outside the Imperium', in *Traditions, Tyranny and Utopias,* pp. 127–62.

[23] This debate is partly summarized in 'Women and Work—A Marxist Perspective' found in my book mentioned in note 3.

be measured in cash terms. Maria Mies traces the capitalist concept of productivity of the predatory ideology of 'man the hunter' and points out that this type of productivity, which is based on violence, is actually only a form of appropriation of nature and of other people's labour, while the subsistence labour of women, slaves and subjugated people is often not acknowledged as 'productive' at all. However, she maintains that capitalist productivity cannot be sustained without the subsistence labour of women, and of contract labour and peasants in the colonies.

One can state the insight in even much simpler terms: without production of life, production of commodities is impossible; people have to *live* in order to produce and consume. Therefore, the criterion for production and consumption needs to be the production and sustenance of life. Use value of products has to override *exchange* value. Obviously, our economy is not organized according to such criteria. Substantial parts of our resources go into the production of means of destruction, and other substantial parts into the production of consumer-goods which are superfluous to the substances of life, wasteful of energy and natural resources and, thus, harmful to the environment.

All over the world, women have been the mainstay of subsistence economy and of production of life, and Maria Mies shows how the destruction of subsistence economy in Europe goes together with the creation of the 'housewife' concept. While, in the West, middle class women are turned into consumers, housewifization in the Third World takes the form of capitalist exploitation of household-based production in the informal sector. Even in socialist societies, the 'housewife' concept, and thus sexual division of labour, has not fully been overcome despite large proportions of women participating in the extended production process. Maria Mies, focusing on Western societies, sees it as strategic to fight housewifization and consumerism, and proceeds from there to plead for a society of much more labour intensive, need-based, decentralized and largely autarkic units of production in which sexual division of labour, class and the polarization between head and hand could be overcome. However, it is not entirely clear how she envisages the overthrow of the dominant development and growth concept.

Vandana Shiva, in her analysis of the Chipko movement and in her evaluation of forest, agricultural and water policies, goes further

further in the reconstruction of a vision of what production of life, in the sense of an ecologically viable subsistence production, means materially as well as spiritually. The situation is movingly depicted in a scene of confrontation between Chipko women and forest officials, in which the women have brought along a lantern in bright day light. Asked about its purpose, they explain that they have to make the forest officials see the light. The male experts need to be taught forestry. The forest officials, of course, scold the 'ignorant' women who do not understand that the forest is a source of profit, resin and timber, but the women obstinately chant in return:

What does the forest bear?
Soil, water and pure air.
Soil, water and pure air
Sustain the earth and all it bears.[24]

In order to understand more fully how production of life has been ousted by production of profit I think it is important to understand the interaction of class and patriarchy a bit more deeply. Since patriarchy by definition operates to upgrade men and downgrade women, it creates a class within a class and, thus, has a certain impact on the question of class and class alliances. The argument that women's struggles divide the working class has to be countered by the argument that it is patriarchy which divides women and men of the working class, while struggles against patriarchy *unite* the working class. Patriarchal working class men tend to make certain class alliances with the exploiter as can historically be seen in the struggles over 'family wage' which account for unequal wages and assume women to be 'housewives'. While women are often accused of spreading 'middle class values' when fighting patriarchy, the line of alliance for women is, on the contrary, one of *de-classing* while the line of alliance for *men* if they uphold patriarchy, is one of alliance with the *upper class*. In the Chipko situation, it is the men who opt to be contractors and thus side with the profit motive, while it is the women who protect subsistence production and ecology by upholding the rights of women and nature, and the right to life for all.

The State uses this interaction between class and patriarchy by trying to co-opt both women and ecology struggles into the existing

[24] Vandana Shiva, op. cit., p. 73.

development concept. Women are promised upward mobility, and ecological crisis is tackled by technocratic means. One of the problems is indeed that, since working class men have a vital interest in women's subsistence labour, they have accepted the predatory concept of labour and productivity. The assumption that it is only wage labour which creates values, neglects the invisible subsistence production of women and the labour of nature as well. It also ignores the fact that the labour of nature can only be sustained if human labour is organized in harmony with nature. Interestingly, it was Marx who, in his *Critique of the Gotha Programme,* vehemently protested against the statement: 'Labour is the source of all wealth and all culture.' He said: 'Labour is *not the source* of all wealth. *Nature* is as much the source of use values (and it is surely of such, that material wealth consists!) as labour, which itself is only the manifestation of a force of nature—human labour power.'[25] He saw it as a bourgeois deception to ascribe 'supernatural creative power' to labour. The industrial concept of dominating and controlling nature, to which much of the working class movement has also subscribed, comes to an end and it will be an end with terrible convulsions of ecological disaster and lethal fights over dwindling resources. It is therefore crucial that the working class struggle incorporates the survival issues of women and nature, and that ecological and women's struggle resist the upward mobility syndrome and orient themselves towards the poorest and most exploited sections like Adivasis, Dalits and the workers of the unorganized sector, of which women anyway form the majority.

The assertion of middle class and upper class patriarchal values and concepts in the field of production connects with a corresponding development in the field of religion and communalism. Communalist ideology and organization has started as a patriarchal, urban middle class, more precisely petty bourgeois, phenomenon but it spreads out into the countryside and attempts to co-opt even dalits and adivasis, and it now tries to co-opt women. It also becomes more and more an explicit ideology of the ruling classes. Apart from offering identity in a situation of uprootedness, it projects perspectives of upward mobility. This upward mobility of course is largely a deception since the existing development concept by its very nature secures privileges only to an élite, while

[25] Karl Marx, *Selected Works* (in three volumes), vol. III (Moscow, 1970), p. 13.

the survival needs of the masses and long-term survival needs to nature are not met.

What makes the situation more complicated is that today communalism not only manipulates working classes and women but it does this by superceding and reasserting caste at the same time. The attraction for low-caste, low-class people is the fact that caste is played down while, at the same time, upper-caste values are asserted. Further, these middle class/upper caste values serve to co-opt and domesticate women. This is important when it comes to spiritual values like those projected by Vandana Shiva. As long as the religious connotation of prakriti, shakti etc., is safely in the hands of the Chipko women, they may indeed express a feminist ecological perspective and the concept of sacredness of life. Picked up by the cross currents of caste and middle class ideology, such concepts are open to communal manipulation and can even by used to manipulate women and ecological issues from a middle class perspective. Patriarchal manipulation of women's-power concepts is, anyway, a sad chapter in the history of religions. The assertion of goddess religion and shakti aspects is full of ambiguities which need to be probed much more deeply. In the Western situation, the 'return of the Goddess'[26] remains a middle class and fairly academic affairs, 'safe' in the sense that goddess religion has ceased to have a material base in subsistence agriculture and in actual organized worship (temples) for centuries. No petty bourgeois communal manipulation is on the agenda. From a psychological point of view, this trend may be quite healing.

Here, in India, things are much more complex. It is good and well to point out that there is a class component in the difference between the Devi as an independent female power-principle and the spouse Goddess, the more domesticated, patriarchal version of the goddess, as Lynn Gatewood does.[27] What she analyses is indeed something like the process of housewifization in the religious field, which certainly needs to be resisted. To go into these differences is important. However, we also know that there is a middle class communalized version of undomesticated, 'unspousified' *devi,*

[26] Edward C. Whitmont, *Return of the Spouse Goddess,* Archana Paperbacks, 1987.

[27] Lynn E. Gatewood, *Devi and the Spouse Goddess,* Manohar Publications, New Delhi, 1985.

projected by some of the terrorists in the freedom struggle and, today, resurrected by communal organizations. There is definitely a world of a difference between 'The Coming of the Devi' as an integral part of an Adivasi uprising during the freedom struggle in Gujarat which David Hardiman has so perceptively and movingly recorded in his subaltern studies[28] and the goddess-worship projected by martial communal organizations. The communalist manipulation of the feminine principle is an area which needs more exploration.

Superfluous to say, goddess worship and projection of a certain middle class type of feminine principle has even turned lethal to women in the practice of and debate on sati. Middle class values, loss in caste status, economic insecurity—all these are cross currents manipulating women, even co-opting them and enforcing both patriarchy and class together.[29] Sati is the supreme logic of housewifization mobilized against the shakti of women as independent producers organized in Chipko, production of profit *versus* production of life.

The Energy Question

From shakti as feminine principle, we have to come back to energy as a productive force in the material sense because both are deeply connected. Besides, the kind of economic system which puts production of life at the centre and which overcomes sexual division of labour, class, and dichotomies between head and hand as projected by both Maria Mies and Vandana Shiva, will need to undo and reconstruct existing socio-economic and political structures to an unprecedented extent. The strength of Vandana Shiva's argument is derived from the fact that she shows that the survival of nature, women and the poor is acutely threatened by the existing policies and that ecological intervention is an *immediate* question of survival. She does not deal with the energy question in a long-term perspective because she considers it virtually a 'Western problem'.

[28] David Hardiman, *The Coming of the Devi: Adivasi Assertion in Western India*, Oxford University Press, 1987.

[29] For the educated urbanized middle class character of the defenders of the Deorala *sati* and the commercial aspects of it see Madhu Kishwar, Ruth Vanita, 'The Burning of Roop Kanwar'; and Prahlad Singh Shekawat 'The Culture of Sati in Rajasthan', in *Manushi*, No. 42–43, 1987, pp. 15–25, 30–34.

However, the question of energy use and energy resource arises in the daily struggles for survival of the marginalized masses in the traditional sector as well. I was alerted to this by a paper by John Kurien which uses the example of the traditional fishermen to illustrate that ecological balance is a question of the *kind* of technology used and not only of who has access to or control over the technology. He argues that overfishing, and thus depletion of the sea, has been caused not only by trawling but, more so, even by outboard motorization of small fishing boats. This means, technology needs to respect the time perspective of nature's growth processes, that there is a limit to 'harvesting' of the sea by more sophisticated technological means within which alone it can yield any result. He pleads for a return to a more labour-intensive technology closer to nature, depending on the traditional knowledge and skills of the fishermen. He argues, among other things, with the law of entropy. Since he describes processes which are extremely similar to those which Vandana Shiva describes for agriculture, I felt compelled to read up on entropy, and felt that this perspective in fact needs to be essentially integrated into the ecological perspective since it strengthens very much the perspective which Vandana Shiva and Maria Mies are trying to develop. It is the perspective of entropy which gives a final blow to the myth of unlimited growth.

I will draw, in the following, on the popularizing presentation of the problem by Jeremy Rifkin, though of course a much more complicated and wider discussion on the subject has been going on.[30] There are two important aspects in Rifkin's book which have a fundamental bearing on our discussion. First, he deals with the first and second law of thermodynamics in order to show that an unlimited growth concept is simply an ideological attempt to negate some basic insights of physics. Second, he shows that history, the organization of society and changes in mode of production, and

---

[30] Jeremy Rifkin with Ted Howard, *Entropy: A New World View.* Afterword by Dr. Nicholas Georgescu Roegen, Bantam Books, New York, 1981. For further reading see Nicholas Georgescu Roegen, *The Entropy Law and the Economic Process,* Harvard University Press, Cambridge, Mass., 1971. Nicholas Georgescu Roegen, *Entropy and Economic Myths,* Pergamon Press, N.Y., 1977. Roger Garaudy, *Appel aux Vivants,* Seunil, Paris, 1979. Juan Martine-Alier, *Ecological Economics: Energy, Environment and Society,* Basil Blackwell, 1987.

science and technology have been marked by what he calls 'energy watersheds'. The last energy watershed before capitalism coincided with the Renaissance and the beginning of the industrial revolution, and the present ecological crisis is seen as the expression of another energy watershed—the transition from fossil energy to the solar age.

The first law of thermodynamics simply states that the energy content of the universe is constant. Energy can neither be created nor destroyed, it can only be transformed from one form into another. If this were all, there would be no problem. However, the snag is with the second law of thermodynamics which says that entropy is ever on the increase. This means, with every transformation of energy a certain amount of energy changes from an available or free state (i.e. available for work) into a non-available or bound state (i.e. some kind of disorder). Rifkin connects entropy directly to the ecological crisis:

That unavailable energy is what pollution is all about. Many people think that pollution is a by product of production. In fact, pollution is the sum total of all the available energy in the world that has been transformed into unavailable energy. Waste, then, is dissipated energy. Since according to the first law, energy can neither be created nor destroyed but only tranformed one way—towards a dissipated state—pollution is just another name for entropy; that is, it represents a measure of the unavailable energy present in a system.[31]

This, in itself, shows the absurdity of a developmental approach which sees low per capita energy production (and consumption) as a sign of backwardness. Of late, great effort is invested in the promotion of more nuclear plants in order to combat this kind of backwardness.[32] However, from the perspective of entropy, energy conservation and low energy use are a sign of hope. Rifkin goes in great detail into the devastating effects of high energy use in overdeveloped industrial society. However, even in our own society,

[31] Rifkin, op. cit., p. 34.

[32] 'Doubts over safety of atomic reactors dispelled', in *Indian Express*, Madurai, 29 October 1988, p. 7. 'Vice Chancellor of the Madras University, Dr. A. Gnanam, said India had one of the lowest per capita energy production of 209 kw equivalent of coal, compared to 693 kw in China, 5362 kw in UK in 11, 625 kw in USA. Under the present circumstances nuclear energy seemed to be a major resource for augmenting power production.'

certain types of high energy use lead to environmental destruction. This is not only a question of cement factories and chemical industries but also of much less centralized technologies like the outboard motors of fishermen or the techniques of the green revolution. With a certain type of energy use, renewable resources like fish, forest, water, soil, become non-renewable.

This has to do fundamentally with the energy watershed at the end of the middle ages when the economy switched from wood to coal, from renewable resource to non-renewable fossil fuel and massive use of non-renewable mineral resources.

What Rifkin describes as an energy watershed coincides with the industrial revolution, rise of capitalism, development of patriarchal science and technology, replacement of an organic world view by a mechanistic one and patriarchal destruction of women's traditional skills. While Rifkin does not go into the analysis of class and patriarchy and of colonialism, he deals with most of the aspects which Vandana Shiva has worked out: specialization and reductionism, the diminishing returns of technology, the self-defeating logic of input-intensive agriculture and reformulation of knowledge and science. Since he lacks political analysis, he sees transformation towards the solar age more in terms of individual conversion in lifestyle and collective experiments in natural agriculture. He also pins his hopes on Third World countries which may not subscribe to the Western development model. Besides, he sees redistribution of existing wealth as an essential prerequisite for an ecologically viable society, but does not really indicate how he hopes to achieve that. Despite such shortcomings, Rifkin's vision of the ecological society in the solar age comes in fact very close to what Maria Mies envisages in her final chapter, and her argument would have been greatly strengthened by the inclusion of the perspective of entropy.

One of the crucial junctures on the road towards an ecologically viable society will be the battle against the multinational corporations which have already monopolized seeds and technologies, and will try to forge ahead in capturing the market for bio-technology and biomass based energy resources. This has been seen very clearly by both Maria Mies and Vandana Shiva, but the future forms of struggle need much more exploration. Maria Mies makes a strong plea for consumer resistance and the politicization of consumption, appealing to women to refuse their expected consumer roles. A much wider question for women is how to recapture production and to assert the production of life concept as the central concept for the reorganization of the production process.

While trying to do this it will also be essential to extend the debate on population and decision making on birth. The present resistance against population control techniques which are violently anti-women, and the struggle against targeting, has to be complemented by ecological struggles which will safeguard children's survival (for example, availability of drinking water) and a critique of the existing pattern of family which makes marriage and child-bearing virtually compulsory. To have and not to have children needs to be a matter of socially responsible choices in interaction with nature. Social support structures which form an alternative to the patriarchal family need to be developed.

The Caste Factor

While grappling with the question of how production of life could have been ousted by production of profit and how the law of entropy could have completely been obscured by a blind faith in an unlimited potential for growth, how the feminine principle is being appropriated and manipulated by patriarchal ideology, caste is an important mediating factor to be analysed. Caste is another cross current in the interaction between patriarchy and class. Caste has had an impact on division of labour which is otherwise determined by class and patriarchy; it has mediated the control over resources and it has vastly encouraged the polarization between labour of head and labour of hand. I have earlier argued that sexual division of labour and sexual violence are among the root causes of ecological destruction[33] and I uphold this argument. I think this aspect is neglected by Vandana Shiva who, in her enthusiasm for the feminine principle, sees women's monopoly over subsistence agriculture as a sign of strength only and not also as a sign of patriarchal extraction of subsistence labour. I am now trying to connect this earlier position of mine with caste as a mediating factor.

Unfortunately, most studies on caste do not apply themselves to the question of patriarchy: they simply take it for granted as a given, similar to the rising and setting of the sun. Also, the older

[33] Cf. note 3.

studies do not normally take ecological aspects into consideration. It, therefore, requires some effort to connect existing caste studies with the focal concerns of this paper: women, ecology and culture. However, as far as the ecological dimension is concerned, the work of Morton Klass is of some help.[34] It is obviously impossible here to go into definitions of caste, the relationships between *varna* and *jati,* or the debate on the origins of the caste system. For our present purpose it may be useful to follow Morton Klass who shows that the one operational unit which maintains the caste system more than all other aspects (like, for example, occupational criteria, hierarchy, purity and pollution) is the functioning of caste as marriage circle.[35] This endogamous body has the power to control the behaviour of the membership. It reflects both territoriality and kinship, and has its own leadership and internal control, submitting to no higher authority. It has the power to expel as well.

Caste as marriage circle has heavily depended on patriarchy, and even in case of intermarriage, caste has been maintained by subsuming women under their husbands' caste. This principle has most clearly been expressed by the principle of hypergamy which is, in itself, an anti-feminist principle since it co-opts women into patriarchal upward mobility and undercuts feminist solidarity of declassing. Since production of life has been controlled by this marriage circle, there has been an in-built mechanism in caste to alienate women from their original skills and to 'uplift' them through ritual upgrading and its ensuing restrictions. Even among Dalits, caste as marriage circle has been in operation and basically it is only among Adivasis that production of life has been organized in a different way. This is not to say that patriarchy is absent among Adivasis but among them it takes different forms, which cannot be explored here.

Since production of life is fundamental to all production, it is also obvious from what has been said above that caste is not just an ideological phenomenon of the superstructure but has a material base to the extent that it continues to function as marriage circle. Of course, there are other material aspects as well to caste, and that is the aspect of appropriation of resources for survival, be these in the form of material or economic resources or in the form of political

---

[34] M. Klass, *Caste: The Emergence of the South Asian Social System,* op. cit.
[35] M. Klass, op. cit., p. 93.

leverage. These wider aspects often go beyond the marriage circle and extend to jati or groups of jatis. Besides, under present conditions, even caste as marriage circle, especially if it follows hypergamous rules, also serves ongoing original accumulation of capital with dowry as a form of plunder, as Maria Mies has pointed out.[36]

In his chapter 'The Economy of Caste', Morton Klass develops an argument which enables us to come closer to identifying the functioning of caste in an ecological perspective. Here it is not possible to go into the intricacies of his argument which draws on Marvin Harris' study on the sacred cow (ecological anthropology) and Polanyl's characterization of socio-economic interaction as reciprocity, redistribution and exchange, which Klass modifies into reciprocal exchange, redistributive exchange and market exchange. Klass also follows Leslie White who sees social systems as 'energy-capturing systems' bound by the laws of thermodynamics and then applies all these insights to the analysis of caste with the help of Neale's application of Polanyi's categories to the study of a North Indian village, comparing it with a study of Kathleen Gough of a village in South India.

To simplify his complicated analysis, we can say that Klass, together with Neale, sees the caste system in traditional village India as 'redistributive exchange system in which the dominant caste in a village, under the authority of the government, controls the production of the crop, the distribution of it, and even the allocation of services.'[37] Participation in this system is not by individuals but by castes in the sense of marriage circles. 'Each of these marriage circles articulates with the total economic system by providing, or controlling access to a specific set of commodities or services, with the dominant caste of the village serving as allocative caste for the redistributive exchange.[38] Klass emphasizes that this system remained largely outside the market, regulated an agricultural production which integrated a vast cattle population and was ecologically wholesome. It depended on the supervision by the dominant castes which were themselves not involved in agricultural labour. Since he is interested only in the origins of

---

[36] Maria Mies, op. cit., Chapter 5.
[37] Klass, op. cit., p. 130.
[38] Ibid.

caste, Klass does not go into the question, what has happened to the caste system under colonialism, and he does not trouble himself with the question, how agriculture could have degenerated from an ecologically eminently viable system to a disastrously destructive one.

If one tries to relate all this back to Vandana Shiva's analysis of traditional agricultural skills controlled mainly by women and maintaining an undisturbed ecological balance, one stumbles over questions which cannot be answered. From Vandana's book one comes away with an impression of a democratically organized collective agriculture dominated by the 'feminine principle' while from Morton Klass, and the many field studies he quotes, one identifies a hierarchical, patriarchal system which was, nevertheless, ecologically functional as long as it did not succumb to the onslaught of market forces.

I find it easier to explain how the model which Klass describes could be superseded by technocratic, patriarchal, Western development concepts than to understand it from Vandana Shiva's analysis which treats caste factors as non-existent. In the model which Klass describes, agriculture is carried out under patriarchal, high caste supervision: head labour controls hand labour. Such a system, under the onslaught of an energy watershed, i.e. substitution of renewable by non-renewable, can easily betray the feminine principle to which it was not committed in the first place. The compartmentalized Brahmin mind has a natural affinity to the reductionist Western mind, with the sole difference that it can resort to reintegration in the spiritual field. This is one of the reasons why the march into the twenty-first century is put forward as going along with Indian spirituality.

There is another factor within the functioning of the caste system which has a bearing on women and ecology. As Louis Dumont has pointed out, purity and pollution in the traditional system was measured by the degree of interaction with organic life.[39] This is why involvement with agriculture and with child birth, including menstruation which is related to fertility, is most polluting. There is, thus, an in-built communality between Dalits, Shudras and women from this point of view. While death is also ritually polluting, the martial castes, who were professionally death-dealing,

[39] Louis Dumont, *Homo Hierarchicus* (Vikas Publications, 1970), p. 47ff.

were not ritually polluted by their occupation. They were ranked above only those involved in production of life. This is ecologically significant because it connects with the pseudo-productivity of the predatory approach which Maria Mies describes vs. the production of life carried out by women, Dalits and Shudras. In an ecologically viable mode of production, interaction with organic life will be of the greatest importance, and this is an additional reason why the recapturing of the feminine principle will have to happen in alliance with the struggle of Adivasis, Dalits and Shudras. This also implies that Dalits and Adivasis have to fight patriarchy in their own quarters if they want to avoid either cooperation by upper caste communal forces or communalization of their own demands.

Having said all this, I hasten to add that I do *not* suggest a position of unity between Adivasis, Dalits and all 'minorities' which is 'anti-Hindu'. Such a position has been floated by various groups as something particularly radical[40] but I consider it to be potentially communalist and bound to create a communal backlash. Even 'anti-Brahmin' is a label which does not sufficiently express what the struggle is all about. All these are externalizations of the problem of caste and patriarchy which obscure the fact that the enemy is in our own midst. Casteism and patriarchy, as well as communalism operate in all of us and we have to tackle this from within. Even the women's movement, the Dalit movement or the ecological movement are not free from patriarchal, casteist and communalist attitudes.

The struggle is much more complicated. This can be seen from the debate on the sacredness of the cow. If cattle are as crucial to Indian agriculture and as ecologically useful as Marvin Morris, Morton Klass and Vandana Shiva assert with a lot of documentary evidence, then it has to be admitted that there is more to cow protection than meets the eye. One has then to distinguish cow protection and worship as a popular belief in an agricultural setting from cow worship as a middle class ideology which may turn communal or anti-women by promoting a docile mother-image of infinite patience. I whole-heartedly agree with David Hardiman when he says,

---

[40] A more detailed understanding of this position can be derived from Vasanti Raman, 'Communalism and the Threat to Diversity', in *EPW,* vol. XXII, No. 5, 31 January 1987, pp. 174–76.

All religions consist, to a large extent, of assimilated folk beliefs. It is this which gives them their mass appeal and great pertinacity over time. Religions are highly ambiguous, with seemingly identical sets of doctrines being made to serve quite contradictory causes. It is an élite form of socialism which can view religion as merely an imposition from above.[41]

This means the debates on sacred cows, sacred forests, vegetarianism and many other issues have to go on in their own rights, while everyone involved tries to use ecological criteria and to fight patriarchy, caste and middle class values from within. There is no ready-made, unambiguous, ecological or feminist folk-tradition to fall back on. The process is dialectical and very painful.

Towards a Sustainable Feminist Classless Society

To summarize, we can return to the initial questions. Firstly, what are the material and cultural skills of women which will be important for building a new society? Secondly, how can the ecological and cultural crises be overcome together.

As far as skills are concerned, it is indeed women's intimate knowledge of forestry, agriculture, water conservation, seeds, herbal medicine which needs to be mobilized against the monopoly of government planning, educated élites, industrial vested interests and multinational corporations. Under the present onslaught of development policies in the countryside, and with the rapid spread of TV, such skills can easily be devalued and destroyed. To preserve them and to make them instrumental to a policy which focuses on production of life is an urgent task. How this can practically be done needs to be explored. Beyond this, women who are still able to transmit such skills need also to be drawn into the debate on multinationals and the coming onslaught of bio-technology and food-processing, which will be ecologically and culturally ruinous in many ways. Food processing will not only drive out traditional subsistence crops but will further de-skill women, impoverish local diets and destroy cultural identities, apart from creating new health hazards. Incidentally, many of the traditional skills of women which are ecologically important are very labour intensive. This is also why they have remained female skills. This aspect reinforces my earlier point that overcoming sexual division of labour will be crucial, not just in the sense of co-opting women into male

[41] David Hardiman, *The Coming of the Goddess*, p. 10.

occupations but for teaching traditional labour intensive skills to men also.

A study needs to be make of the different skills of women in the informal sector from the point of view of what they do to the environment and what they do to women as workers. Where such skills are ecologically useful, they need to be strengthened. Any form of mechanization has to be evaluated under similar aspects. The question of consumer resistance which Maria Mies raises, is an important one in our situation as well, not only in a middle class context but even among the poorer sections where middle class consumer values are spread through media influence. A debate on synthetics and plastics is needed, and consumer resistance has to be built against ecologically damaging goods.

There are also cultural skills, in the more narrow sense of folk forms of song and dance, which need to be rethought in a movement content. In the Tamil Nadu situation, I can think of a simple skill like the *karagattam,* which is a Dalit folk-art carried out by women who dance with water pots on their heads. This is associated with Shakti and water and, thus, with profound production of life symbolism. Today, this dance has become a mere tourist attraction. It has been deprived of meaning, commercialized, and has become a vehicle of sexual objectification and exploitation of women. Do we just write off such skills or can they become part of a counter-culture?

In the light of what Vandana Shiva writes on the popular religion of the Chipko women, and of the ongoing cooperation of ecological issues and women's concerns, the debate on religion needs to be carried further along the lines developed in this paper. Despite being oppressive structures in many of their organized forms, religions have also given inner spaces to women and ecological spaces to larger communities. These aspects need to be rediscovered and weighed against potential communal manipulation. Active struggle against communalism needs to be an integral part of the women's movement, working class movement, ecological movement and Dalit and Adivasi movements. This struggle has to go beyond a narrow bourgeois concept of secularism which can see religion only as a 'private affair'.

Finally, there needs to be a more integrated debate on violence and non-violence since the perception of this question is different in class organizations, in the struggles of Dalits and Adivasis, However, this debate cannot be carried out in the abstract but needs to be developed in concrete struggles.

3

The Gender and Environment Debate: Lessons from India

Bina Agarwal

What is women's relationship with the environment? Is it distinct from that of men's? The growing literature on ecofeminism in the West, and especially in the United States, conceptualizes the link between gender and the environment primarily in ideological terms. An intensifying struggle for survival in the developing world, however, highlights the material basis for this link and sets the background for an alternative formulation to ecofeminism, which I term 'feminist environmentalism'.

In this essay I will argue that women, especially those in poor rural households in India, on the one hand, are victims of environmental degradation in quite gender-specific ways. On the other hand, they have been active agents in movements of environmental protection and regeneration, often bringing to them a gender-specific perspective and one which needs to inform our view of alternatives. To contextualize the discussion, and to examine the opposing dimensions of women as victims and women as actors in concrete terms, this essay will focus on India, although the issues are clearly relevant to other parts of the Third World as well. The discussion is divided into five sections. The first section outlines the ecofeminist debate in the United States and one prominent Indian variant of it, and suggests an alternative conceptualization.

* This essay was originally published in *Feminist Studies*, vol. 18, No. 1 (Spring 1992), and is reprinted here, by permission of the publisher, Feminist Studies Inc., c/o Women's Studies Program, University of Maryland, College Park, MD 20742, USA.

The next three sections respectively trace the nature and causes of environmental degradation in rural India, its class and gender implications, and the responses to it by the state and grassroots groups. The concluding section argues for an alternative transformative approach to development.

Some Conceptual Issues

Ecofeminism

Ecofeminism embodies within it several different strands of discourse, many of which have yet to be spelled out fully, and which reflect, among other things, different positions within the Western feminist movement (radical, liberal, socialist). As a body of thought ecofeminism is as yet underdeveloped and still evolving, but carries a growing advocacy. My purpose is not to critique ecofeminist discourse in detail, but rather to focus on some of its major elements, especially in order to examine whether and how it might feed into the formulation of a Third World perspective on gender and the environment. Disentangling the various threads in the debate, and focusing on those more clearly articulated, provides us with the following picture of the ecofeminist argument(s):[1] (1) There are important connections between the domination and exploitation of nature. (2) In patriarchal thought, women are identified as being closer to nature and men as being closer to culture. Nature is seen as inferior to culture, hence, women are seen as inferior to men. (3) Because the domination of women and the domination of nature have occurred together, women have a particular stake in ending the domination of nature, 'in healing the alienated human and non-human nature.'[2] (4) The feminist movement and the environmental movement both stand for egalitarian, non-hierarchical systems. They thus have a good deal in common and need to work together to evolve a common perspective, theory and practice.

In the ecofeminist argument, therefore, the connection between the domination of women and that of nature is basically seen as *ideological*, as rooted in a system of ideas and representations, values

[1] See especially King, 1981, 1989, 1990; Salleh, 1984; Merchant, 1980; and Griffin, 1978. Also see discussions and critiques by Zimmerman, 1987; Warren, 1987; Cheney, 1987; and Longino, 1981.

[2] King, 1989, p. 18.

and beliefs, that places women and the non-human world hierarchically below men. And it calls upon women and men to reconceptualize themselves, and their relationships to one another and to the non-human world, in non-hierarchical ways.

We might then ask: In what is this connection between nature and women seen to be rooted? The idea that women are seen as closer to nature than men was initially introduced into contemporary feminist discourse by Sherry Ortner who argued that 'woman is being identified with—or, if you will, seems to be a symbol of—something that every culture devalues, defines as being of a lower order of existence than itself ... [That something] is 'nature' in the most generalized sense ... [Women are everywhere] being symbolically associated with nature, as opposed to men, who are identified with culture.'[3] In her initial formulation, the connection between women and nature was clearly rooted in the biological processes of reproduction although, even then, Ortner did recognize that women, like men, also *mediate* between nature and culture.

Ortner has since modified her position which was also criticized by others (particularly social anthropologists) on several counts, especially because the nature–culture divide is not universal across all cultures, nor is there uniformity in the meaning attributed to 'nature', 'culture', 'male', and 'female'.[4] Still, some ecofeminists accept the emphasis on biology uncritically and in different ways reiterate it. An extreme form of this position is that taken by Ariel Kay Salleh who grounds even women's consciousness in biology and in nature. She argues: 'Women's monthly fertility cycle, the tiring symbiosis of pregnancy, the wrench of childbirth and the pleasure of suckling an infant, these things already ground women's consciousness in the knowledge of being coterminous with nature. However tacit or unconscious this identity may be for many women ... it is nevertheless 'a fact of life'.[5] Others such as Ynestra King and Carolyn Merchant argue that the nature–culture dichotomy is a false one, a patriarchal ideological construct which is then used to maintain gender hierarchy. At the same time they accept the view

---

[3] Ortner, 1974, quotes on pp. 72–3.
[4] See the case studies, and especially Carol P. MacCormack's introductory essay in MacCormack and Strathern, 1980, p. 13. Also see Moore, 1989.
[5] Salleh, 1984, p. 340.

that women are ideologically constructed as closer to nature because of their biology.[6]

Merchant, however, in an illuminating historical analysis, shows that in premodern Europe the conceptual connection between women and nature rested on two divergent images, coexisting simultaneously, one which constrained the destruction of nature and the other which sanctioned it. Both identified nature with the female sex. The first image, which was the dominant one, identified nature, especially the earth, with the nurturing mother, and culturally restricted 'the types of socially and morally sanctioned human actions allowable with respect to the earth. One does not readily slay a mother, dig into her entrails for gold, or mutilate her body....'[7] The opposing image was of nature as wild and uncontrollable which could render violence, storms, drought, and general chaos. This image culturally sanctioned mastery and human dominance over nature.

Between the sixteenth and seventeenth centuries, Merchant suggests, the scientific revolution and the growth of a market-oriented culture in Europe undermined the image of an organic cosmos with a living female earth at its centre. This image gave way to a mechanistic world-view in which nature was reconceived as something to be mastered and controlled by humans. The twin ideas of mechanism and of dominance over nature supported both the denudation of nature and male dominance over women. Merchant observes:

The ancient identity of nature as a nurturing mother links women's history with the history of the environment and ecological change.... In investigating the roots of our current environmental dilemma and its connections to science, technology, and the economy, we must re-examine the formation of a world-view and a science that, by reconceptualizing reality as a machine rather than a living organism, sanctioned the domination of both nature and women.

Today, Merchant proposes, juxtaposing the egalitarian goals of the women's movement and the environmental movement can suggest 'new values and social structures, based not on the domination of women and nature as resources but on the full expression of both

[6] See Merchant, 1980, p. 144.
[7] Ibid., pp. 2–3.

male and female talent and on the maintenance of environmental integrity.'[8]

Ecofeminist discourse, therefore, highlights (a) some of the important conceptual links between the *symbolic* construction of women and nature and the ways of *acting* upon them (although Merchant alone goes beyond the level of assertion to trace these links in concrete terms, historically); (b) the underlying commonality between the premises and goals of the women's movement and the environmental movement; and (c) an alternative vision of a more egalitarian and harmonious future society.

At the same time the ecofeminist argument as constructed is problematic on several counts. First, it posits 'woman' as a unitary category and fails to differentiate among women by class, race, ethnicity, and so on. It thus ignores forms of domination other than gender which also impinge critically on women's position.[9] Second, it locates the domination of women and of nature almost solely in ideology, neglecting the (inter-related) material sources of this dominance (based on economic advantage and political power). Third, even in the realm of ideological constructs, it says little (with the exception of Merchant's analysis) about the social, economic and political structures within which these constructs are produced and transformed. Nor does it address the central issue of the means by which certain dominant groups (predicated on gender, class, etc.) are able to bring about ideological shifts in their own favour and how such shifts get entrenched. Fourth, the ecofeminist argument does not take into account women's lived material relationship with nature, as opposed to what others or they themselves might conceive that relationship to be. Fifth, those strands of ecofeminism that trace the connection between women and nature to biology may be seen as adhering to a form of essentialism (some notion of a female 'essence' which is unchangeable and irreducible).[10] Such a formulation flies in the face of wide-ranging evidence that concepts of nature, culture,

[8] For this and the previous quote see ibid., pp. xx–xxi, xix.

[9] King in 'Feminism and the Revolt', 1981 (unlike in her earlier work) does mention the necessity of such a differentiation, but does not discuss how a recognition of this difference would affect her basic analysis.

[10] For an illuminating discussion of the debate on essentialism and constructionism within feminist theory, see Fuss, 1989.

gender, and so on, are historically and socially constructed and vary across and within cultures and time periods.[11]

In other words, the debate highlights the significant effect of ideological constructs in shaping relations of gender dominance and forms of acting on the non-human world, but if these constructs are to be challenged it is necessary to go further. We need a theoretical understanding of what could be termed 'the political economy of ideological construction', that is, of the interplay between conflicting discourses, the groups promoting particular discourses, and the means used to entrench views embodied in those discourses. Equally, it is critical to examine the underlying basis of women's relationship with the non-human world at levels other than ideology (such as through the work women and men do and the gender division of property and power) and to address how the material realities in which women of different classes (castes/races) are rooted might affect their responses to environmental degradation. Women in the West, for instance, have responded in specific ways to the threat of environmental destruction, such as by organizing the Greenham Commons resistance to nuclear missiles in England and by participating in the Green movement across Europe and the United States. A variety of actions have similarly been taken by women in the Third World, as discussed later. The question then is: Are there *gendered* aspects to these responses? If so, in what are these responses rooted?

Vandana Shiva's work on India takes us a step forward. Like the ecofeminists, she sees violence against nature and against women as built into the very mode of perceiving both. Like Merchant, she argues that violence against nature in intrinsic to the dominant industrial/developmental model, which she characterizes as a colonial imposition. Associated with the adoption of this developmental model, Shiva argues, was a radical conceptual shift away from the traditional Indian cosmological view of (animate and inanimate) nature as Prakriti, as 'activity *and* diversity' and as 'an expression of Shakti, the feminine and creative principle of the cosmos' which 'in conjunction with the masculine principle (Purusha)...creates the world.' In this shift, the living, nurturing relationship between man and nature as earth mother was replaced by the notion of man as separate from and dominating over inert

---

[11] See case studies in MacCormack and Strathern, 1980.

and passive nature. 'Viewed from the perspective of nature, or women embedded in nature,' the shift was repressive and violent. 'For women...the death of Prakriti is simultaneously a beginning of their marginalization, devaluation, displacement, and ultimate dispensability. The ecological crisis is, at its root, the death of the feminine principle....'[12]

At the same time, Shiva notes that violence against women and against nature are linked not just ideologically but also materially. For instance, Third World women are dependent on nature 'for drawing sustenance for themselves, their families, their societies.' The destruction of nature thus becomes the destruction of women's sources for 'staying alive'. Drawing upon her experience of working with women activists in the Chipko movement—the environmental movement for forest protection and regeneration in the Garhwal hills of north-west India—Shiva argues that 'Third World women' have both a special dependence on nature and a special knowledge of nature. This knowledge has been systematically marginalized under the impact of modern science:

Modern reductionist science, like development, turns out to be a patriarchal project, which has excluded women as experts, and has simultaneously excluded ecology and holistic ways of knowing which understand and respect nature's processes and interconnectedness as science.[13]

Shiva takes us further than the western ecofeminists in exploring the links between ways of thinking about development, the processes of developmental change, and the impact of these on the environment and on the people dependent upon it for their livelihood. These links are of critical significance. Nevertheless her argument has three principal analytical problems. First, her examples relate to rural women primarily from north-west India, but her generalizations conflate all Third World women into one category. Although she distinguishes Third World women from the rest, like the ecofeminists she does not differentiate between women of different classes, castes, races, ecological zones, and so on. Hence, implicitly, a form of essentialism could be read into her work, in that all Third World women, whom she sees as

---

[12] Shiva, 1988, quotes on pp. 39, 42.
[13] Ibid., pp. 14–15.

'embedded in nature', *qua women* have a special relationship with the natural environment. This still begs the question: What is the basis of this relationship and how do women acquire this special understanding?

Second, she does not indicate by what concrete processes and institutions ideological constructions of gender and nature have changed in India, nor does she recognize the coexistence of several ideological strands, given India's ethnic and religious diversity. For instance, her emphasis on the feminine principle as the guiding idea in Indian philosophic discourse in fact relates to the Hindu discourse alone and cannot be seen as applicable for Indians of all religious persuasions.[14] Indeed, Hinduism itself is pluralistic, fluid, and contains several coexisting discourses with varying gender implications.[15] But perhaps most importantly, it is not clear how

[14] Also see the discussion by Dietrich, 1989. Apart from the religion-specificity of the discourse on the feminine principle, an interesting example of the relationship between different religious traditions and the environment is that of sacred groves. These groves, dedicated to local deities and sometimes spread over 100 acres, were traditionally preserved by local Hindu and tribal communities and could be found in several parts of the country. Entry into them was severely restricted and tree-cutting usually forbidden (see Gadgil and Vartak, 1975). These groves are now disappearing. Among the Khasi tribe of Northeast India, elderly non-Christian Khasis I spoke to identify the main cause of this destruction to be the large-scale conversion of Khasis to Christianity which undermined traditional beliefs in deities and so removed the main obstacle to the exploitation of these groves for personal gain.

[15] For instance, the *Rig Veda,* the collection of sacred Sanskrit hymns preserved orally for over 3,000 years, which constitutes the roots of Brahminic Hinduism, is said to have been traditionally inaccessible to women and untouchable castes, both of whom were forbidden to recite the hymns on the ground that they would defile the magic power of the words (for elaboration, see Flaherty, 1990). In contrast, the Bhakti movement, which began around the sixth century, sought to establish a direct relationship between God and the individual (without the mediation of Brahmin priests) irrespective of sex or caste and gave rise to numerous devotional songs and poems in the vernacular languages. Many women are associated with the movement, one of the best known being the sixteenth-century poet-saint, Mirabai. Today, the Bhakti tradition coexists with the more ritualistic and rigid Brahminic tradition. In fact, a significant dimension of the growing Hindu fundamentalism in recent years is precisely the attempt by some to give prominence to one interpretation of Hinduism over others—a visible, contemporary struggle over meanings.

Similarly, several versions of the great epic, *Ramayana* have existed historically, including versions where the central female character, Sita, displays none of the

and in which historical period(s) the concept of the feminine principle *in practice* affected gender relations or relations between people and nature.

Third, Shiva attributes existing forms of destruction of nature and the oppression of women (in both symbolic and real terms) principally to the Third World's history of colonialism and to the imposition of Western science and a Western model of development. Undeniably, the colonial experience and the forms that modern development has taken in Third World countries have been destructive and distorting economically, institutionally and culturally. However, it cannot be ignored that this process impinged on pre-existing bases of economic and social (including gender) inequalities.

Here it is important to distinguish between the particular model of modernization that clearly has been imported/adopted from the West by many Third World countries (with or without a history of colonization) and the socio-economic base on which this model was imposed. Pre-British India, especially during the Mughal period, was considerably class/caste-stratified, although varyingly across regions.[16] This would have affected the patterns of access to and use of natural resources by different classes and social groups. Although much more research is needed on the political economy of natural resource use in the pre-colonial period, the evidence of differentiated peasant communities at that time cautions against sweeping historical generalizations about the effects of colonial rule.

By locating the 'problem' almost entirely in the Third World's experience of the West, Shiva misses out on the very real local forces of power, privilege and property relations that predate colonialism. What exists today is a complex legacy of colonial and pre-colonial interactions that defines the constraints and parameters within which and from which present thinking and action on development, resource use and social change have to proceed. In

---

subservience to her husband that is emphasized in the popular version (treated as sacred text) and which has moulded the image of the ideal Indian woman in the modern mass media. Feminist resistance to such gender construction has taken various forms, including challenging popular interpretations of female characters in the epics and drawing attention to alternative interpretations. See, for instance, Chakravarty, 1983; and Agarwal, 1985.

[16] See Habib, 1984, and his essay in Ray Chaudhuri and Habib, 1982.

particular, a strategy for change requires an explicit analysis of the structural causes of environmental degradation, its effects and responses to it. The outline for an alternative framework, which I term feminist environmentalism, is suggested below.

Feminist Environmentalism

I would like to suggest here that women's and men's relationship with nature needs to be understood as rooted in their material reality, in their specific forms of interaction with the environment. Hence, in so far as there is a gender and class (caste/race)-based division of labour and distribution of property and power, gender and class (caste/race) structure people's interactions with nature and so structure the effects of environmental change on people and their responses to it. And where knowledge about nature is experiential in its basis, the divisions of labour, property and power which shape experience also shape the knowledge based on that experience.

For instance, poor peasant and tribal women have typically been responsible for fetching fuel and fodder and in hill and tribal communities have also often been the main cultivators. They are thus likely to be affected adversely in quite specific ways by environmental degradation. At the same time, in the course of their everyday interactions with nature, they acquire a special knowledge of species varieties and the processes of natural regeneration. (This would include knowledge passed on to them by, for example, their mothers.) They could thus be seen as both victims of the destruction of nature and as repositories of knowledge about nature, in ways distinct from the men of their class. The former aspect would provide the gendered impulse for their resistance and response to environmental destruction. The latter would condition their perceptions and choices of what should be done. Indeed, on the basis of their experiential understanding and knowledge, they could provide a special perspective on the processes of environmental regeneration, one that needs to inform our view of alternative approaches to development. (By extension, women who are no longer actively using this knowledge for their daily sustenance, and are no longer in contact with the natural environment in the same way, are likely to lose this knowledge over time and with it the possibility of its transmission to others.)

In this conceptualization, therefore, the link between women and the environment can be seen as structured by a given gender and class (caste/race) organization of production, reproduction and distribution. Ideological constructions such as of gender, of nature, and of the relationship between the two, may be seen as (interactively) a part of this structuring but not the whole of it. This perspective I term 'feminist environmentalism'.

In terms of action such a perspective would call for struggles over *both* resources and meanings. It would imply grappling with the dominant groups who have the property, power and privilege to control resources, and these or other groups who control ways of thinking about them, via educational, media, religious and legal institutions. On the feminist front there would be a need to challenge and transform both *notions* about gender and the *actual* division of work and resources between the genders. On the environmental front there would be a need to challenge and transform not only notions about the relationship between people and nature but also the actual methods of appropriation of nature's resources by a few. Feminist environmentalism underlines the necessity of addressing these dimensions from both fronts.

To concretize the discussion, consider India's experience in the sections below. The focus throughout is on the rural environment.

Environmental Degradation and Forms of Appropriation

In India (as in much of Asia and Africa) a wide variety of essential items are gathered by rural households from the village commons and forests for every day personal use and sale, such as food, fuel, fodder, fibre, small timber, manure, bamboo, medicinal herbs, oils, materials for house building and handicrafts, resin, gum, honey and spices.[17] Although all rural households use the village commons in some degree, for the poor they are of critical significance given the skewedness of privatized land distribution in the subcontinent.[18] Data for the early 1980s from twelve semi-arid districts in seven Indian states indicate that for poor rural households (the landless

---

[17] See especially Kerala Forestry Research Institute, 1980, p. 235.

[18] It is estimated that in 1981–2, 66.6 per cent of landowning households in rural India owned 1 hectare or less and accounted for only 12.2 per cent of all land owned by rural households (Government of India, 1987). The distribution of operational holdings is almost as skewed.

and those with less than two hectares dryland equivalent) village commons account for at least 9 per cent of total income, and in most cases 20 per cent or more, but contribute only 1 to 4 per cent of the incomes of the non-poor (Table 3.1). The dependence of the poor is especially high for fuel and fodder: village commons supply more than 91 per cent of firewood and more than 69 per cent of their grazing needs, compared with the relative self-sufficiency of the larger landed households. Access to village commons reduces income inequalities in the village between poor and non-poor households. Also there is a close link between the viability of small farmers' private property resources and their access to the commons for grazing draft as well as milch animals.[19]

Similarly, forests have always been significant sources of livelihood, especially for tribal populations, and have provided the basis of swidden cultivation, hunting and the gathering of non-timber forest produce. In India, an estimated 30 million or more people in the country depend wholly or substantially on such forest produce for a livelihood.[20] These sources are especially critical during lean agricultural seasons and during drought and famine.[21]

The health of forests, in turn, has an impact on the health of soils (especially in the hills) and the availability of ground and surface water for irrigation and drinking. For a large percentage of rural households, the water for irrigation, drinking and various domestic uses comes directly from rivers and streams in the hills and plains. Again there are class differences in the nature of their dependency and access. The richer households are better able to tap the (relatively cleaner) ground water for drinking and irrigation by sinking more and deeper wells and tubewells, but the poor are mainly dependent on surface sources.

However, the availability of the country's natural resources to the poor is being severely eroded by two parallel, and inter-related trends—first, their growing degradation both in quantity and quality; second, their increasing statization (appropriation by the state) and privatization (appropriation by a minority of individuals), with an associated decline in what was earlier communal. These

---

[19] See Jodha, 1986; and Blaikie, 1985.
[20] Kulkarni, 1983.
[21] See Pingle, 1975; and Agarwal, 1990.

TABLE 3.1 Average Annual Income from Village Commons in
Selected Districts of India (1982–5)

State[1] and districts	Per household annual average income from village commons			
	Poor households[2]		Other households[3]	
	Value (Rs)	Per cent of total household income	Value (Rs)	Per cent of total household income
Andhra Pradesh				
Mahbubnagar	534	17	171	1
Gujarat				
Mehsana	730	16	162	1
Sabarkantha	818	21	208	1
Karnataka				
Mysore	649	20	170	3
Madhya Pradesh				
Mandsaur	685	18	303	1
Raisen	780	26	468	4
Maharashtra				
Akola	447	9	134	1
Aurangabad	584	13	163	1
Sholapur	641	20	235	2
Rajasthan				
Jalore	709	21	387	2
Nagaur	831	23	438	3
Tamil Nadu				
Dharmapuri	738	22	164	2

Source: Jodha, 1986, p. 1176.

Notes: [1] 'State' here refers to administrative divisions within India and is not used in the political economy sense of the word as used in the text.

[2] Landless households and those owning < 2 hectares (ha.) dryland equivalent.

[3] Those owning > 2 ha. dryland equivalent. 1 ha. = 2.47 acres.

two trends, both independently and interactively, underlie many of the differential class–gender effects of environmental degradation outlined later. Independently, the former trend is reducing overall availability, and the latter is increasing inequalities in the distribution of what is available. Interactively, an altered distribution in favour of the state and some individuals and away from community control can contribute to environmental degradation in so far as community resource management systems may be more effective in environmental protection and regeneration than are the state or individuals. These two trends I call the primary factors underlying the class–gender effects of environmental change. Several intermediary factors impinge on these primary ones, the most important of which, in my view, are the following: the erosion of community resource management systems resulting from the shift in 'control rights' over natural resources away from community hands,[22] population growth and technological choices in agriculture and their associated effect on local knowledge systems. These also need to be seen in interactive terms. Consider each in turn.

Forms of Environmental Degradation

Although there is as yet an inadequate data base to indicate the exact extent of environmental degradation in India and its cross-regional variations, available macro-information provides sufficient pointers to warrant considerable concern and possibly alarm. Degradation in India's natural resource base is manifest in disappearing forests, deteriorating soil conditions and depleting water resources. Satellite data from India reveal that in 1985–7, 19.5 per cent of the country's geo-area was forested and declining at an estimated rate of 1.3 million hectares a year.[23] Again, by official estimates, in 1980, 56.6 per cent of India's land was suffering from environmental problems, especially water and wind erosion. Unofficial estimates are even higher. In some canal projects, one-half the area that could have been irrigated and cultivated has been lost due to waterlogging,[24] creating what the local people aptly call

[22] I prefer to use the term 'control rights' here, rather than the commonly used term 'property rights', because what appears critical in this context is less who owns the resources than who has control over them. Hence, for instance, the control of state-owned resources could effectively rest with the village community.

[23] Government of India, 1990.

[24] Joshi and Agnihotri, 1984.

'wet deserts'. The area under periodic floods doubled between 1971 and 1981, and soil fertility is declining due to the excessive use of chemical fertilizers. Similarly, the availability of both ground and surface water is falling. Groundwater levels have fallen permanently in several regions, including in northern India with its high water tables, due to the indiscriminate sinking of tubewells—the leading input in the Green Revolution technology.[25] As a result, many drinking water wells have dried up or otherwise been rendered unusable. In addition, fertilizer and pesticide run-offs into natural water sources have destroyed fish life and polluted water for human use in several areas.[26]

The Process of Statization

In India, both under colonial rule and continuing in the post-colonial period, state control over forests and village commons has grown, with selective access being granted to a favoured few. To begin with, several aspects of British colonial policy have had long-lasting effects.[27] First, the British established state monopoly over forests, reserving large tracts for timber extraction. Second, associated with this was a severe curtailment in the customary rights of local populations to these resources, rights of access being granted only under highly restricted conditions, with a total prohibition on the barter or sale of forest produce by such right-holders. At the same time, the forest settlement officer could give considerable concessions to those he chose to so privilege. Third, the colonial state promoted the notion of 'scientific' forest management which essentially cloaked the practice of encouraging commercially profitable species, often at the cost of species used by the local population. Fourth, there was virtually indiscriminate forest exploitation by European and Indian private contractors, especially for building railways, ships and bridges. Tree clearing was also encouraged for establishing tea and coffee plantations and expanding the area under agriculture to increase the government's land revenue base. In effect these policies (a) severely eroded local systems of forest management; (b) legally cut off an important source of sustenance for people, even though illegal entries

[25] See, for instance, Bandyopadhyay, 1986; and Dhawan, 1982.
[26] Centre for Science and Environment, 1986.
[27] See especially, Guha, 1983.

continued; (c) created a continuing source of tension between the forestry officials and the local people; and (d) oriented forest management to commercial needs.

Post-independence policies show little shift from the colonial view of forests as primarily a source of commercial use and gain. State monopoly over forests has persisted, with all the attendant tensions, as has the practice of scientific forestry in the interests of commercial profit. Restrictions on local people's access to non-timber forest produce have actually increased, and the harassment and exploitation of forest-dwellers by the government's forest guards is widespread.[28]

The Process of Privatization

A growing privatization of community resources in individual (essentially male) hands has paralleled the process of statization. Customarily, large parts of village common lands, especially in north-west India, were what could be termed 'community-private', that is, they were private in so far as use rights to them were usually limited to members of the community and therefore exclusionary; at the same time they were communal in that such rights were often administered by a group rather than by an individual.[29] Table 3.2 reveals a decline in village commons ranging between 26 and 63 percentage points across different regions, between 1950 and 1984. This is attributable mainly to state policy acting to benefit selected groups over others, including illegal encroachments by farmers, made legal over time; the auctioning of parts of commons by the government to private contractors for commercial exploitation; and government distribution of common land to individuals under various schemes which were, in theory, initiated for benefiting the poor but in practice benefited the well-off farmers.[30] For sixteen of the nineteen districts covered, the share of the poor was less than that of the non-poor (Table 3.2). Hence the poor lost out collectively while gaining little individually.

[28] See Chand and Bezboruah, 1980; and Swaminathan, 1982.

[29] However, the degree to which the village community acted as a cohesive group and the extent of control it exercised over communal land varied across undivided India: it was much greater in the north-west than elsewhere. See Baden–Powell, 1957.

[30] For a detailed discussion on these causes, see Jodha, 1986.

TABLE 3.2 Distribution of Privatized Village Commons in
Selected Districts of India

States and districts	VCs as per cent of village area 1982–4	Per cent decline in VC area 1950–84	Per cent of land to:		Per cent of recipients among:		Per household area owned (ha.)			
			Poor	Others	Poor	Others	Poor		Others	
							Before[1]	After[2]	Before	After
Andhra Pradesh										
Mahbubnagar	9	43	50	50	76	24	0.3	0.9	3.0	5.1
Medak	11	45	51	49	59	41	1.0	2.2	3.1	4.6
Gujarat										
Banaskantha	9	49	18	82	38	62	0.8	2.0	5.4	8.8
Mehsana	11	37	20	80	36	64	1.0	1.7	8.0	9.8
Sabarkantha	12	46	28	72	55	45	0.5	1.1	7.0	9.8
Karnataka										
Bihar	12	41	39	61	64	36	1.0	2.0	6.4	9.2
Gulbarga	9	43	43	57	60	40	0.8	2.4	4.5	7.7
Mysore	18	32	44	56	67	33	0.9	1.9	4.1	11.6
Madhya Pradesh										
Mandsaur	22	34	45	55	75	25	1.2	2.5	7.7	12.4
Raisen	23	47	42	58	68	32	1.3	2.2	6.2	9.0
Vidisha	28	32	38	62	48	52	1.3	2.5	4.9	6.8
Maharashtra										
Akola	11	42	39	61	58	42	1.0	1.6	3.1	4.6
Aurangabad	15	30	30	70	42	58	1.1	2.2	6.4	6.3
Sholapur	19	26	42	58	53	47	0.7	2.2	3.4	5.6
Rajasthan										
Jalore	18	37	14	86	37	63	0.3	1.7	7.2	12.5
Jodhpur	16	58	24	76	35	65	0.4	1.3	2.3	3.8
Nagaur	15	63	21	79	41	59	1.3	2.5	2.4	5.2
Tamil Nadu										
Coimbatore	9	47	50	50	75	25	0.8	2.5	3.8	5.8
Dharmapuri	12	52	49	51	55	45	1.0	1.9	4.6	7.5

Source: Jodha, 1986, pp. 1177–8.

Notes: [1] Before the distribution of VC land.
[2] After the distribution of VC land.

Similarly, in the tapping of groundwater through tubewells there are dramatic inequalities in the distribution of what is effectively an underground commons. Tubewells are concentrated in the hands of the rich and the noted associated fall in water tables has, in many areas, dried up many shallow irrigation and drinking water wells used by the poor. In some regions, they have also depleted soil moisture from land used by poor households.[31]

Now consider the intermediary factors mentioned earlier: the erosion of community management systems, population growth, and choice of agricultural technology and local knowledge systems.

Erosion of Community Resource Management Systems

The statization and privatization of communal resources have, in turn, systematically undermined traditional institutional arrangements of resource use and management. The documentation on this is growing, but even existing work reveals systems of water management, methods of gathering firewood and fodder, and practices of shifting agriculture which were typically not destructive of nature.[32] Some traditional religious and folk beliefs also (as noted) contributed to the preservation of nature, especially trees or orchards deemed sacred.[33]

Of course, much more empirical documentation is needed on how regionally widespread these traditional systems of management were and the contexts in which they were successful in ensuring community cooperation. However, the basic point is that where traditional community management existed, as it did in many areas, *responsibility for resource management was linked to resource use* via local community institutions. Where control over these resources passed from the hands of the community to those of the state or of individuals, this link was effectively broken.

In turn, the shift from community control and management of common property, to state or individual ownership and control,

---

[31] Bandyopadhyay, 1986.

[32] On traditional systems of community water management, see Sengupta, 1985; Leach, 1967; and Seklar, 1981. On communal management of forests and village commons, see Guha, 1985; Gadgil, 1985; Moench, 1988. On firewood gathering practices, see Agarwal, 1987. Firewood for domestic use in rural households was customarily collected in the form of twigs and fallen branches, which did not destroy the trees. Even today, 75 per cent of firewood used as domestic fuel in northern India (and 100 per cent in some other areas) is in this form.

[33] The preservation of sacred groves described in note 14 is one such example.

has increased environmental degradation.[34] As Daniel W. Bromley and Michael M. Cernea note,

the *appearance* of environmental management created through the establishment of government agencies, and the aura of coherent policy by issuance of decrees prohibiting entry to—and harvesting from—State property, has led to continued degradation of resources under the tolerant eye of government agencies.[35]

Property rights vested in individuals are also no guarantee for environmental regeneration. Indeed, as will be discussed at greater length later, individual farmers attempting tree planting for short-term profits have tended to plant quick-growing commercial trees such as eucalyptus, which can prove environmentally costly.

Population Growth

Excessive population growth has often been identified as the primary culprit of environmental degradation. And undoubtedly, a rapidly growing population impinging over time on a limited land/water/forest base is likely to degrade the environment. However, political economy dimensions clearly underlie the *pace* at which this process occurs and *how the costs of it are distributed.* The continuing (legal and illegal) exploitation of forests, and the increasing appropriation of village commons and groundwater resources by a few, leave the vast majority to subsist on a shrinking natural resource base. Added to this is the noted erosion of community resource management systems which had enforced limitations on what people could and did take from communal resources, and which could perhaps have ensured their protection, despite population pressure.[36]

Population growth can thus be seen as exacerbating a given situation but not necessarily as its primary cause. It is questionable that interventions to control population growth can, in themselves, stem environmental degradation, although clearly, as Paul Shaw argues, they can 'buy crucial time until we figure out how' to dismantle more ultimate causes.'[37]

[34] Also see discussion in Dasgupta and Maler, 1990.
[35] Bromley and Cernea, 1989, p. 25.
[36] Ibid.
[37] Shaw, 1989, p. 7.

What adds complexity to even this possibility is that in the link between environmental degradation and population growth, the causality can also run in the opposite direction. For instance, poverty associated with environmental degradation could induce a range of fertility-increasing responses—reduced education for young girls as they devote more time to collecting fuel, fodder, and so on, leading to higher fertility in the long term, given the negative correlation between female education and fertility; higher infant mortality rates inducing higher fertility to ensure a given completed family size; and people having more children to enable the family to diversify incomes as a risk-reducing mechanism in environmentally high-risk areas.[38] These links are another reminder that it is critical to focus on women's status when formulating policies for environmental protection.

Choice of Agricultural Technology and Erosion of Local Knowledge Systems

Many of the noted forms of environmental degradation are associated with the Green Revolution technology adopted to increase crop output. Although dramatically successful in the latter objective in the short run, it has had high environmental costs, such as falling water tables due to tubewells, waterlogged and saline soils from most large irrigation schemes, declining soil fertility with excessive chemical fertilizer use, and water pollution with pesticides. Moreover, the long-term sustainability of the output increases achieved so far, itself appears doubtful. Deteriorating soil and water conditions are already being reflected in declining crop yields.[39] Genetic variety has also shrunk, and many of the indigenously developed crop varieties (long-tested and adapted to local conditions) have been replaced by improved seeds which are more susceptible to pest attacks. The long-term annual growth rate of agricultural production in India over 1968–5 was 2.6 per cent, that is, slightly *lower* than the pre-Green Revolution, 1950–5, rate of 3.08. Crop yields are also more unstable.[40] All this raises questions about the long-term sustainability of agricultural growth, and more

---

[38] Rosenzweig and Wolpin, 1985.

[39] Under some large-scale irrigation works, crop yields are *lower* than in the period immediately prior to the project (Joshi and Agnihotri, 1984).

[40] Rao, Ray and Subbarao, 1988.

generally of rural production systems, under present forms of technology and resource management in India, and indeed in South Asia.

The choice of agricultural technology and production systems cannot be separated from the dominant view of what constitutes scientific agriculture. The Green Revolution embodies a technological mix which gives primacy to laboratory-based research and manufactured inputs and treats agriculture as an isolated production system. Indeed, indiscriminate agricultural expansion, with little attempt to maintain a balance between forests, fields and grazing lands, assumes that the relationship between agriculture, forests and village commons is an antagonistic, rather than a complementary, one. By contrast, organic farming systems (now rapidly being eclipsed) are dependent on maintaining just such a balance. More generally, over the years, there has been a systematic devaluation and marginalization of indigenous knowledge about species-varieties, nature's processes (how forests, soils and water are formed and sustained interrelatedly), and sustainable forms of interaction between people and nature. These trends are not confined to countries operating within the capitalist mode. Similar problems of deforestation, desertification, salination, recurrent secondary pest attacks on crops, and pesticide contamination are emerging in China.[41]

What is at issue here is not modern science in itself but the process by which what is regarded as 'scientific knowledge' is generated and applied and how the fruits of that application are distributed. Within the hierarchy of knowledge, that acquired via traditional forms of interacting with nature tends to be deemed less valuable.[42] And the people who use this knowledge in their daily lives—farmers and forest-dwellers and especially women of these communities—tend to be excluded from the institutions which create what is seen as scientific knowledge. These boundaries are not inevitable. In Meiji Japan, the farmer's knowledge and innovative skills were incorporated in the broader body of scientific knowledge by a systematized interaction between the farmer, the village extension worker and the scientist. This enabled a two-way flow of information from the farmer to the scientist and vice-versa:

[41] Glaeser, 1987.
[42] Also see Marglin, 1988.

'Intimate knowledge of the best of traditional farming methods was thus the starting point for agricultural research and extension activities.'[43]

Such attempts contrast sharply with the more typical top-down flow of information from those deemed experts (the scientists/professionals) to those deemed ignorant (the village users). The problem here is only partly one of class differences. Underlying the divide between the scientists/professionals (usually urban-based) and the rural users of innovations (including user-innovators) whose knowledge comes more from field experience than from formal education, are also usually the divides between intellectual and physical labour, between city and countryside, and between women and men.

Class–Gender Effects

We come then to the class–gender effects of the processes of degradation, statization and privatization of nature's resources, and the erosion of traditional systems of knowledge and resource management. These processes have had particularly adverse effects on poor households because of the noted greater dependency of such households on communal resources. However, focusing on the class significance of communal resources provides only a partial picture—there is also a critical gender dimension, for women and female children are the ones most adversely affected by environmental degradation. The reasons for this are primarily three-fold. First, there is a pre-existing gender division of labour. It is women in poor peasant and tribal households who do much of the gathering and fetching from the forests, village commons, rivers and wells. In addition, women of such households are burdened with a significant responsibility for family subsistence and they are often the primary, and in many female-headed households the sole, economic providers.

Second, there are systematic gender differences in the distribution of subsistence resources (including food and health care) within rural households, as revealed by a range of indicators: anthropometric indices, morbidity and mortality rates, hospital

[43] See Johnston, 1969, p. 61.

admissions data, and the sex ratio (which is 93 females per 100 males for all-India).[44] These differences, especially in health care, are widespread in India (and indeed in South Asia).[45]

Third, there are significant inequalities in women's and men's access to the most critical productive resource in rural economies, agricultural land and associated production technology.[46] Women also have a systematically disadvantaged position in the labour market. They have fewer employment opportunities, less occupational mobility, lower levels of training, and lower payments for the same or similar work.[47] Due to the greater task specificity of their work, they also face much greater seasonal fluctuations in employment and earnings than do men, with sharper peaks and longer slack periods in many regions and less chance of finding employment in the slack seasons.[48]

Given their limited rights in private property resources such as agricultural land, rights to communal resources such as the village commons have always provided rural women and children (especially those of tribal, landless, or marginal peasant households) a source of subsistence, *unmediated by dependency relationships* on adult males. For instance, access to village commons is usually linked to membership in the village community and therefore women are not excluded in the way they may be in a system of individualized private land rights. This acquires additional importance in regions with strong norms of female seclusion (as in north-west India) where women's access to the cash economy, to markets, and to the marketplace itself is constrained and dependent on the mediation of male relatives.[49]

It is against this analytical backdrop that we need to examine what I term the 'class–gender effects' (the gender effects mediated

[44] For a review of issues and literature on this question, see Agarwal, 1986.

[45] These sex ratios are particularly female-adverse in the agriculturally prosperous north-western regions of Punjab and Haryana, where these figures are respectively, 88 and 87 females per 100 males. For a discussion on the causes of this regional variation, see Agarwal, 1986; and Miller, 1981.

[46] Women in India rarely own land, and in most areas also have limited access to personal assets such as cash and jewellery. See Agarwal, 1988.

[47] See discussions in Agarwal, 1984, 1986; Bardhan, 1977.

[48] See Agarwal, 1984; and Ryan and Ghodake, 1980.

[49] See Agarwal, 1989; and Sharma, 1980.

by class) of the processes of environmental degradation, statization and privatization. These effects relate to at least six critical aspects: time, income, nutrition, health, social survival networks and indigenous knowledge. Each of these effects is important across rural India. However, their intensity and interlinkages would differ cross-regionally, with variations in ecology, agricultural technology, land distribution and social structures, associated with which are variations in the gender division of labour, social relations, livelihood possibilities and kinship systems.[50] Although a systematic regional decomposition of effects is not attempted below, all the illustrative examples are regionally contextualized.

On Time

Because women are the main gatherers of fuel, fodder and water, it is primarily their working day (already averaging ten to twelve hours) that is lengthened with the depletion of and reduced access to forests, waters and soils. Firewood, for instance, is the single most important source of domestic energy in India (providing more than 65 per cent of domestic energy in the hills and deserts of the north). Much of this is gathered and not purchased, especially by the poor. In recent years, there has been a several fold increase in firewood collection time (see Table 3.3). In some villages of Gujarat, in western India, even a four-to-five-hour search yields little apart from shrubs, weeds and tree roots which do not provide adequate heat.

Similarly, fodder collection takes longer with a decline in the village commons. As a woman in the hills of Uttar Pradesh (north-west India) puts it:

When we were young, we used to go the forest early in the morning without eating anything. There we would eat plenty of berries and wild fruits ... drink the cold sweet (water) of the *Banj* (oak) roots.... In a short while we would gather all the fodder and firewood we needed, rest under the shade of some huge tree and then go home. Now, with the going of the trees, everything else has gone too.[51]

The shortage of drinking water has exacerbated the burden of

[50] For a detailed cross-regional mapping of some of these variables in the context of women's land rights in South Asia, see Agarwal, 1994.
[51] Quoted in Bahuguna, 1984, p. 132.

TABLE 3.3 Time Taken and Distance Travelled for
Firewood Collection

Country/region	Year of data	Firewood collection*		Data source
		Time taken	Distance travelled	
India				
Chamoli (hills)				
(a) Dwing	1982	5 hr/day@	over 5 km	Swaminathan
(b) Pakhi		4 hr/day		(1984)
Gujarat (plains)				
(a) Forested		once every 4 days	n.a.	
(b) Depleted	1980	once every 2 days	4–5 km	Nagbrahman and Sambrani (1983)
(c) Severely depleted		4–5 hr/day	n.a.	
Madhya Pradesh (plains)	1980	1–2 times/ week	5 km	Chand and Bezboruah (1980)
Kumaon (hills)	1952	3 days/ week	5–7 km	Folger and Dewan (1983)
Karnataka (plains)	n.a.	1 hr/day	5.4 km/trip	Batliwala (1983)
Garhwal (hills)	n.a.	5 hr/day	10 km	A. Agarwal (1983)
Bihar (plains)	c. 1972	n.a.	1–2 km/day	Bhaduri and Surin
	1980	n.a.	8–10 km/day	(1980)
Rajasthan (plains)	1988	5 hr/day (winter)	4 km	personal observation
Nepal				
Tinan (hills)	1978	3 hr/day	n.a.	Stone (1982)
Pangua (hills)	late 1970s	4–5 hr/ bundle	n.a.	Bajracharya (1983)
WDA (lowlands)				
(a) low deforestation	1982–3	1.5 hr/day	n.a.	Kumar and Hotchkiss (1988)
(b) high deforestation		3 hr/day		n.a.

Notes: *Firewood collected mainly by women and children.
@Average computed from information given in the study.
n.a. Information not available.

time and energy on women and young girls. Where low-caste women often have access to only one well, its drying up could mean an endless wait for their vessels to be filled by upper-caste women, as was noted to have happened in Orissa.[52] A similar problem arises when drinking water wells go saline near irrigation works.[53]

In Uttar Pradesh, according to a woman grassroots activist, the growing hardship of young women's lives with ecological degradation has led to an increased number of suicides among them in recent years. Their inability to obtain adequate quantities of water, fodder and fuel causes tensions with their mothers-in-law (in whose youth forests were plentiful), and soil erosion has compounded the difficulty of producing enough grain for subsistence in a region of high male outmigration.[54]

On Income

The decline in gathered items from forests and village commons has reduced incomes directly. In addition, the extra time needed for gathering reduces time available to women for crop production and can adversely affect crop incomes, especially in hill communities where women are the primary cultivators due to high male outmigration. For instance, a recent study in Nepal found that the substantial increase in firewood collection time due to deforestation has significantly reduced women's crop cultivation time, leading to an associated fall in the production of maize, wheat and mustard which are primarily dependent on female labour in the region. These are all crops grown in the dry season when there is increased need for collecting fuel and other items.[55] The same is likely to be happening in the hills of India.

Similar implications for women's income arise with the decline in common grazing land and associated fodder shortage. Many landless widows I spoke to in Rajasthan (north-west India) in 1988 said they could not venture to apply for a loan to purchase a buffalo under the government's anti-poverty programme as they had nowhere to graze the animal and no cash to buy fodder.

[52] Personal communication, Chitra Sundaram, Danish International Development Agency (DANIDA), Delhi, 1981.
[53] Agarwal, 1981.
[54] Bahuguna, 1984.
[55] Kumar and Hotchkiss, 1988.

As other sources of livelihood are eroded, selling firewood is becoming increasingly common, especially in eastern and central India. Most 'headloaders', as they are called, are women, earning a meagre 5.50 rupees a day for 20 kilogrammes of wood.[56] Deforestation directly impinges on this source of livelihood as well.

On Nutrition

As the area and productivity of village commons and forests fall, so does the contribution of gathered food in the diets of poor households. The declining availability of fuelwood has additional nutritional effects. Efforts to economize induce people to shift to less nutritious foods which need less fuel to cook or which can be eaten raw, or force them to eat partially cooked food which could be toxic, or eat leftovers that could rot in a tropical climate, or to miss meals altogether. Although as yet there are no systematic studies on India, some studies on rural Bangladesh are strongly indicative and show that the total number of meals eaten daily as well as the number of cooked meals eaten in poor households are already declining.[57] The fact that malnutrition can be caused as much by shortages of fuel as of food has long been part of the conventional wisdom of rural women who observe: 'It's not what's in the pot that worries you, but what's under it.' A trade-off between the time spent in fuel gathering versus cooking can also adversely affect the meal's nutritional quality.

Although these adverse nutritional effects impinge on the whole household, women and female children bear an additional burden because of the noted gender biases in intra-family distribution of food and health care. There is also little likelihood of poor women being able to afford the extra calories for the additional energy expended in fuel collection.

On Health

Apart from the health consequences of nutritional inadequacies, poor rural women are also more directly exposed than are men to waterborne diseases and to the pollution of rivers and ponds with fertilizer and pesticide run-offs, because of the nature of the tasks they perform, such as fetching water for various domestic uses and animal care, and washing clothes near ponds, canals and streams.[58]

[56] Bhadhuri and Surin, 1980.
[57] Howes and Jabbar, 1986.
[58] Agarwal, 1981.

The burden of family ill-health associated with water pollution also falls largely on women who take care of the sick. An additional source of vulnerability is the agricultural tasks women perform. For instance, rice transplanting, which is usually a woman's task in most parts of Asia, is associated with a range of diseases, including arthritis and gynaecological ailments.[59] Cotton-picking and other tasks done mainly by women in cotton cultivation expose them to pesticides which are widely used for this crop. In China, several times the acceptable levels of DDT and BHC residues have been found in the milk of nursing mothers, among women agricultural workers.[60] In India, pesticides are associated with limb and visual disabilities.[61]

On Social Support Networks

The considerable displacement of people that results from the submersion of villages in the building of major irrigation and hydroelectric works, or from large-scale deforestation in itself, has another (little recognized) class and gender implication—the disruption of social support networks. Social relationships with kin, and with villagers outside the kin network, provide economic and social support that is important to all rural households but especially to poor households and to the women.[62] This includes reciprocal labour-sharing arrangements during peak agricultural seasons; loans taken in cash or kind during severe crises such as droughts; and the borrowing of small amounts of foodstuffs, fuel, fodder, and so on, even in normal times. Women typically depend a great deal on such informal support networks, which they also help to build through daily social interaction, marriage alliances that they are frequently instrumental in arranging, and complex gift exchanges.[63] Also the social and economic support this represents for women in terms of strengthening their bargaining power within families needs to be recognized, even if it is not easy

[59] Mencher and Saradamoni, 1982; and United Nations Development Program, 1979.

[60] Wagner, 1987.

[61] Mohan, 1987.

[62] These are apart from the widely documented patron–client types of relationships.

[63] See Sharma, 1980; and Vatuk, 1981.

to quantify.[64] These networks, spread over a range of nearby villages, cannot be reconstituted easily, an aspect ignored by rehabilitation planners.

Moreover for forest-dwellers, the relationship with forests is not just functional or economic but also symbolic, suffused with cultural meanings and nuances, and woven into their songs and legends of origin. Large-scale deforestation, whether or not due to irrigation schemes, has eroded a whole way of living and thinking. Two close observers of life among the tribal people of Orissa in eastern India note that 'the earlier sense of sharing has disappeared.... Earlier women would rely on their neighbours in times of need. Today this has been replaced with a sense of alienation and helplessness ... the trend is to leave each family to its own fate.'[65] Widows and the aged are the most neglected.

On Women's Indigenous Knowledge

The gathering of food alone demands an elaborate knowledge of the nutritional and medicinal properties of plants, roots and trees, including a wide reserve knowledge of edible plants not normally used but critical for coping with prolonged shortages during climatic disasters. An examination of household-coping mechanisms during drought and famine reveals a significant dependence on famine foods gathered mainly by women and children for survival. Also, among hill communities it is usually women who do the seed selection work and have the most detailed knowledge about crop varieties.[66] This knowledge about nature and agriculture, acquired by poor rural women in the process of their everyday contact with and dependence on nature's resources, has a class and gender specificity and is linked to the class specificity and gendering of the division of labour.

[64] See Sen, 1990, for a discussion on the bargaining approach to conceptualizing intra-household gender relations, and Agarwal, 1990, for a discussion on the factors that affect intra-household bargaining power.

[65] Fernandes and Menon, 1987, p. 115.

[66] Among the Garo tribals of north-east India in the early 1960s, Burling, 1963, found that the men always deferred on this count to the women, who knew of approximately 300 indigenously cultivated rice varieties. In Nepal, even today, it is women who do the seed selection work among virtually all communities. See Acharya and Bennett, 1981.

The impact of existing forms of development on this knowledge has been two-fold. First, the process of devaluation and marginalization of indigenous knowledge and skills, discussed earlier, impinges especially on the knowledge that poor peasant and tribal women usually possess. Existing development strategies have made little attempt to tap or enhance this knowledge and understanding. At the same time, women have been excluded from the institutions through which modern scientific knowledge is created and transmitted. Second, the degradation of natural resources and their appropriation by a minority results in the destruction of the material basis on which women's knowledge of natural resources and processes is founded and kept alive, leading to its gradual eclipse.

Responses: State and Grassroots

Both the state and the people most immediately affected by environmental degradation have responded to these processes, but in different ways. The state's recognition that environmental degradation may be acquiring crisis proportions is recent and as yet partial; and, as we have seen, state developmental policies are themselves a significant cause of the crisis. Not surprisingly, therefore, the state's response has been piecemeal rather than comprehensive. For instance, the problem of deforestation and fuelwood shortage has been addressed mainly by encouraging village communities and individual farmers to do so.

However, most state ventures[67] in the form of direct planting have had high failure rates in terms of both tree-planting and survival, attributable to several causes—a preoccupation with monocultural plantations principally for commercial use, which at times have been replaced mixed forests; the takeover of land used for various other purposes by the local population; and top-down implementation. Hence, in many cases, far from benefiting the poor these schemes have taken away even existing rights and resources, leading to widespread local resistance. Also, women either do not feature at all in such schemes or, at best, tend to be allotted the role of caretakers in tree nurseries, with little say in the choice

---

[67] For a detailed discussion on these schemes and their shortcomings, see Agarwal, 1986a.

of species or in any other aspect of the project. Community forestry schemes, on the other hand, are often obstructed by economic inequalities in the village community and the associated mistrust among the poor of a system that cannot ensure equitable access to the products of the trees planted.

Ironically, the real 'success' stories, with plantings far exceeding targets, relate to the better-off farmers who, in many regions, have sought to reap quick profits by allotting fertile cropland to commercial trees. As a result, employment, crop output and crop residues for fuel have declined, often dramatically, and the trees planted, such as eucalyptus, provide no fodder and poor fuel.[68] The recent government policy in West Bengal (eastern India) of leasing sections of degraded forest land to local communities for collectively planting, managing and monitoring tree plantations for local use, holds promise. But in several other parts of the country large tracts of such land have also been given to paper manufacturers for planting commercial species.

As some environmentalists have rightly argued, this predominantly commercial approach to forestry, promoted as 'scientific forestry', is reductionist—it is nature seen as individual parts rather than as an interconnected system of vegetation, soil and water; the forest is reduced to trees, the trees to biomass. For instance, Shiva notes that in the reductionist world-view only those properties of a resource system are taken into account which generate profits, whereas those that stabilize ecological processes, but are commercially non-exploitable, are ignored and eventually destroyed.[69]

Indeed, the noted effects of development policies on the environment—be they policies relating to agriculture or more directly to forests and water use—point to a strategy which has been extractive/destructive of nature rather than conserving/regenerative. The strategy does not explicitly take account of the long-term complementarity between agriculture and natural resource preservation and therefore raises serious questions about the ability of the system both to sustain long-term increases in agricultural productivity and to provide sustenance for the people.

[68] Chandrashekar, Murti and Ramaswamy, 1987; and Shiva, 1988.
[69] Shiva, 1987.

But should we see people in general and women in particular solely as victims of environmental degradation and of ill-conceived top-down state policies? The emergence of grassroots ecology movements across the subcontinent (and especially India) suggests otherwise. These movements indicate that although poor peasant and tribal communities in general, and women among them in particular, are being severely affected by environmental degradation and appropriation, they are today also critical agents of change. Further, embodied in their traditional interaction with the environment are practices and perspectives which can prove important for defining alternatives.

The past decade, in particular, has seen an increasing resistance to ecological destruction in India, whether caused by direct deforestation (which is being resisted through non-violent movements such as Chipko in the Himalayan foothills and Appiko in Karnataka) or by large irrigation and hydroelectric works, such as the Narmada Valley project covering three regions in central India, the Koel-Karo in Bihar, the Silent Valley project in Kerala (which was shelved through central government intervention and local protests in 1983), the Inchampalli and Bhopalpatnam dams in Andhra Pradesh (against which 5,000 tribal people, with women in the vanguard, protested in 1984), and the controversial Tehri dam in Garhwal. Women have been active participants in most of these protests.

Although fuelled by differing ideological streams, which Ramachandra Guha identifies as Crusading Gandhian, Appropriate Technology, and Ecological Marxism, these resistance movements suggest that those affected can also be critical agents of change. Common to these streams is the recognition that the present model of development has not succeeded either in providing sustenance or in ensuring sustainability. However, the points from which the differing ideologies initiate this critique are widely dispersed. In particular, they differ in their attitudes to modern science and to socio-economic inequalities. As Guha puts it, under the Crusading Gandhian approach, 'modern science is seen as responsible for industrial society's worst excesses,'[70] and socio-economic inequalities within village communities tend to get glossed over. Ecological Marxism sees modern science and the 'scientific temper'

[70] Guha, 1988.

as indispensable for constructing a new social order, and there is a clear recognition of and attack on class and caste inequalities (although the position on gender is ambiguous). Appropriate Technology thinking, which falls within these two strands, is not as well worked out a philosophic and theoretical position as Gandhism and Marxism. It is pragmatic in its approach to modern science and emphasizes the need to synthesize traditional and modern technological traditions. Although problems relating to socio-economic hierarchies are recognized, there is no clear programme for tackling them. Over the past decade there has been some cross-fertilization of thinking across these different ideological streams.

However, it is important to distinguish here between the perspectives revealed by an examination of *practice* within the environmental movement and the explicit *theoretical* formulation of an environmental perspective. Although dialectically interlinked, the two do not entirely overlap. The three ideological streams, as identified by Guha, relate to different ways in which groups adhering to pre-existing ideological and philosophic positions (Marxist, Gandhian) have incorporated environmental concerns in their practice. In a sense environment has been added on to their other concerns by these groups. This does not as yet represent the formulation of a new theoretical perspective (that an environmental approach to development needs) by any of these groups.

In terms of practice within the movement, women have been a visible part of most rural grassroots ecological initiatives (as they have of peasant movements in general). This visibility is most apparent in the Chipko movement. However, women's participation in a movement does not in *itself* represent an explicit incorporation of a gender perspective, in either theory or practice, within that movement. Yet such a formulation is clearly needed. Feminist environmentalism as spelled out earlier in this paper is an attempt in this direction.

To restate in this context, in feminist environmentalism I have sought to provide a theoretical perspective that locates both the symbolic and material links between people and the environment in their specific forms of interaction with it, and traces gender and class differentiation in these links to a given gender and class division of labour, property and power. Unlike Gandhism and Marxism, feminist environmentalism is not a perspective that is consciously subscribed to by an identifiable set of individuals or groups. However, in so far as tribal and poor peasant women's special concern with environmental degradation is rooted in this material reality, their responses to it, which have been articulated both in complementary and oppositional terms to the other ideological streams, could be seen as consistent with the feminist environmentalist framework.

The Chipko movement is an interesting example in this respect. Although it emerged from the Gandhian tradition, in the course of its growth it has brought to light some of the limitations of an approach that does not explicitly take account of class and gender concerns. More generally too it is a movement of considerable historical significance whose importance goes beyond locational specificity, and is a noteworthy expression of hill women's specific understanding of forest protection and environmental regeneration.[71]

The movement was sparked off in 1972–3 when the people of Chamoli district in north-west India protested the auctioning of 300 ash trees to a sports good manufacturer, while the local labour cooperative was refused permission by the government to cut even a few trees to make agricultural implements for the community. Since then the movement has spread not only within the region but its methods and message have also reached other parts of the country (Appiko in Karnataka is an offshoot).[72] Further, the context of local resistance has widened. Tree felling is being resisted also to prevent disasters such as landslides, and there has been protest against limestone mining in the hills for which the villagers had to face violence from contractors and their hired thugs.

Women's active involvement in the Chipko movement has several noteworthy features that need highlighting here. First, their protest against the commercial exploitation of the Himalayan forests has been not only jointly with the men of their community when they were confronting non-local contractors but also, in several

---

[71] Among the many writings on the Chipko movement, see especially Bandyopadhyay and Shiva, 1987; Shiva, 1988; Jain, 1984; and Dogra, 1984.

[72] I understand there have also been cases of people hugging trees to protect them from loggers in the United States, although they appear to have no apparent link with Chipko.

subsequent instances, even in opposition to village men due to differences in priorities about resource use. Time and again, women have clear-sightedly opted for saving forests and the environment over the short-term gains of development projects with high environmental costs. In one instance, a potato-seed farm was to be established by cutting down a tract of oak forest in Dongri Paintoli village. The men supported the scheme because it would bring in cash income. The women protested because it would take away their only local source of fuel and fodder and add five kilometers to their fuel-collecting journeys, but cash in the men's hands would not necessarily benefit them or their children.[73] The protest was successful.

Second, women have been active and frequently successful in protecting the trees, stopping tree auctions, and keeping a vigil against illegal felling. In Gopeshwar town, a local women's group has appointed watchwomen who receive a wage in kind to guard the surrounding forest, and to regulate the extraction of forest produce by villagers. Twigs can be collected freely, but any harm to the trees is liable to punishment.

Third, replanting is a significant component of the movement. But in their choice of trees the priorities of women and men don't always coincide—women typically prefer trees that provide fuel, fodder, and daily needs, the men prefer commercially profitable ones.[74] Once again this points to the association between gendered responsibility for providing a family's subsistence needs and gendered responses to threats against the resources that fulfill those needs.

Fourth, Chipko today is more than an ecology movement and has the potential for becoming a wider movement against gender-related inequalities. For instance, there has been large-scale mobilization against male alcoholism and associated domestic violence and wasteful expenditure. There is also a shift in self-perception. I have seen women stand up in public meetings of the

---

[73] There is a growing literature indicating significant gender differences in cash-spending patterns, with a considerable percentage (at times up to 40 per cent) of what men earn in poor rural households often going toward the purchase of items they alone consume, such as liquor, tobacco and clothes, and much of what the women earn going toward the family's basic needs. See especially Mencher, 1988.

[74] This gender divergence has also been noted elsewhere. See Brara, 1987.

movement and forcefully address the gathering. Many of them are also asking: Why aren't we members of the village councils?

Fifth, implicit in the movement is a holistic understanding of the environment in general and forests in particular. The women, for instance, have constructed a poetic dialogue illustrating the difference between their own perspective and that of the foresters.[75]

Foresters : What do the forests bear?
　　　　　　　Profits, resin and timber.
Women (Chorus) : What do the forests bear?
　　　　　　　Soil, water and pure air.
　　　　　　　Soil, water and pure air,
　　　　　　　Sustain the earth and all she bears.

In other words, the women recognize that forests cannot be reduced merely to trees and the trees to wood for commercial use, that vegetation, soil, and water form part of a complex and interrelated ecosystem. This recognition of the interrelatedness and interdependence between the various material components of nature, and between nature and human sustenance, is critical for evolving a strategy of sustainable environmental protection and regeneration.

Although the movement draws upon, indeed is rooted in, the region's Gandhian tradition which predates Chipko, women's responses go beyond the framework of that tradition and come close to feminist environmentalism in their perspective. This is suggested by their beginning to confront gender and class issues in a number of small but significant ways. For instance, gender relations are called into question in their taking oppositional stands to the village men on several occasions, in asking to be members of village councils, and in resisting male alcoholism and domestic violence. Similarly, there is clearly a class confrontation involved in their resistance (together with the men of their community) to the contractors holding licenses for mining and felling in the area.

At the same time, ecology movements such as Chipko need to be contextualized. Although localized resistance to the processes of natural resource appropriation and degradation in India has taken many different forms, and arisen in diverse regional contexts, resistances in which entire communities and villages have

[75] Quoted in Shiva, 1988.

participated to constitute a movement (such as Chipko, Appiko and Jharkhand) have emerged primarily in hill or tribal communities. This may be attributable particularly to two factors: the immediacy of the threat from these processes to people's survival, and these communities being marked by relatively low levels of the class and social differentiation that usually splinter village communities in South Asia. They therefore have a greater potential for wider community participation than is possible in more economically and socially stratified contexts. Further, in these communities, women's role in agricultural production has always been visibly substantial and often primary—an aspect more conducive to their public participation than in many other communities of northern India practicing female seclusion.

In emphasizing the role of poor peasant and tribal women in ecology movements, I am not arguing, as do some feminist scholars, that women possess a specifically feminine sensibility or cognitive temperament, or that women *qua women* have certain traits that predispose them to attend to particulars, to be interactive rather than individualist, and to understand the true character of complex natural processes in holistic terms.[76] Rather, I locate the perspectives and responses of poor peasant and tribal women (perspectives which are indeed often interactive and holistic) in their material reality —in their dependence on and actual use of natural resources for survival, the knowledge of nature gained in that process, and the broader cultural parameters which define people's activities and modes of thinking in these communities. By this count, the perspectives and responses of men belonging to hill or tribal communities would also be more conducive to environmental protection and regeneration than those of men elsewhere, but not more than those of the women of such communities. This is because hill and tribal women, perhaps more than any other group, still maintain a reciprocal link with nature's resources—a link that stems from a given organization of production, reproduction and distribution, including a given gender division of labour.

At the same time, the positive aspects of this link should not serve as an argument for the continued entrenchment of women within a given division of labour. Rather, they should serve as an argument for creating the conditions that would help universalize

[76] For a critique of these lines of argument, see Longino, 1987.

this link with nature, for instance, by *declassing* and *degendering* the ways in which productive and reproductive activities are organized (within and outside the home) and how property, resources, knowledge and power are distributed.

Conclusion

The Indian experience offers several insights and lessons. First, the processes of environmental degradation and appropriation of natural resources by a few have specific class–gender as well as locational implications—it is women of poor, rural households who are most adversely affected and who have participated actively in ecology movements. 'Women' therefore cannot be posited (as the ecofeminist discourse has typically done) as a unitary category, even within a country, let alone across the Third World or globally. Second, the adverse class–gender effects of these processes are manifest in the erosion of both the livelihood systems and the knowledge systems on which poor rural women depend. Third, the nature and impact of these processes are rooted interactively, on the one hand, in ideology (in notions about development, scientific knowledge, the appropriate gender division of labour, and so on), and, on the other hand, in the economic advantage and political power predicated especially, but by no means only, on property differentials between households and between women and men. Fourth, there is a spreading grassroots resistance to such inequality and environmental destruction—to the processes, products, people, property, power and profit-orientation that underlie them. Although the voices of this resistance are yet scattered and localized, their message is a vital one, even from a purely growth and productivity concern and more so if our concern is with people's sustenance and survival.

In particular, the experiences of women's initiatives within the environmental movements suggests that women's militancy is much more closely linked to family survival issues than is men's. Implicit in these struggles is the attempt to carve out a space for an alternative existence that is based on equality, not dominance over people, and on cooperation with and not dominance over nature.

Indeed what is (implicitly or explicitly) being called into question in various ways by the movements is the existing development paradigm—with its particular product and technological mix, its forms of exploitation of natural and human resources, and its conceptualization of relationships among people and between people and nature. However, a mere recognition that there are deep inequalities and destructiveness inherent in present processes of development is not enough. There is a need for policy to shift away from its present relief-oriented approach toward nature's ills and people's welfare in which the solution to nutrient-depleted soils is seen to lie entirely in externally added chemical nutrients, to depleting forests in monoculture plantations, to drought starvation in food-for-work programmes, to gender inequalities in ad hoc income-generating schemes for women, and so on. These solutions reflect an aspirin approach to development—they are neither curative nor preventive, they merely suppress the symptoms for a while.

The realistic posing of an alternative (quite apart from its implementation) is of course not easy, nor is it the purpose of this paper to provide a blueprint. What is clear so far are the broad contours. An alternative approach, suggested by feminist environmentalism, needs to be *transformational* rather than welfarist—where development, redistribution and ecology link in mutually regenerative ways. This would necessitate complex and interrelated changes such as in the *composition* of what is produced, the *technologies* used to produce it, the *processes* by which decisions on products and technologies are arrived at, the *knowledge systems* on which such choices are based, and the class and gender *distribution* of products and tasks.

For instance, in the context of forestry programmes, a different composition of the product may imply a shift from the currently favoured monocultural and commercial tree species to mixed species critical for local subsistence. An alternative agricultural technology may entail shifting from mainly chemical-based farming to more organic methods, from monocultural high-yielding variety seeds to mixed cropping with indigenously produced varieties, from the emphasis on large irrigation schemes to a plurality of water-provisioning systems, and from a preoccupation with irrigated crops to a greater focus on dryland crops. A change in decision-making processes would imply a shift from the present top-down approach to one that ensures the broad-based democratic participation of disadvantaged groups. Indeed, in so far as the success stories of reforestation today relate to localized communities taking charge of their environmental base, a viable solution would need decentralized planning and control and institutional arrangements that ensure the involvement of the rural poor, and especially women, in decisions about what trees are planted and how the associated benefits are shared. Similarly, to encourage the continued use and growth of local knowledge about plants and species in the process of environmental regeneration, we would require new forms of interaction between local people and trained scientists and a widening of the definition of 'scientific' to include plural sources of knowledge and innovations, rather than merely those generated in universities and laboratories. This last is not without precedent, as is apparent from the earlier discussion in Meiji Japan's interactive teams which allowed a flow of information not only from the agricultural scientist to the farmer but also the reverse. The most complex, difficult, and necessary to transform is of course the class and gender division of labour and resources and the associated social relations. Here it is the emergence of new social movements in India around issues of gender, environment, and democratic rights, and especially the formation of joint fronts between these movements on a number of recent occasions, that point the direction for change and provide the points of hope.

Indeed, environmental and gender concerns taken together open up both the need for re-examining, and the possibility of throwing new light on, many long-standing issues relating to development, redistribution and institutional change. That these concerns preclude easy policy solutions underlines the deep entrenchment of interests (both ideological and material) in existing structures and models of development. It also underlines the critical importance of grassroots political organization of the poor and of women as a necessary condition for their voices to be heeded and for the entrenched interests to be undermined. Most of all it stresses the need for a shared alternative vision that can channel dispersed rivulets of resistance into a creative, tumultuous flow.

In short, an alternative, transformational approach to development would involve both ways of *thinking* about things and ways of *acting* on them. In the present context it would concern both how gender relations and relations between people and the non-human world are conceptualized, and how they are concretized in terms of the distribution of property, power and knowledge, and in the formulation of development policies and programmes.

It is in its failure to explicitly confront these political economy issues that the ecofeminist analysis remains a critique without threat to the established order.

(This is a substantially revised and abridged version of a paper presented at a conference on 'The Environment and Emerging Development Issues', at the World Institute of Development Economics Research, Helsinki, 3–7 September 1990. A longer version is also available as Discussion Paper No. 8: 'Engendering the Environment Debate: Lessons from the Indian Subcontinent', CASID Distinguished Speaker Series (Michigan State University, 1991).

I am grateful to several people for comments on the earlier versions: Janet Seiz, Gillian Hart, Nancy Folbre, Jean Dréze, Lourdes Beneria, Gail Hershatter, Pauline Peters, Tariq Banuri, Myra Buvinic, and *Feminist Studies'* editors and anonymous reviewers. I also gained from some lively discussions following seminar presentations of the paper at the Center for Population and Development Studies, Harvard University, February 1991; the Centre for Advanced Study in International Development, Michigan State University, April 1990; the Hubert Humphrey Institute of Public Affairs, University of Minnesota, April 1990; and the Departments of City and Regional Planning and Rural Sociology, Cornell University, May 1990.)

References

Acharya, Meena and Lynn Bennett, 1981, 'Women and the Subsistence Sector in Nepal', *World Bank Staff Working Paper No. 526*, World Bank, Washington DC.

Agarwal, Anil, 1983, 'The Cooking Energy Systems: Problems and Opportunities', Centre for Science and Environment, New Delhi.

Agarwal, Bina, 1981, 'Women and Water Resource Development' (photocopy), Institute of Economic Growth, Delhi.

———, 1984, 'Rural Women and the High Yielding Variety Rice Technology in India', *Economic and Political Weekly*, 31 March, A39–A52.

———, 1985, 'Sita Speak' (poem), *Indian Express*, 17 November.

———, 1986, 'Women, Poverty and Agricultural Growth in India', *Journal of Peasant Studies*, 13 July, pp. 165–220.

———, 1986a, *Cold Hearths and Barren Slopes: The Woodfuel Crisis in the Third World*, Zed Books, London.

Agarwal, Bina, 1987, 'Under the Cooking Pot: The Political Economy of the Domestic Fuel Crisis in Rural South Asia', *IDS Bulletin*, vol. 18, No. 1, pp. 11–22.

———, 1988, 'Who Sows? Who Reaps? Women and Land Rights in India', *Journal of Peasant Studies*, 15 July, pp. 531–81.

———, 1989, 'Women, Land and Ideology in India', in Haleh Afshar and Bina Agarwal (eds), *Women, Poverty and Ideology: Contradictory Pressures, Uneasy Resolutions*, Macmillan, London.

———, 1990, 'Social Security and the Family: Coping with Seasonality and Calamity in Rural India', *Journal of Peasant Studies*, 17 April, pp. 341–412.

———, 1994, *A Field of One's Own: Gender and Land Rights in South Asia*, Cambridge University Press, Cambridge.

Baden-Powell, B.H., 1957, *The Indian Village Community*, HRAF Press, New Haven, Connecticut.

Bahuguna, Sundarlal, 1984, 'Women's Non-violent Power in the Chipko Movement', in Madhu Kishwar and Ruth Vanita (eds), *In Search of Answers: Indian Women's Voices in 'Manushi'*, Zed Books, London.

Bajracharya, Deepak, 1983, 'Deforestation in the Food/Fuel Context: Historical and Political Perspectives from Nepal', *Mountain Research and Development*, vol. 3, No. 3.

Bandyopadhyay, Jayanta, 1986, 'A Case Study of Environmental Degradation in Karnataka', paper presented at a Workshop on Drought and Desertification, India International Centre, New Delhi, 17–18 May.

Bandyopadhyay, Jayanta and Vandana Shiva, 1987, 'Chipko', *Seminar*, No. 330, February.

Batliwala, Srilata, 1983, 'Women and Cooking Energy', *Economic and Political Weekly*, 24–31 December.

Blaikie, Piers, 1985, *The Political Economy of Soil Erosion in Developing Countries*, Longman, London and New York.

Bardhan, Kalpana, 1977, 'Rural Employment, Welfare and Status: Forces of Tradition and Change in India', *Economic and Political Weekly*, 25 June, A34–A48; 2 July, pp. 1062–74; 9 July, pp. 1101–18.

Bhaduri, T. and V. Surin, 1980, 'Community Forestry and Women Headloaders', in *Community Forestry and People's Participation—Seminar Report*, Ranchi Consortium for Community Forestry, 20–22 November.

Brara, Rita, 1987, 'Commons Policy as Process: The Case of Rajasthan, 1955–85', *Economic and Political Weekly*, 7 October, pp. 2247–54.

Bromley, Daniel W. and Michael M. Cernea, 1989, 'The Management of Common Property Natural Resources', *World Bank Discussion Paper No. 57,* World Bank, Washington DC.

Burling, Robbins, 1963, *Rensanggri: Family and Kinship in a Garo Village,* Pennsylvania University Press, Philadelphia.

Centre for Science and Environment, 1986, *The State of India's Environment: A Citizen's Report 1985–86,* Delhi.

Chakravarty, Uma, 1983, 'The Sita Myth', *Samya Shakti,* 1 July.

Chand, Malini and Rita Bezboruah, 1980, 'Employment Opportunities for Women in Forestry', in *Community Forestry and People's Participation—Seminar Report,* Ranchi Consortium for Community Forestry, 20–22 November.

Chandrashekar, D.M., B.V. Krishna Murti and S.R. Ramaswamy, 1987, 'Social Forestry in Karnataka: An Impact Analysis', *Economic and Political Weekly,* 13 June, pp. 935–41.

Cheney, Jim, 1987, 'Ecofeminism and Deep Ecology', *Environmental Ethics,* 9, Summer, pp. 115–45.

Dasgupta, Partha and Karl-Goran Maler, 1990, 'The Environment and Emerging Development Issues', paper presented at a Conference on Environment and Development, Wider, Helsinki, September.

Dhawan, B.D., 1982, *Development of Tubewell Irrigation in India,* Agricole Publishing Academy, Delhi.

Dietrich, Gabriele, 1989, 'Plea for Survival: Book Review', *Economic and Political Weekly,* 18 February, pp. 353–4.

Dogra, Bharat, 1984, *Forests and People,* published by the author, Delhi.

Fernandes, Walter and Geeta Menon, 1987, *Tribal Women and Forest Economy: Deforestation, Exploitation and Status Change,* Indian Social Institute, Delhi.

Flaherty, Wendy O., 1990, *Other People's Myths,* Macmillan, New York and London.

Folger, Bonnie and Meera Dewan, 1983, 'Kumaon Hills Reclamation: End of Year Site Visit', OXFAM America, Delhi.

Fuss, Diane, 1989, *Essentially Speaking,* Routledge, New York.

Gadgil, Madhav, 1985, 'Towards an Ecological History of India', *Economic and Political Weekly,* Special Number, November, pp. 1909–38.

Gadgil, Madhav and V.D. Vartak, 1975, 'Sacred Groves of India: A Plea for Continued Conservation', *Journal of the Bombay Natural History Society,* vol. 72, No. 2.

Glaeser, Bernhard (ed.), 1987, *Learning from China? Development and Environment in Developing Countries,* Allen and Unwin, London.

Government of India, 1987, *Thirty-seventh Round Report on Land Holdings—I, Some Aspects of Household Ownership Holdings,* National Sample Survey Organization, Department of Statistics.

————, 1990, *Forest Survey of India,* Ministry of Environment and Forests, New Delhi.

Griffin, Susan, 1978, *Women and Nature: The Roaring Within Her,* Harper and Row, New York.

Guha, Ramachandra, 1983, 'Forestry in British and Post-British India: A Historical Analysis', *Economic and Political Weekly,* 29 October, pp. 1882–96.

————, 1985, 'Scientific Forestry and Social Change in Uttarakhand', *Economic and Political Weekly,* Special Number, November, pp. 1939–52.

————, 1988, 'Ideological Trends in Indian Environmentalism', *Economic and Political Weekly,* 3 December, pp. 2578–81.

Habib, Irfan, 1984, 'Peasant and Artisan Resistance in Mughal India', *McGill Studies in International Development,* No. 34, Centre for Developing Area Studies, McGill University.

Howes, Michael and M.A. Jabbar, 1986, 'Rural Fuel Shortages in Bangladesh: The Evidence from Four Villages', *Discussion Paper 213,* Institute of Development Studies, Sussex.

Jain, Shobita, 1984, 'Women and People's Ecological Movement: A Case Study of Women's Role in the Chipko Movement in Uttar Pradesh', *Economic and Political Weekly,* 13 October, pp. 1788–94.

Jodha, N.S., 1986, 'Common Property Resources and Rural Poor', *Economic and Political Weekly,* 5 July, pp. 1169–81.

Johnston, Bruce F., 1969, 'The Japanese Model of Agricultural Development: Its Relevance to Developing Nations', in Kazushi Ohkawa, Bruce F. Johnston and Hiromitsu Kaneda (eds), *Agricultural and Economic Growth—Japan's Experience,* Princeton University Press, Princeton.

Joshi, P.K. and A.K. Agnihotri, 1984, 'An Assessment of the Adverse Effects of Canal Irrigation in India', *Indian Journal of Agricultural Economics,* 39, July–September, pp. 528–36.

Kerala Forestry Research Institute, 1980, *Studies in the Changing Patterns of Man-Forest Interaction and Its Implications for Ecology and Management,* Trivandrum.

King, Ynestra, 1981, 'Feminism and the Revolt', *Heresies,* No. 13, Special Issue on Feminism and Ecology, pp. 12–16.

————, 1989, 'The Ecology of Feminism and the Feminism of Ecology', in Judith Plant (ed.), *Healing the Wounds: The Promise of Ecofeminism*, New Society *Report 69*, International Food Policy Research Institute, Washington DC, pp. 18–28.

————, 1990, 'Healing the Wounds: Feminism, Ecology and the Nature/Culture Dualism', in Irene Diamond and Gloria Orenstein (eds), *Reweaving the World: The Emergence of Ecofeminism*, pp. 98–112.

Kulkarni, Sharad, 1983, 'Towards a Social Forestry Policy', *Economic and Political Weekly*, 5 February, pp. 191–6.

Kumar, Shubh and David Hotchkiss, 1988, 'Consequences of Deforestation for Women's Time Allocation, Agricultural Production and Nutrition in Hill Areas of Nepal', *Research Report, 69*, International Food Policy Research Institute, Washington DC.

Leach, Edmund R., 1967, *Pul Eliya—A Village in Ceylon: A Study of Land Tenure and Kinship*, Cambridge University Press, Cambridge.

Longino, Helen E., 1981, Review of Merchant (1980) in *Environmental Ethics*, Winter, pp. 365–9.

————, 1987, 'Can There Be a Feminist Science?', *Hypatia*, 2, Fall, pp. 51–64.

MacCormack, Carol P. and Marilyn Strathern (eds), 1980, *Nature, Culture and Gender*, Cambridge University Press, Cambridge.

Marglin, Stephen A., 1988, 'Losing Touch: The Cultural Conditions of Worker Accommodation and Resistance', in Frederique A. Marglin and Stephen A. Marglin (eds), *Knowledge and Power*, Oxford University Press, Oxford.

Mencher, Joan P., 'Women's Work and Poverty: Women's Contribution to Household Maintenance in Two Regions of South India', in Daisy Dwyer and Judith Bruce (eds), *A Home Divided: Women and Income in the Third World*, Stanford University Press, Stanford.

Mencher, Joan P. and K. Saradamoni, 1982, 'Muddy Feet and Dirty Hands: Rice Production and Female Agricultural Labour', *Economic and Political Weekly*, 25 December, pp. A149–A167.

Merchant, Carolyn, 1980, *The Death of Nature: Women, Ecology and the Scientific Revolution*, Harper and Row, San Francisco.

Miller, Barbara, 1981, *The Endangered Sex: Neglect of Female Children in North-West India*, Cornell University Press, Ithaca.

Moench, M., 1988, 'Turf and Forest Management in a Garhwal Hill Village', in Louise Fortmann and John W. Bruce (eds), *Whose Trees? Proprietary Dimensions of Forestry*, Westview Press, Boulder, Colorado.

Mohan, Dinesh, 1987, 'Food vs. Limbs: Pesticides and Physical

Disability in India', *Economic and Political Weekly,* 28 March, pp. A23–A29.

Moore, Henrietta L., 1989, *Feminism and Anthropology,* University of Minnesota Press, Minneapolis.

Nagbrahman, D. and S. Sambrani, 1983, 'Women's Drudgery in Firewood Collection', *Economic and Political Weekly,* 1–8 January.

National Sample Survey Organization, 1987, *Thirty-seventh Round Report on Land Holdings—I, Some Aspects of Household Ownership Holdings,* Department of Statistics, Government of India.

Ortner, Sherry, 1974, 'Is Male to Female as Nature is to Culture?', in Michelle Z. Rosaldo and Louise Lamphere (eds), *Women, Culture and Society,* Standford University Press, Stanford.

Pingle, V., 1975, 'Some Studies of Two Tribal Groups of Central India, Part 2: The Importance of Food Consumed in Two Different Seasons', *Plant Food for Man,* 1.

Rao, C.H. Hanumantha, S.K. Ray and K. Subbarao, 1988, *Unstable Agriculture and Drought,* Vikas, Delhi.

Ray Chaudhuri, Tapan and Irfan Habib (eds), 1982, *Cambridge Economic History of India,* Cambridge University Press, Cambridge.

Rosenzweig, Mark and Kenneth I. Wolpin, 1985, 'Specific Experience, Household Structure, and Intergenerational Transfers: Farm Family Land and Labour Arrangements in Developing Countries', *Quarterly Journal of Economics,* 100, Supp., pp. 961–87.

Ryan, James G. and R.D. Ghodake, 1980, 'Labour Market Behaviour in Rural Villages in South India: Effects of Season, Sex and Socio-Economic Status', Progress Report, Economic Programme 14, International Crop Research Institute for Semi-Arid Tropics (ICRISAT), Hyderabad.

Salleh, Ariel Kay, 1984, 'Deeper than Deep Ecology: The Eco-Feminist Connection', *Environmental Ethics,* 16, Winter, pp. 339–45.

Seklar, David, 1981, 'The New Era of Irrigation Management in India', mimeo, Ford Foundation, Delhi.

Sen, Amartya, 1990, 'Gender and Cooperative-Conflict', in Irene Tinker (ed.), *Persistent Inequalities,* Oxford University Press, New York.

Sengupta, Nirmal, 1985, 'Irrigation: Traditional versus Modern', *Economic and Political Weekly,* Special Number, November, pp. 1919–38.

Sharma, Ursula, 1980, *Women, Work and Property in North-West India,* Tavistock, London.

Shaw, Paul, 1989, 'Population, Environment and Women: An Analytical Framework', paper prepared for the United Nations Fund for Population Activities (UNFPA), Inter-Agency Consultative Meeting, New York, 6 March.

Shiva, Vandana, 1987, 'Ecology Movements in India', *Alternatives,* 11, pp. 255–73.

————, 1988, *Staying Alive: Women, Ecology and Survival,* Zed Books, London.

Stone, Linda, 1982, 'Women and Natural Resources: Perspectives from Nepal', in Molly Stock, Jo Ellen Force and Dixie Ehrenreich (eds), *Women in Natural Resources: An International Perspective,* University of Idaho Press, Moscow.

Swaminathan, Madhura, 1984, 'Eight Hours a Day for Fuel Collection', *Manushi,* March–April.

Swaminathan, Srilata, 1982, 'Environment: Tree versus Man', *India International Centre Quarterly,* 9, Nos 3 and 4.

United Nations Development Program (UNDP), 1979, 'Rural Women's Participation in Development', *Evaluation Study,* No. 3, UNDP, New York, June.

Vatuk, Sylvia, 1981, 'Sharing, Giving and Exchanging of Foods in South Asian Societies', University of Illinois at Chicago Circle, October.

Wagner, Rudolf G., 1987, 'Agriculture and Environmental Protection in China', in Bernhard Glaeser (ed.), *Learning from China?*

Warren, Karen J., 1987, 'Feminism and Ecology: Making Connections', *Environmental Ethics,* 9, Spring, pp. 3–20.

Zimmerman, Michael, E., 1987, 'Feminism, Deep Ecology and Environmental Ethics', *Environmental Ethics,* 9, Spring, pp. 21–44.

II

Work

The first article by Nandita Shah et al., critically examines the argument that structural adjustment will lead to feminization of labour and thus to greater employment opportunities for women. The authors argue that 'feminization' itself is a term which hides more than it reveals, because several contradictory possibilities are conflated in using the word. They show that the trends rather, are towards the declining employment of women due to automation and introduction of technology in a context of structural adjustment, and suggest organizational strategies which will strengthen women's resources in confronting the greater economic pressures they will have to face.

Rohini Hensman takes up two questions, whether human choices are narrowed or enlarged by new technologies and whether the forms of economic expansion currently are leading to job-led or jobless growth. Hensman makes a feminist critique of the sexual division of labour which is assumed to be universal and natural, and which underlies both the location as well as the remuneration of women in the 'public' sphere of work. She argues that feminist philosophy should not be opposed to new technology as such and calls for a far-reaching political agenda that would recast the arena of 'work', using the potential of technology to liberate humans from drudgery while simultaneously breaking down the sexual division of labour and revalorizing the work done by women in the 'private sphere'.

4

Structural Adjustment, Feminization of Labour Force and Organizational Strategies

Nandita Shah, Sujata Gothoskar,
Nandita Gandhi and *Amrita Chhachhi*

This article is a contribution to the ongoing debate on the possible positive and negative impact of the newly-introduced new economic policies (NEP) and structural adjustment programme (SAP) on women workers. The article attempts to link the political and social implications of these economic policies on women's lives and work with the development of strategies for survival and empowerment, focusing on urban working women. Firstly, we would like to state that these policies are not really 'new' in the sense that industrial restructuring since the 1980s had already started affecting industrial workers, and these trends have intensified with the commencement of the IMF-dictated SAP. The second part of the article focuses on the debate on feminization of the labour force under SAP. The final section of the article presents some alternative perspectives and suggests organizational strategies in relation to women's paid and unpaid labour to improve the quality of their lives and lay the basis for empowering them towards transformation of the structures of their subordination.

Different reactions to the NEP and the SAP in India have emerged, ranging from supporters critical of Nehruvian policies to opponents who see it as a surrender of our sovereignty to foreign institutions and countries to the 'we have no choice' pragmatists.

Political parties especially the Left parties have voiced their concern for different sections such as the working class, petty traders and entrepreneurs and indigenous industry through rallies, anti-price rise morchas and swadeshi campaigns. Women's groups have joined other progressive and voluntary organizations to express their fear of the possibility of a severe negative impact especially on the lives of working women.

These reservations and suspicions about NEP have some basis in our past history as well as the experiences of many other countries which have implemented them. With the acceptance of the IMF loan and its conditionalities, it is clear that India has now joined other Latin American, African and Asian countries which had accepted the terms for the IMF–World Bank loans.

However it should be noted that India had begun a process of 'adjustment' quietly since the beginning of the 1980s. Multinational corporations were encouraged to invest by the Indira Gandhi government and even by the Janata Party government. Rajiv Gandhi gave a glimpse of this process when he spoke of moving into the 21st century and brought in indiscriminate computerization.

All three governments continued huge foreign borrowings, deficit financing and indirect taxation. By the time the National Front government came to power, the coffers of the country were more or less empty. Even though failure of their economic approach and the oncoming economic crisis were obvious to all three governments, not one had the political will for making any real radical changes to turn the situation around. They continued with the facade of a mixed, welfaristic perspective whilst opening up a little now and then to the multinationals and the world market. It fell on the Rao government to take this policy forward by publicly announcing liberalization. Its 1991 policy announcements can thus be seen, not as a beginning of economic liberalization but its inevitable consolidation.

It is argued that the Indian economy needs to be 'stabilized' by introducing fiscal and monetary restraint (deflation) and devaluation of currency. This, it is hoped, will reduce demand for imported goods and encourage exports and therefore bring down expenditure. SAP is meant to deal with the supply side by increasing production and efficiency in the production process. Incentives for private sector, privatization of government owned units, delicensing, deregulation and disciplining labour are some of the means of 'adjustment'. In effect adjustment meant jettisoning the older model of the economy and opening up to what has been called the 'magic of the market' or a form of neo-liberalism.

There are several theories on the failure of 'developmentalism' but the alternative posed seems to be worse than the problem. It is feared that the real costs of adjustment will be borne primarily by the most disadvantaged and vulnerable sections of society while the benefits would be limited to a small section. Numerous case studies on the effects of SAP in developing countries have pointed out that even where SAP leads to growth it does not necessarily imply development. For instance, in 1985 the Bolivian economy collapsed and had to be bailed out by a $ 50 million loan by the IMF. Rather than improvement, the economy shrank by 3 per cent in just one year, real wages fell by half; food consumption went down by 40 per cent; number of factories were reduced by 55 per cent. There was a massive march of 7,000 people in Le Paz for Life and Bread in 1986. These were explained away as teething troubles of the painful aspects of adjustment. But things did not improve in 1988 as inflation doubled, real wages continued to decline; and one out of every four Bolivians was out of work. There was mass migration as government departments shut, miners lost their jobs and their wives took up agricultural work (Bank Information Centre, undated).

Even success stories have tragic subplots within them. Ghanaian cocoa production has increased and the income of producers had jumped by 700 per cent in some cases. However the increase was uneven amongst agriculturists. Amongst the cocoa farmers only 18 per cent in the south were favoured versus the poorer ones in the north of Ghana while the majority of non-cocoa producing farmers' per capita income stagnated. There were other more disastrous side effects. The emphasis on cocoa has led to a decline in food sufficiency, deforestation which might mean the disappearance of timber, and a drop in fishing and high prices which has effected the nutritional levels of people. As new crises surface, the Fund blames the government for mismanagement and extends more money for even more 'adjustment' (ibid.).

There are numerous other studies by the ILO and independent scholars which show that SAP in many countries has on the whole failed to generate growth of income and employment. The balance of payments situation may improve, exports may rise given a good world demand, but the majority of the people, especially the poor are no better than what they were before the introduction of these policies.

Where do women feature in the faceless, neutral rows of figures and general indicators of a nation's well-being? Are they affected by SAP in the same way as men? The evidence from a dozen case studies carried out by UNICEF showed that, 'with a few exceptions, children and women of poorer families were the hardest hit by recession'. Apart from the effects on nutrition, workload, mortality, etc., studies have shown how traditional industries which employed a large percentage of women were being closed after introduction of SAP. In Mexico, the 'maquiladoras' industry introduced changes in the labour process which transferred women working in the plant to self-employed work performed at home. According to a document by DAWN, 'throughout different countries there is a growth of the intermittent activities, uncovered by labour contracts or social security.' In Argentina unemployed women who are heads of households find it more difficult to enter the labour market than men (Antrobus, 1990).

Structural adjustment programmes affect sections of working women differentially but the evidence from studies shows that it tends to shrink women's employment opportunities in the organized sector.[1] New employment opportunities are primarily in a small segment of export industries with low wages and extremely adverse working conditions. Under SAP, real wages have declined for labour as a whole and again women have been particularly hard hit. In Brazil, women faced wage reductions ranging from 10 to 30 per cent depending on the sector they were working in (Kriti, 1992). There are many similar examples from other countries in Africa, Latin America, the Caribbean and Asia.

Indian women form a vulnerable and exploited group of people. India has one of the lowest sex ratios in the world of 1,000 males to 923 females. It is a further drop from the 1981 figure of 1,000 males: 934 females. Only 39.4 per cent of women are literate. Less women than men work for a living and for every three men only one woman uses health facilities (Batlivala, 1984). There are

---

[1] The income-tax exemption for women with an annual income of Rs 36,000 in the 1991–2 budget was presented as a major concession to working women. This would benefit a minor section of all working women; the majority (98 per cent) of whom work in the unorganized sector.

depressing figures on the number of rapes, dowry murders, sexual harassment and assaults on women. Some of the basic institutions of society have a shocking record of discriminating against women. For example, banks are reluctant to have women open accounts for their minor children in their names or extend credit for their independent work. Courts, in spite of amendments in the rape and dowry laws, have convicted very few offenders or let them off lightly. In the labour market, the private sector has not been a major employer of women. The government is the largest employer of women but only in 'women-oriented' types of jobs as typists, nurses, teachers, etc. Whatever women require for an independent livelihood and existence such as work, housing, and other resources, are systematically denied to them by the norms of the patriarchal family and society.

Given the existing structure of discrimination against women, the introduction SAP via the NEP with its attendant problems of inflation, recessions, restructuring of industry, fall in real wages, etc., will intensify and worsen conditions particularly for poor women. Many scholars and activists have pointed out that there will be a fall in working women's standard of living, poor nutritional and health level, an increase in the double burden of work and a brake to any improvement of their status in society.

So towards the middle of the 1980s, international agencies such as UNICEF began to express concern at the detrimental effects of SAP on women and children and put forward the proposal for adjustment with a human face. The World Bank too has been forced to respond to the criticisms of the impact of structural adjustment programmes on poor households but the 'compensatory programmes' adopted by it and other agencies to 'alleviate' poverty and inequality intensified by SAP have been shown to be inadequate and limited. Although the proposal for 'adjustment with a human face' highlights the disastrous effects of SAP and suggests protective policies, it does not question the macro-economic policy itself. It suggests improved policies with the expectation that 'enlightened governments' will act on these policies. In practice, governments have tended to ignore or adopt these policies in an indifferent manner. The overall framework within which these ameliorative measures are proposed are paternalistic, treating women only as victims and lack the potential to change the subordination that women face in the economy and society (Elson, 1989). By the end of the 1980s a more systematic effort was made to identify the specific consequences of SAP on women and suggest proposals to protect the position of women as well as incorporate their concerns into the process of adjustment as for instance by the report by the Commonwealth Secretariat, 1989. However, this report also tends to treat women only as victims and focuses on harnessing their 'productive potential' through policy changes rather than through empowering the women themselves.

A major assumption that informs such policy prescriptions is that if women are engaged in employment, i.e., income earning linked to the market, there will be an improvement in their status. Based on this assumption there are a few economists who see the SAP as a ray of hope especially in the context of women's work. They argue that the SAP will introduce flexibility in the organization of industry, in the production process and in the labour market. It will therefore generate low paying jobs which will go to women, thus increasing their work participation rates and generally helping in the alleviation of poverty. It is important for us as researchers and activists to critically look at these arguments as they have a direct bearing on the development of strategies and the empowerment of poor woman in their struggle for a better life.

Feminization Debate

Analysts of present trends in industrialization in developed and developing countries have argued that the characteristic feature of this phase of capital accumulation is 'flexibility', accompanied by a process of 'global feminization' of the labour force. Flexible specialization is based on the diffusion of microelectronic systems in production which overcome the inflexibility of Fordist production systems which were characterized by the assembly line with a high degree of division of labour in which workers were reduced to adjuncts of the machine. Fordist production required long runs of standardized products, large units and the maintenance of large inventories on a 'just in case' basis which increased costs. Post-Fordist or flexible production is based on decentralized small units of production, with subcontracting arrangements, minimum inventories similar to the Japanese 'kanban' or 'just in time' system, with flexible labour deployed over a variety of production tasks. The labour force is used only when required which means workers do not have permanent status, are paid low wages and deprived of statutory rights. The argument for global feminization of the labour force has been put forward by Guy Standing (1989) who notes that the decade of the 1980s is both the decade of 'labour deregularization' as well as a period marked by a 'renewed surge of feminization of labour activity'. This is the period in which 'labour and social rights became perceived increasingly as costs and rigidities' and the growth of very low wage employment. He argues that 'when low wage jobs spread, it is women whose employment in them increases.' Guy Standing uses the term 'feminization' to refer to two processes: a rise in female labour force participation in the face of a fall in male participation rates and the feminization of certain jobs that were traditionally performed by men, i.e. the substitution of men by women.

Applying this thesis to India, Sudha and L. K. Deshpande (1992) state that this tendency towards feminization of the workforce has been observed in official data at national level as well as in the city of Bombay. They argue that feminization through flexible labour practices in urban labour markets over the 80s increased employment opportunities for women.

In elaborating on the direction of female manufacturing employment, they note that employers in Bombay responded to liberalization by employing women or retrenching fewer women than men. Given that trade liberalization is a major plank of the NEP, they estimate that production for exports will increase and since export industries are more labour-intensive, the total demand for labour will also increase. In this context, they argue that the employment for women will increase faster than that of men, since women constitute a cheap and docile labour force.

Sudha Deshpande (1993) goes further to say that:

to the extent that it [NEP] is likely to increase the demand for labour in general and that for female labour faster than in the past; offer wider choice of occupation to women entering the labour market in the near future; and reduce the extent of poverty among families of these working women, the change to NEP should be regarded as a positive change. We must remember for the present that to be exploited in the labour market is bad but not to be exploited is worse.

The assessment elaborated above is based on data gathered from different sources which show the trend towards feminization, particularly in the manufacturing sector. However, a number of questions and problems surface in the utilization of statistical data which show general trends, especially when they are juxtaposed with specific case studies or with the experience of unionists, activists and researchers engaged in micro studies.

In response to the thesis of 'global feminization' projected by G. Standing, Diane Elson has pointed out that although the data in the ILO *Yearbook of Labour Statistics* does indeed show the increase in women's share of total employment in a large number of countries, this need not necessarily imply feminization. It could in fact be 'quite compatible with the disappearance of many jobs of the type traditionally dominated by men, and the expansion of jobs of the type traditionally dominated by women' (Elson, 1996).

To establish the case for feminization of the labour force in India, the Deshpandes use the Annual Survey of Industries for India which puts out a fairly detailed break-up of industry-wise percentage share of female workdays in total workdays in India, 1971 and 1983–4 (Deshpande and Deshpande, 1992: Table 5, p. 2250). Based on this they conclude that '... industries in India used proportionately more female labour in the early 80s than in the early 70s. Whilst this is true in some industries, their table also shows that in silk synthetics, the percentage of women employees declined from 5–10 to 1–5; in the food industry it declined from 21+ to 5–10; in wood products it increased from 5–10 to 10–15; in the chemical industry it increased from 5–10 to 10–15; in food products from 5–10 to 21+. Out of 19 industries, 10 have remained stagnant, two have reduced the employment of women and seven of them register an increase. The data therefore suggests a more mixed picture rather than a definite trend. It also raises the issue of examining such data along with the weight of each sector of production.

A similar problem arises in relation to the next set of data used as evidence which was compiled from the records of the chief inspector of factories, Bombay (ibid: Table 7, p. 2251). It indicates that industries employing more than 50 per cent women have increased from 0.6 per cent in 1975 to 2.5 per cent in 1981 to 3.1 per cent in 1989. The article unfortunately does not go into any details as to which industries employ such large numbers of women. Without this information, the data can be deceptive. For example, there are several units in SEEPZ employing not more than 30–40 employees. Some of these are 90–95 per cent female dominated. However, just down the road Larsen and Toubro and Mahindras employ more than 6,000–8,000 workers with hardly any women workers among them. It is therefore important to know specifically which industries have increased the recruitment of women.

The work participation rate of women in relation to men in manufacturing industry is abysmally low. When assessments are made in terms of percentages, it is important to keep in mind that the relative position of male workers remains high and the increase in female workers in actual numbers is quite low. The interpretation of NSSO and census data for Bombay as indicative of a major increase in women's employment and thereby reflecting a trend towards feminization could be questioned. The Deshpandes argue for instance that male employment during the decade 1981 and 1991 increased at 1.6 per cent per annum while that for females increased at 5.9 per cent per annum [Deshpande and Deshpande, 1992: 2249]. This means that between 1981 and 1982, the employment of men increased from 1,000 to 'only' 1,016 and in the case of women it increased 'substantially' from only 125 to 132 women.

At first glance, it does appear that the number of women employed has risen over the last few decades. The proportion of women in total employment, which includes agriculture, manufacturing, the service sector and informal sector has shown an increase. The total work participation rate for the male workforce at an all-India level fell from 52.65 in 1981 to 51.52 in 1991. The female rate on the other hand rose from 19.77 to 22.69 in the same period (Provisional Census, 1991). However, it is necessary to look beyond these broad trends based on aggregate data and examine complementary data sources in order to qualify and reinforce this generalization.

The Provisional Census categorically states that the higher female work participation rates could be due to the fact that more women were netted. This could have been the result of conscientizing and training census officials and field workers. In addition, the increase in women workers is more in rural areas from 23.18 in 1981 to 27.06 in 1991 while in urban areas it is only from 8.32 in 1981 to 9.73 in 1991 (Provisional Census, 1991). It is also necessary to specify what kinds of jobs are being done by women or are being taken over by them from men. Nirmala Banerjee (1989) points out that while the 1971–81 decadal growth of women in manufacturing (an increase of 60 per cent) could imply a reversal in the earlier trend towards a decline in women's employment as well as entry into new industries, the overall proportion of women workers in urban modern industries was still below 12 per cent in 1981. She points out further that far from a breakdown in the sexual division of labour, 'all that happened was that either women-type occupations had expanded or some occupations had become more identified with women' (Banerjee, 1989).

Qualification of statistical data is also necessary to ward off the problems of contradictory sets of data, especially from government sources. For instance, how does one explain that the figures from the *Statistical Pocket Year Book* of the Government of India (Table 4.1) shows that women's employment in the manufacturing sector has increased from 372,000 in 1961 to 461,000 in 1989 but their proportion in total manufacturing has declined from 11 per cent to 9 per cent or is almost against from 1966 to 1989 at 9 per cent.

Disturbing Observations

So far numerous micro level studies have shown decline in the employment of women. Renana Jhabvala (1985) and Mira Savara (1982) have documented the decline of female employment in the textile mill sector in Ahmedabad and Bombay over the past few decades due to automation. Other case studies in the city of Bombay show how many large-scale industries which employ women in large numbers have replaced their women workers by either men or machines or both (Gothoskar and Banaji, 1984). If there has been a reversal to this trend, it is necessary to specify in which industries this has occurred.

Case studies of particular companies indicate that expansion of production facilities in the 1980s have not resulted in an increase in the employment of women. For example, Hindustan Lever had only two large plants in Bombay and Calcutta for over 60 years. From 1982, Levers decentralized itself to have 20 other plants, besides a network of smaller units which were subcontracted. In the 1960s the Bombay plant employed a substantial proportion of women employees; about 600 women out of a workforce of 1,500. However in 1990, there were only 3 women left. None of Lever's other plants employ women in any substantial numbers except the

TABLE 4.1 Women's Employment in Factories, Mines and
Plantations in the 1960s, 70s and 80s

('000)

Year	Women in factories	
	Numbers	*Percentages*
1989	461	(9)
1988	454	(9)
1987	512	(10)
1986	471	(9)
1985	489	(10)
1984	540	(10)
1983	521	(10)
1982	480	(9)
1981	477	(9)
1980	473	(9)
1979	489	(10)
1978	495	(10)
1977	498	(10)
1976	511	(10)
1975	453	(10)
1974	441	(9)
1973	451	(10)
1971	370	(9)
1970	394	(9)
1966	365	(9)
1961	372	(11)

Source: Statistical Pocket Year Book, Department of Labour, Government of India, Simla, years; 1961 to 1989.

garment plant at the Export Promoting Zone in Kandla, Gujarat
(Gothoskar, 1992).

A similar process has been witnessed in the mining sector (Sen,
1990), the chemical sector and in various sectors in engineering,
toiletries, particularly affecting jobs such as packing where women
are employed (Gothoskar, 1992). A study done by Sharma and
Sengupta (1984) in SEEPZ, the export promotion zone in Bombay
showed that 98 per cent of its workers were women. However, in a

recent interview, the Labour Commissioner said that this proportion has been reduced to about 60 per cent in 1991.

In 'complementary' units or subsidiaries to large industries such as the powerloom industry in Bhiwandi and Surat, women are completely absent. According to a comprehensive study of the powerloom sector conducted at an all-India level by the Ministry of Labour, government of India, women constituted a mere 5 per cent of the labour force in 1988. In the handloom sector however, where the wage levels are much lower, women constituted 44 per cent of the workforce. Here women were invariably paid piece-rates which were very low (GOI, 1986–7). Whereas in the large and organized industries even contract workers are mostly always men.

It has often been argued that when large plants are closed or reduce their operations, the employment is diverted to the small-scale sector so there is a net increase in employment. This is not always the case because the small units, usually ancillary ones of the parent company are automated and require few workers. For example, the Paithan plant of Rhone-Polec (earlier May and Baker) employs 55 workers, mostly men who do the work which in Bombay was done by 300 workers. However smaller units which are exempt from labour regulations do tend to employ women as studies of chemical industrial estates in Ambernath and Kalyan have indicated, although the recruitment of women in comparison with men is low (Gothoskar, 1992). Within the completely unorganized sector, women are employed only in jobs which are seen as women-oriented such as garments or food processing. Small-scale plastic units prefer men giving the usual rationale that hard manual work and night shifts disqualify women from these jobs (Gandhi and Shah, 1992). It is therefore important not to assume an automatic relation between decentralization and increase in female employment.

In examining the data for feminization of the labour force it is useful to make a distinction between different referents of 'feminization' since these are often conflated. Feminization of the labour force has been used to refer to one or all of the following.

(1) Increase in the female participation rate relative to men;
(2) The substitution of men by women who take over jobs traditionally handled by men;
(3) The increase in women's involvement in 'invisible' work, i.e. family labour and homeworking; and
(4) The changing character of industrial work on the basis of new

technology and managerial strategies whereby work is decentralized, low paid, irregular, with part time or temporary labour contracts, i.e. increasingly like 'women's work' (but which is not necessarily done by women) (Chhachhi and Pittin, forthcoming).

An analysis of trends depends on which aspect/s we refer to in identifying 'feminization'. Looking at the shift to export-led growth in large-scale manufacturing in Turkey in the context of structural adjustment policies, Cagatav and Berik (1990) conclude that 'the shift to export-led growth has been achieved without an accompanying or subsequent feminization of employment.' However they do document an increase in homeworking. The role of the state is significant in the discussion on feminization or defeminization. Lack of feminization could be due to gender typing of industries in the context of labour repression, which reduces the labour cost advantage of women workers vis-à-vis men.

A major recommendation of SAP is privatization to make industry more efficient and profitable. Privatization would have significant implications for women's employment. An examination of figures for 1974 and 1988 of women's employment in the public and private sector shows that women's employment has risen more in the public sector rather than the private sector, i.e. in sectors such as electricity, construction, trade, transport, communication finance and insurance and community services. In the mining sector, women's employment increased in the public sector by 149.8 per cent and declined by 86.27 per cent in the private sector. In the finance and insurance sector, women's employment increased in both the public and private sector—by 352.8 per cent in the public sector and by 273 per cent in the private sector. Generally speaking the manufacturing sector is largely privatized. Here too, women's employment increased by 205 per cent in the public sector and 108.8 per cent in the private sector (refer to Table 4.2).

State-owned units are now under pressure to re-organize. Nationalized banks, in which 20 per cent employees are women, have declared 4 lakh people as surplus. Railways have stopped recruitment. The Post and Telegraph Department intends to retrenching 2,00,000 workers (Patel, 1992). Privatization when it does take place will result in a drastic cut in the workforce and women will be the most potential targets.

TABLE 4.2 Women Workers in Organized Industry

(in thousands)

Year	Sector	Agri-culture	Mining	Manufac-turing	Elect-ricity	Const-ruction	Trade	Trans-port and commu-nication	Finance and insur-ance	Com-muni-cation service
1974	Public	18.2	40.3	51.6	19.8	40.6	26.7	48.2	—	823.8
	Private	390.3	20.4	412.2	0.4	22.6	20.7	1.3	—	234.8
	Total	408.3	76.7	483.8	20.2	63.2	47.4	49.5	—	1058.6
1975	Public	14.8	57.7	53.9	10.2	43.2	2.5	50.5	35.2	861.1
	Private	391.0	24.9	399.4	0.3	23.4	16.6	1.8	8.2	236.6
	Total	405.8	82.6	453.3	10.5	66.6	19.1	52.3	43.4	1097.7
1976	Public	36.3	61.7	70.8	10.1	42.6	2.4	55.5	32.6	908.2
	Private	413.2	28.0	443.6	0.4	17.0	12.7	1.6	9.3	251.6
	Total	449.5	89.7	514.4	10.5	59.6	15.1	57.1	41.9	1159.8
1977	Public	62.3	65.9	75.9	10.8	46.3	4.1	58.5	36.8	935.7
	Private	421.5	26.5	450.0	0.4	11.3	12.8	1.6	10.7	262.8
	Total	483.8	92.4	525.9	11.2	57.6	16.9	60.1	47.5	1198.5
1978	Public	116.3	65.8	81.9	11.7	47.8	4.5	62.0	43.5	978.1
	Private	418.1	25.9	490.5	0.3	10.7	13.6	2.0	10.3	272.6
	Total	534.4	91.7	572.4	12.0	58.5	18.1	64.0	53.8	1250.7
1979	Public	171.1	62.0	87.0	13.0	46.8	5.0	65.6	52.8	1011.4
	Private	410.5	24.2	485.3	0.4	12.2	15.7	2.2	13.2	282.7
	Total	581.6	86.2	572.3	13.4	59.0	20.7	67.8	66.0	1294.1
1980	Public	32.6	62.4	92.4	15.7	53.8	5.8	73.2	59.0	1052.5
	Private	428.1	24.0	470.9	0.4	9.8	14.1	2.5	13.1	291.6
	Total	460.7	86.4	563.3	16.1	63.6	19.9	75.7	72.1	1344.1
1981	Public	37.0	63.5	91.2	16.7	49.8	6.1	78.8	68.8	1088.7
	Private	418.9	23.8	503.6	0.5	9.5	14.4	2.7	12.9	307.8
	Total	455.9	87.3	594.8	17.2	59.3	20.5	81.5	81.7	1396.5
1982	Public	29.7	63.5	98.4	17.6	54.4	6.3	86.0	78.6	1145.2
	Private	409.5	24.3	522.0	0.5	10.5	15.3	2.6	14.3	321.2
	Total	439.2	87.8	620.4	18.1	64.9	21.6	88.6	92.9	1466.4
1984	Public	35.8	66.4	100.6	20.0	50.6	8.0	105.4	98.8	1330.2
	Private	462.3	20.3	460.9	0.5	7.3	15.9	2.6	17.0	342.7
	Total	498.1	86.7	561.5	20.5	57.9	23.8	108.1	115.8	1672.9

(Contd.)

(Table 4.2 contd.)

Year	Sector	Agri-culture	Mining	Manufac-cturing	Elect-ricity	Cons-truction	Trade	Trans-port and commu-nication	Finance and insur-ance	Com-muni-cation service
1985	Public	36.3	66.5	102.4	20.7	53.5	8.5	108.4	104.9	1366.4
	Private	403.7	20.8	482.5	0.6	8.1	16.3	2.5	17.6	349.2
	Total	440.5	87.3	584.9	21.3	61.6	24.8	110.9	122.4	1716.0
1986	Public	37.4	66.1	102.5	21.6	57.9	7.7	109.9	110.4	1412.4
	Private	407.3	20.3	485.9	0.6	7.7	16.5	2.7	18.3	358.3
	Total	445.2	86.4	588.4	22.2	65.6	24.2	112.6	128.6	1770.7
1987	Public	46.2	60.8	104.3	25.2	68.5	9.4	123.1	123.2	1520.0
	Private	414.2	15.3	45.9	0.6	6.1	17.6	2.7	21.6	380.0
	Total	460.3	76.1	555.2	25.8	73.6	27.1	125.8	144.9	1906.0
1988	Public	48.3	60.4	105.8	25.6	71.7	9.0	125.9	124.2	1553.5
	Private	465.4	17.6	448.5	0.6	5.1	17.9	2.8	22.4	389.5
	Total	513.8	78.0	554.3	26.3	76.8	26.9	128.7	146.6	1943.0

Sources: Compiled from the *Indian Labour Year Book,* Years: 1975 to 1989, Labour Bureau, Chandigarh/Simla, Ministry of Labour, Government of India.

The Year Book of 1984 does not give these figures for the year 1983.

The issue of women's employment in the context of the NEP has to be seen in the broader context of the rise in general unemployment. Projections on the effects of the economic reforms on the employment situation by economists state that even under the most favourable conditions of growth, unemployment as a result of the present policies of the government will rise from less than 3 per cent in 1990–1 to about 5 per cent in 1993–4. This implies total open unemployment of about 18 million persons in 1992–3 and 19 million the year after (Mundle, 1993). According to this study, in the context of a low growth scenario, additional unemployment will increase to about 22 million in 1992–3, going up to 25 million by 1993–4.

The projection of low growth might be closer to what is likely to happen given the continuing industrial recession, at national and international levels. In addition, government as well as management strategies to handle this recession as well as control labour, through decisions such as increasing automation, shifting production to remote areas, etc., would swell the ranks of the urban unemployed.

Even though the government is ostensibly holding back on the exit policy, the process of job loss has been underway for some time. One form has been through factory closures. There has already been a sharp increase in the number of sick units in the country. The number of sick units had increased by 37,000 between December 1987 and December 1988, and by December 1990 an additional one lakh units had become sick taking the total number of sick units to 3.46 lakh (CMIE, 1992). According to a survey carried out by the Gandhian Labour Institute, 65 units become sick every day and at any time 98 per cent of the total sick units are in the small-scale sector. In the large-scale units, about two million workers are affected by industrial sickness in industries such as jute, cement, textiles, engineering, paper, iron and steel. In the small-scale sector, about 1.5 to 2 million workers are estimated to have been adversely affected. As aspect of the liberalization policy which has intensified this process is the removal of the threat of nationalization of sick units. This threat acted as a significant restraint on unscrupulous activities of business houses. Now there is no check on maltreatment of workers or siphoning off profits into other activities (Thankappan, 1992).

In another survey of 80 large-scale plants in Bombay, 16 had closed down or were on the verge of a closure. The employed workers ranged from 200 to over 3,000. Out of the rest, except in one company, there was a virtual ban on recruitment since the late 1970s and mid-1980s. Amongst these, in 67 plants, the management and introduced 'Voluntary Retirement Schemes' to get rid of the workforce. Most of these schemes were not voluntary in terms of the pressure that employers put on the workers, particularly older workers and women, to leave their jobs. In plants such as Hindustan Ferodo and Hindustan Lever, more than one-third of the workforce was asked to leave and lock-outs were imposed to achieve this purpose (Gothoskar et al., 1991).

What is going to happen to this large mass of unemployed men and women workers? Retrenched workers will enter the unorganized sector, looking for jobs in an already crowded sector. Women workers already constitute the most exploited section of this sector. Ela Bhatt has pointed out that it is the unorganized sector which is being hardest hit by the structural reforms (Bhatt, 1992).

The entry into the unorganized sector of workers who have lost jobs in the organized sector, also has to be differentiated according to skill, gender, marital status. On the basis of research on retrenched workers from the formal sector in Sao Paulo, Brazil, Hirata and Humphrey (1991) point out that it was unskilled men, single parents (mothers usually) and older women who are forced into taking up jobs in the unorganized sector. For women this was primarily in domestic services, cleaning, etc. Adult skilled male workers on the other hand were able to remain in open unemployment till they could return to a factory job. The adult males, with the exception of older, unskilled men, were able to secure their identities as industrial workers, even if this meant periods of unemployment of five months or more. A similar process in relation to male workers from industries which have been recently privatized can be seen in Pakistan. While all workers were retrenched with golden handshakes, skilled workers were re-employed in the same industries while the unskilled entered the unorganized sector.[2]

The evidence emerging from interviews we are conducting as part of an ongoing research project indicate that both male and female workers retrenched from the organized sector are finding it difficult to get new jobs. Shobha was a permanent employee in a pharmaceutical company who took the VRS eight years ago, rather than agree to work as a contract worker when the management initiated a strategy to redesignate existing workers as contract workers and employ new workers on contract paying them much lower wages. She explained that she had been looking after her sister's daughter since the last four years,

...after almost all our money from the VRS got over and all our hopes of getting another job were dashed. My husband was also working for PCL. He too was tricked into taking VRS. He too has tried to get several jobs, but all in vain. See both of us were very good in our work. The management could not point a finger at us, so we were tricked. But in the outside world our skills are meaningless. This we came to know when we began to look for work.[3]

[2] Karamat Ali, Pakistan Institute for Labour Education and Research, Personal Communication.

[3] Interview, 23 November 1993 from the authors' ongoing research project on 'Working Women and Organizational Strategies in India'.

Given the tendencies identified above, we feel it is too premature to state that a process of feminization of the labour force has started in India. Far more research, including case studies and time series data on changing trends in different sectors needs to be carried out before such a generalization can be arrived at.[4]

A major problem, with the notion of 'feminization through flexible labour practices' is that it does not take into account the sexual division of labour, in the production process and in the labour market. Since the inception of industrialization there has been a clear sexual division of labour for instance in textiles, mines, and later, in the chemical industries, engineering and electronics, women workers were assigned to only specific jobs, primarily assembly and packing while men were assigned a wide range of jobs, including supervision, maintenance, etc. The relationship between industrialization and women's employment has never been uni-directional. As Pearson states

...how industrialization affects the gender composition of the labour force within and outside factories depends on the specific context. There are various considerations: the kind of industrialization strategy; the sectoral composition of newly established and expanding industrial production; above all, the supply of men's labour and women's labour for industrial employment.

In India, Banerjee has pointed out that there is an all embracing ideology shared by employers, men workers and even accepted by women workers, which sees the male worker as a 'superior worker'. The jobs that women have got in industry has little to do with skill or capacities but 'went to women ... entirely at the discretion of male workers reflecting the power position men occupied in society (Banerjee, 1991). In cases where men have taken over women's jobs this has usually been associated with a reorganization of production due to technical change or an improvement in wages and working conditions. For instance, Banerjee notes in the electrical industry, women did armature winding for electrical fans but as soon as the wage rates for that job went up, it was taken out

---

[4] The only area where it can be definitely stated that such a process of feminization has occurred is in primary school teaching profession. Women form 70–80 per cent of the teaching force and men by and large avoid such employment. Again given possible cuts in the social sector, including education, which has been part of SAP in other countries, this area of employment could also be hit.

of their hands. Such reversals, also noted in large-scale industries such as pharmaceuticals and toiletries where women-dominated jobs such as packing and assembly have been taken over by men, often lead to a redefinition of these jobs as men's work. On the other hand where management has employed women for jobs previously the exclusive preserve of male workers, these jobs are redesignated as women's work. In relation to flexibility and feminization it is necessary to bear in mind that the '...gender division of labour, which tends to confine women to relatively subordinate and inferior positions in the organization of monetized production, is not overridden by 'flexibility'. Rather it structures the form that 'flexibility' takes' (Elson, 1989).

The projection that NEP will create a demand for the labour of young unmarried girls in the export industries depends on competition in the world market. The shift of capital back to countries in western Europe, the developments in new technology (another feature of 'flexibility') which require closeness to markets, the increased pressure for protectionism in the west, the opening of eastern Europe as a site for labour as well as a market and the requirements of high quality products which demand skilled labour will all impinge on how far India will have access to the world market. There is no guarantee therefore that export industries will expand. In addition, an important factor affecting the possibility of women's employment in these industries, if they do expand, is that given the levels of general unemployment, it is possible that

at least a section of this male labour force will come to bid for those jobs which so far have been allotted to women. In which case, it remains to be seen how far the inherent preference for male labour on the part of employees, that we had earlier noted, will come back into play (Banerjee 1991).

Multiple Survival Jobs

On the basis of the experience in other countries undergoing SAP, the prospects are that women workers would be involved in survival level jobs, probably two jobs, in combination with domestic labour. This will impinge on the time available for their domestic work. Inflation and wage cuts will reduce the family's purchasing power, forcing women to find even more time-consuming ways of cutting expenditure. Data on women's paid and unpaid work in the context of SAP shows that women's unpaid work has been intensified. In a small survey of 400 households in Buenos Aires in 1984, it was found that half of them were spending 40–80 hours week on household tasks (or 7 to 11 hours per day). One-third, especially women with large families were spending 80 hours and two-thirds more than 80 hours on both jobs and family (Carmen and Jelin, 1987).

Economic crisis situations lengthen the total number of paid and unpaid working hours of women. It is possible to inter-relate some of the features of SAP with its economic consequences and effects on women unpaid and paid labour. A modified version of a chart, based on one developed by UNICEF for child welfare and development which shows such linkages, is presented below (UNICEF, 1987). These directly linked relationships are a part of a larger web of inter-relations between production and reproduction, domestic and wage labour, gender construction within the labour process and the sexual division of labour in the household (see the chart).

CHART

SAP features	Effect	Women's lives
* Export-oriented cash crops	High food prices	* more time processing
* Cut in fertilizer subsidy		* purchase in whole sale
* Devaluation of rupee		* low nutritional status
* Cut in subsidy in PDS		
* Underemployment	Low income level	* multiple jobs
* Unemployment		* lower standard of living
* Low paid work		* fall in real wages
* Wage freeze		* longer working hours
* Withdrawal of workers' benefit		* poverty level
* Cut in employment schemes		
* Cut in public expenditure	Poor health services	* no access
* Expensive drugs		* increase in child mortality
		* pre-natal mortality
		* disease/illness
		* more health care at home
* Increased prices of water, fuel, electricity	Deteriorating civic services and housing	* more time fetching water, fuel

(Contd.)

(*Chart contd.*)

SAP features	Effect	Women's lives
* Higher land prices		* longer cooking time
		* longer commuting time
		* scarce housing
		* unhygienic conditions
* Privatization	Insecure livelihood	* subcontracting
* Deregulation		* retrenchment
* Delicensing		* VRS
* Recruitment of flexible labour		* unavailability of credit
		* low bargaining
* Closures and job loss		* Insecure life
* Loss of job opportunity	Increasing crime	* Increase in criminal gangs

The linkages elaborated in the chart are not too far-fetched as India experiences the highest rate of inflation since 1983. The prices of essential commodities have risen from 2.6 per cent in 1984 to 11.8 per cent in 1990 to 16.7 per cent in 1991. The Public Distribution System (PDS) has so far provided the poor with subsidized food but is now in the process of being 'revamped', which means either suspended or restructured. As family income becomes insufficient, women will have to put in more time to make less stretch for more. They will spend more time in domestic labour with little help, except from their older daughters. This burden of multiple jobs and extended domestic labour will sooner or later take a toll on their health. The combination of this with the pre-existing discrimination in food allocation to women and girls will result in a serious health crisis. A fall in nutritional levels will leave them prone to illness, disease and pre- and post-natal complications.

It is possible that working women will reach a point of total collapse but it may not be noticed for their oppression and vulnerabilities are easily masked by the family, explained away by the state and ignored or exploited in the marketplace. Given this situation it is imperative that we also focus specifically on women to develop organizational strategies which can strengthen them in confronting these economic pressures. These strategies could also lay the basis for transforming exploitative relations within the family, in relation to the state and in the market, thereby empowering working women as well as the communities they live in.

Alternative Perspectives

The economic reforms are now entering the second phase. So far the government has devalued the rupee twice (the exchange rate for the dollar went up from Rs 20 to Rs 25 and the second time from Rs 25 to Rs 31), many areas formerly earmarked as public sector units such as leather, chemicals, etc., have been delicensed. The 1993–4 budget has cut duties on consumer and other goods. The exit policy and a new Industrial Relations Bill are being discussed. The government is aware that the poor might be severely affected and has promised safety nets. The National Renewal Fund with its limited budget allocation is inadequate for the number of workers who will be unemployed as well as the number of purposes it is supposed to be used for. Originally seen as providing funds for redeployment as well as retraining, it is now being used primarily for voluntary retirement schemes.

Economists and activists have challenged the government's claim that this form of structural adjustment is the only solution to the balance of payments crisis. The first issue which arises is the manner in which the negotiations with the IMF were conducted and the present policy is being implemented, i.e. the issue of democratic participation. Trade unions, voluntary organizations, women's organizations and concerned individuals have demanded the right to information, specifically on the reasons for the present budget deficit, as well as accountability and acknowledgement of responsibility for the present economic crisis. Negotiations with the IMF were shrouded in secrecy when in fact in a democratic country there should have been a national debate or even referendum on this issue (Open Letter, FFWAP, 1992).

Clearly the new international development discourse on 'transparency' and 'accountability' needs to be actualized as well in the relation between the state and civil society. How can a government claim to express the will of the people when it misinforms, ignores and overrides the alternatives proposed by various groups and individuals. ·

Opposition to the IMF has been combined with proposals for alternative economic policies which could pull the country out of the present crisis. For instance, suggestions have been made for alternative methods to garner indigenous resources, by imposing austerity measures on the rich and their affluent consumption. The government could increase direct taxation on those who can afford to pay. If it summons up the political will, it can bring back capital into the economy by reducing the size of the estimated Rs 1,80,000 crore black economy, freezing of foreign accounts of Indians, including Swiss Bank accounts (an estimate puts this to 150–450 thousand crore) and blocking smuggling and gold imports (NCHR, 1992).

Reduction of defence expenditure which is growing every year is another option. In 1982 India's military expenditure was 53,193 million rupees (US$ 6,325 million) and in 1991 it rose to 1,65,157 million rupees (US$ 9,033 million). In South Asia, India is the largest buyer of conventional weapons.

Rather than expenditure for unproductive and destructive purposes, the same funds could be used for socially useful production and development purposes.

Since globalization under IMF conditionalities and an environment of protectionist tendencies in western markets can only mean a continued subordinate role for developing countries, with the constant threat of being turned into primary producers, efforts could be directed towards building south-south links which will strengthen the developing countries bargaining power vis-à-vis developed countries.[5]

Steps towards such links have been taken by worker leaders and trade union activists who have established networks at a South Asian level. Along with formulating joint strategies in relation to SAP and multinationals for workers' rights, the resolutions also call for opposition to military action by one South Asian country

---

[5] After examining evidence on labour markets in the context of SAP, in 12 countries, Horton, Kanbur and Mazumdar point out '... in response to structural adjustment, labour has moved in the direction opposite to that usually associated with economic development. It has shifted back into agriculture, out of manufacturing and out of the public sector (although one might argue that the latter sector was too large, given the level of development reached). Recession plus adjustment have also resulted in an increase in informalization, greater use of casual labour, decreased worker benefits, and declines in wage differentials for skill and possibly for education. These trends are observed even in the most successful adjustment cases in Asia. Developing countries have long resisted being relegated to the role of primary producers in the international economic order and it is unlikely that structural adjustment which relies on a shift of labour into agriculture is going to be sustainable for long' (Horton, Kanpur, Mazumdar, 1991).

against another and demand that South Asian governments establish economic and political links in the region.[6]

Resistance to attempts towards total control by multinational corporations and international agencies has also shown the possibility of alternatives as for instance the action by the Karnataka Rajya Raitha Sangha, a farmers' organization in Karnataka in organizing a massive demonstration in front of Cargill Seeds to protest against gene theft by multinationals and against the pressures of the Dunkel proposals which led to the withdrawal of Cargill. The debates around the Dunkel proposals has brought to the fore alternative perspectives on agricultural development which would be ecologically sensitive and sustainable.

At a macro level economists have argued that the international monetary system needs to be restructured so that the costs of adjustment are also borne by surplus countries. Mechanisms to ensure that developed countries also take responsibility for the economic crisis have to be evolved as well as ways to ensure that developing countries have more control within the international financial system.

Although alternatives have been presented, the government has not responded to any of these proposals. At the national level, opposition to the NEP by different sections has continued. The established national trade unions have organized massive rallies in the capital to express their opposition to the erosion of workers' rights and the proposed policies. The first general strike was called on 29 November 1991, the second on 16 June 1992. A number of demonstrations have been held against the new Industrial Relations Bill and recently against the new pension scheme.

In resisting the onslaught of SAP on workers, trade unions are following a three-tier approach: struggling against job losses, closures and lockouts, preventing privatization of public sector units; forming workers' co-operatives. In some cases these struggles have been successful. The long and arduous struggle of workers of the UP Cement Corporation against the take over attempt by the Dalmias, forced the government to halt their plans for privatization in October 1991. Workers have presented alternative plans on restructuring their industries without recourse to privatization. National Projects

[6] Final declaration of Conference on Trade Unions Human and Democratic Rights in South Asia, 15 March 1991, Colombo. Joint statement adopted by worker leaders from Multinational Companies in South Asia, 28 March 1992, New Delhi in *South Asia Bulletin*, vol. XII, No. 1, Fall 1992: 104.

Construction Corporation employees have provided an alternative proposal to turn around the sagging company. Kamani Tubes have already shown the possibility of forming a workers' cooperative. The Kamani Union used the support of professionals and management consultants to develop a financially viable alternative plan which was submitted to commercial banks for a loan to assist the buy over. In addition workers invested their gratuity and redundancy claims. After a long legal battle asserting the right of workers to take over the firm, the Kamani Union won and today run a manufacturing plant with over 600 worker shareholders. Subsequently, a number of similar worker-run enterprises were set up.

Such initiatives for worker-run cooperatives in the context of privatization have also emerged in other south Asian countries. For instance in Pakistan there are now 10 successful worker/ employee take overs. A significant development has been the links established between these enterprises at a south Asian level. In November 1993 a team of worker leaders and managers from these enterprises in India and Pakistan visited the Mondragon Industrial Cooperatives in Spain which has been highly successful in reconciling modern industry with ideas of social justice and democratization.[7] Efforts are now underway to develop cooperative relations at the shop-floor level as well as to transform enterprises taken over into truly self-managed cooperatives. Further links are being established with cooperatives in China.

These initiatives are very significant but they are limited since they are concerned with workers in the organized sector. (So far very few initiatives have involved women workers.) Trade unions have yet to respond to the changing pattern of industrialization with its emphasis on decentralization and subcontracting. They have not been able to organize the growing number of workers in the small-scale sector or workers who are casual wage labourers or home-based, a major section of which are women.

Rather than established trade unions or political parties it is other organizations which have taken up the cause of workers in the unorganized sector and particularly of women workers. SEWA's pioneering work in making visible and organizing self-employed women is well known. Annapurna in Bombay has organized the

---

[7] The visit was organized by the Pakistan Institute for Labour Education and Research, Karachi, the Centre for Workers Management, New Delhi, the Dursi Federation of Trade Unions (FNV) and the Institute of Social Studies, The Hague.

phanawalis (women who run home canteens). The Working Women's Forum in Madras has brought together thousands of women by giving them credit for self enterprise. The Tamil Nadu Construction Workers Union has been successful in organizing hundreds of workers to demand benefits and social protection.

There are lesser known examples of small groups or church-based ones organizing domestic servants, construction workers, beedi workers, etc. Most of these organizations have been quite flexible in responding to the varied needs of women workers. The Tamil Nadu Construction Workers Union, for instance, also takes up cases of wife beating, death, health, marriage and other disputes. The Chhattisgarh Mines Sangram Samiti in Madhya Pradesh has set up a hospital. The Chikodi Taluka Kamgar Union in Maharashtra, an organization of tobacco workers has set up a shelter for women in distress. These organizations have formed new structures to allow for greater participation of union members, especially women which has initiated a process of democratization. There are caucuses of women within the larger union, or dual organizations for workers' rights and women's rights, or united fronts for neighbourhood issues and women's rights.

Paradoxical as it sounds, today trade unions can no longer only organize their members on the basis of their identity as workers. Given present trends in industrial restructuring as well as communalism within the labour movement, it becomes essential that organizations recognize the multiple identities of workers, which include gender, caste, religion, ethnicity. The processes whereby these identities are constructed and the shifting basis of identity alliances has to be taken into account in organizing at the workplace, within the community and the household.

Strengthening Survival Strategies

So far women's organizations have joined various forums to protest against the NEP and SAP. In addition it is imperative that we develop strategies to strengthen women workers as they face the onslaught of the economic reforms on their lives. We can learn from the struggles waged by women workers in other countries undergoing SAP. The strategies we develop will have to relate to the specifics of our economic situation and culture of struggle. They will have to constantly bridge the gap between the workplace, community, neighbourhood and household. These would be intermediate strategies which can provide support for women in the present context, yet contain within them the possibility for transforming exploitative relations and lay the basis for self-determination.

Such strategies have emerged as 'spontaneous' responses to the deteriorating standard of living in countries undergoing SAP. Women from low income households have had to evolve various survival strategies. Survival strategies have been seen essentially defensive with little potential to change the general conditions under which individuals and households survive. Concerned with basic survival they are seen to be individualized, and limited to immediate objectives. However, these survival strategies do imply an engagement with the immediate environment and as Daines and Seddon (1990) point out they do have 'the potential for the development of more effective, more sustained and more collaborative forms of struggle....' Cornia has documented and classified the range of survival strategies which the poor, particularly women have resorted to in the context of SAP. Th e are: strategies for the creation of resources which include increasing own production, increasing sale of labour, sales of assets, increasing production through voluntary labour exchanges and cooperative work and transferring income to aid poorer relatives; strategies for conserving and improving the use of existing resources; and extended family and migration strategies.

The potential of these survival strategies to become transformative ones is best seen in the evolution of communal kitchens (comedores populares) in Lima, Peru which emerged in the 1980s as a response to the deteriorating economic situation. Groups of 15–50 households jointly carried out bulk purchase and preparation of food. Women cooked the food on the basis of daily shifts every four or five days, with each household paying according to the number of meals required. Poorer households were either exempted or given food on credit. The communal kitchens thus became 'instruments of redistribution in favour of the poor' (Daines and Seddon, 1990). Women were freed from daily cooking and were able to engage in other activities as well as participate in political meetings. Preparation of meals became a collective task which represented an organization and division of work which was radically different. Entry into public spaces led to interaction with NGO activists and feminists.

Thus women's responsibility towards their families and their children's health and future became a source of energy and action that has permitted them to break with traditional patterns. It has permitted them to enter the public sphere and even, in the last five years, to pass from protest to proposal, and to become active participants in proposing social policies. For example, in 1987 the National Coordinator of Communal Kitchens elaborated a proposal whereby urban family consumption was linked with agricultural production (Dianes and Seddon, 1990).

Similarly the 'mothers clubs' where mothers took turns to manage child care centres have also freed women for other work.

In our own context it is possible to develop similar initiatives. Women's groups can help local women to form consumer cooperatives for wholesale purchase of essential commodities. Organizations working with women in *bastis* have already started organizing around the PDS. The Sabla Sangh in Delhi for instance had a campaign around ration shops calling for controls over corruption, fairer prices and public display of items in stock. Representatives of these organizations could be involved in monitoring the ration shops to ensure fair prices and distribution. This was attempted in Bombay by groups of NGOs and women under the banner of Ration Kirti Samiti.

In a situation where neo-liberal calls for withdrawal of the state are intensifying, women's organizations will have to redouble their efforts to ensure that the state not only continues to subsidize food distribution but also extends support in other areas through the provision of services such as easy access to water, creches, etc. Existing services which are provided usually by NGOs could be extended. For instance running *balwadis* is a common activity for most organizations. However they are usually open only for a few hours for pre-school children. With the same infrastructure it is possible to extend *balwadi* hours for the whole day for small children of home-based workers.

Strategies and policies for working women have to incorporate the various dimensions of women's multiple identities. A policy for women's employment has to support strategies for changing gender ideology both inside as well as outside the workplace. Notions of masculinity and femininity affect skill definitions, wages and working conditions and the location of women within the production process as well as within sectors of industry. The integral link between the household, workplace and community affects women's work as well as their potential for organizing. The issue of the sexual division of labour within the household has to be equally significant as an issue as are strategies to keep jobs for women or get jobs for women. In spite of the highlighting of the double/triple burden of working women, domestic labour as the major responsibility of women continues to be the most resistant to change. In Cuba in the 70s a law was passed which made it possible for women to take their husbands to court if they refused to share in housework. Although there have hardly been any convictions under this law the existence of such a legal regulation could play a role in forcing a questioning of the sexual division of labour.

The present trends towards flexible specialization has led to a discussion on the dual character of flexibility. Part-time work for instance could allow greater choice about hours and patterns of work. However it is then necessary to ensure that flexible workers enjoy parity with full-time works in relation to wages, benefits and rights. A recent ruling in the European Community states that flexible workers should be guaranteed these rights. Employer strategies to reduce labour costs by decentralization and subcontracting could be countered by extending labour legislation along the whole chain of subcontracting and making the large firm responsible for the rights of workers in the smaller units. Similarly the ESIS medical scheme should be extended to all workers.

At a macro level ILO Conventions should be put forward as a non-negotiable conditionality in the context of economic reform. A legal provision for the registration of workers—contract, temporary, home-based, etc., who could be provided with identity cards—could counter attempts to redesignate workers as self-employed and deny them their rights. This strategy has been followed by SEWA for bidi workers. A code of conduct for multinationals and other large companies could help in monitoring production and prices.

Most women perform low skill, manual jobs which gives them a weak position in the labour market. Training women to develop new skills and enhance existing ones has been recommended time and again. Attempts at training women such as the courses in non-traditional skills in carpentry, wiring, masonry, plumbing, etc., run by the YWCA have been very useful, although there have been mixed reactions to these experiments. It takes time for society to accept women as technicians in these fields. In addition to these attempts it is necessary to campaign for the recognition of existing skills.

Training in technical skills could be combined with other educational programmes so that 'if workers lose their jobs, they have acquired something of permanence—more self-confidence, more organizational and advocacy skills, more knowledge of how their society works' (Elson, 1992).

Lack of credit facilities will affect women workers especially the self-employed. Banks will have to be pressured to respond to the poor sections of society. At the same time we have to assist women to gain access to family resources by insisting on joint ownership of land and house, including their names in identity cards, photopasses and ration cards. This could help in gaining access to formal credit sources.

Women in bastis often invest their savings in chit or rotating funds. Community organizations, unions, women's organizations can play a role in seeing that women are not cheated by monitoring these schemes or setting up their own saving schemes.

All these strategies require collective action at different levels: pressurizing the state, supporting working women in their daily survival and developing organizational forms which can empower them within the household, in the market and in relation to the state. A number of voluntary organizations have started programmes on health and provision of services like fodder, banks, credit, etc. given the deteriorating economic situation. While supportive programmes are necessary, these should not become a reason for the state to abdicate its responsibility to provide these services to its citizens. On the other hand, the NEP should be opposed along with presenting alternatives. A double-edged strategy needs to be followed which combines supportive strategies with organized pressure on the government to ensure that the poor do not pay even more for a crisis which was not of their making.

References

Antrobus, P., 1990 *The Impact of Latin American Crisis on Women*, Development Alternatives for Women Network (DAWN), Barbados.

Banerjee, N., 1989, 'Trends in Women's Employment, 1971–81: Some Macro-Level Observations', *Economic and Political Weekly*, 29 April.

Banerjee, N., (ed.), 1991, *Indian Women in a Changing Industrial Scenario*, Sage Publications, New Delhi.

Bank Information Centre (undated), *Funding Ecological and Social Destruction: The World Bank and IMF,* The Other India Press, Goa.

Batliwala, S., 1983, *Women in Poverty—Energy, Health and Nutritional Syndrome*, FRCH, Bombay.

Bhatt, Ela, 1992, 'Structural Reform: View from the Other Side', *The Economic Times*, 15 January.

Cagatay, Nilufer and Berik Gunseli, 1990, 'Transition to Export-Led Growth in Turkey: Is There a Feminisation of Employment?', *Review of Radical Political Economics*, vol. 22 (1).

Carmen M.E. Jelin, 1987, 'The Invisible Adjustment. Poor Women and the Economic Crisis', quoted in speech by R. Jally in Paris on Women Development Group of OECD, June.

Chhachhi, A. and R. Pittin (forthcoming), 'Multiple Identities, Multiple Strategies: Confronting State, Capital and Patriarchy', in Chhachhi, A. and R. Pittin (eds), *Confronting State, Capital and Patriarchy: Women Organising in the Process of Industrialisation*, Macmillan, London.

CMIE, 1992, *Data File on Sickness and Closures*, Bombay.

Commonwealth Secretariat, 1989, *Engendering Adjustment for the 1990s*, Report of a Commonwealth Expert Group, London.

Daines, V. and D. Seddon, 1990, *Survival Strategies, Protests and Resistance: Women's Response to Austerity and Structural Adjustment*, University of East Anglia, UK.

Deshpande, S., 1993, 'Structural Adjustment and Feminisation', in A.N. Sharma, and S. Singh (eds), *Women and Work—Changing Scenario in India*, Indian Society of Labour Economics, Patna and B.R. Publishing Corporation, Delhi.

Deshpande, S. and L.K. Deshpande, 1992, 'New Economic Policy and Female Employment', *Economic and Political Weekly*, 10 October, vol. XXVII (41), Bombay.

Elson, D., 1989, 'Appraising Recent Developments in the World Market for Nimble Fingers. Accumulation, Regulation, Organisation', in A. Chhachhi, and R. Pittin (eds), *Confronting State, Capital and Patriarchy: Women Organising in the Process of Industrialisation.*

FFWAP (Forum for Women and Politics), undated, New Delhi.

Gothoskar, S., 1992a, 'The So-Called Tiny Sector and Women's Employment in India', paper presented at the Seminar on The New Economic Policy and the Tiny Sector, with special reference to Women's Employment, SNDT, November, Bombay.

Gothoskar, S., 1992b, 'Trends in Employment in Major Multinationals in India', unpublished, Bombay.

————1993, 'The Banking Industry in India—Prospects for Women's Employment and Training', paper presented at workshop on 'The Impact of New Technologies on Women's Employment: Horizon 2000', United Nations University in Technology, Maastritch, Netherlands.

Gothoskar, S. and R. Banaji, 1984, 'Making the Workplace a Better Place for Women', *Manushi*, No. 24, September–October, New Delhi.

Gothoskar, S. and P. Halal; S. Dudhat; O. Flavia; and G. Vaidya, 1991, *Job Losses and Closures—Management Strategies and Union Counter-Strategies*, APHD, Hong Kong.

Government of India, (1986–7): *Report on the Working and Living Conditions of Workers in the Handloom Industry in India*, Government of India, Chandigarh.

————, 1988, *Report on the Working and Living Conditions of the Workers in the Powerloom Industry in India*, Government of India, Chandigarh.

Hirata, H. and J. Humphrey, 1991, 'Workers' Responses to Job Losses: Female and Male Industrial Workers in Brazil', *World Development*, vol. 19 (6).

Horton, Kanbur and Mazumdar, 1991, 'Labour Markets in an Era of Adjustment. Evidence from Twelve Developing Countries', *International Labour Review*, vol. 130, Nos. 5–6.

Jhabvala, Renana, 1985, *Closing Doors*, SETU Publications, Ahmedabad.

Kriti, 1992, 'Regular Publication by Society for Participatory Research in Asia (PRIA), No. 2, New Delhi.

Mundle, Sudipto, 1991, *The Employment Effects of Stabilisation and Related Policy Changes in India. 1991–92 to 1993–94*. ILO, New Delhi.

————, 1993, 'Unemployment and Financing of Relief Employment in a Period of Stabilisation: India. 1992–94', *Economic and Political Weekly*, 30 January.

————, 1992, *Against the Stream: India's Economic Crisis and Workers' Alternatives*, Charu, July, New Delhi.

NCHR, 1992, 'Sapping India—Sapping the Indian People: The Impact of IMF–SAP on Housing and Living Conditions in India', National Campaign for Housing Rights, Bombay.

Patel, Vibhuti, 1992, 'Women and Structural Adjustment in India', paper presented at London School of Economics and Political Science, UK.

Rao, Ashok K., 1992, 'Privatisation of the Public Sector—Issues to Consider', paper presented at Workshop South Asian Unionists and Privatisation, March, New Delhi.

Savara, Meera, 1982, *Changing Trends in Women's Employment,* Himalaya Publishing House, Bombay.

Sen, Ilina (ed.), 1990, *A Space Within the Struggle,* Kali for Women, New Delhi.

Sharma, R.N. and C. Sengupta, 1984, *Women's Employment at SEEPZ—Bombay,* mimeograph, TISS, Bombay.

Standing, Guy, 1989, 'Global Feminisation through Flexible Labour', *World Development,* vol. 17 (7).

Thankappan, D., 1992, 'Industrial Sickness and Worker Takeovers', paper presented at a Seminar on Industrial Sickness and Workers' Takeovers, Bombay.

UNICEF, 1987, *Adjustment with a Human Face,* Clarendon Press, Oxford.

5

Impact of Technological Change on Industrial Women Workers

Rohini Hensman

This chapter attempts to take up two of the questions raised in the *Human Development Report 1995*, namely: 'Are human choices enlarged or narrowed by new technologies? Is economic expansion leading to job-led or job-less growth?' (p. 124). Although the focus is on the actual and potential effects of technological change on women workers, these effects have far-reaching implications for human development in more general terms, for present as well as future generations.

Before examining the ways in which technological change affects women workers, it would be useful to look at the situation of women workers prior to and independently of technology, within the context of the currently accepted division of labour in society.

It is an almost universal observation that women workers tend to predominate in certain industries—for example, garments, textiles, food, electronics—while being virtually absent in others (such as steel, machinery and heavy industry in general). Even within the industries which have a substantial representation of women, they are concentrated in certain jobs—cleaning and preparation, packing and checking, sewing, manual assembly and so forth—which are classified as being unskilled or semi-skilled, and are highly labour-intensive, requiring little or no machinery (Banerjee, 1985, pp. 34–35).

That this division of labour is neither natural nor universal is shown by the fact that there are wide variations—between one country and another, or between the formal and informal sectors, or from one time period to another. For example, many offices in India employ men in secretarial and clerical positions which in Europe would be occupied by women, while conversely, in India there are many women construction workers, whereas in Europe this is an almost exclusively male occupation. Again, in the textile industry in Coimbatore, women constituted only 15 per cent of the mill workforce in 1981 and very few worked on the looms, whereas in the informal sector, women constituted 33 per cent of those working on powerlooms (Baud, 1983). And finally, in 1983 women constituted over 25 per cent of the textile labour in Bombay, but by the late 1980s there were virtually no women workers (Hensman, 1988).

The gender division of labour in industry is a *social* division of labour, and therefore can vary according to the situation. What is common, however, is that wherever a job is done exclusively or predominantly by women, it comes to be classified as being less skilled and of lower value, and this is especially so in countries like India where equal pay for work of *equal value* has never been fought for, and therefore the subjective basis on which jobs are evaluated is neither brought under scrutiny nor challenged.

Thus, even where women are working as industrial workers in the strict sense, they earn on average much less than men, for a number of reasons. (1) There is a disproportionately high representation of women in the unorganized sector, where they are paid a small fraction of the wages which would be paid for the same jobs in the organized sector. (2) Wherever unions have not fought for equal pay, women are usually paid less for doing the same work as men, even if equal pay legislation exists. (3) Even where equal wages are paid for the same work, women are segregated into jobs which are regarded as being of less value than most of the jobs done by men.

The unspoken or explicit assumption behind all these practices is that women are less effective as wage-earners than men and have less need of money. The assumption that a woman's wages are merely supplementary persists, despite numerous studies which have shown the large and growing number of women-headed households (Lingam, 1994, pp. 699–704), and the fact that even where both partners are earning, the woman's income is spent almost exclusively on household necessities, whereas a large part of a man's income may be spent on inessential items for himself like alcohol and tobacco (Elson, 1995, pp. 27–30).

On the other hand, where domestic labour is concerned, women are usually assigned exclusive responsibility (even if it is understood that they may delegate some of the tasks to others). Once again this is a *social* division of labour, although its near universality may lead one to believe there is truth in the claim, often advanced, that it has a biological basis. For example, some tasks commonly done by women, such as carrying heavy pots of water, household provisions or babies, sometimes for long distances or time periods, are physically more taxing than many industrial jobs considered too 'heavy' for women. They become 'women's work' not because women are more biologically suited to perform them, but because they belong to the domestic economy which is supposed to be a woman's sphere.

A most important characteristic of work done directly for one's own household is that it is not remunerated in any way. Interestingly, in many third world cultures it is acceptable for these same tasks to be done by men, provided they do them as waged labour—for example, as hotel workers or domestic servants. But these men, like other male workers, would not readily do the same tasks in their own homes for no pay. The assumption here—a corollary of the earlier one—is that women are more suited to unwaged work, and can afford to do it because there is no necessity for them to earn. The reality is that for millions of women who have to combine wage labour with household tasks, the working day is punishingly long—sometimes as long as eighteen hours or more—leaving them no leisure at all and, indeed, insufficient time even to recover from the day's exertion, so that chronic exhaustion and ill-health are the result.

We need not go into the question of the casual connection between these linked assumptions; probably both are the consequence of rigid gender stereotyping which is deeply ideological in nature. What is important to recognize, however, is that *given* the latter assumption, the former necessarily follows. In other words, *if* we assume that women are uniquely suited to doing unwaged domestic labour and therefore must take responsibility for this work and bear the major burden of it, then it follows that women, on average, will be less effective as wage earners than men. After all, women are not superhuman, and no matter how hard they work, they can never be equal to men so long as they have this extra workload at home. Of course, it may be possible for women in exceptional circumstances (for example, single women without children, or those who can afford to pay for home help and child care) to perform as well as men in paid employment over their entire working lives, but for the majority this option will not be available.

I emphasize this because it has important practical consequences —namely, that all attempts to bring about equality for women in paid employment will fail so long as this other inequality is not addressed. This is not to deny the importance of equal pay legislation, and especially legislation aimed at guaranteeing equal pay for work of equal value; nor of equal opportunities policies aimed at ensuring that women are not discriminated against in recruitment and promotion to jobs at all levels including the most skilled and qualified; nor of equal education and training opportunities for women and girls. Similarly, legislation which enables women to combine domestic responsibilities with paid employment has enabled many women to stay on in employment when they would otherwise have had to leave. Restrictions on night work for women, in addition to reducing the probability of sexual assault, prevent employers from insisting that women workers should comply with shift schedules which would interfere with their commitments at home. Maternity leave provisions allow them to get paid while they have babies and recover from the deliveries. And workplace creche facilities provide child care for their pre-school children. All these are crucially important and have to be fought for. But they still leave women at a disadvantage as compared with men.

Three points should be noted. First, it may be the case that in conditions of labour shortage employers or the state or both have proved willing to provide facilities like maternity leave or child care in order to encourage married women to enter the labour force. But these are fragile privileges, easily withdrawn when labour is plentiful, as occurred in post-war Britain. And indeed, from the standpoint of employers and the state, it is absurdly irrational to engage paid employees to do this work when women could be doing it unpaid at home—and, moreover, reducing the numbers of unemployed in search of work. In our labour surplus economies of South Asia, the legal right to child-care facilities remains for most women a dead letter. Even in the formal sector, employers evade legislation by simply refusing to comply with it, or by not recruiting women at all.[1] The bidi industry in India is a case where employers have avoided the obligation to provide workplace creches by dispersing workers to do the work in their homes—that is, by transferring production from the organized to the unorganized sector.

This brings us to the second point, which is that these facilities are really available only to women in the large-scale organized sector. For over 90 per cent of women workers, who work in the unorganized sector, this legislation is more or less irrelevant. If they are required to work at night, they have to do so or face dismissal; they are likely to be dismissed automatically if they marry or get pregnant, or, at best, they may get unpaid maternity leave; and they have to arrange for child care themselves if they want to continue working after bearing children. Paradoxically, this may mean that they are in one way more equal to men than women in the organized sector because employers, unhindered by protective legislation, are often much more willing to take on women for jobs which in the organized sector are monopolized by men.[2] But this 'equality' is won at a heavy cost to a woman's personal life. It may mean, for example, that she cannot get married or have children while she is working or, if she does, her health and family life may suffer serious strain resulting from the absence of any allowances for domestic commitments. Lack of child care has another undesirable side effect: it usually means that girls are kept away from school to look after younger siblings at home, thus extending deprivation and exploitation to the next generation.[3]

Finally, let us assume an ideal scenario (which does not in fact exist anywhere) where women have equal access to education and training, routinely get equal pay for work of equal value, are provided with paid maternity leave and child care, and are guaranteed equality of opportunity with men provided they are equally qualified and equally capable of doing the job. There would

[1] See Rohini 1991, for the various strategies used by employers to avoid recognition of the legal rights of women workers.

[2] For example, Isa Band (1983) notes that women working in the unorganized powerloom sector, where their proportion was much higher than in the organized mill sector, had to work night shifts on alternate weeks.

[3] See Dietrich, 1995, pp. 1551–54, for a graphic description of the apalling conditions under which women are employed in the unorganized sector, and the tragic consequences for their children, especially girls.

still be a large number of women—perhaps the majority—who in the course of their working lives would need to take breaks for having babies, who would find shift-working schedules incompatible with their domestic responsibilities, and so forth. The provision of child care *while they are at work* does not change the fact that they still have an extra burden of domestic work at home, and this affects their employment status in subtle ways. For example, it may prevent them from attending evening classes or training courses which are necessary for promotions, or the continual conflict between divergent commitments may ultimately induce them to simplify their lives by taking early retirement. Those who manage to stay at par with men would still be the exception rather than the rule.

This is the background against which technological change occurs, introduced by the very same capitalists who feel that child care is not something they need to be concerned about. For them, maximizing returns on heavy investment in new technologies which may soon become obsolete due to rapid advances is a compulsion. Some ways of achieving this are shift-working, cutting wage costs by reducing the workforce to a minimum, and preferably getting rid of workers' unions by shifting production to non-unionized workforces.

What does this mean for women workers in the organized sector? Very often it means job losses. Let us take a brief look at a few examples:

(1) In the Indian Leaf Tobacco Division (ILTD) of India Tobacco Company (ITC) in Chirala, Andhra Pradesh, 5,000 women lost their jobs in 1982 when manual stripping of leaves, which was done by women, was replaced by mechanical threshing. Today, only men handle the highly automated machinery. The women who lost their jobs were devastated; some even committed suicide. In the entire ILTD, some 25,000 women lost their jobs in the course of automation.[4]

(2) In open-cast iron ore mining in Chhattisgarh, Madhya Pradesh, raising of ore in manual mines was originally performed by a workforce consisting of almost equal numbers of men and

[4] Verbal communications from J. Banaji and V. Janardhan who interviewed the women in Chirala, and from an ITC trade unionist at the Conference of the International Union of Food and Allied Workers in Goa, November 1995.

women. In the mechanized mines, by contrast, not a single woman was employed for this task. Moreover, as mechanization progressed in the manual mines, total employment declined, but women's employment declined more, so that in 1995 they were only 27.6 per cent of the total workforce in these mines (Sen, 1995).

(3) Bombay's pharmaceutical industry once provided thousands of relatively secure, well-paid jobs for women. But in the 1960s and 1970s, with automation gaining momentum, many employers stopped recruiting women. By the 1990s, most companies had stopped recruitment even of men, and some, like Ciba-Geigy, Proctor and Gamble and Boots, closed down their Bombay operations altogether, either shifting production to highly automated new units with all-male workforces in 'backward' areas, or subcontracting it to small- and medium-scale units, both with non-unionized workforces (Workers' Solidarity Centre, 1995).

It is true that new technologies also create new jobs for women; for example, in the manufacture and use of electronic products or in the small-scale units to which production is subcontracted. But these are not the same women as those who have lost their jobs; typically they are young, single, and sometimes more highly educated or qualified. Further, the vast majority of the new jobs go to workforces which are difficult or impossible to unionize, whereas the jobs lost, in all these three cases, belonged to unionized women workers.

Workers in the unorganized sector too are faced with job losses when their work is mechanized. A government committee set up in 1974 estimated that one powerloom displaces six handlooms; between 1974 and 1981, 2.8 million workers lost their traditional occupations, 43.75 per cent of them being women. Here, again, some new jobs were created—for example, some of the displaced women workers found employment working on mechanized winding machines. But the number of new jobs created was very far from being sufficient to absorb the number of workers displaced (Action India, 1995).

So the women who have lost their jobs are not likely to find new ones with comparable conditions, and even where new jobs are created, they are likely to be fewer than those which have been lost, and under worse employment conditions. Moreover, the new technologies bring with them a whole range of new problems, which non-unionized women workers in insecure jobs are ill-equipped to deal with. Some of the health hazards associated with these technologies—such as chemical hazards in electronic assembly and repetitive strain injury for those working at computer terminals—are not envisaged or dealt with by existing legislation, and in other countries women who suffer from them have had a hard struggle even to get them recognized as work-related injuries. Additionally, employers often use new technologies to intensify work and impose more control over workers.

It looks as if the introduction of new technologies has meant a narrowing rather than enlargement of choices for industrial women workers and possibly also for men, so far as employment is concerned. And this is linked to the fact that industrial production with new technologies involves large investments and very high productivity but creates only a very small number of new jobs while often destroying a much larger number of old ones. If we look to Europe, North America and Japan to show us our future, we can envisage a situation where industrial growth in terms of increasing investment and production is accompanied by growing structural unemployment which refuses to go away.[5] What, then, is the solution to this problem?

One solution which has been argued quite widely is that technological change should be opposed altogether, or at least limited to the adoption of intermediate technologies which are appropriate to labour-surplus countries like ours. One problem with this perspective is that it would not be feasible in an open economy which is part of the world market, since competitive pressures would compel the adoption of advanced technologies as a matter of survival. The alternative would be a state-controlled economy which is isolated from the world market, but maintaining this isolation and depriving people of the opportunity to buy anything produced abroad, especially if it is unavailable or much more expensive domestically, would require a fairly high degree of state authoritarianism, probably linked to corruption and a flourishing black market. At a time when this model has been given up in Russia, Eastern Europe and China, it seems unrealistic to expect it to succeed in India.

Moreover, even if it were feasible, would such a thing be desirable? Do we really want to preserve a situation where the

[5] For example, the engineering industry in Germany was expected to lay off 100,000 workers in 1996 ('German firms, unions inch closer to deal on job creation', 1996).

majority of men as well as women have to labour long hours simply in order to survive, where women have to work even harder to care for children and perform domestic tasks, and at the end of it all have hardly any time to enjoy their children or relax with friends?

If we use our imaginations to separate the way in which new technology is being used to generate vast profits controlled by a tiny minority and think, instead, of its potential uses, we can see that the enormous increases in the productivity of labour achieved by advanced technologies make it possible, for the first time in human history, to satisfy the basic material needs of the world's population. If the work necessary for doing this is distributed equitably among all able-bodied adults, it would be possible to wipe out unemployment and carry out a dramatic reduction in working hours. This would leave plenty of time for domestic tasks which could also be considerably lightened by technology, and if they are shared equally between males and females, everyone would have plenty of time for relaxation.

All this sounds madly utopian at present, yet the main obstacle to it is not technology but human beings. First and foremost, of course, such a perspective would be opposed tooth and nail by the small number of human beings who wield an enormous amount of power under the present international capitalist world order and would lose this power in a more egalitarian system. But even the majority of working people, who would undoubtedly benefit from such a change, would need a major shift in perception before they could even see such a vision, much less adopt it as their goal. Why? Because this vision of a possible future requires a gestalt shift in the way in which we view and evaluate paid work and the time we spend on relationships. Today, typically, a 'full-time job' occupies at least eight hours a day or forty hours a week; the fact that this may leave millions of people permanently unemployed is not seen as anomalous. Technological change may increase the productivity of each person's labour by ten, twenty or a hundred times, yet they must still work just as long. Paid work is seen as the serious business of life, and it must occupy the centre of the stage.

On the other hand, the caring work which is mostly done at home is marginalized so completely that it becomes all but invisible. Many people would not even regard the child care, cooking and cleaning done in the home, usually by women, as real work. When it is done by women in their own homes, it is never remunerated:

in other words, its *social* value—as distinct from its personal value for those who benefit from it—is regarded as zero. The fact that it is done by women is linked with their low status in society; in many communities, a man who did this work would be regarded with contempt.

Yet can we imagine the consequences to society if all this unpaid work is not done? The most vulnerable—very young children and invalids, for example—would simply die, and the lives of everyone else would suffer from severe disruption and deprivation. Alternatively, costs would rise steeply as people substituted paid for unpaid labour, so that no one would do anything for anyone else except for payment. This would be a cold, commercialized world, where the absence of personal care would lead to an increase in mental illness, possibly also manifesting itself in physical symptoms, and society would suffer the consequences.

So can we change our perceptions and see the time we spend cuddling a baby, playing with a child, listening and talking to a spouse or a friend, caring for an invalid—the time we spend being an attentive ear, a soothing voice, a shoulder to cry on—as being crucial for the welfare of society as a whole? Can we see caring and nurturing as activity which humanizes both women and men rather than a burden which is shunted off onto women? It may not be possible—or, indeed, desirable or necessary—to evaluate this 'work' in monetary terms, yet this need not prevent us from recognizing its value in human and social terms, for those who perform it as well as its recipients.

New technologies make such a vision of the future both possible and necessary. They make it possible by achieving a drastic reduction in the labour time necessary for producing the material necessities of life; they make it necessary because otherwise a larger and larger proportion of humanity will be condemned to a life which is regarded as socially useless because there is no employment for them. If we achieve this radical shift in perception, then 'work' in a more conventional sense would not cease to be important, but it would share the stage with time spent on creating and maintaining caring, nurturing, mutually affirming relationships. We would be able to shift from one mode of activity to another without downgrading the importance of either.

Suppose we now come back to the real world of today, where the majority of human beings drudge all their lives to scrape a living, where women work harder and are paid less, and where technological change usually means unemployment and marginalization for more and more people: what strategies would we formulate, what demands would we make, if we adopt such a vision as our goal?

To begin with, we would not oppose technological change as such, but instead would attempt to eliminate its negative consequences and realize its positive potential. This would involve measures such as:

(1) Democratization of the workplace by obtaining information and consultation rights for employees, so that the introduction of new technologies is carried out with consultation of the workforce.[6] This will reduce negative consequences such as large-scale retrenchments (often disguised 'voluntary retirement schemes' [VRS]) by making changes gradually, providing training to existing employees so that they can handle the new technology, and reducing working hours so that fewer jobs are lost. Negotiation can also ensure that technological change is linked with improvements in working conditions and health and safety. One example of this type of bargaining occurred in The Netherlands in the engineering firm Akzo, where in the 1980s the union succeeded in creating 950 jobs by shortening working hours to 38 per week. Examples from India are hard to find, but in Kamani Tubes the union won temporary access to company information in the 1970s, and this proved invaluable in enabling them to form a workers' cooperative and take over the plant when it was facing closure in the 1980s (Banaji and Hensman, 1990, pp. 192–93).

(2) On a national level, it is absurd that we are going into the twenty-first century with working hours which are more appropriate to the nineteenth century! A campaign should be launched to reduce the statutory maximum from 48 to 40 hours per week initially; later, we could think of reducing them further. Likewise, health and safety legislation should take account of hazards associated with new technologies.

[6] This suggestion was made in Union Research Group, 'Automation and Redeployment on Packing Lines' (1983) after an investigation of the effects of automation of the packing lines in the food and pharmaceuticals industries. Women workers had many sensible suggestions on how production could have been improved if they had been consulted about (a) the selection and (b) the layout of the new machines.

(3) Even with these measures, it is likely that not all of those who have been displaced by technological change will find work in the same workplace or industry, and we also have to think of all those who are already unemployed or underemployed quite independently of any technological change. A fund should be created to (a) provide them with subsistence till they are able to find employment; (b) provide them with training and help with finding suitable employment; (c) support the formation of producer groups and cooperatives which will create new employment. Organizations like the Self Employed Women's Association (SEWA) and SSA-Sasha are already engaged in supporting the formation of women workers' cooperatives or producer groups. While most of these are engaged in artisan production, SSA-Sasha has also trained semi-literate women to handle the modern technology necessary for producing herbal cosmetics. The introduction of computers in the SEWA Bank did not render any women jobless, but instead enabled them to spend the time freed from bank work in going out to meet and help other SEWA members. These are cases where new technologies under the control of women have been used to create employment, enrich work and enhance the earning capacities of women.

(4) One way of fighting against the progressive elimination of women from the organized sector workforce is to fight for equal opportunities legislation which will make it illegal for employers to discriminate against women in recruitment at all levels (including skilled and qualified jobs), training and promotions. Such legislation exists in other countries (for example, Britain), but even the concept hardly exists in India. This is anomalous, since the Constitution of India rules out discrimination on the ground of sex, and India has also ratified the International Labour Organization (ILO) Convention 111 (1958) on the elimination of discrimination in employment and occupation. One way to proceed could be to pressurize the government to put this ratification into practice by passing the appropriate legislation.

(5) Domestic labour today is unnecessarily arduous and time-consuming due to the *inadequate* application of technology. To take one simple example, millions of women spend a huge amount of time and energy either carrying water for long distances or waiting for hours at a water tap; the burden could be enormously reduced if every household had its own water tap with running

water for at least a few hours every day. This is an area where technology could well be used to develop equitable water management and distribution systems which will make this vital resource readily accessible to every household.

(6) While it is important to obtin maternity leave and child-care facilities (provided by employers and/or the government) for women workers, it is also important to make it clear that men too have domestic responsibilities. This can be done by demanding paternity leave—at first only a few days or a week, but later increasing the amount of time—and creche facilities for the pre-school children of *all* workers. Night work should be compensated not merely by much higher shift allowances than those available at present, but also by even shorter working hours, so as to partially catch up on their family and social life. Here again, examples from India are hard to find, but the Scandinavian countries have generous paternity leave provisions, and in The Netherlands, shift allowances amounting to 33 per cent of gross salary as well as a 36-hour week for shift workers had been introduced by the 1980s (Banaji and Hensman, 1990, pp. 63–65, 115).

(7) This would need to be accompanied by an awareness-raising campaign to educate people about the social importance of time spent on caring and nurturing, and creating and maintaining mutually affirming relationships; also to make them recognize that this is not simply 'women's work', and that men who lack this experience are emotionally impoverished and dehumanized. Apparently some successful efforts in this direction have been made in Korea.[7] On the other side, it should also be emphasized that women and girls are quite capable of handling advanced technology, and should be provided with encouragement and training opportunities if they show an aptitude for it. There would have to be a movement to reform the content of textbooks as well as the whole education system accordingly.

(8) If reforms are fought for only in the organized sector, it will simply accelerate the transfer of production to the unorganized sector which is already going on. It is therefore essential to ensure that workers in the unorganized sector have the same legal rights, and to find forms of organization and struggle which would enable

[7] There is a fascinating account of how this has been approached in 'This is the way to make a democratic family' (1993).

them to obtain their rights. An encouraging development here is the formation in May 1995 of the National Centre for Labour (NCL), a federation of twenty-seven organizations of informal sector workers including SEWA, National Federation of Construction Labour, National Fishworkers Forum, Anganwadi Karamchari Sangh, Forest Workers' Union, Agricultural Labour Union, and many others. The NCL, in which the large female membership is reflected in the composition of the leadership, will hopefully succeed in making progress towards levelling up the rights of unorganized sector workers to match those of workers in the organized sector (Mukul, 1995, pp. 1422–23). The other positive development is that in 1995 the ILO for the first time voted by a narrow margin for a Convention on home-based workers, the majority of whom are, of course, women. The Convention faces solid opposition from employers, but the very fact that these 'invisible' workers are demanding parity with wage-earners at an international level is a notable event (Jhabvala 1995, pp. 3133–36).

(9) At an international level too, production is being transferred from countries like Korea, where women workers have fought for and obtained better conditions, to countries like Indonesia and Bangladesh, where wages and working conditions are abysmal; thus, workers who have struggled successfully for improvements are faced with unemployment, and the general standard goes down once more. This can only be counteracted by forming links between trade unionists and women workers internationally to fight for common minimum labour standards. In this context, it is worth giving careful consideration to the proposal to link a 'Social Clause' incorporating various ILO Conventions[8] to multilateral trade agreements. While the current proposal for a social clause has serious drawbacks (to mention just one, it only has provisions for penalizing governments, not for penalizing companies which violate these Conventions), it has the merit of suggesting a way in which minimum labour standards can be enforced. The debate on this issue should concentrate on working out ways in which *both* countries *and* companies which violate internationally agreed minimum standards can be penalized in an unbiased fashion, rather

---

[8] On freedom of association and the right to organize, abolition of forced labour and child labour, non-discrimination and equal remuneration.

than simply falling back on the existing ILO machinery which lacks any means of enforcement. We should also give some thought to the content of the minimum labour standards. The provisions for equal remuneration and non-discrimination will certainly benefit women; but shouldn't they also include provisions for workers with family responsibilities, without which women workers would continue to be disadvantaged?

This is, admittedly, a massive agenda, and working on it will take us well into twenty-first century. But unless we begin now, the future which faces women workers as well as workers in general is bleak indeed. If we do take up the challenge, however, it will be possible to use new technologies to enlarge human choices, combat gender discrimination, and enhance the quality of life.

References

Action India, 1995, 'Impact of Technologies on Women's Work: Charkhawalees', paper prepared for the United Nations University Institute for New Technologies.

Banaji, Jairus and Rohini Hensman, 1990, *Beyond Multinationalism: Management Policy and Bargaining Relationships in International Companies,* Sage Publications, New Delhi/Newbury Park/London.

Banerjee, Nirmala, 1985, 'Women and Industrialization in Developing Countries', Occasional Paper No. 71, Centre for Study in Social Sciences, Calcutta.

Band, Isa, 1983, 'Women's Labour in the Indian Textile Industry', Research Project Iris Report No. 23, Tilburg Institute of Development Research.

Dietrich, Gabriele, 1995, 'Women's Struggle for Production of Life: Public Hearings of Women Workers in Informal Sector', *Economic and Political Weekly,* 1 July.

Elson, Diane, 1995, 'Gender Awareness in Modelling Structural Adjustment', Working Paper No. 13, School of Economic Studies, University of Manchester, April.

'German Firms, Unions Inch Closer to Deal on Job Creation', 1996, *The Economic Times,* 20 January, p. 7.

Hensman, Rohini, 1988, 'The Gender Division of Labour in Manufacturing Industry: A Case Study in India', Discussion Paper 253, Institute of Development Studies, University of Sussex.

Jhabvala, Renana, 1995, 'Invisible Workers Reach International Heights', *Economic and Political Weekly,* 9 December.

Lingam, Lakshmi, 1994, 'Women-Headed Households', *Economic and Political Weekly,* 19 March.

Mukul, 1995, 'To Organize the Unorganized', *Economic and Political Weekly,* 17 June.

Rohini, P.H., 1991, 'Women Workers in Manufacturing Industry in India: Problems and Possibilities', in Haleh Afshar (ed.), *Women, Development and Survival in the Third World,* Longman, London and New York, pp. 260–87.

Sen, Ilina, 1995, 'A Case Study from the Mining Sector in India', paper prepared for the United Nations University Institute for New Technologies.

'This is the Way to Make a Democratic Family', 1993, *Working Women* (Journal of the Korean Women Workers Associations United), vol. 1, June, pp. 21–29.

Union Research Group, 1983, 'Automation and Redeployment on Packing Lines: Need for a Union Strategy', *Bulletin of Trade Union Research and Information,* No. 3, December.

Workers' Solidarity Centre, 1995, 'Impact of Technological Changes on Women Workers in the Pharmaceutical Industry in the Bombay–Thane Region', paper prepared for the United Nations University Institute for New Technologies.

III

Law

III

Law

Ratna Kapur and Brenda Cossman argue that the formal model of equality which informs High Court and Supreme Court cases on sex discrimination, has in fact worked against women by disqualifying those who are 'different' from an entitlement to equality. On the other hand, when the 'difference' of women has been recognized by the courts, this has led to their categorization as weaker than men and therefore in need of protection. The authors therefore posit the need for another model of equality, the 'substantive' model, by which the actual conditions of women's subordination will be taken into account, so that 'sameness' or 'difference' will be brought into focus depending on which factor will overcome that subordination.

My paper makes a more fundamental critique of law, arguing that law does not have the capacity to pursue justice. At particular historical moments 'justice' is constituted by specific moral visions, and there is therefore a singularity and uniqueness to justice which is at odds with law, which must take a general form, as norm and as rule. This suggests the need to rethink altogether the terms of feminist engagement with the law.

6

On Women, Equality and the Constitution: Through the Looking Glass of Feminism

Ratna Kapur and *Brenda Cossman*

Introduction

Formal equality for women is explicitly enshrined within Indian law. However notwithstanding formal guarantees of equality, Indian women's lives continue to be characterized by pervasive discrimination and substantive inequality. By examining the judicial interpretations of Indian constitutional law, this chapter will illustrate how the legal system itself contributes to the gap between the formal guarantees of gender equality and the substantive inequality that plagues women's lives. We will argue that with some notable exceptions, the judicial approach to the equality guarantees of the Constitution is informed by a problematic approach to both equality, and gender difference.

Beginning with a review and evaluation of the two competing models of equality—formal versus substantive equality, the chapter

The authors would like to thank Ritu Bhargava, Nikki Cunningham, Geetanjali Gangoli, Radha, Radhapyari, Seetel Sunga, Ashraf Unissa, Leti Volpp, and Donna Young for their comments, support and research assistance. The authors are also grateful to Grace Domingo, Jill Maltby and Christine Wright for their technical assistance. We would also like to thank Professor Rebecca Cook and Professor Devidas for their comments on an earlier draft.

This paper was prepared partly with the aid of a grant from the International Development Research Centre, Ottawa, Canada.

will attempt to briefly illustrate the extent to which Indian constitutional law is informed by a formal model of equality, and how attempts at moving towards a more substantive understanding have been thwarted by the deeply embedded assumptions regarding equality as formal equality. The chapter will subsequently examine three competing approaches to the question of the relevance of gender difference: protectionist, sameness, and corrective and then attempt to contextualize the Supreme Court and High Court case law on gender discrimination within these debates.

Formal versus Substantive Equality

The understanding of equality that has dominated Western thought since the time of Aristotle has been one of formal equality. Equality has been interpreted as 'treating likes alike', its constitutional expression in American and subsequently Indian equal protection doctrine, as the requirement that 'those [who are] similarly situated be treated similarly.'[1] Within this prevailing conception, equality is equated with sameness. Indeed, sameness is the entitling criteria for equality. Only if you are the same are you entitled to be treated equally. Further, within this equal treatment approach any difference in treatment between similarly situated individuals, constitutes discrimination.[2] In other words, if you are the same, then you should not be treated differently.

The similarly situated test requires that the Court begin by defining the relevant groups or classes for comparison. In contrast a substantive model of equality begins with the recognition that equality sometimes requires that individuals be treated differently. This approach is extremely critical of the formal model of equality, and its emphasis is on sameness. Martha Minow, in exploring the problematic connection between equality and sameness has observed:

[1] Tussman, Joseph and Jacobus Tenbroek, 'The Equal Protection of the Laws' 37 Calif. L. Rev. 341 (1949); see also Haragopal Reddy, 'Equality Doctrine and the Indian Constitution' *45 Andhra Law Times* 57, 58 (1982) ['All persons are to be treated alike, except where circumstances require different treatment'].

[2] As Parmanand Singh notes in Singh, 'Equal Opportunity and Compensatory Discrimination: Constitutional Policy and Judicial Control', 18: 2 *Journal of the Indian Law Institute* 300, 301 (1976) '...legal equality requires the absence of any discrimination in the words of the law'; see also, K.C. Dwiredi, *Right to Equality and The Supreme Court* 11 (1990), who defines equality as signifying 'that among equals law should be equal and equally administered.'

The problem with this concept of equality is that it makes the recognition of difference a threat to the premise behind equality. If to be equal you must be the same, then to be different is to be unequal.[3]

This initial definitional step can effectively preclude any further equality analysis. If the Court defines the classes as different, then no further analysis is required; difference justifies the differential treatment.[4] Accordingly, when groups are not similarly situated, then they do not qualify for equality, even if the differences among them are the product of historic or systemic discrimination.[5]

The focus of a substantive equality approach is not simply on equal treatment under the law, but rather on the actual impact of the law.[6] The explicit objective of a model of substantive equality is the elimination of the substantive inequality of disadvantaged groups in society. As Parmanand Singh notes, it 'takes into account inequalities of social, economic and educational background of the people and seeks the elimination of existing inequalities by

[3] Martha Minow, 'Learning to Live with the Dilemma of Difference: Bilingual and Special Education' *48 Law and Contemporary Problems* 157, 207 (1985).

[4] Brodsky and Day, *Canadian Charter of Equality Rights for Women: One Step Forward, Two Steps Back*, 153 (1989) ['The way can make the difference between winning and losing. The Court can justify making a comparison between classes or refusing to make a comparison by the way they define the class, or whether they recognize it at all.'] See also at 155, ['Just as the way the Court defines a class can determine the outcome, so can the way the Court compares or fails to compare the classes it has identified. Sometimes the courts simply fail to make a comparison; and sometimes comparisons are tautological because the courts compare classes only within the terms already set out in the law.']

[5] The problems with the formal approach to equality, and with the similarly situated test have been widely recognized and criticized. For example, the Supreme Court of Canada in *Andrews* v. *the Law Society of Upper Canada* [1989] 1 S.C.R. 43, held: ['The test as stated is seriously deficient in that it excludes any consideration of the nature of the law. If it were to be applied literally, it could be used to justify the Nuremburg laws of Adolf Hitler. Similar treatment was contemplated for all Jews.'] In *A. Laxamana Murthy* v. *State of A.P.*, A 1980 A.P. 293, 298 the High Court similarly observed: ['Hitler's classification of all Jews into a separate category for the purposes of butchering them and Naxalites classification of all landlords into a separate category for purposes of exterminating them cannot therefore be faulted on this theory of equal protection clause'].

[6] As Maureen Maloney has written in Maloney, 'An Analysis of Direct Taxes in India: A Feminist Perspective' 30: 4 *Journal of the Indian Law Institute* 397 (1988) ['Such inequality results from provisions which though seemingly natural in their application (and therefore conforming to notions of formal equality) in

positive measures.'[7] The focus of the analysis is not with sameness or difference, but rather with disadvantage. Substantive equality is directed at eliminating individual, institutional and systemic discrimination against disadvantaged groups which effectively undermines their full and equal social, economic, political and cultural participation in society.[8] The central inquiry of this approach is whether the rule or practice in question contributes to the subordination of the disadvantaged group. Accordingly, discrimination consists of treatment that disadvantages or further oppresses a group that has historically experienced institutional and systemic oppression.

The shift in focus from sameness and difference to disadvantage significantly broadens the equality analysis. Within a formal equality model, the difference between, for example, able bodied and less able bodied persons could preclude an equality challenge. According to this mode, because disabled persons are different, they do not have to be treated equally. Within a substantive equality model, however, the focus is not on whether disabled persons are different, but rather, on whether their treatment in law contributes to their historic disadvantage. Indeed, differences are not seen to preclude an entitlement to equality, but rather, are embraced within the concept of equality. Within this model of equality, differential treatment may be required 'not to perpetuate the existing inequalities, but to achieve and maintain a real state of effective equality.'[9] As such, the failure of a rule or practice to take into

reality result in discrimination. Certain provisions have the effect of discriminating between men and women because in practice they only affect women'].

[7] Singh, supra note 2, at 301. He describes this approach as one of equality in fact, or compensatory discrimination.

[8] Kathy Lahey, 'Feminist Theories of (In)Equality', in *Equality and Judicial Neutrality* 71 (S. Martin and K. Mahoney (eds) 1987) argues that courts must adopt an approach which considers the effect of the rule or practice being challenged, to determine whether it contributes to the actual enequality of women, and whether changing the rule will actually produce an improvement in the specific material conditions of the women affected. See also Colleen Sheppard, 'Equality, Ideology and Oppression: Women and the Canadian Charter', in *Charter Watch: Reflections on Equality* (1986) who argues that the central question to be asked is whether the rule or practice in question contributes to the social inequality of women.

[9] Raj Kumar Gupta, 'Justice: Unequal but Inseparate' 11 *Journal of the Indian Law Institute* 57, 76 (1969).

account the particular needs of disabled persons, and thus perpetuate the historic disadvantage of this group, would constitute discrimination, and violate their equality rights.

Judicial Approaches to Equality Rights in India

The following section will briefly review the judicial approaches to the equality rights guaranteed by Articles 14, 15 and 16 of the Indian Constitution. It will attempt to illustrate the extent to which the constitutional doctrine is informed by a formal model of equality, in which equality is equated with sameness. While some inroads have been made towards a substantive model of equality in recent case law, the continuing hold of the formal model of equality over the judiciary's approach has operated to profoundly limit even these more progressive approaches to the equality guarantees.

A. *Article 14*

Article 14 of the Constitution guarantees equality before the law and equal protection under the law. It has been interpreted as a prohibition against unreasonable classification. The equality guarantee does not require that the law treat all individuals exactly the same. Rather, it allows the State to make classifications. However, this power of classification must be exercised on reasonable grounds.[10] The Supreme Court has expressly adopted a similarly situated approach to equality rights under Article 14.[11]

[10] Article 14 provides: The State shall not deny to any person equality before the law or the equal protection of the laws within the territory of India. The Supreme Court has held that two conditions must be met to pass this test of reasonable classification: ['(i) ... the classification must be founded on an intelligible differentiation which distinguishes persons or things that are grouped together from others left out of the group (ii) ... that differentia must have a rational relation to the object sought to be achieved by the statute in question']: *Budhan Choudhry* v. *State of Bihar,* A 1955 S.C. 191; *State of W. B.* v. *Anwar Ali,* (1952) S.C.R. 340; *R.K. Dalmia v. Justice S.R. Tendolkar,* A 1958 S.C. 538. See also *H.M. Seervai, Constitutional Law of India* 292–3 (3rd ed., 1988); D.D. Basu, *Constitutional Law of India* 32 (10th ed., 1988).

[11] ['The principle underlying the guarantee of Article 14 is not that the same rules of law should be applicable to all persons within the Indian territory or that the remedies should be made available to them irrespective of differences of circumstances. It only means that all persons similarly circumstanced shall be treated alike, both in privileges conferred and liabilities imposed. Equal laws

Accordingly, the first step in determining whether Article 14 has been violated is a consideration of whether the persons between whom discrimination is alleged fall within the same class. If the persons are not deemed to be similarly circumstanced, then no further consideration is required.

The principles adopted by the Court are premised on a formal model of equality. The focus of the analysis is on the question of sameness—on determining whether the persons among whom the denial of equality is alleged are the same, or whether the classification is based on reasonable differences. In this approach, there is no interrogation of substantive inequalities—of such social and economic disadvantages that may have produced differences between persons.[12]

More recently, the Supreme Court has emphasized a 'new dimension' of Article 14, namely 'that it embodies a guarantee against arbitrariness.'[13] While the new doctrine has been harshly criticized as a significant shift away from the reasonable classification approach by some commentators,[14] there has been little if any significant change in the underlying understanding of equality. The new judicial reasoning has incorporated the doctrine of classification into its folds and thus continues to be premised on a formal model of equality.[15]

---

would have to be applied to all in the same situation, and there should be no discrimination between one person and another, if as regards the subject matter of the legislation, their position is substantially the same'] in Dalmia, id. at 539. See also *U.P. Electric Co.* v. *State of U.P.,* A 1970 S.C. 21.

[12] See, for example Basu, supra note 10, at 32 who writes ['When a law is challenged as denying equal protection, the question for determination by the Court is not whether it has resulted in inequality, but whether there is some difference which bears a just and reasonable relation to the object of the legislation']. Basu's description of reasonable classification under Article 14 is explicitly based on the equation of equality and sameness.

[13] *Ajay Hasia* v. *Khalid Mujib,* A 1981 S.C. 487, 499; *E.P. Royapappa* v. *State of Tamil Nadu,* A 1974 S.C. 555, 583; *Ramana Dayaram Shetty* v. *I.A.A.I.,* A 1979 S.C. 1628, 1643. See also *Maneka Gandhi* v. *Union of India,* A 1978 S.C. 597, 624 where the Court held: ['Equality is a dynamic concept with many aspects and dimensions and it cannot be imprisoned within traditional and doctrinaire limits ... Article 14 strikes at arbitrariness in state action and ensures fairness and equality of treatment'].

[14] *Servai,* supra note 10, at pp. 272–9, para 16.

[15] ['The doctrine of classification ... is ... a judicial formula for determining whether the legislative or executive action in question is arbitrary and therefore constituting

B. *Article 15*

Article 15 prohibits discrimination on the ground of religion, race, caste, sex, and place of birth. In reviewing the judicial interpretation of Article 15, we will attempt to identify some of the doctrinal techniques used by the Courts and locate these techniques within the broader context of the competing models of equality.

i. Discrimination

A number of debates have arisen in the case law regarding the meaning of discrimination within Article 15.[16] At a general level, this concerns the context of the judicial interpretations of the treatment authorized by Article 15(3). This article, which allows the State to make special provisions for women, has been interpreted as authorizing the State to discriminate in favour of women. However, a further question is whether Article 15(3) authorizes discrimination against women. In *Mahadeb Jiew* v. *B.B. Sen.*[17] the Calcutta High Court held that Article 15(3) could not be used to authorize discrimination against women but rather, from the language used in the Article, it was clear that the intention of the

---

a denial of equality. If the classification is not reasonable ... the impugned legislative or executive action would plainly be arbitrary and the guarantee of equality under Article 14 would be breached.']: Seervai, supra note 10 at 408.

[16] Article 15 provides:

1. The State shall not discriminate against any citizen on grounds only of religion, race, place of birth or any of them.

2. No citizen shall, on grounds only of religion, race, caste, sex, place of birth or any of them, be subject to any disability, liability, restriction or condition with regard to—

   a. access to shops, public restaurants, hotels and places of public entertainment; or

   b. the use of wells, tanks, bathing ghats, roads and places of public resort maintained wholly or partly out of State funds or dedicated to the use of the general public.

3. Nothing in this article shall prevent the State from making any special provision for women and children.

4. Nothing in this article or in clause (2) of Article 29 shall prevent the State from making any special provision for the advancement of any socially and educationally backward classses of citizens or for the Scheduled Castes and the Scheduled Tribes.

[17] A 1951 Cal. 563.

framers of the Constitution was to protect the interests of women and children.[18] Article 15(3) has thus been limited to upholding legislation that benefits women; not extended to authorizing discrimination against women. This interpretation is useful, as far as it goes. At the level of application, when the Courts must interpret whether legislation benefits or discriminates against women, the doctrine provides little guidance. The absence of a substantive approach to equality that attempts to contextualize the legal regulation of women within gender oppression allows the courts to classify laws as 'protection'. There is little consideration of whether the laws actually benefit women or of the appropriateness of the underlying rationale for the ostensibly protectionist legislation.[19]

This question of the treatment authorized by Article 15(3) is related to a deeper question of the meaning of discrimination within Article 15 more generally. Two approaches to the meaning of discrimination can be identified in the case law. In the first approach, discrimination means any classification or distinction on the prohibited grounds. It is based on a formal understanding of equality as sameness, and thus, of discrimination as any distinction as between similar individuals on the prohibited grounds. This formal approach to discrimination is evident in the court's use of the terms 'preferential' or 'compensatory' discrimination. The courts speak of discrimination in favour of women—a term that only makes sense if discrimination is taken to mean any classification or distinction.[20]

---

[18] According to the Court, Article 15(3) did not use the language 'discriminate against' but rather use 'special provisions for'. In *Dattatraya Motiram More* v. *State of Bombay*, A 1953 Bom. 311, at para 7, the Court held that the effect of the joint operation of Article 15(1) and 15(3) was that the State could discriminate in favour of women against men, but could not discriminate in favour of men against women. See also *Shahdad* v. *Mohd Abdullah*, A 1967 J. & K. 120, *Mr. Choki* v. *State*, A 1957 Raj. 10. Seervai, Supra note 10, at 410, is in agreement with this approach, noting at 410 that ['... it effectuates both the general policy underlying Art. 15(1) and the necessity of making an exception in favour of women and children, whose position requires special protection'].

[19] This approach was also followed in *Anjali Roy* v. *State*, A 1952 Cal. 825.

[20] In *Dattatraya*, supra note 18 at 314 para 7, for example, the Court states: ['The proper way to construe Article 15(3) ... is that ... discrimination in favour of women is permissible, and when the State does discriminate in favour of women, it does not offend against Article 15(1)'].

In the second approach, discrimination means an adverse distinction on the prohibited grounds, that is, distinctions that disadvantage. It is based on a more substantive understanding of equality, concerned not simply with treatment that differentiates, but rather, with treatment that disadvantages. This approach to discrimination was suggested in Anjali Roy, wherein the Court held:

All differentiation is not discrimination but only such differentiation as is invidious and as is made, not because any real difference in the conditions or natural differences between the persons dealt with which makes different treatment necessary, but because of the presence of some characteristics or affiliation which is either disliked or not regarded with equal favour but which has no rational connection with the differentiations made as a justifying reason.[21]

The Court's approach goes some way toward substantive equality, in so far as it directs attention to whether the distinctions drawn by the legislation are invidious. However, this shift is limited by the Court's understanding of difference as effectively precluding equality. Within this framework of formal equality, invidious distinctions would only be those distinctions not based on real differences. The Court's approach thereby remains overly influenced by a formal model of equality.[22]

ii. Relationship between Articles 15(1) and 15(3)

A major issue that has arisen with regard to Article 15 is the relationship of clauses (1) and (2) with clauses (3) and (4). Two

---

[21] Supra note 19, at para 16. This substantive approach to discrimination was also hinted at in *Kathi Ranning Rawal* v. *Saurashtra*, A 1952 S.C. 123, 125 wherein Sastri, CJ stated: ['Discrimination thus involves an element of unfavourable bias and it is in that sense that the expression has to be understood in this context.']

[22] There is no symmetry between the formal approaches to discrimination and to the relationship between the articles discussed in the following section; nor between the more substantive approaches to discrimination and to the relationship between the articles. The difference between these understandings of discrimination and of the relationship between the articles remain unarticulated, and the relationship to the broader models of equality is obscured in both the case law and the commentaries. For examples, in Dattatraya supra note 18, the Court adopted the formal approach to discrimination, yet was also shown to have adopted the more substantive approach to the relationship between the Articles. Conversely, in Anjali Roy, supra note 19 the Court adopted a more substantive approach to discrimination, but the formal approach to the relationship between the Articles. This apparent inconsistency is also evident in the commentaries.

approaches to this relationship have emerged in judicial decision-making. We will refer to them as the 'exception approach' and the 'holistic approach'. In the first approach, Articles 15(3) and 15(4) are interpreted as exceptions to the general equality guarantees. A classic statement of this 'exception approach' is found in *Anjali Roy* v. *State of W.B.*, in which the Calcutta High Court held that Article 15(3):

... is obviously an exception to clause (1) and (2) and since its effect is to authorize what the Article otherwise forbids, its meaning seems to be that notwithstanding that clause (1) and (2) forbid discrimination against any citizen on the grounds of sex, the State may discriminate against males by making a special provision in favour of females.[23]

The 'exception approach' has been overwhelmingly supported by the commentators.[24] In the second approach, Article 15 is seen as a whole, and therefore Articles 15(3) and 15(4) are used to interpret the equality provisions more generally. This 'holistic approach' was endorsed in Dattatraya, wherein the Bombay High Court held:

... Article 15(3) is obviously a proviso to Article 15(1) and proper effect must be given to that proviso.... The proper way to construe Article 15(3) in our opinion is that whereas under Article 15(1) discrimination in favour of men only on the ground of sex is not permissible, by reason of Article 15(3) discrimination in favour of women is permissible, and when the State does discriminate in favour of women, it does not offend against Article 15(1).[25]

[23] Supra note 19 at 830–831.

[24] Seervai, supra note 10, at 396 for example, argues that Articles 15(3) and 15(4) must be seen as exceptions to the general guarantees of equality. ['Article 15(1) prohibits discrimination only on the ground of sex; therefore a discrimination in favour of women would necessarily discriminate against men only on the ground of sex and would be void. The discretionary power in Article 15(3) relaxes this prohibition in favour of women by expressly authorizing such discrimination by way of an exception']. See also Seervai, *Supplement to the Third Edition* (1988) 241. Jain and Basu both argue that Articles 15(3) and 15(4) are exceptions to Articles 15(1) and (2). Basu, supra note 10, at 67, who argues for example: ['Being an exception, clause (4) cannot be so extended as in effect to destroy the guarantee in cl (1) ... ']. See also Jain, M.P. *Indian Constitutional Law* 430 (3rd ed., 1978).

[25] Dattatraya, supra note 18, at 314. See also *Ram Chandra Mahton* v. *State of Bihar*, A 1966 Pat. 214. Basu, supra note 10 at 68 is extremely critical of this approach. With regard to the decision in Dattatraya he writes: ['...such

The 'holistic approach' appears to have been given more general expression by several High Courts, and the Supreme Court.[26]

These two competing approaches to the relationship between the clauses of Article 15 roughly correspond to the two competing models of quality. In the first, 'exception approach' equality is equated with sameness. Any deviation from identical treatment as contemplated by Articles 15(3) and 15(4) must then be considered an exception to equality. In the second, 'holistic approach', equality is understood as sometimes requiring that individuals be treated differently. Therefore, the special treatment contemplated by Articles 15(3) and 15(4) need not be seen as an exception, but as a fundamental part of equality.[27] This approach goes some way toward a substantive model, in so far as difference need not preclude equality, but rather, is embraced within it. This approach, however, stops considerably short of recognizing equality as essentially a question of disadvantage. The shift toward substantive equality is further limited by the extent to which the Court remains overly influenced by a formal model of equality. For example, while the Court in Dattatraya adopted this more substantive understanding

---

discrimination in favour of women would be justifiable only if clause (3) could be regarded as a complete exception to clause (1) of Article 15. The use of the word 'women' in juxtaposition to children at (3)(d) suggests that the special provision referred to in it must be related to such disabilities which are peculiar to women and children'].

[26] An early indication of the Supreme Court's preference for it is evident in *Abdul Aziz* v. *Bombay,* A 1954 S.C. 321. In rejecting the argument that Article 15(3) should be restricted to provisions that benefit women, the Court stated that 'Article 14 is general and must be read with the other provisions which set out the ambit of fundamental rights.' More recently, the Supreme Court has held that Articles 14, 15 and 16 constitute a single code. See *Kerala* v. *N.M. Thomas,* (1976) 1 S.C.R. 906; *Shamsher Singh* v. *State,* A 1970 P. & H. 372.

[27] Such an approach has been advocated by Marc Galanter, in relation to the provisions of both Articles 15 and 16: ['Article 15(4) and 16(4) are undoubtedly exceptions to the constitutional prohibition of State employment of the otherwise forbidden criteria of caste, religion and so forth. But it does not follow that they are exceptions to the policy of equal treatment mandated by Articles 14, 15 and 16. In respect to the general policy of equality they represent an empowerment of the State to pursue substantive equality in respect to the disparities between the backward classes and others']. Marc Galanter, 'Symbolic Activisim: A Judicial Encounter with the Contours of India's Compensatory Discrimination Policy', *Law and Society in Modern India,* 112 (1989).

of the relationship between the articles, it also adopted an approach to discrimination based on a formal model of equality.[28]

iii. On the Grounds Only of Sex

Article 15(1) prohibits discrimination '...on the grounds only of religion, race, caste, sex, place of birth or any of them.' It has been interpreted as requiring discrimination 'only' on the prohibited grounds. As the Court noted in *Anjali Roy* v. *State of W.B.*:

[T] he discrimination which is forbidden is only such discrimination as is based solely on the ground that a person belongs to a particular race or caste or professes a particular religion or was born at a particular place or is of a particular sex and on no other ground. A discrimination based on one or more of these grounds and also on other grounds is not hit by the Article.[29]

According to this interpretation, if discrimination is found to exist on grounds other than those enumerated, then there is no violation of Article 15(1). Even discrimination on the basis of sex, coupled with discrimination on other non-enumerated grounds, would not constitute a violation.[30]

The focus on 'the grounds only of sex' has been used primarily to uphold legislation that provides preferential treatment for

[28] For example, *Seervai* supra note 10, at 404, an advocate of the formal equality approach to the relationship between the Articles, adopts a more substantive definition of discrimination. He notes that the definition of discrimination in the Oxford dictionary is 'to make an adverse distinction with regard to; to distinguish unfavourably from others'. This apparent inconsistency, however, in Seervai's analysis is remedied, in so far as, in his view any preferential treatment of one group can be seen as adverse treatment of another group. Thus, virtually any distinction can be understood as adverse distinction. His concept of discrimination can thereby be seen as premised on a formal model of equality in which equality is equated with sameness, and discrimination with any difference in treatment as between those who are the same.

[29] Supra note 19, at 829 para 16. See also *Purnananda Banerjee* v. *Swapna Banerjee*, A 1981 Cal. 123; *Shahdad* v. *Mohd. Abdullah*, supra note 18.

[30] The Court in Dattatraya, supra note 18, at 313 para 7, similarly held: ['It must always be borne in mind that the discrimination which is not permissible under Article 15(1) is a discrimination which is only on one of the grounds mentioned in Article 15(1). If there is a discrimination in favour of a particular sex, that discrimination would be permissible provided it is not only on the ground of sex, or in other words, the classification on the ground of sex is permissible provided that classification is the result of other considerations besides the fact that the persons belonging to that class are of a particular sex'].

women. In attempting to uphold this legislation the courts have searched for some other ground on which the legislative distinction is based. In their search, the Courts have caste their net widely. They have found, for example, that distinctions based also on the 'backward' social position of women, on the financial need of wives for support, and on public morality constitute grounds other than those stated in Article 15(1).[31] This process by which the courts are attempting to uphold legislation that gives preferential treatment to women is somewhat misdirected. Both the backward social position of women, and the financial need of wives for support are products of the social, economic and political inequality of women. Legislation designed to promote women's position and/or provide for the financial needs of economically dependent women should not be seen as discrimination against women. But the reason is not because these distinctions are broader than the ground of sex. Rather, it is precisely because these provisions are based on ameliorating the conditions that women have suffered on the ground of sex. Sex is a category which has traditionally denoted disadvantage—it has been used as a ground for discrimination and has resulted in women being 'more backward' than men. Yet, the Court attempts to distinguish the ground of sex from other factors, rather than seeing the fundamental relationship between them.

The intention of the Courts in their inquiry into 'on the ground only of sex' is laudable. They can in some respects be seen to be pursuing a more substantive vision of equality, that is, one which is concerned with promoting the social, economic and political equality of women. As such, the courts do not strike down legislation designed to benefit women by calling it discrimination on the basis of sex. However, their focus on the technical meaning of 'only on the ground of sex' obscures this normative vision of

[31] In *Girdhar Gopal* v. *State of M.B.*, A 1953 M.B. 147, the Court adopted this approach to uphold the constitutionality of Section 354 of the Indian Penal Code—the offence of outraging the modesty of women. The Court held at para 5 ['If the discrimination is based not merely on any of the grounds stated in Article 15(1) but also on considerations of property, public morals, decency, decorum and rectitude, the legislation containing such discrimination would not be hit by the provisions of Article 15(1). It cannot be denied that an assault or criminal force to a woman with intent to outrage her modesty is made punishable under s. 354 not merely because women are women but because of the factors enumerated....'].

equality. Indeed, the construction of this issue as a narrow and mechanical question of interpretation is motivated by the prevailing understanding of equality as formal equality. The deeply rooted belief that any special treatment constitutes an exception to equality leads the Court to attempt to avoid the issue (Article 15(3) notwithstanding) by constructing the discrimination as not only on the basis of sex. Moreover, this narrow focus on 'the grounds only' of sex is potentially dangerous. Without an inquiry into disadvantage and substantive inequalities, a search for other grounds could even be used to uphold legislation that disadvantages women. For example, legislation prohibiting women from voting could be found to be based not only on sex, but also on the 'backward social position' of women.

The Delhi High Court, in *Walter Alfred Baid* v. *Union of India*,[32] although dealing primarily with a challenge under Article 16(2), recognized some of the problems implicit in this approach to 'only on the grounds of sex'. The Court observed:

... it is difficult to accept the position that a discrimination based on sex is nevertheless not a discrimination based on sex 'alone' because it is based on 'other considerations' even though these other considerations have their genesis in the sex itself. It virtually amounts to saying that woman was being discriminated against ... not because she belonged to a particular sex but because of what the sex implied....[33]

The Court concluded:

Sex and what it implies cannot be severed. Considerations which have their genesis in sex and arise out of it would not save such a discrimination. What could save such a discrimination is any ground or reason independently of sex such as socio-economic conditions, marital status, and other disqualifying conditions such as age, background, health, academic accomplishments, etc.[34]

The approach in W.A. Baid recognized the connection between sex and the social implications of sex, and thus criticized the narrow doctrinal approach to 'only on the ground of sex'. However, the approach is not unproblematic. The decision is rooted firmly within

[32] A 1976 Del. 302.
[33] Ibid., at 306 para 10.
[34] Ibid., at 308 para 10.

a formal model of equality, and the result of the case was to strike down a recruitment rule that had been advantageous for women.

While the debates within the Article 15 case law reveal a tension between a formal and substantive vision of equality, these underlying normative differences remain unarticulated, and the case law remains overly determined by a formal model of equality. Rather than weaving the various substantive equality threads together, the threads are left to unravel.

C. *Article 16*

A similar tension between formal and substantive equality is apparent in Article 16, which guarantees equality of opportunity and prohibits discrimination in matters of employment.[35] A formal interpretation of equality of opportunity prevaded the early case law. For example, in *All India S.M. and A.S.M.'s Assn.* v. *Gen. Manager Central Railway,* the Supreme Court held that equality of opportunity in matters of promotion guaranteed by Article 16(1) must be interpreted to mean equality among members of the same class of employees, and not equality among members of different classes.[36] The similarly situated test, with its emphasis on sameness

---

[35] Article 16 provides:

1. There shall be equality of opportunity for all citizens in matters relating to employment or appointment to any office under the State.

2. No citizen shall, on grounds only of religion, race, caste, sex, descent, place of birth, residence or any of them, be ineligible for, or discriminated against in respect of any employment or office under the State.

3. Nothing in this article shall prevent Parliament from making any law prescribing, in regard to a class or classes of employment or appointment to an office under the Government of, or any local or other authority within, a State or Union territory, any requirement as to residence within that State or Union territory prior to such employment or appointment.

4. Nothing in this article shall prevent the State from making any provision for the reservation of appointments or posts in favour of any backward class of citizens which, in the opinion of the State, is not adequately represented in the services under the State.

5. Nothing in this article shall affect the operation of any law which provides that the incumbent of an office in connection with the affairs of any religious or denominational institution or any member of the governing body thereof shall be a person professing a particular religion or belonging to a particular denomination.

[36] A 1960 S.C. 384, followed in *Govind Dattatray* v. *Controller of Imports and Exports,* A 1967 S.C.

as the basic entitlement to equality, thus infused the court's understanding of equality of opportunity and reinforced the formal model of equality.[37]

Notwithstanding this formal equality approach, a tension has emerged within the court's approach to equality of opportunity. For example, a similar controversy has arisen over the appropriate relationship between the clauses of Article 16. Within the formal approach to equality of opportunity, the special provisions authorized by 16(4) for 'backward classes' are seen as exceptions to the general equality of opportunity guarantees under Articles 16(1) and 16(2). The commentators again advocate the formal approach.[38] Within the second, more substantive approach to equality of opportunity, the special provisions are seen to be used in interpreting the general guarantees.[39] This approach has been

---

[37] It should be emphasized that the critique is directed at the judicial approach to equality, and not necessarily at the particular outcome of the cases. The All India SM and ASM's Assn case could have been decided by reference to a more substantive understanding of equality, and equality of opportunity. The differential treatment in the case, namely that between roadside station masters and guards, was not discrimination, that is, it was not treatment based on personal or group characteristics and/or historical disadvantage. The ruling of the Supreme Court can be supported, without endorsing the particular model of equality that informed the Court's reasoning.

[38] Basu, supra note 10, at 71 argues for example ['Clause (1) and (2) of this Article guarantee equality of opportunity to all citizens in the matter of appointment to any office or of any other employment, under the State. Clauses (3)–(5), however, lay down several exceptions to the above rule of equal opportunity'].

[39] Marc Galanter has described the formal approach to equality of opportunity as one in which: ['Equality is visualised as identical opportunities to compete for existing values among those differently endowed, regardless of structural determinants of the chances of success or of the consequences for the distribution of values']. Galanter, supra note 27 at 262. Within this view, preferential treatment, or 'compensatory discrimination' is seen as an exception to equality; it 'is accepted as a marginal adjustment to be made where the results of complete equality are unacceptable.' He contrasts this approach with a second, more substantive approach to equality, in which ['... the present is seen as a "transition" from past inequality to a desired future of substantive equality; the purposes of compensatory discrimination is to promote equalization by offsetting historically accumulated inequalities. Thus compensatory discrimination does not detract from equality in the interests of present fairness; rather, it is seen as a requisite to the fulfilment of the nation's long run goal of substantive redistribution and equalization.'] Ibid., at 263.

adopted in the case law. Some High Courts have gone so far as to say that Articles 14, 15 and 16 constitute a single code.[40]

The Supreme Court has addressed this debate. In *Kerala* v. *N.M. Thomas*,[41] the Supreme Court held that Article 16(4) was not an exception to Article 16(1), and further held that Articles 15 and 16 are facets of Article 14. Indeed, in Thomas, the Supreme Court began to articulate a substantive model of equality.[42] The clearest statement of this doctrinal shift is found in the judgment of Mathew, J. which explicitly rejects the formal model of equality.[43] and argues that equality of opportunity will require more than equality in law or formal equality.[44]

Though complete identity [sic] of equality of opportunity is impossible in this world, measures compensatory in character and which are calculated to mitigate surmountable obstacles to ensure equality of opportunity can never incur the wrath of Article 16(1).[45]

[40] See *Shamsher Singh Hukam Singh* v. *Punjab*, A 1970 P. & H. 372. For example, in Shamsher Singh, the Court held: 'Article 14, 15 and 16, being the constituents of a single code of constitutional guarantees, supplementing each other, clause (3) of Article 15 can be invoked for construing and determining the scope of Article 16(2).'

[41] A 1976 S.C. 490.

[42] For a detailed discussion of the doctrinal shift in Thomas, see Galanter, supra note 27, at 265–278.

[43] Justice Mathews argues that formal equality is achieved by treating all persons equally: ['Each man to count for one and no one to count for more than one. But men are not equal in all respects.... We, therefore have to resort to some sort of proportionate equality in many spheres to achieve justice.'] Thomas, supra note 41, at 513 para 78. He continues: ['The principle of proportional equality is attained only when equals are treated equally and unequals unequally. This would raise the baffling question: Equals and unequals in what?'] Mathew, J. notes the formal approach to equality requires criteria by which differences, and thus differential treatment can be justified, and observes that '[t]he real difficulty arises in finding out what constitutes a relevant difference.' Ibid., at 513 para 79.

[44] ['Equality of opportunity is not simply a matter of legal equality. Its existence depends not merely on the absence of disabilities, but on the existence of abilities.'] Ibid., at 515 para 90. A similar shift is evident in Krishna Iyer J.'s decision, who refers, for example, to the need to bring the weaker sections of society ['to a real not formal equality']. Ibid., at 529 para 142. He concludes ['... that the genius of Articles 14 to 16 consist not in literal equality but in progressive elimination of pronounced inequality.'] Ibid., at 537 para 167.

[45] Ibid., at 514 para 82. At 515 para 89, he writes '...if we want to give equality of opportunity for employment to the members of the Scheduled Castes and Scheduled Tribes, we will have to take note of their social educational and economic environment.'

In Thomas, the Supreme Court began to articulate a substantive model of equality. While some Courts have recognized the doctrinal shift in Thomas,[46] other courts and commentators have argued strenuously against it.[47] Not surprisingly, the Thomas case has been most severely critized by those commentators who remain firmly committed to equality as formal equality. Their criticisms, however, are rarely articulated in such terms, but rather, remain focused on the narrow, doctrinal aspects of the case. Indeed, the failure of the Court to go far enough in articulating its substantive model of equality can be seen to have contributed to this critical reaction.[48]

The Supreme Court has continued to approach Article 16 in a manner that is critical of formal equality, and appears to be more informed by a substantive approach. In *Roop Chand Adlakha and others* v. *Delhi Development Authority*,[49] the Court was critical of the doctrine of classification within formal equality, observing that the process of classification could obscure the question of

[46] See *Jagdish Rai* v. *State of Haryana*, A 1977 P.&H. 56, 61, in which the Thomas case is interpreted as having 'introduced a new dynamic and a new dimension into the concept of ... equality of opportunity.' See Singh, supra note 2, at 304–319; and see generally Galanter, supra note 27.

[47] Seervai, supra note 10, at 428–441.

[48] Both the doctrinal techniques and the discourses used by the Supreme Court have restricted the transformative potential of the case. For example, the Court adopted 'the theory of legislative device'. The Court cites with approval the passage from Devadasan's case. ['The expression 'nothing in this article' is a legislative device to express its intention in a most emphatic way that the power conferred thereunder is not limited in any way by the main provision but falls outside it. It has not really carved out an exception, but has preserved a power untrammelled by the other provisions of the article']. While this theory of legislative device can be seen to support the view that Articles 15 and 16 must be broadly construed, the reasoning of the Supreme Court has remained predominantly at the level of technical doctrine. The court has not gone far enough in articulating its substantive theory of equality that ought to inform this doctrine. Opponents of this approach remain free to engage exclusively at the level of technical interpretation from the unstated vantage point of formal equality. Seervai and Basu continue to chip away at the reasoning without having to confront the fundamental differences in their normative vision of equality informing the Constitution. Similarly, the Court continues to invoke the term 'compensatory discrimination'. Discrimination thus continues to mean any distinction, rather than distinctions that disadvantage within the broader understanding of substantive equality.

[49] A 1989 S.C. 307.

inequality.[50] More recently, in *Marri Chandra Skekhar Rao* v. *Dean, Seth G.S.M.*,[51] the Supreme Court recognized that disadvantaged persons may have to be treated differently in order to be treated equally:

Those who are unequal, in fact, cannot be treated by identical standards; that may be equality in law but it would certainly not be real equality.... The State must, therefore, resort to compensatory State action for the purpose of making people who are formally unequal in their wealth, education or social environment, equal in specified areas.[52]

Notwithstanding the critics of this substantive approach, it is important to recognize that the choice between formal and substantive equality is not simply a choice of the correct interpretative techniques. It is a normative choice of the appropriate model of equality informing the constitutional guarantees. Any attempt at framing the issue as exclusively one of mechanical techniques simply masks these difficult normative choices facing the judiciary.

It is, moreover, a normative choice between questions of sameness and difference, or questions of disadvantage. Instead of comparing the relative sameness and/or difference, a shift to a substantive model of equality would require the Court's commitment to explore the question of disadvantage in equality challenges, that is, to interrogate whether the differential treatment reinforces the inequality of historically and systemically disadvantaged groups.

IV. Judicial Approaches to Sex Discrimination

A. *Introduction: The Relevance of Gender*
The case law dealing with sex discrimination reflects the more general judicial approaches to the interpretation of equality rights.

[50] Ibid., at 312 ['The over emphasis on the doctrine of classification or any anxious and sustained attempts to discover some basis for classification may gradually and imperceptibly deprive the article of its previous content and end in replacing the doctrine of equality by the doctrine of classification.... The idea of similarity or dissimilarity of situations of persons, to justify classification cannot rest on merely differentia which may, by themselves by rational or logical, but depends on whether the differences are relevant to the goals to be reached by the law which seeks to classify'].

[51] 1990 3 S.C.C. 130.

[52] Ibid., at 138.

The same tension between formal and substantive equality is apparent, a tension which remains largely unarticulated in the case law. The sex discrimination case law remains overly determined by a formal model of equality. While some inroads to a substantive model of equality are evident, the judicial approaches remain limited by their formal equality discourse. But the case law dealing with sex discrimination raises some issues of its own. The prevailing conception of equality as sameness has led to a focus on the relevance of gender difference. Three approaches are apparent: protectionist, sameness and corrective. The following discussion will first briefly review and evaluate these three approaches to gender difference. It will attempt to reveal the extent to which these judicial approaches are overwhelmingly informed not only by a formal approach to equality, but moreover, by a deeply problematic approach to gender difference.

The first, and most common approach is a protectionist approach in which women are constructed as weak and subordinate, and are thus in need of protection. In this approach, the Court's understanding of women's differences is asserted as justification for differential treatment. While in some circumstances this differential treatment is preferential treatment, more often than not the differences are seen as sufficient justification in and of themselves for differential treatment. This approach tends to essentialise difference, that is to say, to take the existence of difference as the natural and inevitable point of departure. There is virtually no interrogation of the basis of the difference, nor any substantive consideration of the impact of the differential treatment on women. Rather, women's differences are seen to justify differential treatment, and any differential treatment is virtually deemed to be preferential treatment. In the name of protecting women, this approach often serves to reinforce their subordinate status.

The second approach is an equal treatment or sameness approach, in which women are constructed as the same as men, and thus, ought to be treated exactly the same as men in law.[53]

[53] This approach is exemplified by S. Jahwari, 'Women and Constitutional Safeguards in India', 40 *Andhra Law Times Journal,* 11 (1979) who writes: ['The true meaning of the principle of equality between men and women is that certain natural differences between men and women is to be treated as normally irrelevant in law, and that consequently is not to be treated as constituting in itself a sufficient justification for unequal treatment'].

This sameness approach is invoked in a number of different contexts. It has been used to strike down provisions that treat women and men differently. It has, however, also been used to preclude any analysis of the potentially disparate impact of gender neutral legislation. According to the sameness approach, it is sufficient that women and men be treated formally equally.

Some feminist approaches endorse this conception of equality according to which gender difference ought to be irrelevant, and women ought to be treated exactly the same as men.[54] In this approach, any recognition of gender difference in the past has simply been a justification for discriminating against women. Advocates of this approach for example, argue that special treatment has historically been a double-edged sword for women, that is, under the guise of protection, it has been used to discriminate against women. Any admission of differences between women and men, and any attempt to accommodate those differences is seen to provide a justification for continued unequal and discriminatory treatment.[55] For example, the use of gender difference in the past in prohibiting women to vote, to be elected to government, to be admitted to the legal profession, and other such participation in the economic, political and cultural dimensions of society.[56]

The third, and most promising approach is a corrective approach, in which women are seen to require special treatment as a result of past discrimination. Within this approach, gender difference is often seen as relevant, and as requiring recognition in law.[57] Under this approach, it is argued that a failure to take difference into account will only serve to reinforce and perpetuate the difference and the underlying inequalities. Proponents of this

[54] This approach is associated with the work of Wendy Williams 'The Crisis in Equality Theory and Maternity, Sexuality and Women', 7 *Women's Rights Law Reporter* 179 (1982), and Williams 'Equality's Riddle and Pregnancy and the Special Treatment/Equal Treatment Debate', 13 *NYU Rev. L. & Soc. Change* 325.

[55] See generally Williams, 'The Crisis in Equality', ibid.

[56] For example, in *Bradwell* v. *Illinois*, 16 Wall. 130 (1872) 490, the refusal to admit a woman to the legal profession was upheld by the United States Supreme Court, on the basis of women's differences.

[57] See note, 'Towards a Redefinition of Sexual Equality', 95 *Harv. L. Rev.* 487 (1981); Krieger and Cooney, 'The Miller-Wohl Controversy: Equal Treatment, Positive Action and the Meaning of Women's Equality', 13 *Golden Gate U.L. Rev.* 513 (1983).

approach attempt to illustrate how the ostensibly gender neutral rules of formal equality are not gender neutral at all, but rather, based on male standards and values. As Naudine Taub has argued 'rules formulated in a male-oriented society reflect male needs, male concerns and male experience.'[58] In such a model, women will only qualify for equality to the extent that they can conform to these male values and standards. Thus, the corrective approach argues that gender differences must be taken into account in order to produce substantive equality for women.

There are some important similarities between the protectionist approach and the corrective approach. Most significantly, both of these approaches conclude that gender difference can be relevant and therefore must be recognized in law. However, there are important distinctions between these approaches. Most notably, the protectionist approach is more likely to accept both gender differences and special protection as natural or essential. The corrective approach, on the other hand, is more likely to consider the basis of the difference, and the impact of recognition versus non-recognition of the difference, on the lives of women. Gender difference is not essentialised, but rather, its relevance is seen in the context of past disadvantage. In other words, gender difference needs to be recognized because of the extent to which it has historically been the basis of disadvantage and discrimination.

These approaches to gender difference are often seen to roughly correspond to the formal and substantive approaches to equality. Both the protectionist and the sameness approach to gender can be seen to be based on a formal model of equality, whereas the corrective approach to gender is based on a substantive model of equality. It is important, however, that these debates not be collapsed. The adoption of a substantive approach to equality does not automatically resolve the question of the relevance of gender

---

[58] N. Taub, Book Review, 80 *Columbia Law Review* 1686, 1694 (1980). As Brodsky and Day, supra note 4, at 149 further note: ['The extreme and persistent economic and social inequality of women, which is the result of society's bias and oppression, is obscured by a definition of equality that focuses only on differences in the form of law. Women are poorer than men, they work in ill-paid female ghettos, they are the primary care givers for their children and parents, and they are overwhelmingly, the victims of rape and battery. Simple gender neutrality in law based on male standards does not address those major inequalities'].

difference. That is, a substantive approach does not necessarily correspond to a corrective approach to gender. Rather, it might in a particular context determine that treating women differently would further contribute to their disadvantage, and thus conclude that women ought to be treated the same. A substantive approach to equality, while opening the space for gender difference to be recognized, does not eradicate the need to make choices regarding when and how difference ought to be recognized.

The basic inquiry of the substantive approach is whether the impugned provision contributes to or reinforces the subordination of women. In some contexts, this substantive approach will require a sameness approach, whereas in other contexts it will require a corrective approach. For example, in relation to basic civil and political rights such as the right to vote and the right to own land, gender would be considered irrelevant in the pursuit of equality, and any recognition of gender would likely only contribute to, or reinforce, the subordination of women. In relation to employment rights, however, a substantive approach may require a recognition of women's reproductive differences in so far as the pursuit of equality will require that women are provided with maternity leave and benefits.

Employment

Sex discrimination challenges in the employment law context can be divided into two sets of cases. In the first set, women have challenged rules, regulations and practices that restrict or prohibit women's employment. In a second, and smaller set of cases, rules, regulations and practices that treat women preferentially have been challenged on the basis that they restrict or prohibit men's employment.

i. Restrictions on Women's Employment

Many of the rules, regulations and practices that impose restrictions on women's employment have been found to violate the equality guarantees. However, the decisions in this area are not entirely unproblematic. Firstly, some of the rules and practices which restrict women's employment have been upheld. Secondly, the approach to equality and gender difference informing these decisions are often problematic. The courts have overwhelmingly adopted a formal approach to equality. The approach to gender difference, however, is divided. Many judges have adopted a protectionist approach, while others have adopted a sameness approach.

In *Raghuban Saudagar Singh* v. *State of Punjab*,[59] a government order directing that women were ineligible for appointments to all positions in men's jails with the exception of the position of clerks and matrons, was challenged as discrimination on the basis of sex.[60] The Court held that the order did not constitute discrimination only on the ground of sex.

It needs no great imagination to visualise the awkward and even the hazardous position of a woman acting as a warder or other jail official who has to personally ensure and maintain discipline over habitual male criminals.[61]

The Court concluded:

...where disparities of either-sex patently add to or detract from, the capacity and suitability to hold a particular post or posts, then the State would be entitled to take this factor into consideration in conjuncture with others.[62]

The Court upheld the restriction on women's employment.

In the Raghuban case the Court adopts a formal approach to equality, within which the perceived differences between women and men justify the differential treatment, and in effect, preclude women's entitlement to equality. Moreover, the Court adopts a protectionist approach to gender difference. The Court emphasized the differences in physical strength between women and men. While a certain level of physical strength may indeed be a necessary occupational qualification, the Court did not interrogate whether the gender-based classification was the most reasonable means of meeting this qualification. Instead of banning an entire class of candidates, a more reasonable classification might have

---

[59] A 1972 P. & H. 117.

[60] The petitioner was a Deputy Superintendent of a women's jail. As a result of the government order, she was denied promotion.

[61] Raghuban, supra note 59, at 121 para 17.

[62] In further support of this assertion of the fundamental physical differences between the sexes, the Court quoted from a 1907 United States Supreme Court decision, *Curt Muller* v. *State of Oregon* (1907) 208 U.S. 412 'The two sexes differ in structure of body, in the functions to be performed by each, in the amount of physical strength.... This difference justifies a difference in legislation and upholds that which is designed to compensate for some of the burdens which rest upon her.'

been based on ensuring that individual candidates meet the required level of physical strength. The Court, however, did not consider the reasonableness of the classification. Rather, physical difference in strength was put forward as natural gender difference and as applying to all women and all men. Indeed, the Court seemed to be concerned with differences beyond mere physical strength. Without exploring the nature of these differences, the Court concludes that these 'patent disparities' would make it awkward, unsuitable, and indeed, immoral for women to be employed as jail officials. Underlying the decision appears to be a concern with protecting women, as the weaker sex, from male prisoners.

In the recent case of *Omana Oomen* v. *FACT Ltd.*,[63] female apprentice trainees were denied the opportunity to write an internal examination on the basis of restrictions imposed on the working hours of women by S.66 of the Factories Act. The petitioners contended that they could have been accommodated in the day shift in which there were several male technicians and that women technicians had been absorbed in other divisions of the company. The Court held that the restriction was based entirely on the basis of sex, and thus violated Articles 14 and 15.

Many constitutional challenges have been directed to employment rules that specifically restrict the employment of married women. In *Bombay Labour Union* v. *International Franchise*[64] a rule requiring an unmarried woman to give up her position when she married was challenged. The rule only applied to a particular department of the company. The justification put forward by the company for this rule was the need to work in teams, that attendance must be regular and that there is greater absenteeism among married women. The Supreme Court held that there was no evidence that married women were more likely to be absent than unmarried women.

If it is the presence of children which may be said to account for greater absenteeism among married women, that would be so more or less in the case of widows with children also.... The only difference in the matter of absenteeism that we can see between married women...and unmarried women...is in the matter of maternity leave which is an extra facility

[63] A 1991 Ker. 129.
[64] A 1966 S.C. 942.

available to married women. To this extent only, married women are more likely to be absent than unmarried women and widows. But such absence can in our opinion be easily provided for by having a few extra women as leave reserve and can thus hardly be a ground for such a drastic rule....[65]

The Court struck down the restriction on women's employment.

In *C.B. Muthamma* v. *Union of India and Others,*[66] the petitioner, a successful candidate in the Indian Foreign Service, was refused appointment because she was married. The rules of the Indian Foreign Service, prohibiting the appointment of married women, and requiring that unmarried women in the employment of the Foreign Service obtain permission before marrying, were challenged. The Supreme Court held:

If a woman member shall obtain the permission of government before she marries, the same risk is run by government if a male member contracts a marriage. If the family and domestic commitments of a woman member of the Service is likely to come in the way of efficient discharge of duties, a similar situation may well arise in the case of a male member. In these days of nuclear families, intercontinental marriages and unconventional behaviour, one fails to understand the naked bias against the gentler of the species.[67]

The Court held that although the rule is discriminatory, the application should be dismissed in light of the subsequent promotion of the petitioner. However, the Court concluded by strongly urging the Government to 'overhaul all Service Rules to remove the stain of sex discrimination.'[68]

The Court adopted a formal approach to equality, and a sameness approach to gender. For the purposes of employment in the Foreign Service, women and men are to be considered the same. According to the Court, women and men must both balance the demands of work and family. Women and men must therefore be treated the same in law. However, the Court is cautious in its adoption of this sameness approach, and in fact, goes on to limit its applicability:

[65] Ibid., at 944 para 3.
[66] A 1979 S.C. 1868.
[67] Ibid., at 1870 para 5.
[68] Ibid., at 1870 para 9.

We do not mean to universalise or dogmatise that men and women are equal in all occupations and all situations and do not exclude the need to pragmatise where the requirements of particular employment, the sensitivities of sex or the peculiarity of societal sectors or the handicaps of either sex may compel selectivity.[69]

The sameness approach is thus expressly limited to the particular circumstances of the particular case. The Court leaves open the possibility of adopting an approach which recognizes differences. Indeed, the discourse of the decision suggests an underlying protectionism. The references to women as 'the gentler of the species', suggests that the Court does see women as different, as weaker, and as in need of protection. Indeed, the recurring references to women as 'the weaker' and 'the gentler' sex reinforces images of women as weak, and in need of protection.[70]

In *Air India* v. *Nergesh Meerza*[71] air hostesses challenged the discriminatory employment conditions for air hostesses and stewards. The Supreme Court upheld a contractual condition permitting the termination of an air hostess's services on her marriage within the first four years, but invalidated a condition that terminated her services on her pregnancy. The Supreme Court began with a review of the basic principles of reasonable classification under Article 14,[72] and set out the criteria for determining the distinct classes.[73] Based

---

[69] Ibid., at 1870 para 7.

[70] While the Court's references to misogynous and masculinist culture suggest that women's differences are the product of these oppressive relations, (the Court writes, for example, 'This misogynous posture is a hangover of the masculine culture of manacling the weaker sex forgetting how our struggle for national freedom was also a battle against mens thraldom.' Ibid., at para 3.) these references are at least in part undermined by references which suggest that women are naturally and essentially weak.

[71] A 1981 S.C. 1829.

[72] In reviewing the doctrine of reasonable classification, the Court adopts the standard formulation of equality as sameness, according to which likes must be treated alike. The Court writes, for example ['(3) Article 14 certainly applies where equals are treated differently without any reasonable bias. (4) Where equals and unequals are treated differently, Article 14 would have no application']. Ibid., at 1842 para 37.

[73] These criteria include, '(a) the nature, the mode and the manner of recruitment of a particular category (b) the classifications of the particular category (c) the terms and conditions of service of the members of the category (d) the nature and character of the posts and promotional avenues (e) the special attributes

on this test, the Court concluded that Air Hostesses constituted a separate class of Air India employees. The Court considered the list of circumstances, noting the differences in recruitment, terms and conditions of service, the promotional avenues, and other 'special attributes' between Air Hostess (AHs) and Assistant Flight Pursers (AFPs), and concluded that AHs were distinct from the class of AFPs.

The Court then considered the challenge to the restriction on marriage. The restriction was upheld on the grounds that it fostered the State family planning programme, that women would be more mature to handle and make a marriage work successfully if forced to wait four years, as well as on the grounds of the financial hardship the corporation would incur should the bar to marriage be removed.[74] The Court concluded that the treatment of the 'fair sex' in this regulation is neither arbitrary nor unreasonable, and thus does not violate Article 14.

The Court subsequently examined the regulation requiring AHs to retire upon their first pregnancy. According to the Court, the dismissal of a pregnant AH '[a]mounts to compelling the poor AH not to have any children and thus interfere with and divert the ordinary course of human nature.'

It seems to us that the termination of the services of an AH under such circumstances is not only a callous and cruel act but an open insult to Indian womanhood—the most sacrosanct and cherished institution. We are constrained to observe that such a course of action is extremely detestable and abhorrent to the notions of a civilized society. Apart from being grossly unethical, it smacks of a deep rooted sense of utter selfishness at the cost of all human values.[75]

---

that the particular category possess which are not to be found in other classes and the like.' Ibid.

[74] The Court held ['Apart from improving the health of the employee, it helps a good deal in the promotion and boosting up of our family planning programme. Secondly, if a woman marries near about the age of 20 to 23 years, she becomes fully mature and there is every chance of such a marriage proving a success all things being equal. Thirdly, it has been rightly pointed out to us by the Corporation that if the bar of marriage within four years of service is removed then the Corporation will have to incur huge expenditure in recruiting additional AHs either on a temporary or on ad hoc basis to replace the working AHs if they conceive and any period short of four years would be too little a time for the Corporation to phase out such an ambitious plan']. Ibid,. at 1850 para 78.

[75] Ibid., at 1850 para 80.

The Court concluded that the pregnancy restriction was unreasonable and arbitrary, and thus in violation of Article 14.[76]

The Air India case illustrates the problems with a formal approach to equality, as well as with an approach to gender equality informed by the narrow sameness/difference debate. Firstly, the formal approach to equality, and its similarly situated test is used to preclude any analysis of substantive inequality between male and female employees. The Court uses the very discrimination between these two groups of employees to distinguish between them—that is, the practice of institutional discrimination against AHs is used in the very definition of classes. As a result of the history of discriminatory treatment between a group of female and male employees, the Court was able to conclude that the classes are distinct, and that no comparison needs to be made between them for the purposes of Article 14. For example, rather than considering the problematic nature of the distinctions between the recruitment requirements for the AHs and AFPs, the Court uses the difference requirements regarding marital status as between AHs and AFPs as a factor in concluding that these employees are different. The circularity of the approach is evident, past institutional discrimination (AHs/women must be unmarried; AFPs/men need not be) is thereby used to preclude any analysis of institutional discrimination (AHs/women and AFPs/men are distinct classes).

Secondly, while some have looked favourably on the decision,[77] the Court's approach to gender difference is quite problematic. In recognizing differences in the context of marriage, the approach adopted by the Court was protectionist—women need to be treated differently to protect them. In recognizing difference in the context of pregnancy and maternity, the approach adopted by the Court

---

[76] In a more recent case against *Air India*, *Lena Khan* v. *Union of India*, A 1987 S.C. 1515, the regulations which required air hostesses employed in India to retire at age 35, with extension to age 45, but which allowed air hostesses employed outside India to continue employment beyond age 45, was challenged as violative of Articles 14 and 15. The Supreme Court held that such discrimination should not be allowed merely because it complies with local law abroad. However, in light of Air India's submissions that it would phase out air hostesses recruited outside of India at age 45, the Court concluded that no intervention was required at this time.

[77] See Rani Jethmalani, 'India: Law and Women', in *Empowerment and the Law: Strategies for Third World Women* 61 (M. Schuler ed., 1986).

was also protectionist and essentialist. Pregnancy and maternity were not simply seen as a biological difference which, in the interest of treating women equally, must be recognized. Rather, in the Court's view, it was a also difference in the roles of women and men, according to which women are not only responsible for child bearing, but also for child rearing. In this view, women's role as mothers is seen as natural and a product of biology, rather than product of the sexual division of labour. The approach adopted by the Court was based upon, and served to reinforce, the ideology of motherhood that has been constructed around these physical differences.[78] Notwithstanding the fact that the Court struck down the pregnancy restriction on women's employment, its understanding of women as different precluded an analysis of the sexist ideologies that continue to inform systemic gender discrimination.

In *Maya Devi v. State of Maharashtra*,[79] a requirement that married women obtain their husbands consent before applying for public employment was challenged as violating Articles 14, 15 and 16. The Supreme Court held:

This is a matter purely personal between husband and wife. It is unthinkable that in social conditions presently prevalent a husband can prevent a wife from being independent economically just for his whim or caprice.[80]

The Court emphasized the importance of economic independence for women, and the importance of not creating conditions that discourage such independence. The consent requirement was held to be unconstitutional. In this case, the Court was the view that consent requirements were an anachronistic obstacle to women's equality. In order to achieve economic independence women must not, at least in this regard, be treated differently than men. The

[78] Indeed, even the physical difference that is being recognized is one loaded with social meaning—pregnancy is simply a biological difference, but it is seen as 'a natural consequence of married life.' For example in reviewing the American case law on sex discrimination and pregnancy, the court made the following observation: '...pregnancy...is not a disability but one of the natural consequences of marriage and is an immutable characteristic of married life. Any distinction, therefore, made on the ground of pregnancy cannot but be held to be extremely artibrary.' Supra note 71, 1852 para 88.

[79] 1986 1 S.C.R. 743.

[80] Ibid., at 745.

decision might be seen to reflect a formal model of equality, and a sameness approach to gender difference which requires that women and men be treated the same. However, the decision also supports a more substantive approach to equality, that is, a recognition that the consent requirement contributed to the subordination of women. The case exemplifies how a substantive approach to equality may still require a choice to be made about the relevance of gender. In this case, an inquiry into whether the rule contributed to or reinforced women's subordination revealed that in this particular context, gender ought to be irrelevant, and thus, a sameness approach was appropriate.

ii. Preferential Treatment

Several cases have involved challenges to employment rules, regulations and practices that treat women preferentially, on the basis that such preferential treatment discriminates against men. The results of these cases have been mixed. In those cases where the employment rules have been upheld, the Court has adopted a more substantive approach which recognizes that equality may require differential treatment. For example, in *Shamsher Singh* v. *State*[81] the employment practices of the State educational system were challenged as violating Article 16(2). The educational system had two branches, one run exclusively by women, the other, exclusively by men. In the women's branch, Assistant District Inspectors were granted a special pay increase. The educational department was subsequently reorganized, and as a result both male and female Assistant District Inspectors were designated as Block Education Officers. Both the women and men were performing identical duties. The male petitioner challenged the pay increase as sex discrimination, and as violative of Article 16(2). The question referred to the Full Bench of the High Court was whether Article 15(3) could be invoked to interpret Article 16(2). In response, the Court held that Articles 14, 15 and 16 constitute a single code, and that Article 15(3) could thereby be invoked to determine the scope of Article 16(2).[82] The petition was dismissed and the pay increase upheld.

In those cases where employment rules have been struck down, the Court has adopted a formal approach to equality, and a sameness

[81] Supra note 26.
[82] Ibid., at 376 para 19.

approach to gender difference. For example, in *Walter Alfred Baid v. Union of India,*[83] a recruitment rule in a school of nursing, a predominantly female institution, which made male candidates ineligible for the position of senior nurse tutor, was struck down as violating Article 16(2). The Court held that Article 16(2) did not permit a classification on the basis of sex:

Article 16(2) incorporates a concept of absolute equality between the sexes in matters of employment which is underscored by the absence of any saving in the other clauses in relation to sex.[84]

The Court thereby adopted a formal approach to equality, according to which women and men are to be treated the same for purposes of employment. This sameness approach does not allow for any difference in treatment on the basis of sex, including a difference in treatment which may advantage women.

With regard to the relevance of gender difference, the Court further stated that although 'it is true that there are patent physical disparities between the two sexes,' such differences could not justify differential treatment without violating Article 16(2):

It is too late, therefore, for anyone to suggest that there is an area of human activity for which women as a class are ineligible or any work for which all women are unfit.[85]

While recognizing certain physical differences as natural, the Court adopted a sameness approach to gender difference, that is, for the purpose of the law, any such gender difference should be irrelevant.

In concluding that the classification in question was one based on sex, the Court rejected the distinction 'between sex and what it implied'.[86] This rejection of the narrow interpretation of 'only on the ground of sex' opened the possibility of recognizing the extent to which gender differences are socially constructed and bringing

---

[83] Supra note 32.

[84] Ibid., at 306 para 10.

[85] Ibid., at 307 para 10.

[86] ['Considerations which have their genesis in sex and arise out of it would not be saved by such a discrimination. What could save such a discrimination is any ground or reason dependently of sex such as socio-economic conditions, martial status, and other disqualifying conditions such as age, background, health, academic accomplishments, etc.'] Ibid., at 308 para 10.

these social dimensions of difference within the folds of the equality guarantees of the Constitution. In the context of a substantive model of equality, this approach would allow the Courts to address the broad range of socially constructed inequalities that women suffer—from economic dependency to educational disadvantage. However, in the W.A. Baid case, this understanding of gender difference was coupled with a sameness approach, whereby any difference, whether natural or otherwise, ought to be irrelevant for the purposes of the law. As a result of the formal approach to equality, and sameness approach to gender difference, the Court found that the gender specific recruitment rule violated Article 16(2). The effect of this approach was to preclude any analysis of the purpose of the differential in treatment, and thus, any consideration of whether the differential in treatment was intended to advantage or disadvantage women. Further, the particular examples used by the Court to distinguish between those factors implied by sex, and those factors which are not, were also problematic.[87] Socio-economic conditions, marital status, health and education are all factors that may be relevant to sex, if measured in terms of the substantive inequality of women, and in respect of which a corrective approach to gender difference may thus be required.

C. *Civil and Political Rights*

The constitutional challenges to legislation dealing with civil and political rights can be divided into three sets of cases. In the first set, women have challenged legislation that restricts their rights to own land. In the second set of cases, legislation that provides reservations for women have been challenged as discriminatory. These reservations have been upheld. A third set of cases some of the problems in the classification of legislation as preferential.

i. Restrictions on Land Ownership

In *Pritam Kaur v. State of Pepsu*,[88] Section 5(2)(a) of the Pepsu Court of Wards Act was challenged as in violation of Article 15(1). Section 5(2) authorized the government to make an order directing that property of a landholder be placed under the supervision of the Court of Wards, if the landholder was incapable of managing his affairs. Section 5(2)(a) authorized such an order if a landholder

[87] Ibid.
[88] A 1963 P.&H. 9.

'by reason of being a female' was incapable of managing the property. The Court noted:

To be a woman is an additional reason on the basis of which the Government can deprive her of the management of her estate. In other words, if a man mismanages his estate, that mismanagement will not render his estate liable to be taken over by the Court of Wards unless his case falls under any one of clauses (b), (c) and (d) of Section 5(2) of the Act. Whereas in the case of a woman it can be so taken merely for the reason that she is a woman.[89]

The Court concluded that Section 5(2) of the Act discriminated on the basis of sex, and thus violated Article 15.

However, two subsequent cases dealing with restrictions on women's land ownership have been upheld. In *Sucha Singh Bajwa & Sadhu Singh Bajwa* v. *The State of Punjab*,[90] Section 5 of the Punjab Land Reforms Act was challenged as violating Article 15 on the grounds that it allowed the holder or owner of the land to select the separate permissible area in respect of adult sons, but not adult daughters. The High Court held:

The subject of the legislation is the person owning or holding land, and not his or her children...[Since] every person described in Section 5 whether male or female is allowed the same permissible area and there is no discrimination qua one land owner and the other on the ground of sex....[91]

The Court further held that the distinction was not made on the ground of sex alone, but rather 'also for reason that a daughter has to go to another family after her marriage in due course.'[92] The Court upheld the restriction.

The decision highlights the ways in which classification and comparison can be manipulated within a formal equality approach. The Court defines the relevant comparison as one between the landholders. Accordingly, since there is no discrimination between male and female *landholders*, the provision is not seen to discriminate on the basis of sex. While the discrimination as between sons and

[89] Ibid., at 16 para 17.
[90] A 1974 P. & H. 162.
[91] Ibid., at 171 para 13.
[92] Ibid.

daughters on the face of the legislation might be seen to offend even a formal approach to equality, the Court evades this question by simply defining this comparison between potential recipients as irrelevant.

Further, the Court's approach to gender is also problematic. In support of its decision, the Court resorts to the doctrine of 'only on the grounds of sex' and argues that there are other factors not based on sex that justify the differential treatment of a daughter, such as the fact that daughters go to another family after marriage. The reasoning exemplifies the problematic distinction between sex and what it implies, that is, the failure to explore the connections between such customary practices and the social construction of gender. The practice of daughters leaving their natural families on marriage is a product of the social organization of gender, and the roles that women are expected to assume. The practice is, in other words, one that is implied by sex. By focusing narrowly on sex, the Court fails to see the necessary connection between sex and what sex implies. Stereotypes of women are used as justification for differential treatment, without any real analysis of disadvantage, nor any attempt to explore the extent to which these stereotypical roles of women have served to reinforce women's inequality.

In *Nalini Ranjan Singh and others* v. *The State,*[93] Section 2 (e) of the Bihar Land Reforms Act was challenged as violating Article 15. The definition of family in the section did not include an adult daughter, for the purposes of claiming a separate unit of land, and was thus alleged to discriminate as between adult daughters and adult sons. On the basis of principles of Hindu personal law, the Court held that daughters are not members of the coparcenary.

Although a daughter can be a member of a joint Hindu Undivided Family, she cannot be given a status as a coparcener in a coparcenary, even after the commencement of the Constitution.... There are various factors which sanction that while a son may be a member of a coparcenary, a daughter may not. As a necessary corollary it follows that the very same reasons which justify the discrimination between a son and a daughter in a coparcenary apply with force to any attack on the validity of the impugned legislation as being violative of Article 15(1).[94]

The Court thus upheld the restriction.

[93] A 1977 Pat. 171.
[94] Ibid., at 179 para 8-A.

ii. Reservations

The cases dealing with constitutional challenges to reservations for women in political institutions have been upheld. In *Dattatraya Motiram More* v. *Bombay*,[95] Section 10(1)(c) of the Bombay Municipal Boroughs 1925 Act for the reservation of seats for women was challenged as violating Articles 14, 15 and 16. With regard to Article 15, the Court adopted the approach that Article 15(3) must be interpreted as a proviso to Article 15(1), and that Article 15(1) prohibited discrimination 'only on the ground of sex', and that Articles 15(1) and 15(3) together allowed the State to discriminate in favour of women against men, but not to discriminate in favour of men against women. The Court held that the reservations did not constitute a classification only on the ground of sex, but rather, was the result of 'other considerations besides the fact that the persons belonging to that class are of a particular sex.'[96]

There is force in the Advocate General's argument that if Government have discriminated in favour of women in reserving seats for them, it is not only on the ground that they are women, but there are various other factors that come into play. It is said that even today women are more backward than men. It is the duty of the State to raise the position of women to that of men.[97]

The decision can be seen to be informed by a substantive model of equality and a corrective approach to gender, in so far as the Court recognizes that the social and historic inequality of women must be recognized in order to overcome this inequality. However, some aspects of the decision limit this progressive approach. For example, the substantive understanding of equality remains limited by the discourse of formal equality apparent in the narrow technical reading of Article 15(1), and of *only* as well as the use of the term discrimination to imply any difference in treatment. Similarly, the understanding of difference is problematic in so far as the Court separates sex from what sex implies—the recognition of the social inequality of women is not seen as based on sex. This distinction reinforces an understanding of sex difference as natural and biological.

In *K.R. Gopinath Nair* v. *The Senior Inspector cum Special Sale*

[95] Supra note 17.
[96] Ibid., at 313 para 7.
[97] Ibid.

Officer of Cooperative Societies and Others.'[98] the Kerala High Court held that Section 28 A of the Kerala Cooperative Societies Act which provided for the reservation of a seat in the committee of every cooperative society did not violate Articles 14 and 15. The Court held that the provision of special measures for women and children has been recognized in Article 15, as well as being one of the proclaimed directive principles of State policy in Article 38. The Court stated:

Even on a global view, women still suffer the pangs of inequality, though women constitute about 50 per cent of the population, effective participation in the political administration is, to them, still a teasing illusion.[99]

The Court then concludes that

...Section 28A is a small step in the correct and progressive direction in offsetting the ill effects of age old handicaps of women.[100]

The decision can be seen to be based on a substantive approach to equality, in which the Court examines whether the provision in question contributes to women's subordination. The Court's inquiry reveals that the provision, which treats women differently, is specifically intended to eradicate historic discrimination against women, and thus, that a substantive approach to equality in this context requires a corrective approach to gender difference.

iii. Civil Procedure

In *Mahadeb Jiew* v. *Dr. B.B. Sen*,[101] a provision of the Civil Procedure Code, which gave the courts discretion to order security for costs where the plaintiff is a woman, and does not possess sufficient immoveable property in India, was challenged as discrimination on the basis of sex. The Court held that the discrimination was not on the basis of sex alone, but rather, also involved property considerations.

Possession of sufficient immoveable property in India is not a consideration bearing on sex at all.... The basic criterion is...that the

[98] A 1987 Kerala 167.
[99] Ibid., at 168 para 8.
[100] Ibid., at 169 para 13.
[101] Supra note 17.

person who is ordered to secure for costs is one who has not sufficient property out of which to pay the successful litigant's costs.[102]

The Court thus upheld the provision. The Court was unmoved by the fact that men without sufficient immoveable property in India were not required to provide security for costs. It simply insisted that the discrimination could not be said to be on the basis of sex alone, but on the combined grounds of sex and property.

The case exemplifies the problematic and indeed dangerous potential of the 'only on the ground of sex' approach, whereby virtually any factor or characteristic can be added to the sex discrimination and thereby make the discrimination not only on the ground of sex. Moreover, the failure to inquire into the question of the social and economic disadvantage of women precludes any consideration of assumptions informing this rule. The distinction between women and men without sufficient immoveable property can be seen to be based on the underlying assumption that women do not have any source of income—they do not work outside of the home—and therefore, will not be able to pay for costs. Men, on the other hand, are assumed to work outside the home, and thus, presumed to be able to pay for costs. The sexual division of labour has operated to make many women economically dependent. However, the classification is too broad. Some women may well work outside the home; men may be unemployed. The 'only on the grounds of sex' test, fails to reveal and interrogate the validity these underlying assumptions. While the objective of the provision is legitimate—that is, ensuring that plaintiffs have sufficient means to pay costs—this objective is not well served by criteria on the basis of sex.

In *Shahdad* v. *Mohd Abdullah*[103] the provisions of the Civil Procedure Code, which state that service of a summons must be made on a male member of the family, were challenged as violating Article 15. In rejecting the challenge, the Court held:

… we have to analyse the background in which this rule was enacted. The functions of females in Indian society is that of housewives. Until very recently it was in exceptional cases that ladies took part in any other activity than those of housewives. Females were mostly illiterate and some of them Parda Nashin. Therefore in enacting this rule, the legislature

---

[102] Supra note 17 at 568 para 29.
[103] Supra note 18.

had in view the special conditions of the Indian society and therefore enjoined service only upon male members and did not regard service on females as sufficient.[104]

The Court noted that Article 15(3) is intended 'to cover any provision specially made for women' and that the provision:

… does not give them any disadvantageous position but rather exonerates them from the responsibility of fastening notice of service as service of the other members of the family.[105]

After noting other provisions which 'confer special privileges upon a protection to women' which have been upheld by the courts, the Court concluded that the service provisions of the Civil Procedure Code did not constitute discrimination on the basis of sex.[106]

The decision is based on a formal approach to equality, in which any difference can be used to justify differential treatment, and a protectionist approach to gender, in which women are seen as different and as in need of protection. The Court seized upon women as housewives as a difference which justified the differential treatment of women and men in law. The approach did not challenge the stereotype of women as housewives; it did not examine the extent to which these stereotypes of women have served to reinforce women's inequality, nor the extent to which the underlying sexual division of labour has produced such inequality. Rather, the difference is taken as natural. The decision exemplifies the way in which the recognition of gender difference under the guise of protection can perpetuate women's subordination. The recognition of the difference in the sexual division of labour serves only to reinforce the negative stereotypes of women as housewives.

Moreover, in the Court's protectionist view, the fact that women are not subject to service is seen as preferential rather than restrictive treatment for women. The protectionist approach blinds the Court

---

[104] Ibid., at 127 para 32.

[105] Ibid., at 127 para 33.

[106] The Court referred to the decisions regarding the provisions adultery under section 497 of the Indian Penal Code, A 1953 M.B. 147 and the maintenance provisions under Section 488 of the Civil Procedure Code, A 1952 Mad 529. ['These authorities therefore lend support to the view that in enacting Civil Procedure Code of 1908, there is no discrimination between a woman and a man simply on the ground of his or her sex on receiving a notice on behalf of some other member of the family'].

to the fact that such a differential in treatment accords women less than equal rights and responsibilities, and thus renders them less than equal members of the family. From the perspective of substantive equality, the legislation could be seen to disadvantage women. However, even within a substantive approach to equality and a corrective approach to gender, it might be necessary to recognize gender difference in this case. It could be argued that the continuing sexual division of labour and the resulting inequalities of women within the family are such that women ought not be burdened with equal responsibilities until such time as they have equal rights. This was not, however, the approach in Shahdad, where the Court merely seized upon a perceived difference, and justified differentiation of treatment.[107]

D. *Criminal Law*

Constitutional challenges have been brought to the adultery, maintenance, prostitution and bail provisions of the criminal law. Unlike the employment cases, these sex discrimination cases have been largely unsuccessful. The Courts have primarily adopted a formal approach to equality and a protectionist approach to gender difference.

i. Adultery

The Supreme Court has considered several challenges to Section 497 of the Indian Penal Code, which makes only adultery committed by a man an offence, and Section 198 of the Code of Criminal Procedure, which allows only the husband of the 'adulteress' to prosecute the men with whom she committed adultery, but does not allow the wife of that man to prosecute him. In *Abdul Aziz* v. *Bombay*,[108] the accused, charged with committing adultery under Section 497, challenged the section as

---

[107] In *Smt. Savitri Aggarwal* v. *K.K. Bose*, A 1972 All. 305 an order granting a hotel bar licence for the sale of foreign liquor was challenged as violating Article 15. The District Excise Officer had granted the license on the basis of sex, observing that certain applications 'deserve sympathetic consideration as they are ladies.' The Allahabad High Court held that such a preference in the granting of licenses did not constitute a special provision for women pursuant to Article 15(3). 'What Article 15(3) contemplates is the making of special provision for women as a class and not the making of provisions for an individual women.' The Court allowed the petition, and quashed the order granting the licence.
[108] Supra note 26.

discriminating on the basis of sex, and in violation of Articles 14 and 15. The High Court concluded that the difference of treatment was not based on sex but rather, on the social position of women in India. On appeal, the Supreme Court held that any challenge under 15(1) was met by 15(3). The Court rejected the argument that 15(3) 'should be confined to provisions which are beneficial to women and cannot be used to give them a licence to commit and abet crimes.'[109] The Court held:

Article 14 is general and must be read with the other provisions which set out the ambit of fundamental rights. Sex is a sound classification and although there can be no discrimination in general on that ground, the Constitution itself provides for special provisions in the case of women and children.[110]

The Court thus upheld the adultery provisions as beneficial to women.

The Court adopted the 'holistic approach' to Article 15, and thereby seemed to endorse the view that equality may require that disadvantaged groups be treated differently, and in fact, preferentially. However, the Court's understanding of discrimination —that is, of any distinction on the prohibited grounds—is suggestive of a more formal approach to equality. Notwithstanding the Court's statement that the Articles should be read together, it seems to understand the preferential treatment allowed by Article 15(3) as an exception to equality. Moreover, it is not clear whether the adultery laws do in fact treat women preferentially. On one level, there is an obvious benefit to not being subject to criminal prosecution. Yet, at another level, the adultery laws are based on problematic assumptions about women, about women's sexuality and about the relationships between women and men. Women are seen as the passive victims of aggressive male sexuality, incapable of agency in sexual relation, and in need of protection. Within this understanding, adultery is seen as the fault of the man; a woman is simply his hapless victim; and not to be blamed. The failure to interrogate the adultery provisions at a deeper level leaves these assumptions in place, and the adultery provisions continue to reinforce underlying social inequalities. The Court's approach,

---

[109] Ibid., at 322 para 5.
[110] Ibid., at 322 para 6.

wherein any differential in treatment can be seen to be beneficial, and any benefit can be seen to fall within Article 15(3), thus fails to adequately consider the questions of inequality and subordination.

In *Sowmithri Vishnu* v. *Union of India*,[111] Section 497 of the Indian Penal Code was challenged as unconstitutional by a woman whose husband had prosecuted her lover for adultery. She argued that the section was discriminatory because the husband had a right to prosecute the adulterer. The wife, on the other hand, had no right to prosecute either her adulterous husband or the woman with whom the husband had committed adultery. In addition, she argued that the section did not take into account situations where the husband had sexual relations with an unmarried woman. In dismissing the petition, the Court held that confining the definition of adultery to men was not discriminatory as '[I]t is commonly accepted that it is the man who is the seducer and not the woman.'[112]

Again, in the Court's view, a wife who is involved in an adulterous relationship is the victim rather than the author of the crime. The offence is committed against the sanctity of the matrimonial home and it is the man who defiles that sanctity.[113]

The Court's decision was firmly located within a formal equality approach. The challenge was not allowed on the grounds that in the context of adultery, women and men are different. Further, the Court clearly articulated is protectionist approach to gender difference. The man was regarded as the seducer and the author of the crime. The approach essentialises women as passive, as incapable of agency in sexual relations, and as victims. Moreover, in the Court's view, these differences were seen as natural.[114]

---

[111] A 1985 S.C. 1618.

[112] Ibid., at 1620 para 6.

[113] Ibid., at 1620 para 7.

[114] In upholding the adultery provisions, the Court further held that the under-inclusive definition was not discriminatory. Third holding reinforces the courts position on relations between married men and unmarried women, who are often prostitute women. Prostitute women are different from all other women and thus entitled to less legal rights or protection than all other women. Such women belie the patriarchal construction of female sexuality as passive. Their agency is considered a threat to the family and the matrimonial relationship and therefore, the law operates primarily against them.

Yet, even within this view, it is not clear why the wife of the adulterer cannot prosecute him. This question is more directly addressed by the Court in, *Revathi* v. *Union of India*,[115] Section 497 of the Indian Penal Code and Section 198(2) of the Code of Criminal Procedure were again upheld. According to the Court these provisions:

...go hand in hand and constitute a legislative packet to deal with the offence committed by an outsider to the matrimonial unit and poisons the relationship between the two partners constituting the matrimonial unit and the community punishes the 'outsider' who breaks into the matrimonial home and occasions the violation of sanctity of the matrimonial tie by developing an illicit relationship with one of the spouses....[116]

The fact that the wife of the adulterer is expressly prohibited from prosecuting her husband is the only exception to the general rule that anyone can set the criminal law in motion. This exception is based on a particular understanding of the nature of the harm caused by adultery. Adultery is seen as a violation of a husband's property rights over his wife; more specifically, of his wife's sexuality. It is not a violation of a wife's rights since she is not seen as having the same claim to her husband. Thus, it is only the husband who can prosecute an adulterer since he is the only one who is seen to have suffered a harm. This basic difference in the understanding of adultery, a difference that is seen as natural, is used to justify the differential treatment, and thereby uphold the law. The underlying sexist assumptions, again, remain uninterrogated.

ii. Maintenance

Several challenges have been made to Section 488 of the Code of Criminal Procedure which requires men to pay maintenance in favour of their wives, but imposes no corresponding duty on women to maintain their husbands. In *Thamsi Goundan* v. *Kanni Ammal*,[117] this provision was challenged as violating Article 14. The Court, in adopting the reasonable classification approach, held that the classification was based on the difference between men and women:

---

[115] A 1988 S.C. 835.
[116] Ibid., at 838 para 5.
[117] A 1952 Mad. 529.

Women as a whole suffer from several disabilities from which men do not suffer. They have no right at least under Hindu law to participate along with their brothers in the inheritance to the property of their parents ... Instances can be multiplied without number to show how women have not equal rights with men. That as a class they are weaker than men cannot also be disputed. In fact they are even called by the appellation 'Weaker Sex'. The very provision in clause 3 of Article 15, that special provision may be made for women, suggests the existence of disparity.[118]

The Court held that Section 488 'applies to all women in similar circumstances'. that is, to all women deserted by their husbands, and that '(1)egislation in favour of this class of people' is not arbitrary.[119]

The Court adopted a formal approach to equality regarding Article 14, according to which only those who are similarly situated are to be treated the same. Women, and more specifically, wives deserted by their husbands, are not the same as men, and therefore need not be treated the same. Moreover, Article 15(3) allows for special treatment of this class of women. The Court's approach to gender is thus one of emphasizing the difference. The Court recognized that there has been historical discrimination against women insofar as they have been denied property rights. Yet it proceeded to treat the difference between men and women as natural, and in so doing, adopted a protectionist approach. The Court explicitly stated women are weaker than men and thus, in need of protection. There is no further interrogation of the deeper relationships of oppression that create these inequalities, such as the sexual division of labour which renders women economically dependent on men.[120]

In *K. Shanmukhan* v. *G. Sarojini*[121] Section 124(1) (b) of the

---

[118] Ibid., at 530 para 3.

[119] Ibid.

[120] In *Gupteshwar Pandey* v. *Smt. Ram Peari Devi*, A 1971 Pat. 181 the Court again held that section 488 was a special provision designed for the benefit or protection of women or children whose husbands or fathers failed to maintain them in spite of sufficient means, and thus within the scope of Article 15(3). The Court again adopts a formal approach to equality, within which Article 15(3) is understood as an exception to equality, and a protectionist approach to gender difference, according to which section 488 is justified on the basis that women are the weaker sex, and in need of special protection.

[121] 1981 Cr. L.J. 830 (Ker.)

Criminal Procedure Code was challenged as being in violation of Article 14 by discriminating between divorcees and wives whose marriages were subsisting. The provision entitles a divorced woman to maintenance, while a married woman is not entitled to maintenance if she refuses to live with her husband without sufficient reason, lives in adultery or lives separately by mutual consent. The Court adopted the reasonable classification test, and held that the classification was based on intelligible differentia.

In the Court's view divorced women and married women were differently situated. The conditions stipulated in the impugned legislation could only apply to married women; they were, by their very nature, inapplicable to divorced women. Similarly, the Court observed that divorced women were disentitled to maintenance in situations which do not apply to married women, such as, when divorced women remarry. The Court adopted a formal approach to equality, according to which the differences between married and divorced women were deemed to be sufficient to defeat the challenge. There is no interrogation of whether the legal treatment disadvantages wives.

Further, the approach to difference is essentialist, that is, in the Court's view, the differences between married women and divorced women were seen as natural, as part of the nature of the institution of marriage. There was no consideration of the extent to which these differences are in fact a product of the legal regulation of marriage, that is, married women and divorced women are different because the law treats them differently. Rather than considering the question of economic dependence and economic need, a criteria according to which married and divorced women may be similarly situated, the Court justified the differential entitlement of maintenance on the basis of the accepted differences. The case illustrates how virtually any difference, including those differences created solely through law, can be found to be intelligible criteria, and thereby satisfy the reasonable classification test of the formal equality approach.

The constitutionality of Section 125 of the Criminal Procedure Code has been considered in a number of cases. These cases have involved applications for maintenance under Section 125, and although the Courts have referred to the equality provisions, the cases are not strictly speaking, constitutional challenges. In *Mustt. Sahida Begum* v. *Md. Mofizul Haque*,[122] the Court held that if the

---

[122] 1986 Cr. L.J. 102 (Ori.).

personal law was held to be final, with the conclusion that a divorced woman cannot claim any further maintenance beyond the period of iddat, a discrimination would occur between the divorced muslim woman and divorced women belonging to other religions or castes. The court rejected the challenge.

The Court can be seen to have based its decision on a substantive approach to equality in so far as it considered how the difference in this instance disadvantages. Religion cannot be a basis for reasonable classification. The Court upheld the premise on which maintenance was granted, which is economic necessity. It clearly states that the relevant criteria must be economic necessity, and that the section is meant to protect the distresses of all wives, including divorced women, irrespective of religion or castes, for their future life until remarriage. At the same time the Court does not outline the reasons for women's economic dependence. It is stated as a fact, and the implicit assumption is that it is a natural and unalterable condition of women.[123]

iii. Prostitution

Several challenges have been made to the provisions of the Prevention of Immoral Traffic in Women and Children Act (PITA). Two early cases involved challenges to Section 20 of PITA. Section 20 permits the removal of prostitutes from any area in the interests

---

[123] In *Balan Nair* v. *Bhavani Amma Valsalamma*, A 1987 Ker. 110 the Kerala High Court commented, in obiter, on Section 125 of the Criminal Procedure Code:

Though Section 125 benefits a distressed father also, main thrust of the provision is to assist women and children in distress. That is fully consistent with Article 15(3) of the Constitution which states that the prohibition contained in the Article shall not prevent the State from making any special provision for women and children.... This provision is a measure of social justice and specially enacted to protect women and children.

The Court held that the provision was consistent with Article 15(3) and could benefit a distressed father although the main thrust was to assist women and children in distress. The Court cited a Supreme Court decision, *Ramesh Chander* v. *Veena Kaushal,* where it stated that 'the brooding presence of the constitutional empathy for the weaker sections like women and children must inform interpretation if it has to have social relevance.' The Court relied on social justice as an interpretive tool for constitutional provisions. The case does not elaborate beyond stating that 'men and women equally, have the right to an adequate means to livelihood' and that Article 15(3) enables the State to make special provisions for women and children.

of the general public. The Magistrate is further empowered to prohibit the prostitute woman from re-entering the place from which she has been removed. In *Smt. Shama Bai v State of Uttar Pradesh*,[124] Section 20 was challenged by a prostitute woman. She argued that prostitution was her hereditary trade, that it was the only means of her livelihood and that members of her family were economically dependent on her. The writ was filed primarily to prevent her landlord from using the provisions of PITA for evicting her from the premises. The Court held that the unfettered discretion conferred on the magistrate to remove any woman believed to be a prostitute from his jurisdiction by Section 20 violated Article 14. The Court held that prostitute women were subject to a punitive form of surveillance to which other women were not, and that this differential treatment constituted discrimination between persons who were similarly situated.[125]

In *The State Uttar Pradesh* v. *Kaushilya*,[126] Section 20 was again challenged as violating Article 14. The Supreme Court, in adopting the reasonable classification approach, held that the difference between prostitute women and non-prostitute women was a reasonable classification. Further, the Court ruled that there were real differences between a prostitute woman who does not demand in the public's interest any restrictions on her movements, and a prostitute, whose actions in public places call for the imposition of restrictions on her movements and even deportation. The object of PITA was not only to suppress immoral traffic in women and girls, but also to improve public morals by removing prostitutes from busy public places in the vicinity of religious and educational institutions.[127]

The decision in Kaushilya is based on a formal model of equality. The differences between prostitute and non-prostitute women, and the differences between prostitutes in busy localities and prostitutes

[124] A 1959 All. 57.

[125] The decision was progressive in many important respects. Most significantly, the Court was prepared to consider the work of prostitute women as a trade rather than a crime. It recognized that women entered the profession because of social and economic hardship, rather than immorality.

[126] A 1964 S.C. 416; The High Court had held that the delegation of power was unguided and unfettered; and that women who were similarly situated, that is, prostitute women, were being treated differently. It thus struck down the provision.

[127] *Begum* v. *State*, A 1963 Bom. 17 (relied on).

working discreetly, were seen to justify the differential treatment. The effect was to preclude an entitlement to equality for those women who fell into the 'problematic' classification: prostitute women working in busy areas. There was no interrogation of the basis for the ostensible differences. Rather, prostitute women were simply deemed different from other women because of their inherent immorality. The approach not only stigmatises prostitute women by justifying the crimialization of their work, but also uses moral considerations to distinguish them from all other women. Prostitute women thus become inherently bad and immoral, and need to be controlled by harsh penal provisions.

Several constitutional challenges to PITA have been made by brothel owners. The Courts have rejected these challenges, holding that brothel owners should not be allowed to take advantage of the Act.[128] These cases also adopted a formal approach to equality, and a difference approach to prostitute women. In Sayed Abdul Khair,[129] the Court held that the provisions of PITA were a reasonable classification since young women all over the world were special victims of the vice market. In Moainuddin,[130] the Court held that women and girls who solicit for prostitution were different from other women. While Sayed Abdul Khair was based on the need to protect women, in Moainuddin, the Court seemed more concerned with issues of morality. The differentiation is based on assumptions that these women are essentially bad. This differentiation disqualifies them from equality and perpetuates their situation and status as 'bad women'.

iv. Bail

Several challenges have been directed to Section 497(1) of the Criminal Procedure Code which allows the Court to grant bail in

---

[128] In *Sayed Abdul Khair* v. *Babubhai, Jamalbhai and Another,* 1974 Cr. L.J. 1337 (Bom.). the accused, a brothel keeper, challenged Section 15 (4) and 16 (1) of the Act as violating Article 14, on the basis that the sections discriminated between girls and women. The provisions empower a special police officer to enter any premises to remove any girl under the age of 21 years if she is carrying on or being made to carry on or attempts are being made to make her carry on any prostitution. In *Moainuddin* v. *State of 1986* Cr. L.J. 1397 (A.P.l) Section 8 of the Immoral Traffic (Prevention) Act, that punishes women or girls soliciting for the purposes of prostitution, was challenged by a brothel keeper as violating Article 14.

[129] Ibid., Sayed Abdul Khair at 1349 para 14.

[130] Ibid., at 1398 para 4.

non-bailable cases when: the accused is under 16 years of age; a woman; sick; or infirm. In *Nirmal Kumar Banerjee* v. *The State*,[131] the Calcutta High Court held that the constitutional validity of the provision had to be determined against Article 14, a general provision, read together with Article 15(3), a provision where the State was empowered to allow special treatment for women and children. The provision was held to constitute a reasonable classification, as a female, or a person below 16 years of age, or an infirm person, were not likely to interfere with the investigation or to delay the trial by abscondence or interference.

While the Court adopts a 'holistic approach' to the equality provisions, it continues to interpret discrimination in a way that means any distinction, rather than distinctions that disadvantage within the broader meaning of equality. In so doing, the Court's understanding can be seen to be firmly located within a formal model of equality. It upholds the provision by adopting a protectionist position whereby women are to be treated in the same way as a person under 16 or someone with an infirmity. Women are seen as weak, as incapable of exercising basic rights in the same way as children and the infirm, and thereby in need of protection.

Similarly, in *Mt. Choki* v. *State of Rajasthan*,[132] the Court held that Section 497(1) of the Criminal Procedure Code, in providing for special provisions in favour of women and children, was within the scope of Article 15(3). The decision was based on the reasoning that, for the purposes of bail, women and children are different from men. The assumption informing the decision is that women are caretakers of the home and thus need to be accommodated so that the home does not suffer. The reasoning is thus based on an protectionist understanding of gender and or women's roles in the home. There is no inquiry into the institutional and structural discriminations that are responsible for keeping women in the home and in the role of primary care givers.

E. *Education*

The case law in this area has involved challenges to the admission practices of educational institutions. In one set of cases, female students have been denied or restricted access to particular schools

---

[131] 1972 Cr. L.J. 1582 (Cal.).
[132] A 1975 Raj. 10.

and colleges. This restricted access has been challenged as discrimination on the basis of sex, and thus, in violation of Article 15. The Courts have generally upheld the restrictions. The grounds have been varied, but the approaches have predominantly been narrow and technical, focusing for example on the meaning of discrimination and/or the significance of 'only on the basis of sex'. The Courts have generally been unwilling to find such admission practices to be discrimination on the basis of sex. In considering these restrictions under Article 15(3), the courts have emphasized the objective of the practices, namely, the attempt to promote schools and colleges specifically for women. The admission practices are thereby seen as preferential treatment as authorized by Article 15(3). While the result could be supported by a substantive model of equality, the discourse of the decisions remain informed by a model of formal equality.

In *Anjali Roy* v. *State of W.B.*[133] an order of the Director of Public Institution directing that no more women students be admitted to College A, but only to College B was challenged as violating Article 15. The High Court held that there was no discrimination within the meaning of Article 15(1) and upheld the restricted access. The Court adopted the technical approach of 'only on the ground of sex', and concluded that no 'discrimination was made against the appellant only on the ground that she was a woman.'[134] The refusal to admit the appellant was, according to the Court, not only on the ground of sex but 'due to the introduction of a comprehensive scheme for the provision of education facilities to both male and female students.'[135]

The cardinal fact is that she was not refused admission merely because she was a woman, but because under a scheme of better organization of both male and female students at Hooghly, which covered development of the Women's College as a step towards the advancement of female education....[136]

The holding is consistent with a corrective approach to gender difference and a substantive model of equality, that is, women's difference must be recognized to overcome historic disadvantage,

[133] Supra note 19.
[134] Ibid., at 830 para 17.
[135] Ibid.
[136] Ibid.

yet the decision of the Court was firmly located within a formal model of equality. While recognizing that discrimination involves invidious distinctions, the Court adopted the formal equality approach to the relationship between Articles 15(1) and 15(3), and as such, could hold that special provisions for women were legitimate, although they allowed invidious discrimination against men.[137] The Court did not consider invidious discrimination within the broader context of substantive inequalities, but only within a formal equality context, such that invidious discrimination can be directed equally at men as at women. The only difference is that Article 15(3) permits the former, and not the latter.

The Court subsequently noted the exclusion of sex from Article 29(2) which deals specifically with admission to educational institutions:[138]

The framers of the constitution may have thought that because of the physical and mental differences between men and women and considerations incidental thereto, exclusion of men from certain institutions serving women only, and vice versa would not be hostile or unreasonable discrimination.[139]

This passing reference to 'physical and mental differences between men and women' is significant. While the Court does not specifically endorse this explicit statement of natural and essential gender differences, the failure to interrogate the assumptions suggests that it is not seen as controversial, and in fact, reinforces this view of essential differences.[140]

In University of *Madras* v. *Shanta Bai,*[141] and order directing that women students not be admitted to affiliated colleges without

---

[137] Ibid., at 831 para 20.

[138] Article 29 of the Constitution provides:

1. Any section of the citizens residing in the territory of India or any part thereof having a distinct language, script or culture of its own shall have the right to conserve the same.

2. No citizen shall be denied admission into any educational institution maintained by the State of receiving aid out of State funds on grounds only of religion, race, caste, language or any of them.

[139] Supra note 19 at 831 para 22.

[140] Ibid. But the Court declined the rule on the relationship between Articles 29(2) and 15.

[141] A 1954 Mad. 67.

receiving special permission was challenged as violating Article 15. The Court held that the university was not part of the State within the meaning of Article 12, and is therefore not subject to the prohibitions of Article 15.[142] However, the Court then considered the relationship between Article 15 and Article 29(2) of the Constitution,[143] and held:

...The true scope of Article 15(3) is that notwithstanding Article 15(1), it will be lawful for the State to establish educational institutions solely for women and that the exclusion of men students from such institutions would not contravene Article 15(1). The combined effect of both Articles 15(3) and 29(2) is that while men students have no right of admission to women's colleges, the right of women to admission in other colleges is a matter within the regulation of the authorities of these colleges.[144]

The Court further discussed the reasons underlying these admission policies, namely the insufficient number of women's colleges to accommodate the demand.

In a later set of cases, the allotment of seats for female students within educational institutions has been the subject of constitutional challenges. In *Balaji* v. *State of Mysore*,[145] for example, the Supreme Court held that Article 15(4) could not be interpreted so as to render 15(1) nugatory, and therefore, that reservations could not exceed 50 per cent. An issue that has subsequently arisen is whether the allotment of seats for women constitutes a reservation within the meaning of 15(4), and thus, whether the allotment of these seats are to be considered in calculating the permissible 50 per cent. The judicial approach to the issue has been divided. Sometimes this allotment of seats for women has been held to be a reservation.[146]

---

[142] Educational institutions will fall within the scope of Article 15 only if they are state maintained; the University of Madras is state-aided, but not state maintained.

[143] Supra note 141 at 70 para 9 ['...the omission of 'sex' in Article 29(2) would appear to be a deliberate departure from the language of Article 15(1) and its object must have been to leave it to the educational authorities to make their own rules suited to the conditions and not to force on them an obligation to admit women'].

[144] Ibid.

[145] A 1963 S.C. 649.

[146] In *Subhash Chandra* v. *State*. A 1973 All. 295 the Court held that the allotment of seats for women in medical school was a reservation, and thus, to be taken into account in calculating the total reservation of seats. The Court

Other times the allotment has been designated as an 'indication of source', and not a reservation.[147]

F. *Family Law*

Constitutional challenges to family laws on the ground of sex discrimination have met with very mixed results.[148] In some cases, the Courts have held that laws which treat women differently than men are discriminatory and thus, in violation of the equality guarantees. Indeed, some cases recognize that the discriminatory treatment is based on sexist attitudes and practices which reinforce women's subordination. The approach adopted by those courts is one of formal equality and sameness—women and men are the same, and thus ought to be treated the same in law. However, other cases have rejected the challenges to family laws. These cases, though also adopting a formal model of equality, emphasise the differences between women and men, and thus, preclude interrogation of substantive inequalities.

---

held: ['the Sub-articles (3) and (4) of Article 15 classify women and children, socially...as distinct groups. If the State Government makes reservations for these groups it cannot be said that classification is not based on rational differentia. The objective of these reservations in favour of various categories of candidates is obviously to make special provision for their advancement']. The Court thus concluded that such reservations were within the scope of Article 15(3), and did not offend Article 15(1).

[147] In *Sukhvinder Kaur v. State*, A 1974 H.P. 35 the High Court refused to treat the allotment of seats for women, as well as those allotted for other diverse categories which did not come within the definition of backward classes as 'reservation'.In *Padmaraj Samarendra v. State of Bihar and Another*, A 1979 Pat. 266, the Court held that the allotment of seats for female students was not a reservation in the strict sense. Reservations involve the allotment of seats 'for the reasons that the persons for whom the seats are earmarked should be educationally, socially or culturally backward and require protection.' In this case, according to the Court, the allotment of seats for women was not for this reason, but rather, based on the state's need for more female doctors in government hospitals. Thus, the Court held that the allotment was not a reservation, but an allotment of source. The Court further held that since the reason for the allotment was the state need for female doctors, the allotment was not 'only on the grounds of sex', and thus, did not violate Article 15(1).

[148] Challenges to social reform in personal law, on the basis of violating equality rights under Articles 14 and 15 have generally been dismissed by the Courts. See, for example, *Gogireddy Sambireddy v. Gogireddy Jayamma and Another*, A 1972 A.P. 156. As Seervai notes, it has generally been held that ['...the State is entitled to proceed by stages and to consider whether any particular community

i. Divorce

Section 10 of the Divorce Act (1869) which provides that a husband may petition for divorce on the basis of his wife's adultery alone, but that a wife may only petition for divorce on the basis of her husband's adultery coupled with desertion, cruelty, rape, incest or bigamy, has been challenged as violating Articles 14 and 15. In an early case, *Dwaraka Bai* v. *Professor N. Mathews,*[149] the Court held that Section 10 was based on differences in adultery committed by women and men, and thus consituted a sensible classification.

A husband commits an adultery somewhere but he does not bear a child as a result of such adultery, and make it the legitimate child of his wife's to be maintained by the wife. He cannot bear a child nor is his wife bound to maintain the child. But if the wife commits adultery, she may bear a child as a result of such adultery and the husband will have to treat it as his legitimate child and will be liable to maintain that child under s. 488....[150]

According to the Court, these differences justified the different grounds for divorce, and Section 10 was upheld.

More recently, in *Swapna Ghosh* v. *Sadananda Ghosh,*[151] Section 10 was again challenged. After reviewing the justification for this provision, namely, that a husband would not bear a child to be maintained by his wife, but a wife might bear a child to be maintained by her husband,[152] the Court held:

I would like to think that even assuming that the liability to conceive as a result of adulterous inter-course may otherwise be a reasonable ground for classification between a husband and a wife permissible under Article

---

governed by the personal law is ripe enough for reform to proceed']. *Seervai,* supra note 10, at 403. The focus of the subsequent discussion is thus on constitutional challenges specifically dealing with allegations of sex discrimination within particular personal laws, not as between different personal laws.
[149] A 1953 Mad. 792.
[150] Ibid., at 800 para 30.
[151] A 1989 Cal. 1.
[152] The Court noted that the only defence for this provision was that stated in *Dwarka Bai* v. *Mathews,* supra note 149, at para 3, namely, where the Court held that since the husband even by committing adultery 'does not bear a child as a result and make it a child of his wife to be maintained by the wife,' the wife by committing adultery 'may bear a child as a result of such adultery and the husband will have to treat it as his legitimate child and will be liable to maintain that child under Section 488, Criminal Procedure Code....'

14, since a wife conceives and the husband does not only because of the peculiarities of their respective sex, any discrimination on such ground would be a discrimination on the ground of sex alone against the mandatory prohibition of Article 15.[153]

The Court, however, concluded that the case could be decided without a determination of these issues:

My only endeavour is to draw the attention of our concerned legislature to these anachronistic incongruities and the provisions of Article 15 of the Constitution forbidding all discrimination on the ground of Religion or Sex and also to Article 44 staring at our face for four decades with its solemn directive to frame a UCC.[154]

On the facts, the Court confirmed the divorce decree in favour of the wife on the grounds of the husband's adultery, cruelty and desertion.[155]

While the decisions reached in these two challenges to Section 10 of the Divorce Act were different, the reasoning informing the decisions is similar in many important respects. Firstly, both decisions are located within a formal model of equality. In Dwaraka Bai, women and men were seen as different, and therefore as not qualifying for equal treatment. In Ghosh, the Court similarly accepted that the differences between women and men might be the basis for a reasonable classification for the purposes of Article 14. However, the decision in Ghosh turned on the Court's approach to Article 15. The Court adopted the 'only on the ground of sex' approach to Article 15(1), and that any differential treatment on the basis of the reproductive differences between women and men would constitute discrimination 'only on the ground of sex'. In the Court's view, sex was an absolutely prohibited ground for classification, and thus, Section 10 of the Divorce Act which did not treat women and men the same, was in violation of Article 15(1). Further, the two decisions adopt very similar approaches to gender difference. In Dwaraka Bai, the differences between women and men justified the different

[153] Supra note 151, at 3 para 3.

[154] Ibid., at 3 para 4.

[155] Ibid., at 5 para 9. More specifically, the divorce decree was confirmed 'on the ground that the husband-respondent is guilty of adultery coupled with such cruelty as without adultery would have justified a decree of judicial separation and also of adultery coupled with desertion without reasonable excuse for two years and more.'

grounds for divorce. In Ghosh, the differences between women and men did not justify the different grounds for divorce. Notwithstanding these differences, women and men had to be treated the same. Yet, both decisions focus on the same biological differences of reproduction. Both decisions view these differences as natural and as the only possible justification for the differential treatement. Both decisions collapse the biological differences of reproduction with the gender differences that have been socially constructed— differences that have also come to be viewed as natural and inevitable. The decisions are informed by the same understanding of difference, the only distinction between them being the legal significance of this difference. The two decisions, although different in their result, can be seen as located within the same discourse of formal equality and a very similar discourse of gender difference.

ii. Restitution of Conjugal Rights

Section 9 of the Hindu Marriage Act, which provides for the remedy of restitution of conjugal rights, has repeatedly been challenged as violating Article 14.[156] In *Sareetha* v. *Venkata Subbaiah*,[157] the Court held that Section 9 did not meet the traditional classification test, and was thus unconstitutional. The Court noted that Section 9 did not discriminate between husband and wife on its face, in so far as 'the remedy of restitution of conjugal rights' is 'equally available to both wife and husband', and it thus 'apparently satisfies the equality test'.[158] Notwithstanding this formal equality, the Court then turned its attention to the operation of the remedy.

In our social reality, this matrimonial remedy is found used almost exclusively by the husband and is rarely resorted to by the wife.... The reason for this mainly lies in the fact of the differences between the men and the women. By enforcing a decree for restitution of conjugal rights the life pattern of the wife is likely to be altered irretrievably whereas the husband's can remain almost as it was before. This is so because it is the wife who has to beget and bear a child. This is practical, but the inevitable

---

[156] See also *Swaraj Garg* v. *K.M. Garg*, A 1978 Del. 296, in considering the interpretation of Section 9, wherein the Court held that any law that gave husbands the exclusive right to decide the place of the matrimonial home without considering the merits of the wife's claim would violate Article 14.

[157] A 1983 A.P. 356.

[158] Ibid., at 373 para 38.

consequence of the enforcement of this remedy cripples the wife's future plans of life and pevents her from using this self destructive remedy. Thus the use of the remedy of restitution of conjugal rights in reality becomes partial and one-sided and available only to the husband....[159]

The Court thus held:

As a result, this remedy works in practice only as an engine of oppression to be operated by the husband for the benefit of the husband against the wife. By treating the wife and husband who are inherently unequal as equals, Section 9 of the Act offends the rule of equal protection of law. For that reason the formal equality that Section 9 of the Act ensures cannot be accepted as constitutional.[160]

The Court in Sareetha concluded that notwithstanding the gender neutrality of the provisions regarding the restitution of conjugal rights, the law had a disparate impact on women. The law is used primarily by husbands against their wives; not by wives against their husbands. Accordingly, the Court concluded that the law operated 'as an engine of oppression' against women. The Court thus moved beyond a formal equality approach to consider the substantive inequalities which are produced by the operation of the law.

The approach in Sareetha, however, is not entirely unproblematic. Firstly, while the Court seems on the one hand to expressly reject formal equality as inadequate, the language of the decision on the other hand retains this understanding of equality. For example, the Court specifically concludes that women and men are unequals, and therefore ought not be treated the same. The conclusion is cast in the language of formal equality rather than moving beyond it. Moreover, the decision is problematic in its approach to difference. In the Court's view, the inequalities produced by the law are a result of the differences between women and men. The Court focuses on the biological differences of reproductions, and, presents the differences between women and men as natural and inevitable. Yet, there is much more at stake than biological differences. The oppression to which the Court refers is not merely the product of biological difference. It is a product of the sexual division of

[159] Ibid.
[160] Ibid.

labour in general, and the social relations of child rearing in particular, which have been constructed around these biological differences, whereby women have been allocated the responsibility for child care.

While women's role in child rearing is often seen as a natural consequence of women's role in child bearing and thus, as biologically determined, biological differences are relevant only in terms of pregnancy and breast feeding. Beyond these early periods of infancy, women's responsibility for child care is a social, not a natural phenomenon. However, in Sareetha, these differences are collapsed, and women's role in child care is seen as a natural product of biological difference.

The approach of the Court to equality is commendable, in so far as it recognizes the impact of child rearing on women. However, the approach to difference is somewhat problematic in so far as it reduces this difference to a natural one. The decision exemplifies some of the dilemmas presented by difference. If difference exists, and matters in the lives of individuals, then it must be recognized. Yet, in recognizing difference, we risk reinforcing the underlying social inequalities that produce these differences. In the context of Sareetha, the dilemma is how to recognize the impact of child rearing on women, without reinforcing the social inequalities that have produced this sexual division of labour.

In *Harvinder Kaur* v. *Harmander Singh Choudhry*,[161] Section 9 of the Hindu Marriage Act was again challenged. However, in this case, the Delhi High Court rejected the challenge and declined to follow the case of Sareetha. The Court noted that while Sareetha was based on the assertion that 'a suit for restitution by the wife is rare', this was only true prior to the enactment of the Hindu Marriage Act. Since the Hindu Marriage Act was amended in 1964 allowing either party of the marriage to petition under Section 13.

There is complete equality of sexes here and equal protection of the laws.[162]

The Court was only concerned with formal equality, that is, with whether women and men were treated as formal equals under the

---

[161] A 1984 Del. 55.
[162] Ibid., at 75 para 44.

law. There is no consideration of the impact of the law, nor in turn, whether there is a disparate impact of the law on women.

In rejecting the challenge, the Court further held that the Constitution ought not to be applied to the family.

Introduction of Constitutional Law in the home is most inappropriate. It is like introducing a bull in a china shop. It will prove to be a ruthless destroyer of the marriage institution and all that it stands for. In the privacy of the home and the married life, neither Article 21 nor Article 14 have any place. In a sensitive sphere which is at once most intimate and delicate, the introduction of the cold principles of Constitutional Law will have the effect of weakening the marriage bond.[163]

In the Court's view, the application of constitutional law would encourage litigation within the marital relationship. Litigation which should be discouraged as far as possible.

The reasoning in Harvinder Kaur is a classic statement of the understanding of the family as private and of the public/private distinction. The family is understood as private, and thus beyond the appropriate intervention of the law. This public/private distinction has been an important dimension of the legal reinforcement of women's subordination.[164] Women have traditionally been confined to the private sphere of the family, as wives and mothers, sisters and daughters; and their access to the public sphere has been denied. The public/private distinction has been used to insu-

---

[163] The Court further articulated its understanding of the family as private, and thus beyond the scope of the Constitution: ['In the home the consideration that really obtains is the natural love and affect which counts for so little in these cold Courts']. Ibid., at para 45. In support of its view, the Court cited the 1919 English case of *Balfour* v. *Balfour* 2 KB 571 which in its view: ['...illustrates that the house of everyone is to him his castle and fortress. The spouses can claim a kind of sacred protection behind the door of the family home which, generally speaking, the civil authority may not penetrate. The introduction of Constitutional Law into the ordinary domestic relationship of husband and wife will strike at the very root of that relationship and will be a fruitful source of dissension and quarrelling'].

[164] Madhu Kishwar, 'Some Aspects of Bondage: The Denial of Fundamental Rights to Women', *Manushi* 31 (Jan.–Feb. 1983), argues that the family structure in India reinforces the subordination of women in a way that precludes women's access to fundamental rights. At 31–32, she writes: ['The feature which most distinguishes women's oppression is that the denial of their most basic rights takes place first and foremost within the family. This is done so effectively that

late from legal review the discrimination that women face within the private sphere of the family. Discriminatory practices, ranging from unequal inheritance rights, to sexual assault, to dowry death have been, and continue to be justified on the ground that they occur within the private sanctuary of the family, and are thus beyond the scope of the law.

The constitutionality of Section 9 of the Hindu Marriage Act was considered by the Supreme Court in *Saroj Rani* v. *Sudarshan Kumar*.[165] The Court held that restitution of conjugal rights did not violate Article 14, thus affirming the decision in Harvinder Kaur and overruling the decision in Sareetha. According to the Court:

In India it must be borne in mind that conjugal rights, i.e. the right of the husband or the wife to the society of the other spouse is not merely a creature of the statute. Such a right is inherent in the very institution of marriage itself.[166]

In the Court's view, there were sufficient procedural safeguards to prevent Section 9 'from being a tyranny', and that the decree was only intended where the disobedience was willful. The Court further held that the decree for the restitution of conjugal rights 'serves a social purpose as an aid to the prevention of the break-up of marriage,' and thus concluded without any further equality analysis that it did not violate Article 14. While the Court implicitly adopts the approach to equality and gender of the Delhi High

---

the hand of the government or of any similar repressive agency is seldom visible in keeping women oppressed. That is why it is easy to dismiss such violations as private family affairs rather than as social and political issues. But if we examine closely how the family functions in keeping women subjected we can begin to see how an exploitative family structure receives crucial support from the government and the state through various laws and rules of behaviour which legitimate the authority of the male members over the lives of women members of the family']; see also Nandita Haksar, *Demystification of Law for Women* 58 (1986); Nadine Taub and Elizabeth Schneider, 'Perspectives on Women's Subordination and the Role of Law', in *The Politics of Law* (D. Kairyns (ed.), 1982); Frances Olsen, 'The Myth of State Intervention', 18 *Mich. L. Rev.* 835 (1985); Judy Fudge, 'The Public/Private Distinction: The Possibilities of and the Limits to Further Feminist Struggles', 25 *Osgoode Hall L.J.* 485 (1987).
[165] A 1984 S.C. 1562.
[166] Ibid., at 1562 para 15.

Court in Harvinder Kaur, it does not expressly state or develop its own views in this regard.[167]

iii. Succession Laws

Several challenges have been made to the laws of succession. These challenges have overwhelmingly unsuccessful. In *Mukta Bai* v. *Kamalaksha*[168] Hindu personal law which excluded illegitimate daughters from maintenance from the estate of their putative fathers was challenged as violating Article 14. In rejecting the challenge, the Court held:

The fact that the law makes no provision for the maintenance of an illegitimate daughter cannot be said to amount to discrimination against illegitimate daughters, such as would amount to violation of Article 14 of the Constitution.[169]

The reasoning in the decision is entirely conclusory. There is no consideration of Article 14 case law, nor any analysis of why the distinction did not amount of discrimination.

Challenges to the Hindu Succession Act, 1956, on the ground that it discriminated on the basis of sex, brought overwhelmingly by men have been rejected by the courts. For example, in *Kaur Singh* v. *Jaggar Singh*[170] Section 14, which provides a female Hindu with the right of absolute ownership over her property was challenged as discriminatory.[171] While the Court acknowledged

[167] It should be noted that the Supreme Court did not comment on the holding in Harvinder Kaur regarding the non-applicability of the Constitution to the legal regulation of the family. Further, more recent cases involving challenges to personal laws have not strictly followed Harvinder Kaur in so far as the non-applicability of the Constitution to the legal regulation of the family is concerned. For example, in *Krishna Murthy* v. *P.S. Uma*, 1987 A.P. 237. *Swapna Gosh* v. *Sadananda Gosh*, supra note 151; and *Lalitha Ubhayamkar and Another* v. *Union of India and Another*, A 1991 Kar. 186; the courts were willing to consider constitutional challenges to the Hindu Marriage Act, the Divorce Act (1869), and the Hindu Adoptions and Maintenance Act, respectively. The ideology of privacy was not invoked, as in Harvinder Kaur, to preclude an analysis of the operation of the provisions of relating to the legal regulation of the family.

[168] A 1960 Mys. 182.

[169] Ibid., at 183 para 5.

[170] A 1961 Punj. 489.

[171] The plaintiffs argued that the effect of Section 14 was discrimination in the powers of alienation of property between women and men. While women had by virtue of Section 14 absolute ownership and thus absolute rights of alienation,

that the Hindu Succession Act did create an apparent anomaly in the powers of alienation of property, it held that the removal of such remained the prerogative of the legislature, not the courts. The Court held that 'it may well be that in view of the inferior status enjoyed by the females, the Legislature thought fit to put the females on a higher pedestal', which was within the purview of Article 15(3).[172] It further held that women as a class were different from men as a class and the legislature had merely removed the disability attaching to women.

In *Partap Singh v. Union of India*,[173] Section 14(1) was again challenged as violating Articles 14 and 15(1). The Court found that Section 14(1) was enacted to address the problem faced by Hindu women who were unable to claim absolute interest in properties inherited from their husbands, but rather, who could only enjoy these properties with the restrictions attached to widow's estates under Hindu law. As a special provision intended to benefit and protect women who have traditionally been discriminated against in terms of access to property, it was not open to Hindu males to challenge the provision as hostile discrimination. Rather, the Court concluded that the provision was protected by Article 15(3), which in its view, 'overrides clause 15(1)'.[174] While the Court thus upheld the provision, the approach to equality and to gender on which it did so remains unclear. The decision could be informed by either a protective approach (women need special provisions to protect them) or a corrective approach (women have historically been discriminated against and require special provisions to correct). The Court's reference to the traditional problems that women faced in property ownership is suggestive of the latter.

In *Sonubhai Yeshwant Jabhar* v. *Bala Govinda Yadav and Others*[175] Section 15(2) of the Hindu Succession Act was challenged as discriminating on the basis of sex, and thus being in violation of Articles 14 and 15. Section 15(2) (b) provides that the property inherited from a husband of a female Hindu dying intestate will

---

men who were still governed by the Punjab Customary Law were not free to dispose of ancestral immoveable property by will.

[172] Ibid., at 493 para 13.

[173] A 1985 S.C. 1695.

[174] Ibid., at 1697 para 6.

[175] A 1983 Bom. 156.

devolve upon the heirs of the husband, whereas Section 8, dealing with the property of a male Hindu dying intestate does not make any such provision regarding property inherited from his wife. In rejecting the challenge, the Court held that the rules were enacted with the clear intention of ensuring the continuity of the property within the husband's line. The assumption that property should be passed down through the male line is so deeply held that the Court does not question the gender bias of the assumption. The historic discrimination against women in inheritance has created a norm, that property is passed through the male line, and it is against that norm that any challenges to the practice are measured, and ultimately rejected.

iv. Maintenance

Constitutional challenges have been directed to the maintenance provisions of several family law statutes. In *Puranananda Banerjee* v. *Sm. Swapan Banerjee and Another,*[176] section 36 of the Special Marriage Act, which provides for a grant of alimony *pendente lite* to a wife was challenged as violating Article 15. In upholding the section, the Court held that it did not discriminate only on the basis of sex, but rather provided maintenance where the wife had no independent income sufficient for her support. The Court further held that even if Section 36 did discriminate on the basis of sex alone, it would be protected by Article 15(3).

The Court has approached the question of the constitutionality of Section 36 from the perspective of formal equality. In its effort to uphold the provision, the Court first adopted the technical approach of 'only on the ground of sex'. Rather then viewing women's economic dependency as a socially constructed gender difference, the Court severed sex from what sex socially implies. The formal model of equality is echoed in the Court's understanding of discrimination, that is as any distinction on the prohibited grounds, which is justified under Article 15(3).

The objective of the Court in this case is laudable, it sought to uphold legislation specifically designed to address women's economic dependency in the family. However, this objective could be better served by a substantive approach to equality, which directs attention to whether the rule in question contributes to the

[176] A 1981 Cal. 123.

disadvantage of women, and a corrective approach to gender, which acknowledges that women may need to be treated differently to make up for past disadvantage. Within such an approach, the provision could be upheld on the ground that it takes gender difference into account to compensate for past disadvantage. The reality of women's economic dependence, resulting from the sexual division of labour within the family, requires that provisions exist to recognize and compensate women for this dependence.[177]

Conclusion

In this chapter, we have attempted to provide a comprehensive review of the High Court and Supreme Court constitutional cases on sex discrimination. We have argued that this case law is primarily informed by a formal model of equality that is an understanding of equality as sameness, and a disqualification of those who are different from an entitlement to equality. We have tried to reveal the ways in which this understanding of equality has lead to a focus on the relevance of gender difference.

In one set of cases, the courts have held that women are different than men; that women are weaker and in need of protection. This difference is used to virtually disentitle women to any claim to equality. In upholding legislation, this approach cannot distinguish between differential treatment that disadvantages and differential treatment that advantages. It cannot, in other words, distinguish between legislation that further contributes to women's subordination, and legislation that attempts to correct or compensate for that subordination. Rather, any and all differential treatment can be justified on the basis that women are essentially and biologically different.

In the second set of cases, the courts have held that for the purposes of legislation, women and men are the same, and therefore must be treated the same in law. The sameness approach has been

---

[177] In *Krishna Murthy* v. *P.S. Umadevi,* A 1987 A.P. 237, Section 24 of the Hindu Marriage Act was challenged as violating Article 14, on the basis that a spouse's liability for alimony was vague, particularly as compared to the Divorce Act, where a husband's liability for alimony was expressly limited to a maximum of 1/5 of his income. In a brief decision, the High Court rejected the challenge, and held that there was no individious discrimination or undue disability to the wife or the husband.

used to uphold legislation that treats women and men the same, and to strike down legislation that treats women differently. However, in striking down the legislation, this approach cannot distinguish as between differential treatment that disadvantages and differential treatment that advantages. Like the protectionist approach, there is no distinction between protectionist legislation that discriminates against women, and corrective legislation that attempts to compensate for past discrimination. In comparison to the protectionist approach, the sameness approach would strike down both protectionist and corrective legislation.

In contrast to formal equality, we have described a second substantive model of equality, and have attempted to reveal the limited extent to which this alternative vision of equality has informed judicial interpretations. In this model, equality is not a question of sameness and difference, but rather a question of disadvantage. Within a substantive model of equality the central question is whether the impugned legislation contributes to the subordination of the disadvantaged group, or to overcoming that subordination. This model of equality creates space for a third approach to gender difference, that is a corrective approach. This third, though very small set of cases recognizes that to correct or compensate for past discrimination, women *may* have to be treated differently.

By asking different questions, then, the substantive approach to equality can direct attention to, and distinguish between protective and corrective legislation, that is, rules that contribute to women's subordination, and rules that contribute to overcoming that subordination. This model can be used to strike down protective legislation, and to uphold corrective legislation. Moreover, this model of equality still leaves room for a sameness approach; that is, by focusing on the relative advantage and disadvantages of women the inquiry can lead to the conclusion that in a particular context, gender difference ought to be irrelevant, and women and men ought to be treated the same.

7

Rights, Bodies and the Law: Rethinking Feminist Politics of Justice*

Nivedita Menon

It is generally assumed that law should be the institutionalized pursuit of justice, or to put it another way, that 'law ought to try to imitate justice' (Sharp, 1990: 28). Thus, while it is accepted that there would always be an excess of justice which cannot be captured by the law, counter-hegemonic political practices reflect the belief that the processes of the law can be forced to reflect the ideal of justice, however imperfectly, incompletely or unwillingly.

The questions this paper addresses are—does law have the capacity to pursue justice, and more fundamentally, can 'justice' be conceived of in a universal sense as suggested for example, by the term 'social justice'. Both questions seem to require a negative answer.

The first assumes that power, the unequal dynamics of which constitute injustice, is juridically, derived. But as Foucault points out, while many of the juridical forms of power continue to persist, these have 'gradually been penetrated by quite new mechanisms of power that are probably irreducible to the representation of the law.... We have engaged for centuries in a type of society in which the juridical is increasingly incapable of coding power, of serving as its system of representation' (1978: 89). This is why, I would argue, our

* Earlier versions and parts of this paper have been published in Patricia Oberoi (ed.), *Social Reform, Sexuality and the State*, Sage: 1996, and Swapna Mukhopadhyay (ed.), *In the Name of Justice*, Manohar: 1998.

attempts to transform power relations through law tend rather, to resediment these relations and to reassert dominant values.

The second question can be addressed in the following way. In the course of this paper I will attempt to shift the assumption underlying understandings of rights, that these are universal and based on a generally accepted moral order. I argue that rights come into being within specific sets of shared norms of justice and equality. However, legal discourse, through which rights are sought to be institutionalized, is marked by the movement towards certainty and exactitude. What are the implications for the liberatory potential of rights once their meaning is fixed by law? If, as I seek to establish, rights are constituted by the values derived from specific moral universes, there is a singularity to justice, a uniqueness which as Derrida puts it, must always concern 'individuals, irreplaceable groups and lives, the other or myself *as* the other in a unique situation' (1990: 949). This uniqueness however, is at odds with law, which must take a general form, as norm and as rule.

In Derrida's understanding of justice, the very condition of justice is that one must address oneself to the other in the language of the other. There is violence involved in judging persons in an idiom they do not share, perhaps even understand. But this violence is obscured by the appeal to 'justice' as a universal value, as to a third party 'who suspends the unilaterality or singularity of the idioms' (1990: 955). Derrida emphasizes that to recognize this paradox is not to abdicate before the question of justice or to deny the opposition between just and unjust. Rather, it involves a responsibility to a 'historical and interpretative memory' (ibid.), that is, to recall the history, the origin and subsequent direction, of concepts of justice and the law. In this way we would be desedimenting the values embedded in the idea of justice as a universal concept. These values have assumed the status of natural presuppositions and the violence of the moment of their imposition has been rendered invisible through a kind of historical amnesia. To interrogate points of origin constantly, to question the grounds of the norms which underlie notions of justice at historically specific moments, is not to surrender an interest in justice. On the contrary, it 'hyperbolically raises the stakes of exacting justice' (ibid.).

The answer then, to the second question that this chapter engages with, is that the achievement of justice in a universal sense is an impossibility. At particular historical moments 'justice' is constituted by specific moral visions, but the discourse of the law is predicated upon the assumption that justice can be attained once and for all by the fixing of identity and meaning. The meaning delivered by law as *the* just one then gets articulated in complex ways with other discourses constituting identity, and tends to sediment dominant and oppressive possibilites rather than marginal and emancipatory ones.

I will engage with the two questions that I have outlined above, through an examination of the issues of abortion and sexual violence. I argue that unproblematized notions of 'body' and 'self' are embedded in feminist discourse on these two issues. The understanding is that 'the body' is a natural and physical object within which the self is located; and that 'sex' is a phenomenon which exists prior to all discourse, simply distinguishable from other kinds of human interaction.

This essay explores the possibility that what we need to take on board in our struggle to develop a feminist sense of self is that 'the body' and 'sex' are not 'natural' but produced by discourses. This is not to deny their 'reality' but to question the assumption that this 'reality' can be accessible outside of particular contexts. It would then become necessary to rethink the attempt to universalize one particular 'reality' through law.

Legal discourse produces the 'body' as an object that has to be one or the other of a series of binary oppositions—male/female, healthy/diseased, heterosexual/homosexual. On the other hand, the experience of 'self' and 'body' validated by feminism as 'real' acquires meaning precisely through an interplay of contexts, a movement that is halted by the rigid codifications required by legal discourse. The issues of abortion and sexual violence in particular, cast women as 'bodies' for both feminist and legal discourse. An examination of these issues would therefore be fruitful in terms of the questions raised above.

Questioning Rights

Both at a conceptual as well as at a political level, rights and law are quite distinctly connected. On the one hand, a social movement operating in the realm of law is constrained to use the language of rights because legal discourse is animated by the weighing of competing rights. In other words, to enter into the realm of law, rights-talk becomes obligatory. On the other hand, when a social movement makes claims based on rights, at some level these claims are predicated on the assumption that these rights should be protected by law. The language of rights thus tends to privilege the sphere of the state and its institutions.

We can trace the evolution of the understanding of rights from the first systematic development of the concept in ancient Rome, when rights were created by the law. For Roman jurists, rights, law and justice were inseparable, and the law was considered to be an expression of the community's conception of justice. Nevertheless rights did not imply absolute control, nor were they unlimited in scope. Rights operated in the realm of civil society, not in the realm of the state or the family, and governed relationships between individuals, not between individuals and the state. During the centuries of feudalism in Europe, rights continued to be conceived of in much the same way, with both individuals as well as communities and groups being the bearers of rights. Indeed, the 'individual' was not clearly separable from his community, work or land. The process of individuation which was to be both empowering as well as severely alienating, began later. Moreover, rights were derived from customs and traditions as well as from law, and all sources of rights had equal validity.

From the seventeenth century, rights began to be seen as inhering in individuals, rather than in groups or communities. This individual, detached from social context and conceived of as constituted by the limits of the body, was clearly male, as feminist critiques have pointed out (see for example, Landes, 1988). Male bodies, being clearly bounded and solid were considered perfect. Female bodies, on the other hand, were seen as disorderly and penetratable and subject to cyclical changes; their bodily processes were messy and challenged the idea of the closed and controlled body surface; and through reproduction, were divisible, suggesting the unlimitability of their boundaries. Thus they could never be the rational, indivisible, unambiguous individual.

The source of rights shifted to the civil law, with customs, traditions and usages being gradually marginalized. Most significantly, the scope of rights changed radically at this time. The natural world was no longer part of a whole in which human beings acquired their sense of self. Rather, it was external and alien to the individual who was to master it and tame it to his ends. This meant that everything in the external world was an object over which men could have rights. Not only the external world, but each of his capacities became quantifiable and alienable while at the same time, man had somehow to be considered separable from his capacities so that his 'self' could remain 'his' even as he sold or alienated aspects of himself. Man's 'self' then, was seen to reside in his capacity to choose, and as long as he chose freely, he was an autonomous individual, regardless of the ways in which his ability to choose was constrained. (Parikh 1987: 5–9)

The idea then of individuals as bearers of rights in their own capacities is barely four hundred years old. These centuries have seen the expansion of democratic rights to larger sections of people, and the discourse of rights has empowered different kinds of social movements. To this extent, I would reject a totalizing reading of Foucault's reading of governmentality which would deny any emancipatory potential at all to the emergence of the public sphere, for in the movement from feudal communitarianism to bourgeois individualism, the individual was certainly freed from the circumscription of feudal hierarchies. But the idea of the citizen empowered with rights in the public sphere derived its emancipatory potential precisely from its positioning against feudal absolutism. With the completion of the bourgeois revolution in the West, and the mediated and refracted manner in which this transformation takes place in colonial and post-colonial societies, the language of rights has lost its relevance. The extension of this language from rights of the individual against the State, to rights of collectivities against one another and against individuals, as well as rights defined in such broad terms as 'the right to be fully human' (Taylor, 1986: 57)—these rights to be guaranteed *by* the State—has raised contradictions which have not been adequately confronted. This paper points out some of these contradictions and their implications for political practice.

Rights have been attacked on several grounds. Marxists have critiqued 'rights' as juridical conceptions which mask substantial inequality, although maintaining that the rights themselves are not illusions. The formal recognition by the doctrine of equal rights of the equal dignity of all human beings, embodies what Poulantzas calls the 'real rights of the dominated classes', which are the 'material concessions imposed on the dominant classes by popular struggle.'

(Poulantzas, 1978: 84). The struggle then, in Marxist terms, is to transform these empty juridical rights into real rights by transforming the structural conditions which disempower the labouring classes. In this view, rights are considered to have a powerful emancipatory potential, both at the level of rhetoric and symbol as well as substantively, with the revolutionary transformation of material conditions. Christine Sypnowich argues that any worthwhile socialist society would require legal institutions to adjudicate disputes between socialist citizens and between citizen and community. She holds that a socialist jurisprudence must draw from the liberal tradition, and using Ronald Dworkin's phrase, argues that it must retrieve the idea of the individual with rights which 'trump' society's policies (Sypnowich, 1992: 86–7). Thus Marxist critiques attack the illusory nature of rights in capitalist society, but hold that the concept of 'rights' has emancipatory potential.

Another powerful and influential critique of rights, law and the state has come from Catharine MacKinnon who argues that liberalism supports state intervention on behalf of women as abstract persons with abstract rights while in reality 'the state is male in the feminist senses.' Abstract rights only 'authorize the male experience of the world.' As a result, she holds, feminist understandings of the state have been 'schizoid'—on the one hand recognizing the world as patriarchal and oppressive, and on the other, turning to the state to make the law less sexist. She sees the state as embodying and ensuring male control over female sexuality even while it juridically prohibits excesses. In fact the legal prohibition of and controls over pronography and prostitution are meant to enhance their eroticism, 'if part of the kick of pornography involves eroticising the putatively prohibited, pornography law will putatively prohibit pornography enough to maintain its desirability without making it unavailable or truly illegitimate' (MacKinnon, 1983: 643–4). MacKinnon's critique of the law and her understanding of gender *as* dominance of women by men (MacKinnon,1987: 32–45) has certainly served the purpose of radically questioning the myth of the neutrality of law which continues to have a powerful hold over the feminist imagination.

Yet MacKinnon herself makes law the focus of her feminist politics in the USA. She has been the pioneer of legislation against sexual harassment and pornography, formulated in terms of employment rights and civil rights respectively. (MacKinnon, 1987: 103–16, 163–97). Her critique of abstract rights is based on an understanding of 'the intractability of maleness as a form of dominance' (MacKinnon, 1983: 636) which leaves no space for women, let alone for feminist politics. If male dominance is so dauntingly seamless then indeed, 'it may be easier to change biology than society' as she dismally concludes (ibid.). But in that case, where is the feminist critique of MacKinnon generated? Clearly there cannot be a perfect fit between the 'intention' of male dominance as MacKinnon sees it, and its effect.

Ultimately, MacKinnon's rejection of abstract rights and their illusoriness in an overarching system of male dominance from which nothing escapes, only leaves feminist politics in a state of paralysis. Given her analysis, it is impossible to justify or understand her legal activism, where she continues to expect to be able to force 'women's experience' into the law. It would then seem that our vision of political transformation has become so focused on the state, that the most radical critiques of the state and its institutions end up merely realigning themselves once again on its territory.

This is particularly characteristic of analyses which suggest that the purposes of justice would be served better by stressing the relative importance of 'needs' as compared to 'rights'. Upendra Baxi, counterposing human rights to basic human needs, problematizes the liberal conception of rights in a situation of mass poverty. He argues that the notion of human rights must be fused into a discussion of developmental processes, development in the sense of value for human dignity, both in an economic as well as in a political sense. He recognizes that needs are socio-genic and culture-specific, and that questions will therefore arise about the hierarchy of needs, about who determines this hierarchy, and the conflict between human rights and needs. Nevertheless he holds that the needs-approach is still the most proper way of understanding the possibilities of a just society. However, Baxi's analysis continues to focus on the State as the agent of change. For instance, he asks, 'Should not continued drought or famine in one state in India ... justify a nation-wide ban on the conspicuous consumption of food on social events?' (Baxi, 1987: 190–5). There is an inability here to come to terms with the State and the law as deeply implicated in the very processes which make famines, uneven development, and enclaves of wealth intrinsic parts of the Indian system.

Nancy Fraser believes that needs-claims can balance the competing claims of mutual responsibility and individual rights even though there exists the danger of playing into the hands of conservatives who prefer to distribute aid as a matter of need rather than right precisely to avoid any assumption of entitlement. Since her analysis is geared towards retrieving aspects of the welfare State while critiquing its paternalism and androcentrism, she is quite unambiguously state-focused. Moreover she concludes by arguing that 'justified needs claims, must be translated into social rights'. This suggests a heirarchy, that needs must graduate into rights if they are to be taken seriously. It would seem then, that she sees needs-claims not as an improvement on rights-claims but merely as a preliminary stage to making rights-claims (Fraser, 1989: 182–3).

The only arguments that consistently reject that state-centric implications of 'rights' and 'law' come from a position that rejects individualism, but at the cost of valorizing 'the community'. Scholars of the Critical Legal Studies (CLS) Movement hold that rights discourse magnifies social antagonism by pitting one set of rights against another and question whether it can facilitate social reconstruction. They urge recognition of consensus building mechanisms within the community.[1] Such an understanding obscures the fact that 'the community' is marked by exclusion along the axes of caste, gender, class and so on. 'Social antagonism' can only be rendered invisible, not obliterated. Feminists in particular, find this position deeply problematic because the CLS critique of individualism installs the family as beyond justice, as a sphere embodying love, generosity and unselfishness, qualities that are above justice. This mystification of the family as a sphere of love and harmony has been one of the primary foci of feminist critique over the last three decades. The family has been identified as one of the primary sites of oppression for women, based on inequality and injustice which are gender based. If the rejection of rights as individualistic entails reinstating the family as moral community, it would clearly be self-defeating for feminism.

Feminists therefore, have attempted to redefine rights in a manner which would enable them not be understood as purely individualist, but which does not dissolve possibilities of autonomy within 'the community'. For example, Martha Minow and Nancy Fraser have both tried to conceptualize rights in a way that they

---

[1] CLS scholars include Roberto Unger (1983), Michael Sandel (1982), Peter Gabel and Paul Harris (1982–3). For a feminist critique of the CLS position on the family, see Susan Moller Okin, 1993: Ch. 6.

embody connectedness between autonomy and responsibility (Minow, 1985a, 1985b, 1983, discussed in Schneider, 1991: 311; Fraser, 1989: 312–6). Similarly, Elizabeth Schneider argues that the experience of the women's movement has shown that a claim of right is a moral claim about how human beings should act towards one another.

Analyses of this kind, which attempt to rescue the emancipatory impulse of the rights discourse from its individualistic thrust, can only do so by introducing the dimension of morality.

The Moral Basis of Rights

The idea that there are rights sanctioned by a moral order whether or not they have legal existence is not a new one (Weinreb, 1991; Feinberg, 1992). Agnes Heller for example, argues that rights are 'the institutionalized forms of the concretization of universal values.' A value is universal if its opposite cannot be chosen as a value. In this sense freedom is a universal value because 'no one is publicly committed to unfreedom as a value.' She adds 'the value of life' as another value which 'comes close to attaining a universal status.' Rights are derived from these values and stem from the conception of justice. Therefore rights language is and should be, she concludes, 'the lingua franca' of modern democracy (Heller, 1990: 1384). Similarly, Ronald Dworkin's conception of rights as 'trumps'— that is, certain irreducible individual rights as having the moral authority to prevail over what is perceived as the community's interest—is based on the understanding of a shared morality (Dworkin, 1977).

However, the notion of 'universal values' is clearly not the kind of morality feminists have in mind when they reinscribe rights on to moral terrain. Such a notion only obscures the power dynamics by which some values are assigned greater status and others are marginalized and silenced. This kind of analysis also allows no room to conceive of conflict among 'Universal Values' themselves. For instance, it is precisely the contradiction between 'freedom' and 'the right to life', both of which Heller designates as universal values, that operates in the abortion debate. But at the same time when feminists refigure rights through morality, they do invoke what is assumed *should* be universal values, that is feminist values. These values are not at present dominant, but feminists believe they should be, and can be, made universally applicable through law. As Nancy Fraser puts it, rights talk is not necessarily individualistic and androcentric. It becomes so 'only when societies establish the *wrong* rights, for example when the (putative) right to private property is allowed to trump other, social rights' (Fraser, 1989: 183).

Clearly, what one 'ought' to do, or what constitutes a 'moral' action, makes sense only within shared sets of understandings on 'justice', 'equality' and so on. Thus, rights are constituted by shared moral boundaries. What happens to them in the realm of legal discourse? Appeals to the law are made on the assumption that rights are self-evident, universally comprehended and universally applicable, but some slippage in meaning takes place once they are in the legal arena where diverse discourses of rights converge. That is, what appears to be a right empowering women within feminist discourse can have an entirely contrary effect once it is materialized in the legal realm. The manner in which this transposition takes place will be explored with reference to the issues of sexual violence and abortion in later sections.

Elizabeth Kingdom's feminist critique of rights questions the desirability of generalizing on a whole range of issues grouped together under the heading of 'women's rights'. She urges instead that specific legislations be analysed from both 'feminist' and 'socialist' perspectives. She argues that this model allows for a more complex analysis of the issues covered by 'women's rights'. She takes up as an instance, the case of protective legislation (restrictions on the employment of women in hazardous work, night work, overtime, and so on), in which the protection of women's rights is inseparable from the struggle to improve working conditions for both men and women (1991: 26–45).

While Kindgom recognizes the problematic nature of 'women's rights', she fails to take her analysis far enough by problematizing the notion of 'rights' itself. As a result, she assumes that it would always be possible to apply a 'feminist' or a 'socialist' understanding to specific legislations without the possibility of conflict between the two. For instance, the example she suggests, that of protective legislation, has been the focus of other socialist–feminist studies as exemplifying the conflict within the working class between the rights of male and female workers (Alexander, 1976; Barrett, 1984). Michele Barrett, discussing the position taken by British trade unions on protective legislation, that such measures should be retained, argues that this was a deliberate strategy to reduce competition for male workers. She notes that such legislation was introduced in areas of competition rather than in all areas of work (1984: 171).

A more thorough feminist critique of rights is provided by Carol Smart (1989). She holds that first wave feminists needed the concept of equal rights to fight against legally imposed impediments but that in the late twentieth century, while law remains oppressive for women, it no longer takes the form of denial of formal rights reserved for men. Continuing the demand for formal rights now is problematic. She suggests that 'the rhetoric of rights has become exhausted, and may even be detrimental' (Smart, 1989: 139). Rights can be appropriated by the more powerful, for example, the Sex Discrimination Act may be used as much by men as by women, to challenge affirmative action for women. She also points out that rights are often formulated to deal with a social wrong, but in practice become focused on the individual who must prove that her rights have been violated. Any redress too, will affect only that particular woman (ibid.: 145).

Posing a problem in terms of rights simply transposes that problem into one that is defined as having a legal solution. While accepting that rights do amount to 'legal and political power resources', Smart holds that the value of these resources seems to be ascertainable more in terms of the losses if such rights diminish, than in terms of gains if they are sustained (ibid.:143). This distinction that Smart makes is crucial to developing any critique of rights, for it forces a confrontation of the fact that while the existence of a given right does not guarantee its realization, its denial will negatively affect the people who had held that right.

However, Smart's critique remains in the terrain of the state, for she urges in place of rights, a reformulation of 'demands' grounded in 'women's experiences' rather than in 'abstract notions like rights' (ibid.:159). What form will these 'demands' take and on whom will they be made? It is not clear how Smart's 'demands' will differ from 'rights' after all. Moreover the formulation of rights-as-abstract versus experience-as-concrete is misleading. We have seen how rights are derived precisely from within a universe of shared 'experiences'. The difference between 'rights' and 'experience' cannot be sustained.

The next section will examine the manner in which legal discourse operates, seeking certainty and exactitude and bringing to a halt the play of meaning and contexts which give rise to rights.

Legal Discourse and the Fixing of Meaning

In India the understanding of 'law' fundamentally changed with the British conquest, legality replaced authority. Whereas in the classical system, judgement had no other object but to put an end to the dispute, it now began to constitute a precedent, a source of law. Even in the mediaeval period, there was great flexibility in the attachment of particular regions to one or the other school of interpretation. Sastric law was as likely to modify its principles to match local custom as custom was, in deference to Sastric law. Islamic law too, was based on revelation as Dharma was, and in neither were decisions of the court the source of law. In both, interpretation and custom had the same importance (Altekar, 1952; Lingat, 1973; Baxi, 1986).[2]

Under the British system however, the judge fixed interpretation once and for all, and further development of the law could take place only through cases. Even where custom was accepted as prevailing over Sastric law, it was fixed as legal rule. Once identified, 'custom' was understood to be fixed, and rigidly codified. Thus, the dynamic interplay between custom and Sastric law was halted. Upendra Baxi argues that it was with 'ascendant capitalism and its Siamese twin colonialism' that the state appropriated to itself the legitimacy of being the sole source of law. All other forms of dispensing justice then began to be seen as inferior, these became designated as 'custom', 'community justice' or 'unofficial adjudication'. He holds that these should be called 'non-state legal systems' because to deny them the status of law is to accept the colonial devaluing of indigenous institutions (Baxi, 1992: 251–2).

[2] Tahir Mahmood (1965) argues that custom is not an independent source of law in the legal theory of Islam. He claims that British administrators misunderstood custom to have the same significance as within Hindu law. The references to 'usages' may have been inspired, according to him, by the practices of Hindu converts to Islam, who continued to follow certain aspects of Hindu law and custom. But if this was prevalent, then to what extent did a pure Quoranic law operate for Muslims any more than Sastric law did for Hindus? It was only at the beginning of the twentieth century that the ulema began to compulsorily enforce Shari'a law.

However modern legal systems are marked by 'a *quest* for ... certainty, consistency and uniformity', as Baxi himself points out elsewhere (Baxi, 1986). This is not characteristic of pre-colonial indigenous justice-dispensing institutions, and the universal use of 'law' to refer to all forms of 'prescriptions, prohibitions, punishments' (Baxi, 1992: 251) would blur this crucial distinction. Baxi does not consider the goals of certainty and uniformity to be desirable and urges in fact, departures from them to ensure 'legal growth'. However, he does not address the question of how such departures are to be effected. The legitimacy of the law rests on the concept of Rule of Law, that is, the due observance of the procedures prescribed for making a valid decision. Thus when Ronald Dworkin questions the rationalist and positivist certainties of law, affirming law rather, as interpretation and meaning, he is clear that such interpretation has to follow 'the injunctions of a grammar of principles'. Such principles are drawn from the moral ideals of a subject assumed to be universal (see discussion in Douzinas et al. 1991: 24–30). Clearly, any attempt to build into the law, an openness to multivalence, would have to be institutionalized if it is to be legitimate. The paradoxical nature of this formulation itself points to its impossibility. Without such institutionalization, departures from consistency and uniformity can only be at the whim of individual judges.

Such departures are in fact, precisely the focus of one school of feminist critique of the law. The perspective of 'legal realist rule scepticism' is that in actual practice, decisions are at the mercy of individual judges who make 'law' through their interpretation of ambiguous and open-ended practices. These interpretations reflect social and individual biases and practices, and the law is thus distorted from its purpose of neutral arbitration in the interests of social justice (Sachs and Wilson, 1978; Atkins and Hogget, 1984). However, this understanding has been attacked from within feminism for reinstating the assumption that bias and prejudice are external to the law, that law proceeding from its Parliamentary source is just and untainted by the values which influence individual judges (Brown, 1986; Kingdom, 1991).

The fixity of meaning required by legal discourse has generated a dilemma for feminists which has come to be formulated as the difference-versus-sameness approach. When 'equality before the law' is interpreted as men and women being the same as each other, courts do not uphold any legislation intended either to compensate for past discrimination or to take into account gender-specific differences like maternity. Thus the sameness approach cannot distinguish between 'differential treatment that disadvantages and differential treatment that advantages' as Kapur and Cossman put it (1993: 61)[3]. Liberal feminists who subscribe to the sameness approach however, continue to insist that the only way for women to achieve legal recognition of their equal status to men is to deny the legal relevance of their difference to the degree that it exists. Women should be recognized as gender-neutral legal persons.

The opposing position from within feminism is that this accepts the masculine as the norm, and prevents the visibility of the unique experience of women. To consider ourselves as gender-neutral 'persons' can only marginalize us and devalidate our experience. However, the difference approach in law has at best been protectionist, thus denying women the claim to equality altogether. It has also been used by courts to justify discriminatory treatment on the grounds that women are different from men (Kapur and Cossman, 1993; Frug, 1992). To put it in Frug's words, 'Sameness feminists have been thwarted by the repeated recognition of difference; difference feminists by the devaluing of *women's* difference' (Frug, 1992: xv).

In other words, feminists seeking social justice through the law have come up against the limits set by the criterion that law be uniform and consistent. It can either recognize sameness (which disadvantages women) or difference (which justifies discrimination). An alternative approach suggested is that of 'substantive equality' (Kapur and Cossman, 1993: 20–1). The focus of this approach is not on equal treatment under the law, but on the impact of the law. This is an attempt to make the law more sensitive to a more complex notion of equality which takes into account the comparative disadvantages of persons under existing unequal conditions. Its proponents hold that in some contexts, the substantive model will require a sameness approach, in others, a corrective approach to take into account difference as well as disadvantage.

This model quite clearly, is an understanding of how the law *ought* to function, and bears out the argument that is central to this paper, that rights are constituted within shared moral universes. The 'substantive equality' approach is an attempt to universalize

---

[3] Included in this volume.

one such moral universe through law. However, both conceptually as well as in terms of political practice, this approach is illustrative of the problematic nature of the discourse of legal rights. It assumes, to begin with, the independence and separateness of the judiciary and legal system from the institutions of the state and the economic and cultural practices which constitute present conditions of inequality. It seems to suggest that all that is required is for judges to be sensitized to the notion of substantive equality, and social conditions will be gradually transformed by law.

To put one objection to this simply, if the morality underlying the notion of substantive equality were so self-evident and unthreatening to the dominant social order, we would not need the law to bring about social justice. One feminist teacher of law and legal activist has come to the conclusion that legal method may be 'impervious to a feminist perspective' (Mossman, 1991: 297). She urges coming to terms with the fact that

... because there is so much resistance in legal method itself to ideas which challenge the status quo, there is no solution for feminists ... except to confront the reality that gender and power are inextricably linked in the legal method we use (ibid.: 298).

In the context of the Canadian Charter of Rights and Freedoms of 1982, Judy Fudge makes a similar point. She concludes that once the demand for substantive equality for women is translated into legal rights, it becomes divorced from broader political demands, 'instead of directly addressing the question of how best to promote women's sexual autonomy under social relations which result in women's sexual subordination, feminists who invoke the Charter must couch their arguments in terms of the rhetoric of equality rights.' And courts interpret 'equality' as formal equality rather than contextualizing it within a historical framework of current inequalities (Fudge, 1989: 49–50).

At a conceptual level, the substantive equality model presents another problem. Rights, once made legally enforceable, acquire a fixity of meaning that can undermine the very morality on which they are based. For instance, Kapur and Cossman cite the right to own land as a 'basic civil and political right' in relation to which the sameness approach should be used, that is, gender should be considered irrelevant. It bears repeating here that the norms validated by law become relevant and binding in all cases in which similar issues are raised. What then would be the implications of using the sameness approach towards the right to own land, in the context of land reform legislation? Here gender identity would be complicated by class, and the sameness approach would disadvantage the weaker party, in this case, the landless.

Marc Galanter's work (1984) is an acknowledgement of the need to confront the tendency of the law to fix meaning. He attempts to build into the law a conception of 'identity' not as a fixed, natural or inherent quality, but as something constituted by interaction and negotiation with other components of society. It is Galanter's view that this understanding of identity would require courts to adopt an 'empirical' as opposed to a 'formal' approach. The latter sees individuals as members of one group only, and therefore, as having only the rights which that group is entitled to. Thus, for example, one who attains caste status loses tribal affiliation as far as the law is concerned. The empirical approach on the other hand, does not attempt to resolve the blurring and overlap between categories and accepts multiple affiliations. It addresses itself to the particular legislation involved and tries to determine which affiliation is acceptable in the particular context. Galanter accepts that in this approach, some slippage is inevitable between judicial formulations and actual administration, for the courts must make subtle distinctions which must be translated into workable rules capable of being administered at lower levels.

It is clear that Galanter applies his understanding of identity as relative and shifting only to 'people', not to 'courts' or 'government'. The latter are assumed to be outside this grid of affiliations, to have a superior understanding of it, and to be capable of choosing the 'correct' perspective, whether empirical or formal. For example, he writes, 'it is beyond the courts to rescue these policies (reservation policies) from systematic cognitive distortion, for courts cannot control the way that various actors and audiences perceive judicial (and other) pronouncements' (1984: 357). Moreover, government intention in framing and implementing reservations is assumed to be identical with the official stated intention, that is, promotion of social justice. Groups are then seen to relate to these policies in their own particularistic ways, while apparently, the government and courts have the overall and universal picture.

Thus, Galanter's attempt to contest law's rigid codifying procedures is unsuccessful as he must retain the notion of the state and of law itself as the unified and self-transparent agency which will interpret the multiplicity of indentities around it.

If as I have attempted to demonstrate, law functions through the assertion of certainty and the creation of uniform categories, and rights are constituted by particular discourses, this resituates rights in a realm of complexity, ambiguity and undecidability. We come then, to a point where we must go further than saying simply this: the language of rights can be alienating and individualistic but since it refers to some desirable capacities and powers the oppressed should have, it can be empowering. We need to recognize rather, that the experience of feminist politics pushes us towards the understanding that social movements may have reached the limits of the discourse of rights and of 'justice' as a metanarrative. It might even be that trying to bring about positive transformation through the law can run counter to the ethics which prompt entry into legal discourse in the first place.

I will now move on to a discussion of the issues of abortion and sexual violence in the context of the women's movement in India, in the light of the issues raised above.

Female Foeticide and Feminist Discourse on Abortion

In India the issue of abortion has been placed on the feminist agenda in a manner quite different to its positioning in the West. Since the dominant discourses construct poverty as being created by over-population, abortion has long been accepted as a measure of family planning. The Medical Termination of Pregnancy (MTP) Act was passed in 1971 amidst Parliamentary rhetoric of choice and women's rights, but it was clearly intended as a population control measure, as several MPs pointed out during the debate on the Bill. The Act was not passed as a result of campaigning by women's groups, nor did there emerge any concerted anti-abortion stream of opinion in the public arena.

Abortion has become an issue for Indian feminists for quite a different reason over the eighties, with the growing practice of selective abortion of female foetuses after sex-determination (SD) tests during pregnancy. The response from the women's movement has been to urge the state to end the practice through law.

Two crucial questions arise for feminists from the issue, debate on which is far from closed within the movement. At the level of politics is the contradiction involved in pushing for legislation which can restrict the access to abortion itself. Two, at the level of feminist philosophy, if abortion is a right over one's body, how are feminists to deny this right to women when it comes to the selective abortion of female foetuses?

An examination of the history of feminist responses to the practice itself as well as to the government's interventions illustrates the contradictions and dilemmas involved in negotiating these questions.

The Forum Against Sex Determination and Sex Preselection (FASDSP) was formed in 1984, and it has been lobbying for legislation to ban the practice. In 1988, the state of Maharshtra passed an Act banning prenatal diagnostic practices. The FASDSP, a broad forum of feminist and human rights groups, was disappointed with the Act because it was full of 'loopholes' and had not taken on the various recommendations the Forum had made (FASDSP, 1988). FASDSP then continued its campaign in the form of pressing for Central legislation which would be more effective. Parliament passed the Prenatal Diagnostic Practices (Regulation and Prevention of Misuse) Act in 1994.

Women's groups are dissatisfied with this Act, and in August 1994 urged the President to send it back for reconsideration to Parliament. Some of the points that their memorandum raised are as follows (*Saheli Newsletter,* January 1995: 11–13):

(a) All ultrasound machines and other equipment which can be used for SD tests should be registered. The Joint Committee had earlier considered this suggestion and rejected it as unfeasible because such equipment is used for various purposes other than pre-natal testing (*Report of Joint Committee,* 1992: 20–1).

(b) Future techniques for sex determination as well as for sex pre-selection should be brought within the ambit of the Bill.

(c) The Act punishes the woman if it can be proved that she was not coerced and that she went in for the test and the abortion of her own will. The memorandum says that punishing the woman is misguided, even on the presumption that she was coerced unless proved otherwise. This is unjust in a context where women rarely take autonomous decisions. The Act in this respect is anti-women, and would create conditions that would limit its effectiveness.

The Act has come into force, and it is clear that most of the loopholes of the Maharashtra Act of 1988, as perceived by women's groups, persist. However, if SD tests are sought to be entirely delinked from female foeticide, which is necessary in order to protect the MTP Act, they cannot be effectively curbed, because most of the equipment is used for other purposes as well. Only by closing off all possibilities of 'misuse' of existing equipment and technology can the practice of female foeticide be effectively controlled. But this would mean bringing *all* abortions under legal scrutiny as well. This is the double bind into which, I argue, legal discourse pushes social movements like feminism—the more narrow the focus of a piece of legislation, the less it serves its purpose, and the broader it is, the more it subverts the ethics underlying the very demand for legislation. We will find similar dynamics at work when the issue of rape/sexual violence is explored further on.

Another important problem emerges from the point about women's culpability in the memorandum of women's groups to the President. It is true that women may be implicated by families being prosecuted by the state, although women are rarely in a position to make choices. Nevertheless, what are the implications of denying agency altogether to women on the grounds that they are never responsible for their decisions and therefore, should not be considered culpable at all? Within the realm of legal discourse, it is dangerous for feminists to construct women as incapable of taking autonomous decisions—the consequences for women's struggles against legally sanctioned discrimination in other spheres could be fatal.

The FASDSP's position is that women who make this choice are constrained by family and social pressures and are not really exercising their free will (FASDSP, 1988: 7). This argument leaves unproblematized the decisions to abort in all other circumstances. That is, women who go in for abortions for reasons like illegitimacy, economic constraints and so on, surely they are equally influenced by social and cultural values? Why is it assumed that only when a woman chooses to abort a female foetus is she not acting on her 'own' will?

If we unravel the underlying thread of reasoning which makes this position a persuasive one for many feminists, we would arrive at an argument which looks like this: Negative female-to-male ratios in a population are invariably corelatable to the low status of women. So the very constraints of a patriarchal society which make abortions necessary in most cases (including the low priority given to research on safe contraceptive methods) would be much greater if fewer and fewer women were born. Therefore abortion must be available to women who want it, while selective abortion of female foetuses must be stopped.

Clearly 'the right to abortion' and the 'right to end female foeticide' are in a complex interrelationship within feminist discourse. 'Rights' over one's 'own' body then, are not natural, timeless and self-evident. They are constituted as legitimate only within specific discursive political practices. Social movements cannot therefore expect that rights would be unproblematically realized on a terrain where their specificity cannot be retained.

Further, the FASDSP calls for a ban on all technologies which could be used for sex-preselection at the time of conception, and for the regulation of all new technologies in future (FASDSP Note Undated). What does it mean for feminist democratic politics to demand legal and bureaucratic control over entire areas of science and knowledge?

There has been considerable rethinking and reflection on the campaign within the movement, and one activist relocates SD tests in the context of the wider issues of democracy and decision-making:

We would assert that a few bureaucrats and/or scientists/technocrats should not have the right to decide on matters which affect society as a whole. We should try to initiate a process whereby a technology would be allowed to operate within a society only after ascertaining its benefits and risks to all concerned (Ravindra R.P., 1990: 29–30).

This kind of perspective cannot merely be added on to a legalistic and state-centred campaign. It should suggest a radical rethinking of the issues and strategies involved, and a definite move away from demands for more legislation. So overpowering however, is the hegemonic perception of law as a transformative instrument that the same writer concludes his argument by calling for a ban on 'misuse' and 'regulating the proper use' of such techniques (ibid.).

Finally, the new legislation and feminist responses to it establish that we remain unable to confront the ethics of condoning abortions when they are specifically due to 'abnormalities' in foetuses. The FASDSP is clear that it does not want a blanket ban on pre-natal testing, and thus endorses such testing for the purpose of detecting 'abnormalities' and the subsequent abortion of such foetuses (ibid.).

However, once we accept there can be a hierarchy of human beings based on physical characteristics, and that it is legitimate to withhold the right to be born from those at lower levels of this hierarchy, then this reasoning can be extended to other categories, whether 'females', 'inferior races' or others. The work of Rayna Rapp and Veena Das points to the recognition that it is not inscribed in the nature of things that a physically or mentally retarded individual should have a poor quality of life. It is the great value placed on individual autonomy and on competition that makes this seem like a self-evident fact (Rapp, 1987, 1993, 1994; Das, 1986). Neither Das nor Rapp offer facile solutions to the dilemmas involved, but their argument foregrounds the moral and ethical vision of feminism, with all its rich ambivalence and self-doubt, a vision which it would be impossible to strait-jacket into the certainties of legal discourse.

Feminist outrage over technologies to control the sex of foetuses, and over the practice of the selective abortion of female foetuses, arises from the ethical and moral vision of feminism. However, to translate this concern into the language of rights and the law appears to threaten this very vision.[4]

Sexual Violence and Feminism

There are two simultaneous impulses at work in feminist analyses of rape, the one revealing the limitations of the law and its inability to encompass the lived experience of women; the other seeking to legitimate this experience precisely through having it recognized by the law as authentic.

In other words,

(a) Certain experiences assumed to be clearly recognizable as 'sexual', are posited as having a reality and an existence prior to legal discourse, and the latter is seen as limited and incomplete to the extent it is incapable of recognizing these experiences, but at the same time.

(b) These experiences need to be authenticated by law to have

---

[4] For a fuller treatment of this issue, see 'The impossibility of "justice": Female foeticide and feminist discourse on abortion', in Patricia Uberoi (ed.), *Social Reform, Sexuality and the State*, Sage, 1996.

social value and be recognized as 'real'. To this extent then, they are to be constituted as real and legitimated by legal discourse. What are the implications of this, that is, of reinforcing the status of law as the primary legitimating discourse?

Recourse to the law is seen as necessary and inevitable because it is believed that designing a law around an experience proves 'it matters'; law is 'the concrete delivery of rights through the legal system' (MacKinnon, 1987: 103). However, dominant modes of constituting the self—as women, as criminal, as victim—are maintained and reinforced through the conventions of legal language. The rejection of these categories can come about in fact, only through resistance to legal discourse (Bumiller, 1991: 96). As Foucault points out, judgement is passed not only on the 'crimes' defined by the code, but on 'the shadows lurking behind the case', 'on passions, instincts, anomalies....' In short, on the deviations from dominant norms (1977: 17). Thus, what the law legitimates ultimately, is pecisely what feminist practice contests.

Moreover, in post-colonial societies, the establishing of law as the only legitimating discourse has meant the marginalizing and devalidating of other legitimating discourses. A uniformity was imposed which radically transformed indigenous notions of ownership, equity and justice. This is not to valorize pre-colonial communitarian values as egalitarian and just. On the contrary, 'the community' is marked by exclusion along the axes of caste, gender, class and so on; inegalitarian power relations are the fulcrum on which 'the community' turns. Nevertheless it would be simplistic to assume the neutrality of the modern legal system. Social movements tend to work on the belief that even if law is as enmeshed in the power structures of society as 'the community' is, it can be forced into the service of progress and change by the pressure of democratic movements. However, as Upendra Baxi points out, underlying the concept of 'Rule of Law' (the due observance of the procedures prescribed for making a valid decision) is the idea that power should become impersonal and be constrained through rules applied by an independent judiciary and autonomous legal profession. But this formal legal rationality does not always constrain the arbitrary exercise of power; Baxi argues that on the contrary, it often helps to camouflage it (Baxi, 1982: 36–7).

What does it mean for feminists to insist that this 'formal legal rationality' should delimit the contours of a particular experience, and that it should legitimate this experience? (See for example, Purewal and Kapur Undated: 3; Draft, 1993: 1). Are we not by implication, accepting that without such validation, the experience itself has no reality? We need to recognize that legal rationality cannot comprehend the complex ways in which sexual violence is constituted.

An analysis of judgements in rape trials which have come up on appeal to High Courts and the Supreme Court of India, and of legal discourse on rape reveals the impossibility of capturing the complexity of what Carol Smart calls the 'binary logic' of the law. There is no room within legal discourse to conceive of women's sexual experience except in terms of consenting/not consenting to male pressure. 'Consent' itself, a state of mind constituted in a complex way, has to be rigidly pegged to a linear notion of physical growth if it is to make sense within legal discourse. Below *the* Age of Consent a woman cannot be expected to have agency in sexual interaction, she can only be understood as victim or dupe. Above this age, even if it is by a few months, she is radically transformed from victim to accomplice. Thus, while recognizing the relative powerlessness and lack of autonomy that characterize women's relations with men, the point is to question the possibility of addressing this experience in the realm of legal discourse.

Even when justice appears to be done, that is, when conviction is secured, the very demonstration through legal discourse of the violation of the woman re-enacts and resediments patriarchal and misogynist values. In India, feminists have begun to view with concern judgements which take a progressive position on the issue of corroborative evidence in rape trials, but based on notions of women's 'chastity' and 'traditions of Indian society'. The implications however, are more serious than feminist critiques tend to recognize—it is not simply that in such decisions the court passively accepts rather than challenges patriarchal values (see for example, *National Law School Journal*, 1993: 170). The seriousness lies in recognizing that if it is assumed that tradition-bound Indian society would make 'innocent' women reluctant to level false accusations of rape, the same factor can be expected to motivate 'promiscuous' women to hide their promiscuity precisely through such accusations. In other words, convictions can be secured only at the cost of turning the case once more on the axis of the 'guilt' or 'innocence' of the raped woman.

This paradox is what underlies the statement made by a feminist lawyer at a workshop in Delhi, that she would rather lose a rape case if in the process the right kind of debate was made possible.[5] But are these two eventualities compatible with each other? The overwhelming hegemony of the law ensures the synonymity of law with justice. If the case were conducted in such a way that the 'right' issues were raised from a feminist perspective, and conviction was not secured, would this not 'prove' to society that these values are not right but wrong? It would appear to be impossible to engage with legal discourse except on its own terms. At the heart of any exercise to locate sexual violence within the law lies the irresolvable conflict involved in defining the harm of sexual violence so exactly that legal discourse can comprehend it, and so retaining ambivalences that the ethical impulse of feminism is undamaged.[6]

Law and Justice

We return now to the questions we began with. Does law have the capacity to pursue justice? Can justice be conceived of in a universal sense? At this point, having gone through the questions raised for feminist politics by the issues of abortion and sexual violence, I would reiterate the assertions made at the beginning of this chapter. First that the very dynamic of law tends towards the fixing and universalizing of identity. Indeed, the emancipatory potential of law, emerging as a tool of the bourgeois democratic revolution, lay precisely in this dynamic. However, at this historical moment, when democratic aspirations are articulated in a far more complex way, and are no longer simply posed in opposition to an absolutist state, the force of law functions to disable the ethical vision of feminism and of other social movements which seek to bring about 'justice'. This is because, I argue, such movements fail to recognize that their vision of justice is predicated on ambiguity and contextuality, qualities which are erased by legal discourse.

Second, following from this, 'justice' can no longer be conceived of as a metanarrative, representing self-evident and universal values, although in the self-representation of 'justice', these are precisely

[5] Ratna Kapur, at an Action India workshop, December 1993.
[6] This issue has been discussed in greater detail in my 'Embodying the Self: Feminism, Sexual Violence and the Law', forthcoming in *Community, Gender and Violence,* edited by Partha Chatterjee and Pradeep Jeganathan, (OUP).

the values it attributes to itself. It is a characteristic of the discourse of justice that it operates on the same terrain as the harm it seeks to redress. That is, the key terms on which the injustice rests are not problematized. Rather they are further legitimated by attempting to show that in the case in question, the norms of justice are interpeted inadequately or non-inclusively. What our exercise here has indicated is that the radical decentering of such key terms would reveal that in the era of late capitalism, multiple visions of justice have come to coexist, all laying claim to universality. In other words, there is a distinct lack of identification between the value of justice and the force of law which must tend towards eradicating multiplicity.

What does this mean for feminist politics? Clearly the option of abdicating law does not exist, for law will not abdicate us. In every sense that 'I' or 'we' define myself or ourselves, legal discourse is implicated. But precisely for this reason, precisely because the regulating and defining force of law is directed towards the creating and naturalizing of specific, governable identities, the law cannot be a 'subversive site', as Kapur and Cossman put it (1996). At best we may be able to use existing legal provisions creatively in such a way that we might negotiate some spaces outside and around prescribed identities. The term 'subversion', however, is too strong for such a limited exercise.

Here it is useful to consider the distinction made by some feminists between law reform strategies on the one hand and litigation strategies on the other. Law reform strategies seek to bring about new legislation to give legal recognition to rights-claims, while litigation strategies use existing laws either aggressively or defensively to advance such claims. It should be clear that it is the latter strategy which I see as the only possible engagement with the law that will not compromise our ethical vision.

However, drawing upon Archana Parasher's work, Kapur and Cossman hold that law reform despite its limitations, must continue to be an important part of the women's movement's engagement with law. In Parasher's view, feminist critiques of law reforms only come from societies where women have already won formal equality in legal rights (1992: 34). Such a conclusion fails to take into account the fact that the legal campaign as strategy has always been accompanied by doubts and questions even among Indian feminists. The major lines of criticism that have emerged are:

(a) That the law is not enough, that the struggle to transform the patriarchal nature of existing laws can only be part of a wider struggle. Gandhi and Shah argue, for example, that legal campaigns are at most a broad strategy to create public awareness and to secure some short-term legal redress (1992: 268). Similarly, Haksar makes the point that law reform cannot be divorced from the more fundamental struggle to transform social values (1994).

(b) That constant recourse to the law creates a series of new legislations which often mean the increase of state control, while implementation remains unsatisfactory (Kishwar and Vanita, 1980–1, 1986; Agnes, 1991, 1992).

(c) Omvedt holds that lobbying for legal reform by urban-based groups wastes energy without achieving much. Such a strategy in her opinion, offers little challenge to the social, systemic basis of increasing atrocities against women (1986: 39–40).

So it is untenable to hold, as Parasher does, that critiques of legal strategies come only from societies where formal legal equality has been achieved. Further, she evidently sees this as a process which would proceed by similar stages in all societies—that is, legal equality followed by 'demands for the autonomy to control... sexuality or the right to inviolability of (women's) bodies' (1992: 34). There are two problems with this argument.

First, the disquiet about the law among feminists in the West is not simply a matter of 'looking beyond law reform' after equal rights have been achieved, as Parasher sees it. Rather, it reveals a realization that law reform and the notion of legal equality itself has worked against feminist interests, as we have been arguing in this essay (Smart, 1989; Snider, 1985; Fudge, 1987). Second, in post-colonial societies, law, a product of the exigencies of colonial administration, cannot be assumed to have the same emancipatory force it might have had in Europe during the transition from feudalism to capitalism. Indeed, in India, colonial law radically delegitimized indigenous notions of ownership and equity which were in many cases more just to women than the laws which replaced them (Agarwal, 1989; Kishwar, 1994; Arunima, 1992).

In other words, the critique made here suggests that the contradictions involved in engaging with the law to produce *new* legislation goes beyond mere 'limitations'. Nevertheless, it must be reiterated that the argument here is not that we ought to abandon legal strategies altogether. In this context, it is useful to draw upon Derrida's insight that deconstruction does not create 'new' terms entirely free of the discourse being deconstructed. Rather, it functions with borrowed terms which are reinscribed in such a way that 'the term's heterogeneous network of references and allusions, its system of possibilities, is revealed' (Lawlor, 1989: 6). Thus deconstruction always remains related to the discourse being deconstructed while transforming the terrain on which it operates, revealing that which had been repressed.

This philosophical insight has clear implications for political practice: in deconstructing legal discourse, we would not be abandoning the terrain of law altogether. Rather, by making visible what has been repressed by emancipatory discourses of the bourgeois democratic revolution, we can recognize the extent to which engagement with the law continues to be inevitable and sometimes fruitful, but also in what ways such an engagement can run counter to our emancipatory vision.

In the final section I explore alternative political practices around the issues of abortion and sexual violence, which might better reflect the feminist ethical vision.

Disembodying the Self

I would begin with a consideration of the pioneering essays of Sharon Marcus and Mary Poovey, which sought to dislocate abortion and rape from 'the body' (Marcus, 1992; Poovey, 1992). Marcus, writing about sexual violence, urges that we rewrite the 'rape script' in which 'a single sexual organ identifies the self' (398). She argues that we do not need to 'defend our "real" bodies from invasion but to rework this elaboration of our bodies altogether,' and 'to revise the idea of female sexuality as an object, as property, and as inner space' (399). The rewriting of the script will also enable a transition from sexual violence to what the calls 'subject–subject violence'. Sexual violence constitutes the target as fearful, defenceless victim, while in subject–subject violence 'each interlocutor expects and incites violence in the other' (396).

Similarly Poovey, in the context of the abortion debate in the West, makes a case for a politics which would not be based on 'the individual sexed body', but rather on the individual conceptualized as 'a heterogeneous rather than homogeneous entity' located in a complex network of social relations. This would relocate 'choice' in a social arena and would require the existence of options not only to safe and legal abortions but to pre- and post-natal care and to day-care facilities (252–3).

The tentative recognition advanced in this essay is that we need to rethink the naturalness of the body for our political practice. We have so far assumed as 'natural' the symbolic order which produces this identity, which inscribes the body as body, as separate from other bodies, as healthy/unhealthy and so on, and which constructs the gendered and heterosexual body as the norm. Can we begin to conceive of a feminist politics which radically contests the production of this identity?

It is useful to consider here Judith Butler's discussion of Freud's *The Ego and The Id* (1923) in which Freud argues that the body does not precede and give birth to the idea of the body but rather it is the idea that makes the body accessible as a body (1992: 135–43). If we work on the belief that it is the idea that makes the body phenomenologically accessible, feminist practice would be liberated from the stranglehold of the discourse that designates the body as the site of selfhood. The boundaries of the stable, gendered, heterosexual self would be seen to be cultural and historical constructs, and not the natural immutable 'reality' that we are apparently irrevocably faced with.

What can this mean for us in our very real struggle against constant dehumanization and humiliation through our reduction to our bodies? The discussion in this paper seems to point to the possibility of realizing that the emancipatory impulse of feminism lies, not in concretizing and more fully defining the boundaries of 'our bodies' through law, but in accepting 'the self' as something that is negotiable and contestable. The indeterminacy of identity need not lead to political paralysis; on the contrary, it could dislocate feminist practice productively, from sterile engagement with legal discourse and hegemonic cultural productions of selfhood, to a realm of radical doubt and constant negotiation of what constitutes 'me' as a 'woman' in some contexts. Emancipation itself must be recognized as disaggregated, split along different axes, just as identity is not just a positive conglomerate of different subject positions, but an ever-temporary construction, forming anew at the intersections of shifting subject positions.

It might be possible then to see the feminist project, not as one of 'justice' but of 'emancipation'. As we saw earlier, the discourse of justice leaves unproblematized the key terms upon which it rests. The term 'body' is one such key category in the issues we have discussed. In the case of sexual violence, it is assumed by all the discourses (including feminist discourses) which circulate around and produce 'sexual violence' as a category, that the body of woman is 'naturally' rapable. The assumptions that only women's bodies are penetratable, that 'sexual violence' is clearly distinguishable from other forms of violence, and that such violence in particular constitutes an attack on the very self-hood of women, is never questioned. The issue then becomes one of 'proving' the magnitude of rape or sexual violence, and the fact that it did in fact take place. Such a recognition has to be forced from the state, and justice secured by conviction of the perpetrator. This leaves the ever-open possibility of other (all) women continuing to get raped. In other words, feminist and patriarchal discourses are agreed on this—that rape is 'a fate worse than death.'

Similarly, with female foeticide and its relationship to 'women's rights over their bodies', we have seen how it becomes necessary to destabilize given notions of 'bodies' and 'women' to understand apparently contradictory positions taken by feminism. Could it be that the way out of this dilemma too, requires a relocation of 'selfhood' *outside* the body?

What if our struggle were to emancipate ourselves from the very *meaning* of 'rape' and 'abortion'—indeed, of hegemonic conceptions of what it means to 'be a woman'? Does the ever-present threat of sexual violence and of other gendered violence (directed at women whether born or unborn), proceed from the locating of the 'female' self inside the sexually defined body of woman? The attempt then should be to redraw the map of our body to make it accessible to new codes, to new senses of the self, so that at least some of these selves would be free of the limits set by the body.

To conclude, if social movements have reached the limits of the law, does it mean that they have also reached the limits of the state? To the extent that law is the language in which state power is exercised, the answer would be in the affirmative. However, if we explore the possibilities opened up by refusing to accept that 'the state' is exhausted by 'Law' and 'Rights', the answer could be in the negative. We need to refigure rights outside the domain of the state, which might render 'rights' unrecognizable in present terms. Simultaneously, we need to reconceptualize the state as exceeding 'Law' and 'Rights'. What would a political practice which is radically decentred from the arena of the state and the law look like? I would end this essay on this question.

I would like to express deepest gratitude to Manoranjan Mohanty (my Ph.D. superviser), Uma Chakravarty and Tanika Sarkar. Continuous discussions with them over a period of time, during which they have expressed sharp disagreements with many of these ideas, have helped me both to rethink as well as to clarify my argument.

References

Agarwal, Bina, 1989, 'Rural Women, Poverty and Natural Resources', *Economic and Political Weekly,* 28 October.

Agnes, Flavia, 1991, 'A Critical Review of Enactments on Violence Against Women', in Maithreyi Krishna Raj (ed.), *Women and Violence: A Country Report,* SNDT University, Bombay.

———, 1992. 'Protecting Women Against Violence? Review of a Decade of Legislation 180–9', *Economic and Political Weekly,* 25 April.

Alexander, Sally, 1976, 'Women's Work in Nineteenth-Century London; A Study of the Years 1820–50', in Juliet Mitchell and Anne Oakley (eds), *The Rights and Wrongs of Women,* Penguin, Harmondsworth.

Altekar, A. S., 1952, *Sources of Hindu Dharma,* Institute of Public Administration, Sholapur.

Arunima, G., 1992, *Colonialism and the Transformation of Matriliny in Malabar: 1850–1940,* Ph.D. Dissertation, Department of History, Cambridge University.

Atkins, S. and B. Hoggett, 1984, *Women and the Law,* Basil Blackwell, Oxford and New York.

Barrett, Michele, 1984, 'Rethinking Women's Oppression Today: A Reply to Brenner and Ramas', *New Left Review* 146, July–August.

Baxi, Upendra, 1982, *The Crisis in the Indian Legal System,* Vikas, New Delhi.

———, 1986, *Towards a Sociology of Indian Law,* Satvahan, New Delhi.

———, 1987, 'From Human Rights to the Right to be Human', in Upendra Baxi (ed.), *The Right to be Human,* Lancer International, New Delhi.

———, 1992, 'The State's Emissary: The Place of Law in Subaltern

Studies', in Pratha Chatterjee and Gyanendra Pandey (eds), *Subaltern Studies VII*, Oxford University Press, Delhi.

Brown, Beverley, 1986, 'Litigating Feminisms', *Economy and Society*, vol. 20, No. 4, November.

Butler, Judith, 1992, 'The Lesbian Phallus and the Morphological Imaginary', in *Differences, A Journal of Feminist Cultural Studies*, vol. 4, Spring.

Bumiller, Kristin, 1991, 'Fallen Angels: The Representation of Violence Against Women in Legal Culture', in Martha Albertson Fineman and Nancy Sweet Thomadsen (eds), *At the Boundaries of Law*, Routledge, New York.

Das, Veena, 1986, 'Deciding on Moral Issues: The Case of Abortion', in Diana L. Eck and Devaki Jain (eds), *Speaking of Faith*, Kali For Women, New Delhi.

Derrida, Jacques, 1990, 'Force of Law: The Mystical Foundation of Authority' (tr. Mary Quaintance), in *Deconstruction and the Possibility of Justice*, a special issue of *Cardozo Law Review*, vol. 11, nos. 5–6, July/August.

Douzinas, Costas, Ronnie Warrington and Shaun Mcveigh, 1991, *Postmodern Jurisprudence: The Law of Texts in the Texts of the Law*, Routledge, London.

Dworkin, Ronald, 1977, *Taking Rights Seriously*, Duckworth, London.

FASDSP, 1988, *Note About Proposed Central Legislation to Ban Sex Determination Tests* (Based on workshop 'Legal Aspects of Sex Determination Tests' held in Bombay, 24 September 1988. On file with Jagori Women's Resources Centre, New Delhi).

Fraser, Nancy, 1989, *Unruly Practices: Power, Discourse and Gender in Contemporary Social Theory*, University of Minnesota Press, Minneapolis.

Foucault, Michel, 1977, *Discipline and Punish: The Birth of a Prison*, Vintage Books, New York.

———,1978, *The History of Sexuality: An Introduction*, Penguin, Harmondsworth.

Frug, Mary Joe, 1992, *Postmodern Legal Feminism*, Routledge, New York.

Fudge, Judy, 1987, 'The Public/Private Distinction: The Possibilities and Limits to the Use of *Charter* Litigation to Further Feminist Struggles', *Osgoode Law Journal* 25:3.

Gabel, Peter and Paul Harris 1982–3, 'Building Power and Breaking Images: Critical Legal Theory and the Practice of Law', *New York University Review of Law and Social Change* 11.

Galanter, Marc, 1984, *Competing Equalities. Law and the Backward Classes in India,* Oxford University Press, Delhi.

Gandhi, Nandita and Nandita Shah 1992, *The Issues at Stake,* Kali for Women, New Delhi.

Haksar, Nandita, 1994, 'Dominance, Suppression and the Law', in Lotika Sarkar and B. Sivaramayya (eds), *Women and the Law. Contemporary Problems,* Vikas Publishing House, New Delhi.

Heller, Agnes, 1990, 'Rights, Modernity, Democracy', in *Deconstruction and the Possibility of Justice,* a special issue of Cardozo Law Review.

Kane, John, 1996, 'Justice, Impartiality and Equality: Why the Concept of Justice Does Not Presume Equality', *Political Theory,* vol. 24, no. 3, August.

Kapur, Ratna and Brenda Cossman, 1993, 'On Women, Equality and the Constitution: Through the Looking Glass of Feminism', *National Law School Journal,* vol. 1.

————, 1996, *Subversive Sites: Feminist Engagements with Law in India,* Sage, New Delhi.

Kingdom, Elizabeth, 1991, *What's Wrong with Rights? Problems of Feminist Politics of Law,* Edinburgh University Press, Edinburgh.

Kishwar, Madhu, 1994, 'Codified Hindu Law. Myth and Reality', *Economic and Political Weekly,* 13 August.

———— and Ruth Vanita, 1980–1, 'Why Can't We Report to Each Other?', *Manushi* No. 37.

———— and Ruth Vanita, 1986, 'Using Women as a Pretext for Repression: The Indecent Representation of Women (Prohibition) Bill', *Manushi,* no. 37.

Landes, Joan, 1988, *Women and the Public Sphere in the Age of the French Revolution,* Cornell University Press, Ithaca.

Lawlor, Leonard, 1989, 'From the Trace to the Law: Derridean Politics, *Philosophy and Social Criticism,* 15, 1.

Lingat, Robert, 1973, *The Classical Law of India* (tr. J. Duncan M. Derrett), University of California Press, Berkeley.

MacKinnon, Catharine, 1983, 'Feminism, Marxism, Method and the State. Towards Feminist Jurisprudence', *Signs,* Summer, vol. 8, no. 4.

————, 1987, *Feminism Unmodified,* Harvard University Press, Cambridge and London.

Mahmood, Tahir, 1965, 'Custom as a Source of Law in Islam', *Journal of the Indian Law Institute,* vol. 7.

Marcus, Sharon, 1992, 'Fighting Bodies, Fighting Words: A Theory and Politics of Rape Prevention', in Joan Scott and Judith Butler (eds), *Feminists Theorise the Political,* Routledge, NY and London.

Menon, Nivedita, 1996, 'The Impossibility of "Justice": Female Foeticide and Feminist Discourse on Abortion', in Patricia Uberoi (ed.), *Social Reform, Sexuality and the State,* Sage Publications, New Delhi.

————, (forthcoming), 'Embodying the Self: Feminism, Sexual Violence and the Law', in *Community, Gender and Violence,* edited by Partha Chatterjee and Pradeep Jeganathan, OUP.

Minow, Martha, 1983, 'Book Review', *Harvard Education Review,* 53.

————, 1985a, 'Book Review', *Harvard Law Review,* 98.

————, 1985b, 'Book Review', *Studies in American History,* 13.

Mossman, Mary Jane, 1991, 'Feminism and Legal Method. The Difference It Makes', in Martha Albertson Fineman and Nancy Sweet Thomadsen (eds), *At the Boundaries of Law,* Routledge, New York and London.

National Law School Journal, 1993, 'Rape: Challenging the Pedestals of Patriarchy', vol. 1.

Omvedt, Gail, 1986, *Violence Against Women. New Movements and New Theories in India,* Kali for Women, New Delhi.

Parasher, Archana, 1992, *Women and Family Law Reform in India,* Sage Publications, New Delhi.

Parikh, Bhikhu, 1987, 'The Modern Conception of Right and Its Marxist Critique', in Upendra Baxi (ed.), *The Right to Be Human,* Lancer, New Delhi.

Poovey, Mary, 1992, 'The Abortion Question and the Death of Man', in Joan Scott and Judith Butler (eds), *Feminists Theorise the Political,* Routledge, NY and London.

Poulantzas, Nicos, 1978, *State, Power, Socialism* (tr. Patrick Camiller), New Left Books, London.

Purewal, Jasjit and Naina Kapur, Undated, *Have You Been Sexually Assaulted?,* New Delhi.

Rapp, Rayna, 1987, 'The Power of Positive' Diagnosis: Medical and Maternal Discourses on Amniocentesis', in Karen Michaelson (ed.), *Childbirth in America: Anthropological Perspectives,* Bergin and Harvey, South Hadley, Massachusetts.

————, 1993, 'Accounting for Amniocentesis', in Shirley Linderban and Margaret Locke (eds), *Knowledge, Power and Practice: Medical Anthropology,* University of California Press, California.

————, 1994, 'Risky Business: Genetic Counselling in a Shifting World', in Jane Schneider and Rayna Rapp (eds), *Articulating Hidden Histories: History, Anthropology and the Influence of Eric. B. Wolf,* University of California Press, California.

Ravindra, R.P., 1990, 'Campaign Against Sex Determination Tests', *Lokayan Bulletin* 8.

Renhabib, Seyla, 1987, 'The Generalized and the Concrete Other: The Kohlberg-Gilligan Controversy and Feminist Theory', in Seyla Renhabib and Drucilla Cornell (eds), *Feminism as Critique,* Polity Press, Cambridge.

Saheli Newsletter, 1995, vol. 5, no. 2.

Sachs, A. and J.H. Wilson, 1978, *Sexism and the Law: A Study of Male Beliefs and Judicial Bias,* Martin Robertson, Oxford.

Sandel, Michael, 1982, *Liberalism and the Limits of Justice,* Cambridge University Press, Cambridge.

Schneider, Elizabeth H., 1991, 'The Dialectics of Rights and Politics: Perspectives from the Women's Movement', in Martha Albertson Fineman and Nancy Sweet Thomadsen (eds), *At the Boundaries of Law,* Routledge, New York and London.

Sharp, Andrew, 1990, *Justice, and the Maori,* Oxford University Press, Melbourne.

Smart, Carol, 1989, *Feminism and the Power of Law,* Routledge, London and New York.

Snider, I., 1985, 'Legal Reform and Social Control: The Dangers of Abolishing Rape', *International Journal of the Sociology of Law,* 13(4).

Sypnowich, Christine, 1992, 'The Future of Socialist Legality: A Reply to Hunt', *New Left Review,* 193.

Taylor, Charles, 1986, 'Human Rights: The Legal Culture', in *Philosophical Foundations of Human Rights,* UNESCO and International Institute of Philosophy.

Unger, Roberto, 1983, 'The Critical Legal Studies Movement', *Harward Law Review,* vol. 96.

Vance, Carole S., 1984, 'Pleasure and Danger: Towards a Politics of Sexuality', in Carole Vance (ed.), *Pleasure and Danger,* Routledge and Kegan Paul, Boston.

Weinreb, Lloyd L., 1991, 'What are *Civil* Rights?', *Social Philosophy and Policy,* vol. 8, Issue 2, Spring.

VI

The Women's Movement

IV

The Women's Movement

The extract from Nandita Gandhi and Nandita Shah's book, *The Issues At Stake*, reviews the various kinds of organizations the authors see as forming part of the present phase of the women's movement and analyse these in terms of ideology, organization principles and agendas. The extract is remarkable for the honesty with which it explores the struggle of women's groups to build alternative organizational structures. The issue of funding which has become the subject of intense debate, also comes up for discussion.

Radha Kumar's essay is an analytical account of the women's movement as it re-emerged in the 70s and 80s. It offers a broad overview of the significant issues for the movement and the relationship of these issues to mainstream politics in India.

Ilina Sen's essay is a response to a Marxist critique of feminism made in the 80s by an ideologue of the women's wing of the CPI(M). Sen's argument marks out the classic debate between Marxists and Socialist feminists in the Indian context and is a valuable contribution to the political interaction between the two.

8

Organizations and Autonomy

Nandita Gandhi and *Nandita Shah*

All issues, campaigns and social movements are sustained by the zeal and energy of a large number of people. In looking at them, however, the focus is usually on organizations: they are the ones that project beliefs, ideologies and strategies in a collective manner and indeed often become synonymous with the movement. But organizations are not just instruments for the implementation of certain objectives: they shape and are shaped by people, in their actions and ideas and histories are contained memories of their past, their origins, of traumatic splits, of dramatic campaigns, of hope and despair. The selection of a particular kind of structure, as well as the internal processes followed by any organization are statements of political consciousness.

The Indian Women's Movement has hundreds of organizations but no single one can be called representative of it. Equally, there are no accepted prototypes. How then do we perceive these organizations which give the movement a voice in the political arena? Why are some called 'new' or 'autonomous', others criticized as 'separatist' and why have women felt the need to experiment with organizational structures and debate the need for funding? There is no way we can enumerate the number of organizations which form part of the IWM. Several may belong in the register of public charities/trusts, others may be listed with the Welfare Board as *mahila mandals,* some recorded as trade unions, co-operatives, media organizations, or even as one of the hundreds of unofficial, unregistered groups in the court. Some are caucuses which function from within mixed organizations. The few existing directories of women's organizations give such sparse information that it is not possible to differentiate welfare groups from the more political ones.

Often, it is difficult to know if an organization is a hundred years old, or recently established, alive only on paper or a mature group. What can be said however, on the basis of historical evidence, is that the largest number of organizations emerge during the peak phases of social movements. A national seminar on 'A Decade of Women's Movement in India' (SNDT, 1985) which attracted women from different parts of the country, concluded that the last decade seemed to have been one such period.

The variety of organizations usually listed as belonging to the present phase of the IWM are support groups, agitational groups, grassroots groups, wings of political parties, professional women's groups and research and documentation centres (Desai and Patel, 1985). These are not distinctive or 'new' to this phase as most of them have counterparts in the earlier two phases. Today's support groups or those providing shelter, legal aid etc., were earlier called rescue homes. Several such homes were established during the social reform movement for housing widows, unwed mothers, battered women and destitutes. For example, Bapnu Ghar, Bombay, specifically caters to women with marital problems. The 100-year old Arya Mahila Samaj was one of the first organizations to provide space for women to meet and hold discussions and functioned as an indigenous YWCA with hostels and training classes. Its very existence was a protest in the face of stiff resistance from orthodox forces. The AIWC (1927) was more 'political' in its agitational forms and demands. Trade unions, mass organizations and women's wings of political parties have existed since the emergence of the multi-party system in India.

Most of the women's groups, new or old, service or agitational, had to opt for an organizational structure which best suited their politics. Many chose models based on the principles of centralized power and leadership. The selection of a formal structure with a pyramidical hierarchy seems 'natural' in a society which has, as its smaller unit, the family, while its highest governmental body concentrates of power in the hands of a few people. As the Women's Voice, Bangalore said,

It happened almost naturally. When we started organizing women in slums, each place would choose a few women to take the lead and act as organizers and they, with their counterparts from different slums, would decide on a joint action. So we standardized this by forming units and committees.

Lenin, often called the organizer of the revolution, reformulated this structure with built-in democratic mechanisms. His concept of a democratic centralist party has a tightly structured body, with members, including those elected from fronts, mass organizations and unions, and a small representative powerful congress. Each member has the right to freely voice his or her opinion at their respective levels but once decisions are made by the supreme body they are binding on all the members. The principles of democratic centralism have been widely accepted by political groups such as trade unions and mass fronts. But they have also been severely criticized by the Bolsheviks and Utopians in Europe as well as by the Gandhians, Socialists and women's groups in India. However, it has been mainly women's groups which have seriously tried to work out alternative organizational structures based on the principles of decentralization and collective participation.

Little Democracy and too much Centralism?

The Leninist Model

Based on the Leninist model is the Nari Mukti Santha, Assam, a mass women's organization of landless and small middle peasants which was set up in 1979 after the peasant struggles in Sibsagar which were organized by the Khetiak Santha and CPI(ML) (Santosh Rana Group). Its broad objectives, as stated in the programme adopted at the Biswanath Charali Conference on 23 and 24 June 1979 are:

To organize mass movements against all sorts of exploitation and oppression and against all sorts of social and domestic discrimination against women so as to establish equal rights for women and men in all fields.

Its organizational structure begins with the local level village unit, whose general body meets every three years or sooner to elect the district and state committees which, in turn, elect the president, vice president, joint secretary and treasurer. Each member has to pay a subscription of six rupees for one year of which half is retained by the local unit and the rest forwarded to the state committee. The organization's leader is a dynamic young woman who is also a member of the party. It is mainly due to her untiring efforts that the Santha has mobilized thousands of women in struggles for wages, against atrocities on women and for the rights of unwed mothers. In an interview with her, we discovered she was totally dedicated to her party and the Nari Mukti Santha. She firmly believes in the former's political ideology, its democratic centralist structure and the necessity of a women's wing. The latter allows the raising of relevant women's issues and the former encourages women's participation in the internal functioning of the organization as well as in the larger revolutionary struggle. If there was a problem, it was not so much with the time tested Leninst organizational structures as with the leaders and members. As an example she pointed to the success of the Nari Mukti Santha, the dedication of its leaders and the militancy of the masses of women members. To stress her point she recalled Lenin's words in a conversation with Clara Zetkin:

...real freedom for women is possible only through communism. The inseparable connection between the social and human position of the woman, and private property in the means of production, must be strongly brought out. We must win over to our side the millions of toiling women...there can be no real mass movement without women.... Our ideological conceptions give rise to principles of organization. No special organizations for women: a woman communist is a member of the party just as a man communist with equal rights and duties. Nevertheless we must not close our eyes to the fact that the party must have bodies whose particular duty it is to arouse the masses of women workers, to bring them into contact with the party and to keep them under its influence.... So few men, even among the proletariat, realise how much effort and trouble they could save women... if they were to lend a hand in 'woman's work' (Lenin, 1978).

Lenin's suggestions for the political involvement of women are taken very seriously by leftist trade unions because they usually have women members. Unfortunately they have found that although women often participate in demonstrations, they are hardly ever interested in involving themselves in union work. The Centre of Indian Trade Unions (CITU) is one of the oldest national unions in the country which still has a sizeable following. Its women's wing, the All India Co-ordination Committee of Working Women (AICCWW) was formed in 1979 in Madras in a meeting prior to the CITU convention, and was established as a national body with a membership of all CITU women's wings. The AICCWW has no formal constitution of its own but has separate state level meetings, holds elections from a general council of 500 members and has a working committee of 300 members who represent 42 industries and services. Its objective is to provide a national forum for the problems of working women and influence their trade unions to encourage the participation of women in union activities.

The AICCWW recognizes that more and more women are forced to seek work due to economic compulsion but are faced with closures, mechanization and retrenchment. The committee has consistently taken up issues related to employment, wages and conditions of working women. Its other area of concern has been the participation of women in trade unions. The CITU and the AICCWW have spared no pains in urging men and women at all meetings to take up women's issues and encourage their participation. B.T. Ranadive, the president of the CITU, asked leaders of the Railways and Post and Telegraph in 1982 to appoint special women's committees to work among women because unions are not meant only for men. Vimal Ranadive quotes him as saying: 'the dual role of a husband in the house and union leader in the office must end' (Ranadive, 1987). However, the AICCWW very frankly admits that there is still a great deal of work to be done.

The membership of the women in the union under socialism is about 45 per cent to 50 per cent of the total...in GDR the TU membership is 51 per cent...in the first convention it was found that women, even in industries and occupations where they formed a sizeable section were hardly represented in the leading bodies of the unions. After seven years we are not in a position to say that the situation above has changed considerably (Ranadive, 1987).

After years of experience in unionization and sincere efforts at increasing women's participation in unions, the CITU reiterates Lenin's comments: women need to be educated, freed from domestic drudgery and encouraged to overcome their diffidence.

Parallel Structures

Some of these problems have been addressed by another union, the Construction Workers Union which was formed in 1979 in Madras. This union has rallied together men and women working in the construction industry in almost all parts of Tamil Nadu. After an intense period of lobbying and public demonstrations, the union was able to introduce a Bill in the State legislature to regulate wage terms, bring better working conditions and introduce welfare schemes. Like the AICCWW, it was aware that women were inactive in unions because of their domestic responsibilities and lack of organizational experience, that they were losing jobs because they were unskilled and were being deprived of basic necessities such as creches and maternity benefits. Women also formed half of the union's constituency:

Construction workers come from traditional earth workers communities which built the earlier dams and ponds. Women have always been a part of the construction team. We formed a women's wing because it is necessary for women to have organizational experience which does not come through only participating in morchas. The Construction Workers Union's women's wing has its own committees and elected office bearers at the village, district and state levels. It was made compulsory for the main body of the union to have at least one woman on each of its committees.

As women do not have sufficient free time to attend meetings or as men may be working on different shifts, the union declares a holiday each month for all units and women's wings to meet as a general body. Each unit has a graded system of contribution towards union expenses. A unit can be formed with a minimum of 30 members who elect a committee with at least one woman member. Instead of level wise elections, the district, state and the council committees are directly voted in by all the units.

The parallel structures of the union with women office bearers and the women's wing both separate and integrate women's problems and 'general' issues. Women who may be reluctant to come to union meetings for any reason bring their problems to the informal women's wings. Everything from wages to desertion to lack of water supply is discussed, analysed and decided upon. Some of the issues are once again raised in the union meetings for action and consolidation. For example, women are aware that they do not get well paid jobs because they are not skilled. When they raised the issue in the union, it was impossible for men to oppose their being taught masonry. The second commonly quoted reason for women's retrenchment is protective legislation.

We had a huge demonstration of men and women to oppose the restriction on night shifts for women. This is not applicable to the construction industry because the laying of slabs has to be finished without a break. If women cannot work at night they will be laid off.

The third important issue for women workers is their wages, one that is usually ignored by the male dominated unions. A union activist narrated an incident when some women workers very hesitantly approached her with a complaint about *mistries* (foremen) hiring local women to work for lower wages.

It was a serious complaint and the women were afraid because the *mistries* had the power to recruit labourers and could take their revenge by not employing them at all. We did not want a men versus women or higher paid workers versus labourers fight. So we had a series of meetings with the women, then with the men and finally decided that as the local women were also workers they should be made union members and be paid minimum wages. The *mistries* realised that they should employ union women.

At another level, the union has also taken the responsibility of tracing errant husbands who try to avoid paying maintenance to their wives and children. The secret of blending what are called 'women's' and 'general' issues seems to be:

We don't see ourselves as a trade union. So everything connected with construction workers and not only with their wages is taken up. Ours is a construction workers struggle which is more of a movement for basic rights in society.

Overcoming Tokenism

The tradition of male encouragement and benign patronage towards women in politics was established at the time of the nationalist movement when many women emerged as leaders and politicians. Jayprakash Narayan (JP), a collegue of Gandhi, a socialist and later a Sarvodaya leader, spearheaded the Bihar movement in 1973 to protest against corruption and inflation. The Chhatra Yuva Sangarsh Vahini emerged as a student wing after the Tarun Shanti Sena, Samta Yuvjan Sabha, and several individuals merged to form an organization for men and women below 30 years who wished to support the movement. The Chhatra Yuva Sangharsh Vahini established itself as a mass organization with statewide branches in most parts of the country. After the lifting of the Emergency and the death of JP, the Bihar movement disintegrarted but the Vahini continued to initiate campaigns and work in different communities. Several of its women members also became active in the anti-obscenity and dowry campaigns, as well as those for land rights for dalit women. Today, the Vahini defines itself as an organization with a class, caste and woman-oriented perspective.

The Vahini is similar to most mass organizations in the sense that it has a national council as its highest decision making body (over the national, state, district and village level committees) which is re-elected every year. However, it has rather creatively introduced special provision which gives mass movement organizations like the Bodhgaya Andolan Sanchalan Samiti direct membership in the Council without having to go through the tiered elective process of representation. When women voiced the need for a Mahila Vahini, the organization agreed to form women's cells at each level to enable women to hold discussions and provide its members with shelter and financial support. Women were also given representation in the national committee. The women activists were happy at the quick response but troubled at why it was that, in spite of special provisions and encouragement, very few women gained entry into the central decision-making bodies of most organizations. From their own experience, they found that the criteria set for top leadership dissuaded all but a few determined women. Firstly the tiered elective path to the top was full of hurdles which could not be cleared by most Vahini women. The Vahini insists that women who wish to get in do at least a month and a half of rural work in a year or have one camp experience. The reality, however, is that having done a stint of rural activity most women return to their towns because of the very real problems of transport, the toll of living as single women or because of marriage. There are no provisions which take into account the work of those women who live in urban areas and have been active in the anti dowry, rape and obscene posters campaigns. So women do not have the same political stature as their male colleagues or the requisite mass influence. Secondly, in theory, organizational procedures guarantee every member an equal voice which, in practice, may actually mean the domination of the most assertive or articulate. Sometimes women find themselves outnumbered by men whose insistence on 'objectivity' and 'rigorous theory' as the only mode of expression ensures that women's voices and issues have a low priority.

If the Vahini was serious in its attempts to encourage women's leadership it should, argued its women cadres, have given women direct representation in the Council as in the case of mass organizations such as the Bodhgaya Andolan Sanchal Samiti. This would have ensured them a voice in the decision-making process, facilitated the raising of women's issues and strengthened women's political participation.

The Body and Its Parts

Another problem in democratic bodies is the tension which invariably develops between the party or main body and the 'wing'. A case in point is the Textile Labourers Association (TLA) and SEWA (Self Employed Women's Association) split. The TLA is the biggest single union of textile workers set up by Gandhi in 1917 in Ahmedabad. Several decades later, it was approached by some women head loaders and asked to take up their problems. The head loaders were referred to the women's wing which decided to procure credit facilities for them. In 1971, with the help of TLA, some 8,000 women were enrolled as members for drawing bank credit. In ten years time SEWA had already established a series of programmes for the self employed, for example their own bank, welfare schemes such as maternity benefits, widowhood and death relief, health security, creches, a small housing project, a production unit for making quilts, and a rural wing in colloboration with the TLA's Agriculture Labour Association.

Alongside these programmes, SEWA had staged some militant protests of hundreds of women (1978), moved the courts and appealed to the state government to set up an Unorganised Labour Board (1980). Though most of SEWA's programmes were developed jointly with TLA, its rapid growth strained its relationship with the main body.

One of TLA's major concerns and areas of conflict was SEWA's development programme. Such programmes, it was felt, would hamper SEWA's union activities. SEWA, however, saw the self-employed as a section which was exploited by different groups such as dealers, moneylenders and the police. If they were unconventionally called workers then their union too would have to be unusual in its approach to their problems. In 1977, a struggle for minimum wages for women *chindi* (rag) workers, handblock printers and bamboo workers provoked merchants to harass women by refusing to give them work. SEWA felt that women on the brink of survival could not struggle endlessly. A year later it set up the SEWA Arthik Vikas Nigam for setting up worker owned cooperatives. 'Pressure and development or union and cooperative—by linking the two, both the arms (of SEWA) have been able to uplift the worker from exploitation and unemployment.' (Bhatt, E. 1979) The debate between SEWA and TLA continued until SEWA made a public declaration supporting the dalits during the 1981 anti-reservation riots in Ahmedabad. Charging the organization with indiscipline, the TLA expelled it from its fold. The differences between TLA and SEWA were not irreconcilible but an organizational split would have taken place sooner or later. Though both have their roots in Gandhian philosophy, one had remained static whereas the other had developed an independent status, its own style of functioning and politics. SEWA's growth, popularity and dynamism was slowly influencing the hierarchical and paternalistic relationship between the two. SEWA's composition had compelled it to rethink its understanding of the formal and informal sectors, of unionization and development and men and women workers. Would TLA have allowed SEWA to experiment and grow, would it have accommodated it as a partner rather than as a wing, indeed, would it have transformed itself, democratized its structure and methodology and been willing to debate its theoretical inadequacies? Without such changes in the parent organization, it is only a matter of time before an organization's 'wings' spread themselves, and it breaks away.

Considering Equality

A group of social workers involved in organizing dalit labourers in Tamil Nadu have pre-empted the TLA–SEWA situation. They have set up two groups: the Landless Labourers Movement (LLM) and the Rural Women's Liberation Movement (RWLM). The two are organizationally linked as well as separate, autonomous bodies. The RWLM has been organizing women in over 55 villages of Arkonam and Tiruttanl areas in Tamil Nadu since 1981. 'The fundamental aim of this movement is to establish women's associations in town and village areas in order to create a socialistic pattern of society and economic upliftment.' Like the Assamese Santha, it too begins with the village unit which elects two members each for the area and general body committees. The general body, which is an elected body of 110 members, elects the executive body. Membership is one rupee per year. The RWLM works closely with the Landless Labourers Movement (LLM) in taking up what are called 'general' issues like wages, caste atrocities, and it meets for common discussions and planning of strategies. Each organization works independently of the other but the internal hierarchies of the RWLM and the LLM stop at the apex of their respective organizations. Then both are on an equal plane. 'Once some LLM members wanted to join the RWLM. All the women were firm: no, they said, we want our own organization.' By giving equal theoretical importance to class and patriarchy, the RWLM and the LLM have questioned the accepted sovereignty of the 'general' body or party as leader of all mass fronts. The RWLM have also organizationally responded to one of the most frequent criticisms made against mass organizations: the issue of leadership. Not many women in general and especially rural landless women have the confidence or want the responsibilities of leadership. It is relatively easier for middle class leaders to head and control mass organizations of the landless, peasants and workers. The RWLM's middle class activists are called 'organizers' and their main activity is to catalyze people.

There are different people: activists, villagers, non-activists etc. at different levels of consciousness. We have been slowly motivating and involving them. If women don't call their own meetings we try to find out the reasons, help organize them and show them the procedures. The tough part is decision-making. Women are not used to taking decisions without their husbands or fathers.

By deliberately withdrawing from formal posts, RWLM middle class activists encourage and train local, landless women to develop the skills and confidence to manage and run their own organizations.

The RWLM is also conscious of the problems of entrenched leadership so common within parties and mass organizations. Leadership, whether it is middle or working class, has its own problems and tensions within a democratic framework. Leadership when concentrated in one person's hands gives him or her total control of information and decision-making. No effective opposition can be organized and dissidents either have to toe the line or simply drop out of the group. Secondly, leadership also places a formidable burden on leaders which requires total dedication and time. Women are rarely supported by their families and therefore have very little free time, which makes it difficult to make a commitment. There are numerous examples of women leaders having chosen to remain childless or give their child rearing responsibilities to their parents.

The RWLM tried to form a collective leadership of eight women to distribute the tasks and responsibilities of a leader. It is significant to note here that the men in the LLM refused to participate in such an experiment, although they were not averse to bearing the burden, and the glory, of leadership. After a few months, it was found that it was not always possible for the women leaders to come from their villages, meet, share tasks and formulate plans. Eventually one of them took over the tasks and, as a result, the leadership. The experiment did not succeed so the RWLM adopted the yearly rotation system; interestingly, the present president has quite come to like her exalted position. For the RWLM the opposing pulls between encouraging dalit women's leadership and preventing them from becoming too established still continues.

Grappling with 'Space'

Apart from these attempts to re-create and modify the Leninist mode, there were others which stepped right out of its framework. The late 1970s were especially conducive for such alternative attempts because some women were dissatisifed with the marginalization of women's issues, as well as the hierarchy and bureaucracy in left and progressive organizations. Others who were influenced by or evolving a feminist understanding retained a dual membership in their mixed and women's groups. In addition, there was also the intangible but real factor of political euphoria, feelings of sisterhood and enthusiasm which moved them towards an alternative based on a different set of values and beliefs. Organizationally, it meant the rejection of large structures in which individuals became alienated cogs caught in the well-oiled mechanisms of traditional leadership patterns. Even in institutions like the family or at the workplace, women have always been at the receiving end of violence and injustice. They needed what was then popularly called a 'space' where they could relate to each other equally, develop their skills, share responsibilities and work out their theory and practice. It seemed natural for women then to turn towards an antithesis: the concept of a decentralized organizational structure. Without any precedents to go by, the decentralized organization was visualized as a leaderless collective with decision making by consensus, a voluntary rotation of tasks, emphasis on inter-personal relationships and an acceptance of political diversity instead of adherence to a prescribed political position.

These collectives declared themselves 'autonomous' or independent and undertook a variety of activities such as support functions, publishing magazines, cultural programmes, agitations and propaganda etc. They gave themselves names which recalled women's power, equality and struggle: Vimochana, Nari Samta, Chingari. Some registered themselves as trusts with a conventional structure but in actuality (like Saheli, New Delhi, Women's Centre in Bombay and Pennuramai Iyyakam in Madras) functioned according to their own set of rules. These groups, mainly urban based, form a very small part of the IWM but their existence is important as they make a political statement and project a vision of an alternative. For them, the struggle has not been easy: it has been like paddling upstream against a hostile current of tradition. Soon after the first protests, when women's groups had settled down to sustained action, many began to feel a persistent pressure from different sources to conform, adjust and fall in step. The media never quite grasped the idea of the collective. Intent on projecting the latest newsworthy topic, they would select women from the new groups and turn them into leaders and celebrities. A woman activist belonging to an underground Marxist Leninist group in Kerala found, to her utter amazement, that she had been transformed into a heroine. Another such uncomprehending projection landed an activist of the Chhatra Yuva Sangarsh Vahini in deep trouble with her colleagues. They were very disturbed that her part in the collectively planned campaign against a Muslim fundamentalist ban on women seeing commercial films had been widely publicized at the expense of the group. The police would often approach a group of women or an organization and want to speak to the 'leader'.

Unregistered groups have no status or standing with the law courts. Women and men who would come to these groups for support and help were often confused about their functioning. Then there was a more insidious pressure from within the groups that suggested that it was necessary to put the informal phase behind and move towards a formalization of structure and functioning. The women's wings of both Communist Parties asked the Forum

Against Rape, Bombay to reconstitute itself as a federation of women's organizations with elected office bearers. Others wanted it to officially register itself, seek accommodation and streamline its functioning. The rationale behind such demands was that spontaneous action has to consolidate itself in organized action and develop other projects for which there should be structures, programmes and a democratic electoral process. Actualizing an alternative decentralized structure has been a slow and difficult process marked by unanticipated problems, interminable debates and some painful splits. Some groups have returned to hierarchical forms and others have re-structured themselves. Unfortunately, these processes have not as yet been sufficiently documented. Perhaps these groups feel it is too early to evaluate and analyse themselves. In the National Conference on 'Perspectives for Women's Liberation Movements in India' Bombay, 1985, three groups out of a total of 85 opted to present their organizational functioning. One gave an oral presentation, the other wrote a factual report and only one probed and candidly questioned its organizational behaviour (*Report,* 1985). Perhaps the intermixing of personal and working relationships within groups makes these processes difficult to document; equally it could be the fear of being misunderstood or misrepresented that keeps women from speaking up. To maintain a public silence on internal organizational matters is not uncommon or surprising. Most organizations demand it by a dictate, or members themselves keep silent out of loyalty. Perhaps time and emotional distance from one's organization will show, as has been shown in the case of family conflicts, that organizational problems and processes, are political too as they reflect ideology, strategy and vision. Sometime now or in the future they will have to be discussed in an open forum with courage, sensitivity and objectivity. At present there is very little material to document. We have mainly relied on our experiences as members of women's groups to characterize the main features, strengths and problems of collectives.

Unity in Diversity?

Women have often formed political platforms and alliances with mainstream parties. The 1980s however saw the birth of several autonomous women's groups. In 1979, for example, the Forum

Against Rape in Bombay (later, Forum Against Oppression of Women) was informally created by women who had come for a discussion on the Open Letter written by four lawyers against the Supreme Court judgment on what came to be called the Mathura rape case. Saheli, in New Delhi, was started by a group of eight women who had protested together in several dowry murder cases.

We began to feel strongly that the women's movement had to provide an alternative support structure for women.... We did not start with a manifesto. Too many groups had fallen apart on ideological differences before they could even get started. There were (and are) different levels of feminist consciousness in our group but all of us share a common concern (Saheli, 1985 *The First Four Years*).

Many such groups proliferated, mainly in urban areas in different parts of the country. Some, like the Nari Nirjatan Pratirodh Manch, Calcutta, brought together a range of women from sympathizers of the ruling Communist Party of India (Marxist), to different Maoist groups, socialist feminists and activists of voluntary agencies. The Mahila Utpidan Birodhi Sangarsh Samiti, Ranchi, has brought together Maoist sympathizers and apolitical housewives.

Ideological heterogeneity exists in political parties too but is set aside by the willing submission of the majority to the party line which, the majority believes, analyses the present political trends and helps in planning strategy. Here, experimentation or debate are not encouraged, rather, what is stressed is adherence to tenets and policies. What probably made women activists of the 1980s more amenable to submerging their political differences and making common cause in the 'autonomous' movement was the realization that no political party had understood or realized the latent militancy and consciousness of women which had so resoundingly revealed itself throughout the 1970s. Perhaps it was necessary for women to distance themselves from traditional, accepted theories and practices, draw on each other's political experiences, to go back to the subjective and rethink their positions and actions. This gave them a collective strength, a spirit of militancy and a fresh approach to theory which became so evident that left organizations were forced to take cognizance of these groups.

However, there were also some unforeseen consequences. While some activists left these groups because of ideological differences, others felt that maintaining such diversity meant a reluctance to

have any ideological debate within the group. In Pennuramai
Iyyakam, Madras, some of the younger members complained that
the older ones were not interested in an ideological debate with
them. The older members felt that often theory which was
developed outside the group became a reference point and
influenced its working. In many groups discussions begin with an
issue and end with strategic planning; theory may find a place, but
theoretical discussions are mainly confined to women engaged in
research. There have not been many attempts to devise ways of
breaking the theory/practice divide and forming alternatives so that
different women can hold theoretical discussions. A study circle
formed by Shakti, a Bombay based resource centre, to discuss
analytical concepts such as partriarchy, feminism and its various
streams, had to close down for want of people.

Conferences and discussions, especially large ones, consciously
confine themselves to empirical findings and experiences for
maximum participation, while smaller meetings are often viewed
as élitist or irrelevant. As a result, most groups have produced papers
which mainly recount their activities and describe campaigns,
programmes or events. Women's groups cannot neglect to formulate
their own theory and praxis. If the collective cannot do so as a
group, it will require individuals from among its own members to
do this work. Another way this difficulty can be overcome is through
a co-ordinated effort by women's groups and women's studies
researchers and academics.

Formal and Informal Members

What makes one a member of an organization? Informal bodies
usually have no restriction on membership, their dues are nominal,
there are no party identity cards and no statutory attendance. Some
members prefer not to attend meetings, others come only for
demonstrations, others may be interested in particular campaigns.
One woman proclaimed herself a member of a group because she
felt she needed a group identity at a conference! In April 1983,
some women, tired of the Forum Against Oppression of Women
(FAOW)'s ad-hocism, asked for a formalization of the group into
a federation with representatives and voting rights. The majority
of the group rejected the proposal as they felt that as an agitational
group, the FAOW should be open to whoever wanted to be part
of it and was willing to work on the basis of collective decision

making. In practice this discouraged women belonging to political parties or groupings who could not take decisions in their individual capacities, that is, without referring back to their party. For Saheli, New Delhi the question of dual identity came up in a different way.

Due to certain circumstances, support for individual women is what Saheli got known for and before its other activities were fully developed.... At a personal level, it did pose a dilemma: to get absorbed into the task of helping individuals or to carry out other issue-oriented activities and campaigns.... Some members chose to resolve this dilemma by taking on campaign work in other organizations. For the rest of us it mean having a reduced collective strength and practically no choices (*Saheli*, 7th Anniversary, 1988 brochure).

Some of the older members saw no contradiction in having a dual membership in Saheli and in other groups because Saheli was an open organization and also because they felt their work in other groups aided rather than hindered Saheli's functioning. In the ensuing heated debate, it was decided that no member of Saheli could have dual membership which prompted five of its older members to leave the group. What makes an organization 'open' and how does such openness help or hinder its members and their efficiency? Some claim that an open policy gives ample opportunity for anyone who would like to join in or propose an action.

There is no exclusion of any woman from whichever part of the world, whichever group she may come from. A genuine lack of caste/class/political/religious bias and a true spirit of cosmopolitanism is something even the most ardent critics of the FAOW have appreciated (FAOW, 1985).

But there have been problems too. Journalists and researchers have attended the group's meetings and given distorted versions without understanding the context or background of decisions and actions. Some have given press statements on current topics which the majority have not discussed or agreed upon. Most important and disturbingly, such an open door policy has not encouraged a growth in membership. On the other hand, semi-open bodies too have lost members as well as the input of those from other groups who may want to give some of their time and energy. Perhaps collectives need to reconsider their membership policies.

Sachetana, Calcutta, which also works as a collective, has worked out its own method: they have retained the more conventional method of formal application, recommendation and acceptance of a new member by the group. This is based on their conviction that women should consider their membership and involvement in a group seriously and consciously. This gives them a sense of identity, responsibility and commitment. Formal membership also eliminates the problem new women may have in joining a group. They need not depend on older members or 'cultivate' them to be accepted into the group.

Subtle Hierarchies

Collectives have rejected hierarchies; they oppose the belief that there are some people with leadership qualities who ought to carry the responsibility of leading others. The leader, seen as a superior, talented person, can exercise considerable power over his or her followers. Collectives see this as an unequal, often oppressive relationship that denies others the room to develop their abilities and ideas. It is hoped that by removing the official post of a leader and decentralizing the structure each member will be able to relate to the other equally as well as assume the collective responsibility of leadership. It is easy to banish leaders and an administrative hierarchy but more difficult to maintain a non-hierarchical structure because of the presence of the subtle, invisible forms of hierarchy. In a group of volunteers, for example, there may be some who can afford to spend more time, take more responsibility and therefore have more access to people and decision-making. Women with full-time jobs and/or family responsibilities who may be equally committed, feel hesitant to intervene or opine on issues or actions. Sometimes, full time or paid workers had an edge over the part time volunteers. In other groups, volunteers, because of their non-remunerative 'social work' based on notions of altruism or sacrifice, were given a special status with no accountability. Then there are groups within groups which usually consist of people who have certain things in common such as education, social class, tastes, language or a political tendency. They can, at the same time be friends who share similar ideas and values and/or political comrades. This can be both a help and a hindrance to the group. For example work allocation is often swift and easily executed if people are personally close, but this can also lead to the formation of an inner circle which can become an élitist force and which often has control of the decision-making.

Most groups function so casually that they unconsciously follow procedures which prohibit free access to information. The combination of experience and information which founder members usually have can sometimes become the basis of hierarchy and power. Decentralization does not mean the complete rejection of procedures such as writing minutes and maintaining reports, rather it should mean the development of other, newer, methods. The problem of hierarchy most sharply comes up in deciding a salary structure. According to the concept of collective functioning, each member should get paid an equal amount.

Organizationally we need to ask whether a uniform salary structure is possible given that skills and experiences differ. Flavia Agnes, one of the founder members of the Women's Centre, Bombay says that the group battled with this problem for almost three years. The centre had followed a policy of employing women in distress who needed work as fulltimers, volunteers and part time workers. But it was not easy to decide how each worker should be paid. The idea of a need-based salary structure was rejected because women perceived their basic needs according to their class and education. A middle class woman for example, would find it difficult to live in a low rent *chawl*, or she may aspire to an expensive education for her children. The concept of seniority in terms of the number of years spent with the organization had its own problems: it could mean a disparity which need not be commensurate with people's skills, while differential incomes for different inputs were also not acceptable all round. Another dimension of this problem is the question of commitment to the women's movement. Should women's groups recruit their staff from the movement or should they also include professionals? Women from the movement and those from social work schools not only have different perspectives but different expectations of social/job mobility and salaries. For them, political commitment and expertise are not mutually exclusive. Nonetheless, it is true that women's groups have traditionally shied away from discussing details such as working hours, salaries, holidays, increments and other job conditions. But these form an important part of a harmonious working relationship. More discussion is necessary on these important issues as the survival and effective functioning of the group will depend on it. It has become increasingly clear that it was idealistic to imagine that there could be complete equality within a group. There are class, caste, cultural differences: some women have more stamina, others more time and fewer responsibilities, some have special skills or personality traits. The collective had set out to provide a space for the participation and development of capabilities of all women. On the basis of our experiences, we need to ask again: if we want a leaderless structure how are we going to undertake all the functions usually performed by the leader? Secondly, can we have rotating leaders or convenors who are more accountable to the group? Can we prevent the abuse of leadership by acknowledging everybody's contribution, by sharing access to money and information as well as teaching and sharing skills?

Allocation of Work

All organizations require a division of work in order to be able to function. Such categorizations often become rigid and prevent people from learning and developing their skills. They also place a value tag on each type of work which prevents mobility or promotion. Conventional organizations usually follow the job hierarchy which exists in society: for example, leaders perform high profile jobs such as public speaking, representation; educated middle class members might be involved in theorizing or debating; grassroots level activists usually mobilise people, organize demonstrations or do administrative work. The professed aim of the collective is to break these divisions and share work equally among the members. Instead, this often leads to problems: tasks are not completed on time, correspondence may or may not be prompt, and, occasionally, someone takes charge and pulls up everyone when the level of disorganization gets unbearable (Saheli, 1985).

As a magazine, *Manushi* could not afford to be leisurely about time. They found that from a group of 30 women with differing commitments and ideology, some took on specific tasks, others did but often did not meet their commitments and eventually the burden fell on a core group. This group then asked why those who did not work, should have any say in the decision making. Immediately after its first issue, there was a heated and disturbing controversy in which *Manushi* split and reconstituted itself. (Manushi Prakashan, 1987). However, what is also clear is that tasks are assigned to those who have some experience. This then leaves the less interesting tasks for others to pick up, thereby reinforcing hierarchies. Another aspect of shared responsibilities is the pressure on members of the group to undertake tasks they may not be comfortable with. Those who have never theorized before are asked to write papers because everyone should express themselves. Or those who had never climbed a public platform in their lives are firmly though gently asked to deliver lectures. In many groups women are often so apprehensive of task rotation that they disappear when they know their turn is coming round. Others find that their special talents like writing or acting are often simply ignored by the group. A good orator will not be asked to speak because she may seem to be taking over this important task. Ironically, task work-rotation in its literal sense can itself become oppressive for individuals.

Usually the load of work in collectives has not permitted the problems of work rotation and distribution to surface. Accountability has been an issue which has often led to quarrels and splits. Voluntary work done over and above regular, full-time jobs often means it has been hastily performed. Collective members are hesitant to pull up such defaulters, for who can say who is responsible for what. Some groups have established a system of deadlines and evaluations for paid as well as unpaid members. This persistent dilemma is central to the survival of collectives.

The Group Decision-making Process

To break the hierarchy between decision makers and administrators, informal and collective groups decided against executive or elected bodies and involved all their members in the decision-making process. Soon enough it was noticed that collective decision-making, especially in large groups, tended to either become painfully long (too many issues being handled in too short a time) or ineffective (delayed or repeatedly changed). Groups were then impelled to establish procedures for decision-making which would not prevent them from being open to people and their involvement.

For example some groups set up sub-groups which could meet, decide and implement programmes thus leaving the larger group to act as a policy making group. *Manushi* made a definitive link between work responsibility and decision-making.

Despite much unpleasantness, it was decided that in future only those women who were willing to make a regular time commitment and take on specific responsibility would be involved in the decision-making process. Others were welcome to give as much casual help as they wanted, but could not insist on taking part in every decision-making process (Manushi Prakashan, 1987).

Some groups which started informally later formalized their decision-making structures by co-opting serious and committed volunteers into a central body. Members of the formal body of the Women's Centre, Bombay who were accountable to the Charity Commissioner wondered why a collective method should place more responsibility on them. They asked all those interested in decision-making to join the formal group and share responsibilities as well as policy decisions.

Differences between group members in terms of their personalities, class, political experience, etc., also play an important part in the level of their participation. Newer members may need time to think or prepare before they make up their minds. We were once in touch with Maitreyi, Bombay, a seven-member research and training group which takes almost all its decisions unanimously. A group of like minded people? Perhaps, but its composition pointed to another factor. One of them, a pioneer in the women's movement, is vocal, resourceful and performed most of the groups administrative work and also suggested programmes. The rest were professionals who did not have her experience or time. Such a lopsided division of work and responsibilities created a situation in which she became the mainstay of the organization and its unofficial leader, and by virtue of this, dominated the decision-making process. Any views that were different from hers were unconsciously avoided or rejected. For decision-making to be truly collective and equal, it seems that not only is a common background of skills, political experience and time a prerequisite, but also respect and value for each other's views which overcomes the various differences between women and encourages each to be fully involved in the group and its processes.

Returning to the Basics

If more attention has been given to the discussion on collectives, it is because setting up collective structures is a brave step; it is more difficult to be non-conformist and search for alternatives. The process is slow, painful and arduous. The last 10–14 years have taught us invaluable organizational lessons which we need to now put together, clarify our concepts and realize our strengths and mistakes. We need to build ways which will encourage this search without extracting a heavy emotional toll from us. This is our contribution to such a beginning.

In the Indian context, 'space' for women to speak, empathize and share experiences has never meant rap sessions or small discussion groups which became so popular in the Western Women's Movement in the 1960s. For many of us, the organizational translation of this concept took place in different ways. It meant the creation of a 'space' for women within organizations to make them (the organizations) more flexible, accessible and sympathetic to women. It also meant the establishment of such a conceptual and political space through autonomous groups. We made a division between the formal or the more traditional structured groups and the informal structureless or newly emerging groups. But there is no such thing as a structureless group. Wherever there is a group that carries on some sustained activity and has a purpose, the group can be said to have a structure. The real difference is in the explicit or implicit nature of the rules and norms of the group. What are usually called structured groups have their rules in the form of constitutions and manifestos whereas the informal ones have tacit and flexible rules. Some of the problems which have plagued collectives have their origin in informality. In the late 1970s, when several women decided to come together and consciously play down their political differences in order to work together, they needed a flexible, non-bureaucratic and open body. They were willing to experiment with the setting up of a 'space' for women, collective decision-making and action.

However, over time, many of these groups, without much debate or conscious re-structuring, shifted from their earlier organizational form—that of a coalition—to being an organization. Coalitions are temporary, single issue, open groupings in which each member has an equal voice, status and responsibility. Organizations are member oriented and conduct a range of activities. While ideologically, women may prefer the open egalitarian nature of coalitions, practically they are often pushed into a more streamlined functioning with long-term objectives.

Many of us now believe that the painful transition from an

informal to a formal structure could have been easier if we had been more open in discussing our own norms and procedures. Informality need not mean no rules. Nor can hierarchy and power be wished away or banished so easily. Indeed, we now know that only experiments and discussions, long and arduous as they may seem, will create new guidelines and approaches. *Manushi* began as a broadbased collective and went through numerous changes.

It was only through a long, painful struggle that we came to know that merely using a label like 'collective' does not automatically create the reality of a truly egalitarian structure...we were a set of people with widely varying commitments, skills, time...women did not even know each other....' (Manushi Prakashan, 1987).

Eventually, the group dropped the notion of voluntary functioning and labour, as well as the notion of a 'collective'. In other areas, however, it continued to retain its links with the movement. It remained a non-commercial venture, refusing to accept advertisements or organizational funds. This meant Manushi's commitment to women required it to have a policy that the group needed volunteers to work on the magazine; the group has resisted using a set of individual names with defined tasks as commercial magazines do, it encourages women, regardless of their political persuasion, to work and learn in *Manushi* and maintains a vigorous network of friends and activists.

Saheli, in Delhi, feels it is necessary to have more discussion and conceptual clarity.

There is little understanding of the concepts of hierarchy and authority. Often, co-ordination by an individual is mistaken for authoritarian behaviour. Accountability as well as responsibility is mistaken for hierarchy. Disciplining by a group is seen as curtailment of individual initiative. Formal structures and procedures are avoided, either they are not established at all or there is a definite hesitation to use them even on democratic principles (Saheli, 1985).

This realization reflects a certain political maturity as well as a shift away from emotional reactions to experimenting with alternative forms of organization. Many women's groups now accept the inevitability of organizational chaos, emotional traumas, disillusionment and splits which come with the desire to change and re-structure on the basis of experience. There are several other dilemmas which need attention and debate: these relate to the familiar efficiency and hierarchy debate, the standards groups set for themselves in terms of working etc. as well as the possibility of resolving our conflicts without personalizing them and with the least amount of organizational and emotional damage.

In spite of all their problems and dilemmas, women's collective organizations have had an impact in as much as they have initiated a democratization process in mass and other organizations. Women's caucuses within mass organizations have demanded and created spaces for dialogue and representation, as in the case of the Chhatra Mahila Vahini. Mass organizations such as Women's Voice, Bangalore, maintain a more loose and egalitarian relation with their different units: the sister concern, the Domestic Worker's Union, functions autonomously with its own activists. The RWLM has established an equal, if not a more prominent status with the LLM. And groups which still function as collectives have not only re-structured themselves but revised their expectations and concepts without abandoning the broader goals of collectivism.

Funds for the Organization

Some amount of money is necessary for any group or organization to function. 'Going to the streets', a common enough protest action in any social movement, requires money for pamphlets, placards, loudspeakers, not to mention the time and effort which goes into getting press releases, police permission and contacting a variety of participants and officials. Organizations which provide services or work at the grassroots level have to pay salaries and bear the costs of office space and other administrative expenses. No movement can sustain itself for long without formulating a policy on money, its generation and utilization. During the nationalist movement, centrist organizations, unlike those of the left, were heavily funded by the emerging Indian industrialists, traders and big farmers. An activist posed the question thus:

Today, some extreme Marxist Leninist groups generate their funds from donations and raids on banks and rich landlords; this is a policy as well as a matter of ideology. The question of funding remains a sensitive one, and one on which it has been difficult to have an open dialogue without people's prejudices and moral stances coming to the fore. Today there are three camps, the ideal one which raises its own funds, the untouchables which take foreign funds and the tolerable ones which take State funds. At the most there is a debate like in the Patna Conference on the advantages and disadvantages of taking foreign funds. But have we ever discussed what are the problems in generating funds, in taking different types of funds, the subtle influences, the fear of co-optation and most importantly the utilisation of funds?

Organizations have to grapple with this dilemma: the need for some funding as against the need for autonomy. They have to ensure both their ideological as well as organizational survival. One without the other has no meaning and to look after both brings undeniable strain. Whatever be the source of the money: the people, government or foreign organizations, there is no denying that this will have some influence, however indirect, on the organization. Ideally, all organizations would prefer that their own members sustain the organization and control its policies. Small groups, coalitions and trade unions sustain themselves on the subscriptions given by their members. However, often, groups may have a very small membership or members may be many in number but may not be able to afford even a minimal membership fee. How these organizations will make up their funds is the crucial question for them. And how will such fund raising tie in with the organization's ideology and objectives?

Collecting from the People

The fear that outside organizational funding usually comes with strings attached has led several organizations to adopt the path of raising money from individuals, or holding charity shows. In 1988, Saheli, New Delhi, raised Rs 100,000 through a cultural show and sale of brochures. 'This process of reaching out gave donors an opportunity to give us ideas, criticise our work and give us referrals to other resources. We found this to be a very positive way of collecting funds for our work' (*Saheli*, 7th Anniversary brochure, 1988). *Manushi*, New Delhi, says,

We saw collecting subscriptions and persuading people to give donations as an important political task....In the process we were simultaneously linking many of them to *Manushi's* future...this seemed the best way of not only ensuring the reader's sense of active participation...but of ensuring its [the magazine's] autonomy....

There is no denying that donations are the best way of raising money for organizations. By going to the people with one's ideas and work, the organization seeks and receives a validation of its objectives and work. However, in spite of the general agreement on the usefulness and political correctness of collection drives, very few organizations have been able to depend on them over a period of time. The Women's Centre, Bombay has not ventured to repeat its massive 1983 effort of organizing a film premiere which enabled them to raise almost Rs 250,000. They found that a group of two fulltime activists and six volunteers had to suspend all their other work to concentrate on fund-raising for over two to three months. Sometimes this kind of effort is a break in an organization's daily activities and the massive effort it takes hardly seems worth the results that accrue from it. Insufficient or irregular income means insecurity for the workers and uncertainty for their programmes. This often dissuades experienced people, professionals or those with family responsibilities from joining the staff. Most of the time, fund-raising is a labour intensive and unpredictable task which often puts a small group of workers under tremendous pressure. It is common to find cases of 'burnout' among them, or a desire to shift to more secure, mainstream jobs. And finally, the common problem with donation drives is that the same group of progressive individuals is contacted year after year: activists and volunteers usually do not have many commercial contacts which can yield advertisements and large donations. In addition, it is also difficult for the few activists to reach a large number of people who are willing to give small personal donations unless they have done some community or trade union work. This vicious circle also works in another way. The Lawyer's Collective, Bombay, a group of lawyers involved in public litigation, was able to raise the initial amount needed to start publishing a legal magazine. They had hoped that, once established, subscriptions and a few advertisements would make the magazine self sufficient. But this specialized subject appeals only to a small audience of activists and progressive lawyers. A limited circulation raises its per copy production cost which then makes the magazine expensive for its activist readership.

Parting with Some Profits

Advertisements from business houses usually constitute a substantial income for charity shows. Organizations are sometimes able to persuade business houses to advertise particularly as companies can often write such expenditure off against tax. Business houses can also take advantage of special tax concessions for donations and for rural development and welfare schemes. Whether for tax benefits or welfare, many industrialists have made quite a name for themselves as philanthropists and social workers. The name of Tata is connected with numerous hospitals, research institutes, schools etc. Bajaj worked closely with Gandhi during the national movement to promote his 'constructive programmes'. Hindustan Machine Tools, Kirloskar Brothers and many others have set up ancillary workshops to provide employment for destitute or needy women. Organizations seeking aid from business houses have found that through personal contacts they can receive generous amounts and support. But, converting these one-time gestures into commercial transactions such as regular advertisements has proved difficult. In the early days of Manushi, its activists ruled out advertisements as a form of soliciting support because,

... we were likely to be reduced to promoting detergent powders and fashion garments and because there was pressure from advertisers to make the magazine more glossy and 'attractive', we decided to stop wasting our energies chasing advertisements (Manushi Prakashan, 1987).

Then there is the matter of ideology. Earlier, business houses funded Gandhi and the Indian National Congress because they believed in nationalism, its modernization policies and the reconciliatory Gandhian approach towards labour-management problems. Today, business houses have political empathy not with the new and progressive groups but parties and forces which are opposed to the Congress party. Goenka and his Indian Express group has supported Jayprakash Narayan, the Bihar Movement and more recently the alliance of opposition parties. By and large they are uninterested in small 'non-aligned' groups and their alternative development models. At best they might employ social workers at attractive salaries and design programmes which are usually aimed at looking after their own workers or to augment their production processes. How else can one understand the behaviour and attitude of Hindustan Machine Tools in Bangalore or Kirloskar in Pune? Both sought to perform two tasks at the same time: to provide employment for needy or widowed women and take care of the marketing by linking it with their factories. Eminent personalities, wives of top executives and social workers set up and supervised these workshops. When the women workers found that they were doing the same work as the main factory's permanent staff but at a much lower wage, they went on strike. Both managements had public opinion on their side when they advised the strikers to be grateful rather than militant.

Vimochana, Bangalore could only provide moral (and some financial support) to these workers. Eventually, some workers left and the strike was discontinued. Unable to explain the disparity in wages, Kirloskar put forward a righteous and pained front. The editor of the company's Marathi magazine *Stree* was advised not to carry any articles on the strike.

The Taxpayer's Money

State funds are often referred to as 'our or the tax payer's money' to which organizations feel they have a right. Voluntary and political bodies include themselves as representatives of particular sections of the people. Voluntary groups think it is not only their right but also their duty to get State funds and supervise the implementation of the State's welfare schemes. The whole question of the relationship of voluntary groups and the State, and whether groups should exert pressure on the State to use people's money carefully, is a much debated one. Nationalist Indians criticized the older reformists for wasting their time collaborating with the British on social reforms. Some even forcefully disrupted their meetings. Gandhi, in his characteristically shrewd way, combined reform and revolution to follow each other in phases. Since then the Congress Party has continued to rely on voluntary bodies such as the Rashtriya Seva Dal (now almost extinct), Sarvodaya, youth and student bodies and voluntary groups for implementing its social and welfare programmes. In 1975, women's organizations were hopeful that the new National Committee on Women, with its special bureau to monitor implementation of laws, would usher in an era of collaboration between the government and the groups. Almost ten years later, the Rajiv Gandhi government held out another hope in the form of a separate Department of Women and Child Development within the Human Resources Development Ministry. It indicated that for the first time women were assuming importance in governmental plans. Programmes were impressively drawn up and huge budgets allocated for things such as a series of hostels in every major city and town, employment schemes emphasizing non-traditional work for women, short stay shelters and women's development corporations. Women's groups found an echo of their concepts and language, coupled with a genuine sympathy. But actually getting State funds was quite another matter. While some groups were relatively successful, others found that the bureaucratic tangles and delays were too time consuming to deal with as the new department had neither political clout nor an implementation machinery. Saheli, New Delhi says, 'Initially we made use of government funds for running our short stay home, but found the attitude of the government far from satisfactory.... There was a keen desire on their part to supervise our work rather than support it. So we stopped taking these funds.' SEWA found that the government's maternity benefit scheme was lying unutilized and undertook to implement it. Laboriously it registered hundreds of pregnant women and carried the scheme through. It was not long before State officials began, at first subtly, and then overtly, demanding that SEWA enforce the two child policy of family planning if it wished to continue the maternity benefit scheme. The government reserves the right to not only supervise and intervene but brooks no opposition from the recipients of its funds. In 1974 some of the Sarvodaya and other Gandhian organizations decided to involve themselves in the Bihar movement against corruption in the ruling party. The Congress government showed its ire by setting up the Kudal Commission to investigate what it called their acts of treason and other misdemeanours. Justice Kudal went on what can only be called an 'obviously partisan witch hunt' (*Times of India,* 9.8.89) and blacklisted 1000 groups. Finally after years of harassment, he referred 116 cases to various departments out of which 57 were dismissed for lack of evidence.

In 1985 the government declared that Rs 150–200 crores were earmarked in the Seventh Five-Year plan for the voluntary sector. Attached to this carrot was the proposal for a Code of Ethics and a Draft Bill for a Council of Rural Voluntary Agencies. There were several organizations which approved of a National Council of representative voluntary organizations which could strengthen the 'voluntary movement' by streamlining its relationship with the government in terms of funds and support. The Code would regulate the groups, keep a check on ostentatious life styles, give norms of performance and make organizations more accountable. Many others criticized the planned code as yet another way of controlling voluntary groups and depoliticizing them. Lastly, several groups point out that it is not only state bureaucracy and interference but the fact that the bulk of state funds allocated for development and welfare come, in any case, from foreign governments on the basis of bilateral agreements, which pushes them (the groups) into applying for foreign funds. The Norwegian, Dutch, German and US governments have generously funded wasteland, water, environmental, educational and women's programmes. For example, the Ford Foundation, with the agreement of the government, has funded the University Grants Commission in setting up women's studies cells in almost every major university.

The Foreign Hand

The government estimates that roughly Rs 230 crores is received annually from foreign donors by about 4000 organizations all over India (*Indian Express,* 23.9.86). This large and systematic inflow of money has drawn different reactions from the Hindu fundamentalist parties, the Communist parties and the government. It has also generated much fear and debate on the interventions of the 'foreign hand' or interference by foreign countries in the internal affairs and political processes of the country. Unfortunately, instead of giving serious consideration to these arguments, people have tended to take moralistic and righteous stances which have resulted in closing off all avenues for discussion.

Hindu fundamentalists were perhaps the first to raise their voices against foreign funds because of their opposition to Christian and Islamic organizations and their proseletyzing activities. As they could not ask for a ban on these organizations or their welfare activities, they constantly watched them for indiscretions, opposed individuals and maligned them.

Since the 1970s the Communist Party of India (Marxist) has vociferously taken up cudgels against voluntary agencies who receive foreign funds. For the CPI(M) foreign funds 'means foreign influence and that means foreign allegiance' (G. Dasgupta, CPM Member of Parliament). One of their members, Prakash Karat, has written an elaborate document on the grand imperialist conspiracy to 'harness the forces of voluntary agencies/action groups to penetrate Indian society' (1985). It is true that fronts have been used to channel funds for political purposes. 'Project Brahmaputra' which was exposed in 1979, involved CIA agents posing as researchers but clandestinely working in the turbulent North East region of the country. Co-opting voluntary groups and influencing them by easy money can be one strategy in the many different ways of covert subversion. But if we are concerned enough to go beyond the rhetoric of a grand imperialist design we will have to investigate different layers of the strategy of subversion. Will it not be easy for a power or powers to influence a country steeped in debt and heavily reliant on aid in the form of finance, grain and technology? Bilateral governmental agreements channel crores of foreign funds into particular countries and these funds are then used for development programmes, education etc., which can, if effectively used, break the back and rationale of local actions and movements. Similarly, new and sophisticated technologies help in gathering information on various subjects and areas. Equally, information and personal details are used to blackmail and pressurize governments. The evidence of the 'foreign hand' is all around us, so it becomes difficult to link it only to foreign funding. It is too simplistic to assume that all organizations are tools or agents.

The British Socialists maintain a worldwide network with other socialist groups, parties and programmes. The anti-Marcos movement in the Philippines, the anti-apartheid movement in South Africa or the erstwhile left government of Nicaragua welcome help from sympathizers. Many of the small groups supportive of these movements survive on outside help and finance. Those who provide this help see the process of soliciting and giving as a way of raising public consciousness and influencing their government's policies.

Marxist–Leninist groups believe that all voluntary work 'even the most progressive, is reformist in character and not revolutionary...volags [voluntary agencies] undermine the need for people's organizations in actual practice...'. (Swaminathan, 1985). The reform or revolution debate is an ongoing one but of late, political developments and people's militancy have forced voluntary agencies to take a more anti-State stand and the left to introspect about why movements seem to be developing outside parties. In fact, most of the recent actions of militancy, from tribals, dalits, students, women or informal sector workers have come from outside the organized left parties. This has raised a number of questions: can it be that left parties are losing their areas of influence to more dynamic, younger political groups which are critical of them? Why have they consistently refused to recognize them as left and democratic forces? And why have they chosen to so vociferously and aggressively attack voluntary groups rather than influence their conformist and incorrect ideology? Does not such a stand project that theirs is the only correct politics? Indeed, if any benefits have been derived from this fear and mistrust they have been derived by the state. All foreign funds, no matter where they come from, are monitored by the Home Ministry and the Foreign Contributions Regulations Act (FCRA), 1976. The FCRA prohibits foreign money being used for election purposes, or by the press, government servants or political parties (Clause 4). A lsit of 141 organizations of a 'political nature' such as unions, civil liberties groups, friendship groups and religious ones identifies those who have to seek permission prior to receiving funds. This Act came at a time when the government sensed the increasing politicization of the new non-government, non-party groups which were emerging from the church and voluntary sector along with the more political trends of Marxist Leninism, Trotskyism, radical dalit organizations etc. The FCRA provided an ideal way of keeping tabs on all groups, and by keeping the debate on funding alive the government was able to play off voluntary groups against the left parties and religious groups against each other by assuming the role of a neutral mediator.

If the voluntary sector is receiving large amounts of foreign money it is only because the government has agreed to this international transfer. On the one hand, this lessens the demands on its own exchequer and, on the other, it controls the 'type' of organization which receives funds. Organizations like AVARD which were earlier favoured by the Congress Government, soon earned the latter's wrath for their connections with the Bihar movement. The Gandhian rural development agency was charged with supplying maps to EZE, a German Christian funding agency. It is necessary for all public organizations, political or otherwise, to be accountable, yet neither the government nor the ruling party has attempted any such accountability. Also, the entire debate on foreign funds puts all foreign agencies into the same category. An investigation of a particular funding organization may perhaps provide some clues as to its motivation and ideology. Organizations such as Ford Foundation have a large fund controlled by business executives, government officials and other influential people. Their financial resources (for which they are not accountable to anyone but themselves) make them powerful in their relations with their own governments and those of other countries. Such funding organizations are usually at best status quoist or, at worst, fundamentalist. They are likely to be more interested in influencing and effecting change at state policy levels as in the area of health in which all sorts of dangerous foreign drugs and contraceptives have been advocated or in the field of education. None of them would, for example, suggest the Paolo Frierian method of non-formal literacy training which motivated thousands of Latin American Indians to take up issues related to their oppression. Then, there are smaller organizations which raise funds through donation drives, wealthy individuals, church-going parishioners and businesses. And even smaller ones which appeal to special groupings such as trade unions, socialists, environmentalists or students. These are, in a way, more accountable to the people or their constituencies. There are numerous examples of links between groups of donors, the funding organizations and the recipient voluntary groups. Such organizations usually have a liberal and humanitarian approach and are often under the scrutiny of their own governments.

Women's groups in the Nari Mukti Sangarsh Sammelan, Patna 1988, pointed out that the easy availability of foreign funds could lead to things such as co-option by funders, or lack of accountability to the group, particularly where funding (as with the Norwegians) is easily available to individuals, or it can create hierarchies and differences within the organization; freely available funds also attract all sorts of people such as professional social workers, or opportunists who take up stopgap work in order to gain experience before graduating to a more lucrative job. Usually such a mix of people coming to work together can lead to internal ideological and organizational problems. There is thus some truth in all the criticisms levelled at foreign funding. At the day-to-day organizational level, it is undeniable that easy availability of foreign funds brings changes in the group and the politicization process. On the other hand, it is also true that without funding many groups may not have been able to survive for too long or take up issues and research which have fed into the movement. Perhaps it may help this debate to step out of the boundaries of the pros versus cons and the either/or approach and shift to the importance of understanding and retaining one's autonomy, both financial and ideological. Trade unions, which were considered models of self sufficiency, also had to struggle for things such as office space, money and time. It is clear that it is not easily possible to take purist positions. Organizations connected to the left are proud of not receiving any foreign funds though they do receive some indirect support in the form of subsidized books, advertisements and free visits or medical treatment for their cadres in socialist countries. What they receive in large quantities is ideology, the correct line and international party directives. Several older members of the Communist Party of India still regret the heavy price they had to pay for following a pro-British policy during the nationalist movement. Time and several political reversals have forced at least some of the Marxist–Leninists to break their ideological dependency and formulate their own strategies.

Women's organizations have attempted to handle the conflicting pulls of control and autonomy in several different ways. *Manushi* has worked out a two-tier system of subscription in which foreign subscribers subsidize Indian ones. This, however, does raise the question of how far *Manushi*'s survival is likely to be affected by its foreign readers, the changing face of the Western and Indian movements and the organization's own theoretical development. So far, *Manushi* has succeeded in building its own identity and retaining a fiercely independent stand. As a service organization, Saheli, on the other hand, requires more money, equipment and people to maintain its many activities. At different times it has received funds for different purposes from the State, foreign agencies and through donations. It is therefore in a position to reject any one of them without the fear of collapsing. The Rural Women's Liberation Movement in Tamil Nadu functions as an autonomous political organization headed by dalit women leaders. It does draw some support from a few middle class organizers who are attached to a development and training agency. These kinds of linkages and interdependencies are becoming more and more common.

Our discussions with women's organizations brought forward several important points: First, organizations which have a strong political identity, an ideological direction and clear aims and objectives are the least susceptible to national or foreign, subtle or more direct influences. SEWA, for example, is not likely to succumb to any foreign donor or the government. When the Reserve Bank tried to pressurize SEWA to give credit to men or to organize men in the informal sector, the mass of women and their representatives firmly refused. Second, all organizations must strive to be somewhat self sustaining. Usually women's organizations provide free services to women. Can we instead have a graded fee so that those who can afford to pay can subsidize those who cannot? Not all sympathetic women have the time to belong to organizations or to donate their time to them. But perhaps some of them can donate a percentage of their income to an organization of their choice. The Manipur women have a tradition in which each woman is expected to donate one evening to the local women's organization's activities or for night patrolling for drunkards and drug addicts. Defaulting members are charged a fine.

Living One's Politics: The Question of Autonomy

What individuals within an organization are searching for is the freedom for the organization to function without restrictions. This search links up at a broader level with the quest for individual autonomy or self realization and independence. The concept of autonomy is not new for the Indian political scene. It can be traced to the influence to liberalism on the reform and nationalist movements.

Liberalism propagates the unreserved right of the individual to freedom and equality. Individuals as owners of their own mental and physical capabilities should determine their own lives. From all the reformers and leaders who spread this notion especially in the context of women, Gandhi was the most forthcoming, clear and radical. He advocated that women had a right to their individuality and should resist any form of force or violation of their personal dignity. He urged women to 'refuse to deck yourself for pleasing men'. He challenged Hindu social tradition by saying that women should not surrender their bodies and minds upon marriage. When asked what should be done if women opposed the removal of untouchability, or nationalism, Gandhi said that husbands cannot deny their wives a right to their own views even if the views were not progressive. Throughout the reform and nationalist movements, this idea of individual freedom was accepted by women in their personal and organizational lives, where they often met with resistance, and discouragement, from their families and colleagues. This has also been generally true for other oppressed people who are given no political space to assert their rights, for example tribals, dalits and ethnic minorities. Each such grouping has broken away from mainstream organizations and politics. Yet, in spite of the familiarity of the idea, the formation of a few new women's groups in the early 1980s and the assertion of autonomy on their part caused a commotion. Autonomous groups were considered an oddity, popularly denigrated as anti-male and attacked by the left parties as 'separatists'.

Verbal explanations and a few hastily written papers did nothing to clarify the concept of autonomy or its usage. Vimal Ranadive, one of the leading members of the All India Working Women's Co-ordination Committee, and the Delhi Janwadi Mahila Samiti, derisively quotes a definition of autonomy, 'Autonomy may be defined in terms of men, the State and political parties. In effect, it is a safeguard against patriarchy within all the concerned institutions' (Datar, 1983). Randive then goes on to declare all such autonomous organizations as feminist, ideologically misguided and potentially dangerous on the political scene. The concept of autonomy is nothing but another attempt to put all men into a 'patriarchal class' and all women into a separate class. As propagators of autonomy, feminists were encouraging a struggle between men and women, 'forgetting' the fact that unless both fight against the feudal bourgeois system both remain exploited (Ranadive, 1986). This 'men versus women' understanding has led feminists to concentrate on alcoholism, wife beating and dowry rather than issues such as price rises, war etc. She further states that by distancing themselves from political parties, feminists 'would not like women to be politicized so that they can march ahead....' Finally, she insinuates that the new groups are agents of the State, 'We have not come across any criticism on the economic and political policies of the government made by these groups. The question is raised why and what are the reasons?' This oversimplification and the attack on feminists is surprising as most of the left women leaders of today were influenced by the reform movement and had begun their political careers during the nationalist movement. They have often echoed Gandhi in urging women towards inner realization, strength and self confidence.

These women have themselves taken bold and unconventional

decisions in their lives. They have overcome numerous barriers, displeased their families, defied social customs, opted for inter-caste or inter-religion marriages, and survived as political activists in a male dominated party. Most of them have not only internalized the very essence of individual freedom, and courageously implemented it in their lives but have supported women and built up women's organizations (Gandhi, 1985), Why then is there so much antagonism to the concept of autonomy and the new women's groups? There is so far no single definition of autonomy which can be debated, critiqued and questioned. Perhaps this is because the concept has emerged from and is still being developed through political practice. Undoubtedly, there is a need to deepen the existing understanding on women's oppression and their political participation.

A major theoretical body of thought on women's oppression has come from the early socialists, Engels and Bebel, and has been reinforced later by the organizational principles of Lenin. It therefore becomes necessary to distance oneself from Marxist theory and practice on the women's question. This means critically reviewing Engels, interpreting Marx, re-defining and suggesting different concepts and developing a praxis apart from that of the left political parties through separate women's organizations. Autonomous organizations were visualized as spaces by women where they could come together to share their feelings, thoughts and experiences, voice their protest, formulate their own theory, strategy and demands, develop organizational skills, and create an environment of support and solidarity. Actualising this meant maintaining some independence and distance from men, political parties and the State. In practice we found that hardly any group maintained such autonomy. It was more a matter of keeping this picture before them as an ideal to help them develop a sense of autonomy. A closer look at the composition of the new groups shows that the majority of these have members who have either come from mixed groups or continue to maintain personal or organizational links with them. It is also common for women to have dual membership in women's and civil rights or mass organizations. Apart from this, many women are married, sometimes to men in progressive groups. Secondly, a large number of the new groups are not only women's groups but caucuses such as the Mahila Vahini within the Chhatra Yuva Sangarsh Vahini, or structurally linked like the RWLM to the LLM. Sympathetic men have always been involved and groups such as the FAOW, Bombay, earlier invited men to their public demonstrations. Chingari, Ahmedabad organized separate meetings for men. Women's Voice, Bangalore, spent hours debating whether middle class women should be admitted but never bothered about the few men who helped out and attended their meetings. It seems that the flag waving, anti-men, hysterical caricature of feminists has been drawn from the biased descriptions of the Western media and quite falsely applied to the Indian situation. Indeed, no women's group has so far denounced men or male organizations.

Men have been excluded from women's organizations not because they are men but because women need to overcome their dependency on them and build confidence and organizational skills for themselves. The formation of women's groups as separate from either the State or political parties is a statement about their desire to remain independent. This however does not mean that they wish to remain separate and in isolation from mainstream politics. Given the situation and issue, they have co-operated with and challenged both the State and political parties. Many women's groups have participated in the special efforts made by the State in setting up women's cells in police stations, education programmes, research units or committees for recommendations. They have also accepted funds from the State for their programmes. The broad trend however has been to form alliances with left women's wings and other progressive organizations to demonstrate against and take the State to task. Vimal Ranadive herself cites several examples of joint actions between the Janwadi Mahila Samiti and autonomous groups. The Marxist Leninist party, the Indian People's Front, included autonomous women's groups in its convention in Calcutta in 1986. It could be asked that if members of the autonomous groups are linked with mixed and mass organizations and believe in joint action and coalition why do they insist on organizational independence? Is not such an independence purely notional? Women's groups believe that organizational autonomy is a prerequisite for ideological reviewing and for any experimentation that may be necessary for the development of a different theory and practice. They have, however, discovered that even with organizational autonomy it has not always been easy to shed their earlier patterns of thinking.

Stree Shakti Sanghatana, Hyderabad, in a candidly written

article admitted that, 'Initially we...were extremely anxious to emphasize the Marxist component in our Marxist Feminist approach' (Kannabiran et al., 1986). It took the group a good many years to realize that in spite of organizational distance it was still working within the same paradigm set by the left and taking the same issues such as custodial or landlord rape in the same form. Yet it was because of its autonomy that the group could maintain a loose structure and a more participatory and democratic decision-making process.

For women's groups being autonomous seems to mean proclaiming independence without disturbing one's dual membership; rejecting male-dominated organizations; being conscious of the hold of prevalent ideology and praxis along with the desire to review it; and choosing to make common cause with like-minded organizations. Given all of these, is there any one way in which we can define autonomy? Which groups can be called autonomous? Obviously there is no one brand of autonomous groups which believe and follow a particular ideology. The women's wings of the Chhatra Yuva Sangharsh Vahini and the Indian People's Front as well as the smaller new groups unhesitatingly call themselves autonomous. On the other hand, certain left party women's organizations which go out of their way to declare themselves autonomous are rejected by others as mere 'wings'. Are there degrees or levels of autonomy which groups accept or reject? Some of the confusion around the concept of autonomy can be cleared if we differentiate autonomy from separatism. Separatism means the policy of keeping away from certain people, things or organizations whereas autonomy is a complex political concept.

The difference between the two is not mere semantic hair splitting. One might ask whether leaving the home and family can be placed alongside taking *sanyas* or renouncing the world. Can abstaining from meat take the place of vegetarianism? In both cases simplification would rob the terms of their spiritual and political dimensions. As autonomy is a developing concept it should be viewed more as a process or a state of being one aspires to rather than a set of conditions which, if fulfilled, give an individual or organization the label of autonomous.

Gandhi had called autonomy becoming conscious of one's inner strength and purity, having the determination to assert one's beliefs and becoming self confident. He urged women to shed their mental shackles. Self realization was, for him, the first step in taking responsibility for oneself, one's rights, body, ideas and work. However, liberal thinking emphasizes individual judgement so much that it fails to take into account that beliefs, desires and choices are socially constructed and can often lead to self deception or conditioned responses. As social beings, women relate with other women, men, institutions, classes, the State, etc. Autonomy has therefore to be viewed in relation to other people, relationships, institutions and different aspects of life.

Individual freedom is a part of society's freedom, personal responsibility merges with the social, the private with the public, the family links to the State, etc. It is this integration of different aspects of life which gives the concept of autonomy a complexity, depth and contemporary connotation. This added dimension to the very individual and narrow perception and autonomy or self assertion moves it out from its specific individual framework. It can no longer be applied to only personal lives as Gandhi and many women leaders had done earlier but has to be so internalized that it fuses with every aspect of one's life. Striving for individual autonomy then means striving for autonomy for all women, realizing it within the family, asserting it with the State, changing the unequal balance in relationship with men and in general with other organizations.

Organizations do not become autonomous because they are dominated by women or because they do not accept State or foreign funds. There are several which keep the decision-making in their hands but are not yet independent. Rather, it is the internalization of this integrated and intricate concept and the continuous effort for its actualization which gives them a different dynamism and methodology.

Such organizations, whether they are part of larger bodies or separate, will keep women's individual and collective autonomy as their primary goal and build strategies around this. The concept of patriarchy explains the control of women's labour, fertility and sexuality by men, and if capitalism explains control at the material and ideological levels, then autonomy negates this appropriation by hope, self assertion and freedom. Autonomy means reclaiming what women have lost: their identity, their freedom and their rights. It means not delegating or entrusting responsibilities but taking them up oneself no matter how hard and impossible the task may seem. Women (with or without sympathetic men) will have to resist marginalization of women's issues, fight for equal participation, create alternative structures and develop their own analysis and programmes to realize their liberation. The attack of left party women is not so much on the concept of autonomy or their organizational autonomy, both of which they themselves have accepted. Rather, it is related to what the left sees as feminists' audacity to question Marxism and organize outside of the framework of left parties and trade unions. Perhaps it is time to break away from the Leninist suspicions of feminism and the conflict of nineteenth century European feminism and socialism and begin a dialogue based on the reality of Indian women's oppression and Indian women's groups. The concept has emerged and developed through a felt need and will inevitably disappear when women reach a stage of confidence and power and when they think that their theory, issues and organizations are accepted and are allowed to transform mainstream politics.

References

AIWC, 1986, Annual Session Seminar paper.

————, 1983, 'Women's Movement: A Feminist Perspective', paper presented at the Workshop for Research Project on Women's Movement at Lonavala, April.

Desai, N. and V. Patel, 1985, 'Change and Challenges in the International Decade 1975–85', Popular Prakashan, Bombay.

Forum Against Oppression of Women, 5 August 1980, *Police Terror on Women,* pamphlet, Bombay.

————, 1985, *Sharing Our Problems in the FAOW—Its Organizational Structure and Functioning,* paper presented at the conference on perspectives for Women's Liberation Movement in India, Bombay.

Gandhi, N., 1985, 'When the Rolling Pins Hit the Streets—The Anti-Price Rise Movement 1972', manuscript, Bombay.

Kannabiran V. et al., 1986, 'The Relocation of Political Practice—The Stree Shakti Sangathana Experience', *Lokayan Bulletin* 4: 6, New Delhi.

Lenin, V.I., 1978, *Women and Communism,* New Book Centre, Calcutta.

Manushi Prakashan, 1987, *Manushi,* New Delhi.

Ranadive, Vimal, 1986, *Feminists and the Women's Movement* (All India Democratic Women's Association), New Delhi.

————,1987, *Problems of Working Women and Their Participation in Trade Unions,* All India Co-ordination Committee of Working Women (CITU), New Delhi.

Saheli, 1985, *Saheli the First Four Years,* New Delhi.

————, 1988, 7th Anniversary Brochure.

Swaminathan, Srilata, 1986, 'A Letter on Voluntary Agencies and the Code of Conduct', Rajasthan.

9

From Chipko to Sati: The Contemporary Indian Women's Movement

Radha Kumar

In this chapter I offer a selective description of the contemporary Indian women's movement. I am selective partly because space is limited, partly because I want to cover a range of campaigns from urban to rural and radical to reformist, and partly because I describe key moments in the development of the movement since the early 1970s. Inevitably, my discussion is partial.

The phrase *the contemporary Indian women's movement* is itself debated in India. Many would argue that the campaigns described here do not fall under the rubric of one movement and indeed that the women who engaged in some of the campaigns did not regard themselves as part of an overarching women's movement. There is some truth in this criticism, and it is not my intention to misappropriate activity. Nevertheless, social theory would be that much poorer—and so, for that matter, would we—if we were always to restrict our definitions to those offered by the social actors. My justification here for using the article *the* (women's movement) to describe a sum of campaigns around issues of importance to women is that the campaigns fed into a network of women's groups and were part of a process of change and development in feminist thinking: As far as the public impact of women's campaigns is concerned, awareness of women's problems and rights has accumulated through these campaigns.

I have tried to find a concise way of describing this process by dividing the chapter into four sections. The first provides the context in which contemporary feminist ideas developed. The second describes the early feminist campaigns, which were largely city based. The third describes the period of growth and maturing when a host of movements and campaigns, both historical and contemporary, fed into Indian feminism. And the fourth deals with the years in which feminists faced a series of attacks and challenges.

WOMEN'S STATUS
Date of women's suffrage: 1950
Economically active population: M 84%; F 29%
Female employment (% *of total workforce*): 25
Life expectancy; M 57: F 58
School enrollment ratio (*F/100 M*)

primary	71
secondary	55
tertiary	37

Literacy: M 64%;   F 39%

The Context

After India gained independence in 1947, the Congress government made partial attempts to fulfill the promises it had made to women by declaring in the constitution the equality of men and women, setting up various administrative bodies for the creation of opportunities for women, and inducting a number of feminists into the government. In the 1950s and 1960s, therefore, there was a lull in feminist campaigning. The movement that started in the 1970s was very different from its predecessors, for it grew out of a number of radical movements of the time.

In the early 1970s, the Indian Left fractured, and some factions began to question their earlier analysis of revolution. New leftist ideas and movements developed, albeit on a smaller scale. Among these the most interesting movements for feminists were the Shahada and anti-price rise agitations in Maharashtra and the Self-Employed Women's Association (SEWA) and Nav Nirman in Gujarat. The Shahada movement, in Dhulia district of Maharashtra, was a Bhil tribal landless labourers' movement against the exploitative practices of non-tribal local landowners. Drought and famine in

Maharashtra during this period exacerbated the poverty already created by invidious rates of sharecropping, land alienation, and extortionate moneylending charges, and these conditions contributed to rising militancy among the Bhils. The Shahada movement began as a folk protest (through radical devotional song clubs) in the late 1960s. It took on a more militant campaigning thrust when the New Left joined the movement in the early 1970s and helped the Bhils form an organization, the Shramik Sangathana, in 1972. Accounts of the Shahada movement say that women were more active than men and that as their militancy grew, they began to take direct action on issues specific to them as women, such as the physical violence associated with alcoholism.[1] Groups of women began to go from village to village to storm liquor dens and destroy liquor pots. If any women reported that her husband had beaten her, other women would assemble, beat him, and force him to apologize to his wife in public.

Meanwhile in Gujarat, what was probably the first attempt at forming a women's trade union was made in Ahmedabad by Gandhian socialists attached to the Textile Labour Association (TLA). Formed in 1972 at the initiative of Ela Bhatt, who worked in the women's wing of the TLA, the Self-Employed Women's Association was an organization of women who worked in different trades in the informal sector but shared a common experience of extremely low earnings, very poor working conditions (most of them either performed piecework in their homes or toiled on the streets as vendors or hawkers), harassment from those in authority (the contractor for home workers and the police for vendors), and lack of recognition of their work as socially useful labour. The aims of SEWA were to improve these working conditions through training, technical aid, and collective bargaining and to 'introduce the members to the values of honesty, dignity and simplicity of lifegoals reflecting the Gandhian ideals to which TLA and SEWA leaders subscribe.[2]

Conditions of drought and famine in the rural areas of Maharashtra in the early 1970s led to a sharp rise in prices in the

[1] Maria Mies, 'The Shahada Movement: A Peasant Movement in Maharashtra, Its Development, and Its Perspective', *Journal of Peasant Studies* 3, No. 4, July 1976, p. 478.

[2] Devaki Jain, 'The Self Employed Women's Association, Ahmedabad', *How* 3, no. 2, February 1980, p. 14.

urban areas. In 1973, Mrinal Gore of the Socialist Party and Ahilya Ranganekar of the Communist Party of India–Marxist (CPI–M), together with many others, formed the United Women's Anti Price Rise Front, 'to mobilize women of the city against inflation just as women ... of the rural poor had been mobilized in the famine agitations.'[3] The campaign rapidly became a mass women's movement for consumer protection and its members demanded that the government fix prices and distribute essential commodities. So many housewives were involved that a new form of protest was invented: At appointed times housebound women would express their support for demonstrators by beating *thali*s (metal plates) with *lathi*s (rolling pins). The demonstrations themselves were huge, comprising between ten and twenty thousand women. Commonly, demonstrators would protest rising prices and hoarding by going to the offices of government officials, members of Parliament (MPs), and merchants, surrounding them, and offering them bangles as a token of their emasculation or by going to warehouses where goods were being hoarded and raiding them.

Soon after, the movement spread to Gujarat, where it was known as the Nav Nirman Movement of 1974. Nav Nirman, originally a students' movement against soaring prices, corruption, and black marketeering, became a massive middle-class movement joined by thousands of women. In its course the movement shifted from protesting these issues to mounting an all-out criticism of the Indian state. The methods of protest ranged from mass hunger strikes to mock courts passing judgment on corrupt state officials and politicians, mock funerals celebrating the death of those condemned by their courts, and *prabhat pheri*s, or processions to greet the dawn of a new era. Women also 'rang the death knell of the Legislative Assembly with rolling pins and thalis.' It took the police some three months to subdue the Nav Nirman movement, and between ninety and one hundred people were killed.[4]

In the same year as the Nav Nirman movement developed and was subdued, the first women's group associated with the contemporary feminist movement was formed in Hyderabad. Comprising women from the Maoist movement, the Progressive Organization of Women (POW) exemplified rethinking within

[3] Gail Omvedt, 'Women and Rural Revolt in India', *Journal of Peasant Studies*.
[4] Vibhuti Patel, *Reaching for Half the Sky*, Bombay: Antar Rashtriya Prakashan Bawda, 1985, pp. 8–10.

the Left. As in the Shahada movement. Maoist women were beginning to stress the existence of gender oppression and to organize women against it; but whereas in the former the question came up through the single issue of wife beating, the POW attempted an overarching analysis of gender oppression in its manifesto, which was largely influenced by Friedrich Engels and August Babel.[5]

The year 1975 saw the sudden development of a whole spate of feminist activities in Maharashtra. This has been seen by some feminists as the result of the United Nations' declaration of 1975 as International Women's Year. Perhaps the declaration did provide a focus for activities centering on women. But it seems likely that these activities would have taken place even without the declaration; for an interest in women's problems had been developing in Maharashtra since the early 1970s, as we have seen through the Shahada and anti-price rise agitations. Influenced by the POW, Maoist women in Pune formed the Purogami Stree Sangathana (Progressive Women's Organization), and Maoist women in Bombay formed the Stree Mukti Sangathana (Women's Liberation Organization). March 8, International Women's Day, was celebrated for the first time in India by both party-based and autonomous organizations in Maharashtra; the Lal Nishan (Red Flag) Party commemorated it with a special issue of the party paper. In August, the Marathi socialist magazine *Sadhana* brought out a special women's issue; in September *dalit*s and socialists organized a conference of *devadasi*s (literally, servants of the gods; or temple prostitutes); and in October a number of organizations that had developed out of the Maoist movement, such as the Lal Nishan Party and the Shramik Sangathana, organized a 'United Women's Liberation Struggle' conference in Pune. It was attended by women from all over Maharashtra, including some from left-wing political parties such as the CPI–M, the Socialists, and the Republicans.[6]

Especially interesting was the connection now being made between the anticaste dalit movement and feminism. The dalits, classified as untouchable under the Hindu caste system for their association with such polluting tasks as curing leather or clearing excreta, had a long history of anticaste protest in Maharashtra. In the late nineteenth century, under the leadership of Jyotiba Phule,

[5] Gail Omvedt, *We Will Smash This Prison*, London: Zed Books, 1980, Appendix II.
[6] Omvedt, 'Women and Rural Revolt'.

dalits had also espoused women's rights to education, against purdah, and for widow remarriage. *Janwedana* a dalit Marathi newspaper, brought out a special women's issue entitled 'In the Third World Women Hold Up Half the Sky,' a slogan borrowed from the Chinese Revolution to make clear its departure from First World feminism; some months later women from the dalit movement formed an intriguing new group called the Mahila Samta Sainik Dal (League of Women Soldiers for Equality). The name itself, which stressed equality and conjured up images of a women's crusade, drew on the Black movement in the United States, and the Dal's manifesto claimed African—American activist Angela Davis as a sister. Both the Dal and POW emphasized women's oppression; the Dal additionally emphasized the oppressive character of religion and the caste system.[7]

The declaration of a state of emergency in 1975 by Prime Minister Indira Gandhi interrupted the development of the fledgling women's movement. Many political organizations were driven underground, thousands of activists were arrested, and most who remained at liberty focused on civil rights, such as freedom of speech and association, the right to protest, and the rights of political prisoners. The lifting of the emergency in 1977 and the formation of the Janata government in 1978 led to a renewal of some of the earlier movements. Women's groups were formed all over the country but mainly in the major cities.

Early Feminist Campaigns

The distinguishing features of the new women's groups were that they declared themselves to be 'feminist' despite the fact that most of their members were drawn from the Left, which saw feminism as bourgeois and divisive; that they insisted on being autonomous even though most of their members were affiliated to other political groups, generally of the far Left; and that they rapidly built networks among one another, ideological differences notwithstanding. All three features were, however, defined and in certain ways limited by the history of these groups, whose first years were spent mainly in attempts at self-definition. The fact that most of their members were drawn from the far Left and belonged to the urban educated middle class influenced the feminist movement of the late 1970s

[7] Omvedt, *We Will Smash This Prison*, p. 174.

and early 1980s in complex ways. For example, one of the main questions that feminists raised in the late 1970s was, how could women be organized and represented? While there was a general agreement that it was not the role of feminist groups to organize or represent women, there was considerable disagreement on why this was so. For some, feminist groups were in essence urban and middle class and so could neither represent Indian women as a whole nor organize them; others believed that, although autonomy was necessary for the development of feminist theory, in practice it would divide existing organizations and movements. The role of feminist groups, therefore, was to raise feminist issues in mass organizations such as trade unions or *kisan samitis* (peasant committees), which would then be in a position to organize and represent women as well as men. Yet others believed that once a women's movement began, it would naturally spread and grow in multiple ways, creating its own organizations and representatives, and so it was superfluous for feminist groups to debate whether they should organize and represent women.

Many groups opted for autonomy, which they defined as separate, women-only groups without any party affiliation or conventional organizational structure, which they considered hierarchical, self-interested, and competitive. By contrast, the women's groups that were formed in the late 1970s were loosely organized and without formal structures or funds. The only party-based women's organization to be formed in the late 1970s was the Mahila Dakshata Samiti (Women's Self-Development Organization), which was founded in 1977 by socialist women in the coalition Janata Party.

While there was therefore a feminist critique of party politics, the terms of criticism varied widely: Some feminists were critical of party practices but believed that parties could enact valuable reform and fulfill feminist aims; others were critical of entrenched political parties, and yet others argued that political parties, even of the Left, were so centralized that they would never fulfill feminist aims. Meanwhile, the influence of feminist ideas was growing. Though the feminist campaigns in the late 1970s and early 1980s were dominated by the new city-based groups, a similar growth of feminist consciousness had taken place in certain rural movements. The 1950s sharecroppers' movement in the Telengana area of Andhra Pradesh was again renewed in the late 1970s, and the area was declared a 'disturbed zone' by the government. In Telengana's Karimnagar district, where women had been especially active in the landless labourers' movement from the 1960s on, the new wave of agitation began with a campaign against the kidnapping of a woman called Devamma, and the murder of her husband, by a local landlord. According to the Stree Shakti Sanghatana formed in the late 1970s in Hyderabad, the demand for independent women's organizations came from the women themselves, who raised the issues of wife beating and landlord rape through the *mahila sangham*s (women's committees).[8]

At around the same time, in the Bodhgaya district of Bihar feminist issues were raised by women in the socialist students' organization, the Chhatra Yuva Sangharsh Vahini (Young Students' Struggle Organization), which was involved in an agricultural laborers' movement for land reclamation from the temple priest who owned most of the land in the area. As in the Shahada and Telengana movements, women were active in the struggle, and in 1979 a women's camp in Bodhgaya decided that Vahini campaigns to reclaim plots of land would demand that plots be registered in the names of men and women.

The Movement Against Dowry

The first campaigns of the contemporary Indian feminist movement were against dowry and rape. Protests against dowry were first organized by the Progressive Organization of Women in Hyderabad in 1975.[9] Although some of the demonstrations numbered as many as two thousand people, the protests did not grow into a full-fledged campaign because of the imposition of the emergency, which drove most activists underground. After the lifting of the emergency, a new movement against dowry started in Delhi. This time it was against violence inflicted upon women for dowries, especially against murder and abetment to suicide. There have since been protests against dowry harassment and murder in several parts of

[8] Stree Shakti Sangathana, 'The War Against Rape', in Miranda Davies (ed.), *Third World, Second Sex*, London: Zed Books, 1984, p. 201.

[9] Dowry is the sum of money as well as other items (jewellery, furniture, car, other consumer durables) given by the bride's family to the groom's family at the time of marriage. Dowry is practised mainly by Hindus of all classes but has increased most significantly in recent years among the urban middle classes. At the same time, the size of dowries has increased, as well as the practice of the groom's family demanding additional dowry after the marriage.

India, but Delhi has remained the site of sustained agitation against dowry and dowry-related crimes, largely because it seems to have the highest number of murders of women for dowry in the country.

Although the Mahila Dakshata Samiti was the first women's organization in Delhi's contemporary feminist movement to take up the issue of dowry and dowry harassment, it was Stri Sangharsh, a fledgling feminist group founded in 1979, that drew public attention to dowry-related crimes. On 1 June 1979, Stri Sangharsh organized a demonstration against the death of Tarvinder Kaur, a young woman from Delhi who had left a deathbed statement saying that her in-laws had killed her because her parents could not fulfill the in-laws' ever-increasing demands. The demonstration was widely reported by the national press, and in the next few weeks there was a spate of demonstrations against dowry deaths, one of the biggest ones led by the Nari Raksha Samiti (Women's Rescue Committee) on 12 June through the alleys of old Delhi. Each demonstration was headline news, and a public debate on dowry and dowry-related crimes began.

Until this time women's deaths by fire (women doused with kerosene and set on fire, often by the in-laws and husband) had been termed suicide, and even these suicides were rarely seen as being due to dowry harassment. No one (including the police) had ever bothered to investigate them or even categorize them. And mostly they had been passed off as private affairs that took place within the family and were of no concern to the state. Within weeks, however, feminists reversed the indifference of decades, linking death by fire with dowry harassment and showing that many official suicides were in fact murders. Feminists recorded the last words of the dying woman, took family testimony, and encouraged friends and neighbours to come forward with their evidence. As a result, many families began to lodge complaints with the police against the harassment of their daughters by the in-laws for more dowry.

Campaigns against dowry deaths now began to be taken up by neighbourhood groups, teachers' associations, and trade unions. Within feminist groups a series of strategies was devised to enhance public awareness of the problems associated with dowry: Stri Sangharsh produced a street play, *Om Swaha* (priests' incantation around the ritual wedding fire), that attracted large crowds all over the city and continues to be performed by different groups today;

Manushi, a Delhi-based feminist magazine, organized a series of public meetings at which people pledged neither to take nor give dowry.

In 1980, a year after the antidowry agitation began, the government passed a law against dowry-related crimes that recognized abetment to suicide because of dowry demands as a special crime and made mandatory a police investigation into the death of any woman within five years of marriage. However, the law was a considerable disappointment to feminists. Although it acknowledged that dowry harassment could be construed as abetment, it did not specify the kinds of evidence that could be used to prove harassment, nor did it make abetment a cognizable offence. And though the law was passed in 1980, the first positive judgment under it did not occur until 1982, when a Delhi Sessions Court magistrate found two people guilty of dowry murder and sentenced them to death. The judgment was reversed by the Delhi High Court in early 1983. Women's groups from the party-affiliated Left and autonomous groups protested and were held for contempt of court. In 1985, the Supreme Court upheld the verdict but converted the sentence to life imprisonment. Moreover, the storm that women's groups raised in 1983 had some indirect effect: In December 1983 the Criminal Law (Second Amendment) Act was passed, which made cruelty to a wife a cognizable, non-bailable offence punishable by up to three years' imprisonment and fine; the act also redefined cruelty to include mental as well as physical harassment. In addition, Section 113-A of the Evidence Act was amended so that the court could draw an inference of abetment to suicide. Technically this shifted the burden of proof and thus lessened the burden upon the complainant. Finally, the act amended Section 174 of the Criminal Procedure Code, requiring a postmortem examination of the body of a woman who died within seven years of marriage.

In practice most of these amendments do not make it much easier to secure convictions for dowry death. Hearsay evidence has to be overwhelming for an Indian court to convict, as people will say anything to gain a point, even before a court of law. Traditionally most women are raised with the belief that after marriage they have no source of support—including livelihood—other than their in-laws. So the women themselves are loath to bring charges of harassment. Similarly, postmortem examinations do not necessarily give evidence of murder. As most dowry deaths are the result of burns, generally with kerosene, it is difficult to prove that they resulted from murder, which is why so many dowry deaths were put down to stove accidents before women's groups began to argue otherwise.

Overall the agitation against dowry-related crimes led feminists to varying conclusions. On the one hand, they discovered they could get massive public support for campaigns against certain kinds of crimes against women, such as dowry-related murder. On the other hand, they found how difficult it was to work with the law against such crimes. This latter experience was repeated in regard to rape.

The Agitation Against Rape

Beginning just a few months after the campaign against dowry-related crimes, the agitation against rape started with campaigns against police rape. The scale and frequency of police rape are quite startling in India: Police records themselves show that the number of rapes by government servants in rural and tribal areas exceeds one a day.[10] This figure vastly understates the actual number of such rapes, for it does not cover incidents of mass rape by the police (i.e. the rape of groups of women by groups of policemen, generally as a reprisal to subaltern movements for redress in rural areas); even in the case of individual or gang rape, the figure cannot cover unreported incidents, which are likely to be at least as numerous as reported ones.

When the new feminist groups were formed in the late 1970s, they were already familiar with the categories of police and landlord rape, for both, especially the former, had been addressed by the Maoist movement. Moreover, the issue of police rape achieved new significance in 1978, just as feminist groups were in the process of formation, through an incident in Hyderabad where a woman called Rameeza Bee was raped by several policemen, and her husband, a rickshaw puller, was murdered when he protested his wife's rape. A popular uprising ensued: Twenty-two thousand people went to the police station, laid the man's dead body in the station veranda,

[10] Figures of reported rapes in India, year by year, are provided by the Bureau of Police Research and Development in Delhi. Evidence for the statements made here is in the bureau's report in the *Times of India, Statesman, Indian Express,* and *Patriot,* 2–12 April 1978.

set up roadblocks, cut the telephone wires, stoned the building, and set fire to some bicycles in the compound. The army had to be called in, and the uprising was quieted only after the state government had been dismissed and a commission of inquiry into the rape and the murder had been appointed.[11]

In 1979, there were women's demonstrations against incidents of police and landlord/employer rape in many parts of the country. Campaigns against these incidents, however, remained isolated from each other until 1980, when an open letter by four senior lawyers against a judgment in a case of police rape in Maharashtra sparked off a campaign by feminist groups. Known as the Mathura rape case, the incident had occurred several years earlier, when a sixteen- or seventeen-year-old girl, Mathura, was raped by local policemen. Under pressure from her family and the villagers, a case was registered against the policemen, who were acquitted at the Sessions Court, convicted on appeal at the High Court, and later acquitted by the Supreme Court. The defence argument for the policemen was that Mathura had a boyfriend and was thus a loose woman who could not by definition be raped. The open letter was in protest at the Supreme Court's acceptance of this argument.

The campaign against rape marked a new stage in the development of feminism in India. The networks that had begun to form in 1978–9 were now consolidated and expanded and used to coordinate action. Finding this letter in the left-wing journal *Mainstream*, the Bombay feminist group Forum Against Rape (FAR, which is now called the Forum Against Oppression of Women) decided in February 1980 to campaign for the reopening of the case and wrote to feminist groups across the country to propose that demonstrations be held on International Women's Day (8 March) to demand a retrial. In effect, this was the first time that feminist groups coordinated a national campaign. Groups in seven cities responded to the FAR letter and organized demonstrations on 8 March demanding a retrial of the Mathura case, the implementation of relevant sections of the Indian Penal Code, and changes in the rape law. In both Bombay and Delhi, joint action committees were formed of feminist groups and Socialist and Communist Party affiliates to coordinate the campaign.

[11] This account compiled from reports in the *Times of India, Statesman, Indian Express,* and *Patriot,* 2–12 April 1978.

Meanwhile, protests against police rape were reported from all over the country, only some of which were organized by feminists. As in the agitation against dowry, the first protests against police rape sparked off a series of protests by neighbourhood and trade union-based groups in different parts of the country. The kind of press coverage that was now given to incidents of police rape and protests against them encouraged national parties to use the issue as a political lever against their rivals. When in June 1980 policemen arrested a woman called Maya Tyagi in the small town of Baghpat in Haryana state, stripped her naked, raped her, and paraded her through the streets, the incident aroused such furore from women's organizations and political parties that Home Minister Zail Singh went to Baghpat with ten women MPs and ordered a judicial inquiry into the incident. While they were in Baghpat, the Lok Dal, an opposition political party, staged a noisy demonstration (according to the newspapers) against the incident, claiming it underlined Congress misrule. Roughly a week later, Parliament debated the large-scale increase in the incidents of rape and atrocities against women, and several MPs used the issue to demand the resignation of the home minister and suggested that the death penalty be introduced to punish rapists.

Within months of the agitation, the government introduced a bill defining the categories of custodial rape and specifying a mandatory punishment of ten years' imprisonment, *in camera* trials, and a shift of the onus of proof onto the accused. The clause over which controversy raged was the burden of proof clause, which said that if the women could prove intercourse with the accused at the time and place she alleged, and if it had been forced upon her, then the accused would be presumed guilty until he could prove otherwise. Immediately there arose the cry that this violated the legal principle that a man was innocent until proved guilty, and the papers were full of articles vehemently protesting the clause, some of which exclaimed that this paved the way for every revengeful woman to frame innocent men.

The government had taken the wind out of feminists' sails by responding to their demands with such a radical piece of legislation. But this was only one of the reasons the agitation faded so rapidly. The highly publicized nature of the campaign and the speed with which rape was used by mainstream political parties in a welter of accusation and counteraccusation placed feminists in the invidious position of having to rescue the issue from political opportunists. Moreover, the nature of the issue, the kind of social sanction accorded to rape, and the problem of acquiring medical evidence to prove it in a country where only the big cities are technically equipped to provide such evidence constituted formidable obstacles.

Indeed, a 1988 Supreme Court judgment in another case of custodial rape, the Suman Rani case, showed how clauses in the law that were intended to ensure fairness allowed scope for interpretations that ran contrary to the purpose of the law. The sentence against Suman Rani's rapists was reduced because of the supposed conduct of the victim—in this case the fact that she had had a lover was held to militate against the crime of the rapist. This issue of conduct was especially important given the circumstances under which much urban custodial rape takes place. In Delhi, for example, the People's Union of Democratic Rights discovered that in several cases the victims had run way from home with the men they loved against their families' wishes; then the police had tracked them down in cities to which they had fled and used their 'runaway' status as a reason to separate them from their partners and rape them.[12]

The Supreme Court judgment was a staggering setback for the feminist movement, which in 1980 had appeared to have at least partially gained its point that character and conduct should be deemed irrelevant. Feminists reacted with a storm of protest. The National Front government responded promptly with the promise of yet another amendment of the rape law, this time concerning the rules of evidence. But the key question, of implementation and interpretation of the law, remained open.

However, the judgment also led to a renewed debate on the definition of rape in which feminists stressed that the technical deninition of rape obscured the fact that it was an act of violence because the definition treated forcible penetration by anything other than a penis as 'molestation' and applied a similar distinction to forcible penetration of any organ other than the vagina (except for anal rape, which it deemed an 'unnatural act'). Molestation, in fact, was much more common than rape according to police reports, but was generally regarded benignly as 'Eve-teasing' and rarely punished.

[12] People's Union for Democratic Rights, *Custodial Rape*, Delhi: People's Union for Democratic Rights, March 1990.

These early years of the contemporary Indian women's movement taught women's groups a series of lessons, of which the foremost was that there was considerable public support—from men as well as women—for campaigns against gender oppression. In effect, a handful of feminists discovered that they could garner public support and influence policy even though their numbers were small and their groups weak. However, this discovery did not bring unmixed pleasure, for it also entailed having to deal with the political exploitation of feminist campaigns, as in the movement against rape.

Growth and Maturing of the Movement

The mixed experiences of the campaigns against rape and dowry led many feminists to question their methods and tactics. The discovery that there was little and faulty connection between the enactment and the implementation of laws left many feeling rather bitter that the government had easily sidetracked their demands by enacting legislation. This gave rise to further questions about the efficacy of basing campaigns around demands for changes in the law and, by extension, around demands for action from the state. On the one hand, this questioning strengthened decisions to take up individual cases and follow them through the intricacies of the courts, no matter how long it took. On the other hand, feminists began to move away from their earlier methods of agitation, such as public campaigns, demonstrations, and street theatre, feeling that these had limited meaning unless accompanied by attempts to develop structures to aid and support individual women. In the early 1980s, women's centres were formed in several cities. These centres provided a mixture of legal aid, health care, and counselling; one or two of them also tried to provide employment, but they foundered for lack of sufficient resources.

Though centres to provide women with aid, counselling, health care and employment had existed from the early twentieth century on, these new centres were different in several important ways. First, most of the earlier centres had concentrated on one or two issues, whereas the new ones attempted to provide help on a range of interrelated issues. Second, the earlier centres had had a social welfare ideology, whereas the new ones were explicitly feminist. For example, earlier centres providing health care had concentrated on maternity and child welfare alone. The new centres, in contrast, took a more holistic view, looking at how women treated their own bodies.

Third, the new centres represented an effort to put feminist concepts of sisterhood into practice as well as to redefine these concepts by basing them on traditionally accepted structures of friendship among women. In both Delhi and Kanpur, for example, the names of the centres symbolized moves to locate notions of sisterhood in a specifically Indian context. Both chose to focus on and thereby reinterpret the traditional concept of a girlfriend; in Delhi, the name chosen was Saheli (Female Friend) and in Kanpur, Sakhi Kendra (Centre for Women Friends). Saheli, with its association of playfulness, was chosen by the Delhi feminists who set up the centre to signify that they were concerned not only with helping women in distress but also with sharing moments of play and pleasure. The centre's founders wished to give due weight to the positive aspects of women's lives, particularly their forms of celebration and creativity. This led Saheli to host a 1983 workshop for feminists from all over India at which there were sessions on song, dance, drama, and painting.

Attempts to appropriate symbols of women's power grew in the 1980s through reinterpreting myths, epics, and folktales and unearthing historical forms of women's resistance in India. To some extent an interest in tradition had been present in the Indian feminist movement since the 1970s. The street plays *Om Swaha* and *Mulgi Zali Ho* (A Girl is Born, performed in Bombay in 1979–80) had both used traditional songs and dances; many exhibitions mounted by feminists had similarly used traditional images. At that stage, however, the main effort was to detail traditional forms of women's subordination in India, from birth to puberty, marriage, maternity, work, old age, and death. In the 1980s, the emphasis changed to looking for traditional sources of women's strength rather than simply suffering. For some, this consisted of identifying images of women warriors to be used as a battle cry for latter-day women and to appreciate and recast Kali, the all-powerful mother goddess, in a feminist mould.

If the interest in tradition led some feminists to reinterpret images, others were more interested in defining the ways in which ordinary women used the spaces traditionally accorded them to negotiate with their husbands, families, and communities. Special attention was now paid, for example, to the way in which women appropriated specific religious practices such as spirit possession, simulating possession by the *devi* (goddess), particularly during pregnancy, to wrest concessions from their husband or families that would otherwise have been impossible. Accounts now began to circulate of women who had simulated possession to reform alcoholic husbands or get money for household expenses, and this tactic began to be highlighted as a means of gaining power.

The search for historical examples of women's resistance led feminists to scrutinize the distant and immediate past, to look at the role women played in broader movements for social transformation, and to reclaim some of the movements predating contemporary feminism. One example was the Chipko movement against deforestation in the northern Indian mountain tracts. Beginning in the mid-1970s, Chipko (literally, cling to) was a movement to prevent forest destruction by timber contractors and was carried forward largely by women, who were traditionally responsible for fuel, food, and water in the family. There was little or no discussion of it as a women's movement until the early 1980s, when feminists began to celebrate it as a mass women's movement and theories of women's special relation to their environment began to be advanced.[13] A new awareness of women's role and problems developed within the movement, and the hitherto defunct government-sponsored village- and district-level *mahila mandals* were revitalized.

By the early 1980s, feminism had branched into a series of activities ranging from the production of literature and audiovisual material to slum-improvement work, employment-generating schemes, health education, and trade unions. New attempts to organize women workers' unions were made. Interestingly, these attempts focused largely on the unorganized sector, as SEWA had done; unlike SEWA, however, they grew out of campaigns for an improvement in living conditions. By this stage the feminist movement had diversified from issue-based groups into distinct organizational identities. The first professions to feel the influence of feminism were journalism, academia, and medicine. Soon after the feminist movement began, most of the major English-language

[13] A classic example is Vandana Shiva, *Staying Alive: Women, Ecology, and Survival in India*, Delhi: Kali for Women, 1988. (An extract from the book is included in this volume).

dailies had deputed one or more women journalists to write exclusively on feminist issues, and a network of women journalists evolved. In Bombay, this network was formalized into a women journalists' group in the mid-1980s, with the purpose of lobbying for better reporting on women's issues, such as dowry, rape, and widow immolation. Feminism thus had a much wider audience than before.

Women's studies took off in the 1980s, initially under the aegis of independent research institutes such as the Centre for Women's Development Studies (CWDS) in Delhi, though an attempt to fund research at the university level was made by the S. N. Damodar Thackersay (SNDT) Women's University in Bombay, which set up a women's research unit. The SNDT and CWDS began to jointly host annual national women's studies conferences, and interest in women's studies grew so rapidly that today the University Grants Commission, a central government body, plans to set up women's studies courses at the college level.

While the influence of feminism in medicine has been less effective than in journalism or academics, the connection between theory and activity has been closer here than in the other two. For example, radical medical organizations such as the Voluntary Health Association of India and the Medico Friends' Circle have worked closely with women's organizations in campaigns against harmful pregnancy testing and contraceptive drugs such as Net-en and Depo-Provera, which transnationals have dumped in developing countries such as India. Because of this close cooperation, feminists have been able to generate much more detailed information on issues of health (such as the effects of Net-en and Depo-Provera and the alternatives to them) than on most other issues. And though feminists have been unable to eliminate some of the more glaring abuses of medicine, such as the use of amniocentesis to abort female fetuses, the connection between radical doctors and feminist groups has allowed them to use a wider range of tactics than in other campaigns. For example, in the campaign against the widespread use of abortifacient drugs for pregnancy testing, doctors' groups and women's groups were able to jointly argue their case before the government-appointed drug controller in 1986–7 and to pressure him into holding hearings about these drugs all over the country. They were also able to produce lists of doctors and medical centres that prescribed these drugs without warning patients of the side effects, which include damage to the fetus.

During the same period, the far Right began to organize its own bases among women. The Maharashtra-based Hindu chauvinist Shiv Sena (Shiva's Army) activated its women's wing to engage in anti-Muslim propaganda. Interestingly, its main argument was one advanced in the nineteenth century that had had enduring success in India: that the Muslim rate of reproduction is so prolific that it will outstrip that of Hindus.

An even more worrying development took place between 1982 and 1983 in Delhi, Rajasthan, and parts of Bengal, where attempts were made to revive sati, the practice of immolating widows on their husbands' funeral pyres. Under the aegis of the Rani Sati Sarva Sangh (an organization to promote sati), feminist discourse was used to propagate a cult of widow immolation. Women's demonstrations were organized in various parts of the country to demand women's 'right' to commit sati. In Delhi, feminists decided to hold a counter demonstration along the route of a pro-sati procession. This was the first time that feminists were forced to confront a group of hostile women, which was in itself so shocking that it took the heart out of the counterdemonstration. Most distressing of all, however, was the way in which the processionists appropriated the language of rights, stating that they should have the right, as Hindus and as women, to commit, worship, and propagate sati. At the same time, they also appropriated feminist slogans on women's militancy, for example, '*Hum Bharat ki nari hain, phool nahin, chingari hain*' (We, the women of India, are not flowers but fiery sparks). The feminists who attended that demonstration experienced a humiliating sense of loss on discovering that their own words could be so readily used against them.[14]

The early 1980s witnessed a series of countermovements against feminist ideas by sections of traditionalist society. The rise of these countermovements was partly related to the spread of feminism and the influence it was beginning to have on women's attitudes, especially within the family. The kind of support that women's centres gave women who were being harassed for dowry or forced into arranged marriages, for example, provoked a considerable degree of public and private hostility, and feminists began to face attacks from irate families in person and through the police and the courts. However, where earlier such attacks would have led to

[14] This experience was recounted to me by Nandita Haksar and Sheba Chhachi, December 1983.

a wave of sympathy for the feminists, from the mid-1980s on they were accompanied by a public, and increasingly sophisticated, critique of feminism. Much of this criticism took place in a context of growing communalism.

Challenges to the Movement

The issue of personal, or religion-based and differentiated family law became especially controversial for feminists in 1985 in what is now referred to as the Shah Bano case. In India, personal law falls under the purview of religion, though individuals can choose secular alternatives. This choice is, however, circumscribed: A woman married under Muslim or Hindu law, for example, cannot seek divorce or alimony under secular law; she has to abide by what is offered by the religious laws by which she was married. Neither Muslim nor Hindu personal law entitles a woman to alimony. Under Muslim law she is entitled to the return of her engagement gift *(meher)*; under Hindu law she is theoretically entitled to the gifts that went with her at marriage *(stridhan)*. Finding an abnormal number of destitute divorced women in India, the British colonial government passed a law under the Criminal Procedure Code (Section 125) entitling destitute divorced women to maintenance by their husbands. It was Section 125, which remains in Indian criminal law, that was at issue in the Shah Bano case.

Shah Bano was a seventy-five-year-old woman who had been abandoned by her husband and had filed for maintenance under Section 125. While her claim was being considered, her husband divorced her, using the triple *talaq*.[15] The Supreme Court, in its judgment, upheld Shah Bano's right to maintenance from her husband under both Section 125 and Muslim personal law.[16] It

---

[15] One of several methods of divorce permitted by Islam, the triple *talaq* is the easiest, requiring only that the husband say 'I divorce you' thrice.

[16] In upholding her right to maintenance under Muslim personal law, the Supreme Court referred to two verses from the Koran that had been cited by Shah Bano's counsel, Daniel Latifi:

Ayat 241	*English version*
Wali'I motallaqatay	*For divorced women*
Mata un	*Maintenance (should be provided)*
Bil maroofay	*On a reasonable (scale)*
Haqqhan	*This is a duty*
Alal muttaqeena	*On the righteous*

asserted that Section 125 transcended personal law. The court was critical of the way women had traditionally been subjected to unjust treatment, citing statements by both Manu, the Hindu lawmaker, and the Prophet as examples of traditional injustice. And the court urged the government to frame a common civil code because the constitutional promise of a common or uniform civil code would be realized only at the government's initiative.

The judgment was widely criticized by feminists,[17] liberals, and secularists as well as by Muslim religious leaders for what were held to be unduly weighted critical comments on Muslim personal law. The ulema (scholar-priests) issued a *fatwa* (proclamation) that the judgment violated the teachings of Islam. Wide publicity was given to the *fatwa*, and within a few months the whole issue took the form of a communal agitation claiming that Islam was in danger. One hundred thousand people demonstrated against the judgment in Bombay and at least as many in Bhopal, both cities with large Muslim populations. Supporters of the judgment were threatened, stoned, and beaten up.

Demands began for legislative action against Section 125. In August 1985, a Muslim League MP, G. M. Banatwala, offered a bill in Parliament seeking to exclude Muslim women from the purview of Section 125. Though the ruling Congress Party opposed the bill, as Muslim public protest against the Shah Bano judgment mounted, the party began to backtrack. To understand why the issue became so heated, one has to look at the context. In October 1984, the Vishwa Hindu Parishad (World Hindu Organization) launched an agitation demanding that a shrine in the precincts of Muslim mosque, the Babri Masjid, in Ayodhya be declared the birthplace of the god Ram and a temple be built on the spot. The VHP led demonstrations all over the country between 1984 and 1985, drawing as many as two hundred thousand people. The Babri Masjid issue and the Shah Bano case began to be linked as

---

Ayat 242

Kazaleki yuba
Iyyanullaho   *Thus doth God*

Lakum ayatehee la
Allakum   *Make clear His Signs*

Taqeloon   *To you: in order that you may understand*

[17] See, for example, Madhu Kishwar, 'Pro-Women or Anti-Muslim?: The Shah Bano Controversy', *Manushi* 6, No. 2, January–February 1986.

representing a Hindu communal onslaught on Muslims. The threat of Hindu communalism appeared especially strong in the wake of the November 1984 riots against Sikhs following the assassination of Indira Gandhi.[18]

In the 1985 state elections, the Congress lost in a number of Muslim constituencies. Alarmed by this, it announced that the government would consider a bill along the lines of Banatwala's bill, and in 1986 the Muslim Women's (Protection of Rights on Divorce) Bill was enacted. At the same time, the government let a local magistrate's judgment that the shrine in the Babri Masjid be given over to Hindus go unchallenged.

For feminists, the agitation around Muslim women's rights to maintenance consisted of a series of bitter lessons. They discovered the ease with which a 'community in danger' resorts to fundamentalist assertions, among which control over women is one of the first. Feminists also confronted the ability of the Indian state to accommodate the reactionary elements of both communities—on the one hand by taking no action against the Vishwa Hindu Parishad agitation and on the other, allowing personal law to cut into the application of uniform laws such as Section 125.

At the same time, the agitation posed certain issues that were to become increasingly important for feminists in the years to follow. There were the questions of secularism; its definition and practice, particularly by the state; and its relation to religious freedom. By and large, opponents of the Muslim Women's Bill espoused a classic liberal democratic view of secularism as a system that separated religion from politics, that disallowed religious definition of the rights of the individual, and that allowed freedom of religious practice only insofar as it did not curb the rights of the individual. A 1986 petition against the bill jointly organized by feminists, social reformers, and Far Left groups, for example, argued that all personal laws 'have meant inequality and subordinate status for women in relation to men' and that therefore religion 'should only govern the relationship between a human being and god, and should not govern the relationship between man and man or man and woman.'

As against this, the government definition of secularism appeared

---

[18] See 'The Muslims: A Community in Turmoil', *India Today*, 31 January 1986.

to be radically different. According to Prime Minister Rajiv Gandhi, 'secularism is the right of every religion to co-exist with another religion. We acknowledge this by allowing every religion to have its own secular laws.'[19] This statement seemed to imply that personal laws were defined as secular—presumably on the grounds that as religion in this instance defined the relationships between human beings rather than between humans and god, it was on 'secular' terrain. Religion, then, could formulate secularism. Another implication of this statement was that all religions had the right to representation within the law and the right to make their own laws. While to a certain extent these rights were not new, the supremacy they accorded to personal law reaffirmed the colonial codification of religion-based family laws and ran counter to the constitutional promises of offering alternatives to personal laws and moving toward uniform rights.

So much pressure was put on Shah Bano that she gave up the right she had long fought for, abjuring the maintenance the court had accorded her. As in the agitation against rape, the problems and needs of women were soon submerged by the discourse of 'community'. Even worse, in this agitation, setting a trend for others to follow, the individual woman was smothered by a newly constructed symbol of woman, the 'real woman' who followed men in demonstrations organized by Muslim religious leaders, who signed petitions against Shah Bano, who abhorred claims for maintenance because they were against her religion, and who saw feminists as unnatural creatures attempting to wrest her identity from her. This positing of the real woman in opposition to the feminist began to be widely made for the first time in the history of the contemporary women's movement in the mid-1980s, and it is revealing that this symbol arose in the course of communal–fundamentalist self-assertion. In the 1987–8 agitation around sati that followed on the heels of the Muslim Women's Bill agitation, the issues of secularism, religious representation, the Indian nation-state, and the symbol of the real woman were expanded even further.

In September 1987, an incident of sati in the village of Deorala in Rajasthan sparked off a campaign that gave rise to a furious debate that spanned not only the rights and wrongs of Hindu women but also questions of religious identity, communal

---

[19] Quoted in a brochure for the film *In Secular India*, by Mediastorm.

autonomy, and the role of the law and the state in a society as complex and as diverse as India. Within a couple of weeks of the incident of sati, several articles appeared that engaged in a polemic against Indian feminists, accusing them of being agents of modernity who were attempting to impose crass, selfish, market-dominated views on a society that had once given noble, spiritual women the respect they deserved.[20] These market-dominated views of equality and liberty were portrayed as being drawn from the West, so Indian feminists stood accused of being Westernists, colonialists, cultural imperialists, and, indirectly, supporters of capitalist ideology.

Given that there has been, on average, only one reported sati a year in post-independence India, the extraordinary debate that the 1987 sati incident aroused was puzzling. In a way it can be understood only as part of a process of political reorganization in which the death of Roop Kanwar, the girl who was immolated, became the symbol of Rajput identity politics. In contrast to some of the other areas in which sati had been attempted, Deorala was a relatively highly developed village. The family was well off. Roop Kanwar's father-in-law was headmaster of a district school, while she herself was a graduate. A Rajput family, the Kanwars had links with influential Rajputs and mainstream state-level politicians.

Roop Kanwar had been married only a short while before her husband died. When her marital family decided that she would become a sati, the event was announced in advance because sati is always a public spectacle. Yet her natal family was not informed. Evidence pointed to murder: Some of her neighbours said that she had run away and tried to hide in a barn before the ceremony but was dragged out, drugged, dressed in her bridal finery, and put on the pyre, with logs and coconuts heaped upon her. The pyre itself was lit by her brother-in-law.[21] Reports indicated that the local authorities knew of the planned sati, yet their only action was to dispatch a police jeep, which was overturned on its way to the site. Following this debacle, three more days elapsed before a government representative visited Deorala.[22]

[20] These articles appeared first in the Delhi-based Hindi- and English-language national dailies *Jan Satta*, 'Banwari', 29 September 1987, *Indian Express*, Ashis Nandy, 10 May 1987, and *Statesman*, Patrick D. Harrigan, 22 May 1987.

[21] *Statesman*, 18–20 September 1987.

[22] *Times of India*, 17 September 1987.

Immediately after the immolation, the site became a popular pilgrimage spot, and a number of stalls sprang up spelling auspicious offerings, mementos, and audiocassettes of devotional songs. Her father-in-law, prominent men from the village, and members of a newly formed organization, the Sati Dharm Raksha Samiti (Organization for the Defence of the Religious-Ethical Ideal of Sati), together formed a trust to run the site and collect donations. Within some three weeks the trust had collected around Rs 50 lakhs (close to $ 200,000).[23] The leaders of the Samiti were urban professionals or businessmen from landowning families whose sphere of influence extended over both rural and urban areas. Their propaganda was illuminating. Policy-markers and the intelligentsia argued that a representative state should recognize and legitimate Rajputs' claim that sati was a fundamental part of their traditions; a refusal to legitimize sati, they said, was a deliberate attempt to marginalize the Rajputs. The women's groups, for example, were represented as using the issue as a means to attack Rajputs. In the 1990 state elections, several leaders of the Samiti won seats in the state legislature.

As the pro-sati campaign developed, the argument about Rajputs was extended to Hindu identity. The head priests of the major Hindu temples in such centres as Benares and Puri issued statements that sati represented one of the most noble elements not only of Rajput culture but also of Hinduism and claimed that issues such as sati should be placed under their purview as arbiters of Hindu personal law and not that of the state. At the same time, they also raised the bogey of 'Hinduism in danger' from the opponents of sati.

The Hinduism in danger cry was echoed by far Right Hindu nationalists, spearheaded by the Shiv Sena, which organized a series of pro-sati demonstrations and argued that the Indian state was particularly biased against the Hindus, for it was willing to accede to the demands of minority communities for representation but was unwilling to do the same for the majority. The particular point of reference here was the Muslim Women's Bill, and, as in the Muslim Women's Bill agitation, the pro-sati agitation also posited real women against feminists.

The pro-sati agitators mobilized considerable numbers of women in their support. This allowed them to claim that they

[23] Ibid.

represented the 'true' desires of Hindu women and to accuse the feminists of being unrepresentative. So the feminists were placed in the anomalous position of appearing to speak in the interest of women whom they could not claim to represent and who defined their interests differently.

The tradition versus modernity argument further isolated feminists. The bogey of modernism was so successful that it masked the fact that sati was being used to create a 'tradition', despite feminist efforts to emphasize this. Tradition was defined so a historically and so self-righteously that it obscured the fact that the pro-sati campaign was run on 'modern' lines, with modern arguments, and for modern purposes, such as the reformation of electoral blocs and identity-based community representation within the state.

However, a closer look at the nature of women's support for the pro-sati agitation revealed that this was ambiguous and at many points consisted of firmly differentiating between the worship and the actual practice of sati. An examination of the women who were mobilized for the pro-sati demonstration made clear that they were not, in fact, the women who were most directly affected by the issue. Widows were conspicuously absent.

For most feminists, the campaign around sati revealed the growing opposition to feminism and spelled a considerable setback for the movement. Yet the challenges it posed to feminist self-definitions yielded some valuable insights: a more complex understanding of the ways in which different groups and communities saw themselves and a recognition that it is not helpful, especially at moments of crisis, to view the state as a monolithic entity, for it is important to assert that women have the right to a voice in the administration of their society. Representation consisted not merely of a show of numbers but also in the encouragement of a plethora of voices, which was to some extent taking place through the feminist and associated movements. Opposition to sati came from a variety of sources: Both the right-wing Hindu reformist tradition and maverick left-wing Hindu reformers such as Swami Agnivesh of the Arya Samaj opposed it. In fact, Swami Agnivesh challenged the head priests of the Puri and Benares temples to a debate on the scriptural 'sanction' of sati. His challenge was declined. Opposition also came from sections of the Gandhians and from the anticaste movement. Within Rajasthan, considerable opposition to both sati and state inaction on Roop Kanwar's death was voiced by huge numbers of women, largely rural, who joined demonstrations to protest against the glorification of her death.

Conclusion

The contemporary Indian women's movement is a complex, variously placed, and fertile undertaking. It is perhaps the only movement today that encompasses and links such issues as work, wages, environment, ecology, civil rights, sex, violence, representation, caste, class, allocation of basic resources, consumer rights, health, religion, community, and individual and social relationships. It is also one of the rare networks that encompasses party-based, professional, and independent groups and is flexible enough to bring old enemies, such as the orthodox Left and the Maoists, onto a campaign platform and allow traditional rivals among the socialists and the communists to forge a common alliance against the politically uninformed autonomous groups. An index of the movement's influence is the extraordinarliy large participation of women in most radical campaigns, particularly in urban areas. One of the most notable examples of the radicalization of women is that of the Bhopal gas victims. Following the tragic explosion of MIC gas from the Union Carbide plant in Bhopal in 1984, the one organization of gas victims that emerged as strong and sustained was the Bhopal Gas Peedit Mahila Udyog Sangathana (Bhopal Gas-Affected Women Workers' Organization). Though the organization is not feminist (indeed, it is headed by a man), a number of feminist groups work with it, and it is linked to the women's movement.

Structurally the women's movement has a vertical as well as horizontal reach: From a horizontal network of autonomous feminist groups, issue- and occupation-based women's organizations, development groups, radical professional associations, and party-affiliated organizations, it reached upward to administrative institutions, state functionaries, members of Parliament, and political leaders. Feminists are now invited to lecture at the Indian Administrative Services Academy, the training school for Indian government servants; they provide courses for the police, who have considerably expanded their employment of women; and many state governments have invited them to organize women's development programmes. In many ways it is the horizontal reach of the women's movement that has allowed it to have policy influence; in particular, the combination of the networking capacities of the autonomous groups and the mobilizing capacities of the Left party-affiliated organizations has often given women's campaigns a cutting edge.

These strengths are yet to be fully recognized. The attacks of the 1980s and the rise of communal women's organizations such as Rashtra Sevika Samiti, and the women's wing of the far Right Hindu Rashtriya Swayam Sevak Sangh have overshadowed the often quiet work being done locally and regionally and have brought political divisions to the fore. Relationships between Left party-affiliated organizations and autonomous women's groups are frequently strained by differing organizational interests, and each is wary of making concessions to the other. Moreover, the spread and diversity of the movement have coincided with a period of growing atomization, so that campaigns can sometimes be dissipated by the existence of numerous overlapping but separate lobbies.

Acutely as these problems are felt, they are minor. Of the roughly three thousand women who attended the all-India women's liberation conference in 1990 in Kerala, some 60 per cent were rural women, in groups ranging from development to church to leftist. In many areas women are pioneering literacy campaigns. Increasing numbers of women are taking advantage of cooperative credit facilities. New avenues for women's political participation have opened at village and district levels. It may be that in the next few years national level feminist campaigns will lie relatively fallow but that work at the institutional level will be locally and regionally strengthened.

Another development to watch with interest is the diasporic links among Indian women's groups. Both Britain and the United States already have fairly active Indian women's groups, with strong reltionships to women's groups in India. South Africa is even more interesting, for feminists of Indian origin are integrated not only in women's groups but also in politics overall.[24] This diasporic network is unusual and could become an important source of mobilization against communal identity politics.

[24] To cite but one of the most notable examples: Frene Ginwala, a South African ANC feminist of Parsi origin, is now a leader of the House in Mandela's government.

10

Feminists, Women's Movement, and the Working Class

Ilina Sen

About a year ago, a document titled 'Feminists and Women's Movement' authored by Vimal Ranadive and published by the All India Democratic Women's Association (AIDWA), became available to the reading public.* Because Vimal Ranadive is known to have been working in the cause of women's rights for a long time, and since AIDWA is a federation with a large base of working women, one expected that the document would explore and comment on the relationship between the working class movement and the women's movement.

Having gone through the document however, one is bound to admit that one is disappointed. For not only has the author not recognized the positive aspects of the relationship between the working class and the women's movements, she has chosen to focus almost entirely on feminism's 'destructive' potential. Her presentation contains so much obvious prejudice and betrays such distrust and fear that some of the valid questions she raises, about the role of funding in women's organizations for example, lose their impact. The women's movement, at least in our country, is relatively new. The dangers and pitfalls facing it are many. It is only right that we question the form and content of women's organizations constantly. But when the process of rational questioning is suspended, and distrust substituted in its place the result is not merely confusing; it is misleading as well.

Let's take up Ranadive's main arguments one by one.

* *Feminists and the Women's Movement*, AIDWA, New Delhi, 1986.

In the nineteenth and early twentieth centuries, women in Europe, Britain and America faced blatant discrimination in wages, employment, and received unequal treatment in several spheres. The feminists of this period, Ranadive argues, justifiably fought for rights to education and the vote, for equality under law in matters of marriage, property rights and child custody. Feminists of this period turned the edge of their attack against the policies of discrimination of capitalist society which wanted to utilize women's cheap labour while denying them their rights. However, Ranadive concludes, while the demands of the feminists were justified in those times, they are today directed against men and hence uncalled for.

It is of course perfectly true that the demands for women's equality were first articulated in a modern context in Europe and America in the aftermath of the general democratic currents raised in society in the wake of the industrial revolution. In the late nineteenth and early twentieth centuries women in the West fought for the vote, for the right to legal equality and education. The constitutional equality that Indian women (and women in many other countries) today enjoy is the result of the struggles waged by these women. The constitutional guarantees that women in socialist countries enjoy also originate from these struggles, and many of the early socialists were also strong fighters for women's rights and saw the two struggles as linked. The names of Engels, Bebel and Zetkin come most obviously to mind in this context, but there were many others.

At the same time not all those who fought in the cause of women's rights were necessarily socialists. The liberal feminist current was strong in the England of 1880 and subsequent years, and middle class women agitated for higher education, the vote, legal changes and birth control. The women from the Pankhurst family (Sylvia, her mother and sister), Marie Stopes and Margaret Sanger were among those in the vanguard of this movement, and the issues these women raised could not be ignored by the socialists. The extent and nature of the interaction between feminists and the various socialist groups affected both. Sylvia Pankhurst in a later phase attempted to link up women's issues with those of the working class and was rejected in the process by her family and many of her former comrades.

While this long history has helped to achieve in practice many of the demands of women for equality in liberal democratic and socialist political structure, can the same be said for the situation in our own country? Is it not true that in our country these rights exist often only in name? Do women here have, in practice, equal access to education? Do personal laws for women in different communities see them as equal under law? Is it not true that for the majority community in our country the natural guardian of the child is assumed to be the father? And as for exploitation of cheap labour, is it not true that women's paid work in agriculture and most sector of unorganized industry (where over 80 per cent of 'working' women toil) is undervalued, and that sex-based wage discrimination is rampant? What then is Ranadive saying? Is she saying that it is unreasonable to struggle against such discrimination? These are the issues feminists in India are taking up, and precisely such struggles she finds justifiable in the West in a historical context. Or does she say that these struggles are not justified outside the sphere of left and trade union politics? In which case one can ask whether these structures have breadth and depth enough to take these issues up fully, or if not, whether one should ask Indian women to shelve their demands until such time as left structures are capable of shouldering the complete responsibility for voicing them?

Next, Ranadive says that feminists today, while they have differences among themselves, are united in attributing the exploitation of women to patriarchy. This, she goes on to explain, means that unless women fight men, they will not achieve emancipation. It is true that feminists today have many differences among themselves. What they do have in common however is a commitment to equality and social justice for women. The analysis of patriarchy and the structures of patriarchal dominance has developed through feminist practice, but once again details and precise positions vary depending on positions the feminists take vis-à-vis the rest of society. To define it as 'fighting men' is both malicious and ridiculous and hardly befits the author's attempts to be taken seriously. As a matter of fact here, and elsewhere in the document Ranadive shows her extreme discomfort with the term 'feminist' and appears to interpret it in an oversimplified way to mean radical feminists only. At least in India radical feminists are a minority.

Ranadive further equates feminists with action groups who work among backward sections of women with the idea of disrupting the left and the organized women's movement. It is true that many 'action groups' are today working among backward sections of the population. Many of them began with religious affiliation or as charitable organizations and developed through their experience and acquired a gradual understanding of the structural reasons for social injustice. Many of them were and are funded by foreign donor agencies, and from what one knows of the ways of Uncle Sam, it is quite possible that some are bolstered to play the proverbial destabilizing role. The scale of their operations is, however, often of ludicrous proportions before the might of the Indian state. What often brings these groups into conflict with the organized left is not that they are working in the interests of the ruling class, but that many of them, while they use a Marxist methodology and analysis, remain for historical reasons outside the party fold. Class action launched by such groups from non-party platforms challenges the hegemony that the organized left feels it has in these areas, and the result is often confrontation and hostility between the official left and the 'pretenders'. To come back to the question of feminists and action groups, there are, of course, many action groups which do no work on women, and many feminists outside of action groups. It is true, however, that small non-party groups are often more supportive of work with women. This is both because the groups' small size enables them to be more open and flexible than large monolithic structures, and also because women activists in such groups often push for and achieve a distinct space for their work with women. Such actions often pose further problems for the left, for the official left is often structurally unable to adapt to these newer issues and can only respond by branding them as heresy.

Ranadive goes on to accuse the feminists of being critical and distrustful of left parties and trade unions, and especially of being critical of patriarchy in these organizations. The official left's hostility to the articulation of women's issues from independent platforms has been commented on above. Feminists, including socialist feminists do sometimes respond with counter hostility. Once again the practice of left parties and trade unions provided them with ready ammunition. The uncomfortable fact is that for many years left parties and trade unions have ignored and suppressed the women's questions and assigned a peripheral role to women activists. These structures have thus become open to charges of patriarchy. It must not be forgotten that the promises of socialism extend to women as much as to men and that women have just as many expectations from socialist liberation as men do. Hence the criticism levelled at left formations by women and women's groups should not be regarded as disruption but rather as the anger born of disappointment and frustration.

Ranadive is also critical of the feminist demand that women should organize independently, that their organizations should be autonomous, and that decision-making in such organizations should be in women's hands.

The issue of the 'autonomy' or otherwise of the women's movement and of women's organizations is an old one. It dates back to the early days of both socialism and feminism. Revolutionary theory has had a strange dichotomous position on this, and this is nowhere more clearly illustrated than in Lenin's famous interview with Clara Zetkin. For, Lenin says at one point, 'Our ideological conceptions give rise to principles of organization. No special organization for women. A woman communist is a member of the party just as a man communist with equal rights and duties.' But more or less in the next breath he adds

The unpolitical, unsocial, backward psychology of ... (women) ... their isolated spheres of activity, these are facts. It would be absurd to overlook them. We need appropriate bodies to carry out work among women, special methods of agitation and forms of organization. That is not feminism, that is practical revolutionary expediency.*

This illustrates beautifully both the fear and the need of the left of separate forms of organization for women. These two trends have continued to guide the thinking of left organizations on the women's question, and have stunted the growth of political work with women from a class perspective. Decision on how far to take or not to take the women's question at any particular time have been taken in accordance with 'larger' considerations.

Socialist states have similarly taken extremely contradictory positions on state policy regarding women. In the Soviet Union the stress on releasing women for social production and decreasing her family responsibility in the early years of the republic contrasts with the pro-natalist policies following the devastations of the Second World War. All this in practice has meant that the democratic women's movement has not proceeded smoothly in

---

* *Editor's note:* This passage can be found in *On The Emancipation of Women*, Progress Publishers, Moscow 1977, p. 110.

association with revolutionary politics, and that revolutionary organizations have continued to be myopic about women's issues. Part of the reason also why such organizations have continued to be dominated by men is that their half-hearted attempts to bring the masses of women into the fold of revolutionary politics have not been too successful. The demands for autonomy and independence of decision making arise from here. However, while acknowledging its historical importance and relevance, it is important to keep in mind that this can only be a principled stand. It is equally important for feminism to clarify its relationship with broader social movements and political currents. If all women took all decisions only for and by themselves, the only political solution for them would be a lesbian state, and this certainly does not form part of the vision of every feminist for a just society.

Ranadive criticizes feminists for making the question of women's unpaid labour in the home an issue and finds their attempts to ascribe value to it absurd. While some of them presumptuously attempt to rewrite Marxist theory to ascribe value to house-work, others demand wages for housework. Is it possible that she means this as a serious criticism? Women's exclusive responsibility with housework has been recognized as a major reason for her unequal participation in social life by all those who have dwelt for a moment on the present situation of women. Lenin refers in his interview with Zetkin to women growing 'worn out in petty, monotonous household work, their strength and time dissipated and wasted, their minds growing narrow and stale....' And, of course, the most sensitive exploration of this issue from within the socialist tradition is to be found in the writings of Alexandra Kollontai. In several places she discusses these issues, for e.g.

The wife, the mother who is a worker sweats blood to fill three tasks at the same time; to give necessary working hours as her husband does, in some industry or commercial establishment, then to devote herself as well as she can to her household and then also to take care of her children. Capitalism has placed on the shoulders of the women a burden which crushes her: it has made of her a wage worker without having lessened her cares as a housekeeper and mother. We, therefore, find the woman crushed under her triple insupportable burden, forcing from her often a swiftly smothered cry of pain... (Kollontai, A., *Communism and the Family*, 1918, Bookmarks, London, 1984).

That communism has no ready-made solution to these problems is also acknowledged by Kollantai, viz., 'These problems ... derive from the fact that the question of motherhood is being tackled but has yet been completely solved' (Kollantai, A., *Selected Writings*, Allison and Busby, London, 1977).

Once we accept the fact that women's exclusive and unrecognized preoccupation with housework is a problem, the next question is what our stand on this should be. Women have taken many different positions, depending on their understanding. The wages for housework position is only one of several stands on this issue. Other feminists have tried to ascribe 'value' to domestic work theoretically. Ranadive ridicules this effort, but the argument is at least worth listening to seriously. Yet other feminists have demanded equal and joint responsibility for domestic work by domestic partners, and yet others have advocated a rejection of heterosexual family life. Feminists have all recognized the problem, and have worked towards ascribing freedom of choice and dignity to household work that is crucial for sustenance and survival.

Feminists are further accused of denying the educative and liberative importance of the participation by women in large scale social production.

Given the sacramental relationship of women with housework and domestic labour, to what extent public productive labour liberates her and to what extent it crushes her further is really an open question. Nevertheless equality of employment opportunity and access are no doubt important demands. As such it is amazing how, with the left and trade unions supposedly committed to this equality, the shrinkage in the female labour force has taken place to the extent that it has. Leaving aside for a moment all estimates of female employment in the agricultural and unorganized sectors, large scale reduction in the female workforce has taken place in independent India in mining and textiles, the traditional female-intensive industries, along with the workforce in general.

Vimal Ranadive's own writing (*Women Workers of India*, National Book Agency, 1976, Ch. II, 'Dwindling Job Opportunities') documents this trend. Between 1963 and 1972, the percentage of women in total employed in factories decreased from 10.36 to 8.73. Jhabvala has shown how women's retrenchment in the Ahmedabad textile industry was preceded by an agreement in 1933 (to which the majority trade union was party) which stipulated that the unemployment resulting from rationalization would selectively apply to married women whose husbands are benefited by the rationalization process. (Jhabvala, *Closing Doors; A Study of the Decline of Women Workers in the Textile Mills of Ahmedabad,* SETU, 1985.) Similarly it has been documented that the percentage of women workers in the entire mining sector declined from 20.1 to 11.9 between 1951 and 1971. Even today, in the captive mines of the Bhilai Steel Plant, details of the voluntary retirement scheme are circulated to women workers by the recognized union which is affiliated to the AITUC. If equal participation in public productive labour is liberating for women, what is one to make of a left trade union's stand on this? On the other hand, much of the defence of women's rights to paid employment has come from non-party women activists, the feminists.

Another point that is raised is that feminists ignore the major advance made by women in socialist countries. Feminists also ignore major enemies like imperialism and the danger of war. Not only women, but all people in socialist countries have achieved major advances and tremendous improvement in their levels of living. If feminists or the upholders of any other cause negate this, it is, of course, incorrect. However, socialist countries have by no means solved all the problems in the way of awakening human-kind to a truly liberated existence and are themselves trying out new strategies. In the past, self-righteous dogmatism has led to tremendous human misery and oppression in several socialist states, and if it is not constructive to ignore positive developments, it is also not constructive to eulogize the socialist states as paradise on earth. And since the democratic duty of the women's movement is to struggle for women's rights, one should not fault it or feminists for criticizing the socialist states if they feel the socialist states have fallen short of expectations on the women's question.

Imperialism and war are today major dangers facing humankind and its survival. Not only feminists but all people should fight these trends but the platform of the women's movement is meant to fight women's oppression, and even if feminists confine their struggle to women's issues from this platform, nothing is seriously wrong. There can be other organizations to oppose imperialism and war, which feminists may join or support. Can one blame the feminists for taking their own work seriously?

Ranadive contradicts herself, on the one hand she says that feminists are not willing to join united fronts of toiling people and raise issues of the relationship of the women's movement to wider revolutionary politics, and on the other hand accuses them of trying to disrupt organizations like CITU and AIDWA by entering them and subsequently trying to subvert their work. Contrary to what Ranadive says, women from many walks of life and from several organizations did take part in mass movements like the anti-price rise agitation. A mutual wariness between feminist and class organizations is, of course there for all kinds of reasons; which we have been discussing above. Ranadive goes on to add that feminist groups like the ones based in Bombay and Delhi limit themselves to taking up individual cases of women in distress and discourage mass action and politicization of these issues. This allegation has greater substance, but one must remember that the city-based groups represent a particular type, and that they do, through legal forms and the media, achieve a different kind of political action.

The coverage that the activities of the feminists receives in media comes in for criticism next. The motives of the bourgeois press in giving such coverage are questioned, and Ranadive goes on to add that feminist magazines like *Manushi* are expensively produced, indicating access to (dubious) funds.

When we are talking of media coverage, is it not the publicity that certain issues get that is important rather than which groups gets a mention in the press? If city-based feminists have done a service to the interests of women by drawing public attention to issues like amniocentesis and uneven personal laws, what should be our problem be with such a situation? The questions of funding and the 'professionalization' of activist intervention in the cause of women are, of course, serious issues. But the particular example chosen is not a good one. *Manushi* focused attention on Indian women's contributions and struggles at a time when no other such paper existed. To deny credit to *Manushi* for this is churlish. And can one seriously criticize *Manushi* for being well-produced. In fact, the Hindi edition of *Manushi* has had to close down for financial reasons. The pity is that today there is very little open debate taking place on these issues. What we do have is hardline attitudes, and reactions and counter-reactions. Even the present reply to Ranadive's document reads necessarily like a reaction whereas it should really have been in the spirit of a dialogue. The relationship between feminism and socialism is an old one, but the modalities are not defined on either side. The issues of family, sexual relations and organizational structures for women are important and must enter public debate. At the same time it is not possible to confine women's politics to 'the personal'. The tasks are incomplete, and both have a long way to go. Being living ideologies, both contain within themselves much variety, diversity and room for growth. The dialogue between them has as much potential for mutual enrichment, provided we are able to enter into it with honesty and openness. If this essay goes even a small way in setting such a process in motion, it would have been more than justified.

V

Women, Community, Rights

Sudesh Vaid and Kumkum Sangari's essay is a study of the ideology of sati, the incidence of widow immolation and its embeddedness in the political economy. Their essay explicitly rejects the use of the word Sati to describe the practice of widow immolation, and uses 'sati' in quote marks to indicate a set of ideologies, beliefs and orientalist stereotypes that legitimate the violent practice of widow immolation. Their paper unravels the complex interaction of patriarchy, class and caste in the construction of widow immolation as a sign of women's own will and agency. It offers an account of how local elites, contending and collusive groups, administration, belief systems, institutional mechanisms, regional and metropolitan ideological formations come together to shape the practice of immolation and its interpretation. It offers a feminist critique both of the subordination of women's rights and of the meaning of community.

Veena Das, in her analysis of the two most significant cases which highlight the tension in the triad of Women/Community/Rights—Shah Bano and the sati of Roop Kanwar—places them in the context of three sets of relations. The relationship between state and community, between citizen and state, and between community and ('its') women. Set within this context, it becomes possible to see that the culture of a community creates the resources for questioning ideologies of the state while at the same time in most cases homogenizing the imagining of the community and silencing alternative perceptions. Thus we are enabled to make a feminist critique both of imaginings of 'community' as well as of state practices which deny validity to any other loyalties than to the state itself.

11

Institutions, Beliefs, Ideologies: Widow Immolation in Contemporary Rajasthan

Kumkum Sangari and
Sudesh Vaid

Widow immolation is one of the most violent of patriarchal practices, distinct from other forms of patriarchal violence, first in the degree of consent it has received, and second in the supportive institutions and ideological formations that rationalize and idealize it. In fact the violence, the consent, and the complex of institutions and ideological formations are mutually interrelated. The event is mythologized precisely because of, and proportionate to, the intensity of violence inherent in it.

It is analytically useful to distinguish between two kinds of ideological formation—general ideologies and 'religious' belief in widow immolation as 'sati'. Although such beliefs are indeed transmuted ideologies, distinguishing between religious beliefs and other ideological formations helps to understand how events of widow immolation are locally structured by belief systems. It also helps to clarify and dismantle the popular ideological category called 'the faith of the masses'.

In this paper we have tried to use the term 'widow immolation' to designate the primary violence, and the word 'sati' to indicate those structures of belief and ideology that gain consent for widow immolation. In doing so, we have tried to distinguish our usage first from the religious aura of the word 'sati', second from the discrete set of cultural values separate from the event that contemporary ideologues claim 'sati' represents, and, finally, from the voyeuristic discourse that widow immolations have produced in colonial spectators and their contemporary progeny.

Events of widow immolation have emerged from caste, class and gender relations as well as from different kinds of sectional struggles for power (political, cultural, familial, community). However, each event is quite specific and produced through a disparate and variable set of factors; that is, each event is structured differently in different contexts. Except for the central fact of the immolation of the widow, events are not identical. However, their ideological representations function to homogenize them. These are formalized first at the site of the event and later through institutions, wider ideological formations and belief structures. The institutions, ideologies and beliefs that cluster around widow immolation serve to transform widow immolation into 'sati'. They function simultaneously as structures *representing consent* (of the woman, family, community) and *wresting consent* (from the same). As such they develop a casual, generative relation to the recurrence of widow immolation.

Changes either in class formation or in the intersecting histories of specific social groups interlock with changes both in the practice of widow immolation and in corollary institutions, ideologies and beliefs. Their interrelated histories, common constituents and functions produce several overlaps as well as internal differences. Contemporary institutions, ideologies and beliefs characterize widow immolation in differing ways through a set of centralising notions: the volition of the widow, the potency of *sati* (essence of purity) or *satitva* (virtue, chastity), and the assignment of suitable roles for family and community.

Institutions centred on widow immolation function as an organized site for the production and reproduction of ideologies and beliefs, and represent well-defined sectional interests. Institutionalization works to normalize and canonize widow immolations, and situates them as part of a regional 'history' in the public memory; a widow immolation cannot cross over either into public, patriarchal discourses, or into belief systems without the assistance of institutions. The 'sati' temple which sacralizes violence is the crucial intermediary between the event and the renewal of attendant ideologies and beliefs. Without the assistance of institutions, widow immolation could not perhaps be made to provide a locus either for the organization of interests or for ideological and political mobilization.

Beliefs and ideologies are mutually dependent and interpenetrative as well as discrete and internally differentiated. 'Religious' belief in widow immolation as 'sati' constitutes a specific kind of ideological formation, which because of its existential emphasis on pain, suffering, death, and their utopian dimensions, can draw on wider, more varied areas of social life for legitimacy. Beliefs have a long cumulative history which carries the sediment of previous events and earlier representational structures; it is partly from their longer duration that they are able to efface the modalities of their constitution and appear to be more autonomous than they are (thereby enabling contemporary ideologies to encash them in various ways). Finally, those gender, caste and class differences or wider political processes to which beliefs have a specifiable relation repeatedly reconstitute beliefs within changing social formations; they can thus function, paradoxically, to temporarily enhance or renew the relative autonomy of beliefs.

Although ideological formations that function in the name of anything other than religious belief have a narrower time frame, they also have a specific history related to previous and present ruling groups, intra-class conflicts and political, economic conjunctures. They, too, enclose histories of contestation; but whereas this is fairly easily discernible in the terrain of general ideologies, the 'rules' for the changing symbolic constitution of the immolated widow within belief systems encode the histories of contestation in different and more obscure ways.

The maintenance and reconstitution of patriarchies is the material basis common to widow immolation, related institutions and ideological formations. Therefore domestic ideologies are central to this entire constellation. Here too, however, it is possible and ever necessary to make certain distinctions. (Or, to put it differently, remaking patriarchies is at once the common ground and the space for internal differentiation between ideologies and beliefs.) Beliefs carry patriarchal values and practices around widow immolation in the direction of prescription, ritual, salvation schemes, supernaturalism, sanctification and worship: that is, simultaneously towards forms of fixity and memorialization and dispersal into different social and religious spheres. Ideologies, at least since the nineteenth century, have tended to bring such values into active relation with broader, contestatory formations that address concepts such as Hinduism, tradition, nation or Indian history; these situate widow immolation in relatively 'historical' frames and tend to affirm the family or traditions as units of social order whereas beliefs tend to affirm domestic ideologies by sacralizing them. Because of the location of ideological formations in contemporary patriarchal practices and values, the 'sati' cannot exist at a purely symbolic or mythic level: the actual widow appears to be central to the pedagogy of both ideologies or beliefs. Indeed beliefs and ideologies can coexist in structural and historical relationship and use each other for self legitimation, as in the case of contemporary Rajasthan where local beliefs centre on miracles performed through the agency of satt, while middle class ideologies produce high traditions.

Although formed in reponse to the same social realities, the perceptual modes, historical duration, forms of address and engagement of beliefs and ideologies with these realities is different. The particular interaction between specific patriarchies, events, ideologies and beliefs is one of the factors which acts to *resubstantiate* social belief in widow immolation as 'sati' at any given moment. The particular location of the patriarchies concerned in caste and class formations determines for which women 'sati' acts as a general ideology and for which women it can function as a material force. The theories of female subjectivity which attempt to separate and reify the woman's volition—that is to represent violence either as a product of female agency or as being anything than violence—are in fact, methodologically speaking, working on the same model as the ideological formations that structure the practice of widow immolation. Essential to both is the suppression of the materiality of the event and of the processes that inform the immolation.

The processes of the formation of institutions, ideologies and beliefs, take place in relation to caste and class groups whose interests and involvement can be differentiated in a number of ways. But whereas events, and to a lesser extent, institutions and active worship are localized, ideologies spread across regional boundaries and have acquired a middle class, urban character. In this essay we propose to discuss one such history of contemporary renewal, composed of the recurrence of events, the construction of ideologies, the emergence of institutions and the constitution of belief in a specific conjuncture. The question of the women's violation is central to all of them and can be understood only in relation to them.

The essay attempts to elicit several interrelated dimensions of the localized phenomenon of widow immolation in the Shekhawati region of Rajasthan.[1] The paper is divided into three sections. The first section introduces the Shekhawati region and then offers a detailed account of a widow immolation at Jhardli village in 1980 in order to locate its commonalities with other immolations in the area, including Deorala where Roop Kunwar was immolated in 1987. These commonalities include the role of Rajput and other elites of the village; the role of the police and administration; the centrality of belief in satt which mediates between the social and the supernatural; and the local operation of institutional mechanisms and ideological structures. The second section describes the recent history, present location, and contradictory and collusive relationship of the group involved: Brahmins, Rajputs and Banias. It also examines the influence of the Rani Sati temple which commemorates the immolation of a bania widow and analyses the contemporary popular narratives generated around this 'medieval' event. The third section discusses the overlaps and distinctions between regional and metropolitan ideological formation; and concludes with an analysis of the interrelated issues of popular belief and the question of consent.

Shekhawati

Culturally the Shekhawati region includes the contiguous areas of Churu, Nagaur and Bikaner[2] but present day Shekhawati

---

[1] Stray cases of widow immolation have occurred in Uttar Pradesh, Madhya Pradesh and Maharashtra, but the largest number have taken place in Rajasthan—no less than 28 of an estimated total of 40 in the past four decades.

The primary material on widow immolation in this area was collected in investigative visits to Rajasthan between March 1981 and October 1988. For earlier essays based on fieldwork see K. Sangari and S. Vaid, 'Sati in Modern India: A Report', *Economic and Political Weekly,* 16: 31, 1 August 1981, pp. 1284–88; Sangari and Vaid, 'The Politics of Widow Immolation', *Imprint,* October 1987, pp. 27–31; and Sudesh Vaid, 'Politics of Widow Immolation', *Seminar,* no. 342, February 1988, pp. 20–23. An earlier version of the present essay appeared in *Economic and Political Weekly,* 26: 17, 27 April 1991.

[2] According to colonial records, Shekhawati was the largest *nizamat* (an administrative district) covering 4,200 square miles, bounded by the Rathor states of Bikaner and Jodhpur, and by Patiala, Loharu and Jaipur (*The Imperial Gazetteer of India,* Oxford: Clarendon, 1908, vol. 22, pp. 268–70).

administratively consists of the districts of Jhunjhunu and Sikar in the Jaipur division of Rajasthan. Adjoining Jaipur district, they lie within fairly easy reach of both Delhi and the state capital, Jaipur. Traversed by the Aravalli hills, Shekhawati consists of two zones, one semi-arid and desert, the other relatively fertile and densely populated. Most of the immolations have taken place in the latter zone, stretching from Danta Ramgarh to Neem ka Thana. The districts of Jhunjhunu and Sikar, though administratively separate, are closely interconnected, physically through road and rail transport, culturally through their peoples and history. Jhunjhunu was an important trading centre even before the fifteenth century and a stronghold of the business community; Udaipurvati, in the same district, was a stronghold of the Shekhawat Rajputs. Both communities, as we will discuss later, have played a decisive role in the recurrent immolations. At present, while most of the actual widow immolations are taking place in Sikar district, the nearby town of Jhunjhunu with its Rani Sati Temple commemorating a medieval widow immolation, has become central to consolidating and propagating a cult around 'sati'.

The history of this region suggests that widow immolation was not widely practised in the past. The Rajput chieftains of Shekhawati, part of the ruling Kacchwaha clan of Amber (Jaipur) managed to gain some local power only in the renewed struggles for political power prevailing in eighteenth-century Rajasthan. Even then, however, they continued to be vassals of the Amber rulers who did not encourage widow immolation. In only a few instances were ranis (queens) and women of the zenana (attached to the royal household) immolated with the body of a deceased ruler. This is in sharp contrast to the rulers of Marwar (Jodhpur) and Mewar (Udaipur) who gave a wide legitimacy to widow immolation. In these states, the practice of burning some of the ranis and attendant women on the pyre of a deceased ruler became a virtually obligatory and institutionalized practice and was emulated even by minor chieftains.

Unlike them, the Amber rulers did not make the practice a recurrent royal event and one ruler in the eighteenth century even tried to abolish it altogether. During the colonial period, Jaipur was the first of the 18 states of the Rajputana Agency to abolish widow immolation and to make it a penal offence (1846).

Significantly, leading Shekhawati chieftains gave their public assent to this abolition legislation.[3] Of the sporadic instances of widow immolation that regional records show occurred during the colonial period, only a few took place in Jaipur state. The overwhelming number were in Mewar and Marwar. There is both direct and indirect testimony to the absence of an active legacy of widow immolation. The decay and neglect of memorials for widows immolated during the medieval and colonial period indicate that the social or religious significance attached to the practice had become attenuated by the 1950s. Not even all rajput memorials have been accompanied by steady worship: it appears that the decline of ruling families has been accompanied by a decline in worship. The evidence we have gathered reveals ad hoc attempts beginning in the 1950s to piece together a set of beliefs and rituals which have now become part of the standardized 'plot' of widow immolation in the Shekhawati area.

Jhardli

The specific constellation of social, religious and cultural meanings that are currently being attached to widow immolation can be seen in the case of Om Kunwar who was immolated in Jhardli village, Sikar district on 30 August 1980. Jhardli, located seventy kilometres from Jaipur, is an extensive village with a metalled road leading to it, a post office, electricity, a high school and two new primary schools. Most of the population of about 10,000, consists of jat peasants, lower caste agricultural labourers and artisans. However, the village is socially dominated by Rajputs and banias (traders). The social structure continues to be caste based, but infringements and changes have begun to occur. For instance lower castes now build houses of brick or stone, which Rajputs had not permitted earlier. Due to lack of employment opportunities, large sections of both the high caste and low caste population gain their livelihood from urban areas and services—construction work in Delhi; trading

---

[3] Sutherland to H.H. Greathead, 18 August 1846, RAO, f. 43, Gen II 1846, National Archives of India (hereafter NAI); Ludlow to Sutherland, ibid., NAI. See also R.K. Saxsena, *Social Reform: Infanticide and Sati*, Delhi: Trimurti, 1975, pp. 127–31; and V.N. Datta, *Sati: Widow Burning in India*, Delhi: Manohar, 1988.

in Jaipur, Delhi and Calcutta; employment in the police and the army.

On our first visit to Jhardli in 1981, we learnt from the villagers that they knew of no widow immolation except one which took place 'about two hundred years ago'. One small memorial with a story of adolescent love attached to it marks the place where an *unmarried* girl of the Gujjar caste is supposed to have immolated herself for an Ahir youth two centuries ago.[4] There is, however, little room for idealisation in the facts concerning the immolation of Om Kunwar, a 16-year-old Shekhawat Rajput girl. Her husband Ram Singh, aged 22, a truck driver in Bombay, had been suffering from tuberculosis. The *gauna* ceremony, marking the time when a bride begins to live with her husband,[5] had taken place six months before his death; the couple did not have much of a conjugal life together since Ram Singh was being treated in various hospitals outside the village. Shortly before his death Om Kunwar is said to have written to her brother describing the misery of her married life in her in-law's house.

The story, as told to us by those who were closely implicated in the event, began with the death of Ram Singh in a Jaipur hospital. His body was brought to the village by early afternoon. The funeral procession was already on its way to the cremation ground when Om Kunwar suddenly ordered that the body be brought back. She had decided to become a 'sati'. The sensational news quickly spread, a four foot high pyre was built with offerings of wood, etc., made by relatives and some of the villagers. Thousands watched the event with shouts of *'sati mata ki jai'* ('glory to mother sati'). The sarpanch (administrative head of the village) set out to inform the police at Thoi police station eight miles away, but needless to say the immolation had taken place by the time he returned at sunset with the police party. Some villagers said, however, that he was one of the *arthi* (funeral bier) bearers, so the veracity of his claim is by no means established. Cases were subsequently registered against six people for abetment to suicide. The ashes were guarded from both tantrics and lower castes for thirteen days by young armed Rajput

---

[4] In this region the Ahir and Gujjar castes are cultivators.

[5] This ceremony involves taking a bride to her husband's house, where she takes residence for the first time, and the marriage is consummated, and may take place several years after the wedding ceremony.

volunteers.[6] This was followed on the thirteenth day by the post-funeral *chundri* ceremony,[7] performed not as it customarily is with relatives and friends, but with great publicity and fanfare. Two hundred thousand people are reported to have converged on the village that day. A trust was formed to build a dharamshala (resthouse for pilgrims and travellers) and a commemorative temple, and soon after, donations began to come in.[8]

Like most Shekhawat Rajputs, Richpal Singh, the father-in-law of Om Kunwar, has a small landholding, a bare five bighas (regionally varied unit of land measurement) of unirrigated land which yields only one annual crop. Like other such small landholders, both he and his sons have taken to army service. Richpal, now retired, was in straitened circumstances. Tensions over financial matters are said to have occurred with the deceased Ram Singh. He had been adopted by a widowed paternal aunt married into the Richpal family and both were being supported for several years by Richpal Singh. The aunt, a child widow, had adopted Ram Singh in the hope of having a provider in her old age.

The immolation of Om Kunwar was represented as a 'voluntary' act. We should note at the outset that every successfully carried out immolation is *always* narrated as a story of pure volition on the part of the dead woman. Hence the specific nature of the 'volition' must be ascertained according to the particular exigencies of each case and should be seen in relation to determining social, cultural and religious factors existing in this region. In other words a discussion of the woman's agency must be related both to the

[6] *Tantras* are teaching occult rituals for the worship of deities to gain superhuman power. Tantrics are followers of the tantra, an anti-brahminical, shakti worshipping religious sect who have at times opposed widow immolation. In Jhardli, the ashes were believed literally to *contain* the satt which had earlier possessed the women; and since the ashes had the ability to *confer* their power, they were guarded to ensure that no tantric could steal or misuse them. We were also told that the living 'sati' of Jodhpur could not become a 'sati' because a sunar (person from a lower artisan caste) robbed her of her satt by throwing a blue veil over her. This colour was said to have 'Muslim' associations in the district.

[7] A chundri is a length of tie-and-dye cloth used to cover the head on festive occasions and in marriage rituals, and is never worn by a widow.

[8] A businessman donated 30,000 rupees towards the dharamshala and another built a well costing 40,000 rupees.

situation and to ideologies. There are indications that Om was already subject to various kinds of pressure. She was in a state of acute emotional tension and had a hysterical fit ten days earlier. During her short stay in her in-law's house she had gauged the hardships of a widow's life visible in the position of her mother-in-law. A local brahmin priest, Jamnalal Shastri, had already presided over an earlier immolation in the neighbouring village of Hathideh in 1978 and written a propagandistic booklet deifying the widow and eulogizing that event as an example of the purifying force of *nari dharma* (moral and social obligation of a woman). It is not possible to ascertain the extent to which Om's immolation was premeditated by the priest and the family, and to what extent it was 'improvized' by them at the last minute; what is clear from their *contradictory* and *contradicted* accounts is that far from preventing it, they were central to the decision-making process at every stage.

Many of the rites which could only have been performed with the assistance of the family and other people, were projected in local accounts as miracles. *Mehndi* or henna has to be ground into a paste,[9] trunks have to be unlocked and bridal clothes taken out. In Om's case some isolated instances of such assistance were privately acknowledged—her elder sister brought her ornaments to wear, gave the *pujari* (temple priest) 20 rupees to buy a chundri, which was then actually provided by her *dharmapita,*[10] a tailor. However, such details are submerged in the broader, public story in which miracles are assembled into a seamless, virtually self-creating series of events: water turns into mehndi, trunks unlock themselves, Om's bridal attire rises to the top, Om leaps unassisted on to the tall pyre, the fire lights by itself. The projection of mundane events as miracles has a dual function: it becomes a means of concealing and denying individual assistance and community responsibility (miracles by definition are 'unperformed'), and the miracles become the evidence of the presence of satt.

These miracles and satt are complicit and mutually reinforcing and it is difficult to ascertain which comes first. However, possession

---

[9] A Rajput widow customarily leaves mehndi hand prints on a wall of the house prior to immolation.

[10] A dharmapita or 'godfather' is adopted for brides, in certain exigencies, from the village of her husband's family. He performs ritual functions in lieu of her own father.

of a widow by satt is a prerequisite for being 'eligible' for immolation. Kappu Kunwar, Om's sister-in-law, described satt as a trance-like state in which the woman behaves as one possessed: in this state, the woman's interest in material life ceases, she is now in direct communication with god. What is remarkable is the unquestioning co-existence of Kappu's description with her own memory that Om had behaved in a similar manner ten days earlier when her husband was still alive. At that time her behaviour was seen and treated as a demonic possession; but later, when Om became widowed, the same behaviour was seen as evidence of her possession by satt. The notion of satt appears to be flexible enough to incorporate and redefine any extreme emotional state. The chief arbiter of whether Om Kunwar was possessed by satt seems to have been the priest, Jamnalal Shastri. He asked Om Kunwar to reveal her satt and allegedly *his own* hands started to burn. Shastri also undertook to interpret her gestures, for example, he told us that Om had raised her arms above her head in the posture of one who had given herself up to god. (Om Kunwar's brother was said to have doubted Shastri's diagnostic powers.)

Since a woman who is possessed by satt is believed to have special powers to bless and curse, fear of her curse becomes a useful explanation for not crossing 'her will' or preventing her immolation: all decisions are henceforth ascribed to the woman. Satt is also supposed to endow her with the power of prophecy, the power to cure diseases and exercise evil spirits, and the ability to will the pyre to light itself. The family recounted the blessings Om bestowed on them while the priest described her blessings to the village and her promise to grant boons to her devotees. The blessings conveniently absolve family, priest and village of all blame—they function as a reassuring sign of the widow's good will and their own good intentions in obeying her behest, i.e. carrying through the immolation. The statements of the pujari of the present temple dedicated to Om, as well as of Shastri, were in keeping with this rationale. The pujari maintained that Om told *him* to perform the last rites. Thus, obtaining the coveted position of the salaried pujari of the temple became the alleged outcome of the widow's *own* wish. Shastri and other's professed to have asked Om, once she was on the pyre, *'ab aapka kya hukum hai?'* ('what is your command now?'), and claimed merely to have obeyed her orders. Even in their own account, however, Om did not answer any of the questions related to prophecy and disease that were put to her before she was on the pyre; nor had anyone in the village either been cured or had their wish granted.

As for the pyre that lights itself, family and villagers admitted privately that this fire was lit with matches by a school-going nephew.[11] The myth of the self-lighting pyre was sought to be maintained, however, by other narratives—that of the headmaster, for example—which claimed that the fire went out after half an hour and *then* relit itself. And, according to Shastri, when the fire went out Om took an *agarbatti* (incense stick) from the pujari, waved it over the pyre and the flames re-appeared. Doubts had been and were still being expressed by some villagers as well as visitors to the village about whether this was a 'genuine sati' since a match had been used. Further, a harijan (low caste) woman told us that other witnesses reported Om pleading, 'Don't light the pyre!'

The satt supposedly makes the woman immune to the fire and enables her to sit composedly on the burning pyre. The absence of pain proclaims the presence of superhuman power, signals the transformation of women into goddess: ironically, the ultimte and incontrovertible proof of satt can be had only when the woman is actually burning. In Jhardli, the idealized versions (headmaster's, priest's, shoemaker's) emphasize Om Kunwar's calm expression, composed behaviour, unmoving body as proof of her immunity to the fire. Movements which could not be ignored were rationalized: Om's swaying to and fro and saying she was in pain, and her pushing away of the brambles which were being thrown on the pyre in the attempt to relight it, were all explained as the pulling away of her satt by an evil *dakait*—a low caste worshipper of the god Shani (Saturn). The relatively less idealized versions were provided by a harijan family, who claimed to have seen signs of her pain and noted her efforts to move, which were impeded by the arrangement of the logs and by the throwing of brambles on her. In their perception the brambles were deliberately thrown to prevent her from running away—it seems she was throwing off the brambles even as onlookers kept piling them back on. The narrators of these less idealized versions did not doubt the validity of satt as a concept, they only doubted its presence in this particular case.

[11] A minor cannot be prosecuted for abetment to murder under present criminal law.

The whole question of 'voluntary' widow immolation hinges on the *local* acceptance of the presence of satt. Satt structures the interrelated, mutually generative factors of community participation in widow immolation as well as its wider perception. As is evident from the immolation of Om Kunwar, if even a theoretical space exists for the exercise of a woman's volition it would be restricted to a stage in the proceedings *before* the proclamation of satt. Once a woman is proclaimed to be possessed by satt, an inexorable logic is set into motion and she has barely any scope to protest, to change 'her' mind or even to grasp the full implications of 'her' decision, assuming that she ever made such a decision. Once proclaimed, satt only creates a space for the woman's consent not for her resistance—for not only does the declaration of satt itself depend on others who can *attest* to the miracles, it opens the way for wider community participation.

The transformation from an inauspicious widow to a goddess begins with the utterance of the word satt, long before the actual burning. As soon as this virtual transformation has taken place, the coercive pressure of the crowd's collective will to witness the 'actual' moment of transformation—namely the burning—shapes the event. For the woman, satt only provides the space for reflecting or accepting the will of others; she is swept on the wave of the gathered community's 'religious' feeling, compelled to die according to the dictates of satt. Satt makes the public burning of the woman possible by obliterating the horror of the act. Any visible evidence that she is struggling against immolation is itself construed as a struggle within her, between her satt and whatever is supposedly antagonistic to satt around her. Because her unwillingness to be burned is *seen* as an expression of the influence of elements antagonistic to her satt, it can be censored from the meaning, the experience and later the dominant narratives of the event. Crucially the concept of satt submerges the material and social bases of the event and gives a sense of religious euphoria to the mass witnessing of the immolation. At every stage, belief in satt becomes the religious equivalent of physical force.

Through the conception of satt the entire event of widow immolation is construed as an epiphany of divine intervention projecting its victim as the embodiment of *shakti* or divine feminine power. The power of satt is created in inverse proportion to and reinforced by the low status of women as well as by patriarchal ideologies. Without the prescriptive ideal of a *pativrata* or a devoted self-sacrificing wife the notion of satt would lose much of its potency. Significantly, local accounts of satt implicitly acknowledge its relation both to the social position of widows and to the patriarchal perception of widowhood as a continuation of wifeliness, particularly for the upper castes. The reasons given by local women as to why *only* widowed women are possessed by satt, embodied this acknowledgement either as an experience of victimisation (Om's widowed mother-in-law felt that god chooses as vehicles of satt those widows who have no one to care for them) or as an expression of mild cynicism (a harijan woman said that satt possessed women and not men because men can remarry). Local men placed satt as an expression of female virtue that is either innate or socially inculcated. While the headmaster said women in general have greater spirituality and fortitude, hence they, not men are the vehicles of satt, the priest ascribed it to the good, correct *samskara*[12] of the woman. The belief in satt functions to elevate what would otherwise be seen either as ritualized murder or as 'suicide' into a supremely holy act of wifely devotion.

The value which accrues from satt obtains both at the ideological and material levels. Traditionally widow immolation increased the honour and prestige of the family and clan. In Jhardli this has benefitted mainly the village which has become a sacred and well-publicized place. The power axis of the village—its panchayat,[13] priesthood, traders and the literati—seems to be in a better position to exploit the event than the family. Richpal Singh in fact complained that he had been denied his 'rightful' place in the temple trust (with its attendant advantages) because his political affiliations differed from those of the panchayat. The temple trust, consisting of eleven men, had amassed one hundred thousand rupees in donations within a few months. The village has profited from increased transport facilities, trade, inflow of money, avenues for the employment of labourers. These benefits evidently had been foreseen to some extent. Some deliberation had gone into the choice

[12] Samskara is literally, that which purifies; here it refers to the history of conduct and the formative influences which mould a person in this life as well as previous lives.

[13] A panchayat here is a statutory village council under the Rajasthan Panchayat Act but it can also refer to non-official, caste or community-based councils.

of a site that could become a pilgrimage place. In recounting the event, the local headmaster represented Om's ability to lead the funeral procession to an appropriate site as another proof of her special power; but other accounts, including Shastri's own, indicate that she was in fact *led* to the site by Shastri and others: she walked *behind* the bier carrying her husband's corpse. They chose this site instead of the usual *shamshaan* (cremation ground), for its accessibility from the main road linking it to Jaipur; its proximity to the older Ahir–Gujjar 'sati' site, and its suitability as an undisputed, unclaimed property. The eye to publicity was evident in the unavailing effort to procure a camera to commemorate the event.

On our second visit to Jhardli in 1986 we found that, as the villagers had anticipated, legal action had petered out. The case against the culprits had been dropped after a year for 'want of witnesses'. The village still had the same bania sarpanch. We also found some gain for the family; the temple established as a collaborative and profitable institution functioning along the joint axis of class power and caste grouping, complete with idealized and ideological representations of the event; as well as visible and invisible reinforcement of a patriarchal model for women. The gains for Richpal's family were petty and personal. A small memorial shrine had been set up within their modest dwelling. A set of bridal clothes, purporting to be Om Kunwar's, were on display, while a sword and sheath, emblematic of rajput valour, were newly hooked on the wall. We learned that Richpal and his brother no longer cultivated their small landholding themselves; the land was now leased to sharecroppers. This was a step up since it is considered to be beneath a Rajput's dignity to touch a plough. The large marble commemorative temple which had been built, and financed by both Marwari businessmen and Rajputs, represented a broader-based institutionalization of the event. A marble statute of Om Kunwar on the pyre with the body of her husband in her lap had been ceremonially installed in 1983, graced by the presence of Sawai Bhawani Singh, the ex-maharaja of Jaipur. The composition of the temple committee was exclusively male and upper caste. However, the majority of the pilgrims were rajput women arriving in chartered buses to the temple, and donations came from towns and cities, not from the village itself, indicating in part the organized though invisible spread of 'sati' as an ideology. This same upper caste patriarchal model embodied in the temple and its activities was being visibly reinforced among lower castes. The old memorial of the Ahir–Gujjar 'sati' was freshly painted, a boundary wall had been built to mark the site of the 'proper' temple which was to be constructed by the caste groups in question. This temple was now positioned to face Om Kunwar's.

Scenes of the 'glory' of a rajput Rajasthan were painted on the walls of the temple dedicated to Om: Padmini of Chittor leading women to *jauhar*[14] and Rana Pratap with his famous horse. This was in keeping with wall paintings in other contemporary rajput temples which primarily draw not on local Shekhawati or Jaipur based legends or history, but on the glorified past of a 'Hindupat' Mewar, aligning widow immolation to previous rajput and nationalist constructs.[15] Also painted on the walls was a woman on a pyre with the rays of the sun miraculously lighting the flames, alongside various gods and goddesses from the Hindu pantheon.

Two propaganda booklets soliciting donations, one introduced by a local rajput lawyer, Raghubir Singh Rathor, and the other by Jamnalal Shastri, were available.[16] These printed booklets, containing prose and verse, biographical narratives and devotional songs, seek to *finalize* the formulaic public story of Om's immolation. However, they find it difficult to synchronize Om's volition with community sanction. Significant deviations and discrepancies—from the verbal accounts, from each other, as well as within each booklet—remain. In *Mahasati*, introduced by Rathor, Om is said to be publicly planning immolation long before her husband dies. This prior announcement is intended to accentuate Om's will, but contradictorily it enlarges the space for family and community participation. Shastri's cautious effort to blur his personal involvement is apparent in his introduction to the *Bhajanmala* where it is not Om but the community which has 'premonitions'! In Shastri's account, well *before* the funeral

---

[14] A jauhar was a mass immolation of women, sometimes along with male servitors, in the context of imminent defeat in battle.

[15] The term Hindupat means committed to Hindu ideals and faith and itself reflects a retrospective hinduisation of medieval rajput history.

[16] Kunwar Narayan Singh, *Mahasati Om Kunwar, Jhardli, Sikar*, intro. Raghubir Singh Rathor, Jhardli: Mahasati Om Kunwar Trust, n.d; Surendratt Diwakar, *Mahasati Om Kunwar Ma Bhajanmala*, intro. Jamnalal Shastri, 3rd ed., Jhardli: Shri Satimata Samiti Trust, 1982.

procession left, at a point when all Om had purportedly done was to put a coconut on the corpse and say 'Hari Om', people were already whispering, *'Sati hone ka mahaul dekh'* ('See, this is the scenario for being a sati'). When Om called back the procession a crowd of thousands is said to have already gathered to praise her. Elsewhere, however, the *Bhajanmala* claims the procession was called back not by Om herself but by local children.

Though the details vary, the two booklets work within a similar ideological framework, situating the immolation in a structure of different levels and forms of consent. Both place Om in traditions of patriotic Hindu nationalism and in the line of the heroic jauhars and widow immolations of Rajasthan including the Shekhawati region. Both seek to revive pativrata behaviour as a familial ideal in order to counter the decline of nari dharma and the evils of westernization; and both describe Om as a *roop* (manifestation) of the goddess Durga; both establish Om's satt as miraculous, thereby rendering legal intervention irrelevant if not sacreligious. Both build up the absence of pain: in *Mahasati* Om delivers an *updesh* (edifying speech) as she burns while in *Bhajanmala* she chants as she burns. Both depict a happy, elated and worshipful community; *Bhajanmala* establishes the community's approval or participation at every stage. Both contain lengthy accounts of the dissuasion of Om by family and village elders. None of these dissuasions express doubt about widow immolation as an event or about 'sati' as an ideology, only about Om's capacity and *will* to become a 'sati'. Indeed in both narratives, the dissuasions are a formal stage in the process of asking Om to prove her satt through miracles *before* the family and villagers concerned can 'permit' immolation. In sum, both booklets try to *disperse* the responsibility of individuals into the sanction of the community or crowd, as well as *concentrate* agency for the immolation in Om Kunwar.

Deorala

Like Jhardli, Deorala, where Roop Kunwar was immolated on 4 September 1987, is a village dominated by Shekhawat Rajputs. With a population of 13,000 it is located only 30 minutes off the main Delhi–Jaipur highway. Deorala falls under the same police jurisdiction as Jhardli and Hathideh. During her eight months of marriage, Roop had lived for less than a month with her husband

and in-laws. When preparations for her immolation began, according to some witnesses, she ran and hid but was dragged back; she was surrounded by armed guards on the way to the funeral, and her struggle to escape when the pyre was lit was prevented by these guards as well as by the logs and coconuts piled on her. Eyewitness accounts attest to her struggle, her shouts for help and her abnormal physical condition at every stage of the 'event'.[17]

The 'plot' or public account of the Deorala case replays what is by now an established formula for immolating a woman and representing it as 'sati'; it reveals a family resemblance to the public accounts of Om Kunwar's immolation as well as those of other widow immolations in the region, and runs as follows. The husband's death occurs after a long illness and is usually anticipated. The widow proves her eligibility by dressing unaided in her bridal finery, and by mysteriously producing henna marks on her palms and on the walls of her house. She asks her family to inform as many people as possible, leads the procession, personally chooses a site near the entrance of the village, instructs the 'ignorant' family pundit in the correct rites. It is impossible to prevent her because of the power of her satt (in this case evinced by the scorching heat of Roop's body attested to by an aunt)[18] and for fear of her curse. The senior male members and/or her father-in-law are inexplicably called away at the time, or as in the case of Roop's father-in-law, conveniently fall unconscious for three hours. The village patwari (revenue and land records official) or sarpanch is either missing or on his way to the police station, which he never reaches in time. The funeral rites are performed with undue haste, nevertheless several thousand people gather to watch. The movement of hastening crowds remains invisible to the police or, if they notice it, they do not have a sufficient police force to intervene. The hapless woman always leaps unaided onto a four or five foot high pyre and commands a minor relative (in Roop's case the 15-year old brother-in-law) to light it. Soon after, when perfunctory police proceedings

---

[17] See *Trial by Fire: A Report on Roop Kanwar's Death* by the Women and Media Committee, Bombay Union of Journalists, Bombay: Bombay Union of Journalists, 1987.

[18] And also by the Shankaracharya of Puri who was not present but who claimed in an interview that Roop's father-in-law was trying to save her by holding her back but 'there was lightning effect from her body and he was thrown back', *Sunday Observer,* 20 September 1987.

begin, the child criminal is either transformed into a miraculous ray of sunlight or a whiff of incense that lights the pyre. Sometimes the igniter is eliminated altogether and, in retrospect, the pyre is said to have lit itself (here in response to Roop's raised hands). In either case the woman suffers no pain as she burns. By a strange collective amnesia the event, though photographed by a few and seen by thousands, is witnessed by no one. However, it is instantly commodified and converted into petty cash and large donations. The woman's life is recast as a hagiography, with eager help from her natal family, representing her as being pious or possessing satt from her childhood. (In this case Roop was established as a pious devotee of Rani Sati.) A temple commemorating successful murder is constructed.

This was the 'plot' of the Jhardli and Deorala immolations as well as the dozen others we have investigated. Everywhere, the onus for orchestrating the entire event is everywhere put on the widow. All verification is made to rest on the unavailable testimony of the dead woman. Every detail of the event is selected to disguise premeditation and to make the helpers and colluders invisible. Their invisibility is then represented as a divine miracle. In reality, of course, divine miracle is legal alibi. Not only is the crime consciously structured in *full knowledge* of the prohibitory law, it is also assembled around the *inability* of existing law to deal with community crimes, to take cognizance of and contend with patriarchal ideologies or to recognize and act on the nexus between religion and patriarchal ideologies. The political will to enforce even the existing law has been conspicuously absent.

Most of the immolated women in this region have been married into relatively 'impoverished' families. Roop Kanwar's Jaipur-based natal family seems to have been exceptionally affluent;[19] her inlaws were not. Her father, among those Rajputs who have gone into business, owns a transport agency. Her father-in-law holds an M.A. degree and teaches Hindi at the Khejroli secondary school. His brother is a city dweller (Jodhpur) while his nephew is studying medicine. Both sides of the family, whether in business or in education, have taken a leading role in glorifying her immolation

---

[19] Roop's dowry is reported to have consisted of 25–40 *tolas* of gold, fixed deposits worth 30,000 rupees, a television, a radio, fans, a refrigerator and some furniture. Her father donated one lakh rupees to her temple in Deorala, and the expensive chundri ceremony was performed by her Jaipur-based brother.

as a 'sati'. The village itself has eight schools, a literacy rate of 70 per cent, electricity, radio and TV. Soon after the event, the village literati analysed news reports of the crime, disseminated printed pamphlets, composed eulogistic songs and poems; local headmasters and teachers took pride in the event and attested its 'miraculous' nature. In Jhardli, too, the school headmaster (a kayasth by caste) felt honoured to be the first to put a chundri on the fourth day, while a schoolteacher had assisted in the rites. A large number of Rajputs from Deorala, as from many other villages in the area, join the army. Significantly, the village that undertook to celebrate the Deorala immolation in a *mela* (fair) on 29 September 1987, in defiance of government orders, was Mawda Kalan. A widow was immolated here on 11 October 1975, and subsequently deified; half the Rajputs (who constitute about 90 per cent of the total population) in this highly literate village are employed in the armed forces. Similarly, relatives of other immolated widows—the father in Madhav-ka-Vas (24 March 1954), the deceased husband in Surpura (25 February 1975) and the father-in-law and brother-in-law in Jhardli—were employed in the army.

The persons involved from an amorphous group, difficult to define sharply in class terms. Not being either cultivating farmers, large landholders or agricultural labour, they are at once structurally peripheral to the local agricultural economy and integrated into urban orbits through trade, education or the armed services. Most of them have petty landholdings but their primary occupations are non-agrarian. Due to their upper caste status and their integration in the professions, the bureaucracy and the wider economy, they form an influential social stratum and are able to call on the local police and administration, many of whose members belong to the same set of families and economic stratum. Again, as an important section of the rural electorate they also attract political patronage.[20] Further, regional and community ties give them access to the more privileged classes in the cities. Almost every contemporary temple has influential patrons and donors:

[20] Among the politicians who vociferously supported the right to worship and glorify the immolation in Deorala were: Kalyan Singh Kalvi (State Janata Party President), Om Prakash Gupta (Bharatiya Janata Party), Hukum Singh (BJP), Jai Singh (Lok Dal) and Chan Singh Pradhan (Lok Dal).

ex-maharajas, politicians, and most important, industrialists and traders.[21] Without their financial support, not a single 'sati' temple would either have been built or be able to sustain its propagandistic function. Significantly, it is the successful immolation of a widow, which pulls the village out of mundane anonymity and elicits both social support and financial patronage from sections of the middle and upper classes in urban and metropolitan areas.

II

Brahmins and Rajputs

The village élite who orchestrate the event on site are clearly connected to and represent a wide and interlocking set of forces. The most central of these are sections of the brahmin, rajput and bania communities, who otherwise constitute a minority of the population. They have differential histories, internal class contradictions, as well as interlocking roles in the formation of supportive ideologies and disseminating institutions (temples, schools, melas, committees, societies).

Historically, the brahmins as priests, and the *bhat*s and *charan*s as genealogists, bards and eulogizers attached to courts, were important social groups in rajput kingdoms. Apart from their roles in the political domain, they were important in the social sphere and in family life. They regulated and maintained clan and caste superiority, arranged matrimonial alliances and played a determining role in the lives of women, particularly among the rajputs.[22] They also assisted in the production of the ideology of rajput male *veerta* (martial valour), with all its prescriptive implications for rajput women—especially in the patriarchal practices and supportive ideologies of jauhar and widow immolation.

The contemporary role of brahmins, although less visible than that of rajputs and banias is also important—where as involved individuals, as part of local religious organizations, as forming regional networks that 'influence' and instigate events or as

---

[21] As in the case of earlier immolations in the region, the Deorala committee was instantly assured financial support by an official representative of an industrial group. (*Times of India*, 17 September 1987).

[22] See K.L. Qanungo, *Studies in Rajput History*, Delhi: S. Chand, 1969.

functionaries presiding over commemmorative temples. For instance, the so-called 'living sati' (her immolation was prevented in 1985) at Devipura, a few kilometres from Deorala, had asked for instructions from her guru at the Triveni temple located near the village. A guru from the same temple was associated with the immolation at Hathideh and the priest who officiated at Jhardli had links both with the Hathideh family and the Triveni temple. Since at least the mid-1980s local brahmin networks have tied up with other religious and educational institutions (*peeth*s, *math*s) or, increasingly, with militant Hindu organizations for *prachar* (propaganda), *yagna* (ritual to make offerings to gods and purify the environment) and other forms of ideological reinforcement.

The brahmins, however, form an ancillary social group to both the rajputs and the banias. By the late nineteenth century widow immolation had almost ceased among the rajput ruling class and reported incidents are very rare within Rajasthan as a whole. But although this period was marked by the virtual cessation of widow immolation as a social practice, at a symbolic and ideological level it garnered fresh reinforcement, and acquired new shapes. Assertions of the 'exceptional' nature of the history of Hindu Rajputs as a 'race' and cultural group in part revolved around the immolation of their women. This construct was partly encouraged by British valorization of Rajputs as one of the 'martial races'. Such cultural valorization coincided not only with the kshatriya (warrior caste) self-image of Rajputs but, ironically, was coincident with rajput submission to British paramountcy. This submission, which ensured for the aristocracy a continuation of their position as a ruling class in Rajasthan, simultaneously enabled a mythical aura to be created around 'martial qualities'. A symbolic cohesion, which glossed over internal occupational, economic and cultural stratification among Rajputs, came to be maintained as group 'identity'. In part this colonial construct was a product of the romanticization of Rajputs by Colonel Tod who incorporated the already idealized charan narratives of jauhar and widow immolation into the *Annals and Antiquities of Rajputana* (1829). The emblematic figures of these tales—the martial rajput and his consort, the brave rajputni—with their attendant ideologies, were re-used by sections of the emergent middle classes and became a staple of their cultural Hindu nationalism from the late nineteenth century (especially in Bengal) to the present. In this process the historical specificities of both

jauhar and widow immolation were repressed and both practices
became exemplars of willed self-sacrifice.[23] The defence, by sections
of the nationalist intelligentsia, of widow immolation as symbolic
of the cultural and spiritual glory of 'Indian womanhood', is part
of a long history, takes many involuted shapes and has differing
ideological locales that we cannot trace here. In its broad contours
it produced a constellation of meanings which fuse a notion of
'sati' as volition with nationalist aspirations and with a specific
idea of the nation. 'Sati' comes to signify an inviolable womanhood
comprising ideal wifeliness, heroic death and ascetic self-sacrifice—
grafting a set of patriarchal ideals into nationalist aspirations.

Soon after Independence, nationalist reconstitution of rajput
legend and history became potent ideological weapons within
Rajasthan for another set of reasons and within an altered social
configuration. At this time, a connection was frequently made
between the mutually supportive nature of rajput cultural authority
and rajput political power, in which the former, centred largely on
male heroism and its female counterparts, was held to be the *basis*
for both right to property and right to rule. The defence of rajput
patriarchy became one basis for the defence of patrimony. The
political articulation of this appeared in an agitation opposing land
reforms that took place during the Fifties in the wake of the Rajasthan
Land Reform and Resumption of Jagirs Act (1952, amended 1954).
Initially the agitation was led by the Kshatriya Mahasabha, an
organization comprising ex-rulers and big *jagirdars* and the mass of
petty landholders.[24] Their defence of the *jagirdari* system of land
entitlement, which had been in use since Mughal times, was based
on, among other things, a claim to its extreme antiquity (it was said
to date back to 'the dawn of civilization' and to the Vedas) and on
the claim that jagirs had been acquired in return for 'unparalleled
heroism and sacrifice. . .in devotion to the cause of the Ruler, Country
and Religion.' Finally members of the Kshatriya Mahasabha claimed

---

[23] See for example, Romesh C. Dutt, *Pratap Singh: The Last of the Rajputs: A Tale
of Rajput Courage and Chivalry*, Allahabad: Kitabistan 1943.

[24] A jagir was a territorial assignment for land revenue purposes, and grantees
had to provide military and other feudal services; jagirs were also granted in
recognition for administrative service, and granted without military and tax
obligations for charitable and religious purposes. A jagirdar is the holder of a
jagir while the jagirdari system refers to the system instituted during the Mughal
period under which such assignments were made.

to be a class of hereditary landholders with a historical record of and potential for leadership in rural India—a class with martial traditions now in the service of the defence forces. Upholding the right of private property they condemned land reforms as 'partial communism', and claimed that such economic discrimination against 'one class of income' amounted to cultural discrimination against 'one race or religion or language'.[25]

Later, the petty landholders formed their own organization, the Bhuswami Sangh, to carry on the agitation when the princes and big landowners withdrew in 1954, after arriving at a favourable settlement with the government. The epicentre of the Bhuswami Sangh agitation was Udaipurvati, the bastion of the Shekhawat rajputs. The Bhuswami Sangh like its parent organization, also mediated its opposition to land reform through a powerful cultural ideology combining rajput 'identity' with militant Hinduism. A contributory factor in promoting this ideology was its support by the Rashtriya Swayamsewak Sangh (RSS) which had become active in Shekhawati during the forties. One supporter of the Bhuswami Sangh explicitly conflates Indian, Hindu and kshatriya history identifying them with a nationalist defence of *'bhartiya sanskriti'* (Indian culture) which always had and must continue to rest on caste stratification and inegalitarian social relations.[26]

The Bhuswami Sangh represented not only the existing class contradictions within the rajput community, but also specifically, the emergence of a middle class, with links both to modern professions and agrarian society. The majority of Shekhawat rajputs were and are petty landholders or *bhumias*,[27] needing to supplement their income from non-agrarian sources. Some have taken to

[25] Memorandum submitted to the Rajasthan-Madhya Bharat Jagir Committee by the Special Organization of Rajasthan and Madhya Bharat Jagirdars, 18 November 1949, Jaipur. See also *Report of the Rajasthan Madhya Bharat Jagir Enquiry Committee*, Delhi: Govt. of India, 1949; *Report on Rajasthan Jagirdari Abolition*, Jaipur: Govt. of Rajasthan, 1953; Deol Singh, *Land Reforms in Rajasthan: A Report of a Survey*, Delhi: Govt. of India, 1964.

[26] See Ayuwan Singh, *Rajput aur Bhavishya*, 2nd ed., Jaipur: Ayuwan Singh Smriti Sansthan, 1981.

[27] A *bhumia* is a landholder under the *bhumichara* tenure system; bhumias claim that land held under this system was, unlike the jagir, personal hereditary property. For a history of bhumias and jagirdars see Dilbagh Singh, *The State, Landlords and Peasants: Rajasthan in the 18th Century*, Delhi: Manohar, 1990, pp. 42–50, 144–57.

business and academic professions, but from the mid-nineteenth century onward, when the Shekhawati Brigade was formed, they have joined the army and police in large numbers. This service has helped them maintain a sense of their 'martial' tradition as a 'kshatriya' caste group. The leadership of the Bhuswami Sangh was drawn from the bhumias and jagirdars who in 1947 had formed the Ram Rajya Parishad, a militant Hindu organization closely associated with several religious leaders.[28] This urban middle class leadership was able to mobilize small landholders in massive numbers in the 1950s to fight with 'religious dedication in the defence of ancient rights to the soil ... in the name of a kshatriya's religiously sanctioned claim to power and state and society.' The leaders exhorted tens of thousands of lathi wielding, saffron clad rajputs to remember that their 'ancestors' had fought for 'dharma' and 'their wives had committed jauhar.'[29] The higher ranks of upper class rajputs had betrayed them. On themselves, therefore, rested the responsibility to preserve rajput tradition. Thus the ideology of the erstwhile rajput ruling class was, militantly propagated under transformed conditions, to defend the economic and social interests of small proprietors.

Although the agitation was finally called off in 1958, the claims to tradition and the heritage of Rana Pratap, Mewar and Chittor—consisting of the heroic rajput man defending the motherland while the heroic rajput woman committed jauhar or 'sati'—accrued a special strength from the militancy of the movement. Female immolation was vociferously regrounded in a kshatriya *parampara* or grand tradition, described as resting on the material basis of the jagirdari system (linked to clan ownership), political power and martial violence.[30] Though belied by the long history of rajput alliances with the Mughals and the British, the eulogistic representation of widow and mass female immolation as patriotic acts in defence of Hindu religion and custom aligned itself with certain nationalist tendencies and drew its emotional resonance

---

[28] K.L. Kamal, *Party Politics in an Indian State*, Delhi: S. Chand, n.d., pp. 76–79.
[29] Suzanne Rudolph and Lloyd Rudolph, *Essays on Rajputana: Reflections on History, Culture and Administration*, Delhi: Concept, 1984, pp. 60–61. A lathi is a wooden staff; dharma refers to a combination of duty, righteousness, faith and religion.
[30] See Singh, *Rajput our Bhavishya*.

from them. Significantly however, these were now directed against an indigenous, not a colonial, government. At one level the ideologies of the Kshatriya Mahasabha, and more sharply, of the Bhuswami Sangh represent their respective self-perception and consciousness as classes. At another level—even as the land reforms affected the class-divided rajput community differentially—a certain cohesiveness was nevertheless achieved regarding patriarchal ideologies. These ideologies of the Kshatriya Mahasabha and Bhuswami Sangh, linking 'cultural' revitalization to a hoped for rajput return to political power,[31] have played a part in activating social sanction for widow immolation as an exemplum of female *veerta* or heroism.

The grounds on which ideological cohesion was sought by the rajputs in the 1950s, apart from the broad assistance it received from and rendered to militant Hindu forces, was also crucial in the local self-definition of 'rajput' versus other castes at a time when the cultural power of rajputs coexisted in contradictory fashion with economic and political decline. Yet, significantly, a supporter of the Bhuswami Sangh, acknowledging class distinctions among rajputs, argues that Hindu power must now be sought on a class basis while retaining caste distinctions and community identity.[32] In mobilizing rajputs in defence of the Deorala culprits, the present (Sati) Dharma Raksha Samiti (SDRS) draws on this legacy. The same class fraction that constituted the Bhuswami Sangh now leads pro-'sati' agitations and stages rallies reminiscent of the Bhuswami Sangh rallies of the 1950s.[33] Its ideological position on widow immolation both draws on and constitutes a development from the 1950s. Significantly, the ideologies produced in that decade have been in live interaction with the recurrent widow immolations carried out with impunity in this area for the past 35 years, starting with the immolation of young Taradevi in Madhav-ka-Vas in 1954 right until the Deorala incident.

The ideological formation as it has now crystallized is marked by the attempt of pro-'sati' rajputs to broaden the social base of

[31] Ibid.

[32] Ibid.

[33] The richer Rajputs now also have business interests and a public school education. For instance, the convenor of the SDRS, Narendra Singh Rajawat, is in the leather export business.

support for widow immolation. This is in striking contrast to the attempt in earlier periods of rajput hegemony to preserve it as a 'privilege' of rajput women. There is a history of contestation of the 'privilege' to carry out widow immolation by other upper castes (and in isolated instances by a few lower castes) in the erstwhile rajput principalities. Nevertheless, it continued to be claimed as a special mark of rajput blood and rank. Now however, rajputs are attempting to elicit ideological support from a broad range of upper and lower castes. Regional, religious and patriarchal commonalities are invoked to give other castes groups a stake in the eroding cultural hegemony of the rajputs. In this attempt, patriarchal norms governing women are being widened and redistributed by bestowing upon widow immolation a central position, in simultaneous relation to rajput history and caste identity on the one hand, and to the purported essence of a homogenized Hinduism on the other. This can be seen in the pamphlets distributed and in the speeches at rallies organized by pro-'sati' groups and organizations in the wake of nationwide protests at the Deorala immolation and the new legislative prohibition of widow immolation and its worship (Commission of Sati Prevention Act, 1987).

In 'Hinduon se Apeel', as in the speeches delivered at the 8 October 1987 rally in Jaipur,[34] widow immolation is made to represent a Hinduism whose patriarchal content cuts across caste and class. The pamphlet makes a simultaneous bid to create a regional identity and an overarching Hinduism: forced widow immolation is acknowledged as a crime, but voluntary widow immolation is said to have the sanction both of the Shastras in general and of their *own* local traditions in Rajasthan in particular. The pamphlet asserts that the present government, worse than the Muslim or the British, is the antagonist of a generalized Hindu dharma and of the constitutional right of freedom to worship. The men and women who dare worship Roop Kanwar are described as valiant *vir*s and *virangan*s. The sanctioning power of rajput

[34] 'Hinduon Se Apeel', a pamphlet attributed to the SDRS and written to mobilize Hindus in 'traditional attire' for the 8 October 1987 pro-'sati' rally in Jaipur; transcript of speeches made at the same event. In these speeches the RSS, BJP and Vishwa Hindu Parishad were upheld as political organizations symphathetic to their cause.

tradition is claimed on two distinct grounds. First, identifying widow immolation with jauhar, they claim its practice in Rajasthan as superior to its counterpart in nineteenth century Bengal on the illusory grounds that widow immolation in Rajasthan was always voluntary and therefore was too noble to be banned. Second, since rajputs are claimed to be both a martial race and historic defenders of Hindu dharma, the legislation is construed as a direct challenge to which they must collectively respond. Widow immolation is used simultaneously as a locus for community cohesion and for universal 'appeal', for the pamphlet claims, the 'sati' 'tradition' is the property of many different non-rajput castes. This attempt to universalize the practice and ideology of widow immolation was also represented by the presence of various non-rajput speakers at the Jaipur rally.[35] Similarly, the statement of Devi Singh Mandawa, President of the Rajasthan Kshatriya Mahasangh, represents 'sati' as not merely the heritage of rajputs but also of brahmins, oswals, mahajans, menas, sunars, malis and nais.[36] These social groups probably have little sustained interest in maintaining rajput cultural hegemony in actual practice; any cohesion across caste/class lines becomes precarious in the face of the rajputs' assiduous efforts to maintain caste distinctions in most areas of social life ranging from worship at temples, to use of village well and marriage arrangements. However, such alliances serve the double ideological purpose of keeping women in place and reinforcing a Hindu militancy that can generate greater consensus; moreover they often benefit the particular individuals and groups who take a leading role in mobilizing them.

The indigenism of the SDRS pamphlet and the speeches at the rally is displayed in their abusive attacks on irreligious and westernized individuals, especially women—*azad kism ki auraten* (free/immoral women)—who are characterized as opponents of

[35] The speakers included representatives of other communities—meena, gujjar, dholi, kayasth and brahmin as well as a token Muslim. Some were representatives of organizations like Akhil Bharatiya Hindu Mahasabha, Akhil Bharatiya Gujjar Mahasabha, Chittor Jauhar Samiti, Bharatvarshiya Dharma Sangha, and the Math of the Shankaracharya of Puri.

[36] *Hindustan*, 26 September 1987. Devi Singh Mandawa, a member of the Rajput Sabha, active in organizing pro-'sati' rallies, the author of a history of the rise of Shekhawati power, takes pride in the land reform agitations of the Bhuswami Sangh.

Hindu dharma. A sharp opposition, both regional and ideological, is constructed between the sexual immorality and independence of such women and the *patibhakti* (dutiful worship of the husband) demonstrated in widow immolation. Finally, all women of Rajasthan are upheld as exemplary: unmarried girls are virtuous, wives are faithful, never seek divorce, and widows do not remarry.

However, the social degradation of the widow is the patriarchal substratum of the ideologies of female valour and 'sati'. Economically dependent, most rural rajput women live in such strict seclusion that they are not permitted daily outdoor tasks such as fetching water or gathering fuel, let alone taking up remunerative employment. Unlike women from the majority groups, the jats and lower castes, rajput widows are not permitted to remarry. They are expected to be maintained by their in-laws and are deemed to have only a moral right to the deceased husband's share of property. Even if the in-laws abide by their responsibility to maintain her, the widow's life, stripped of the protection and status accorded by a husband, is often miserable. If treated badly by her in-laws a widow may return to her parents; but after their death she can expect little from the natal family. Often a widow adopts a male child to provide for her when he grows up. Widows must still remove all symbols of marital status, give up jewellery, suffer dietary restrictions, and wear only certain colours and fabrics. Although the severity of social opprobrium has decreased, even now a woman is required to sit for fifteen days in a corner on the death of her husband; and because widows are considered inauspicious, their movements are restricted to certain times of the day. The actual situation of the majority of contemporary rajput women is in inverse relation to the idealizing myths created on their behalf.

Banias

The colluding role of a section of the corporate business sector consisting of leading industrialists, entrepreneurs and traders hailing from the Shekhawati area has been crucial to the recurrence of widow immolation in the region. One group, chiefly of Agarwals and their subcastes, either resident or migrant from the area, is actively engaged in propagating 'sati' worship.

The enterprising bania community of this area (as of other parts of Rajasthan), collectively known as marwaris, has continuously migrated to other places and prospered. For instance, out of the 101 top business houses in India at present, 27 are of Shekawati origin.[37] The local traders are 'poor' compared to their urban counterparts. It is the latter, along with metropolitan business houses, that provide a strong financial base for 'sati' worship. Through such financing worship has been extensively institutionalized in recent decades within the region and to a lesser extent, in different parts of the country. Institutional modes, centred around newly built temples, have widened the spatial reach and diversified the channels for propagating ideologies and beliefs in widow immolation as 'sati' through ritual ceremonies, annual religious fairs, welfare activities, the induction of print, audio and visual media.

The Shekhawat Agarwal business community has more difficulty than the bhumia rajputs in negotiating its past history to claim the cultural symbols of the former ruling classes. There were some instances of widow immolation in this community during the medieval period but these may simply have been symptoms of proximity to rajput life styles and a kshatriya ethos. For leading *sahukar*s and *mahajan*s (bankers, moneylenders and traders) were usually close to the court, and as financiers and administrators, they received various honorific titles from rajput rulers. Some of them maintained a princely style of living with armed retainers who guarded their goods on caravan routes. There are also some scattered instances of their participation in battles. Alternately, widow immolations among some bania families may have been early manifestations of a desire to appropriate rajput patriarchal practices and acquire higher cultural status.

The formation of a regional network, which has figured prominently in the support of 'sati' in the past few decades, dates back to medieval times. As traders, bankers, financiers and moneylenders, they were encouraged by local chieftains and village thakurs (landlords) to establish commercial centres within their territory. Among such centres were Sikar, Ramgarh, Lakshmangarh, Fatehpur, Nawalgarh and Jhunjhunu.[38] Despite large scale

---

[37] D.K. Taknet, *Industrial Entrepreneurship of Shekhawati Marwaris*, (Jaipur: Taknet, 1986), p. 103. Apart from heading large industrial houses, migrants from Shekhawati have developed numerous smaller-sized businesses and firms. By 1940, 156 firms belonged to Agarwals from this region alone, pp. 179–211.

[38] Taknet, *Entrepreneurship*, pp. 36–37; Thomas Timberg, *Marwaris: From Traders to Industrialists*, Delhi: Vikas, 1978, pp. 111–12.

migration to the cities, the trading community continues to have a substantial presence in these towns and the adjoining villages.

The colonial period, often termed the 'golden age' of the banias, gave a tremendous boost to the fortunes of both impecunious banias and rich mahajans, and it saw the formation of a community network that now encompasses large parts of India. With the opening of the Delhi–Calcutta railway route in 1860, thousands of Agarwals from this region spread along the Gangetic belt to Assam, Bengal, Orissa, and farther east into Burma and South-East Asia. Calcutta became the headquarters of marwari capital amassed through cotton, jute, oil seeds, opium trade as well as banking and speculation.[39] To a lesser extent, fortunes were also made in Bombay. From these fortunes huge havelis (mansions), with their now famous wall paintings (some of which commemorate widow immolation) were constructed in the home villages of the entrepreneurs.[40] This widespread network has determined both the mode of institutionalization and the proliferation of 'sati' temples in several parts of the country and abroad (Singapore, Hong Kong). The period of marwari expansion was also the period of their sectional involvement in nationalist versions of pan-Hinduism of the one hand and on the other in *goraksha* (cow protection) movements in the 1890s and 1910s, and in engineering Hindu–Muslim riots in urban Bengal in the 1920s. Also around the 1870s they began to take a growing interest in tracing their own genealogy and origins, an activity that represents the contradictory face of expansion—the search for community solidarity and cultural authority.

Post-Independence policies provided further opportunities for expansion to Shekhawati businessmen. Families such as the Jhunjhunwalas, the Poddars, the Khaitans, now head leading industrial houses. Although these industrialists and businessmen no longer have the local economic interests they had in colonial times, they maintain their cultural and religious links with the Shekhawati area; one form this has taken in the past four decades has been the construction of huge 'sati' temples. The wide network

[39] By 1900, 280 out of the 444 family firms from Shekhawati were located in Calcutta, Timberg, *Marwaris*, pp. 116–17.

[40] See Francis Wacziarg's and Aman Nath's introduction to their *Rajasthan: The Walls of Shekhawati*, Delhi: Vikas, 1982.

of small traders especially from northern, central and eastern India, has joined the representatives of metropolitan business concerns in their support for 'sati' by making donations, setting up local temples, propaganda and annual pilgrimages to Jhunjhunu and other 'sati' temples in Rajasthan. Here we will confine our discussion to the Rani Sati temple in Jhunjhunu, the largest and most influential of bania temples dedicated to Aggarwal woman said to be immolated in medieval times.

Rani Sati Temple

The contemporary institutionalization of 'sati' worship by the bania community has three major aspects: the re-formation of belief and ideologies through contemporary narratives about medieval immolations and their dissemination in various forms; the relation between the ideologies produced and contemporary immolations; and the collusive material and ideological interaction between banias and rajputs.

The history of Rani Sati temple indicates that the participation of marwaris in a nationalist construction of 'sati' with its accompanying patriarchal values and Hindu chauvinism, began quite early but acquired a substantial shape in this region only after Independence. The commemoration of Narayani Devi, hitherto worshipped as a *kuldevi* or family goddess within the privacy of Agarwal homes, was converted into public worship sustained by massive amounts of money. The original shrines were small *mundh*s (memorials) in a forest at some distance from Jhunjhunu town which later expanded. According to the Census of India (1961) an annual mela, a temple managing committee and plans for minor expansion were all introduced in 1912. The main gate was completed in 1936 but the *mundh*s were not converted into temples until 1956—two years after the immolation of a rajput widow in Madhav-ka-Vas in this region. The Rani Sati temple trust is privately controlled by Shekhawati Aggarwals settled in Bombay and Calcutta, and the 105 'sati' temples the Rani Sati Sarva Sangha has supervised in building all over India, consolidate a formidable network of donors within the trading-manufacturing community. While the present shape of the the temple dated to 1960, the temple has continued to expand.[41] No longer a family

---

[41] In 1986 a new section to the temple and a 51 kilogram gold *kalash* (cupola) were added, and by 1988 it had acquired more land.

deity of the Jalans, Rani Sati is now worshipped by many castes. Years of propaganda in the form of cultural programmes, commemorative and eulogistic meetings have paid dividends. Ostensibly a philanthropic venture, the adjacent Rani Sati Girls Primary School was established with 175 students in 1961. According to local accounts, hardly anyone came to temple in the 1950s; with the establishment, of the school, students could be and were made to line up for daily homage at the temple—an activity suspended only after the Deorala incident.

The historical veracity of the legend of Narayani Devi, alias Rani Sati, is difficult to prove. The two dates given for her immolation—1295 and 1595—do not match either with the history of Jhunjhunu or with the number of generations of Jalans descended from her. What is significant here is not only the claim to historical veracity but also the ostentatious concern with historical legitimization through alleged facts, research and evidence displayed by the official annual journal of the Rani Sati Sarva Sangh. This concern stems partly from the attempt to manufacture long genealogies to compete with those of rajput families and to emulate the rajput worship of *shakti* (divine female energy). More important, it reflects a need to institutionalize worship not merely of 'sati' as an embodiment of shakti—the defensive bania claim—but rather of a real immolated woman as 'sati'.

The ideology of the prachar and legends has much in common with that of rajput temples. More significantly it reproduces the same configuration—a compound of domestic ideology for women, voluntaristic versions of the event centred on satt and a relocation of family and community responsibility—which makes immolations possible. A large quantity of supportive narrative literature has been directly produced by the temple trust in Jhunjhunu and in its branch in Delhi and much more has been sold in the temple precincts, and distributed at public meetings arranged by the trust or its subsidiaries, in the past two decades.

These biographical narratives of Narayani Devi substantially negotiate the legal and social contours of contemporary immolations and their representations, a problematic that could scarcely have been carried over from the medieval period, i.e. presenting the woman's agency as orchestrating the event, the problem of the witness being an interested even culpable participant in immolation yet without whom the miraculous nature of the event cannot be established, the difficulty of squaring widow immolation as a product of the woman's own volition with the necessarily public and participatory nature of the funeral, and finally, the need to cite, establish and generate consent and belief as a basis of institutionalized worship of widow immolation as 'sati'.

The basic narrative of Narayani Devi is as follows. After the death of Narayani's husband in battle, the servant Rana, the lone survivor, gathers wood from the jungle and builds the pyre. She puts her husband's body in her lap, sits on the pyre, and then instructs him that she is henceforth to be called Rani Sati, and that in the temples dedicated to her there will be no *murti* (idol) but only a *trishul* (trident, weapon of Shiva).

However, there are essentially two versions of this story as well as several variations of each version in both prose and verse which contain different emphases. In the more common version, Narayani's life resembles the hagiography of contemporary immolated widows and the event is more or less 'spontaneous'. In the other, semi-mythicized version, reflecting kshatriya aspirations, Narayani is an avatar (incarnation) of Uttara (Abhimanyu's widow in the Mahabharata who is not permitted concremation because she is pregnant), and Narayani's immolation is predestined, being a boon granted to Uttara by the god Krishna.

Although neither version is fully mythical, the first version, unsupported by the predestination or semi-mythical paraphernalia of the Uttara version, is not only more involved in establishing a context for historical veracity but also with addressing the agency of those—family, servant—involved in the immolation. Both versions, however, are engaged though differently, in the struggle to free from responsibility those involved in the immolation.

In the semi-mythicized Uttara version Narayani is determined to be 'sati' from her childhood; she and her parents know through Krishna, who has had the event planned to the last detail from centuries, that soon after she marries, her husband will be killed[42] Krishna, disguised as a religious mendicant or *sadhu* (accompanied by his similarly disguised consorts, Radha and Rukmini) here functions as a surrogate brahmin and so provides a divine precedent

[42] Ramdev Sharma, *Shri Rani Sati Mangal (Byavala)*, Jhunjhunu: Satyanarayan Goenka, 15 August 1986; Ramakant Sharma, *Shri Narayani Charitmanas*, Varanasi: Nand Kishore Jhunjhunwala, n.d. [sold in the Delhi Rani Sati temple, 1987], hereafter referred to as *Narayani Charitmanas (1)*.

for similar contemporary intermediaries! Krishna is an arbiter of Narayani's satt, i.e. he tests her will and determination to be 'sati'. The job of dissuading her falls to him and to her mother. However, the dissuasion functions only to confirm or establish Narayani's agency and simultaneously constitute Narayani (as yet unmarried) as the spokesperson of patriarchal values that seem to emanate from her.[43] In one of the two variations of the Uttara version, once Narayani proves her determination, her mother shifts from weeping and scolding to joy, and later at the wedding, addressing her daughter as *'amar suhagin'* ('one who is eternally married'), bids her be a dutiful wife and to bring glory to both families.[44] The consent of the natal family to Narayani's future immolation being established, the celebration of the wedding becomes simultaneously a celebration of 'sati'. The Uttara versions thus not only spread satt across the whole of Narayani's life but are studded with miracles: the infant Narayani lights a fire magically, joins the severed head and body of her husband's corpse, stops the sun at ten past six so that wood for the pyre can be gathered, causes a well to dig itself in order to rectify the absence of water, and speaks while burning. The semi-mythicized Uttara versions acknowledge family and other participation more openly since they are able to displace individual and family responsibility onto predestination. Of course, Rana, who collects wood and builds the pyre, asks for and is given instructions in all versions. However, in one of the Uttara versions, he is not only represented as a loyal, feudal retainer of Narayani's marital family, but Narayani elevates him to the status of being Abhimanyu's charioteer and servant in every birth. She even changes her name so that he will be worshipped before or with her.[45]

The non-mythicized versions contain no scenes of family dissuation and only one contains a miracle—Narayani restores a wounded Rana to health so that he can assist her.[46] The immolation is represented as a spontaneously improvised incident for which the only preparation is the pious childhood of Narayani, thereby reducing the space for family or community participation. In these

---

[43] *Mangal: Narayani Charitmanas (1).*
[44] Ibid.
[45] Ibid.
[46] *Shri Rani Sati Charitamrit: Pramanit Jivan Charitra evam Stutian,* Jhunjhunu: Shri Rani Sati Mandir n.d. [sold 1988].

accounts satt is confined to the time of battle and burning. In most, Narayani is made to declare, either after the pyre is alight or when she reappears after her death, that she is obeying her wifely duty and going with her husband of her own free will.[47] In one of the non-mythicized variations, where Rana is a bystander, Narayani discovers him worshipfully singing her praise before she has declared her decision to be a 'sati'; here, not only is Rana described as fortunate but participation in immolation is equated with worship and devotion so the man who actuates immolation is sanctified as a blessed witness. While Rana ecstatically watches the pyre, the gods rain flowers on it.[48] The trauma-free happiness of the 'witnesses' establishes the very mode of 'seeing' an immolation.

Thus the narratives of both the semi-mythicized Uttara version and the non-mythicized version, without acknowledging it, revolve around the contradiction between female volition and community participation, which they manage to displace but do not resolve. In attempting to do so, however, they reveal their own social agency in mediating the contradiction between 'spontaneity' and premeditation of contemporary widow immolation. The social agency of these narratives is also evident in the elements they share with actual immolations as well as with subsequent accounts and visual depiction of these immolations. These common elements involved are either replicated or remodulated by the narratives of Narayani Devi which are indelibly marked and shaped by the history of past and contemporary immolations. These narratives thus provide a mediating middle ground between the violence of actual immolations and the euphemisms of subsequent worship. We will take up only a few significant aspects that are common to most of the Narayani Devi biographical narratives.

The representation of Narayani Devi consciously establishes a continuum between a domestic ideology of husband worship and wifely fidelity for women, popular beliefs, a kshatriya version of nationalist notions of female heroism, transformational myths of satt and specific ways of institutionalizing worship. These are especially significant because the banias have claimed, after the

[47] *Charitamrit; Amar Virangana Shri Rani Sati Ji,* Jhunjhunu: Rani Sati Mandir, n.d. [sold 1988].

[48] Verse narrative in Gopigram Joshi, *Shri Rani Sati Ji Chalisa,* Jhunjhunu: Om Printers, n.d. See also *Shri Rani Bhajan Pushpmala,* Delhi: Shri Rani Sati Sarva Sangha, n.d. [sold 1987], and hereafter referred to as *Pushp Mala (I).*

legal ban on the glorification of widow immolation in 1897, that their versions of satt 'sati' and shakti are unconnected to widow immolation. Yet all of the narratives function equally as description of and prescription for patriarchal obedience; in all of them Narayani is taught her duty by her natal family, while in one narrative Narayani herself prescribes patriarchal conduct for her family.[49] The annual journal of the Rani Sati Mandir unequivocally states that the highest ideal for a Hindu wife is to maintain her contract with her husband upon his death which is what Narayani fulfils when, in obedience to her pativrata dharma, she burns on the pyre.[50] This high ideal cannot be achieved by all women but only by exceptional women such as Narayani Devi. Therefore her worship cannot be confined to the family alone. In this way the journal prepares a basis both for inclusion and exclusion of non-banias. Narayani is claimed as a *kuldevi*, a goddess for a bania subcaste, while for all others she can be a universal *muradi* goddess, that is a granter of boons.

Satt as a rational for belief and the representation of the woman herself orchestrating the event are replicated in all versions. In most biographical narratives[51] the pyre is lit by her own *tej* (inner heat) or by supernatural shakti. In one variation, the servant is eliminated; Narayani herself prepares a pyre on the battlefield sits on it, taking her husband's body in her lap. She then prays to the fire god to turn them into ashes and the fire breaks out by itself.[52] As soon as the fire is extinguished, she appears in the form of a trishul-bearing shakti or Durga to the servant Rana and instructs him to carry her

---

[49] *Charitamrit.*

[50] *Shri Rani Sati Mandir, Varshil Karya Vivran,* 1983–84. Pativrata dharma is the code of obligations for a devoted wife.

[51] *Shree Rani Sati Bhajan Pushpmala,* Delhi: 1985, distributed by the Rani Sati temple at Jogibara, Delhi and hereafter referred to as *Pushpmala* (2); *Shri Rani Sati Charit Manas: Pramanit Jivan Charitra evam Stutian* (Jhunjhunu: Shri Rani Satiji Mandir, n.d. [sold 1988]); Ramakant Sharma, *Shree Narayani Charit Manas* (Bombay: Shri Rani Satiji Mandal: 15 August 1986), hereafter referred to as *Narayani Charitmanas* (2); Vijay Laxmi Aggarwal, 'Jhunjhunu Mela', *Kulpali,* Delhi: 1984, pp. 11–13; *Charitamrit; Chalisa.*

[52] Kailash Jatia, 'Shree Rani Satiji is Our Ancestor. We Worship Her as Our Family Goddess'. This pamphlet was distributed at a public meeting organized in Delhi on 6 March 1988 by *Kulpali,* a weekly magazine brought out by the Rani Sati temple in Jogibara, Delhi, which is an organ of the Delhi and Jhunjhunu trusts.

ashes to Jhunjhunu. She saves her husband's soul, becomes a protectoress of her kul (lineage) and lights the undying flames of satt.[53] In this variation, the other meaning of the word satt, eternal truth—is intended. However, this truth or purity only comes into existence and becomes available through her immolation. Consequently its separate or general philosophical meaning becomes, in practice, both subsidiary to and inseparable from widow immolation.

Similarly, the visual depictions encash the same set of beliefs centred on satt which underwrote the immolations at Jhardli and Deorala. Picture prints that show Narayani Devi as a woman on a burning pyre holding her husband on her lap have been selling rapidly outside the temple. The cover of a book of devotional songs shows a lighted pyre with a trishul planted on it while poised above is a woman receiving blessing and power from Krishna.[54] The forty feet long *jhanki* (sequential tableaux) in the temple enclosure depicting Narayani Devi's life and death, had an explicit, gimmicky transformation scene. The figure of a woman holding her husband's head in her lap, bobs up and down burning in red crepe-paper flames worked by a hidden mechanical device and a fan. As the figure subsides into the flames, goddess arises behind her with a trishul in one hand and a revolving *chakra* (halo) around her head.[55] As we were watching, a peasant woman exclaimed '*dekho satt kaise hota hai*' ('see, this is how satt happens'). The next two tableaux show the reception of Narayani Devi in heaven and her subsequent deification in Jhunjhunu with the help of a detailed model of the temple including the shrines of twelve women of the same lineage who were subsequently immolated. What the banias attempt to obfuscate is that the entire meaning of both the trishul as a symbol and shakti as a concept rests on the material fact of the immolation of a widow.

The significance of this reiterated narrative is enormous. Without the support of this story, Narayani Devi can neither earn her title of 'sati' or gain such status with her devotees. The meaning of the word 'sati' in this context derives from the story of her

---

[53] *Narayani Charitmanas (2).*

[54] *Pushpmala (2).*

[55] The *chakra* here carries the resonance of the disc, a weapon of Vishnu and his incarnations.

immolation and it has had this fixed connotation over the years. In all the narratives, the worship is instituted by the marital family, and not only the immolation itself but the entire modality of worship—site of temple, nature of worship, the kind of goddess she will be and the rewards for worshipping her—is presented in a woman's voice. The immolated widow becomes the voice of social sanction and provides a composite justification for the temple as an institution, even to the point of herself explaining the time lag between her immolation and the institutionalization of worship. As in accounts of contemporary events, the widow *herself* seeks deification and publicity, but whereas the participation of crowds in the actual event is seen to exalt the immolation, here it is more the participation of crowds in temple worship that justifies and exalts immolation. The temple becomes the chief end-product of immolation.[56] The stress falls on darshan (sight of divinity) or paying homage by visiting her temples, i.e. not just on individual belief but on structures which reflect and solicit belief and crystallize it into public worship.

In addition to 'voluntary' immolation dictated by the woman and the self-lighting pyre, other similarities between the bania's defence of widow immolation and that by the perpetrators in Jhardli or Deorala also emerge from this literature. Both use ancient and medieval episodes to defend contemporary episodes of widow immolation, and both claim that opposition to the glorification of widow immolation past and present is anti-Hindu and anti-national. In *Sati Parampara ki Jvalant Jyoti Shikhayen* by Ram Chander Vir,[57] not only does the introduction explicitly approve of 'voluntary' widow immolation, but a large number of widow immolations, both contemporary and historical (of which Rani Sati is one), are minutely described. Eighteen of the twenty contemporary immolations described in Vir's book have occurred in Rajasthan, and all but three of these occurred in the Shekhawati area. Not only is the proportion of historical to contemporary half and half, but past episodes serve only to legitimize the contemporary re-emergency of widow immolation in the area. Further, Rani Sati

[56] *Mangal; Amar Virangana; Charitamrit; Chalisa; Pushpmala (1).*
[57] Mahatma Ram Chander Vir, *Sati Parampara ki Jvalant Jyoti Shikhayen* (Virat Nagar, Rajasthan: Panchkhand Peeth, 1986) with an Introduction by Acharya Shri Dharmendra. Distributed at the meeting called by *Kulpali* in 1988.

is placed at the head of coherent 'tradition' of which the contemporary incidents are but a continuation. Thus despite Vir's disavowal of supporting the practice of widow immolation, and being concerned only with the 'pure' and purifying ideology of 'sati', the two mesh at every level.

Further Bania and Rajput Convergence

In their legends the banias have appropriated the rajput ideology of veerta, particularly female veerta. The explicit axis of assimilation is of course Durga and her trishul, more covertly it is a nationalist paradigm of the brave, self-sacrificing woman or virangana (a surrogate for all Hindus),[58] who dies in an actual or symbolic confrontation with Muslims. Most written versions of the narrative insert veerta into domestic ideology. Narayani is projected as a virangana who engages in battle herself after her husband has died fighting the soldiers of a Muslim ruler. Her heroism is represented as a product of wifely devotion or satt;[59] in some variations she is shown fighting with a combination of *vir ras* (heroic passion) and *satt ka tej* (strength of satt).[60] In other versions 'sati' and virangana are conflated *'sati roop se shatru sanhaare'* (she killed her enemies with the power of her manifest form as 'sati').[61] Narayani's heroism displayed *after* the death of her husband and *prior* to her immolation is bounded on either side. Contained, it does not present a challenge to patriarchal norms. The 'sati' produces the virangana who also carries traces of Hindu nationalism. Narayani's contemporaries are represented as a 'Hindu *jati* (race) protecting their dharma by maintaining the pativrata tradition.[62] In one variation Narayani even fights the nawab (Muslim governor) herself; the nawab who is now elevated to shah (ruler), threatens her chastity and she kills him.[63] *Amar Virangana,* written after the recent anti-'sati' legislation

---

[58] For a discussion of the overlaps between the virangana, Durga and the 'truthful, just' woman capable of self-sacrifice in other North Indian narrative traditions see Kathryn Hansen, 'The Virangana in North Indian History', *Economic and Political Weekly,* vol. 23, no. 18, 30 April 1988, pp. WS 28–29.

[59] *Mangal; Amar Virangana.*

[60] *Narayani Charitmanas (1).*

[61] Verse narrative in *Chalisa.*

[62] *Charitamrit.*

[63] *Narayani Charitmanas (1).*

to disapprove legal charges of glorification, recasts the devoted wife more emphatically as the heroic warrior of a quasi-nationalist parable, without obliterating her wifeliness. The story does this by first purposively omitting the description of the servant building the pyre, and second by omitting the pyre itself in the accompanying illustration. Narayani is shown sitting in mid-air holding her husband in her lap with a blank, empty space underneath; the narrative proceeds to describe the self-lighting fire and her transformation into trishul-bearing shakti who appears to the servant and instructs him to carry the ashes. An invoked tradition is clearly a tradition in-the-making.

The trishul, Shiva's weapon, also carried by Durga as shakti, has now become an insignia of 'sati' in bania temples. Not only does it carry resonances of Durga worship in Bengal with Narayani being compared to *'Calcutta ki Kali'*[64] but, as used by banias, the trishul also attempts to approximate the murti used by rajputs. It is made to represent a married woman, young and distinctly bridal in appearance: eyes are painted on while the *bindi* (vermilion mark), *nathni* (nose ring) and red *chundri* draped below or behind the insignia of the trishul, all indicate marital status.

The changing symbologies of 'sati' worship have a wider significance. At one level, the present cult is assimilative, and has marauded many existing modes of worship for its symbols. Further, if marwaris have capitalized on rajput culture and innovatively merged 'sati' with shakti, recent rajput and other temples have also begun to share the symbol. All recent temples have adopted the trishul as an appendage to the murti of a woman sitting on a pyre and holding her husband on her lap. Here too, in imitation of the marwari temples, 'sati' and shakti are coalescing. In the Kotdi temple, the altar virtually replicates the Rani Sati trishul. The temple office had a large framed print which represented Savitri, immolated two decades ago, as Durga astride a lion, carrying a trishul similar to the Rani Sati insignia. At the bottom corner was another such trishul along with wood, a small flame and the words *jyoti prakat* (flame manifesting itself) in reference to the self-lighting pyre. The site of Roop Kunwar's immolation in Deorala was also marked by a trishul with a red chundri draped over it to resemble the figure of a woman.

[64] *Chalisa: Charitamrit.*

The present iconography of 'sati' in the area, the feminized trishul, embodies the convergence of several ideological currents and interest groups: assertions of a 'glorious' rajput community identity, aspirations to kshatriya status by the business community militant Hindu revivalism (where the trishul is frequently used as a symbol of an aggressive Hinduism),[65] and the attempt to retain hegemonic control by the upper castes. Separately and together, they all fuel a reassertion of patriarchal norms for women. Some marwaris may be appropriating the 'heroic' medieval narratives of rajput culture, and some rajputs may now be vocally defending contemporary widow immolation, but the supporting ideology of both is directed towards binding women within a restrictive domesticity which can interlock with an aggressive Hinduism. In this sense they reinforce each other.

The marwari enterprise is interacting with contemporary widow immolations in a variety of other ways. Individuals from the community have been donors and participants at most incidents and members of this community frequently serve as treasurers and/or members of the committees formed to raise commemorative temples after a widow immolation has taken place.[66] The palatial Kotdi temple memorializing the immolation of Savitri, a widow from a sonar (a lower artisan caste) family, in April 1973, has been built principally through donations from Calcutta and Bombay businessmen. A photograph of a jhanki bearing procession lauding Savitri in Calcutta was displayed on the temple office wall. Reciprocally, booklets glorifying the Kotdi immolation have been sold in the Rani Sati temple precincts at Jhunjhunu. Family members and other persons from villages where immolations have occurred in the past 15 years have visited and been inspired by the Rani Sati temple. At least four bania widows, all belonging to relatively poor families in the community, were propelled into immolation in the late 1970s in

---

[65] In this context it is significant that *Amar Virangana* carried a picture of a map of India that shows a goddess carrying a trishul in the centre, and also that recently a section of the Marwari community has been actively supporting the Vishwa Hindu Parishad.

[66] Some Aggarwals set up a reception pandal (tent) for Rajputs in Deorala, defying the ban on the chundri ceremony, *Indian Express,* 11 September 1987. The treasurer of the Jhardli temple belongs to this community.

this region.[67] The Jhunjhunu temple is the model for the Kotdi and Jhardli temples. Recent 'sati' temples imitate its modes of public worship, its organization, means of prachar, and its performance of mahayagyas (large scale yagyas). Pilgrims to the Jhunjhunu temple invariably go to nearby Kotdi on the way and perceive little difference between the commemoration of medieval and contemporary widow immolation, or between the legend and the reality. The visual, symbolic and ideological overlap renders the time gap between the two indeterminate. In fact contemporary cases of widow immolation are swiftly being recast as legend, their dates are already blurred in popular recall. It is no coincidence that most contemporary incidents of widow immolation have taken place within a small radius of the Jhunjhunu temple.

All three groups—brahmin, rajput, bania—are anxious to manage the entry of women into a changing society in which the situation of women is also changing. The ideologies interact with events and operate differentially depending on a range of factors such as class, urbanization, caste and affluence. The rajputs' ideological propagation has resulted in the immolation of many rajput women; the banias' ideological propagation has resulted in the immolation of relatively few women from their own community; but given their wider networks, economic power and support for enshrining immolated women of other castes, they have been far more influential. Like the rajputs the banias, too, are interested in a cross class/caste ideology.

These two groups have specific relations of collusion at several levels as well as a wide complicity in the scale of values. At other levels, they retain a distance from each other. Each group worships its own immolated widows, and banias publicly deny that they support rajput immolations. At local levels, rajputs express resentment at the success of bania 'satis', cast doubt on their 'authenticity', claim that the government has 'favoured' the Jhunjhunu temple above their own and retain different interests as a community. However, the inclusion of Jhunjhunu into the 'sati' canon by the 8 October

---

[67] One of these was in Hathideh, adjoining Jhardli, and the immolation of two of these women was prevented. When one of the women whose immolation was prevented at Depolia, Chirana, was brought to the Jhunjhunu police station by the police, she reportedly said that she too wanted the glory of Rani Sati.

1987 SDRS pamphlet, constitutes a thinly veiled appeal for marwari bania support and in fact, recognizes their complicity.

In some indirect ways bania organizations have come out in defence of contemporary rajput immolations with the help of intermediary priests. The Aitihasik Sati Mandir Bachao Committee, formed by banias in defense of the Rani Sati temple, issued a pamphlet by Dharmendraji Maharaj. This pamphlet claimed, on the evidence of Maharaj Ram Chander Vir, that there have been no contemporary cases of instigated or forced immolation—they are all products of purity, wifely love and female volition.[68] The contents of the book by Ram Chander Vir have been described already. Interestingly, Vir has been a participant in at least one local immolation. On his own admission, he was imprisoned for three months for abetting a widow immolation near Virat Nagar in Rajasthan several years ago. While Dharmendra, who conducted a Bhagwad Gita recitation for Roop Kanwar's death anniversary in defiance of the government ban, has been part of the vicious anti-Muslim campaign on the Babri Masjid versus Ram Janam Bhoomi issue,[69] and was a chief speaker at the thinly attended Aitihasik Mandir Bachao Committee meeting in Delhi in 1989.

At a practical level, the legislative ban on glorification has, for the time being, led to an increased confluence of interests. Significantly, the Burrabazaar area of Calcutta, a business locality dominated by trades from Shekhawati and other areas of Rajasthan was the scene of pro-'sati' demonstrations following the legislative ban on the glorification of widow immolation after the Deorala incident.[70] The committee formed in Jhunjhunu to defend the continuation of the mela and worship of Rani Sati has been in open conference with a similar committee formed in Deorala to defend and expand the worship of Roop Kanwar.[71] The Deorala Committee has openly acknowledged that its future plans for building a temple and its legal strategy depend upon the success of

[68] Dharmendra Ji Maharaj, *Hinduon ki Divya Sati Parampara evam Vartman Sandarbh*, distributed at a meeting called by *Kulpali* in Delhi on 6 March 1988, Calcutta: Aitihasik Mandir Bachao Committee, n.d.

[69] *Times of India*, 10 September 1989. At the time this revised essay goes to press, Babri Masjid has been destroyed by the combined action of the BJP, VHP and RSS, leading to widespread violence mostly against Muslims in the country.

[70] *Times of India*, 12 November 1987.

[71] *Indian Express*, 30 August 1989.

the Jhunjhunu case now pending in the Supreme Court. The Deorala committee tacitly acknowledge the Rani Sati temple as a major ideologue of the area and recognizes the practical need for such a centralizing ideology in order to institutionalize worship.

The Metropolitan Ideologies

With the strong protests following the Deorala event initiated by the courageous action of Jaipur-based women activists, widow immolation had become a controversial issue involving increased subterfuge and obfuscation by its covert and explicit defenders. As the legislation affects both the perpetrators of the Deorala immolation and the trustees of the Rani Sati temple, their petitions and counter petitions at the Rajasthan High Court and the Supreme Court represent the alignment of sections of urban rajputs, banias and allied upper castes with those involved in widow immolation or its glorification at the mofussil (small town) centres. These ideologies emanating at the sites of immolation and glorification overlap or align with metropolitan ideologies producing an overarching ideological formation cutting across regional boundaries. This functions as a counter to urban-centred protest by liberal, left and democratic sections and organizations, including the feminist.

The first overlap is a consensus around the concept of 'authentic' or 'voluntary sati'.[72] There are, however, gradations and differences in the way volition is constituted. As we have pointed out, at the local village level, the widow's volition is its own opposite since it is embedded in belief in the agency of a supernatural power. For the urban supporter, volition usually rests on the liberal notion of rational choice. Here the notion of agency rests centrally on the woman herself, while in the former it is subsumed under divine agency. This transference of volition and agency to the woman makes the immolation simultaneously deplorable and admirable: deplorable because it is a sign of the miserable social status of the widow, but nevertheless admirable as representing courage to

---

[72] *Rajasthan Patrika*, 20 September 1987; SDRS pamphlet and transcript of speeches, ibid., and as reported in *Indian Express*, 30 September 1987; *Rashtradoot*, 6 September 1987; Ashis Nandy, 'The Sociology of Sati', *Indian Express*, 5 October 1987; Om Prakash Gupta (BJP) in *Trial by Fire*. For an earlier analysis of some of these tendencies see Kumkum Sangari, 'Perpetuating the Myth', *Seminar* no. 342 (February 1988).

undergo 'self-immolation', For conservative ideologues, the concept of volition is traversed by structured notions of cultural identity. They construct the immolation as a symbolic event which has the power to hold together all that seems to be in danger of falling apart: the extended family, female obedience to patriarchal norms, sectional group identities, Hindu tradition, Indian spirituality and the nation itself. Further, by representing 'sati' as definitionally opposed to modernity, westernization and materialism, defending it is construed as combating the colonial legacy.[73]

The second ideological overlap occurs in the arguments centering on concept versus practice. When the practice of widow immolation is, tactically or otherwise, considered, 'sati' is defended as a glorious civilisational concept or even philosophy: the idea is maintained as a purified realm.[74] But can the 'idea' of 'sati' be isolated from the changing variables of custom, belief, practice? Are these separate compartments in the social lives of people? Do they not interact? As it turns out metropolitan ideologues themselves confront this difficulty.

This is evident in their recurring anxiety over the 'true' meaning of the word 'sati'. There is an active debate on whether 'sati' is simply a good wife, or an immolated widow or the divine female principle of shakti. Each of these terms has a complex social history, but all three meanings are compressed in the present social meaning of 'sati' as it inheres in incidents of immolation, modes of worship and domestic ideologies. Ironically therefore, to uphold any single meaning does not serve the desired ideological purpose and becomes a self-contradicting enterprise. The anxiety to preserve the three meanings as separate comes from several directions. It comes, of course, from those who wish to resist legal action on the charge of glorifying 'sati'.[75] It comes also from those who are interested in

---

[73] SDRS pamphlet and speeches; Nandy, 'The Sociology of Sati'; Banwari, 'Narnari Sambandh', *Jansatta*, 29 September to 1 October 1987.

[74] Speeches at a meeting organized by the Aitihasik Mandir Bachao Committee in Delhi, 1989; Ashis Nandy, 'The Human Factor', *The Illustrated Weekly of India*, 17 January 1988, pp. 20–23.

[75] This position is to be found in the publications of the Rani Sati Sarva Sangha, the speeches of the Aitihasik Mandir Bachao Committee, the *Kulpali* editorial (1987), and the pamphlet entitled *Kulpali Saptahik dwara 6 March 1988 FICCI Sabhaghar mein ek 'Sati Nivaran Vidheyak Sambhavnae' Vishay par Ayojit Sammelan mein Vicharniya Mudde.*

maintaining unviolated enclaves of tradition, heroism, asceticism or abstract self-sacrifice and in preserving the concept—alternately named 'satitva' and 'sati'—as sacrosanct while condemning the practice.[76] It is impossible, however, to separate the concept from the practice by intellectual fiat since the practice itself gives substance and social legitimacy to the concept.[77] Finally, the concept being primarily patriarchal, even the compartmentalization of the meaning of 'sati' continues to use immolation prescriptively, i.e. to define what a woman should be. Paradoxically, those insisting on a separation of meanings are in fact deeply implicated not only in the conflation of these meanings, but also in the patriarchal ideology that such a conflation represents.[78]

The third aspect, common to both local and metropolitan ideologues is a domestic ideology centred on the good wife as upholding familial ideals, with its implicit or explicit regulation of female sexuality. The patriarchal family is upheld as an ideal unity of complementary gender roles and as the prime practitioner of tradition, thereby evading the issue of family involvement in immolation.[79] The regulatory potentials of the ideology rests on representing widow immolation as an exceptional or stray event, not as a custom; otherwise, most widows would burn. This 'stray' event is then neatly aligned with a grand tradition or parampara that in turn is composed of a series of such exceptional events![80] The argument that it is a stray event is based on the statistically lower incidence of widow immolation as compared to dowry deaths. In this way, beginning with the SDRS, an attempt has been made to delink widow immolation from other forms of violence and crimes against women. This manoeuvre is based on the recognition

---

[76] For example, Banwari, 'Nar-nari'; Nandy, 'The Human Factor'.

[77] Thus Nandy is reduced to locating 'the authenticity of the idea behind sati' in mythological times or in 'historical times read mythologically' and gives the example of medieval Rajasthan! ('The Human Factor', p. 22).

[78] The *contrast* between the legal defence by the Rani Sati Temple Trust in the Supreme Court, based on the claim of only worshipping shakti in the form of Durga, and the actual activities of the Rani Sati Sarva Sangha and the Aitihasik Mandir Bachao Committee, does not need reiteration.

[79] SDRS pamphlets and speeches; Banwari, 'Nar-nari'.

[80] Acharya Dharmendra, speech at Aitihasik Mandir Bachao meeting, ibid.; SDRS pamphlet and speeches; Banwari, 'Nar-nari'; Nandy, 'The Human Factor' and 'The Sociology of Sati'.

that as the most public and publicized of crimes, widow immolation has enormous normative and symbolic value—is indeed more serviceable as an exceptional event.

Fourth, local and metropolitan ideologies are based on a common historiographic model which refines the distinction between custom and incident, and localizes the distinction between voluntary and coerced widow immolation. Epidemics of widow immolation, as opposed to incidents, are said to be the product of either cataclysmic social transitions or foreign rule—Muslim or British. The onus is put, in a typically communal historiography, on 'external' elements. Bengal under the British is a hotbed of coerced immolation, while Rajasthan is proved to be (now and/or in the past) the sanctified home of voluntary ones.[81] Both claims are based on a species of anti-colonialism which makes a violent patriarchal practice the gift of an invader, and then uses this as a rationale to defend a terrible and recurrent abuse of women. The idealization of immolations in Rajasthan remains possible because, unlike Bengal, the violence involved was not demystified by a reform movement in the colonial period.

Finally, the sections of the intelligentsia engaged in constructing pro-'sati' ideologies claim to be defending authentic Indian traditions—especially the culture, tradition and faith of the worshippers in Rajasthan. These traditions are seen as existing from time immemorial within Rajasthan where a religious world view has miraculously remained intact; they give a new lease of life to the static, self-validating sociological model of tradition versus modernity.[82] There is a direct investment here in an indigenist, populist notion of 'Bharat' and her tradition-led masses which can function profitably to maintain India as a backward enclave and as a cultural spectacle favoured by neo-colonialism. The worshipful community is perceived as an undifferentiated mass that is inert in all but its faith. While this faith is represented as centred on 'sati' as a concept and on voluntary widow immolation, it is at the same time disconnected from the actual events of immolations and from

[81] Statement of Rajawat, SDRS convenor in *Trial, by Fire*, Acharya Shri Dharmendra, 'Hinduon ki Divya Sati Parampar Vir', *Sati Parampara, Jvalant Jyoti Shikhayan;* Nandy, 'The Sociology' and 'The Human Factor'.
[82] Editorial, *Jansatta*, 18 September 1987; *Rajasthan Patrika*, 18 September 1987. In 'The Human Factor' Nandy assures his readers that the natural moral discrimination of villagers ensures that they will only worship authentic 'sati's.

supportive institutions. The worshipful community in these accounts seems to have little volition regarding the immolation of the widow. This is not surprising, since like local worshippers, metropolitan ideologues also set out to erase the fact that widow immolation is a community crime. Evidently such populist idealization of the faith of the masses is quite selective because it obliterates from past and present historical memory not only those vast numbers of Indian people who have *never* practised widow immolations, but also those who did *not* and still do not share its assumptions.[83]

Popular Beliefs and the Question of Consent

As we have seen, not only are assumptions of the mystique of rural backwardness or of an isolated village community in the grip of immemorial custom or indeed any argument resting on the 'belief of the masses', ideological in character, but local institutions and metropolitan ideologies obscure the constitutive and generative relation of ideologies (including their own) to belief. They create a receptive environment for those beliefs.

There can be no originary moment in the constitution of faith—it is a specific process which interacts with and is activated by forces within a particular social formation and with specifiable patriarchies. Belief is socially constructed; it is at once freshly constituted and has pre-existing or pre-structured constituents which can be re-attached to familiar and new objects. If faith was not labile, new cults would never emerge. Though existing constituents are remodelled or re-attached, faith in 'sati' is also constituted by the immolation, or as in this region, by a series of

---

[83] Interviews with women from Rajasthan, mostly working women, reveal that many are aware of the factors which come together in a widow immolation: the control and oppression of women within the family; the inculcation of certain patriarchal beliefs in women themselves; the dependent status of widows which determines the *family's* actions; the self-interest of priests and members of the village; and the commercialization of religion. The women interviewed recognize the fact that pro-'sati' attitudes are anti-women, that religious cults can be fabricated, and show various degrees of scepticism, though not entire disbelief, about the miraculous powers of satt. Among lower caste men and women there was some indifference towards both the worship and the ideology centred on widow immolation. (This is based both on our interviews and on Kavita, Shobha, Shobhita and Sharda, 'Rural Women Speak', *Seminar*, no. 342, February 1988, pp. 40–44.)

successive immolations rapidly institutionalized and commodified. Pre-existing symbols, existing and evolving structures of feeling, and modes of belief, enter into new relations with each other.

There are crucial questions of faith and consent which need detailed and rigorous examination. In this section we will only look once again at some of the issues we have already raised, the re-activation of faith in widow immolation and the various forms of consent to it, in the light of those new relationships which enable a reformulation of its pre-existing constituents as pure 'continuity'.

To some extent faith in 'sati' has been kept alive by nationalist and rajput patrimonial ideologies which have maintained the concept of 'sati'. Private family worship of immolated women, mainly rajput and bania, has also played a part. However, contemporary institutions reconstitute these elements and represent 'sati' as a sign of unbroken continuity by eliding the new elements within the old. All institutions represent 'sati' as a sign of continuity—of wifely virtue, of tradition and of belief. Belief, whether rajput, bania or popular, is thereby represented as pre-existing. For it would be a contradiction in terms to take credit for authoring a goddess. So despite indisputable evidence of the contemporary expansion and reconstitution of worship, the goddess is represented as one in continuing series of such objects of worship.

Belief is inextricable from the social processes that generate it; it has no autonomous origin; but once articulated in rituals and institutions it acquires an aura of autonomy much greater than other ideological formations have. And in this case the aura of autonomy from the material realm is partly generated by the very forces which play a determining role in the practice of contemporary widow immolation. Marwari finance is one element that generates an 'autonomous' realm for the parampara of 'sati' in the region. The divine miracle, among other things, also makes for an eminently commodifiable event. Belief in 'sati' is partly fostered by the spectacular and systemic commodification of the event. The best evidence for this, pointed to earlier, are the neglected, scantily worshipped 'sati' memorial stones which lie adjacent to some of the temples of recently immolated widows. Villagers often do not even remember the legends of small dilapidated 'sati' memorials which lie close to home and they flock in large numbers to the recently built huge, ostentatious marble temples. Without the glamour, recognition and institutionalization of a palatial temple the meaning of immolation would neither circulate nor gather 'value'. The big temples legitimize the event, fix it visibly in public consciousness and memory, popularize worship. They give the final stamp of 'religion' to the event. The huge sums of money spent in construction and acquired through donations appear like proofs of faith and belief. Faith and profit appear to run parallel to each other, intersect, depend on each other.

The circulation of reified values allied to the persuasive vocabulary of popular culture transforms the institutional mode of address. Commodification catches the gimmickiness of popular, especially cinematic culture. All the pictorial representations of immolated widows, including the jhanki in the Rani Sati temple, depict the instantaneous deification of the woman. The neon and kitsch of the Rani Sati and other bania temples do not visually represent the authority of timeless tradition, rather they represent the authority of flashy technologization.

To some extent, the effectivity of 'sati' as a universalizing ideology depends both on the syncretic nature of belief and of popular modes of worship, which enable it to touch the lives of different people in various ways. Significant overlaps also exist with a wide range of other forms of worship. The connections of 'sati' worship with a popular composite culture are mainly limited to the belief in the new 'sati' goddess as muraad (boon) giver which overlaps with the already syncretic pir traditions in Rajasthan. Votive offerings at the tomb of a pir, usually a holy Muslim man, are made by people of all communities. Syncretization from various Hindu customs and traditions include innumerable private and public ritual: festivals like Gangaur and Teej which are structured around acquiring or preserving women's *suhaag* (marital status), and other rituals performed on occasions such as birth and marriage, overlap in content, method and assumptions with those now built around 'sati' worship. Both Gangaur and Teej are popular Rajasthani festivals in honour of Parvati, the consort of Shiva; they are observed by unmarried girls to obtain a good husband and by married women to preserve marital happiness.

We would, however, like to stress the problematic nature of syncretism both as a general concept as well as in 'sati' worship. As a concept, the positive connotations of liberal pluralism which syncretism acquired during the nationalist period (especially in the struggle against communalism) tend to obscure its transactional aspects. Further, the much applauded internal flexibility or adaptability of Hinduism acquires another meaning in the matter of widow immolation. Here, an intra-Hindu syncretism functions, through specific transactions, to normalize 'sati' worship by drawing it into active relation with other adjacent modes of worship. For example, the narratives and devotional literature about the Jhardli immolation (like those that surround other contemporary immolations as well as Narayani Devi of Jhunjhunu) place the widow in traditions of puranic Hinduism, ascetic renunciation, yog, bhakti,[84] Durga worship, local gurus, recent cults (e.g., Santoshi Ma) and simultaneously into a composite regional and national tradition comprising Mirabai, Padmini, Lakshmibai, thereby amalgamating bhakti with anti-Muslim and anti-British sentiments. Such syncretism functions on a variety of fronts—drawing on generally acceptable pantheons, new and old, Shaivite and Vaishnavite—to fit 'sati' worship into generalized worship, easing cross-caste participation. In both rajput and bania temples, the use of popular bhajans (devotional songs), some of them specially adapted to 'sati' worship, as well as 'sati' bhajans based on Bombay film songs and marriage or *bidai* songs (the latter sorrowfully bid farewell to the departing new bride), relates the 'sati' worship to a customary sphere and inserts it into popular culture. The syncretism draws into its ambit even those traditions which are indifferent or hostile to widow immolation. For instance the incorporation of Mirabai as emblematic of ascetism or renunciation and thereby an ancestress in the 'sati' tradition, obliterates the sharp opposition that Mirabai's corpus contains to widow immolation and to some other patriarchal practices. The overlaps with other forms of worship cannot therefore be interpreted in a formalist language which ignores their contextual and substantive nature.

In the assimilation of 'sati' into other forms of worship, not only does 'sati' worship *retain* its ideological character, the ideology of 'sati' actually *facilitates* certain forms of affiliation. Those modes of worship which exist in dispersed form and are related to structuring the lives of women and obtaining their consent to

[84] Yog is a school of philosophy emphasizing rigorous control of the body to enable concentration on transcendental reality; bhakti is a form of unmediated, personalized worship associated with specific individuals and movements.

patriarchal values, have come to be concentrated in 'sati' worship. Whatever be the similarity with adjacent modes of worship (and the domestic ideologies inhering in them) the 'sati' goddess is singular, because unlike any other goddess she never transcends the violent event or narrative which gives her birth and assigns her a specific, exemplary female role. For instance, there are overlaps between worship at the new medieval 'sati' temples and Durga worship both in symbols and in rituals. However, as we have shown, the perception and meanings of this worship continue to be contextually determined, and depend on the immolation of a woman. All the villages in this area where widows have been immolated in recent decades are known as 'sati dhams' (abodes of 'sati', places of worship)—widow immolation is the fulcrum around which other meanings or connotations of 'sati' revolve. The identity of the dead woman is certainly reinforced by her affiliation to Durga but the fact that she only acquires this affiliation from having been immolated remains at the forefront of common perception. Further, socially sanctioned symbolic modes for women—shakti, motherhood, asceticism inspired by devotion to (future) husband—cluster around Durga, simplifying if not assisting the affiliation of 'sati' to Durga. In short, of the neighbouring modes of worship that are synthesized in 'sati' worship, many are specifically grounded in the everyday maintenance of patriarchies—in a form in which many women themselves consent to their own oppression. It is this consent to 'everyday' religious forms of patriarchal legitimization which opens the way and eases the consent to the exceptional form of such legitimization that 'sati' represents.

Belief in 'sati' can transform everyday consent to patriarchy into a menacing form of social agency during an immolation, ranging from more or less passive forms of involvement to active perpetration. The double nature of an event of widow immolation seems on the surface to compartmentalize perpetration from belief: the actual event which is premeditated and conspiratorial seems to split off from consent and faith, which operate along diverse lines differentiated by caste, gender, closeness to and distance from event. However, the division that this seems to imply between perpetrators and colluders is, as we discussed in our account of Jhardli, difficult to maintain with any rigidity. The division inhabits much popular perception too, partly because it complements the division of a pure Hinduism from its corrupted versions, which prevails in contemporary liberal positions opposing communalism; this tends to obstruct critical examination of Hindu traditions and practices as a whole.

At the local level there are no simple demarcations between so-called participants and believers, given the fact that the event itself, after the declaration of satt, is structured by mass participation. The *active* pressure of the witnessing crowd shapes the event; indeed, the desire to witness is itself coercive. The crowd represents a closure of alternative options for the woman, it approves, supplements and finalizes the machination of families, priests etc. The widow's immolation becomes a public spectacle, the property of persons of all ages and social groups. The line between perpetration and belief can be thin—perpetration itself both rests on and creates a substratum of belief. The relation between faith and coercion comes up repeatedly in the case of the family, of the witnessing crowd, or of a village.[85] The belief in miracles which is empowering for the crowd and allows them to witness the event, is a form of coercion, sanctioning their active and passive participation in an immolation. Reciprocally, coercion, both physical or ideological, plays a part in re-constituting faith. Hence it is difficult to neatly compartmentalize the faith of those who perpetrate the crime self-servingly from those who watch it done, and those who later worship.[86]

The social character of divine intervention can be seen from the nature and function of miracles. The 'primary' miracle is of a woman turning into a goddess. The 'subsidiary' miracles establish the *prerequisites* for and *authenticate* the primary miracle, and at the same time they *structure* the event around its illegality.[87] What

[85] The rajputs of Mawda Kalan, whom one could represent as attached to 'tradition', neither preserve nor worship the ruins of a small 'sati' memorial adjoining the village. They have however, built a marble temple for a widow immolated in the mid-1970s. They organize melas, go to Jhunjhunu, are raising donations to construct a dharmashala, and came out in vociferous support of the immolation in Deorala. Are these 'traditional' villagers?

[86] A small Aggarwal trader admitted to lighting the pyre to burn his own mother (Hathideh, 1977) but claimed in the next breath that there were witnesses who stated the fire lit by itself. If this man did not have faith in some of the empowering myths of 'sati' he could hardly have set about burning his own mother. And if witnesses did not have some kind of 'faith' they could not have claimed that the fire lit itself even as they watched the son light it.

[87] These subsidiary miracles can be subdivided into five groups. The first group establishes the eligibility of the woman. These miracles are usually banal, such as the woman raising her arms above her head, or a woman telling her son that his

is striking in these is the adaptability of faith—not its traditional character or purity. A criminal mystification—the self-lighting pyre—forms a substratum of popular belief. The fact that divine intervention is said to take place at the precise moment when somebody is *about to* light the pyre says something about agency and belief. Those who have participated as perpetrators and collaborators, *know* that it is a crime even if they continue to *believe* in its religious character. We know, too, from the frequent presence of armed guards at immolations, that reliance on supernatural powers is limited. It is difficult in the circumstances to make a mystique of faith or to hold as infallible a faith which supports a crime, and rests in large part on structures of belief which directly conceal the facts of the crime.

People do not simply lie or tell the truth about the event. They often see what they expect to see, since individual, narrative and institutionalized agencies authorized to interpret 'religious experience' who guide the act of seeing, already exist. In some sense, then, faith precedes sight and enters into a dialectic of expectation and re-interpretation. And yet even this powerful process cannot produce a 'final' version of the event. The ideal plot is overlaid on the real one which in fact constantly slips out at interviews— admissions of human agency compete with the intervention of divine agency. Even local perception of the widow reveals its own inconsistencies: she seems to vacillate between being human and superhuman. She is seen as a heroic woman because she can *bear* the pain of the fire as well as be believed to be immune to the pain of burning because of her satt and goddesshood. Finally, as far as the apparent split between participation and belief is concerned, structures of belief exist simultaneously with structures of use and exploitation, faith is inseparable from instrumentality.

---

missing watch is in the pocket of his shirt. The second group establishes more direct alibis which erase signs of participation. The third group distances the guilt of the event—the woman appears in a dream to the family and tells them she has suffered no pain in the fire, or it is said that her nylon sari does not burn first but along with the woman, thus making the fire untrue to its 'nature'. The fourth group explains why the family did not prevent immolation—proofs of the widow's ability to curse, the fact that she cannot be touched because her body burns with satt. The fifth group are deterrents to police or legal action— the tyres of the police jeep puncture, making it impossible for them to arrive in time to prevent immolation, or the son of the police commissioner falls ill until the family is released.

It is worth emphasizing that the idealised miracle-laden 'plot' suffers a major breakdown in the case of prevented immolations. In Devipura, where the police prevented the immolation of Jaswant Kunwar in April 1985, verbal interviews and the commemorative booklet contain not only relatively direct admission of the agency of relatives, family and community but, most significantly, there is not a single miracle. The help of Jaswant's sister-in-law and other persons is acknowledged. Even the crowd is represented differently. A newspaper report describes the crowd as being aggressive, angry and infuriated, and the booklet, in a departure from the norm, describes the crowd around the pyre as fearful and worshipful, and, after police intervention, as disappointed, saddened and frightened.[88] The joyful crowd then is an effect of successful immolations. Although the explicit theme of the booklet is the autonomy of religion from law, its own description of the attempted immolation is shorn of all religious markers—except the woman's devoutness. Significantly, the disappointed sons of Jaswant attributed to the police the same role that tantrics and evil dakaits were given at Jhardli: they accused the police of destroying their mother's satt.[89]

This brings us to another important mechanism of belief in widow immolation as 'sati'. In both Jhardli and Devipura, opposition to widow immolation—whether material or ideological—is construed as threat and danger to satt. Whereas in Jhardli the so-called threat posed by tantrics and dakaits provided a reason for guarding the pyre and acted to maintain the facade of Om's volition, in Devipura, the snatching of satt by the police provides a rationale for an unsuccessful immolation that allows belief structures to remain intact. In both cases we can discern a mechanism by which forms of social opposition to widow immolation, past and present, are transformed and appropriated by or incorporated into structure of belief. This not only forecloses (for many) ideological contest, but functions to erase the *history* of these very forms of social opposition. However, the history of such opposition becomes the hidden history of structures of belief themselves insofar as they have condensed and transformed histories of earlier opposition into their own assimilative mechanisms.

---

[88] *Times of India*, 7 April 1985; *Mahamahim Mahasati Jaswant Kunwar Chandrawat* (No publisher or date, sold at the temple in Devipura in 1987).
[89] *Times of India*, 7 April 1985.

As an aspect of belief, popular consent involves consent both to the supernatural and to the social values implicit in the belief. In this sense consent works through consensus as in the matter of satt. Though satt is activated by an impending immolation, it depends on a prior substantive belief that what is being witnessed is a deification, and that the viewer embodies the beneficence by watching. As we have shown, satt translates and sublimates actual social agency—of those involved in invoking satt, family, villagers, other women—into something external or beyond control. Satt is manufactured and gains consent partly because it first elides human participation, then 'benevolently' re-inducts the participants who can express the pride of participation without feeling the guilt of collusion.

Consent can also work through contradiction: satt gains consent partly because it acts as a system of *exclusion*. As a principle of selection satt also guarantees that *not* every woman will be possessed. So, by virtue of its exceptional character, it gains consent in the form of religious belief from other women. The very concept of satt is infused with domestic ideology albeit in the ironic form of exceptionalism. The exceptional character of satt works to maintain patriarchal ideology—the exceptional event is made to do ideological work in the everyday sphere. The satt that gains consent at once legitimates the patriarchal and the supernatural, and more especially, the former through the latter. Since women themselves are often invested in these patriarchal structures, as for example through the ideology of *suhaag*, social structures of voluntary and enforced consent to everyday patriarchal practices can be drawn into public consent.

There are wider social parameters to the relation between patriarchies and beliefs. Patriarchal values not only gain consent for the event, rather the need to reformulate them in part informs the modalities of both the rajput defence of their patrimony and bania assertion in the cultural realm through the expansion of 'sati' temples. One mode of reformulating patriarchies is precisely to locate them in a configuration of religious event, community history and popular belief. Then in turn patriarchal values themselves become a sanctioned mode of building a wider social consensus—one not confined to these communities—which can then play a part in the constitution of militant Hinduism through other issues.

What is the object of popular consent? It is consent for the patriarchal subjugation of women within wider ideologies of permanence and change. What is sought to be preserved is what is seen to be changing: monogamous fidelity, the woman inside the domestic role the woman as the preserve of 'truth' and 'tradition', the arena on which to defend personal religion against the law. The universalizing definition of the pativrata is not mechanically tied to a caste or class, but to what *may* be a class consciousness shared by those who do not physically belong to it. The pativrata woman is being defined against women who work (in the Shekhawati area, women in agricultural labour), non-Hindu women (only Hindu women can be 'sati'), the popular caricature of the westernized woman (the model that urban banias have to contend with), women in marriage arrangements other than monogamy (most likely to belong to lower caste groups), widows who may seek remarriage, divorced and unmarried women, educated women who may seek employment, urban feminists, and any women who challenge their given role. It is to these women and the complex, changing forces which they appear to embody that the consent to widow immolation, together with attendant ideologies and beliefs, is addressed. Clearly this address goes beyond any single social group or class though it may originate in them. The domestic jurisdiction of pativrata dharma enlarges into a powerful patriarchal discourse which performs a range of functions in the public domain which are not restricted to either women or widow immolation. It is a discourse that marks within itself both contestation and the changes to which it is addressed. As far as women are concerned it is a discourse which challenges the notion of the woman as a citizen, i.e. in the consciousness of democratic rights and individual abilities, in the right to choice, and in the right to an identity not governed by religious denomination.

The internalization of ideologies and beliefs produced by the event is thus related to a wider social process and not confined to the narrower stakes in the practice of widow immolation or to the patriarchies of the specific groups involved. However, once internalized, these ideologies and beliefs become a part of the objective forces and structures which can produce further widow immolations or carry over into other forms of violence against women. For these reasons we need to explore the wide range of relationships between patriarchies, the systemic violence which inheres in them, the consent they need to generate and contemporary processes of social change.

12

Communities as Political Actors: The Question of Cultural Rights

Veena Das

At the time of Partition, over the question of recovery of abducted women and unwanted children, the nation state was invested with a new agency—it was addressed by the people as the agency for setting right grievous wrongs suffered by family and community. The two cases which I examine in this essay relate to a transformation of this relationship between people and the state. Here, what we witness is not a tactical alliance between state and community but a contest over the issue of cultural rights, especially the right to regulate the spheres of law and memory.

One of the symbols used by the community to mobilize political support in modern India in recent years is couched within the phrase 'cultural rights'. Despite the apparent similarity of phrasing, however, I believe that cultural rights cannot be thought of as parallel to, or analogous to, political rights, for the term 'cultural rights' includes a variety of situations with very different moral implications. Further, cultural rights cannot be understood exclusively within a framework of a theory of interests, for they refer primarily to political passions. Before I explore this relationship between cultural rights and political passions further, let us see the political and juridical contexts in which the problem of cultural rights has been formulated.[1]

[1] I am grateful to Upendra Baxi for intensive and extensive discussions on the subject of cultural rights, and for many ideas most generously shared.

The Subjects of Cultural Rights

The question of cultural rights has been formulated in national and international forums primarily in the context of the rights of minorities. The Indian Constitution grants minorities the right to preserve and develop their culture as well as make institutional arrangements for this, for instance by establishing educational institutions. As formulated in the Constitution, this right is in the nature of a restriction on the powers of the state.

A similar concern with the preservation of minority culture is evident in the formulations of various provisions of international law concerning the rights of persons belonging to minorities.[2] The Commission on Human Rights, established in 1946 by the United Nations assembly, appointed a Subcommission on Prevention of Discrimination and Protection of Minorities. Between 1947 and 1954 this Subcommission attempted to define the concept of a minority. Although most members agreed that the definition must include an objective and a subjective element, it failed to arrive at an agreed definition of this crucial concept. This was partly a reflection of the dualistic character of international law in relation to human rights—for which the state and the individual form the two poles around which legal personalities are organized. In international law it is states which mutually recognize each other. In certain cases groups of individuals have the right of petition, but there has been great hesitation in granting legal personality to groups. In part, this approach is a result of the specific historical circumstances under which the international community recognized that the most gross violations of individual rights can occur within lawfully constituted states, for example the attempt to exterminate Jews in Nazi Germany. Thus the first formal recognition of the crime of genocide (*crimen lesae humanitus*) was made in Nuremberg in 1945. This concrete context, within which the concern with human rights came to be articulated in international opinion, naturally emphasized the rights of individuals against the overwhelming power of the state.

According to Sacerdoti (1983), these rights fall into the following five clusters:

[2] On the question of rights of minorities in international law, see Copotorti, 1985 and Sacerdoti, 1983.

1. Rights of individuals, peoples, groups, and minorities to existence and protection from physical suppression. At the individual level this is expressed as the right to life, of which an individual may only be deprived through due process of law. At the collective level this is recognized through the Convention on Genocide which makes the physical suppression of a group punishable.[3]

2. Rights of individuals not to be discriminated against on grounds of membership of a minority group.

3. Rights of persons belonging to racial or ethnic groups not to be the objects of hate or hostile propaganda.

4. Prohibitions against actions meant to destroy or endanger the existing character, traditions and culture of such groups.

5. Rights of persons belonging to ethnic, linguistic, or religious minorities to preserve their culture and language, and rights of persons belonging to religious minorities to practise and profess their religion.

It is quite clear that the subjects of all these rights are individuals. Especially important in this context is the right of an individual not to be discriminated against on grounds of membership of a group, or not to be made the object of hatred or hostile propaganda. Yet it is also evident that the subjects of these rights cannot be treated as isolated, atomized individuals, because, in order for them to preserve and enjoy their culture, the collective survival of traditions becomes an important condition. To understand the complexity of the issues involved, let us pay close attention to Article

---

[3] It has been noted that the Convention on Genocide made physical killing and forcible control of biological reproduction punishable, but could not reach any agreement on cultural genocide. Further, the provisions of the Convention were not applicable to groups whose members were recruited on the criterion of choice, such as political groups on homosexuals [cf. Lodor-Lederus, 1983]. On major examples of genocide in the twentieth century, see Baccianini, 1987. Crawford 1988 has noted that 'peoples' or 'groups' protected by the rules on prevention and punishment of genocide include groups which could not be classed as beneficiaries of the right to self-determination. He also notes that the Genocide Convention is directed at offenders rather than victims, emphasizing the *duties* of legal persons, whether these be rulers, public officials or private individuals. But to the extent that the Convention has as its object the preservation of groups, it is meaningful to talk of their rights. As we shall see later, it is precisely on the question of the preservation of a group as a cultural entity that serious conflicts may come about between the rights of groups and those of individuals.

27 of the International Covenant on Civil and Political Rights:

In those states in which ethnic, religious or linguistic minorities exist, persons belonging to such minorities shall not be denied the right, in community with other members of their groups to enjoy their own culture, to profess and practise their own religion, or to use their own language.

It should be noted that the subjects of these rights in Article 27 are persons; yet we have to ask whether the rights promised to minorities can all be derived from the fundamental human rights of individuals, or whether it becomes necessary to evoke additional criteria of a collective nature for the protection of minorities. The crucial phrase in this article is *in community with other members of their groups*. It would seem from this phrase that a collective dimension of rights is being recognized only in the form of associational rights, so that individuals can, in community with other individuals with similar characteristics, enjoy these rights. Yet how can this community of individuals be preserved if the cultural traditions or language or religion of the group is allowed to disappear? Can one define a group as a mere aggregate of individuals? Would a Chinese, an Indian and a Bantu when aggregated make up a group with a culture, and can each such individual be said to be enjoying their culture in community with other members of their group?[4]

The discussions which took place among members of the Subcommission on Protection of Minorities, it seems, reflected some of the difficulties mentioned here. For instance, it was recognized that the definition of minority cannot be arrived at by enumerating objective criteria. It was stated that the members of a minority group must show a subjective will to preserve the traditions of their group; also that if a group became numerically depleted it might not be able to show the will to preserve and live by these traditions. It was repeatedly stated in different contexts that the issue was not only of biological survival, nor only of ensuring that minorities did not suffer discrimination, but also that, in order for individuals to be able to enjoy their culture, it must be preserved in the conscience collective.[5]

[4] On the difference between an aggregative notion of totality and a distributive one as applied to human societies, see Das, 1989a.

[5] In its attempts to define minorities, the UN Subcommission on Prevention of

The following theoretical issues, then, seem to me crucial in developing a conceptual framework within which we may think about cultural rights. First, if we divide rights according to their adjectival qualities into (a) individual rights, and (b) collective rights, then we need to ask what relation this distinction has with the one between the individual and the collective as morphological categories as well as subjects of rights. Second, in granting individuals the right to enjoy their culture, what obligations does the state have towards ensuring the survival of that culture? Is the state simply required to abstain from interference, or does it have positive obligations towards these groups?[6] Is the dualistic structure of human rights—which is organized around the state and the individual as the two poles with legal personalities—adequate in the context of cultural rights? In other words, is the state the only possible organization of human collectivities that can be bestowed with legal personality in the matter of rights, or is it possible for groups and communities to be recognized as legitimate expressions of man and woman's collective existence? Finally, if we consider it necessary that the rights of collectivities, as distinct from the collective rights of individuals, be recognized, then how would relations between different collectivities on the one hand,

---

Discrimination and Protection of Minorities discussed, in 1950, the following text:

(1) The term minority includes only those non-dominant groups in a population which wish to preserve stable ethnic religious, or linguistic traditions or characteristics markedly different from those of the rest of the population.

(2) Such minorities should properly include a number of persons sufficient in themselves to preserve such traditions.

(3) Such minorities should be loyal to the states of which they are nationals. The suggested definition came up for sharp criticisms. Bruegel commented that all obligations against any positive steps have been collected in a resolution which is supposed to define desirable positive steps. Similarly, the representative of a Jewish organization commented that no minority of any kind could get any rights under these provisions. See Sacerdoti, 1983.

[6] Capotorti, 1985 favours the interpretation that the state has positive obligations to protect the culture of minorities. To quote him, 'If real equality of treatment is to be assured—only tolerance pure and simple will not achieve it.' He goes on to say that Article 27 would be superfluous if it only granted rights that could be basically deduced from human rights. 'With particular reference to the cultural field, it should be recalled that the obligations imposed on states by Articles 13 and 15 of the Covenant on Economic, Social, and Cultural Rights (concerning every individual's rights to education and to take part in cultural life) have the features of positive obligations to be implemented through appropriate measures.'

and the collectivity and the individual on the other, be governed? A strong fear has been expressed by many scholars to the effect that since there is no legally acceptable definition of 'people', the recognition of such entities as legal beings may lead to a gross violation of human rights enjoyed by individuals in the interest of an abstraction such as the nation, the community, the masses, the economy or even the state.[7]

Given these questions, I would suggest that just as the experience of the Second World War was of crucial importance for European and American societies to arrive at a conception of human rights—which has its foundation in natural law theories and which essentially tries to empower the individual against oppressive state structures—so the experience of contemporary Asian societies with struggles over culture is crucial to develop legal structures within which the collective dimension of human existence takes clearer shape. This collective dimension is recognized in the Universal Declaration of Human Rights, when reference is made to the 'community in which alone the free and full development of personality (of everyone) is possible.' It seems important, therefore, to apply our intellectual resources towards developing our concepts of culture and community.

What is Culture?

Definitions of 'culture' are contested. In anthropological usage the word refers to a system of shared meanings through which collective existence becomes possible. However, as many recent critiques of this position point out, this sense of culture gives no place to the idea of judgement, and hence to the relations of power by which the dominance of ideas and tastes is established. As Said says about Matthew Arnold's view of culture:

what is at stake in society is not merely the cultivation of individuals, or the development of a class of finely tuned sensibilities, or the renaissance of interests in the classics, but rather the assertively achieved and *won* hegemony of an identifiable set of ideas, which Arnold honorifically calls culture, over all other ideas in society (1983, 10).

The implications of Arnold's view of culture are profound; they lead us towards a position in which culture must be seen in terms

[7] See Sieghart, 1988 and Crawford, 1988.

of that which it eliminates as much as that which it establishes. Said argues that when culture is consecrated by the state, it becomes a system of discriminations and evaluations through which a series of exclusions can be legislated from above. By the enactment of such legislation the state comes to be the primary giver of values. Anarchy, disorder, irrationality, inferiority, bad taste and immorality are, in this way, defined and then located outside culture and civilization by the state and its institutions. This exclusion of alterity is an important device by which the hegemony of the state is established; either certain 'others' are defined as being outside culture, as are 'mad' people; or they are domesticated, as with penal servitude—Foucault's monumental studies on the asylum and the prison demonstrate this.

It is this context which we must understand in order to fully appreciate the challenge posed by the community to the hegemony of the state, especially to the notion that the state is the sole giver of values. At the same time, the danger is that we may in the process be tempted to valorize the community as somehow representing a more organic mode and therefore a more authentic method of organizing culture. Many scholars feel that culture is more organically related to the traditions of groups, whereas traditions are falsely invented by the hands of state.[8] The issues are by no means as simple, for culture and tradition are not instituted in society once and forever, but are subject to the constant change and flux which are an essential feature of every society. Indeed, the very attempt to freeze and fix cultural traditions may be inimical to their survival. Finally, in the contests between state, communities and collectivities of different kinds on the one hand and the individual on the other, we can see the double life of culture: its potential to give radical recognition to the humanity of its subjects as well as its potential to keep the individual within such tightly defined bounds that the capacity to experiment with selfhood—

---

[8] This, for example, appears to be the case in Unger's conception of 'community', as he acknowledges in a postscript to *Knowledge and Politics*. 'But the vision of empowerment in the classical doctrines of emancipation is clouded by unjustifiably restrictive assumptions about the possible forms of social life and in particular about the possible institutional definitions of market and democracies. *In place of the theory of organic groups, I would put a programme that extends the ideal of empowerment*, and relates it to ideals that it seems to exclude, by freeing it from unnecessarily confining premises', Unger 1984a, 339–40, emphasis supplied.

which is also a mark of humanity—may be jeopardized.

So, we arrive at this double definition of culture. By this I mean that the word culture refers to both a system of shared meanings which defines the individual's collective life, as well as a system for the formulation of judgements which are used to exclude alterities, and which thus keep the individual strictly within the bounds defined by society. It is in view of this that the question of cultural rights seems to me to be placed squarely within the question of passions rather than interests. It is time now to define passion.

After the classical work of Hirschman on political passions, it was usual to think of passions as obstructions in the path of reason. Passions had to be overcome for enlightened interest to emerge. This view of passions is extremely limited. Indeed, certain kinds of revelations, including the recognition of oneself as human, become possible only through passion.[9] If the self is constituted only through the Other—so that desire, cognition, memory and imagination become possible through the play of passion—then the revelatory role of passion must be acknowledged not only in the life of the individual but also in the life of the collective. Passion then must play a role in politics. It is my argument that it is precisely through the life of the passions that culture and community have become entangled in the shaping of public culture within modern India.

As we have seen, the demand for cultural rights at this historical moment is in a context where cultural symbols have been appropriated by the state, which tries to establish a monopoly over ethical pronouncements. The state is thus experienced as a threat by smaller units, who feel that their ways of life are penetrated, if not engulfed, by this larger unit. The situation is quite the opposite of the relation between the part and the whole in hierarchical systems, a relation seen as the characteristic mark of traditional polities in South Asia.[10] In a hierarchical system, *differences* between constituent units were essential for the 'whole' to be constituted.

[9] This view of passion has been developed in recent years primarily by Unger, 1984b, although the history of the concept is complex.

[10] A systematic elaboration of this view may be found in Dumont (1971). Dumont's view has been criticized for its idealist orientation, and recent studies of kingship point to various complexities both within the ideology of hierarchy as well as in the categories of the polity. See especially Shulman, 1985; Kulke, 1978; Dirks, 1987 and Stein, 1984.

In other words, small units came to be defined by being bearers of special marks in a hierarchical entity. And although by definition they could not be equal in such a system, the very logic of hierarchy assured that they could not be simply engulfed into the higher totality. This was both a source of their oppression as well as a guarantee of their acceptance (though not a radical acceptance) of their place in the world. My argument is not an appeal for a return to hierarchy as a principle of organization. Rather, it is an effort to locate the special nature of the threat which smaller groups feel in relation to the modern Indian state.

Community and State

In order to understand contests between the community and the state in India, and thus to clarify key concepts, I focus upon two different events which are taken as exemplars.

The first of the two events is popularly known as the Shah Bano case. This case, as is well known within India, raised the entire question of the relationship between on the one hand secular law, as formulated and implemented by institutions of state, and on the other the rights of minorities as well as rights of women. The second event concerns the occurrence of sati in 1987, in a small town of Rajasthan. This has come to be called the Roop Kanwar case after the eighteen-year-old girl who was consigned to the flames upon the death of her husband. Her sati led to a severe contest between women's groups and some Hindu organizations on the nature of her death, which threw up questions about violence against women on the one hand, and the rights of a community over its religious customs on the other.

In both cases the state intervened and passed new legislation, though the direction of the legislative provisions was quite different in each case. A comparison between the two cases will help us see the kinds of questions which arise in India's political culture, specially as regards issues of cultural rights. The contradictions and conflicts between different kinds of community on the one hand, and the state and community on the other, appear starkly in such events.

The Shah Bano Case

The Shah Bano case refers to events which followed from a criminal appeal by an appellant, Mohd. Ahmad Khan, against respondents

Shah Bano Begum and others, in the Supreme Court in 1985.[11] The appeal arose out of an application filed by the divorced Muslim woman, Shah Bano, for maintenance under Section 125 of the Code of Criminal Procedure. The appellant, an advocate, was married to the respondent in 1932; there were three sons and two daughters born of their marriage. According to the respondent, she was driven out of her matrimonial home in 1975. In April 1978 she filed an application against her husband under Section 125, in the court of the judicial magistrate, Indore, asking for maintenance at the rate of Rs 500 p.m. On 6 November 1978 the appellant divorced the respondent by an irrevocable *talaq* (divorce) permitted under the personal law of Muslims. His defence of Shah Bano's petition for maintenance was that she had ceased to be his wife after the divorce, that he had paid a maintenance allowance of two years and deposited a sum of Rs 3000 by way of dower during the period of *iddat* (which normally is three menstrual cycles, or the passage of three lunar months for post-menopausal women). The pre-history of the case does not concern us; what is important is that the husband was in the Supreme Court by special leave, and the court had to give its ruling on the question of whether the provisions of Section 125 of the Code of Criminal Procedures were applicable to Muslims.

The judgement, given on 25 April 1985, has a heterogeneous structure. The court decided that the provisions of the Code of Criminal Procedure were indeed applicable to Muslims, and therefore upheld the High Court decision on the provision of maintenance to Shah Bano. In the course of giving the judgement, however, Chief Justice Chandrachud also commented upon several other issues. These included the injustice done to women in all religions, the desirability of evolving a common civil code as envisaged by the Constitution, and provisions in the Shariat regarding the obligations of a husband to provide maintenance to a divorced wife. In a way, it was this very heterogeneity which allowed the judgement to become a signifier of issues which touched upon several dimensions, including the nature of secularism, the rights of minorities, and the use of law as an instrument of securing justice for the oppressed.

I do not wish to suggest that the judgement by itself created

---

[11] A voluminous literature exists on the Shah Bano case, only some of which has been directly referred here. A very useful compilation of this literature is available in Engineer, 1987.

these issues; in fact the Muslim community was in the midst of debating these issues itself. (The fact that an eminent lawyer, Yunus Saleem, had appeared as counsel on behalf of the Muslim Personal Law Board and not as counsel for the defendant attests to this interpretation.) The issue had become contentious at both the legislative and adjudicatory level. Baxi (1986) summarized this well:

What has caused this insecurity [among the Muslims]? Surely not the affirmation by the Supreme Court of India of an order raising the maintenance of Shah Bano from about Rs 70 to Rs 130 from a husband whose earnings as a lawyer were very substantial indeed? Ahmad Khan did not resort to the Supreme Court because maintenance amounts caused great financial hardship to him. The real meaning of the Shah Bano litigation was an attempt to secure reversal of two earlier decisions of the Court allowing maintenance to divorced Muslim wives under Section 125 of the Criminal Procedure Code. The litigation was devised to reinstate the Shariat. And it succeeded in the first round when Justice Fazal Ali explicitly referred to a five-bench judge the question whether the earlier decisions were in consonance with the Shariat Act, 1937, which laid down that in all matters of family, including divorce and maintenance, courts will decide the questions in the light of the Shariat.

Thus it was not the judgement which created the issues, but certain complications were introduced as a result of the lack of restraint in judicial prose.

Following this judgement there was great agitation within the Muslim community, heated debates between 'progressive' and 'fundamentalist' Muslims, arguments between women's groups and Muslim leaders, and argumentation on the floor of parliament. The political debates, pressures and counterpressures finally led to the passing of the Muslim Women (Protection of Rights on Divorce) Bill, 1986. This bill was hailed as a victory for fundamentalists by some and as a triumph for democracy by others; it was alternatively seen as a betrayal of women's rights and as a document which had vindicated the position of women in Islam—which, it was alleged, had stood questioned in the Supreme Court judgement. Although in 1985–6 it was perhaps not possible to delineate the complexity of the issues, so that the debate was seen in terms of a confrontation between secularists and communalists, it should now be possible to break out of this battle of shadows to see the varied and complex nature of the question.

The first matter to address is the nature of the judgement itself.

On legal issues the judgement was quite clear. The judges stated quite categorically that earlier decisions of the Supreme Court had referred to whether Muslims were exempt from the application of Section 125 of the Criminal Procedures Act. They said that Section 125 referred to all cases in which a person of sufficient means refused to maintain a wife, including a divorced wife who was unable to maintain herself. Incidentally, the provisions of the act also applied to aged parents, children and handicapped adult children. The purpose of the act was to see that, where relatives could maintain a destitute relative of these categories, they fulfilled this duty, preventing the destitute person from turning vagrant.

The judges quoted from the speech of Sir James Fitzjames Stephen, who had piloted the Code of Criminal Procedure, 1872, as Legal Member of the Viceroy's Council. They did this to establish the purport of the relevant sections of the code within which Section 125 occurred: Stephen had described this particular section as a 'mode of preventing vagrancy or at least of preventing its consequences.' Supporting this interpretation, the judgement stated that 'the liability imposed by Section 125 to maintain close relatives who are indigent is founded upon the individual's obligation to society to prevent vagrancy and destitution. That is the moral edict of the law and morality cannot be clubbed with religion.'

One may differ on some counts with the seal of approval given to this piece of colonial legislation, for the precise concern in Stephen's pronouncement was not with individual rights but rather with 'prevention of vagrancy' as a threat to public order. The creation of a legal category of vagrants, as well as the criminalization of 'close relatives' who could be held responsible for supporting indigent relatives, reflected the basic opposition of colonial rulers to the maintenance of unproductive populations.[12] That the judges should have invested this clause with such moral fervour without considering at any point the state's responsibility towards the maintenance of the indigent is another story.

---

[12] Responsibility for maintenance of pauper lunatics and pauper lepers was similarly placed upon the family in the Lepers Act and the Lunatic Act. It is interesting to observe that in the metropolitan countries the problem of indigent populations was sought to be resolved by institutional solutions. For a masterly account of poor laws, the category of vagrants and its relation to the growth of capitalist market systems in England and Wales, see Scull, 1977.

To return to the strictly legal issues, the judgement did not raise questions which could have become symbols of the contests that were to follow. The judges baldly stated that Section 125 was part of the Code of Criminal Procedures and not of civil law. They further stated that they were not concerned with the broad and general question of whether a Muslim husband was liable to maintain his wife, including a divorced wife, under all conditions. The correct subject matter of Section 125 related to a wife who was unable to maintain herself, and their ruling was limited to such a case. Clearly, given the fact that there is a uniform criminal code to which all Indian citizens are subject, the court could not take into account the religion of the persons involved. Had the judgement stopped at this point, the issue would only have been restricted to whether the criminal and penal codes applied to all citizens of India, regardless of religion.

But the judgement went beyond this issue. It considered questions relating to interpretations of the Quran and Islamic law on the issue of maintenance of divorced wives. The judges also made several comments on the desirability of evolving a common civil code as a means of achieving national integration and gender justice.

The opening paragraph of the judgement said that the appeal did not involve questions of constitutional importance; however, it did raise issues of another kind that were important: 'Some questions which arise under the ordinary civil and criminal law are of a far reaching significance to large segments of society which have been traditionally subjected to unjust treatment. Women are one such segment.' The judges then quoted from Manu—the famous line which acts like a signature for all discourses on Manu— namely *na stri swatantryam arhati*, i.e. a woman does not deserve autonomy. Having shown their critical capacity in relation to Hindus, they then criticized Islam, taking for their authority a statement by Sir William Lane, made in 1843, to the effect that the fatal point in Islam is its degradation of woman.

The semiotic function of this framing paragraph in the judgement was to establish the secular and learned credentials of the judges for, by a time honoured tradition in our political culture, secular credentials are signalled by handing out in an even manner criticisms of the majority community and minority communities.[13] The second purpose was to show a concern for gender justice:

[13] I have noted the function of this rhetoric elsewhere. See Das and Nandy, 1986.

This appeal . . . raises a straightforward issue which is of common interest not only to Muslim women, not only to women generally, but to all those who, aspiring to create an equal society of men and women, lure themselves into the belief that mankind has achieved a remarkable degree of progress in that direction.

Thus, we have two moral ends posited in the judgement: first, the creation of a society of equals between men and women; and second, the moral duty of the individual to support destitute relatives in order that society does not bear the consequences of vagrancy. The two ends, however, do not belong to the same moral plane.

The third relevant set of observations are on the importance of evolving a common civil code. 'It is a matter of regret', state the judges, that 'Article 44 of our constitution has remained a dead letter.' They deplore the absence of any official activity for framing a common civil code. 'A common civil code will help the cause of national integration by removing disparate loyalties to laws which have conflicting ideologies.' The case of Shah Bano becomes in this way the occasion for an attack on conflicting ideologies of family and marriage among the different communities in India. There is no attempt in the judgement to explain why different ideologies in the sphere of personal life are seen as intrinsically threatening to national integration. This is taken to be 'self-evident'. To an anthropologist this appears puzzling, for the self-evidence of one culture is often the puzzle of another. One must recall that personal law concerns not only Hindus and Muslims but also tribal communities whose family affairs are regulated by their own customary laws, and on which intellectual discourse in India, with a few honorable exceptions, remains silent.[14]

At one level then, the judgement is about Shah Bano and the applicability of the provisions of the Code of Criminal Procedure

[14] For one instance of this silence, see the paper by Krishna, 1986, in which the debate on personal law is constructed primarily as a problem concerning the Muslim community. Krishna argues that according to Islamic political theory the relation between Muslims and a non-Muslim state is contractual, devoid of any moral obligation on the part of the former towards the latter. He singles out Muslims as 'the one community' that felt threatened by the integrative process initiated by the Constitution. Krishna's paper is remarkable for lack of analysis of the ideology of integration, or the processes through which the state may establish a hegemony over smaller communities. But it must be said, in all fairness, that Krishna is not alone among social scientists in his unquestioned support to nation-state ideologies.

to all citizens, regardless of religion. It is not about civil law or national integration. At other levels, however, it is about the unquestioned allegiance to legally created semiotic objects, such as the category of 'vagrants', who are defined by the danger that they supposedly pose to public order. Second, there is a complete rejection of legal pluralism in the judgement, for it is taken as self-evident that conflicting laws create conflicting ideologies which are inimical to national integration. Finally, there is the question of the rights of women. This is raised but then totally eclipsed by the allegiance to abstractions like public order and national integration.[15]

From the perspective of secular and progressive opinion, the opposition to the judgement of the Supreme Court was led by 'fundamentalists' and 'communalists', and their rise to power indicated 'regressive' threats to Indian society—a somewhat simplistic characterization of the complex issues that were raised.

The Response of the 'Community'

The first such complex issue was the relation between community and state. I do not think that a claim was ever made, on behalf of any section of the community, that Muslims should be ruled in accordance with Islamic laws in matters pertaining to crime and punishment. It was, however, aggressively asserted that in civil matters pertaining to family and marriage the Muslim community recognized only the authority of the shariat.[16]

From some of the responses given by Muslim leaders it seems clear that laws pertaining to crime and punishment were seen as

[15] The allegiance to the idea of public order is a little surprising, given that there is widespread recognition among many jurists that hypothesizing about a danger to public order rather than showing its existence in concrete terms is often a pretext for the state to use its police functions illegitimately. See also Barham, 1984.

[16] See, for example, the comments of Syed Shahabuddin in Engineer, 1987. He had criticized the competence of the judges to interpret the shariat which, he said, was an exclusive right of the ullama. When questioned if he would advocate the Islamic punishment for theft, i.e. amputating the arm of the thief, he replied that such punishments could only be given by an Islamic state and under Islamic rules of evidence which were not applicable in the Indian case. Unfortunately, most such statements were made in a highly adversarial context, whereas what is needed is one or several comprehensive position-pictures on the varieties of relationship possible between the shariat, non-state customary law and state law in matters pertaining to both criminal and civil law.

coming under the jurisdiction of the state; laws pertaining to family and marriage were seen as coming under the jurisdiction of the 'religion' or 'culture' of the community. One way to interpret this claim of the community over its civil matters is to see it as part of a worldwide pattern, a pattern connected with the decline of the idea of the nation state which pretends full ideological and political loyalty to its own value. In challenging the state as the only giver of values, the community may be seen from one point of view as claiming authority over its private life. Nevertheless, the all-pervasive presence of the state was acknowledged in the very act of the new legislation and the widespread support it received from 'fundamentalist' sections of community. In giving their support to the new bill, such sections were paradoxically reiterating the authority of the state to legislate and the courts to interpret the shariat,[17] while simultaneously asserting their own obligation to give direction to state law. The bill postulated that a divorced woman was to be supported by those relatives, such as sons or brothers, who were in the category of heirs, and that if such relatives were unable to support a divorced and indigent woman, then it was the responsibility of the community to support them through its *waqf* boards. In other words, though the category of relatives who were to support an indigent woman was altered, the right of a woman to have these provisions endorsed by courts of law in a

[17] It should be recalled that codification of the shariat for purposes of adminstration of personal law by British courts, through the Shariat Act of 1937, was a piece of colonial legislation that took away the customary rights of Muslims and created an area of 'tradition' suited to the British. The élitist assumptions behind such legislation are obvious, as also the attempt to create a homogeneous community that which could be administered with greater ease.

In the case of the Muslim Women (Protection of Rights) Bill 1986, also, varying interpretations of the shariat were manifest within the Muslim community which were homogenized through an act of state. For example, the Islamic Shariat Board of Kerala stated in a memorandum to the Prime Minister, dated 1 February 1986: 'views expressed by the commentators of the Quran and eminent theologians recognized by the Islamic world corroborate the verdict of the Supreme Court.' For this and other dissenting views, see Engineer, 1987.

It is not surprising that there should have been differences in interpretation within the Islamic community itself on the interpretation of the shariat, for this is at the heart of the hermeneutic enterprise to which all revelation is necessarily subject. Even among these different voices, however, folk interpretations of theology are given no voice among contemporary Islamic theologians. On the conflict between élite and folk interpretations, see Das, 1985.

modern state were not challenged. One could say that the forms of legal mediation instituted by the modern state were endorsed, even as the contents were being directed via mobilizations of the Muslim community in a particular direction. The community, then, can be seen not as claiming sovereignty in competition with the state, but informing the state on the direction of laws in the field of marriage and the family.

The second question which arose from the judgement was whether it was legitimate and proper for personal laws to reflect the differences between different communities on the nature of conjugality. It was argued by some Muslim scholars that a Hindu woman, upon marriage, lost her rights in her natal family and became fully incorporated in the family of her husband: this is reflected in several institutional practices, including the fact that divorce is not recognized in the Dharmasastras.[18] Under such conditions, it was argued, even when the laws were developed and provisions for divorce introduced, the liability of the husband to maintain his abandoned or divorced wife was of a piece with the concept of marriage and conjugality. In contrast, marriage under Islamic law was a contract, and a woman was never fully incorporated in the husband's group. She continued, for instance, to exercise rights of property in her natal family. It was therefore considered proper that a woman should be maintained by those relatives, namely sons and brothers who expected an inheritance from her share. This argument had also been put forward in the court and been rejected as contrary to 'law' and 'life'. When codified in the new law on the Rights of Muslim Divorced Women, it was criticized by several women's group as equivalent to taking away the rights of maintenance from women, for it was felt that a woman would never drag members of her natal family or her children to a court of law.

There were several implicit assumptions about law and life in the judgement, as well as in some of the responses of women activists. These are presented as being self-evident, which again appears puzzling seen from the eyes of another culture. Certainly, the central place given to conjugality in the life of a woman, and

[18] Divorce was recognized in the customary regulations of many castes, but it is part of the same élitist discourse, referred to earlier, for jurists and scholars of Islam who wrote on this issue to have equated Hindu law with rules in the Dharmasastras.

her primary definition as a wife rather than a daughter or a sister, is not a principle one can derive from 'life' if we mean by this that it derives from nature. Seen in the cross-cultural context, in many societies where marriages are hypogamous a woman may be seen by her natal family as simply 'lent' to the husband's family (cf. Leach, 1968).[19] She is never incorporated in the conjugal family and continues to exercise all her rights in her natal family. Yet there is no evidence that her status is lower than that of women in societies which practise hypergamous marriages, and in which the rights of the husband override any claims by her natal kin. One must not assume that the concepts of marriage and sexuality enshrined in 'secular' laws are somehow derived from principles of life. In fact, it would be interesting to enquire the extent to which some 'secular' laws relating to marriage, conjugality, sexuality and family bear the stamp of ecclesiastical laws and reflect a Christian understanding of marriage and family, rather than being unmediated reflections of the 'law' of 'nature'.

As to the question that women are reluctant to take their natal family and children to a court of law, I think this reflects the unspoken assumption in our society, among both Hindus and Muslims, that conjugality may become a site of conflict but that conflicts between a woman and her natal kin should be covered by a shroud of silence.[20] In fact violence against a woman by her natal family, including attempts to deprive her of her property rights, are by no means uncommon. In the Muslim case, many studies show that although women have a theoretical right over property in their natal families, they rarely get to exercise this right, exchanging it for the right to visit and receive gifts.[21] Thus, if women's rights are to be strengthened against those of the family, there is no reason to exclude rights as a daughter or sister from this arena of conflict. The very emphasis on the woman as wife reflects the preoccupation with her role as wife, to the exclusion of her other roles.

[19] This unfortunate vocabulary has to be applied here because women are invariably seen as 'exchanged' between men at the level of ideology although they subvert this ideology, in many ways, in the practices of their everyday life. For a masterly account of both—forms of laws of exchange and their limits—Levi Strauss, 1969 is still unequalled.

[20] This silence does not apply to conflicts between brothers over property.

[21] See Eglar, 1967 and Das, 1973.

It should be evident that I believe the real issue in this case is not secularism versus communalism or national integration versus national disruption.[22] It is rather a question of whether powers of the state should be extended to encroach into the sphere of the family. In the colonial period, this encroachment was justified on the grounds that the state was engaged in the creation not only of a civil society but also a 'good' society (Spivak, 1985). This is why although many interventions by the colonial state concerned the rights of women, these were so enmeshed in a network of other concerns that women themselves seemed almost peripheral to the issue. This is why if the state is to intervene in order to correct injustices against women in institutional structures such as the family, the focus of its legislative and adjudicatory labour has to be women themselves. The conflict between the rights of subordinate groups, such as women, to break the power of traditions which subordinate them to men on the one hand, and the radical recognition of the right of minorities to exist as cultural entities on the other, are not capable of being resolved through easy solutions. But minimally, it is necessary that these issues are addressed on their own terms, and that they do not become a contest between the passions of the state (national integration, patriotism) and the passions of the community (its cultural survival in the form given to it by the dominant male culture).

In the context of the debate in the Shah Bano case, several women activists pointed out that the issue was not whether women enjoyed a high status in Islam at the level of ideas. The question was whether women were able to obtain reasonable security for themselves under existing institutional structures. The large number of petitions for maintenance from women (including Muslim women) which came up every year under Section 125 of the Criminal Code were clear indication that the family or the community were not protective institutions, as scriptural quotations from religious traditions would have us believe.

We know the family to be a site of conflict. So, when a community claims that the right to its own culture includes the right to legally govern its members in the sphere of the family, where do women or children who may be oppressed by the

---

[22] I hope it is clear from the form of my argument that I am not implying there are no real battles on the issues of secularism and communalism, but rather that it is a mistake to frame the Shah Bano case in terms of these polarities.

pathologies of the family and the community go for redress? Can the right of a community to preserve and develop its culture exclude the right of individuals to move out of the community, or critique and even reject its norms through an exercise of other options? Clearly not. Meanwhile, one must note that the appropriation of the issue of justice to women under the master symbols of state and community almost made them disappear from view, except in the title of the new legislation.

This eclipse is best seen if we pay attention for the moment to Shah Bano. The facts of her personal case were as follows: married to her first cousin, she was the mother of three adult sons, the eldest being fifty-four. Her husband had taken as his second wife another first cousin. It seems likely that her sons had asked this seventy-six-year-old woman to sue her husband for maintenance as a move in their ongoing dispute with their father (and another of his sons, by his second marriage) over property. After the Supreme Court decision, Shah Bano was persuaded by 'leaders' of the community to reject the court's decision. Her letter speaks most eloquently of the way in which a woman may simply become the means by which various contests between men are conducted: contests between father and son; between adherents of different schools of interpretation of Islamic law; between state and community. A passage from her letter says:

Maulana Mohammad Habib Yar Khan, Haji Abdul Gaffar Saheb and other respectable gentlemen of Indore came to me and explained to me the commands concerning *nikah*, divorce, dower and maintenance in the light of the Quran and hadith...since women were getting maintenance through law courts, I also filed a suit for the same in the court of law and was successful...till then I had no idea about the shariat's view in this regard.

She then goes on to say that after the provisions of the shariat had been explained to her, she rejected the judgement of the Supreme Court which upheld her plea for maintenance from her divorced husband. Thus, from the lowest to the highest levels of male society, she became nothing more than a pawn through whom men played their various games of honour and shame.

As ought to be evident from this discussion, the Supreme Court judgement raised several conceptual issues regarding culture and community. These may be summarized as follows:

1. Does the constitutional right given to minorities to preserve and enjoy their culture, as well as the rights of minorities enshrined in the international instruments of the UN (such as the Covenant on Human Rights), include their right to live according to their own civil laws of family and marriage? Does the existence of conflicting ideologies of marriage and family in itself pose a danger to the sovereignty of the state?

2. If legal pluralism in civil matters is considered acceptable or even desirable, so that the norms of particular communities are given not only the status of custom but of law—what Baxi (1985) calls non-state law[23]—then what are the limits to the control that such communities may exercise over their individual members? In other words, how does one take into account heterogeneity *within* a community for the purpose of recognizing 'non-state law'?

3. How would one resolve conflicts posed by the desire to preserve culture by a filiative community (such as an ethnic or religious minority) and a similar but affiliative community (such as the community of women) which wishes to reinterpret that culture according to a different set of principles?

4. We have seen how the human rights movements empowered the individual against the power of the state. If a commitment to cultural rights leads us similarly to empower the community against the state, how can one ensure that the individual is not totally engulfed by the community?

The Question of Sati

I turn now to the second incident, which involved the wilful ritual consignment to flames of an eighteen-year-old girl. This incident took place in Deorala, a small town of Rajasthan, on 4 September 1987, when Roop Kanwar ascended or was forced to ascend the funeral pyre of her husband. The continuance of sati which had stigmatized India's identity in the eyes of the British, and the fact that it happened at a time when women's groups had been engaged in combating violence against women in the family (especially the violence against young brides in their conjugal families on account

---

[23] The expression 'non-state law' hardly commends itself on grounds of elegance but has the great advantage of steering debates away from normally sterile discussions on the difference between law and norms, or law and custom. It also disputes the claim of the state as the only legitimate maker of law.

of inadequate dowry) made Roop Kanwar a very volatile issue. It would be a mistake, though, to suppose that the opposing political formations which emerged around this issue could be summarized as 'tradition' versus 'modernity' or 'men' versus 'women'. For one thing, Hindu religious leaders were themselves sharply divided on the issue of the place of sati in Hinduism. Thus, the Shankaracharya of Puri appeared as a strong supporter of the custom, whereas reform groups such as the Arya Samaj, led by Swami Agnivesh, challenged both the Shankaracharya's authority as well as his understanding of Hinduism. Similarly, in the so-called modern sector, there were those who saw sati as a pathology of Hinduism and those who saw it as a pathology of colonialism.[24]

It is not possible to discuss all the complex issues in the various public discourses and their implications for the political culture of India today. I only wish to point out here that there is a long tradition of two hundred years in which sati came to be regarded as the symbol by which the whole of Indian society could be characterized as either a land of miracles or of savagery (cf. Prinz, 1988). My attempt is to disengage from this debate in order to pose the problem of cultural rights in the contemporary context. The question of the history of the institution of sati is important, but as we shall see it stands transformed here into the issue of how popular memory is organized.

Some of the problems raised by Roop Kanwar on the relationship between cultural rights and law were similar to those raised by Shah Bano; therefore I shall concentrate on those issues which raised new problems on the question of cultural rights. The object of my analysis is the text of the Commission of Sati (Prevention) Act, 1987, which the government enacted in order both to prevent incidents of sati and to devise adequate instruments for the punishment of those responsible for inducing the commission of sati. Although this act was designed to punish those responsible for the death of a widow, it paradoxically defined the woman herself as also punishable.[25]

An important feature of the act was to make criminal the 'glorification' of sati. It defined 'glorification' as any of the following:

---

[24] It is not possible to refer to the large and complex literature that grew out of this event. But see Das, 1986b; Nandy, 1975; Ray, 1985; Mani, 1986, 1989, Weinberger-Thomas, 1989; and the Special issue of *Seminar*, 1988.

[25] See Dhagamvar, 1988.

(a) the observance of any ceremony or the taking out of a procession in connection with the commission of sati

(b) the supporting, justifying or propagating the practice of sati in any manner; or

(c) the arranging of any function to eulogize the person who has committed sati

(d) the creation of a trust or the collection of funds, or the construction of a temple or other structure or the performance of any form of worship or of any ceremony with a view to perpetuate the honour of or to preserve the memory of any person who has committed sati.

It is this aspect which raises questions different from those raised by the Shah Bano case.

As in Shah Bano, it was the semiotic excess of the judgement as well as the manner in which orthodox reactions were characterized by 'progressive' opinion that converted the issue of women's rights into secularism versus communalism. In Roop Kanwar, as in Shah Bano, the language of criticism reveals much more than people's attitudes to women's rights.

In terms of the political unconscious, I believe that one of the confrontations was over the nature of time-consciousness in the discourses of the state and the community. This may seem at the outset a very abstract issue, and one unlikely to raise strong passions on either side. I hope to show, however, that the ideologies of modern states do try to control the time-consciousness of communities, and impose upon them a single, monolithic view of time. This then gets translated into issues of how to control and organize one's own history, as well as how far a community is willing to submerge its biography in the biography of the nation state.

From the viewpoint of the state which enacted this legislation, time is valued as a scarce resource for a future-oriented mastering of problems left over from the past. In this time-consciousness, there are no exemplary models from the past. Modernity does not borrow standards from the past—it draws its normativity from itself. In many of the speeches made in parliament, as well as in the way in which this particular episode was inscribed, frequent references were made to the fear of returning to a barbaric age. Indeed, the bill itself made this observation:

The recent incident of the commission of sati in the village of Deorala in Rajasthan, its subsequent glorification and the various attempts made by the protagonists of this practice to justify its continuance on religious grounds had aroused apprehension all over the country that this evil social practice, eradicated long back, will be revived. A general feeling had also grown in the country that the efforts put in by social reformers like Raja Rammohun Roy and others in the last century would be nullified by this single act in Rajasthan.

As this statement about the objectives of the bill shows, an act of sati comes to signify an anxiety about time which is typical of modernity, namely the return to a regressive past which would cancel all progress made by the modern state on behalf of society. This past has to be rigorously controlled and eliminated. The new legislation not only sought to control and punish future incidents of sati and abetment to commit sati, it also tried to control the past—i.e. its resurgence in the present.

Criminalizing the glorification of sati obviously belongs to an order of events different from the actual commission of sati. This is because in all modern forms of governance the state establishes an absolute right over the death of its citizens. Within modern state structures it is only through due process of law that a person may be deprived of her life. In ordinary cases, no death is legitimate unless certified by agencies of the state, and as far as heroic deaths are concerned it is the nation which has a monopoly over what constitutes sacrifice. The glorification of a particular social or religious practice, however, is open to a greater range of freedoms and merges with the right to practise one's religion. Interference with this custom raises the question of whether the state has a right to control the future or whether it can also redefine, and in this sense control, the past. Given these difficult questions, it was only to be expected that bringing the glorification of sati within the purview of legislative acts would not go uncontested.

The contest I will now examine is the litigation between the trustees of the Rani Sati Mandir and the Indian government over this very question. The Rani Sati temple is located in Jhunjhunu, about 190 km from Jaipur. It is owned by the Rani Sati Mandir Trust with its head office in Calcutta. According to oral tradition, the temple is dedicated to the memory of Narayani Devi, the wife of a merchant of Jhunjhunu who, during his travels with his young wife, was attacked by Muslims and died. His wife, according to legend, fought with the Muslims, defeated them, and then having constructed a funeral pyre consigned herself to the flames alongside her dead husband.

As this legend shows, the sati myth has been appropriated here by merchant castes as a challenge to Rajput legends which asserted that only Rajput women could become true satis. These merchant castes now found their position being challenged by the new ruling. Their temple had for long organized an annual mela on Bhadra Amavasya, in the month of September. After the passing of the act, the district magistrate of Jhunjhunu banned the glorification of sati in any manner whatsoever all over the district by any individual or group,[26] and accordingly the temple was closed in August. Preparations for the annual mela on 10 September were halted. The Rani Sati Mandir Trust in Calcutta challenged this order in the High Court there, on the grounds that the order interfered with the freedom to practise one's religion, and was therefore unconstitutional. The High Court, in its order of 17 August 1988, upheld the right of the Rani Sati Temple in Jhunjhunu to conduct daily worship (*puja*) and service (*seva*), and also restored the right of individuals to worship in the temple. The court order also stated that the respondents should not cause interruption or harassment to visitors and devotees during the daily worship of deities located in the temple. However, as far as the annual public mela was concerned, the position of the court was ambivalent. It allowed individual notice to be given to members with respect to the Annual General Meeting but did not permit public announcement of the mela in newspapers. In its judgement the court clearly made a distinction between public and private religion; the public aspects of religion were to be regulated by the state as 'law and order' issues, leaving religion in everyday life to the individual conscience. This division, by which public festivals, routes of processions, and the regulation of noise in sacred places were to be treated as 'law and order' issues, has been part of the state's repertoire for the management of crowds and the protection of public order since the early nineteenth century.[27]

Not surprisingly, the Supreme Court, when hearing a special leave petition filed by the state of Rajasthan, said that 'Offering of puja inside the temple and holding of mela outside are certainly two different aspects and the mela may give rise to problems of

---

[26] This was reported on 22 August in all the major national dailies. For an analysis of the legal issues, see van den Boch, 1989.

[27] See for example, Das, 1990a and Roberts, 1990.

law and order.[28] While presenting their case in the Supreme Court, the trustees of the Rani Sati Mandir claimed that the offering of puja within the temple did not constitute a glorification of sati, whereas a writ petition filed by the All India Democratic Women's Association and the Janvadi Mahila Samiti questioned this particular interpretation.[29] These organizations requested a prohibition of *chunari mahotsava,* the event in honour of the sati goddess Narayani Devi.

The questions raised by the new legislation exist on two different planes. There is first the concern with preventing future occurrences of sati and punishing offenders who aid and abet such acts. Yet ambiguity is built into the heart of the legislation, for it does not quite know whether to treat the woman 'with respect to whom sati is committed' as victim or criminal. This difficulty is not insurmountable, for in all cases defined as 'hard' a thin line has to be maintained between legitimacy and law. From a simply legal point of view, suicide is a punishable offence in the Indian Penal Code, and symbolic recognition has to be given to this. The act, however, clearly lays out that in determining the extent of punishment (imprisonment up to a year, a fine, or both), the Special Court shall 'before convicting any person take into consideration the circumstances leading to the commission of the offence, the act committed, the state of mind of the person charged of the offence at the time of the commission of the act and all other relevant factors.' Such acts must remain suspended between legitimacy and legality, and only at the adjudicatory level shall we be able to see the working of the act. In contrast with the woman, stringent punishment, including life imprisonment, is laid out for those who abet or aid such acts, which means moving from the definition of sati as suicide to its definition as murder.

The second question relating to the glorification of sati as well as preventing the veneration of sati matas raises the entire issue of whether a community has the right to construct its past in the mythic or the historic mode, in accordance with its own traditions, or alternatively whether the state may exercise complete monopoly over the past. That no straightforward answer is possible must be

[28] Special Leave Petition (civil), no. 9922 of 1988, in the Supreme Court of India, Civil Appellate Jurisdiction.

[29] Writ Petition, Supreme Court of India, no. 913 of 1988.

clear from the earlier discussion. For on the one hand we have a hegemonic exercise of power by the state, which acts as the only giver of values—and this is affirmed when even its most vocal critics turn for help to the state; and on the other hand we witness constructions of past time in such a way that all new events are sought to be understood as mechanical analogies of a limited stock of past events, a process which often leads to hegemonic control being established over the individual by the community. This is especially so when the community draws its energy from the symbol of a divine sacrificial victim, as in the case of sati.[30]

Finally, I suggest that there is a new participatory model of legislation which is introduced by the act. This is a model in which the state acknowledges the role of women's groups when giving direction to legislation. In the earlier case of the Muslim Women's Bill, no acknowledgement was made of the legitimate interests of women. There the community was defined solely as a filiative community—i.e. those born as Muslims. In this later case of the Commission of Sati (Prevention) Act, women's groups and the interests they represented were given a legitimate place, making legislation at least a triangular contest between state, community, and women's groups.

There are two aspects of the community that I have identified with reference to the two cases discussed here. In the first case the contest between community and state was over the realm of law and the possibilities of the pluralism in the conduct of personal life. In the second case it was the right to organize memory. Both cases challenged the hegemony of the state as the only giver of values, but also showed deep-rooted contests between different definitions of 'community' itself. There was a particular polarization between the community defined on the basis of filiation and the community defined on the basis of affiliative interests. It is to the implications of this polarization that we need to briefly turn.

In debates between women's rights and the rights of a community, an implicit assumption which seems to have crept in is that the culture to which the community lays claim is essentially a male

[30] I am not unaware that the bazaars which came up on the *chunri mahotsava* to celebrate Roop Kanwar's sacrificial death show how even scared victims cannot escape commodification. See in this context Sangari and Vaid, 1988 (included in this volume).

creation. Indeed, there is a long tradition in the social sciences which asserts that the dominant public culture—what Simmel called the 'objective culture'—is historically a male creation. In a debate with Marianne Weber, Simmel denied the possibility of a female culture. Women, he said, could contribute to the private and subjective spheres but not transcend these, whereas for Marianne Weber the representation of male culture as objective and female culture as subjective was a result of historical circumstances, and therefore alterable.[31]

The Shah Bano and Roop Kanwar cases raise the further possibility of interrogating male definitions of the community. Since the organization of memory is a crucial issue for definitions of the community, it is necessary to define memory as both an archive and a history. Thus, women's practices have been historically suppressed in the public culture of all communities but they continue, both in the private spheres of life and as archive. If these were to be revived and given recognition in public self-portraits of the community, it would become necessary to address questions about the heterogeneity of the community and the multiplicity of identities. For instance, in the case of sati, women's narratives among many Rajput communities have emphasized the everyday presence of sati matas in the lives of women and dwelt rather less on their violent deaths. Would such a construction alter the community's portrait of its own culture? What appears now as a conflict between two different kinds of communities (e.g. Muslims and Rajputs) on the one hand and women's groups on the other, could well become a conflict *within* a community if women were to lay greater claims to the public cultures of filiative communities themselves.

The relation between a community and its culture brings two distinct sets of preoccupations in creative tension with each other. These are: (a) how does the culture of a community create a shared vision of the world—a resource for questioning ideologies of the state, including an unquestioned allegiance to the state; and (b) does this shared culture homogenize the community to the extent that other definitions of culture and community are effectively denied and silenced? At the heart of culture we saw an enormous conflict, not only between state and community but also between different definitions of community.

[31] See Marianne Weber, 1971.

A resolution to this problem can only occur if the state ceases to demand full ideological allegiance from the various collectivities which constitute it; and if communities, instead of demanding complete surrender from individual members on the pretext of preserving their culture, recognize the paradoxical links of confirmation and antagonism from its members. An individual's capacity to make sense of the world, as I said earlier, presupposes the existence of collective traditions; but individuals must be able to experiment with these collective traditions by being allowed to live at their limits. A simultaneous development of the rights of groups and individuals will depend upon the extent to which these paradoxes can be given voice, both in the realm of the state and in the public culture of civil society.

We have taken important, symbolic instances to examine how the relation between state and community, between alternative definitions of the community, between filiative communities and affiliative communities and finally between community and individual may all be seen as located within a web of creative or destructive tensions in the matter of cultural rights. This allowed us to consider the problem from the perspective of two major communities, Muslims and Hindus, in modern India. In the Shah Bano and Roop Kanwar cases the institutional context entailed a dramatic use of agencies of the state—mainly law courts, as well as a mobilization of the community through which the public sphere was sought to be transformed. In a sense *cultural memory*, as it embodies a portrait of the self, and *desire,* as it is embodied in sexuality and marriage, were brought out from the domain of the private into the public sphere.

References

Barham, Peter, 1984, *Schizophrenia and Human Value*, Basil Blackwell, Oxford.

Baxi, Upendra, 1986, Text of observations made at a public meeting on the Muslim Women (Protection of Rights) Bill, 1986, Bombay, Hindustani Andolan.

Boch, P. van den, 1989, 'A Burning Question: The Sacred Centre as the Object of Political Interest'. Paper presented at a symposium on *The Sacred Centre as the Object of Political Interest,* University of Groningen, 5–8 March.

Copotorti, F., 1985, 'Minorities', in *Encyclopaedia of Public International Law,* vol. 4, Max Planck Institute, Berlin.

Crawford, James, 1988, 'Introduction', in *Right of Peoples* (ed. James Crawford), Clarendon Press, Oxford.

Das, Veena, 1973, 'The Structure of Marriage Preferences', *Man* 8 (1), pp. 30–45.

———,1985, Towards a Folk Theology and Theological Anthropology of Islam', *Contr. to Ind. Soc.* (n.s.), (18, 2), pp. 293–300.

———,1989a, 'Difference and Division as Designs for Life', in *Contemporary Indian Tradition: Voices on Culture, Nature and the Challenge of Change* (ed. Carla Borden), Smithsonian Press, Washington.

———,1990a, 'Introduction: Communities, Riots, Survivors', in *Mirrors of Violence: Communities, Riots and Survivors in South Asia* (ed. Veena Das), Oxford University Press, Delhi, pp. 1–37.

Das, Veena and Ashis Nandy, 1986, 'Violence, Victimhood and the Language of Silence', in *The Word and the World: Fantasy, Symbol and Record* (ed. Veena Das), Sage Publications, Delhi, pp. 177–97.

Dhagamwar, Vasudha, 1988, 'Saint, Victim or Criminal', *Seminar* (342), pp. 34–39.

Dirks, Nicholas, 1987, *The Hollow Crown: Ethnohistory of an Indian Kingdom,* Cambridge University Press, New York.

Eglar, Z., 1960, *A Punjabi Village in Pakistan,* Columbia University Press, New York.

Engineer, Asghar Ali, 1987, *The Shah Bano Controversy,* Orient Longman, Delhi.

Krishna, Gopal, 1986, 'Islam, Minority Status and Citizenship: Muslim Experience in India', *Arch. Europ. Social* (XXVIII), pp. 353–68.

Kulke, H., 1978, *The Devaraja Cult,* New York, Ithaca.

Leach, E.R., 1966, 'Asymmetric Marriage Rules, Status Difference and Direct Reciprocity: Comments on an Alleged Fallacy', *Southwestern Journal of Anthropology* (17), pp. 49–55.

Levi-Strauss, Claude, 1969, *The Elementary Structures of Kinship* (Rev. edn. tr. by J.H. Bill and J.R. von Sturmore, ed. by Rodney Nedham). George Allen & Unwin, London.

Mani, Lata, 1986, 'Production of an Official Discourse on Sati in Early Nineteenth Century Bengal', *Economic and Political Weekly* (XXI 17).

Prinz, Christina, 1988, *Sati: Ideologie und Praxis,* Magisterarbiet zum

Thema, Südasien Institute der Universitität Heidelberg, Seminar for Ethnologie.

Ray, A.K., 1985, *Widows are Not for Burning*, ABC Publishing House, Delhi.

Roberts, M., 1990, 'Noise as Cultural Struggle', in *Mirrors of Violence: Communities, Riots and Survivors in South Asia* (ed. Veena Das), Oxford University Press, Delhi, pp. 240–86.

Sacerdoti, Georgio, 1983, 'New Developments in Group Consciousness and International Protection of the Rights of Minorities', *Israel Year Book on Human Rights* (13), pp. 46–146.

Scull, A.T., 1977, *Decarceration*, Prentice-Hall, New Jersey.

Shulman, David, 1985, *The King and the Clown*, Princeton University Press, Princeton.

Sieghart, Paul, 1983, *The International Law of Human Rights*, Oxford University Press, London.

Spivak, Gayatri Chakravarti, 1985, 'Can the Subaltern Speak? Speculations on Widow Sacrifice', *Wedge* (7/8).

Stein, Burton, 1984, *All the King's Manna,* Manohar Publications, Delhi.

Weber, Marianne, 1971, *Ehefrau und Mutter in der Rechtsentwicklung: Eine Einfuhrung,* Aalen, Scientia Verlag (first published in 1907).

Weinberger-Thomas, Catherine, 1989, Cendres d'immortalite: La cremation des veuves in Inde, *Archives des Sciences Sociales des Religions* (67/1), pp. 116–46.

VI

Victimhood/Agency

Vidya Rao's article examines *thumri* as a space within Indian classical music in which women have extended the confining space allotted to them by reclaiming unexpected realms of richness. Her argument is that while one feminist strategy has been to reject and break out of the confines of the roles and spaces allotted to women, an equally creative way of subverting confined spaces has been to extend such spaces without surrendering to them.

Susie Tharu and Tejaswini Niranjana address the impasse arising from the appropriation of feminist language and symbols by political initiatives inimical to the democratic and ethical vision that has animated feminist politics in India. The authors feel that this kind of impasse indicates a fracturing of the 'humanist subject' assumed to be at the core of feminist politics, while at the same time opening up possibilities for new political alignments.

13

Thumri as Feminine Voice*

Vidya Rao

As women in patriarchal societies we are familiar with limitations, constraints, and small, confining spaces. We live in confining spaces—both physical ones—the *char divari*—and ideological ones—appropriate jobs, notions of family honour, chastity.

Women have dealt with these limiting and confining spaces in many ways—by enduring them, by claiming them to be meaningful and powerful, by acquiring some power through manipulation of what is available, by breaking out of and rejecting them and moving into the wider space of the world. Sometimes, however, these interactions arise out of an understanding of woman as victim of the patriarchal order; such an understanding, in turn, can only be dealt with by surrender, or rescue operations through reform or confrontation.

I believe that women can and have extended their limited spaces in dignified, creative encounters, and in ways that I think are qualitatively different from surrender, manipulation or destructive confrontation. I think one way of doing this has been to extend this space without rejecting or vacating it but by exploring and working with what is available within it, by re-interpreting its constraints to discover unexpected richness. This paper focuses on one such encounter—*thumri* singing. I attempt here to explore and understand the structure of the form thumri which I see as the feminine voice in Indian music.

Parita Mukta speaking of the padavali of Meerabai, tells us that through singing and hearing these *pads*, the world now becomes

* This is the revised version of an article, 'Thumri as Feminine Voice' which appeared in *Economic and Political Weekly,* 28 April, 1990.

streemay—feminine (Mukta, 1994). I understand her to be saying that dominant values, dominant ways of seeing, dissolve before the loving gaze of this poetry. I believe that this is a quality of thumri too. It, too, is *streemay*, feminine; it makes the world *streemay*. I hear it therefore as a feminine voice. Moreover, I see this feminine voice as being deeply subversive, though not confrontative.

Thumri is the small space traditionally given to women in the world of Indian classical/*margi* music. This is a fine cameo form which uses specific poetic themes, musical embellishments, ragas and talas. It is considered light and attractive but lacking the majesty and range of forms like khayal and dhrupad and is best heard or appreciated in small intimate *mehfil*s. Though there have been many very fine male thumri singers, this form is primarily associated with the female voice—with the *bai*s and *tawaif*s of the nineteenth and early twentieth centuries.

I consider thumri to be the feminine voice in music not because of its evident indentification with women singers, nor with the fact that the poetic text articulates female desire (albeit constructed in the male gaze) but because of its interrogative/subversive quality. I understand this quality to be inherent in its structure and to manifest in the ways in which it extends its space by playing with ambiguities, layers of meaning, and in its use of humour. I understand it also to inhere in thumri precisely because of the way this form, focusing squarely on love, speaking in the voice of the yearning, pining nayika, articulating this love in apparent consonance with its representation in patriarchal feudal society, yet presents us with another vision of love, of ourselves and the world.

Thumri is one stylistic form of traditional Indian music. While it seems to have very old roots—its origins lie in the *desi* (or folk) music of the region known as *purab* (eastern U.P. and Bihar)—it was only in the nineteenth century that it was elevated to margi (roughly classical) status, though it never really lost its strong desi flavour. Wajid Ali Shah's is a name that is linked in musical lore with this transition. Nawab of Avadh, poet, singer and dancer, 'Akhtar Piya', as he signed the many thumris he composed, like all rulers before and after him, maintained a coterie of singers and dancers for his amusement and indeed for the enhancement of his prestige. A specific style, a gharana, might be said to develop through the interaction of desi voices singing *margi sangeet* interpreting it in their own way (Erdman, 1978). The singers at Wajid Ali Shah's court sang their *desi kajris*, *horis*, *chancharis* and *dadras* but 'elevated' them to margi status by a self-conscious use of raga—naming of ragas and employing some degree of *ragadari*. But more importantly the new *sangeet* came to be 'heard' differently—as margi and courtly, rather than as the desi music of household and village, of life cycle and calendrical rites. With Wajid Ali Shah's exile in 1856 to Matia Burj, there ensued a diaspora of musicians—to princely states in other parts of India, apart from those who followed the nawab, into exile, making Calcutta an important centre of thumri singing. Thumri spread to places as far away as Hyderabad (At the turn of this century there were still tawaifs in Hyderabad singing thumri—remembered now nostalgically by today's *ghazal* singers and patrons). Both Shukla (1983) and Manuel (1989) have described in detail the evolution of thumri as a form. Here I will only focus on and understand thumri as it heard today, how singers and listeners together construct its meaning, and how also regardless of this contextualized meaning, *in itself*, thumri seems to me to be, in performance, presenting us with another voice, another vision.

Notions regarding thumri echo our ambivalence regarding the erotic and those aspects of our history and culture that have been seen as problematic. Wajid Ali Shah himself poses a problem. Both lay opinion and historical research are confused as to how to 'read' this monarch who has been variously seen to be somewhat pleasure-loving and effete, a careless administrator, a debauchee, and equally, a monarch sensitive to his subjects' needs, non-communal (though this is itself a later construct imposed on nineteenth century behaviour patterns) a fine poet, and a great patron of the arts. Thumri's main performers, and the contexts of their performance, the *kotha*, or the darbar are difficult for us to swallow. What sense is one to make of a form sung by women who entertained a group of élite men with songs of romantic love—some of the lyrics explicitly sexual. There is little escape from the fact that thumri is a form constructed squarely in the male gaze. Women sing, articulating female desire, but desire as patriarchally-constructed. Their audience consists entirely of men, and the singers will later, entertain these men not only musically but sexually as well. This situation has been deeply embarrassing to the 'modern' notion of Indian 'culture' that has attempted to construct music in an otherworldly, spiritual mode; much of the early twentieth century 'reform' in music had been aimed at 'rescuing music from the disrepute into which it had fallen as a result of its association with the professional class of singing girls' (Deshpande, 1972). But apart from the embarrassing erotic poetry of thumri, there is its musical structure which defies classification—not quite desi any more, nor clearly margi, using raga but in very different ways from khayal—the exemplar form today.

When musicologists, listeners and singers—even thumri singers themselves—speak today of thumri, this ambivalence is the overpowering emotion one encounters. There is often total rejection (several singers will not sing thumri—though some are not averse to introducing elements of thumri singing into khayal itself), condescension and grudging acceptance of it as a pretty and charming form, but lacking depth, as a form that is easy to sing, requiring no special teaching or learning.

Thumri's aficionados will equally vociferously defend this form asserting its 'difficulty', the years of training required before the voice is even ready to begin attempting the fluid *ang* of thumri, the long years of *riaz* taken to arrive at not just *taiyari* (technical perfection) but *mizaj* (a state of mind, an attitude); the assertion that thumri too has its own *taleem*, that it too draws on margi music's grammar and vocabulary. They will point to the most technically complex forms of the repertoire—*tappa*, and *bandish ki thumri* and ask if the virtuosity required in these forms is not equal or greater than that required in khayal singing. They will stress that without emotion, thumri is dead. And finally, tackling thumri's poetic text and traditional performing context, they will tell you that the earthly love described in these songs is but a metaphor of the yearning of the *atma* for the *parmatma*. It is, after all, deeply religious.

It is generally acknowledged that difficult or easy to sing, classical or not, the canvas of thumri is a small one. Thumris are usually set in only a few ragas of the traditional repertoire; they range therefore over only a small number of ragas. These ragas are considered 'light' and 'sweet', characterized by *madhurya guna*. They are recognized and distinguished from other ragas primarily by their *chalan* (movement) and *ang* (phrases with their specific weightage, pauses and tensions) rather than by clearly articulated *aroha-avaroha* (ascending and descending note structure). Thumri's origins in *desi dhuns* (melodies) are evident in the very similar movements of several thumris set in the same raga. Not having a clear structure but rather *chalan* or *ang* as the identifying feature rules out logical or linear development of the raga in thumri.

Many thumris, moreover, take *madhyam* as the tonic—a note half-way up the normal scale, effectively giving the singer only five notes (from *madhyam* to *upper shadja* on her normal scale) to work with. In the realm of *tala* too, thumri works with small, light talas—*dadra, kaharwa*. The slow 14 beat (sometimes 16 beat) *deepchandi*, while having the expanse and dignity of *khayal's vilambit laya*, does not possess the complexity or weight of talas like *jhoomra* or *dhamar* (also of 14 matras). And thumri is restricted to shringara rasa—its lyrics are invariably romantic.

As a student of music and supposedly a 'modern' woman, I often found myself embarrassed at thumri's excessively romantic lyrics, and its heavy orientation to the male gaze. I found too that was no escaping the fact that this was a form that directly addressed itself to its audience—traditionally all élite men—and could not, therefore, be easily redeemed by such ideas as the inherent spirituality of music, the protestation that a singer sings only for herself/himself or for 'god', and that the audience is irrelevant. It was when I began to learn thumri and experience it for myself in my own voice that I began to discover some rather interesting things about its composition and elaboration, and what it seemed to be articulating. Thumri seemed to be always extending the space available to it—but doing this not lineally or in the normal, logical way that khayal employs, but in a kind of lateral way—extending itself inwards perhaps, rather than outwards and upwards. There were also many planes along which thumri moved to extend its space. And finally, both because of what it was doing and the ways in which it was doing this, thumri appeared to be relentlessly questioning the established and accepted structures of music and indeed of our ways of understanding the world.

Because it so relentlessly questions the established order, I see thumri as deeply subversive, while yet being an integral part of the corpus of traditional music and sharing in the consensus of ideas about what is musical and what is not. So that it is both part of and outside of this order. Indeed this is apparent even at a very mundane level; thumri is often devalued as a form of little significance relegated to the last few minutes of a concert of 'serious' music. Yet few musicians will disregard it completely, many will include at least a few thumris in their repertoire, and most will praise it for its lyrical, evocative charm.

Singers and musicologists often consider thumri to be a feminine form because it has traditionally been heard in women's voices, because its lyrics articulate a woman's emotions (the narrator is always a woman—even if the composer is a man), and also because thumri's lightness and sweetness are considered to be suited to the female voice. But most composers of thumris were men (even the teachers were often men), female emotions are expressed, but squarely in the male gaze, and women have, of course, no monopoly over lightness and sweetness. And finally, speaking to any singer today you will hear a string of male names as well—from Bhaiya Ganpat Rao to Bade Ghulam Ali Khan.

It is not, therefore, the sex of the narrator, composer or singer that makes thumri a feminine form, but rather some other quality that inheres within the form. It is this other quality that I will attempt to try and understand.

Extending Space: Moving Out

In the early years of this century women—those from families of professional women singers, as well as the new aspiring recruits to the field of professional music—sought to extend their limited space by moving out of the confines of thumri into the wider world of khayal, even *dhrupad*. Music had begun moving out of the kotha, the mehfil and the élite private soiree to the wider, more ambiguous space of the concert platform, and the even more public 78 rpm record. Music and its function, and both thumri and the female singer began to be consciously—and unconsciously—redefined, and re-interpreted.

The traditional singers of thumri faced a precarious future. With the loss of the old sources of patronage, thumri's performing space and context were changing. A thumri's singer could no more be sure of an educated listener who would understand the subtle nuances of her art. While all music has been similarly affected, a form like khayal has managed to negotiate this shift better, perhaps because of its more clearly articulated rules and structures, the possibilities it provides a singer for a display of virtuousity, and— at one level—its clearer, more accessible use of music's vocabulary and grammar. Thumri's most fragile, more intimate ambience can barely survive in the impersonal vastness of some of our auditoria or the metallic absences of the pre-recorded cassette. In thumri more than in any other form perhaps the singer and the listener must see each other—even the actual physical space in which it is performed must be small, intimate. The form was at a disadvantage in the new milieu.

But this apart, it was also deliberately pushed out. Much of our current sense of what is music, what is appropriate music, and how to listen to it has been shaped by what happened in the turbulent, early years of this century when social reform, a revivalist vision, a wish to reclaim India's spiritual and cultural traditions, and also a recasting of women's roles resulted in an attempt to 'purify' music and rescue it from its earlier associations.

Given this notion of what music ought to be, thumri, already affected by the change in performing context, suffered badly. Its erotic poetry and 'unorthodox' musical structure might be redeemed somewhat by highlighting its possible spiritual, 'real' meaning—but this did not help very much. Women who might have been singing thumri began to do other things. Many became actresses, in Parsi and Marathi theatre and in films. Some became known as classical artists. This was not always easy. Musicians will repeatedly tell how, in the early years after independence, few traditional thumri singers were heard on All India Radio since 'no one whose private life was a public scandal' was patronised by this body. Women tell of how they had to produce marriage certificates or give an undertaking that they had given up their *pesha* before they were allowed to sing. Women moved out or were pushed out of thumri's miniature canvas into the expanses of khayal or into the world outside music.

Thumri and tawaifs may not be uppermost in the minds of most feminists. But thumri, what it is, its history, and the stories of its singers do encourage us to ask questions that, to me, are pertinent to understand how we are to be—modern women, who yet are not totally cut off from our histories.

For me, thumri, how to sing it, what sense to make of it, how to understand it in relation to the world I live in, how to reconcile my singing self and my ordinary, somewhat beleagured-in-the-modern-world self—these questions were not just academic ones. As a woman, I had to make sense of all of this. I had to ask how I, and women like me (and men) could try to understand a form like thumri. Was I to abandon a form if it seemed small and constraining, if it appeared to be light, pleasing and romantic, if it did not fit current notions of what was serious music? Was I to abandon it because the image of woman it presents is ostensibly the negative one of the coy nayika, because it seems not to meet current expectations and constructions of woman's image and role, of what is 'progressive'? Could I erase totally the cultural forms I have inherited? What sense was I to make of them?

Jagah—Musical Spaces

When learning to sing, a student learns many things—raga and tala structure, laya, correct swar and shruti (perfect pitch), the many alankars (or ornamentations), how to combine these alankars aesthetically and appropriately. But a student also learns how to recognize and use jagah in the musical composition to create improvised patterns that are both pleasing and correct—that make musical sense. A student learns to recognize and use the appropriate points of departure in the composition—places in the composition's structure from where improvised flights into other spaces are possible, and, moreover aesthetic. Primarily these spaces are yielded by the musical and rhythmic pattern. In khayal, for instance, the badhat or development of the raga takes place basically according to the swar structure and patterns ascribed to it by musical convention. In doing so, no doubt, the singer is influenced by the poetic content of the composition, but the poetry itself never acquires a separate importance. To the jagah of swar and rhythm, thumri adds others—the jagah of the poetry, the bol, and the jagah of body movement and bhav (the jagah of dance). Consider then the levels on which thumri plays, unfolding itself simultaneously, and explicitly so, along musical, rhythmic, poetic, physical and expressive planes. To the jagah of swar and laya, thumri adds the jagah of the infinite possibilities and meanings yielded by the poetry. And traditionally (though rarely now) thumri singers used body movements, hands and mudras, eyes and gestures, to create new jagah and extend these musical and poetic meanings still further. So a thumri singer singing the beautiful Khamaj thumri '*Kaun gali gayo Shyam, bata de sakhi*' (Tell me my friend, which road did Shyam take? Where has he gone?) would develop the composition along the appropriate (paths) rastas available to it in Khamaj's swar structure, in accordance, too, with the special modes possible in the form of thumri. The singer would also spin out the words 'kaun gali' using not just words and swar, but also eyes and hands to show the many possible (and impossible?) galis, real and metaphorical; then focus on 'bata de'—tell me—a question to which, of course, there is no answer. In performance, then what was just a simple line of poetry set in a 'simple' raga like Khamaj grows beyond our wildest imaginings. The bandish almost explodes with meaning.

Should this begin to sound as if thumri is merely a tune pegged onto poetry, it is not so. Shabda-pradhanta, the importance of shabda, here does not reduce it as music. I think, in fact it adds to it. There is a fusion of word and swar—Manuel says 'poetry gives up its literary status and becomes a purely musical element' and that the aesthetic meaning of the text (i.e. the poetry) in thumri itself becomes musical, not, literary ... (Manuel, 1989). To my mind it is not without reason that traditionally the phrase 'shabda-pradhanta' was not used to describe thumri: the phrase used was 'bol banao'—to *make* 'bol', but also to make '*bol*'. Bol, I think, are different from shabda. I hear the word 'bol' as more dynamic—'bol' means' both word, sound or syllable, but is also an entreaty to speak (it is both noun and verb). This dynamism is compounded by the word *banao* or *banana*—to do, to make. Both the music and the singer are active.

Musical Textures

It is not inappropriate to speak of the textures of the voice or of the musical text as all forms and styles of singing use texturing. In thumri this texturing acquires an importance and significance that is quite unique. Texturing of the voice brings into play many voices. This is most clearly, most literally heard in the *dohre daane taans* of *tappa* (one of the forms—included in the thumri repertoire) and in *kaku prayog*. Dohre daane taans are intricately worked double—'dohre'—taans. The voice very swiftly shifts from a tight, 'held' one to a soft, loose one. The effect is one of the swiftness of taan, but there is a curious swinging sound to it. The taans themselves do not cover a large area but move in and out of a small note space. Dohre daane taans sound sensuous and full, even soft and sweet, at the same time as being intricate; there is a strange harsh–sweet quality to them, a sense of loosening the voice's reigns and pulling them in again. In kaku, the singer 'shifts' the physical voice. The same line may be repeated (and with the same swar notation) but in different 'voices'—now loud, now soft, now almost crooning—the voice from the pit of the stomach, from the chest, the throat or the head. The same swar notation may also be sung with different stress, emphases and pauses—and of course these two (i.e. the different voices and the differently stressed passages) may be combined to further increase space and meaning. I hear this as not merely an exercise in voice control or laya patterns, but the creation of drama. By shifting the voice, by introducing many voices we move from simple first-person narrative to dramatic narrative; a hundred voices and perspectives on the same idea, note, pause, silence. Thumri uses this drama very effectively, in many ways—with the voice (the physical voice), with the body (eyes, hand, movements of the torso)—but also in more subtle ways as the shifting of the voice in the use of *sanchari* and *sambodhan*. An intertextuality is also introduced by an entire shifting of the gaze of the another text, placed here as a quotation. Frequently singers interweave verses—*dohas* in Brijbhasha or *sher* in Urdu—in dadra. This is not merely the addition of some more poetry, but juxtaposes very different structures, textures, sounds and moods to the original text. The dadra's rhythmic movement is cut by the doha's arhythmic flow. Should the chosen couplet be in Urdu there is then the knitting together of the very different sounds of ornate Urdu and earthy Brijbhasha. The couplet allows the singer to simultaneously refer to, play with, subvert the meaning(s) of the doha and the original dadra, play on emphases, fix perhaps on one meaning implicit in the text, then move onto the ambiguity of the main text, or the way around—a play then with ambiguities and certitudes.

Texturing—Sanchari

All art forms in India use sanchari. The theories of aesthetics as put down in *Natya Shastra* still inform the performance of dance, music and drama. Very briefly (and simplistically), *rasa* (sentiment/emotion) is that which leads the artist and the audience to *ananda* (supreme bliss). Rasa is created by the interaction of *sthayi bhavas*, and *sanchari bhavas* (also called *satvika bhavas*). Sthayi bhavas are dominant states of mind such as desire, anger, fear, amusement, sorrow, etc. These are expressed, made manifest, made concrete through sanchari bhavas (transitory states). Sanchari is the movement of the bhava, in a sense its articulation. In dance, for instance (where sanchari is more clearly 'seen') a dancer moves from a literal interpretation of a line of song to associative interpretations of each word, and of the entire line, and text, even introducing an intertextuality by referring to other song or dance texts.

An old thumri (in the raga variously known as Misra Tilak Kamod, Manjh Khamaj or Bihari) goes thus:

Aangan ma mat so sundarva
Aaj ki ratt chaand gahe bahiya....

Through singing and through bhav the singer might play on the word *sundarva* (who is this sundarva, sundarva's many qualities, the many moods in which I speak these lines to sundarva), but also on 'chaand gahe bahiya'—and the many possible interpretations of an ambiguous line: 'the moon enfolds/is enfolded'.

Through sanchari the singer achieves another less literal shifting of the voice, and also a shifting of the identity of the narrator and of the one being addressed (sambodhan). Who is the listener? Is it at all the listener who is being addressed—or is this a case, as in the popular thumri, of '*tirchhi najariya ke baan*'? If it is not the listener who is being addressed, then who is?

In the dadra '*Hamse no bolo*', the world '*na bolo*', and '*bolo*' can be sung in ways that imply an entreaty to speak, rather than the anger of the nayika. Similarly in the dadra in Pilu '*Gori baanke nainon se chalave jaduva*' we see this ambiguity—who is speaking and to whom?

This verbal ambiguity is echoed in the melodic structures—Pilu *will* slip into Shivranjani—and what the voice does with swar and words, the eyes, hands and body extend further. And suddenly this tiny dadra—three lines of poetic text and a brief scale from madhyam to upper shadja—set in the 'light', 'small' raga Pilu takes three small steps and encompasses the universe.

This is only at the level of poetry and movement. The most important aspect of thumri singing is its very interesting and unique use of raga-space and the ways in which it extends this.

Sanchari and Bhav

In its use of, and articulation of bhav, thumri seems to disorder the usual ways of performance. Thumri's explication creates an almost unbearable dramatic tension—a disordering of accepted motions of time, space, identity of raga, tala, bhava, nayak-nayika. Consider the thumri *Nindiya no jagaao raja gaari doongi*. As composed, in this bandish, the word 'gaari' falls on the *sam* (the first, and therefore stressed beat), but the phrase '*gaari doongi*' circles around a sweet movement of ni-sa-dha-*ni*.

Although the bandish appears to be in the voice of an angry nayika, the musical composition belies this—'gaari doongi' is expressed in the tender phrase ni sa dha ni. The thumri is primarily playful and there is a self confidence here, despite the reproach. However, elaborating the bandish, the singer goes through many emotions. The identity of the nayika shifts from the self assured woman to the inexperienced mugdha, to the angry khandita to the sorrowing vipralabdha.

In one version of this bandish, the voice shifts in the antara (the second part) from being that of the playful nayika to one of genuine reproach at a genuine betrayals. This shift, this play of different voices does more than enunciate the nayika's confusion, torment and ambivalence. It sets up a time-frame as well. The bandish becomes not only the voice of the nayika in the here and now, but also as recounting the agony of the past, of the long night of betrayal and separation. Temporality is created, experiences are recounted one by one, so that what one thinks is 'happening' now, has really already happened a long time ago, and is being relived in the telling. Nor has any of this happened at all—this is what the nayika will say when in some never-to-be-reached future, when the eternity of 'viraha' will by convention (though not now, not in this life, not in this *yug*) end in lovers' meeting. These eternal presents and continuous pasts, and futures that have already happened, create more times, more ambiguity. All these times co-exist simultaneously; this drama takes place in a magical time which is not past, present or future.

Raga and Musical Spaces

Thumri finds musical spaces in many ways. There are, as with khayal, the jagah yielded by the swara pattern of the particular bandish—these explore, in keeping with the spirit and 'feel' of the bandish, the raga's special quality, its angs, its magical moments, pauses, stresses and silences. In addition to this raga-based exploration, thumri finds other musical jagah to unfold itself. If thumri plays with ambiguities though its poetic text, this play is even greater in the musical 'text'.

The swar structure of a raga is given. There may be variations according to gharana as to how this structure is set up at all, but there is a common consensus that a raga has a specific structure and pattern; much of musical 'correctness' lies in understanding and presenting this structure as accepted by convention. Thumris are however often (though not always) set in ragas which do not have such a clear structure, nor a very clearly articulated aroha-avaroha. Thumri's elaboration is based not just on exploring the ragas 'structure', but equally of exploring the ambiguities and many meanings available in this structure. To this extent khayal is a more 'closed' form. A khayal singer singing *Jaijaiwanti* would take great care not to allow shades of a similar raga like *Gara* or *Hameer* to creep in and 'pollute' the purity of the raga. A thumri singer singing Gara would, on the other hand, revel in these points of danger and explore just how far and how much otherness can be introduced into the body of the raga. A swar in the raga becomes the door that leads to other ragas; a swar as it is heard in one raga is deliberately punned upon to give it the meaning and jagah of that swar in another raga. Gara's two gandhars yield spaces for Jaijaiwanti, Bhairavi's *komal rishabh* and *gandhar* just slightly lowered are made to mean Todi.

This punning on the meaning of the swar phrase and the *raga-ang* is what is called thumri's tendency to mix ragas. Classical music defines two ways of mixing ragas. In *raga-sankar*, two (or more) ragas are mixed so that a third, separate identity is created—ragas such as Madhukauns. Another kind of mixing of ragas, *sansrishti*, is where the two or more ragas do not dissolve to create a new one. Here the identities of the original ragas remain impermeable and distinct. But thumri uses neither of these methods. It is not so much that ragas are mixed to create a third new raga with its own new identity and personality. Instead the points of weakness, the margins and boundaries, in the raga's structure are used as points at which other ragas are allowed to enter into the body of the main raga. To me this seems to be playing with notions of mixing, and pollution, of transgressing boundaries, of dealing with dangerous thresholds. But also, there is a kind of humour here—a play on, and an exploiting of the different meanings that a single swar or swar pattern (for instance re-pa or ni-dha-ni) can have.

Talking of the body's boundaries and rules governing purity and pollution, Mary Douglas observes that the structure of its (pollution's) symbolism uses comparison and double meaning like the structure of a joke; she talks of the 'sad wit', the 'unfunny wit' of pollution symbolism (Douglas, 1984). It is this 'sad wit' of pollution that I think is involved in the 'mixing' of ragas in thumri.

Thumri seems to equally make use of *moorchhana*. In moorchhana, a new raga is created by shifting the tonic to another note. Thus Bhoopali's moorchhana on gandhar gives us Malkauns; Craras moorchhana on pancham becomes Khamaj. By using the technique of moorchhana, the thumri singer deliberately awakens the unconscious scales in any given raga. What happens here is that unless one is very aware of these musical nuances, one may miss the point completely, lose one's bearings in the ocean of swars and in fact find no clear *shadja* (tonic) to anchor one's hearing of the raga, and make musical sense of it. Several 'scales' seem to co-exist at the same time.

I am practising the *chaiti 'Sej chadhat dar laage'*. I have been told by my guru that this is in the raga *Jogiya*. Though this chaiti uses shadja as the tonic, my tanpura is tuned not to sa-pa but to sa-ma and deliberately so, to play up the moorchhana *bhed* possibilities in this chaiti, and the ambiguities of madhyam as vadi/madhyam as tonic. Because of this bandish's emphasis on madhyam, and the tanpura tuned to madhyam, this swar seems to dominate; it vies for place with shadja. A sense of madhyam as the tonic is created. If this feeling is given expression, the perspective of the raga shifts; the raga 'becomes' Pilu. Or was it always also Pilu? This shift in perception is simultaneous with the primary recognition of the raga as Jogiya. The scale is no more a clear identity, but a riddle, a permanent question mark. It seems to me that this, rather than any other reason, is why many singers and teachers do not allow notation of thumri even today—there *is* no fixed notation, only possible meanings and perspectives—and why sargam singing is considered highly inappropriate in thumri.

I see all this as an example of musical humour, *hasya*, the rasa that is closest to *shringar*. Simultaneously I see it as standing outside and laughing ironically at the differences set up between one raga and another, at rules and methods, and indeed at the lines drawn between one rasa and another.

No singer has ever spoken to me explicitly about puns or

humour in thumri. However I find that their approach to the
singing very often supports this view. Any one who has watched
Birju Maharaj dancing a thumri would have noticed and enjoyed
the humour which he cuts his own sancharis of viraha with irony
and humour. And I once had the opportunity of watching Shobha
Gurtu in an informal session with her students singing the dadra
'*Thade rahiyo*'—pleading with a moustachio twirling '*yaar*', or
threatening an imaginary cowering '*banke Shyam*' with dire
consequences if he should dare to leave—all to some exquisite
examples of *bol banao* singing.

And as an example of deliberate play on mistaken identities—
of ragas, talas or people, there is this story, told to me by one singer,
eyes twinkling mischievously. There was once a nawab who prided
himself on the number of *nath utarwais* he had sponsored, and,
therefore, also, on the number of young tawaifs he had 'launched'
on their careers. (The first sponsor and patron of a young tawaif
has the right to remove and keep her nath, nose-ring. In return he
had to give her the smaller laung, or nose stud, and this ceremony
was known as nath utarwai.) The tawaifs of one kotha he
frequented, however, had an answer to this. Not protest, not suicide.
They merely got the nawab very, very drunk, and then sent to him
each time the same tawaif with, of course, a brand new nose ring
for his collection.

Thumri and the Female Body

It seems to me that there are resonances between these qualities of
thumri and its articulation, and the Hindu discourse on the body.

The body as metaphor for society is not a new idea. It is central
to much traditional imagery and iconography and has been
recognized and studied by social scientists. The body itself also has
multiple meanings and references—it is not merely the corporeal
body, or the body of 'scientific' medical discourse. 'Just as it is true
that everything symbolises the body, so it is equally true (and all
the more so for that reason) that the body symbolizes everything
else' (Das, 1988). To see the body as a metaphor for music is
therefore not so far-fetched. Even music's vocabulary of *ang,
mukhra, shakl, chalan,* etc. indicate different aspects of a raga,
bandish or tala, in terms of parts of the body. Parts of an instrument
are named as parts of the body. Conversely, bandishes which liken

the body to an instrument deepen and further this body/music metaphor.

One can also ask, *which* body is this? There is the body that is beyond gender or age, beyond attributes—and that *is* music. But there is also the specific body—male or female, young or old, pre-pubertal, pregnant or whatever. It appears to me that thumri shares with all music a sense of the *nirgun* undifferentiated body, while also being simultaneously analogous to the female body.

Hindu discourse on the body treats it as a space that must be protected from pollution that may enter through the liminal extremities, and as a space requiring periodic purification when transgression of its boundaries does take place. Commenting on Srinivas' data on the Coorgs, Douglas (1984) says,

The ritual life of the Coorgs ... give us the impression of a people obsessed by the fear of dangerous impurities entering their system. They treat the body as if it were a beleagured town, every ingress and exit guarded for spies and traitors.

The margins of the body are liminal and dangerous. They are the doors through which pollution can enter, or through which, matter issuing forth, can transgress the body's boundaries. The body is therefore bounded, the extremities marked, and closely guarded.

The female body on the other hand, is almost incapable of total closure. It is the open body, the body that is irreversibly polluted every day (through sexual intercourse) and periodically polluting and dangerous, with every menstrual period, or with birth pollution. Yet it is precisely this polluting and pollutable quality that reflects the *rta* of the universe, and also ensures its continuity and that of the patrilineage (Das, 1988).

There is of course, no *one* Hindu discourse on the female body. Even Manu's is a highly ambiguous text—speaking of menstrual pollution in one breath and of a return to purity through menstruation in the other. Das sees

two major concerns in these rules, both of which are expressed through the metaphor of impurity. The first set of rules relates to the periods of purity and impurity which regulate sexual access to a women. The second is with rituals of purification, including purification and expiation for a woman who has engaged in adulterous sexual relationships.

According to Das, 'the law texts which present the place of woman in a patriarchal universe, emphasize the woman's accessibility to the male, her return to purity, and her obligation to increase the lineage' (1988). So the 'different' discourses are not so much contradictory, as expressing a practical concern for continuance of the patrilineage, and thus the social order, while articulating codes regarding women's sexuality simultaneously stress also the *transformative* (rather than simply polluting or purifying) power of menstruation and sexual intercourse.

Das sees this internalization of the obligation to be sexually active and procreate as 'a third person perspective' on the body. Underlying this is 'a first-person discourse' which articulates the irreversibility of the pollution that a woman is obliged to incur through the process of sexual relations. 'A woman's body, they say, is made jhuti every day, and such pollution cannot be terminated— that which has been made jhuta ... can never attain purity again' (Das, 1988). Such a view of the female body leads to its perception as the body (the persons) that can absorb pollution, sin and danger:

We can now see how polyvalent is the symbol of pollution. On the one hand, the engagement with sex leads to the perspective on the female body as being constantly transformed by use, as being progressively polluted. On the other hand, it is the very capacity of the woman to absorb the negative forces of the cosmic and social world that allows men to be regenerated' (Das, 1988).

In the light of this I find it not the least surprising that tawaifs, whose music seems to me an analogue of the female body should be not only singers, but also should at one time, have had a sexual role to play—voice and body articulate the same truth, and the sexuality of the tawaif is only symbolic of the open-ended quality of her music.

In a beautiful and evocative paper on Bankim Chandra's novels, Sudipta Kaviraj (1987) speaks of the interplay of desire and denial: '... desire seen as man's (or mostly woman's) elemental inclinations, and denial as the system of prohibitions constructed by society to bind and channel them and render them safe.' It is in this interplay of, and conflict between, desire and denial that thumri stands. It is here that it articulates female desire, not in the overt articulation of such desire as evinced in its poetry. This latter is female desire constructed through the male gaze—male desire reflected back to the listener (but an active, not passive listener) in the guise of female desire. Thumri's play with this construction masks a deeper, more fundamental, desire, a desire moreover that seems to have no object. Nothing is known any more; all certainties, all order is questioned, is disordered. And as with Bankim's *Indira*, it appears that what is being questioned is not just the identity of an individual—a raga, bhava, rasa, the singer or the listener—but more radically, the nature of such identity itself. Such questioning 'ties the immaculate definitions of the Hindu moral system into knots,' says Kaviraj— he could well be speaking of thumri, where, too, 'the luminously clear, unfringeable relationships are bent out of shape, sent into a mysterious abeyance'.

The endeavour of khayal is to guard its thresholds and gates, watch all points of danger, allow for no transgression of the purity of the raga. Thumri on the other hand—like the female body—is entirely open. The style of singing is based on this openness of the form. It is a small form with small scales, small, light ragas, small talas. But it leaves itself, wide open and vulnerable. As a result it is able, constantly, to expand the space available to it in quite unique and unexpected ways.

Thumri cannot be 'closed'. Were this to happen it would cease to be thumri; it would, in a sense, die. The margins, dangerous, liminal points, the extremities of the human/musical body from where pollution can enter, where one raga can enter another, where meanings can be collided and blurred, these are welcome in thumri. This however does not mean that other musical forms are not interrogative, subtle or polyvalent—they are. It is only that forms like khayal embody an accepted musical dicourse more clearly. Thumri stands outside of this, gently interrogating it. Nor is thumri's an anarchic, unstructured voice. Here too, there are subtle 'rules' for negotiating these transgressions across the boundaries of raga, sahitya, tala and bhava.

As female body, thumri is open, dangerous—yet fecund and regenerative. As the feminine voice it is the liminal voice, the voice that relentlessly interrogates the order, asking over and over again, the question that has no answer. While I see this quality as subversive, I do not see it as destructive. It is in seeing (or hearing) the otherness of thumri that we come to know our ordinary selves. 'Nothing', says Kaviraj (1987) 'could be more important to someone wishing to know the structure of the universe than to know these limits ..., to come to the edge of the world and peer at the darkness beyond, to acknowledge our 'other' nature, and to see ourselves and our limits as fallible and provisional.' 'We accept', he says, 'the provision of our happiness. We learn to forgive. We grasp the secret of kindness.' And so it is with thumri.

References

Das, Veena, 1988, 'Femininity and the Orientation to the Body', in Karuna Chanana (ed.), *Socialisation, Education and Women: Explorations in Gender Identity,* Orient Longman and NMML, New Delhi.

Douglas, Mary, 1984, *Purity and Danger: An Analysis of the Concepts of Pollution and Taboo,* Ark London: (First published 1966).

Erdman, Joan, 1978, 'The Maharaja's Musicians: The Organization of Cultural Performances at Jaipur,' in Sylvia Vatuk (ed.), *American Studies in the Anthropology of India,* Manohar, New Delhi.

Manuel, Peter, 1989, *Thumri in Historical and Stylistic Perspectives,* Motilal Banarsidass, Delhi.

Mukta, Parita, 1994, *Upholding the Common Life: The Community of Mirabai,* Oxford University Press, New Delhi.

Shukla, Shatrughna, 1983, *Thumri ki Utpatti,* Vikas and Shailiyan, Delhi University, Delhi.

14

Problems for a Contemporary Theory of Gender*

Susie Tharu and
Tejaswini Niranjana

I

Suddenly 'women' are everywhere. Development experts cite 'gender bias as the cause of poverty in the Third World'; population planners declare their commitment to the empowerment of Indian women; economists speak of the feminization of the Indian labour force. In 1991–2, for instance, the People's War Group of the CPI (M–L) found themselves drawn increasingly into women's campaigns against sexual and domestic violence, dowry, and the sale of arrack or country liquor. Upper-caste women thronged the streets in the anti-Mandal protests; women are among the best-known leaders of the Ramjanmabhoomi movement; the BJP have identified women and Dalits as the principal targets of their next election campaign. Film after film features the new woman, who also figures prominently in Doordarshan programmes. In overwhelming numbers, women joined the literacy campaigns in Pondicherry and parts of Andhra Pradesh. The anti-arrack

* This chapter was first presented as a paper at the Anveshi/Subaltern Studies conference on Subalternity and Culture held in Hyderabad in January 1993. An earlier version has appeared in *Social Scientist*. We thank K. Lalita, Veena Shatrugna, Mary John, V. Geeta, Parita Mukta, and Lata Mani for discussing the paper with us, Mr Dasgupta and the staff of the *Eenadu* library for letting us use their collection of press clippings, and Anveshi Research Centre for Women's Studies for creating a context where such issues are engaged. Our thanks to Dipesh Chakrabarty and Shahid Amin for useful editorial comments.

movement initiated by rural women destabilized the economy of Andhra Pradesh.

How might we 'read' the new visibility of women across the political spectrum? What does it represent for gender theory and feminist practice today? For all those who invoke gender here, 'women' seems to stand in for the subject (agent, addressee, field of inquiry) of feminism itself. There is a sense, therefore, in which the new visibility is an index of the success of the women's movement. But clearly this success is also problematic. A wide range of issues rendered critical by feminism are now being invested in and annexed by projects that contain and deflect that initiative. Possibilities of alliance with other subaltern forces (Dalits, for example) that are opening up in civil society are often blocked, and feminists find themselves drawn into disturbing configurations within the dominant culture. We attempt in this chapter to understand the implications of this phenomenon. We feel our task is all the more urgent since the crisis in feminism is clearly related to the crisis of democracy and secularism in our times.

In the 1970s and 1980s, an important task for feminist theory was to establish 'gender' as a category that had been rendered invisible in universalisms of various kinds. In Hyderabad, for example, the campaign against 'eve-teasing' taken up by women students in the early 1970s brought into the open the hostile and sexually threatening conditions all women had to deal with everyday, not only in the university, but also on the streets and in every kind of work-place. Through public interest litigation, as in the cases of injectable contraceptives (Net-Oen) and police rape, and appeals against a variety of judgements—on custodial rape, family violence, restitution of conjugal rights—we demonstrated the asymmetries and inequalities in gender relations that underwrote the notion of rights and the legal process. We demanded changes that would make the law more sensitive to the cultural and economic contexts of women's lives. Women's groups investigating 'dowry deaths' demonstrated how the designation of the family as private domain restricted women's access to protection against domestic violence. They exposed the collusion of the law, police, medical system, and the family in classifying these deaths as suicides. Feminist scholars worked to salvage gender and women's issues from being subsumed by class analysis, sought to extend the Marxist understanding of labour to include domestic production, and pointed out the marginality and vulnerability of women in the workforce; disciplinary formations such as history or literature were critically discussed, and alternative narratives produced that foregrounded women. We demonstrated gross inequalities in women's access to health care systems or to 'development', and examined patriarchal ideologies as they worked across a wide range of institutions. These initiatives extended our understanding of the micro-politics of civil society, showing how pervasively mechanisms of subjugation operated, and how processes of othering functioned in relation to women.

In the late 1980s and the early 1990s—the Mandal/Mandir/ Fund-Bank years—however, we face a whole new set of political questions.[1] Entering into new alliances we have begun to elaborate new forms of politics. These have demanded engagement with issues of caste and religious affiliation/community and with new problems emerging from the 'liberalization' of the economy, creating contexts in which the contradictions implicit in earlier initiatives have become increasingly apparent. For example, feminists calling for a uniform civil code in the context of the Shah Bano case soon realized the difficulty of distinguishing their position from that of an aggressively anti-Muslim lobby, and began to downplay the demand as 'Shah Bano' become the rallying cry for Hindutva. Similarly, in Chunduru, sexual harassment was cited as justification for the punishment meted out to Dalits by upper-caste men. More recently, leftist women's organizations in Hyderabad were placed in a dilemma about joining in a protest against the arrest and torture of a Muslim student accused of 'eve-teasing'. Debates around the introduction of hormonal implants and injectables into the national family planning programmes reveal analogous contradictions that underlie notions such as women's freedom, self-determination, or their right to choose. We feel that the kind of contradictions that confront gender analysis are structurally similar to those that face class analysis, caste initiatives and, more broadly, democracy and secularism today. In this chapter, our concern is to investigate the relationship of these contradictions

---

[1] We use 'Mandal' to refer to the anti-Mandal (anti-reservation) agitation, 'Mandir' to refer to the Ramjanmabhoomi movement to build a Ram temple in Ayodhya–Faizabad, and 'Fund–Bank' to refer to the era of structural adjustment policies promoted in India by the International Monetary Fund and the World Bank.

to the gender, caste, class, and community composition of the 'subject' in the dominant order. Historically, this citizen–subject has been underwritten, and naturalized, by the 'humanism' that presents it as politically neutral.

II

Gender analysis, like class analysis, had revealed how the humanist subject and the social worlds predicated onto it functioned in such a way as to legitimize bourgeois and patriarchal interests. What has never been really apparent, however, is the way in which both Marxist and feminist politics continue to deploy other dimensions of the hidden structuring (such as caste or community) of the humanist subject, as well as the premises of secularism–democracy invoked by it. We have been unable, therefore, to critically confront inequalities of caste or community implicit in that subject or its worlds. We have also found it difficult to radicalize the concepts of secularism and democracy to meet the political requirements of our times. We shall be arguing in this chapter that these tasks call for an investigation and critique of the humanist premises that not only underwrite the politics of dominance but also configure the 'subject of feminism'.

The notion of the 'human' as it appears in political theory, and more importantly in humanist common sense is inextricable from what has been termed the metaphysics of substance. Framed by this metaphysics, the human appears as a substantive base that precedes and somehow remains *prior* to and outside of structurings of gender, class, caste, or community. In liberal political theory, it is this human core that provides the basis for legal personhood. Humanist Marxism offers a critique of the class investments of liberal individualism, but preserves the normative idea of a human essence, principally in the concept of alienation and in teleological notions of history but also in the notion of ideology as false consciousness. Humanist feminism, too, is predicated on notions of female alienation from a putative human wholeness. Even across significant political and theoretical divides, the notion of a human essence that remains resolutely outside historical or social coding continues to operate as 'common sense'. It is not difficult to see that these theories, and their politico–legal derivatives, actually produce what they claim to recognize. For example, by basing the *rights of the individual* on the fiction of a substantive human core,[2] the law creates that core, or more precisely, a core-effect; the idea of *alienation* gains force only as it measures itself against a human fullness; *teleological narratives of history* find resolution only in a fully and recognizably human world.

This produced, this human subject, on whom the whole question of 'right' is predicated, was imaged as the citizen–subject and the political subject. This imaging, (a) articulated gender, caste and community (and initially even class) only in the realm of the social; (b) marked these as *incidental* attributes of *human* self; and, (c) rendered invisible the historical and social/cultural structuring of the subject of politics. The shaping of the normative human–Indian subject involved, on the one hand, a dialectical relationship of inequality and opposition with the classical subject of Western liberalism and, on the other, its structuring as upper-caste, middle-class, Hindu, and male. The structuring was effected by processes of othering/differentiation such as, for example, the definition of upper-caste/class female respectability in counterpoint to lower-caste licentiousness, or Hindu tolerance towards Muslim fanaticism, and by a gradual and sustained transformation of the institutions that govern everyday life.[3] Elaborated and consolidated through a series of conflicts, this structuring became invisible as this citizen–self was designated as modern, secular, and democratic.[4]

[2] For a relevant discussion of the metaphysics of substance and the question of rights, *see* Mary Poovey, 'The Abortion Question and the Death of Man', *in* Joan Scott and Judith Butler (eds), *Feminists Theorize the Political*, Routledge, London, 1991.

✳[3] The historical emergence of the citizen–subject in India has been explored in the impressive work of scholars like Kumkum Sangari, Uma Chakravarti, Lata Mani, Partha Chatterjee, Gyanendra Pandey, and others. *See* Kumkum Sangari, 'Relating Histories: Definitions of Literacy, Literature, Gender in Nineteenth-Century Calcutta and England', *in* Svati Joshi (ed.), *Rethinking English: Essays in Literature, Language, History*, Trianka, Delhi, 1991; Sangari and Sudesh Vaid, 'Introduction' to Sangari and Vaid (eds), *Recasting Women: Essays in Colonial History*, Kali for Women, Delhi, 1989; Uma Chakravarti, 'Whatever Happened to the Vedic Dasi? Orientalism, Nationalism and a Script for the Past'; Lata Mani, 'Contentious Traditions: The Debate on Sati in Colonial India'; Partha Chatterjee, 'The Nationalist Resolution of the Women's Question', all in *Recasting Women*; Gyanendra Pandey, *The Construction of Communalism in Colonial North India*, Oxford University Press, Delhi, 1990.

[4] For a fine account of how Satyajit Ray effects the consolidation of this human citizen–subject in the freshly-minted realism of the Apu trilogy, *see* Geeta Kapur,

Our strategy in this chapter will be to examine certain 'events', such as Mandal or the rise of the Hindu Right, in which contemporary feminist analysis is coming up against certain impasses. These impasses indicate, on the one hand, a fracturing of the humanist consensus that has been the basis of left- as well as right-wing politics and, on the other, an opening up of possibilities for new political alignments and initiatives. These events, it seems to us, characterize the moment of the contemporary and might he investigated as metonyms of gender in which cultural meanings are being contested and refigured.

Obviously, each of these metonyms has a separate and particular history. But since our focus here is on the contemporary moment, we are concerned less with the emergence of these 'events', more with the impress of history on the present. In a strict sense, then, our approach is genealogical. We wish to explore historical conflicts as they structure everyday life and affect political initiatives in our time. The aim is to initiate a polemic that will render visible the points of collision and the lines of force that have hitherto remained subterranean, and construct instruments that will enable struggles on this reconfigured ground.

III

Our first metonym is Mandal–Chunduru, where we investigate the articulation of the gender question in the hegemonic culture of the 1990s. In both Mandal and Chunduru, 'women' were foregrounded, although in different ways. 'Women' came to be invoked here as, in a sense, feminist subjects: assertive, non-submissive, protesting against injustice done to them *as women* (Chunduru) or *as citizens* (the anti-Mandal agitation). An examination of the hidden structuring of this feminist subject would, we believe, reveal its similarities with the subject of humanism, marked—in a way that requires the occlusion of the marking—by class, caste, and community.

Mandal

The background is one familiar to most of us. The then Prime Minister V.P. Singh's announcement on 7 August 1990, of the

---

'Cultural Creativity in the First Decade: The Example of Satyajit Ray', *Journal of Arts and Ideas* 23–24, January 1993, pp. 17–50.

implementation of the Mandal Commission recommendations for reservations of 27 per cent for Backward Castes, apart from 22.5 per cent for SC/STs in government service and public sector jobs, sparked off student riots, primarily in North India, but also in Hyderabad and a few other places. The methods of protest ranged from street-cleaning and boot-polishing to self-immolation; the discourses deployed most significantly were those of Unrewarded Merit and the Salvation of the Nation.[5] The actual course of events is too well-known to require recounting here. What we would like to focus on is the imaging of women in the anti-Mandal agitation, preceded by a brief discussion of the way in which the agitation itself was represented in the media.

Indian Express editor Arun Shourie, rousing the upper-caste youth to action in his editorials, spoke of 'the intense idealism and fury' of the students (*Indian Express*, 29 September 1990). A well-known intellectual denounced the reservations for OBCs as a 'transgression of moral norms' and as a political practice that would 'destroy the structure of democratic politics' (Veena Das, *Statesman*, 3 September 1990). She spoke of the 'hidden despair' of the 'youth', and the government's refusal to recognize that 'people' 'may be moved by utopias, not interests'. The media's invocation of *students, youth,* and *people* was marked by a strange consensus on usage—these terms were obviously unmarked, yet referred only to those who were upper-caste or middle-class. An editorial in the *Independent* bemoaned the fact that the middle-class now had no place in India (4 October 1990), suggesting that somehow they were the only legitimate political subjects/actors in a democracy. Only the subject of humanism could claim the utopias of the Enlightenment.

The Nation was a central figure in the anti-Mandal discourse. Claiming the heritage of Jawaharlal Nehru (a 1950s speech of Nehru's was widely circulated, asserting that reservations would produce a 'second-rate' nation), the anti-Mandalites saw themselves as the authentic bearers of secularism and egalitarianism. Equality, they argued, would be achieved by a transcendence or a repudiation of caste, community, and gender identifications. For feminists who had struggled for years to inscribe gender into the liberal model, the Mandal issue posed a difficult question. Young middle-class

[5] These activities were designed to signify that meritorious men and women, who would otherwise occupy white-collar positions, would be forced as a result of the reservations policy to earn a menial's livelihood.

women began to declare that they were against the reservations for women that had been announced in Andhra Pradesh for instance, as well as against the idea of reserving seats for women in public transport. Reservations (like subsidies) were *concessions*, and would make women 'soft', they said, reducing their ability to be independent and strong. In the anti-Mandal protests women often appear not as sexed beings but as free and equal citizens, as partners of the rioting men, jointly protesting the erosion of 'their' rights. The nearly unanimous media celebration of the upper-caste students framed them within a non-sectarian nationalism and humanism; these young men and women were truly egalitarian and therefore anti-Mandal, whereas pro-Mandal groups were accused of supporting a resurgent casteism.

We asserted earlier that 'the Indian' comes into being in a dialectical relationship of inequality with the Western subject of humanism. In the first two decades or so after Independence, the post-colonial 'Indian' lays claim to a more egalitarian liberalism than that produced in the age of empire and in the heart of empire. Nehruvian socialism takes shape after the Soviet example of state planning, although allowing for a 'mixed' economy that retains large numbers of middle-class professionals in the public sector. In the global configuration that has emerged after the collapse of the second world, in the context of economic 'liberalization' in India and the gradual erosion of the public sector, the neo-nationalist Indian subject proclaims its Indianness even as it internationalizes itself. Now claiming equality with the Western subject of humanism on the latter's own terms, the 'Indian' aggressively demands the rejection of everything that would come in the way of its achieving an equal place in the new world order.

Whereas in the Nehru years the retarders of progress were seen as casteism, fundamentalism, or feudalism, and the role of the state was to help overcome these, in the Fund-Bank years these 'evils' are imaged as being located in welfarism and in the state-controlled public sector itself. The 'failure' and 'inefficiency' of the public sector is seen primarily as the outcome of the reservations policy; if becoming 'efficient', therefore, is the only way of integrating India into the world economy, then the obvious means of achieving this is to abolish reservations and establish a meritocracy. The sociologist André Beteille argued recently that no one wants to defend a caste hierarchy today;[6] but what he did not add was that the new secular hierarchy—a meritocracy premised on efficiency—

refigures, transforms, and redeploys caste. In an artical written during the anti-Mandal agitation, BJP leader K.R. Malkani mentioned 'a vice president of the IBM' who 'joked that they have so many Indians, and they are so good, that they in the IBM have decided not to employ any more, since they could just take over the IBM! Read the Brahmin for the educated Indian, and you have some idea of our wealth and brain power' (*The Daily*, 11 October 1990). After the self is marked upper class/upper caste, the process of marking, as we have already suggested, becomes invisible. The recomposition of the middle class, the secular class that stands in for the nation, is thus predicated on the redeployment and othering of caste.[7] Professing secularism enables a displacement of caste (and also community) from the middle class sphere, so that it gets marked as what lies *outside*, is *other* than, the middle class. In the consolidation of the middle class and in the othering of caste, 'women' play a crucial role.

Not only were women visually foregrounded by the media during the agitation, they also took part in large numbers in the struggle to do away with reservations for backward castes and Dalits. A report in the *Free Press Journal* says: 'The girls of Jadavpur University were the most militant and wanted to blockade roads and defy the law' (15 October 1990). In many cities, hitherto 'apolitical' women students participated enthusiastically in demonstrations and blockades, mourning the 'death of merit' and arguing the need to save the nation. Wives of IAS officers demonstrated in the capital on behalf of their children, who they claimed were being denied their rightful share in the nation. The fact of women 'taking to the streets' became in the hegemonic culture iconic of an idealism that recalled the days of the freedom struggle. The marking of 'women' as middle class and upper caste has a long genealogy that, historically and conceptually, goes back into nationalism as well as social reform.[8] Marked thus, 'women' are seen as morally pure and uncorrupted—hence the significance

[6] In a public lecture on caste in modern India, delivered at the University of Hyderabad, January 1992.

[7] The media always uses the term 'caste groups' or 'caste organizations' to refer to *lower-caste* groups. As K. Satyanarayana has pointed out, 'caste' usually refers only to lower caste.

[8] *See* the articles in *Recasting Women* by Partha Chatterjee and Uma Chakravarti, as well as the introduction to Susie Tharu and Lalita K. (eds), *Women Writing in India: 600 BC to the Present*, vol. 2, Feminist Press, New York, 1993.

of their protest, which becomes a 'disinterested' one since they have no place in the organized political process.[9] However, as a powerful strand of nationalism asserts, it is women who are entrusted with the task of saving the nation. In actuality, the nation is frequently imaged as 'woman' (Bharatmata, Mother India).

The re-emergence of women in the public sphere as claimants to the nation and to citizenship results in a masculinization of the lower castes. To rephrase the title of a well-known feminist book, in Mandal-Chunduru, all the women are upper caste (and, by implication, middle-class Hindu) and all the lower castes are men. As we argued earlier, in the anti-Mandal agitation, 'women' feature as citizens and not necessarily as gendered beings. But the representation in the media of their well-nourished faces and fashionable bodies visually defined the lower castes as Other. The photographs of the anti-Mandal women suggested that caste (read lower caste) is defined against 'women', and against the assertive and articulate humanist–feminist subject. As Sangari and Vaid have agrued, 'the description and management of gender and female sexuality is involved in the maintenance and reproduction of social inequality.'[10] Sexuality was a *hidden* issue in Mandal, as an interview with an anti-Mandal woman student suggested. The student had held in a demonstration a placard readings: 'We want employed husbands.' When asked why, she said that reservations would deprive their men of employment. In that case, why should they not marry 'backward' boys? '"But how can that be ...", her voice trailed off' (Jyoti Malhotra, *The Independent*, 26 August 1990). The anti-Mandal women had learned to *claim* deprivation and injustice, now not as women but as *citizens,* for to ground the claim in gender would pit them against middle-class men. The claiming of citizenship rather than sisterhood now not only set them against Dalit men but also against lower-caste/class women.

Chunduru

Interestingly, it is the claim to sisterhood that accomplishes the same effect in Chunduru. To sketch the context: in the culmination

[9] That 'this student movement' 'articulates political processes that lie outside the domain of organized politics' was Veena Das's characterization of the anti-Mandal agitation in 'A Crisis of Faith', *Statesman*, 3 September 1990.
[10] *Recasting Women*, p. 5.

of a series of hostile encounters spread across at least two to three years, on 6 August 1991, in the village of Chunduru in coastal Andhra Pradesh, thirteen Dalits were murdered by upper-caste Reddys. The catalyzing 'event' appeared to be the incursion into the cinema hall space reserved by tradition for members of the upper castes by a young Dalit graduate, who was later beaten up, forced to drink liquor, and marched to the Chunduru police station, where he was 'accused of harassing upper-caste women in an inebriated condition.'[11]

After the carnage of 6 August, the mourning Dalits organized a funeral procession, during which some haystacks and thatched roofs were set on fire. Most of the Reddy males had left Chunduru to avoid arrest. The upper-caste women who stayed behind complained loudly of harassment by the Dalits, suggesting that their present accusations stemmed from a long history of grievances against Dalit men. The women claimed that they had been tied to trees and kerosene poured over them, and only the arrival of the police saved them from death.

Shortly after, the Reddys of the region formed a 'Sarvajana-bhyudaya Porata Samithi' along with the Kammas, Brahmins, Kapus, Rajus, and Vaishyas, and organized processions, *dharnas*, and roadblocks to protest their 'oppression' at the hands of Dalits.[12] The upper-caste women, they contended, had been systematically harassed by Dalit men. Accusations of eve-teasing and assault multiplied, post-Chunduru. On 13 August in Kollipara village near Tenali, a Dalit boy was beaten up by upper-caste boys for teasing 'a schoolgirl'; a report dated 11 August 1991, said that earlier in the month, a Dalit student was stabbed on the pretext that he had teased 'three girls'. The original cinema hall story was recorded as one about 'a Harijan youth putting his feet up on the seat in front in the cinema hall occupied by a caste Hindu girl' (*Statesman*, 9 August 1991). In Chunduru itself, the story went, just before 6 August, when Dalit labourers were no longer employed for transplantation and women from the landlords' family had undertaken the task, Dalit men were supposed to have accosted

[11] We base this narrative of the events on Samata Sanghatana's report, published in *Economic and Political Weekly*, XXVI: 36, 1991, pp. 2079–84.

[12] For this information, we are indebted to K. Balagopal's report, 'Post-Chunduru and Other Chundurus', in *Economic and Political Weekly*, XXVI: 42, 1991, pp. 2399–405.

the women one day, quarrelled with them, stripped them naked, and forced them to remove the transplanted seedlings and re-plant them. Enraged upper-caste women attacked the convoys of Chief Minister Janardhana Reddy and former Chief Minister N.T. Rama Rao, blaming the State for not providing them protection from the Dalits.

Years of sexual abuse of Dalit women by upper-caste men appear under the sanction of 'custom' while the alleged 'eve-teasing' of upper-caste women by Dalit men invokes the horrors and prohibitions/punishments of major transgression, the penalty of death. Chunduru drew the attention of urban women's groups, but especially for those feminists who had refused to be part of the anti-Mandal agitation and were attempting to build fragile alliances with Dalit organizations, the hegemonic articulation of the gender issue as one of 'molestation' (of upper-caste women) was deeply problematic. But to counterpose this against the molestation of Dalit women was equally problematic.

Feminists can grapple with this problem only by addressing the key role played by caste in the making of the middle-class woman. In the nineteenth-century *bhadralok* campaigns against Vaishnav artistes, as much as in the anti-nautch initiatives in Madras Presidency, the virtue and purity of the middle-class woman emerged in contrast to the licentiousness of the lower-caste/class woman. It is a logic that continues to operate, as for instance in the cases of Rameeza Bee and the Birati rapes: the women crying rape were 'prostitutes' and therefore had no right to complain of sexual harassment.[13] A woman's right over her body and control over her sexuality is conflated with her *virtue*. So powerful does this characterization become that only the middle-class woman has a right to purity. In other words, only *she* is entitled to the name of woman in this society. Again we see, as in Mandal, the masculinization of the lower-castes— the Dalits only male, the women only upper-caste. The category of 'woman', and therefore in a very important sense the field of feminism as well as the female subject, emerge in this context by obscuring the Dalit woman and marking the lower caste as the predatory male who becomes the legitimate target of 'feminist' rage.

[13] *See Report of the Commission of Inquiry into the Rameeza Bee and the Ahmed Hussain Case*, Government of Andhra Pradesh, 1978; and Tanika Sarkar, 'Reflections on Birati Rape Cases: Gender Ideology in Bengal', *Economic and Political Weekly*, XXVI: 5, 1991, pp. 215–18.

IV

The introduction into national 'family welfare' or population control programmes of long-acting hormonal implants and injectables, and possibly also of RU 486, the abortifacient pill, is the metonym through which we would like to explore contradictions implicit in feminist demands for freedom, choice, and self-determination.

Women's groups and health activities in India have opposed these contraceptives on several grounds. They have commented on the dangerous side-effects (disturbed menstruation, hypertension, risk of embolism, nervousness, vomiting, dizziness, etc.) and contra-indications (these drugs may not be used by women with any history of liver or heart problems, diabetes, clotting defects, cancer, migraine, recent abortion, irregular cycles, or smoking). They have pointed out that the administration of such contraceptive technologies depend on well-equipped health-care systems. Existing public health facilities in India are nowhere near adequate for screening potential users, inserting and removing implants, and providing continued monitoring of user health. They warn of the risks involved in using drugs not developed or standardized for women in India. They argue that hormonal contraceptives should not be introduced before conducting epidemiological and biochemical studies that take into account differences in weight, diet, and so on, between Indian women who will use these contraceptives and the 'average' Western woman.[14] All told, it becomes evident that considered as contraceptives for Indian women who are not part of the urban middle class, the profiles of Norplant, Net-Oen and RU 486 are abysmal.

International organizations such as Planned Parenthood and the Population Council who fund research on these contraceptives and promote their use, as well as the multinational corporations that manufacture them, invoke the founding demands of the women's movement itself as they market these drugs. Women's lives, rights of self-determination and choice, privacy, autonomy, and empowerment is now on the agenda of multinational capital.

[14] The high costs of the contraceptive (one set of Norplant implants will cost the Indian government around Rs 750) and the profits that will accrue is also an important issue, but was not raised by activists.

What is more, powerful feminist lobbies such as the Feminist Majority in the USA endorse these claims. Consider a widely publicized statement by Werner Foros, president of the Washington-based Population Institute, released in Bombay as part of an initiative to counter efforts by Indian women's groups to oppose Norplant. While Foros does cite resource shortage in third world countries as an important factor in population planning, he seems far more distressed that a majority of women in such countries had no control over their fertility, that the important right of 'choice' was not available to them. In the same statement, he quotes a survey in which 300 million women worldwide had said that they hadn't wanted their last child; 'women today do two-thirds of the work, earn only one-tenth of the money and own less than one per cent of the property. So the empowerment of women is perhaps the most important intervention we can pursue.' His goal was a population programme in which the poorest of poor couples has the means to make a choice.[15]

Similarly, the scientist Etienne-Emile Baulieu—consultant and spokesperson for the multinational Roussel-Uclaf who have developed the abortifacient pill, RU 486—speaks of it as the 'moral property of women'. It is a duty, he claims, to make the right to this property available in the third world: 'Denying this pill is basically signing the death warrant for the 200,000 women who die [worldwide] annually from abortion,'[16] Fred Sai, president of Planned Parenthood, feels that the most serious problem facing India's otherwise praiseworthy efforts at population control is the

[15] 'Men's attitudes are big hurdles', interview with Sonora Jha Nambiar, *The Sunday Times (of India)*, 1 November 1992, p. 11. In what appeared to be a well organized campaign, Fornos, Sai, and other functionaries of these and similar organizations seemed to have been brought to India principally to endorse the government's Norplant programme, stalled by a writ filed by some feminist organizations. They were provided high profile coverage in the press (Rahul Singh, Bachi Karkaria, Darryl D'Monte, Rashme Seghal interviewed them and discussed Norplant). The articles invoked the horrors of an expanding India, welcomed scientific advances such as Norplant and decried women's protest against it as 'vociferous and clearly misguided', misinformed, 'unfortunate and politicized', and as holding up progress when the country was on the brink of disaster.

[16] Fern Chapman, 'The Politics of the Abortion Pill', *Washington Post*, 3 October 1989, p. 13. Cited in Renate Klein, Janice G. Raymond and Lynette J. Dumble *RU 486 Misconceptions, Myths and Morals*, Spinnifex, Melbourne, 1991.

lack of 'contraceptive options' that are offered to the Indian woman and the consequent limits to the choices she can make as an individual with an individualized profile of requirements.[17]

The feminist credentials of those who research into and promote these contraceptives are further consolidated when their initiatives are presented as enabling and empowering women in conservative or religion-bound contexts. Thus the campaign for the abortifacient pill stressed the fact that women would initiate and control the abortion process themselves, and that they could do so without telling anyone else in the family. In brief, the promise was of technologically bypassing social or legal prohibition: 'What could be more private than taking a pill, how could a state control swallowing?'[18] In the USA the Feminist Majority spoke of anti-abortionists as the common enemy of women and science, since 'both women's health and freedom of research are being sacrificed by allowing anti-abortion extremists to block the production and distribution of RU 486'.[19] Proponents of Norplant and Net-Oen in India argue that long-acting implants or injectables that do not interrupt intercourse and do not require women to do anything on a regular basis are particularly suitable for an illiterate and backward population. They also point out that these drugs expand the options open to women, and allow Indian women to take decisions about contraception that do not require the cooperation of their husbands or the sanction of their families. Choice and privacy are both invoked in the battle which is set up as one between the good, progressive, pro-woman scientists and promoters of these contraceptives, and their conservative, anti-woman opponents. Thus the 'limited options' offered by our population programme are attributed 'to the conservative Indian medical mindset, which has reservations about hormonal contraceptives' (*Times of India*, 1 November 1992), while the stalling of Net-Oen and Norplant, first by feminist litigation and later by the drug controller who has called for fresh trials, is decried respectively as 'unfortunate and politicized' (*The Independent*, 22 October 1992), the handiwork

---

[17] Quoted by Sara Adhikari in 'Countdown to Disaster', *The Sunday Times (of India)*, 1 November 1992, p. 11.

[18] Ellen Goodman, 'Moral Property', *The Boston Globe*, 17 July 1989, p. 11. Cited in Klein et al., p. 25.

[19] Klein et. al., pp. 5–6. The recent decision to make RU 486 available in the USA was seen as a feminist victory.

of a few 'vociferous and clearly misguided' groups (*The Week*, 16 November 1992), and as inefficiency and 'procrastination that hinders real progress' (*Times of India*, 1 November 1992).

The figure of the woman that is being liberated and endowed with rights in these discourses requires scrutiny. The use of these contraceptives is premised on the notion that wise planning and scientifically developed products can fulfil women's demands for liberty and self-determination (and catapult them into modernity) without changes in existing family relations or in society at large; in other words, the promise is of a technological fix that can bypass sexual politics and indeed the network of relations in which women are gendered and subjugated. For example, most of the women worldwide who die attempting abortion die not because existing methods are unsafe but because abortion is *illegal*, and has to be done furtively in ill-equipped places and possibly by untrained personnel. This fact finds no place in these statements; neither does the fact that problems arise even in countries like India where abortion is legal, because a 'standardized' medical education does not train doctors to perform abortions. The abortifacient pill is not going to change that situation; indeed, as a technology it is designed to evade such issues and ends up, (a) placing the entire burden for what continues to be a difficult and often illegal procedure on the individual woman; (b) putting women's health in considerable danger; and (c) ruthlessly expanding what might be thought of as 'reasonable' risk and 'tolerable' pain or discomfort to make up for the irrationality of the system.

Norplant was developed as a durg that could be used on unruly and recalcitrant populations not only in the third world but also in the First. It targets the woman, is long-acting, does not need a literate or numerate user, does not require the user's cooperation after it has been implanted, and can be monitored by the authorities with just a glance at the woman's arm. Despite the huge investments in propaganda about woman's choice, Norplant's potential as an instrument of control was clearly recognized. In the USA, less than a month after it was passed by the Food and Drug Administration, a judge ordered that a convicted woman should not be let out on probation unless she agreed to have the implant. A newspaper editorial suggested that because of growing poverty among the blacks, welfare mothers should be offered incentives to use Norplant (*Philadelphia Inquirer*, 12 December 1990). Norplant is now promoted in much-advertised population control programmes in some of the most coercive regimes in the third world—Chile, Indonesia, the Philippines, China—and the somewhat less obliging Indian government is described or 'lacking political commitment' or indulging in 'procrastination … that hinders real progress' when the country is 'hurtling towards disaster'.

Women's freedom, agency, and choice is invoked only within the closed-off, private domains of the family and of reproduction, which are in turn imaged as extremely—and unchangeably—conservative and chauvinist. These assumptions underlie the production and marketing of the contraceptives, but they are socially endorsed, elaborated, and reproduced in the family welfare programme as a whole through advertising campaigns, institutional arrangements and attitudes. In addition, the wide range of sexual and familial relations that exist in the country and the variety of subject-positions that are therefore available to a woman are, in the process, homogenized and naturalized in a conservative mode. For example, these contraceptives assume that women have no control over the conditions in which they get pregnant; that contraception cannot be negotiated or discussed by the couple; that the woman has no right to refuse sex. No attempt is made to reinforce or envisage more egalitarian relationships or place responsibility on the man. In the world of the family welfare programme, a man who is not a male chauvinist is a contradiction in terms. No questions are asked about the nature and quality of existing health care systems and the complex factors that mediate different women's access to them. The politics of the private is not addressed, and no questions are asked about the contradictions between various women's requirements and the national and internationalist agendas of population control. Women's freedom begins to look alarmingly like the freedom to consume these expensive and dangerous products in a climate of disinformation that makes a mockery of 'consent'. These discourses continue to address the question of women's rights and invoke women as free agents in vocabulary drawn from feminism, but only within the once again depoliticized and privatized domains of the family and of reproduction.

The problem is that a whole range of issues that constitute the subjugation of women, and indeed their differential subjugation in relation to class, caste, and community, are naturalized in the 'woman' whose freedom and right to privacy is invoked and who becomes the bearer of the 'right' to choose. The very same move also makes it possible to bring this individual's rights into alignment with the interests of population control and multinational profit. For instance, hormonal injectables/implants might be considered as expanding contraceptive options for women in situations where they have ready access to an efficient and well-equipped medical set-up. To put it in different terms, for a woman whose caste, class, and community positioning matches that of the citizen–subject, hormonals might be regarded as genuine 'choices'. Yet, ironically, these contraceptives were never developed for this woman. They were intended for 'less desirable' demographic groups: the teeming millions of the third world, non-white immigrants in the first world, criminals. Corresponding, in our national context, are the rural 'masses' and the urban poor, a majority of whom are Dalits and Muslims, and of course Muslims in general. Feminists using arguments about women's health have been able to drive a wedge into one fault-line in this structure. Yet untouched however are issues of caste, class, and community that require us to expand the problematic beyond that of the 'rights of the liberal body'. Women— as individuals or in groups—have to bear the increasingly heavy burden of these contradictions as they invent resources with which to negotiate their ever more demanding citizenship and to survive.

V

Hindutva Women

Women on the Right have also opened up a space that might in many ways be regarded as feminist. As Tanika Sarkar points put in a study of the Rashtrasevika Samiti (the women's wing of the RSS), women are 'active political subjects' not only in the Samiti, but also more generally in the domain of communal politics.[20] The women leaders of the BJP are not daughters, wives, or mothers of deceased male leaders. They are there in their own right and seem to have carved out distinctive political roles and identities for themselves. Equally significant is the articulate and often passionate involvement of women who otherwise seem to have little interest

---

[20] Tanika Sarkar, 'The Woman as Communal Subject: Rashtrasevika Samiti and Ram Janmabhoomi Movement', *Economic and Political Weekly*, XXVI: 35. 31 August 1991, p. 2062. Henceforth cited in the text as TS.

in public life in issues such as reservations, the appeasement of Muslims, or corruption in the bureaucracy. Riots now have a new profile, with women, sometimes even middle-class women, actively participating as in Bhagalpur in 1989, Ahmedabad in 1990, or Surat in 1992. News photographs showed a sizeable number of women among those arriving for the 1992 Ayodhya *kar seva*. Several papers carried reports of Sadhvi Rithambara and Uma Bharati cheering on the crowd that tore down the Babri Masjid.

More striking—and in some ways more disturbing—than the appearance of this militant individual on the public battlefields of Hindutva is her modernity and indeed her feminism. The new Hindu woman nearly always belongs to the most conservative groups in Indian society—upper-class/caste, middle-ranking government service or trading sectors—but she cannot be regarded as traditional in any simple sense of the term, any more than Hindutva can be read as fundamentalist.[21] There is very little talk of going back to tradition. The focus is on injustice, for which the Babri Masjid serves as symbol. At issue in the war of Hindutva, which is defined after Savarkar as love for the motherland, is not Hinduism, but the Indian nation.

Predictably, self-respect is an important theme. However, hitched onto women's aspirations for self-respect is the idea of Hindu self-respect. One account of the origin of the Samiti is that Lakshmibai Kelkar founded it after she saw *goonda*s (interestingly not Muslims) raping a woman in the presence of her husband. Since Hindu men (who are in this story both lustful and weak) could not protect their wives, Hindu women had to train to do so themselves (TS 2061). As in authoritarian politics the world over, the emphasis is on discipline and on purging or cleansing the social body of corruption, using force if necessary. While the immediate object appears to be Indian society, the Muslim enemy is very close to the surface here. In the RSS/VHP/BJP imaginary, the *matrabhumi* is presented as a repeatedly raped female body and the myth of the enemy within and of Muslim lust play key structural roles. Thus,

---

[21] Each one of the office-bearers of the Rashtrasevika Samiti, Tanika Sarkar points out, denounced sati. What about voluntary sati? A young activist said with genuine revulsion: *Woh ho nahin sakta. Aurat jalegi kyoon?* (That can never happen. Why would a woman burn herself?) Shakha members do not use their caste names and everybody eats together. The Samiti is not against inter-caste or even inter-community marriage—provided the families agree (ibid.).

for Muslims *aurat matrabhumi nahin hai, bhog bhumi hai* (Woman is not the motherland, but an object of enjoyment).[22] The violence women experience and their need to fight against and gain respect within their own society is all but obscured as the well-made enemy steps in, suggesting that self-respect is best gained in the protection of the motherland. The fact that in the projected Hindu *rashtra* Muslims would not be allowed four wives was regarded by *karsevikas* at Ayodhya as index of the respect women would receive in that utopia (TS 2062).

Like the anti-Mandal agitation, Hindutva would seem to have enabled an articulate, fighting individualism for women and for men. Its power is productive in the Foucauldian sense, inciting its subjects to speak out and act, to become independent, agentive, citizen-individuals. One notices increasingly the confident exponents of Hindutva (students, otherwise unremarkable middle-class men and women) who intervene at seminars and public meetings. These subjects are marked as authentically Indian and as having found an ethos within which their natural—and national—expressive selves can emerge and be sustained.

It is important to understand that though this new Hindu self is represented as discriminated against and embattled, it has the confidence of occupying a 'neutral' ground that provides the basis for a new moral authority. Hindutva, for example, is represented as a potential national ethos within which all other religions and communities might be justly housed. The claim is commonly backed by two arguments. One, a redeployment of nationalist versions of Indian history in which Hinduism is represented as having a long tradition of tolerance; the other an invocation of Western nation-states and their endorsement of dominant religious traditions in the secularism they practice. The history of violence through which those national bourgeoisies established authority is never discussed. The new Hindu subject speaks the voice of a reason that opposes false dogmas (such as Western theories, pseudo-secularism), challenges the bias of existing institutions (the courts, the constitution) on the ground that they are not sensitive to the desires of the majority and appeals to truths that are self-evident to genuine Indians. Thus Girilal Jain writes about the 'bloated rhetoric

---

[22] Pradip Datta, Biswamoy Pati, et al., 'Understanding Communal Violence: Nizamuddin Riots', *Economic and Political Weekly*, XXV: 45, 10 November 1990, p. 2494.

of secularism, constitutionalism and the law' (*Times of India*, 12
December 1992), while Swapan Dasgupta comments after the
demolition of the Masjid:

In effect the *kar sevak*s presented Hindu society with a *fait accompli*.
They could either disown the illegal act on account of both politics and
aesthetics. Or they could come to terms with their own assertiveness,
equate it with the storming of the Bastille and the collapse of the *ancient
regime*, and prepare to face the consequences. [*Sunday*, 20–26 December
1992, p. 9.]

In moves that are surprisingly quickly effected and apparently hold
conviction for increasingly large numbers of Indians, the virulent
anti-Muslim history of Hindutva, a political agenda focused on
pulling down a mosque and building a temple, and a record of
communal violence, is gilded over and legitimized as Hindutva
reoccupies the discourses in which bourgeois nationalism
established authority in its European birthplace—and, more
important from the point of view of our argument in this chapter,
the forms of subjectivity that emerged in tandem with it. Thus
L.K. Advani (invariably represented in the press as mature, soft-
spoken, and charming) insists that his is actually the only 'secular'
party. The demolition of the Babri Masjid is only a 'temporary
setback'. A.B. Vajpayee (honourable, reasonable, cultured) exonerates
the real BJP by locating communalism only in its 'young and
overenthusiastic party workers' (*Indian Express*, 26 December
1992).[23] The angle on neutrality that appears in the context of the
gender question is more telling. Members of the Rashtrasevika
Samiti distinguished their position from that of other women's
organizations by saying, 'when we arbitrate we do not always take
the woman's side. We are neutral.... *Hum ghar torne-wale nahin
hain*' (We are not home-breakers) (TS 2062). Similar evidence of
'neutrality' in relation to caste or class is not difficult to locate.

The politics of this neutrality-effect demands closer scrutiny.
The BJP/VHP/RSS combine are pressing in on a whole set of
existing figures, logics, and institutions as they lay claim to the
nation and to neutrality. As their allusions to European history

[23] The Left Front government in West Bengal distinguished itself at the time of
the Bantala and Birati rapes by very similar evasions. See Tanika Sarkar,
'Reflections on the Birati Rape Cases: Gender Ideology in Bengal', *Economic
and Political Weekly*, XXVI: 5, 2 February 1991.

and to first world nationalism also indicate, a figure that is repeatedly referenced is the bourgeois citizen–subject and the world that was 'legitimately'—and ruthlessly—recast in his interests and in his singular image. Closer home is the neutrality of the Nehruvian state and of planned development in which the 'social' problems of caste, class, and gender, and colonialism are addressed and analysed by scientific planners and handed over to the bureaucracy for redress. The problem, briefly summarized, is that though this state acknowledges social disbalances and accepts responsibility for righting them, it functions on the basis of an executive centrality in which the state is authorized to speak and act for the people. It is becoming increasingly clear that the task of shaping this executive centrality and a social imaginary that authorized it, dominated cultural politics in the immediate post-Independence period. Identities that had taken shape in major pre-Independence class, caste, and gender struggles, and which might have provided the basis for another social imaginary of the nation, were fractured and disorganized as they were rewritten into narratives of humanity and citizenship. The task, however, is an ongoing one, for hegemony is continuously under threat. Films, novels, histories, television programmes, the press in general, the curricula, and a range of institutions of civil society address potentially rupturing questions of caste, gender or community and rework them into narratives that legitimate the middle-class, upper-caste Hindu, patriarchal and internationalist markings of the hegemonic subject.

As a result of this alliance with the subject of humanism, the common sense of the new Right has a much greater hold than the formal/electoral support received by the BJP might suggest. Thus, whether one looks at the mainstream press or at the apparently non-political programmes put out by Doordarshan (the morning chat shows, the evening serials, the children's programmes, the afternoon women's programmes), or ways of thinking, feeling, reasoning, and arriving at conclusions that govern the daily lives of the growing consumer population, Hindutva seems well set to becoming hegemonic. Powerful new discursive articulations are thus effected between this individualism and organic–conservative themes of religion, tradition, nation, family, personal integrity, order, and discipline. The discussion on minorityism, injury/appeasement, pseudo-secularism, and nationalism have brought these subjects into focus in a virulently anti-Muslim frame and as it feeds directly into a genealogy of modern Indian womanhood that marks it not only as Hindu, but as upper caste/class, the Muslim woman is caught in a curious zero-zero game. Either way she loses. She cannot really be woman any more that she can be Indian. As woman and as Indian, she cannot really be Muslim. As for the women on the Right, they are indeed empowered by these new movements, but in a way that sets up the feminist project as one that endorses caste/class hierarchies and the othering of Islam.

VI

We have been arguing that the hegemonic articulation of the gender issue sets up the feminist subject in an antagonistic relationship with, for example, class–caste (Mandal–Chunduru), or religious identity (women on the Right), and in such a way as to aid the reabsorption of this subject into consumer capitalism. We now turn to our last metonym, the anti-*arrack* movement in Andhra Pradesh. The various ways in which the movement has been interpreted and 'women' have been represented seem to work in such a way as to erase and delegitimize earlier feminist initiatives. The process is not a simple one, and we do not claim that we have been able to map all—or even most—of its complicated strategies and effects. Media depictions of the anti-arrack movement annex its initiative into a variety of contemporary discourses about the nation, its women, and the purification of the former by the virtue of the latter. Feminist theory and practice are caught in a curious set of contradictions. The portrayal of the anti-arrack women as the only authentic feminists, paradoxically also involves, (a) a denial that their struggle is concerned specifically with *women's issues,* and (b) a reinscription of it as an anti-feudal struggle, or as a struggle to cleanse the body politic and save the nation. What seems to enable both the denial and the reinscription is the invoking of the anti-arrack woman as the subject of humanism. Interestingly, in terms of the positions offered to the female/feminist subject, there is little to distinguish the articulators of the women's issue in a conservative, high nationalist mode from those who invoke it as part of the class (or specifically anti-feudal) struggle. As these diverse writers seek to separate the anti-arrack movement from historical feminism, they obscure crucial dimensions of the radical egalitarian potential of actually existing feminism. At the same time, they make invisible dimensions of the anti-arrack movement that find resonance with other feminist initiatives.

What are the facets of the anti-arrack struggle that became visible as we contest these dominant representations of it? What implications do they have for contemporary feminist practice and gender theory? We begin with a brief narrative of the movement.

A series of struggles centred around government-backed sales of arrack (*sara* in Telugu) have been taking place over the past decade or so in various regions of Andhra Pradesh. In each region, different local configurations have sustained arrack as an issue; while in the Telengana region and in a few other districts the CPI (M–L) groups have initiated or supported the agitation, in some of the coastal Andhra districts the movement seems to have emerged in conjunction with other events, such as the adult literacy programme. Women all over rural Andhra Pradesh attacked excise department jeeps and police, burned arrack packets, punished arrack sellers, and fined the men who continued to drink. After September 1992 the movement appears to have gathered rapid momentum, spreading from village to village in a manner that no organized political party has been able to predict or control. Since the article which was the basis for this chapter was originally written in December 1992, there have been further developments: the Andhra Pradesh government announced a ban on arrack in Nellore District from 15 April 1993, and throughout the state from 1 October 1993. The ruling Congress-I claimed the ban as a pro-people initiative on its part. Enormous coloured hoardings depicted the evils of arrack, portrayed smiling rural families freed from the menace, and Chief Minister Vijayabhaskara Reddy gazed benevolently on the scene from gigantic cut-outs towering above the hoardings, which were put up at major interesections in the capital city of Hyderabad.[24] The audio-visual publicity machinery of the government ventured into remote areas of Andhra Pradesh to spread propaganda about the need to stop drinking arrack. In the Assembly elections of November 1994, the Congress suffered a major defeat, and the Telugu Desam Party (which had earlier introduced the government-sponsored distribution of arrack)

---

[24] Government Order (G.O.) No. 402 dated 24 April 1993. Announcing the ban, Vijayabhaskara Reddy said that total prohibition was the 'policy of the Congress Party right from the start' and the ban had nothing to do with the crusade launched by the Telugu Desam.

returned to power. The new Chief Minister, N.T. Rama Rao, declared within minutes of taking office that prohibition of all liquor would immediately come into force in the state. He was only acceding, he said, to the demand of the sisters who had voted for him.

Each political organization, however, seemed to appropriate the *sara* women, laying claim to their struggle, and configuring them as the true subjects of feminism. The range is an astonishing one: from the Gandhians to the Lohiaites to the Telugu Desam to the BJP/RSS; from the Marxist–Leninist parties to the traditional Left (CPM and CPI) to the Dalit Mahasabha; not to mention women's organizations across the spectrum: from the Arya Mahila Samiti to the socialist Mahila Dakshata Samiti, from the A.P. Mahila Sangham to the two Progressive Organizations for Women backed by different M–L parties. The woman in the anti-arrack struggle appeared as a Romantic subject, and predicated onto her were an assortment of complex narratives of which she was sole heroine.[25]

The BJP MP, Uma Bharati, praising the anti-arrack women, wanted 'women also [to] campaign against dowry, craze for foreign goods and corruption'; she felt they should 'help create national awakening (*swadeshi jagran)' (The Hindu*, 20 October 1992). The BJP in Nellore District where the movement was very strong are said to have named the women as Shakti, Kali, and Durga, just as the all-India vice-president of the BJP, Jana Krishnamurthy, declared that '*matru shakti* [mother's strength, power] had caused others to fall in line' (*The Hindu*, 12 October 1992). Taking a slightly different but related stand, Dalitbahujan theorist K. Ilaiah spoke of the movement as asserting 'the mother's right to set the family right'.[26] Vavilala Gopalakrishnaiah, an elderly freedom fighter, argued that the anti-arrack movement was 'similar to the freedom movement' and that 'care should be taken to see that it will not be politicized' (*The Hindu*, 16 October 1992).[27] Mothers with babies

[25] They use the word 'Romantic' as shorthand for the free, agentive, expressive, spontaneous rebel subject typical of the nineteenth-century literary-cultural movement of Romanticism.

[26] K. Ilaiah, 'Andhra Pradesh's Anti-Liquor Movement', *Economic and Political Weekly,* XXVII: 43, 1992, p. 2408.

[27] There are interesting parallels with the anti-Mandal agitation, which many intellectuals acclaimed as a manifestation of nationalism, at the same time warning against any attempt to 'politicize' it.

in their arms walk miles to come for demonstrations, wrote Vimala of the POW (*Nalupu*, 1–31 October 1992). The imagery was that of woman 'who has come out into the street [*veedhiloki vacchindi*]' (film actress Sharada, in *Eenadu*, 5 October 1992); and, as in the anti-Mandal agitation, or in the nationalist movement, this woman became the icon of purity and idealism.

In trying to explain why women were out on the streets, writers seem to obscure many factors that might have enabled the rebellion to find articulation, such as the withdrawal of the rice subsidy, the carefully planned increase in arrack sales, the literacy classes and the stories about arrack in the literacy primers. What is offered instead is the picture of the village woman's eternal tears and suffering, and how *sara* 'sucks the blood of the poor' (*Nalupu*, 1–31 October 1992). When driven to extreme despair, suggest the dominant narratives, the woman's human essence asserts itself and allows her to claim the status of citizen–subject.[28] Interestingly, the assertion of her 'civility' is premised on her being wife and mother, on her concern for her children and husband. What the woman desires, as Sharada would have it, is 'happiness in the family' (*Eenadu*, 5 October 1992) and that the auspicious marks of her marriage (*paspu-kumkumam*) not be taken from her. This refiguring of the authentic subject of feminism seems to be an implicit critique, for example, of urban feminists as they are customarily imagined in the dominant cultural representations of our time. This authentic feminist subject is characterized by a retired judge as a rural woman with 'a specific nature of her own'; 'she lives as a slave to custom as long as she can, and when she cannot tolerate that life any more and begins to break barriers, neither men nor the urban women can imagine the manner in which she will struggle. She has nerve' (Justice Arula Sambasiva Rao, in *Eenadu*, 6 October 1992). The woman's militancy is coded as that spirit which makes her a good wife and mother; the true sati demonstrates her *paativratya* or devotion not by being passive but by acting aggressively to save her husband from an untimely death.

By emphasizing the 'familial' impulse behind women's militancy, dominant explanatory narratives deny the status of the *political* to their actions and seek to contain their scope. A celebratory report in *Indian Express* (13 October 1992) described the anti-arrack issue

---

[28] 'The tears of thousands of families are pushing them into the struggle', says the actress Sharada, *Eenadu*, 5 October 1992.

as 'a burning social question'; N.T. Rama Rao of the Telugu Desam Party invoked the memory of Gandhi's desire to impose prohibition and his (Gandhi's) opinion that 'only womenfolk could bring about this social change' (*Indian Express*, 15 October 1992). Ramoji Rao, editor and publisher of *Eenadu* Telugu daily that gave extensive coverage to the *sara* struggle, said: 'Every individual who keeps trust in the values of social life should wholeheartedly welcome the Great Movement [*Mahodyamam*].... Everybody with flesh and blood, who has a sense of shame, and humanism, is cheering the struggle' (*Eenadu* editorial, 25 October 1992). Analysts on the Left seemed to veer between interpreting the movement as one for social reform (personal conversation with CPM members) and seeing it as 'part of the anti-feudal struggle' (*Nalupu*, 1–15 November 1992). That the movement was perceived by some as 'leaderless' helped to push towards a characterization of it as 'non-political'. As Ramoji Rao put it in an editorial, the movement had 'transcended caste, religion, class and party' although after it had gathered momentum various 'political parties and women's organizations are now hurrying after it' (*Eenadu* editorial, 13 September 1992).

The obverse of the refusal to image the women as political actors is the bestowal on them of a social role, that of rescuing not only their families but also 'saving the nation'. The hegemonic narratives *authorize* the women, give them 'moral authority' to *cleanse* a body politic 'stinking of *sara*' (*Eenadu* editorial, 13 September 1992). Once again, the consensus in terms of analysis and solution is stunning. Across the political spectrum, writers set up an elaborate demonology in which the valiant women battle the forces of evil, represented by the politicians, the arrack contractors, government officials, industrialists, and the whole 'corrupt' apparatus of state and civil society.[29] The meaning of *sara* (K. Balagopal calls it the 'obscene fluid') here becomes that which is unnameable and disgusting beyond belief, standing for the 'uncivilized politics'[30] abhorred by the enlightened secular humanist. Repeatedly, *sara* is evoked not only as being 'responsible for all the violence and atrocities on women' (Suman Krishna Kant, Mahila Dakshata Samiti chair, in *Eenadu*, 3 October 1992) but also as signifying the

[29] See, for instance, civil liberties activist K. Balagopal's 'Slaying of a Spirituous Demon', *Economic and Political Weekly*, XXVII: 46, 1992, pp. 2457–61.

[30] The phrase is from the AP Civil Liberties Committee press statement, issued by K.G. Kannabiran and K. Balagopal, *Eenadu*, 18 September 1992.

source of all evil and corruption; and it is rural women who are 'blowing the conch-shell of battle to destroy the atrocious *sara* demon' (*Eenadu* editorial, 25 October 1992). As K. Balagopal puts it, 'The supreme courage and tenacity of thousands of rural women has pitted itself against the abysmal humbug of the state's rulers ... [and the women] have taken up sickle and broomstick to drive the obscenity out of all our lives' (*Economic and Political Weekly*, 14 November 1992, p. 2457). The anti-arrack movement will 'cleanse us of corruption' (a CPM supporter, in personal conversation); a polity that has fallen away from the idealistic days of nationalism will have its moral impurity washed away by the *sara* women.

What other readings might be possible both of the problem and the struggle? We would want to contest the dominant representations, for example, by suggesting that the *sara* movement is a significant elaboration of the politics of everyday life, and that in such a reading questions of gender, class, caste, and community come into a radically different configuration, where the emphasis shifts from moral purity to economic exploitation or the aspiration for physical well-being.

The observations that follow, necessarily impressionistic, are based on our visit to twelve villages in three *mandals* of Nellore District in November 1992.[31] While the women's success in reducing or even preventing arrack sales directly affected the State and can be seen without much effort as a 'political' action, the movement also seemed to have resulted in a reconfiguring of power—and gender relations—within villages. Women did not usually confront individual men in their homes but attacked the local *sara* shop and the excise jeeps that supply liquor. The women also seemed to articulate many domains of their life in political terms or as political issues (even areas that class analysis would see as 'economic'). As Kondamma of Thotlacheruvupalli put it: 'Why does the government send us *sara*? Let them give us water instead, and we could have two crops a year. Now we have nothing.' Commenting on the State's indifference to their lives, she pointed out that while they had 'home delivery' of arrack they had to go nearly twenty miles to the nearest town to treat a simple case of diarrhoea. In this village (Udaygiri Mandal, Nellore District), the women had pulled

---

[31] We were part of a team sent to Nellore by Anveshi Research Centre for Women's Studies, Hyderabad. Our account of the movement draws heavily on the Anveshi report of the visit.

down the arrack shop and collected donations to build a stone platform over it which they used for public meetings. 'Why should we care', said Kondamma, 'if the government is losing money on *sara* because of us. When they had profits, did we see any of it? If the government has losses, let them cut *your* salaries.' Marvelling at the state's obtuseness, she remarked: 'You should feed a buffalo before you milk it, otherwise it'll kick. And we've kicked.' This year we won't vote for anyone,' she continued. 'They're all the same. And if our men want to vote, there'll be war between us.'

Other women, in the village of Kacheridevarayapalli (Anantsagar Mandal, Nellore District), drew up a figurative balance sheet that assigned a different set of meanings to *sara*. The *cost* of the government's Rs 850 crores of excise revenue was death (caused by the men's drunkenness—the deaths were those of themselves as well as of the women, the latter often suicides), hunger, ill-health, lack of education for the children, constant debt, their belongings— all the pots and pans and all their clothes—pawned for buying *sara*, their mental anguish. When they got rid of *sara*, said the women, they began to eat twice a day, the village streets were clean ('no drunks vomiting all over the place'), everyone's health improved ('the men are getting fat and contented'), they had peace of mind (*ippudu manasushanti undi*), freedom from abuse, and solvency. The village landlords expressed the fear that labourers who had stopped drinking *sara* and were now able to save a little would not come to them for loans. Agricultural wages would now have to be paid in real money rather than partly in packets of *sara* obtained at a discount. Women's growing control over wages was beginning to undermine long-standing structures of dependency. What is seldom noted in the celebratory accounts of the origin-stories of the anti-arrack movement is the Congress government's withdrawal of the rice subsidy for low-income families. The movement could be seen then as a critique, in a sense, not only of the State but also of the priorities of the globalizing economy and the effects on everyday life of structural adjustment and the contemporary reorganization of markets.

Many of the women in the movement spoke of the significance education, or literacy, has for them. One of the stories we heard about the beginnings of the movement was about an inaugural function in Ayyavaripalli village for the government-initiated Akshara Deepam programme designed to eradicate illiteracy. The function, attended by a State Cabinet Minister and the District Collector, was disrupted by some drunken men. The women of the village, as in all other villages the only ones who attended the night classes, demanded the closure of the local *sara* shop so that their classes could be held in peace. Willing to promise anything to ensure the success of the literacy programme, the officials complied. This and other narratives about women's achievements were written into the post-literacy primers; stories such as the one about Dubagunta village (*Adavallu Ekamaithe*—If Women Unite) where three drunken labourers lost their way and drowned in a tank. A hundred women first stopped the local arrack cart from entering the village; then they turned back 'a jeep full of *sara* packets'; after this, the lesson goes, the police arrived to enforce the right of the contractor to sell arrack. The women stood their ground, saying they would go to the Collector if necessary. 'This year,' the lesson concludes, 'no one came forward to bid for arrack in our village.'[32] Women also spoke of other lessons, charts, and topics for discussion in their literacy primers, such as 'Seethamma Katha', 'Unity', and 'Who's Responsible for this Death?', which inspired them to join the struggle against arrack. 'We want our children to go to school,' said Kondamma of Thotlacheruvupalli. This claiming *from below* of the right to education makes evident one of the most important agendas of the anti-Mandal agitation, the denial of education to the lower castes.[33] The upper-caste anxiety about educated Dalits, as in Chunduru, is to prevent them from occupying the space of the modern as it has been marked out in the post-colonial nation. The *sara* women's claiming of education seemed to recognize this logic and challenge the exclusions of modernity itself. The Dalit and Muslim women engaged in the struggle seemed to be articulating a claim on the rights of the citizen, from a critical perspective not necessarily predicated on their 'human essence'.

In spite of the fact that the women in the movement were predominantly from the Scheduled Caste, Backward Caste, and

[32] *Chanduvu Velugu* and *Akshara Deepam* literacy primers. We are grateful to T.S.S. Lakshmi and K. Sajaya for providing translations of the lessons.
[33] A popular anti-Mandal refrain was that educational opportunities for lower caste people would wean them away from their traditional occupations, turn them into clerks, and thereby destroy the handicrafts and textiles that symbolized Indian culture.

Muslim communities, their jointly undertaken efforts to stop the excise officials received the tacit support of the upper-caste women of their village. Although it is an understanding obtained from the women's perspective that allowed them to claim *sara* as 'their' issue, the movement seldom pitted them against individual men, or against women from other castes/communities.

A unique feature of the anti-arrack movement was the refusal of the women to take up initiatives beyond their village. As Mastanbi of Kacheridevarayapalli put it, 'Are the women of the other villages dead? Why should *we* go there to fight against *sara*?' In relating their initiatives to the specificity of their location (their slogan is *Maa ooriki sara vaddu*—'We don't want sara in our village'), in demarcating a domain over which they can exercise control, the anti-arrack women seem to be envisaged, and engaged, in a politics of the possible.[34]

VII

It seems to us that the early 1990s represent a turning point for Indian feminism. Each of the metonyms we have chosen for analysis focus on hegemonic mobilizations of a 'feminist' subject specific to our times. Each displays the contradictions that emerge within feminist politics and the challenges that confront gender analysis in the context of the refiguring of dominance in a rapidly globalizing Indian economy. Clearly the metonyms evidence an undertow in existing Indian feminism, of structures of domination. Yet the anti-Mandal agitation, the politics of contraceptive choice, the feminism of the Hindu Right, or the representations of the anti-arrack movement provide us also with configurations that crystallize and precipitate the possibilities of new and more radical alliances. This chapter has been primarily concerned with the exploration of factors that disable alliances between feminism and other democratic political initiatives, but we regard this as a crucial first step in the shaping of a feminism capable of a counter-hegemonic politics adequate to our times.

[34] We take this phrase from Kumkum Sangari's well-known article, 'The Politics of the Possible', reprited in Tejaswini Niranjana, P. Sudhir and Vivek Dhareshwar (eds), *Interrogating Modernity: Culture and Colonialism in India*, Seagull Books, Calcutta, 1993.

It is possible that in this essay this concern has not allowed us to focus richly enough on the democratic potential of actually existing feminism. Yet it is clearly this potential that both demands and empowers the kind of critical engagement evident in our argument. It is also precisely this democratic potential that has enabled us as feminists to support Dalit movements or take part in anti-communal initiatives today. By confronting the specific genealogy of the woman-subject and its impress on contemporary politics, we have tried also to open up for investigation the subject of democracy—secularism in India.

VII

Sexuality

Ruth Vanita urges the need for any women's movement to fundamentally rethink gender and sexuality to liberate both men and women into developing different notions of the self and alternative kinds of family or collective living. The rigid 'normality' of the gender divide, of heterosexuality and of an anthropomorphism alienated from other species is challenged by Ruth, who argues that there is a large body of narratives in Indian languages and in Indian culture historically, which offer alternative possibilities of conceiving of the self.

15

Thinking Beyond Gender in India*

Ruth Vanita

The words 'man' and 'woman' are universally translatable into most known languages. Although there are important differences in the ways the man–woman relationship is structured in different societies, these differences are less important than the basic similarity of the relationship, premised upon a normative heterosexuality, geared towards reproduction of a dominant group (men) and a subordinate group (women).

Witness the case of Nicole Simpson whose history of enduring violence at the hands of her husband, concealing its extent from the public gaze, suffering pressure from her family to try and save the marriage, is so startlingly similar to the numerous cases of wife-beating that often culminate in wife-murder in India.[1] That more

* A version of this paper was first presented at a conference on Indian women organized by the South Asia programme at Cornell University, 1 April 1995. Another version was presented at the South Asian programme, Syracuse University. The paper presents some of my reflections on women's situation and women's movements in India, based on 13 years of working as founding co-editor of *Manushi*—a journal about women and society, for which I wrote a regular legal column, and as a feminist activist involved in many campaigns relating to violence against women. I left *Manushi* in 1990, and not all the views expressed in this paper represent those of *Manushi*.

[1] The similarity, in the US and in India, of media and public reaction to atrocities, especially those perpetrated by celebrities, is evident in the recent Naina Sahni case. Her husband, Sushil Sharma, a Congress politician, is alleged to have murdered her and burnt her body in the kitchen of a restaurant. Sharma's public profile and the gruesome way the body was disposed of, has led to the case being

Indian than American women may end up dead in such situations has a lot to do with the greater affluence of American society which makes it possible for women to find a job and a place to stay and leave before they are killed.

Focusing on issues like sati and the so-called dowry deaths in Indian society or, conversely, on the high rate of abandonment of women and children by men in western societies, tends to foster a syndrome of what might be called 'Our patriarchy is better than yours'.[2] This syndrome functions both at the collective and at the individual level, and within women's movements as much as in society at large, if more insidiously in the former than the latter.

The direction of activist, media or governmental energies, which are directed only (or mainly) towards prevention or redress of atrocities, functions both as a threat and a reassurance for most women. The average woman is subliminally persuaded that she has nothing to complain of if her husband does not batter her. The atrocity, constructed as such by media, legal terminology and protestors, functions to legitimize rather than to undermine the structures of male–female relationships. For every one reported police rape taken up by women's groups in India, there are hundreds of unreported routine marital rapes: for every one case of severe wife beating there are hundreds of cases of more routinized, less severe violence in marriage as well as hundreds of routinely unhappy, tedious marriages.

In the late '70s, one of the main theoretical differences between party affiliated women's organizations and autonomous women's groups was supposed to be that the former emphasized class over gender and the latter gender over class. Twenty years later, the differences seemed far less important because in actual practice all

---

in newspaper headlines everyday, and to several protest demonstrations by women's organizations.

[2] I refer to the deaths as 'so-called dowry deaths' because *Manushi*'s experience of dealing with these cases over the years showed that several other factors, primarily that of the powerlessness of a wife whose natal family abandon her to the mercies of her marital family, contribute more to the escalating violence that leads to wife-murder than dowry in itself. The deaths are frequently projected as caused by dowry because the law makes it easier to prosecute cases so classified. See Madhu Kishwar, 'Rethinking Dowry Boycott', *Manushi*, 48, 1988, and 'Towards More just Norms for Marriage', *Manushi*, 53, 1989, Madhu Kishwar and Ruth Vanita, 'Inheritance Rights for Women', *Manushi*, 57, 1990.

of us were doing the same work—what could be called firefighting and band-aid application. We were constantly responding in various ways to two kinds of requests: first, to change a violent marriage into a routinely unhappy one; second, and less often, to change an unhappy marriage into a happy one; third, to take revenge for a marriage that had ended in frustrating, injuring or killing a woman.

Although different organizations had started out with different agendas and political positions and although these differences remained in theory, women activists in general, if to different degrees, ended up functioning as marriage counsellors, retrievers of dowries and legal aid providers. Families frequently demanded of the organization in which I worked that we function like a macabre wedding band and demonstrate and protest the demise of a marriage. What is more, we were criticized for resisting such pressure.

Overall, unless themselves the targets of protest, most families and most men who came in contact with our women's organization, as also most government agencies and officers including the police, applauded our work and thought we were doing very useful social work, as indeed we were. We were keeping heterosexual structures in repair by functioning as unpaid relief workers, even though this wasn't quite what we had set out to do. In a society where women suffer so much pain, such relief work needs to be done—and perhaps everyone should contribute a certain number of years of their life to doing it—like a sort of tithe or tax.[3]

However, if think that by doing this work we will end violence against women, or preserve the institution of heterosexual monogamy and at the same time end such violence, we are under the same delusion as the wife who appeals to women activists to reform her husband. Despite their political differences, today, most feminists and non-feminists, rightists and leftists, Hindus, Muslims and Christians in India share the basic assumption that, although there are many abuses within heterosexual monogamy, this system in nevertheless the best available.

Let me illustrate this via an example of reform in the marriage law. A couple of years ago some women's organizations were drafting proposals for changes in the Hindu Marriage Act and the Special

[3] See Ruth Vanita, 1987, 'Can Police Reform Husbands? The Crimes Against Women Cell', Delhi; *Manushi*, 40.

Marriage Act, a process that is still underway. It so happens that the Hindu Marriage Act (no doubt inadvertently) does not, in its initial definition of the parameters of the act, specify the sex of the partners involved. Last year, two young women tried to take advantage of this when they filed an application to marry under the act. They could not be legally prevented but were pressured by officials to give up the idea.[4] But women's organizations have not taken note of this feature or pressed to write it more clearly into the body of the act. Nor have they even considered challenging the system of monogamy enforced by this act.

Why should not three or four or more people of any sex be able to marry? If this were allowed, the institution of marriage would be open to such radical alteration that it would no longer be the same institution. Different communities in India have practised polygamy and polyandry, practices now outlawed. The undesirability of the economic and other inequalities built into these practices tends to be confused with the practices themselves; a residual puritanism makes these inequalities more visible than those that are built into heterosexual monogamy. Monogamy as an absolute principle is full of holes, since if it is an absolute, as some would argue, then divorce and remarriage are wrong. Conversely, if serial monogamy is acceptable, why should group marriage not be acceptable?

I am not raising these questions merely as a theoretical exercise: they have a direct bearing on practice. For instance, the desire to abolish verbal *talaq* often confuses the inequality built into it with the practice itself which is merely the practice of divorce on the basis of irretrievable breakdown of marriage. That one partner should be able to end the marriage unilaterally without citing reasons is based on the idea that no one should be forced to live with someone they do not want to live with. They should not have to prove anything or to vilify the person concerned before deciding to leave. What is undesirable about verbal talaq is that under Indian Muslim law only men have this right. In fact, Islamic law has a

[4] The case was widely and sympathetically reported in national dailies. While there have been several cases of women marrying each other in temples and proceeding to live as spouses (for example, the police women Lila and Urmila in Bhopal, 1987; Neeru and Meenu in Faridabad, 1993), this was the only one I know of where two women proposed to take advantage of the lacuna in the Hindu Marriage Act and have their marriage registered in court.

provision in operation in some Muslim countries, called *khula*, whereby a woman can exercise a similar right. She can leave her husband even if he does not want to leave her, merely by making a certain payment, just as on talaq, a husband is supposed to pay *mehr*.

Introducing khula and building economic safeguards into talaq, which is easily done because Muslim marriage is a contract and any kind of safeguard or provision can be written into the *nikahnama* or marriage contract, would transform Muslim marriage law into the most progressive law in the country. No marriage law in India allows divorce on grounds of irretrievable breakdown which most other democracies allow. In India, if one partner wants to leave and the other does not, the one who wants to leave has to prove that the other is an undesirable person rather than alleging simple incompatibility. Why does abolishing talaq have an appeal that introducing khula does not? Because the near-universal assumption that heterosexual monogamy is the best practice makes it easier for people to accept the idea of imprisoning men within monogamous marriage in the same way as women already are, but difficult to accept the idea of providing women and men with easy escape routes from marriage.

In fact, no society practises only heterosexual monogamy. Indian society certainly does not. This is because most people are dissatisfied, to different degrees, with being men or women. I agree with Monique Wittig that the word 'woman' is no more redeemable than the word 'nigger' or, I might add, the word *chamar* or *choora*, and the word 'man' than the word 'white'.[5] The categories 'woman' and 'man' are illogical categories based on certain parts of the body which may or may not be used to certain predefined ends. We might as well divide all human beings into big-eared and small-eared people and hope to work out a sane society based on such a division.

At some point in its development, any women's movement must take one of two directions both at the level of thought and of action, or, more likely, must work out some combination of both directions: (i) that of repairing the structures of heterosexual marriage and family, making them somewhat more equitable or

[5] 'The Straight Mind', 1980, in *The Straight Mind and Other Essays*, Boston: Beacon Press, 1992, pp. 29–30.

(ii) that of rethinking gender and sexuality to liberate both women and men into developing different kinds of family or collective living. People in any society always, incipiently, work out alternative forms of familial living. What a movement can do is to foreground and validate these forms and encourage others.

Women's movements in India have, by and large, only taken the first direction—that of reforming marriage and the laws and social codes related to it. Their concentration on people as victims rather than agents and their reluctance to question gender and sexuality categories has fostered a stress on equity rather than liberation. Their self-characterization as 'women's movements' and dropping the word 'liberation' is not fortuitous. Today, many people outside of women's movements are far more advanced in thinking through and enacting liberatory modes of life, relationship and community.

In all societies, persons who are dissatisfied with the heterosexual system to the point of not wishing to gain the rewards of fitting into it, have devised different ways of opting out, individually and/ or collectively. As Wittig says: 'The refusal to become (or to remain) heterosexual always meant to refuse to become a man or a woman, consciously or not.'[6] Serena Nanda has examined *hijra* (eunuch) communities as experimenting with such ways of opting out. Hijras function as one model of difference. More than one older woman friend has told me, half playfully, half seriously 'I'm a hijra', which reminds me of Virginia Woolf's statement that she was neither a man nor a woman. Young Indian lesbian friends have expressed to me feelings similar to my own, to the effect that they do not think of themselves as women or as men. As an experiment I have asked many non-feminist women friends of differing classes, age and marital status whether they would like to be reborn as men or women, and have received the answer: 'Not as a woman.' Some have said they would like to be birds.

Unfortunately, the articulation of such feelings has often been silenced in feminist circles, by ascribing it to low self-esteem or even self-hatred. On the contrary, I would argue that it is related to high self-esteem, to the perception of oneself as not the complementary of a man, not wishing to play any role vis-à-vis a man that could be defined as womanly, and therefore, not being,

[6] 'One is Not Born a Woman', 1981, in *The Straight Mind*, 13.

for any practical purpose, a woman. Emphasizing one's womanhood while opting out of a bad marriage produces the kind of victim narrative which so many modern Indian women fiction writers have endlessly repeated, where the body of the text is taken up with the struggle to get out and the text ends as soon as the heroine does get out, because there is logically nowhere for her to go except another marriage, suicide or lonely depression.

I shall briefly look at some other kinds of narrative produced historically by persons who opted out of heterosexual structures, and at the inheritance of these traditions by some modern Indian writers. Working on women *bhakta* and *sant* poets was a very enlightening experience for me (as is my current experience of working on the lives of European medieval saints), because it showed how their lives and work followed a trajectory of critique, protest and opting out of the heterosexual system, followed by the forming of alternative community and friendship networks. That *bhakti* movements criticized class, caste and religious differences and defied institutional authority of various kinds has often been demonstrated.[7] Many inheritors of such movements exist today; for example, throughout the period of terrorism and police brutality in Punjab, the Radhaswami Satsang continued to function as a mass forum where Hindus and Sikhs met and worshipped together.

What is common to the legends of almost all bhaktas and sants, men and women, is that they refused to be good spouses and good parents. Many women refused to marry; those who were married left their husbands. This feature is also found in the lives of medieval mystics in Europe, women who chose to be nuns rather than wives. Frideswide in medieval England is supposed to have performed a miracle which blinded her prospective husband and ended his pursuit of her; Avvaiyyar in medieval Tamil Nadu is supposed to have performed a miracle which turned her into an old woman so that her prospective husband would stop pursuing her.[8] Both men

---

[7] Devotional movements which began in south India in the 6th century, spread to almost all regions of the country. There was much regional variation but the movements shared a mystical tendency to stress the oneness of all life. Bhaktas usually expressed devotion to an incarnate god or goddess and sants to a disembodied divine principle.

[8] Another medieval English saint Wilgefortis miraculously grew a beard to discourage a prospective husband. Women worshipped her under the name of 'Uncumber' because they hoped she would uncumber them of their husbands.

and women altered gender categories by trying to strip them of meaning—by walking naked, by growing their hair long, and by rethinking the terms. Thus 12th century Kannada Virashaiva poet Dasimayya writes:

Suppose you cut a tall bamboo in two;
make the bottom piece a woman, the headpiece a man;
rub them together till they kindle: tell me now
the fire that's born,
is it male or female, O Ramanatha?[9]

A new relation to the universe is often envisaged through the idea of being an animal. The last boundary to be crossed is that of the species. To acknowledge that we are animals and that that is the most important thing we have in common across class, caste, nation, gender lines is perhaps a necessary first step towards dissolving those lines. As the 14th century Sufi Nizamuddin Auliya remarked: 'When a lion emerges from the forest, no one bothers to ask whether it is male or female.'[10] Hindu thought provides the space for such a move—all the deities are accompanied by non-human creatures, and some like Ganesh, are combinations of animal, human and divine. Mahatma Gandhi suggested that we look past our contempt, inherited from the British, for cow-worship, and consider the cow as a symbol of nature, a reminder of the need to respect other species from whom we take so much. In the writings of women sant poets, deer and cows often figure as images of victimized women: conversely, small creatures that can fly are symbols of the powerless that become powerful. The 13th century Varkari sant poet Muktabai writes:

An ant flew to the sky
and swallowed the sun.
Another wonder—
a barren woman had a son.
A scorpion went to the underworld,
set its foot on the Shesh Nag's head.
A fly gave birth to a kite.
Looking on, Muktabai laughed.[11]

[9] A.K. Ramanujan, *Speaking of Siva*, Harmondsworth: Penguin Classics, 1985, p. 110.
[10] *Manushi*, special issue on Women Bhakta Poets, January–June 1989.
[11] Translated by me with Champa Limaye, in Ruth Vanita, 'Three women sants of Maharashtra', *Manushi*, January–June 1989.

The barren woman's son here may well be an image for the text itself, as in the popular saying about Mirabai:

One's name will live on through one's work
Consider this if you are wise.
Mira did not give birth to a son
Nor did she have any disciples.[12]

Outside of institutional structures of the family and the formal educational system, these women nevertheless wrote narratives of power and creativity. They functioned as models for other women. Mahatma Gandhi cited Mirabai as an example for women. When a little girl was born to a follower, he said he hoped she would become a Mirabai. This is interesting because normally a divorcee and a widow would not be cited as model. There is a continuous tradition of such models and forums that women can appeal to, to legitimize opting out.

For instance, a friend's grandmother who did not get along with her husband, joined the Brahmakumaris. This took up most of her time, she was almost never in the house; since she had taken a vow of celibacy she had no further sexual relations with her husband and as the special food she cooked was unacceptable to the palate of the family, she ended up not cooking for anyone but herself. While the family resented this behaviour, they found it hard to forbid it. Another friend's aunt left her husband to join a Jaikishen ashram in Maharashtra. In India today, as in medieval Europe, the institutions of fasting and pilgrimages provide women with ways of controlling and accessing familial and individual patterns of life and mobility.

These traditions have also been inherited and transformed textually, for instance, by contemporary poets Suniti Namjoshi and Vikram Seth. These two writers have immense popularity and appeal; they are readable and widely accessible. Their writings show a blend of various traditions, Indian and non-Indian, and they often use animal tropes to suggest crossings of the boundaries of race, gender, culture, nationality and sexuality. Less containable than human beings in categories of nationality and gender, animals as they have figured in western and eastern mythologies, literatures,

[12] Translated by me, in Ruth Vanita and Madhu Kishwar, 'Poison to nectar: the life and work of Mirabai', *Manushi*, January–June 1989.

and even popular jokes and stories, often reveal the surprising commonalty of apparently distinct traditions.

Suniti Namjoshi is a feminist writer from Maharashtra who has lived in Canada and England for a large part of her creative life. In her writings, the protagonist is generally named 'Suniti' and inhabits a world populated by various human and non-human creatures and literal and mythical beasts who are in communication with one another. The Sanskrit first name functions in English as a marker of strangeness, while Suniti and those she meets are often rendered even stranger by unexpected attributes, as with the blue donkey who is the ultimate embodiment of meditative wisdom and Bhadravati, the lesbian cow—a comic send-up of the way Indian lesbians are often invisible to non-Indians. The attempts of cows and donkeys to interact with or keep their distance from lordly tigers suggest the difficulties of survival in and struggle with the dominant culture.

In one preface, Namjoshi connects her choice of a beastly persona with her questioning of gender stereotyping, and also with her pantheistic Hindu background wherein a beast is not inherently inferior to a human being because the same spirit may in various reincarnations inhabit both human and non-human bodies. She concludes this meditation by asking, 'But what sort of beast was I?'[13]

Vikram Seth's narratives also draw on old Indian traditions of friendship between human and non-human animals such as Yudhishthir and his dog, Ram and Jatayu, and western traditions such as St. Francis and his wolves and lambs. In *Beastly Tales from Here and There* (Penguin, Delhi, 1992), each of the ten narrative poems is named for two creatures of different species. The asymmetry of these unconventionally matched pairs suggests the oddness of alliances that are not within normative paradigms. These are poems about friendship—same-sex friendship and love, and also cross-sex friendship and love; in all of them, however, the question of gender, of 'he' or 'she' is rendered unimportant by the use of species sameness and difference to mask it. One has to go back to check whether the elephant or tragopan were both male or the two mice both female.

---

[13] Preface to 'The Jackass and the Lady', *Because of India: Selected Poems and Fables*, London: Only Women Press, 1989, p. 29.

In Seth's 1994 libretto, *Arion and the Dolphin*, the human–non-human friendship narrative, briefly and comically explored in *The Golden Gate*, appears centrally and seriously. It can be read as an ironical version of the old story of the faithful animal who dies for a human being; however, its romantic and passionate tone makes it susceptible to being read as a coded homoerotic text.

Thus, Indian society like other societies, has continuous traditions of creating non-victim narratives, narratives of opting out of gender categories and forming new kinds of alliances across various boundaries. We need to make these narratives, past and present, more visible, by researching them, writing about them and celebrating them.